MW01278408

God's Seven Ways To Ease Suffering

By Ronald D. Anton

God's Seven Ways To Ease Suffering
by Ronald D. Anton

Printed in the United States of America

ISBN 978-1-60477-267-8

Unless otherwise indicated, Bible quotations are taken from the American Standard Version (New Testament). Copyright © 1901 by Thomas Nelson & Sons, and the King James Version (Old Testament), Copyright © 1940, by A.J. Holman Co. Portions of Scripture have been italicized for emphasis by the author.

In thanksgiving, praise and worship of my Lord and Saviour, Jesus, Christ, "who for the joy that was set before him endured the cross" (Hebrews 12:2).

Cover Design by Kathy Bridgeman, Grand Island, New York

www.xulonpress.com

DEDICATION

THIS BOOK is gratefully dedicated to Jacob Hyman, Dean Emeritus of the University of Buffalo School of Law, whose intellect and integrity have inspired generations of lawyers. A Constitutional Law scholar of incomparable erudition, his life has honored God's call to serve righteousness and ease suffering by wise and faithful application of the Law. My gratitude persists after half a century for this mentor and friend, who broadened my horizons in the quest for truth; confirming my belief in a benevolent, Supreme Law-Giver in Sovereign control of the universe.

I also appreciate this opportunity to express my gratitude for the friendship and assistance of Donna Winstanley during the preparation of the manuscript, and Kathy Bridgeman, who designed the front cover. I thank God for the encouragement of my faithful prayer partners, Rev. Elwood Mann and Rev. Frank Bongiovanni, whose exemplary lives have inspired more of the manuscript than I could ever attribute to them.

Ronald D. Anton, 2007
Niagara Falls, New York

TABLE OF CONTENTS

INTRODUCTION

"Weeping may endure for a night, but joy cometh in the morning."

- Psalm 30:5

When I was a boy I learned it was unmanly to cry. Indeed, it was difficult to envision John Wayne in tears, no matter how much torture he endured. However, after decades of feminist encouragement, and mellowed by the distillation of time and experience. I have concluded one can weep manfully. After all, the Bible records that the most perfect man who ever lived wept three times. The shortest verse in the Bible is "Jesus wept" at the tomb of Lazarus, over man's sorrow and fear of death. Jesus wept over the lost souls of Jerusalem, who refused to receive Him as God's cure for sin. And He wept tears of revulsion over mankind's horrible sins, so odious to God, which He alone could propitiate by His sacrificial and vicarious atonement (Hebrew 5:7).

Every Easter I weep over this awesome love of Christ on the Cross, first with tears of remorse at His Crucifixion, and then with tears of joy at His Resurrection. My eyes mist whenever righteousness is nobly expressed in selfless acts of love, kindness, and sacrificial devotion to the needs of others. I get a lump in my throat when a believer courageously stands firm in the integrity of his conviction; defends the weak; exhibits mercy, or any Godly trait.

I am moved to weep with those who mourn, or suffer from infirmity, grief, affliction, fear, imprisonment, or deprivation of any kind. I groan for the hard-hearted stubbornness of those who refuse to accept the gift of salvation in Christ, but prefer to follow the broad way leading to eternal destruction.

I know, because the Bible says so, that God is Sovereign, totally good and benevolent, and bestows blessings on men. The sun shines and the rain falls on wicked as well as good men. We inhabit a congenial planet beneath a firmament created for man's comfort and well-being. We are surrounded by beauty, abundance, and basic harmony, despite occasional aberrations in nature. Most men are born healthy and rational, with broad capacities for growth, knowledge, productivity, and appreciation for God and the gifts He has reserved for us.

Christians are heirs to a panoply of far more significant spiritual blessings, available to all willing men from a loving and caring Father. Man's sin separates him from God, but God so loved and valued man that he arranged for His Son, Jesus Christ to enter into history as a sinless man, to suffer and die as the sinner's substitute. Jesus so loved us He sacrificed himself to torture and death on the Cross in the place of every sinner, each of whom needed salvation from sin. By the shedding of His sinless Blood and death on the Cross, Jesus atoned or made reparation for the sins of all men. He reconciled sinners to a right relationship with a holy God by removing the cause of enmity. He redeemed us from slavery to sin. He ransomed us from the penalty of sin, which is damnation and death, reserved for, and deserved by, all unsaved sinners. He justified or vindicated sinners by thus satisfying the affront of sin to God's Justice.

By His sheer grace and determination to love us, God makes salvation available in every generation to willing believers using the ABCs of faith: Acknowledge you are a sinner; Believe Jesus died for your sins; Confess Him as Lord and Saviour. By His grace in love, God convicts wrongdoers of sin, making them ashamed of their iniquity, and prepares the hearts of sinners to receive their Lord and Saviour through faith, by hearing the Gospel Word of salvation preached by Christ.

Faith in Christ not only brings about salvation, but also a New Birth, which involves a spiritual regeneration or total transformation of the believer's inner, spiritual being into a changed, new man, reconstituted, and completely replacing the old, or natural man, who will grow progressively into the very nature, character, and image of Christ. At the New Birth the Holy Spirit literally comes to indwell a believer, and begins an ongoing process of sanctification and growth, by setting regenerated men apart from the world, and implanting divine holiness within them. The Spirit imparts Christ's character to us, manifested in the Fruit of the Holy Spirit: love, joy, peace, patience, goodness, kindness, faithfulness, gentleness, and self-control. He provides supernatural faith, repentance, and obedience for good works, consistent with our new nature. God promises to complete our earthly sanctification with glorification at the Second Coming of Christ. Then our purification will be perfected, and believers will be able to share all eternity basking in His love; praising and worshipping Him as His marvelous character and creativity continue to unfold through unspeakable wonders.

At the New Birth, we are also baptized into the Church, the Body of Christ, consisting of all believers in Christ, of whom Jesus is the Head. The Church has the ongoing incarnational task, as the fleshly body of Christ, to minister to the needs of both saved and unsaved men through special supernatural endowments. Every member receives a ministry gift from the Holy Spirit, such as wisdom, knowledge, faith, healings, miracles, prophecy, discernment of spirits, tongues, or interpretation of tongues, to assist the Church in fulfilling its mission. Christ gives ministry gifts to some believers to serve as apostles, prophets, evangelists, pastors, and teachers.

God anoints members of the Body to provide strength, encouragement, edification, exhortation, education, and support by ministering to the needs of others throughout our worldly pilgrimage. God's power accomplishes the growth and effectiveness of the Body, which thrives by concerted effort and magnified power of believers united with one another in prayer and action. Weaker members can draw strength from those who are stronger in the Lord, and when they are strengthened, they can, in turn, help other weaker members and minister to the unsaved. God comforts us in our sorrow so that we may comfort others with His same consolations which have comforted us.

Jesus said He came to bring fuller, more abundant life to believers, both here and Hereafter. This includes some material, earthly, and temporal blessings, and some eternal and spiritual ones. Some blessings involve health, sufficiency, and spiritual prosperity in Christian life and growth. God promises that we can know Him; have the mind of Christ; follow Jesus; fellowship with Him; effectively pray in the name of Jesus; grow in holiness; render loving service to others for the sake of Jesus; witness with conviction for Jesus; and develop faithful obedience, as He did. Christ is the object of this life, and Christ-likeness is the object of Christian disciple-ship, for which God's grace anoints and equips us. Knowing God is the object of our worship; to love, serve, and glorify Him; as we prepare to be with Him for eternity.

With such an array of promised blessings, it is little wonder that believers embark upon the faith life with joyful anticipation that God lavishes good things in the world upon Christians. Yet, in rejoicing over God's promised resources to enjoy, cope with, and overcome the world, we should remember that such victories will be preceded and accompanied by trials, temp-tations, troubles, torments, tribulations, pains, privations, persecutions and suffering for believers. While the opening Chapters are a celebration of God's Sovereignty, Providence, and loving kindness toward His children, the later Chapters examine the processes intended to bless believers, which have inherent potential to produce suffering when they are distorted by irresponsible human freedom.

God's love regularly provides us with protection and deliverance from evil; suffering inflicted by the world, the flesh and the devil, and other sinful men driven by power, lust, greed, and pride. As He did for Job, God provides believers with a hedge of protection against worldly assaults, and offers haven in the shelter of His arms. He furnishes us with guardian angels, charged with ministering to the earthly needs of the faithful. He provides His own spiritual armor, which, if faithfully worn, protects us from the assaults of evil and repels all the fiery darts of the evil one. We are given the authority of the name of Jesus, by which we can enter into prayer, as well as resist the devil, so he must flee from us.

Until the travail passes, God assures believers that any suffering, temptation, or persecution inflicted by the world will be regulated by Him in intensity, impact, duration, and frequency. He will allow only temptations common to man; circumstances will never by beyond our strength to endure; and will always be followed by a way of escape provided by God. If He does not help us to escape, evade, or elude every worldly consequence of our sin, He will miti-gate the severity of the suffering by abbreviating it, or helping us to reverse, remedy, or endure adverse conditions in the strength and comfort of His presence. We can rely on strength from Jesus, Who promises to be with us always, and to bear or lighten our cares. We are supported by other believers, even as we sustain them, for we are all called to bear one another's burdens. The example of Christ's life and of the martyrs of the Church whose faith was unyielding, can also inspire our own fidelity to God in the face of persecution.

To facilitate our sanctification, God has promised that when we sin in this life, He is merciful and will forgive us, and cleanse us of all unrighteousness when we repent and turn from our sins. God promises to forget our confessed transgressions, and wash us in the precious Blood of Christ, so we may continue to be freed from the weighty burden of sins. He gives believers a peace which passes all understanding, based on the certainty of our security in Christ.

God has also promised to respond to prayers of petition and intercession, by which Divine intervention is invited into the affairs of men. When we intercede by prayers invoking God's mercy on behalf of others, we are doubly blessed, as Jesus intercedes on behalf of His faithful and the Holy Spirit transforms our desires and prayers so they can comply with God's will and response. As Sovereign God Almighty, He foresees, inspires, and factors our prayers into His divine Providence so that His perfect will and intent for believers is always accomplished.

God has given us His Word, divinely authored and inspired, though written by the hands of men, to reveal and detail the perfect and awesome beauty of His character and creativity, which are worthy of our worship, praise, and thanksgiving. The Word proclaims His purposes and sets forth God's instructions for acceptable living, which He has ordained for our welfare, so we might avoid sin. The Holy Spirit elucidates the Scriptures so we can know God, fellowship with Him, and have understanding to ease our journey in this world and prepare us for the next. When Satan attacks us, if we resist him and cite the Word as Jesus did, we are empowered to have a direct, victorious response to his challenges. As absolute truth, the Scriptures are intrinsically joyful when studied and digested.

The New Birth occurs through faith in God's Word, and our New Born spirit is fed, grows, and continually washed clean by the water of the Word. Jesus, the Word, is the author and finisher, pioneer, and perfecter, creator and sustainer of our faith, which comes by hearing the preaching of Christ in the Word. Our faith is generated as we experience the dependability of God's Word, and rely upon God's integrity, power, and goodness to deliver the blessings promised in His Word. Belief in the Word is the key to God delivering on His promises. Jesus revealed that the measure of faith which a believer has in God's Word determines the measure by which the Word will bear fruit and fulfill God's specific promises in his life. We reap the fruit of faith in direct proportion to the extent of our sowing faith in the Word.

While Christians are aware of all these blessings which attest to the absolute goodness of God, they are still perplexed by the existence of evil and suffering which are allowed to co-exist in a good world under the total control of a perfect, all-wise, all-powerful, and all-loving God. There is no imperfection or weakness in God, so, since evil is a reality, He apparently has voluntarily relinquished some of His Sovereign power and control over the affairs of men in the world. The more we understand God's reasons for this, the better we can endure, profit from, and overcome the affliction, torment, persecution, and pain which Jesus reveals are the companions of believers in this world.

The phenomenon of evil is explained in part by the fact that spiritual blessings and gifts from God, bestowed in His perfect love and goodness to benefit believers, also have intrinsic properties, operations, and consequences, which can inflict suffering whenever man fails to use the blessing properly. God purposes to favor man with the privilege and joy of active participation in these activities. This collaborative effort, based on trust between God and man, dignifies and exalts man if he acts as God has prescribed. For, man is greatly blessed by God's grace when he is allowed to participate, strive and contend for the accomplishment of God's purposes.

We are exalted as sons by sharing the joys of accomplishment, victory, and maturity when we are entrusted with duty, responsibility, accountability, and obligation. God's grace gives man the opportunity to render obedience for the sheer joy of pleasing his Father. However, if man fails to fulfill God's trust by disobedience, rebellion, and uncooperation, then painful consequences can result. God has summoned believers to participate in improving their world, and thereby reduce suffering, privation, and unspirituality among men. Man is free to respond or not, and when he mis-uses his God-given free choice, he can momentarily delay and frustrate God's purposes, resulting in loss to oneself and others.

We can understand how benevolent spiritual blessings have the potential to produce distress, by observing the natural order and operations of nature, which are patently benevolent, yet carry an incidental potential for harm without God intending that result. For, the constituent processes of nature inherently allow for occasional injury under certain conditions. The operation of these natural laws and their properties and characteristics are benignly intended and ordained by a good God only for good. Their potential for risk or harm to believers from natural disasters and catastrophes is not planned, necessitated, or desired by God, who is incapable of evil. The processes and relationships which God has established to accomplish a superior and supervening good, <u>may</u> intrinsically, but unintentionally, produce distress.

Consider the law of gravity, for example. Gravity is a benevolent natural law which serves the needs of the universe. Gravity holds the planet in orbit, so that the exact distance required from the sun's heat and flames is maintained to sustain life. Gravity also attracts and holds men to the surface of the earth, lest they drift off into space unintentionally. Yet, gravity also has innate potential to harm one who falls and fractures a limb. It can blindly and mechanically operate to cripple or kill the unfortunate victim who falls from a great height, without any intent by God to cause harm.

Fire warms us from the cold, cooks the food which sustains us, and provides light for illuminating the darkness, yet it has inherent properties which can also asphyxiate by smoke, or consume burning flesh. It is ridiculous to infer that a benevolent God intends fire to harm one who carelessly touches the flames, simply because fire's constituent elements behave in the manner God designed for benevolent purposes.

The same soil which provides plant food to sustain life can smother humans buried in an avalanche. The same warm breeze which brings temperature comfort to one hemisphere, can set destructive tornadoes in motion when it encounters frigid air in another part of the world. Similarly, water is an intended blessing to sustain life, quench thirst, cleanse, provide natural beauty and recreation for boating, ice-skating, and swimming. Yet, the inherent properties of water to occupy space, boil, or freeze at precise temperatures, can also harm by drowning, flooding, scalding, slipping or skidding on ice. We cannot say God intended or orchestrated every harmful result, when the normal, unique properties of water provide so many more benefits by the hand of a good, loving, and giving God.

Consider God's blessing of freedom, which pervades and transports many other blessings from God. When we obediently and responsibly use God's gift of freedom, we are blessed and can bless others. It appears God has relinquished some autonomy by giving man the glorious gift of genuine free choice and self-determination to accept or reject Him. In this blessing, God is glorified by rational men willing to respond to His love, choose to be holy like Him, act responsibly, and intelligently appreciate and worship Him. God is not glorified by pre-programmed automatons who are incapable of making a moral choice to love or obey God. Thus, God intends to give man dignity, stature, and virtue by allowing him freely to receive Jesus and choose God out of love, rather than fearful subservience, implanted instinct, or imposed coercion.

Freedom of human participation makes God vulnerable to temporary failure because of man's imperfection. Whenever we distort, abuse, or corrupt our precious freedom of choice out of pride or stubbornness, it always produces harm for us, or inflicts suffering on others. Yet, the essence of freedom is ability to choose, evaluate, discern, and decide, even if exercised wrongly. Although the risk of error is intrinsic to freedom, God never intends, compels, or urges wrong choice, and God could not remove the incidental error inherent in genuine free choice, without destroying the very character of freedom.

Freedom is apparently so superior, paramount, and important in God's hierarchy of values that in order to endow all men with freedom, He will even allow an individual man freely and willingly to lose his salvation, and condemn himself to an eternity without God. God has chosen not to withdraw freedom because of its potential for harm; but to empower and train men in the proper and responsible use of freedom, to accomplish God's plans and purposes.

Despite the possibility of corrupt consequences by the perverse use of freedom, God exercises self-restraint, honors His concession of authority to believers, and tolerates, corrects, and works for good, any results of man's abuse of freedom. God honors His gift of participation, despite the potential of incidental harm or loss to men. Genuine choice defines freedom, and freedom curtailed is no freedom at all. Pre-determined or forced results would mean choice has been eliminated for the actor, which would erase freedom to respond to God out of love.

God blesses His children with freedom to respond, collaborate, and participate in seven divine processes intended to benefit the believer and others. When we freely and willingly receive and apply these seven blessings, we will know joy, for they enhance our fellowship with God; express our love toward others; and develop our spiritual capacities to enjoy more abundant life. Irresponsibly choosing to disdain the blessings in our exercise of freedom, produces suffering for oneself and others, as it harms our fellowship, love, and development of holiness. Thus, the first blessing is freedom; itself, to participate by obediently and rightly choosing to cooperate in all of God's revealed plans and purposes.

The second blessing is freedom to respond to God's grace by the exercise of faith or belief in the promises of God contained in Scripture. Faith is also a blessing bestowed by God upon believers, by which man is authorized to invite and activate God's power. God promises many things to believers through the Holy Scriptures, which reveal His plans and purposes for believers. When a person believes what God's Word has promised, and that it is intended for and applies to him, he is privileged to appropriate and invoke personally that promise for his benefit. God gives every believer a measure of faith, and that faith comes by hearing the Word. Faith becomes operative when we trust God to act according to His Word, with every expectation and reliance that God will perform His revealed intent, when we petition Him to intervene in our lives. By faith we activate, evoke, effectuate, and petition for the promised blessings of God's Word.

Thus, it is by God's grace through faith we begin the Christian life by trusting God's promise of a New Birth when we personally accept Jesus as Lord and Saviour of sinners. By faith, God authorizes us to seek and expect His designated activities of healing, prosperity, deliverance, or any promise expressed in His Word. Yet, if we fail to exercise that free choice to accept Jesus, we are cut off from the New Birth, baptism into the Body of Christ, and all other blessings promised believers for the abundant life in Christ, here and Hereafter.

If we fail to exercise faith because we do not believe God's promises extend to us, or because we cannot believe God intends to be so merciful and gracious to sinners, we cannot receive the benefits which God has promised to us or to others through us. We may even be responsible for affliction in the world from lack and deprivation allowed to continue because our faith was never applied to benefit others according to God's plan. For without faith, we and others may have not, because we asked not.

The third blessing is sustained obedience to all of God's commands, which guide, develop, and position us along God's way, for the fuller, more abundant life of divine blessings. God intends freedom to be used responsibly and in obedience to God's instructions. Obedience to God's Word expresses and evidences one's faith in God's will, and acknowledges His superior intelligence and wisdom, which entitle Him to guide and direct our conduct. We are promised blessings when we are obedient, and denial of blessings when we are stubbornly disobedient and rebelliously out of God's will for us. There are harmful consequences for disobedient wrong-doing, as well as rewards for obedient right-doing, and our carnal expressions of unforgiveness, hatred, envy, strife, jealousy, pride, and self-righteousness will interfere with our blessings.

The fourth blessing God has given man is the privilege of prayer, or direct contact with God, by which we draw comfort, courage, wisdom, and power to defend and maintain holiness and fulfill every blessing bestowed by God. The privilege of prayer is a conferral of dignity upon man by allowing and entrusting him to participate in promoting the welfare of oneself or another by inviting the resources and power of God to effect change, whether it be salvation, health, prosperity, or relief from affliction, guilt, bereavement, or persecution.

God allows us the privilege of intercessory prayer offered on behalf of and for the good of others by seeking God's intervention to supply their needs and bless them. God wills only good for all men, and delegates its effectuation to faithful men in prayer. God has promised to answer our prayers offered in faith when they are in accord with His will. Our prayers can invite Him to intervene in worldly affairs in answer to prayer. When we are filled with God's love, we yearn to share His love and goodness with others, especially the afflicted, down-trodden, and unsaved. Such intercessions are selfless and other-oriented. Their motive is not personal gain, but love for others, which blesses us with experiencing the love of God, and the joy of sharing that gift with another.

Man's involvement in prayer does not prevent God from relieving or delivering another person despite man's neglect to pray. God is able to factor into His Sovereign governance of Creation the effect of believers' prayers freely offered up, and His will and purposes will always be accomplished, despite man's failure to pray. Yet, since God has called us to trigger or invite His intervention in the world through our prayers, who knows how much healing, prosperity, deliverance, or salvation has been delayed, lost or denied because we failed to respond freely and responsibly to God's delegation of authority through prayer.

The fifth blessing from God is the Body of Christ, the Church of all believers in the Lord, from which a believer can draw strength in the unity, gifts, and fruit of the indwelling Holy Spirit. In turn, God allows His children to be exalted by fulfilling the Great Commission to witness to others about the Good News of salvation for sinners by grace through faith in Jesus. We are privileged to participate joyfully in the authentic, modern miracle of spiritual New Birth, whenever unsaved men are convicted, converted, regenerated, and made new men. The Church is given authority over all the power of the evil one, and ordained to loose those in bondage to sin, by witnessing the Gospel to the unsaved, and freeing those who respond to God's grace.

Yet, if we do not share the Good News of the Gospel with the unsaved, they may never come to know Christ personally, We will have left them in their natural, sinful, and carnal state, unchanged by the transforming love of Christ, and pre-disposed to be unloving and resentful toward Christians. If we do not obey the Great Commission, we will be surrounded by an unbelieving, sinful world, and persecuted for the Word's sake when we do venture to witness, worship, or exert the moral authority of Christ.

The sixth blessing with which God entrusts His children is the service of Good Stewardship; actively ministering good to the needs of others, both saved and unsaved, by sharing the love and other resources provided by God. A steward knows he holds God's blessings in trust as a co-worker for God's glory, by sharing and distributing to others as they have need; as agents of, and in the name of Jesus. As in all obedience, we are immediately rewarded with the joy of giving; of rightly using God's gifts as he directs, as we seek to please and glorify Him by conforming to his will. We also participate in God's love by sharing it with others, so that we enjoy a special, close experience of God, Who is love, as we are immersed in His love through giving. Even as we are blessed, we are called to bless others by sharing.

God provides abundance so we may do good works. Blessings are to accomplish God's purposes of sharing spiritual values and gifts with others, and not exclusively for one's own comfort or personal advantage. There is no prosperity apart from serving God in good stewardship. There is no reaping of what we sow in faith without motives of gratitude to God and love for others, rather than selfishness and avarice. God will not favor His child who selfishly indulges his own passion in disregard of his stewardship to share God's blessings with others.

When we fail to render mercy and compassion to the suffering and bereaved, or fill any lack of the needy in the world, we have denied them the love God intends to impart through us. For, He has constituted and empowered us as His agents by use of spiritual and material gifts, to facilitate another's relief and release from privation, disappointment, frustration, and guilt. Clearly, God will always fulfill His will, with or without our participation, but who can measure the suffering and lack caused by our resistance, reluctance, recalcitrance, or sloth in heeding God's call to stewardship and spreading the blessings of the Lord to others.

The seventh blessing from God is our privilege to participate in the acceleration and perfecting of our actual holiness and righteousness. As we are progressively transformed to the likeness of Christ, we are better fitted to enjoy more abundant life and fellowship with God and other believers, which Jesus promised. There is no question that God's power alone accomplishes our growth in righteousness. He begins the process of holiness with our regeneration and completes it with our glorification in the Hereafter. In the interim process of sanctification, He allows man to collaborate in becoming literally and increasingly like Jesus. It seems likely God grants this grace to promote man's dignity through participation and sharing in the divine activity of holiness, rather than simply bestowing unlearned, unearned, and finished qualities of Christ-like character upon us. He allows us to experience the joy of accomplishment in the creative process of our spiritual transformation, and to cherish that for which we have worked and to which we have contributed. Just as we had to choose to embrace Jesus as Lord and Saviour, we must also choose to become like Him in this life by being receptive to the transforming work of the Holy Spirit, and striving to be pure.

If we are obedient to God's commands and try to think, speak, and act like Jesus, our spiritual lives will be fuller and richer in this world because they are in harmony with God's purposes. We are also specifically promised rewards in heaven for obedience in righteousness. If we do not collaborate in growing holy, we forfeit mature enjoyment of God's fellowship here on earth, and we may fail to set the best example for others who observe our Christian walk. When we neglect obedience in righteousness, neither will we store treasures in Heaven. We may all be glorified and perfect in Heaven, but one would expect a perfect gold piece to be of more value to God than a perfect copper penny, fashioned by the extent of our cooperation here on earth. When we fail to collaborate in sanctification from the Holy Spirit, we lose access to spiritual blessings, and invite suffering, since God must then refine our character and prune away the sin in our lives by corrective discipline. The sooner we learn the lessons of chastisement contained in the suffering which comes our way, the sooner we will ease our suffering.

Because we are called to cooperate in our growth in holiness, we will experience the discomforts and sufferings of training which are intrinsic to the very process of developing purity which God entrusts to believers. Just as boxers, athletes and marines must prepare rigorously to become qualified and ready, so Christians must be trained for spiritual struggle in the world. We need to be strengthened and steeled for our encounters in battle, struggle, resistance, danger, sacrifice and persecution inherent in a world which constantly tempts the flesh away from the righteousness for which we contend.

Although a believer is no longer compelled to sin, he is still tied to sin by the temptations of the fleshly body in which his new spiritual being resides. A believer's flesh is still susceptible to the allures of the world, the flesh, and the devil; of wealth, power, success, prestige, sex, and pride. The world's attractions can impede one's spiritual growth, so we need God's grace to empower our resistance to the ongoing enticements and struggles of this world. We need to be trained for combat with evil, and the thorough discipline required is intrinsically painful. If we ignore our training, we will never achieve the necessary proficiency in this world to attain the goal of personal holiness. If we seek the Kingdom of God and His righteousness, we must experience the hardships of growing to spiritual maturity, but the result is well worth the effort.

Evil and affliction are not the determiner of our destiny, but God is! Whatever the origin of our suffering, it is a great comfort to know that if God did not expressly send, orchestrate, manipulate, or intend it, He will divert or modify potential harm and work all things for ultimate advantage and good for those who love Him and walk according to His purposes.

If we continue to have faith God's blessings will come in His own, good time, then we can focus on the lessons He would have us learn during the delay in answering prayer or providing blessings. We can better appreciate the need for discipline in discipleship. We can have confidence that God is aware of our exact status, and will provide precisely what we need, neither too early nor late, according to His timetable. He will be there in your sorrow: never too late to be of comfort, nor too early to provide what you do not yet need.

While all temptations and most afflictions are the product of human and demonic origin, God has revealed His benevolent intent to use chastening, chastisement, testing, and training to promote the spiritual and eternal good of His children. Because God's nature is perfectly good we may be sure any punishment He originates, or allows toward wrongdoers cannot be evil or unjust, but intended for some higher good purpose. God's Judgment on sinners must be affirmed or it would mean nothing. His Justice must be demonstrated or it would have no deterrent effect on sinful conduct. The extermination of unrepentant, unredeemably wicked men at the time of Noah, Sodom and Gommorah both satisfied God's Justice, and preserved His Church pure and free from the contamination, gangrene or cancer of Godless beings.

While the consequences may inflict substantial damage upon the ones being penalized, God always exercises great restraint and forbearance, with clear warnings and opportunity to repent, before administering punishment to evildoers. He has provided Jesus as the Saviour by Whom our sins can be forgiven and forgotten, and proclaimed His wish that all men come to repentance and to Jesus for salvation. He spares sinners even up to the midnight hour, so each may have full opportunity to hear and respond to God's grace through faith in Jesus.

Nevertheless, in the interim, while God mercifully and lovingly forbears in applying His Justice against rebellious sinners, the evil they perpetrate against others continues to inflict harm, suffering, and persecution in the world. Indeed, if God eliminated all evil which existed at any given moment, He would also destroy those unsaved sinners who would later come to repentance, conversion, and forgiveness in Christ. Yet, God's benevolent intent to give sinners every opportunity to be saved, has the intrinsic hazard of allowing ongoing suffering to be initiated by unredeemed men.

When our sins harm us or others, God may lovingly inflict pain and deprivations to deter repetition of the sin which destroys character. When we are forced to take responsibility and suffer from our own actions, we are chastened, chastised, instructed, corrected, and rehabilitated so as not to repeat such sinful conduct. God may require the worldly hardship of making restitution and reparation to our victims. He may send failure to crush prideful arrogance, self-sufficiency, and other ungodly traits we may be developing. He may use delay to cultivate patience, or humiliation to develop humility.

He may use travails as a chisel to transform us to the likeness of Christ, or as a force to develop and train our resistance to evil. Whether or not God ignites the fire or flame of suffering, He will use it to refine us into the holy children He intends us to be.

God may deny blessings and visit suffering and persecution on believers to strengthen their faith by trying and testing it. Faith is especially needed in helpless situations where deliverance by human contrivance is impossible, and we can rely upon the Lord alone for rescue. Much faith is born out of seemingly incurable misery and absence of worldly means for relief. God may be driving us, through the desperation of our plight, to remember Him, cultivate trust in Him as our last resort, and strengthen our faith in Him.

God may send the trials we encounter to help us see how far we have come in our faith, or how great the distance yet to be traversed. Suffering may seem inconsequential in the world, and yet have cosmic implications. Job never understood why he fell victim to so many misfortunes. Yet, God was proving Job's faithfulness through his tribulations, and Job responded by focusing his total trust in God, regardless of what happened. Trials can make us appreciate that God is our greatest ally in the transformation of character, and we are empowered to grow from faith to faith when we rely on Him and spend increasing time with Him.

God may use pain to turn our attention to Him so we can rediscover the sweet pleasures of His fellowship and communion. He may knock us flat on our backs to force us to look upwards and remember His presence and our need for Him and His comfort, wisdom, and strength. Presuming upon God's love for easy forgiveness can lead to the ruinous attitude that it is easy to escape consequences, which makes it easier to yield to sin the next time we are tempted.

God may allow some suffering so He can be glorified by His deliverance of the one afflicted. Jesus used the healing of a man blind since birth, and the raising of Lazarus from the dead to glorify God. Suffering can confirm and remind us of God's glory and grace, and stimulate an appreciation of His blessings. It can teach us to turn all our crosses into a witness of God's love and testimony of God's faithfulness toward believers and sinners. God may also allow suffering to continue in order to prove to the believer or the world, the strength of the believer's faith, and patience in affliction, enabled by the power of God's grace.

God allowed St. Paul to endure the suffering of a thorn in the flesh, delivered by a messenger of Satan, to prevent Paul from becoming too elated over the divine revelations he had received. God turned Paul's focus toward Him, and affirmed that God's strength was sufficient for Paul to overcome his suffering. God may use suffering to engender appreciation of all other blessings of God's grace enjoyed by the one afflicted, as well as those observing, but spared such affliction.

God may sustain a believer with the revelation nothing worldly is of any significance compared to Christ and the blessed hope of His return. If He does not give us the desires of our hearts, He will relieve our longing by transforming our desires to conform to His. We will want no blessings on earth, save His fellowship; we will gladly surrender our crowns in Heaven to Him, as long as we can anticipate the greatest reward of being with Him for eternity.

God may also use, though not initiate, catastrophes, natural disaster, and human negligence, producing multiple deaths and infirmities, to remind us that the wicked rebels who reject Him will be punished, and that their prospect of eternal destruction is far worse than mortal death. The reality of loss visited by natural calamities may highlight our mortality, and motivate repentance to avoid the punishment of separation from God for eternity.

Our hopes that God will give us what we ask for in the name of Jesus must always yield to our faith God can be depended upon to do what is right and in our best interests as a member in the Body of Christ. We need to replace hope that God will give us worldly blessings we desire, with faith in God as benevolent Sovereign, Who is all-wise, all-powerful, perfectly good and kind, and Who can provide for our needs or rectify the suffering and persecution inflicted by oneself and others.

May the lessons learned here enlarge our coast, so we can receive and lovingly share God's gifts of freedom, faith, obedience, intercessory prayer, witness, stewardship, and growth in holiness. May we increasingly share in the joy of other Christians' righteous and loving acts; in recognizing there are others who are right with God, serve God rightly, and rejoice in expressing God's love toward others. May these words encourage the righteous, loving response of Christians to God's grace, and transform the weeping of suffering and sorrow into tears of joy and praise as we consciously fulfill God's purposes, to His glory. May the transition from weeping at night to joy in the morning be received not only as an augury of Heaven, but a recurrent earthly event designed by God.

CHAPTER 1

A CELEBRATION OF GOD'S GOODNESS

"We know that in everything God works for good with those who love him, who are called according to his purpose... For I am sure that neither death, nor... anything else in all creation, will be able to separate us from the love of God in Christ Jesus our Lord."

— Romans 8:28–39

Whenever personal affliction visits us, or a tragedy of monstrous proportions occurs, the vulnerability of human existence is exposed, and gives rise to doubts about God's goodness or omnipotence. Terrorist attacks unfolding in the 21st Century have revived these questions, but the dilemma of evil in God's creation is not new. Victims throughout history have wondered how God could allow the ferocity and carnage wrought by the Assyrians, Mongols, Vandals, Huns, Goths and Saracens. The horrors of 20th Century death camps and genocides carved unforgettable images of human depravity which the God of the Flood would never have tolerated.

In World War II, German Nazis exterminated six million Jews, while Russian Communists eradicated two million Polish patriots. Fifty million souls were killed or wounded, and the entire world suffered massive deprivations. Even though America had won the war, a generation which had lost its innocence asked, "Where was a good, all-powerful God in the midst of all this?" Could God have really initiated or endorsed such evil as His instrument to chasten the world for some good reason, incomprehensible to man? Spiritual faith in God's revealed goodness and Sovereign power, wrestled with natural doubt and disillusion in the face of overwhelming evil, carnage, and atrocities. Was it possible God was not only impotent to prevent evil, but also irrelevant, finally overcome by the prospect of human self-sufficiency and corruption?

Throughout history, believers have seen evil men persecute Christians for their faith, and careless men injure or kill believers as randomly as non-believers. We see faithful Christians, indwelt by the Holy Spirit, denied blessings of health and prosperity contrary to God's promises in the Scriptures. Worse, we see believers throughout the world enduring unhappiness, anxiety, pain and torment as a regular part of their Christian walk. It seems likely some of the passengers aboard the ill-fated airplanes which became terrorist weapons on September 11, 2001, had embarked covered by prayers for their safety, which apparently were unheeded.

If God could be so indifferent to the needs of His people, then perhaps He could routinely be detached from the affairs of Christians and disinterested in their well being. If so, then perhaps God was also irrelevant for other practical purposes. In fact, following the horrors of World War II the exclusion of God from American experience replaced our dependence on Him, and eventually resulted in the expulsion of Godly values from public and educational activities.

A God no longer protecting His people, might also have suspended His exercise of Sovereignty, activity, or involvement in the affairs of Americans. Such a God offered no relevant laws or morality for our guidance. Consequently, without a divine moral compass, we tolerated relaxing the divorce laws; the deterioration of the family; alternative life styles where unmarried couples lived together; gay couples married; and legalized abortion which embraced a fiction that life in the womb was not human prior to birth. Godlessness also produced a drug culture; disaffection; distrust of authority by youth alienated from 'the establishment'; over a million Americans in prison; rampant sexual promiscuity and disease; pornography; gambling; and half the world ignorant of the Gospel of Christ.

This litany of how we have disobeyed and abandoned God simply recognizes the phenomenon that doubt about God's care and relevance has separated us from Him. It reminds us how much we need some clear reconciliation of pain with God's omnipotence and goodness, to explain why evil can reach even the righteous. Pain and tribulation seem incompatible with the blessings intended for believing children by a benevolent Father. Suffering seems to contradict the faith life and belie divine providence because it usually involves deprivation, denial, and loss of the material and temporal blessings we are promised by faith.

If God were only as good as the average man, He would recoil from harming others, so it is preposterous to attribute heinous acts to a God who reveals Himself as perfectly good, prodigious in His benevolence, and providential in His concern. It is inconceivable God has authored or authorized these evils, for God reveals He is perfectly good and the dispenser of only benevolence to His Creation. Yet, Since God has also revealed He is all–powerful, we wonder how He could have allowed subordinate beings to perpetrate such evils.

This chapter is not about suffering, but about God's perfect goodness, despite the apparent contradiction of affliction, persecution, and evils perpetrated in the world. God exhibits and discloses such goodness that it becomes impossible to attribute evil to Him, except by dishonest, contorted logic.

Our vulnerability to terrorism and other evils at the start of the third millennium prompts us to re–examine all our assumptions, and evokes a self–analysis, which hopefully will sustain a return to Christian activism and involvement in contesting evil in the world.

We cannot have faith in God's Word if we conclude God is dead, irrelevant, or unconcerned about human needs. We cannot depend on His deliverance if He is rendered vincible or enervated. We cannot glorify God if we believe He is irreconcilably angry because of one's sin; that He is unfair, untrustworthy, or vengeful toward believers; or that He ignores one who failed to pray or have enough faith.[1] We need a major reaffirmation of God's Sovereignty, Providence, and benevolence, more than ever in the midst of current afflictions.

Because Jesus warns us to expect and accept suffering and persecution in this world, despite being Christians, and often, because we are Christians, almost everyone has pondered why there is suffering in the world if God is both good and all–powerful. Next to the mystery of God's own beginnings, probably the most perplexing question for believers is how evil can exist in a Creation which is presided over by a perfect and perfectly good God. One possibility is that God is not omnipotent and cannot control all evil. John Stuart Mill searched for some rational reconciliation between God's goodness and apparent tolerance for evil, and concluded that God is either not good or not almighty. Either He wants to stop suffering, but cannot, or He could stop suffering but will not.

Voltaire reasoned that since God is good, yet allows evil to exist alongside good, then God must be limited in His power to control evil. Otherwise, God would destroy evil before it had opportunity to afflict man. The argument concludes that even imperfect human parents would, if they were able, save a child from his own folly by rescuing him from harm's way. Any parent who saw his child about to fall from a height would intervene to warn or physically prevent the occurrence. The parent may not have contributed to the potential risk, but if he knowingly fails to prevent it, then he has allowed it. What parent, capable of only imperfect love, would allow his child to suffer when it is in his power to relieve the cause of suffering, and the child was ignorant of, or truly repented his errors? Should we expect any less from a God of perfect love? Therefore, it is concluded, a good God would surely keep His children from evil — unless it were not in His power to do so.

At the other extreme, some conclude that God has the power to end evil, but chooses to loose it into creation and inflict it upon man. In other words, God shares the anthropomorphic human trait of being less than perfectly good. To justify this conclusion, the argument is sometimes made that the fierce God of the Old Testament resembles an ironfisted Judge, capable of bruising His creatures to punish them. Man angers God, and elicits a retributive or punitive response; vindictive, vengeful, recriminating, and retaliatory, which endorses taking an eye for an eye.

Advocates of the view that God is not always or totally good, claim the Old Testament depicts God as a vengeful Shylock, implacably collecting the last ounce of Justice due Him from sinners. They will point to His wholesale destruction of cities and nations, exhibiting an inconsideration of human life whenever it suited His purposes. They note especially the penalty exacted from Jesus to bear mankind's sins in His sacrificial atonement for every sinner's affront to God's justice.

The classic idea of punishment, unless mitigated by mercy, involves infliction of pain or suffering; the deprivation of freedom, pleasure, health, or wealth to re–pay wrongdoers with the coin of retribution. In the world, even a Christian who breaks the secular law can expect to be called to account at the bar of justice for his personal transgressions. In the vernacular of the street, "if you do the crime, then you do the time." Such punishment, no matter how deserved, will be regarded as evil and painful by one who endures it at the hands of an avenging God.

Let us keep in mind as we study these instances of God's apparent disdain or cruelty toward mankind that He was often preserving a remnant of the righteous by removing what was actually evil from their midst. Other times, what appeared to be evil, were merely the rigors inherent in the process of training for righteousness. Sometimes, it was lovingly intended as a deterrent to harmful conduct which would be otherwise freely pursued unless God made sinning a painful exercise for us. And there will be times we cannot fathom the goodness in God's discipline or chastisement because we lack capacity to discern or appreciate the transcendent and supervening good which God is working. In such cases, we must remember that God's ways and thoughts are so much higher than ours (Isaiah 55:9), and His ways are unknowable and unfathomable: "Verily thou art a God that hidest thyself" (Isaiah 45:15). Deuteronomy 29:29 says: "The secret things belong unto the Lord our God: but those things which are revealed belong to us and to our children forever, that we may do all the words of this law." We must rely on the total goodness and righteousness of His character which is revealed in His Word.

There may be more things we cannot understand than we can, when it comes to God's plans, strategies, and operations. When Job was suffering, God did not explain how Satan's accusations had prompted Job's series of ordeals. Rather, God charged Job to accept the rightness, wisdom, and omnipotence underlying whatever God had permitted to happen. He reproved Job's pride in attempting to defend or justify his innocence, which impliedly accused God of injustice. God reminded Job of how little he knew about creation, much less had any participation in fashioning it (Job 38:1–41).

God challenged Job to explain the what and how of creation: "Canst thou lift up thy voice to the clouds, that abundance of waters may cover thee? Canst thou send lightnings, that they may go... Canst thou draw out leviathan with a hook... None is so fierce that dare stir him up: who then is able to stand before me? Who hath prevented me, that I should repay him? Whatsoever is under the whole heaven is mine" (Job 38:34–35, 41:1–11). Since Job had no idea of how the physical universe was formed, though totally subservient to God, he could hardly question God's management of the moral universe. For, the power revealed in God's material creation suggests the same power is connected and available to govern wisely the spiritual realm, including coordinating man's wellbeing.

Romans 11:33–35 concludes: "O the depth of the riches and wisdom of God! How unsearchable are his judgments and how inscrutable his ways! For who has known the mind of the Lord or who has been his counselor? Or who has given a gift to him that he might be repaid?" (citing Isaiah 40:13–14).

GOD'S PROVIDENCE EQUALS HIS OMNIPOTENCE

God's goodness is inferable from the fact of creation; for if He declares the world worthy of being created by Him, then that which He was pleased to bring into existence is worthy of being sustained by Him. Providence includes the idea that God will preserve and keep in being what He was pleased to create. Christians overwhelmingly believe in God's Sovereignty, inextricably tied to his goodness: that He not only created the universe, but also preserves, governs, designs, influences, and exercises dominion over every aspect of it. He sustains, guides, and controls all creatures, developments, and sequences to their appointed end. God's will determines our destiny, and His providential purposes and plans for mankind have been clearly revealed and assured from before time.

God reveals that he intimately knew, created, and cared for each one of the billions of humans in the world, even before conception. "For thou hast possessed my reins; thou hast covered me in my mother's womb" (Psalm 139:13). Psalm 139:16 attests: "Thine eyes did see my substance, yet being unperfect: and in thy book all my members were written... when as yet there was none of them." At Jeremiah 29:11 God reveals: "I know the thoughts that I think toward you saith the Lord, thoughts of peace, and not of evil, to give you an expected end."

God has plans for each of us from our beginning to the end, and remains concerned over us as he continues to care for us. God is everywhere His children find themselves. God's sovereignty is in His providence as His caring hand touches our lives completely. Psalm 139:8–10 says: "If I ascend up into heaven, thou art there: If I make my bed in hell, behold thou art there.

If I dwell... in the uttermost parts of the sea; Even there shall thy Hand lead me, and thy right Hand shall hold me."

Although creation gives God the right of absolute control, He chooses to exercise His Sovereignty benevolently. Nehemiah 9:6 proclaims: "Thou art Lord alone; thou hast made heaven... the earth, and all things that are therein... and thou preservest them all." Job 7:20 refers to God as "preserver of men," and Psalm 36:6 recognizes: "O Lord, thou preservest man and beast." Providence incorporates the idea of God providing everything needed by his Creation (Psalms 104:27–32; 145:15–16; and 147:9; and Matthew 10:29–31).

Hebrews 1:2–3 refers to Jesus, the "Son, whom he appointed the heir of all things, through whom also he created the world. He reflects the glory of God and bears the very stamp of his nature, upholding the universe by his word of power."

God's Providence is particular, as well as general. This means that He cares for daily details, as well as eschatologic and universal tendencies, and moral triumph over evil. We may become so occupied with a general activity, that we have no time for specifics, or we may be so involved in a specific task that we ignore world events. But God is not so limited. He can attend to particular events, as well as superintend empires and worlds. In fact, the general Providence of God reaches to every particular, minute object, and event. And the particular Providence of God becomes general because it embraces every particular.[2] God neglects neither the government of the world, nor the welfare of the individual. His general and particular Providence are so intertwined, that one cannot exist without the other.

Consequently, God's providence orders all events: directs the destiny of mankind, regulates good and evil, establishes the time and place of one's birth, in which we have absolutely no say; sets occurrences during life, and the time and manner of our death. (See Hebrews 9:27 and Psalm 103:15). Consequently, we must look elsewhere than God's deficiency, if we are to find a reconciliation of evil in the world with God's goodness and power. For, if God is so gracious in His loving ministrations toward man, then we can trust His benevolence with our lives and future. The One who knows you best, still loves you most, despite your faults. God never tires of giving His best and seeks us out to do it. His spiritual gifts are magnificent, and He, "By the power at work within us is able to do far more abundantly than all that we ask or think" (Ephesians 3:20).

God's intention for His creature, man, is awesomely benign: "For he has made known to us in all wisdom and insight the mystery of his will, according to his purpose which he set forth in Christ, as a plan for the fullness of time, to unite all things in him, things in heaven and things on earth" (Ephesians 1:9–10).

The well–being and blessings of creatures are determined by the character of their Creator. A Creator Who is disinterested and forsakes his creation, or worse, is malevolent and tortures his creatures, will be the provider of few blessings and comforts. But a Creator Who is perfect life, light, and love, as God is revealed to be (John 1:4, 5:26; I John 1:5, 4:8, 4:16), can intend and provide only good things for His creation. His life preserves, rather than destroys. His light illumines and shares knowledge, rather than confuses or confounds. And His love is expressed in Providence, grace, benevolence, and deliverance of His creatures from their own folly. All sin results from demonic or human activity: our own or that of others, initiated by creatures exercising the freedom allowed by God.

God is inherently incapable of initiating or endorsing temptations to sin, from which most suffering proceeds. His nature and works cannot have or be intended to have, any hatred, death, or darkness in them. James 1:13 declares that God does not use temptations to sin in the spiritual rearing of His children: "Let no man say when he is tempted, I am tempted of God; for God cannot be tempted with evil, neither tempteth he any man." God may use a trial to test the faith or obedience of a child, but it is Satan who turns the test into a worldly temptation. However, even when we are tempted by the world, the flesh and the devil, God empowers our resistance: "No temptation has overtaken you that is not common to man. God is faithful, and he will not let you be tempted beyond your strength, but with the temptation will also provide the way of escape, that you may be able to endure it" (I Corinthians 10:13).

The Old Testament declares that God is perfectly and totally good. Psalm 5:4–5 declares: "For thou art not a God that hath pleasure in wickedness; neither shall evil dwell with thee... thou hatest all workers of iniquity." Psalm 31:19 proclaims: "oh how great is thy goodness, which thou hast laid up for them that fear thee." Psalm 34:8 invites: "O taste and see that the Lord is good: blessed is the man that trusteth in him." Psalm 52:1 says: "the goodness of God endureth continually." Psalm 107:8 declares: "Oh that men would praise the Lord for his goodness, and for his wonderful works to the children of light." Jeremiah 31:14 adds: "my people shall be satisfied with my goodness, saith the Lord." (See also, Genesis 18:25; I Chronicles 16:34; Lamentations 3:25; Proverbs 21:12; Psalms 45:7, 69:16; Zechariah 9:17; Romans 12:2; 2 Thessalonians 1:11; and I Timothy 4:4).

It is self–evident that God, Who is perfectly good, is incapable of any evil which might harm His creation or creatures. Jesus puts it: "A sound tree cannot bear evil fruit, nor can a bad tree bear good fruit" (Matthew 7:19). Jesus proclaims: "there is none good but one, that is, God" (Matthew 19:17 KJV). God's perfect goodness absolutely prevents Him from doing anything evil. He cannot tolerate looking upon sin, and even turned away from Jesus when he bore all of mankind's sins on the Cross, causing Jesus to cry out: "My God, my God, why hast thou forsaken me?" (Matthew 27:46). God's desire is that "the wicked turn from his way and live" (Ezekiel 33:11); and God in his goodness, always warns the wicked before visiting destruction upon them (Proverbs 29:1; Ezekiel 3:19, 33:8).

It is impossible to reconcile God's perfect goodness with evils which are senseless and contrary to God's loving character. Thus, most suffering cannot originate in God's Sovereign will for the very reason that any evil consequences totally conflict with His nature. God cannot have intended or instigated every affliction which befalls man, because we cannot ascribe really harmful acts to God, which are totally inconsistent with His revealed goodness. In defense of God's absolute sovereignty we ought not be driven to ridiculous extremes which attribute horrible tragedies to the design of a loving, caring Father.

God's Word is clear that He "hatest all workers of iniquity" (Psalm 5:5). He hates wicked thoughts (Zechariah 8:17; Proverbs 6:18). God "lovest righteousness, and hatest wickedness" (Psalm 45:7; see also, Psalm 26:5). If you trust in God, "The Lord shall preserve thee from all evil" (Psalm 121:7; see also, Isaiah 57:1; Galatians 1:4; 2 Timothy 4:18; and 2 Thessalonians 3:3). Jesus prays that His followers be kept by God "from the evil one" (John 17:15). He teaches us to pray God "deliver us from evil" (Matthew 6:13), and Jesus would never prescribe futile prayers for us.

Psalm 97:10 instructs believers: "Ye that love the Lord, hate evil." The righteous are to hate evil and love good; to do good even to those who hate them; and to hate corruption because it violates God's Law (Proverbs 8:13, 11:23, 16:6; Amos 5:14,15; 2 Kings 21:16; Psalm 34:14; Jeremiah 7:31; 3 John 11; Jude 23; and Matthew 5:44). I John 3:4 says: "Sin is the transgression of the law." Sin is defined as "doing that which was evil <u>in the sight of the Lord</u>" (2 Kings 21:16), and sin is primarily against God "Against thee, thee only, have I sinned, and done this evil in thy sight" (Psalm 51:4).

God twice declined to harm Job, rejecting Satan's incitations to put forth His hand against His faithful servant (Job 1:11–12, 2:5–6). God remonstrated with Job's friends for wrongly attributing Job's suffering to God (Job 42:7). Satan initiated Job's suffering, although only to the extent allowed by God (Job 1:11–12; 2:4–6). Satan tries to deceive men that God is the cause of evil which Satan has initiated.

Human love can be lustful, consuming, self–gratifying, and exploitive of its object of affection. But God's love is always perfect, graciously benefiting the beloved, and a testament to God's perfect goodness. God never lies (Titus 1:2), and in Him "There is no variation or shadow due to change" (James 1:17). God avows at Job 36:4: "For truly my words shall not be false."

CREATION AFFECTED BY MAN'S FALL

After God had created man, and blessed him, "God saw every thing that he had made, and, behold, it was very good" (Genesis 1:31). A sinless Adam was included in God's appraisal of His creation as "very good." God intended man to enjoy happiness, harmony, and fellowship with Him in the Garden of Eden. Adam was created in God's image and likeness, filled with God's own life, that he might have a life as much like God's as was possible for a created being. The original creation provided only bliss, innocence, freedom from pain, and exemption from death for man. God bestowed His grace for peace, happiness, comfort, guidance, and protection upon Adam and Eve and gave them dominion over the earth (Genesis 1:28). "And God blessed them and said unto them, Be fruitful, and multiply, and replenish the earth, and subdue it; and have dominion over... every living thing that moveth upon the earth" (Genesis 1:28).

Although this original loving relationship between God and man was impregnable against external assault, it could be shattered by Adam's disloyalty through disobedience. Adam could signify his desire for God by trusting God's word and obediently submitting to His will. Conversely, disobedience and disloyalty indicated Adam honored some lesser value above God's guidance, grace and love. God not only gave Adam dominion over the Garden, but also told him "to dress it and <u>to keep it</u>" (Genesis 2:15), implying there were forces of deterioration against which Adam must be alert. The principal destructor was Satan, against whom Adam should have been on guard in God's first test ever of man's fidelity.

Man is identified as the corrupter of his innate goodness: "God hath made man upright; but they have sought out many inventions" (Ecclesiastes 7:29). I Timothy 4:4 affirms that "everything created by God is good." Adam was invested with genuine freedom of choice in the Garden of Eden, but he was capable of wrongly exercising his freedom by choosing wrongly. When Adam disobeyed God, he fell from God's grace, and could not extricate himself from the consequences of sin without a Savior. Consequently, New Testament salvation does not jettison Genesis, since it is not possible to understand the need for individual re–creation without understanding the Fall of man in Adam. It is not possible to understand the need for a Savior, without understanding the sin from which we must be rescued.

God had warned Adam that he may not eat of the tree of the knowledge of good and evil, "for in the day that thou eatest thereof thou shalt surely die" (Genesis 2:17). Tasting of this tree held peril for Adam because in his pre–fall state of innocence, he perceived only good in everything. But acquisition of knowledge about good and evil would make Adam aware of choices between them, and provide opportunities to depart from total reliance on God's benevolent counsel. Adam would make decisions and mistakes according to his own imperfect knowledge, by presuming to be as wise as God, and no longer needing to consult God.

Satan, the father of liars, deceived Eve and said that she and Adam would not die if they ate of the forbidden tree, but "be as gods" (Genesis 3:5). Adam and Eve succumbed to an appetite to eat something forbidden; to a lust for power to be as God, knowing good and evil; and to a desire to accomplish something independently, although specifically forbidden by God. By yielding to the serpent's temptations to be as gods, Adam exhibited pride, repudiated God's commandment not to eat of the tree, and asserted a rebellious self–sufficiency apart from God. Adam had become a sinner, by showing loss of faith in, and stubborn contempt for, God's guidance. For, "sin is lawlessness" (I John 3:4), and Adam's disobedience to God broke fellowship with a righteous, faithful, and loving God. Loss of fellowship with God was a consequence of sin, initiated by man's guilt. Adam was aware of his disobedience, and knew guilt and fear for the first time. He severed his relationship with God symbolically by hiding in the Garden to conceal his newly appreciated nakedness (Genesis 3:8).

Each participant in original, sinful disobedience was punished for disregarding God's laws. God cursed Satan: "I will put enmity between thee and the woman, and between thy seed and her seed; it shall bruise thy head, and thou shalt bruise his heel" (Genesis 3:15). "Unto the woman he said, I will greatly multiply thy sorrow and thy conception; in sorrow thou shalt bring forth children" (Genesis 3:16). "And unto Adam he said... Cursed is the ground for thy sake; in sorrow shalt thou eat of it all the days of thy life" (Genesis 3:17; see also, Hebrews 9:23). Adam and Eve were expelled from the Garden, denied access to the tree of life, and to God's grace and protection. Yet, at the same time, redemption was mercifully granted, since God promised the bruising of Satan's head by Jesus, the seed of woman (Genesis 3:15).

As a result of Adam's original sin and Fall, "sin came into the world through one man and death through sin, and so death spread to all men because all men sinned" (Romans 5:12; and see I Corinthians 15:22). Satan seized dominion over the earth and all mankind. Ephesians 2:1–3 reveals that even Christians formerly "were dead through the trespasses and sins in which you once walked, following the course of this world, following the prince of the power of the air, the spirit that is now at work in the sons of disobedience. Among these we all once lived in the passions of our flesh, following the desires of body and mind, and so we were by nature children of wrath, like the rest of mankind."

Only those in Christ escape this subservience to Satan in the world. Ephesians 2:12 reminds us that all men without Christ "were at that time separated from Christ, alienated from the commonwealth of Israel, and strangers to the covenants of promise, having no hope and without God in the world." Jesus characterized the Jews who rejected him as evil, and "of your father the devil, and your will is to do your father's desires" (John 8:44). St Paul observed: "for I have already charged that all men, both Jews and Greeks, are under the power of sin... None is righteous, no, not one" (Romans 3:9–10). Until we are converted by the Gospel, we remain children of the devil. Indeed, "the whole world is in the power of the evil one" (I John 5:19, and see also, Romans 7:23, 8:23; Ephesians 5:8; Colossians 1:13; and Titus 3:3).

Satan apparently had legitimate authority over the world when he tempted Jesus on the mountain and offered, without being challenged, to "give... him all the kingdoms of the world and the glory of them" (Matthew 4:8). Satan was able to afflict Job in the world, albeit with God's permission, granted for purposes of vindicating Job's faith. Satan had power to afflict Peter, according to Jesus: "Simon, Simon, behold, Satan demanded to have you, that he might sift you like wheat, but I have prayed for you that your faith may not fail; and when you have turned again, strengthen your brethren" (Luke 22:31–32).

I Peter 5:8 warns believers: "Be sober, be watchful. Your adversary the devil prowls around like a roaring lion, seeking someone to devour." Ephesians 6:12 confirms that "we are not contending against flesh and blood, but against the principalities, against the powers, against the world rulers of this present darkness, against the spiritual hosts of wickedness in the heavenly places." Hebrews 2:14 recognizes "him who has the power of death, that is, the devil." 2 Corinthians 4:4 refers to the "god of this world (who) has blinded the minds of the unbelievers, to keep them from seeing the light of the gospel of the glory of Christ." Jesus compares Satan to a thieving bird who snatches the Word of God from a man and devours the seeds of salvation "sown in his heart," so they would not take root and bear fruit (Matthew 13:19).

Church Fathers, such as Origin, Irenaeus and Augustine saw that sin imposed a double servitude. The disobedience of man's fall was not only a process of detachment from holiness and deprivation of God's fellowship and gifts, but also a bondage to sin by attachment to Satan, the instigator of sin. By turning from God, man did not become his own master, but lost his freedom, falling captive to evil powers. Man became subordinate to Satan, ensnared, and in servitude by trusting Satan's lie rather than God's truth. Instead of subduing the earth, as originally directed by God, man became an addict and a slave to its harvest as he wrongly used grain and fruit for alcohol, plants for narcotics, and tobacco for smoking.

The Bible does not specify the mechanism by which Satan seized dominion of the earth from Adam. It may be that Adam forfeited supernatural gifts of sanctifying grace, virtue, and integrity which he had originally enjoyed, and without which, mankind was doomed to sin repeatedly, because helpless against the wiles and power of Satan. Genetic discoveries that DNA in every cell carries the blueprint for life, by which characteristics are transmitted from one generation to another, help explain how sin could have become inherently and constituently a defect in fallen man, so that by inherited nature he became a sinner. His will had become vulnerable to the flood of insatiable worldly appetites and sensual temptations which Adam had released by deliberately surrendering to temptation. Man's fallen nature then developed with an innate pre–disposition and predilection to sinfulness. It may be that Adam had faith in, and submitted to Satan's contrary assurances and thereby preferred and exalted his counsel and rule over that of God. Perhaps Adam's doubt, distrust, and disobedience to God constituted a transfer of allegiance as he chose to believe in the word of Satan rather than of God.

THE PROBLEM WITH SIN

Sinful man needed to be saved in many ways. He needed to be rescued or ransomed from the power of Satan to whom he had relinquished the earth. He needed to be transformed in his sin nature, released from his bondage to sin, isolation, and loneliness, and made constituently righteous. But above all, sin had alienated man from a righteous God, and man needed to be restored to fellowship and right relationship with God. Isaiah 59:2 proclaims: "Your sins have hid His face from you, that he will not hear." A sinner's heart is "evil from his youth" (Genesis 8:21). "For there is no man that sinneth not" (I Kings 8:45). "They are all together become filthy: there is none that doeth good, no, not one" (Psalms 14:3, 53:3). Isaiah 64:6 concludes: "But we are all as an unclean thing, and all our righteousnesses are as filthy rags." See also, Psalms 51:5, 58:3; Proverbs 20:9; Ecclesiastes 7:20; Jeremiah 17:9; and Isaiah 48:8.

Man's predicament as a sinner was necessitated by God's Justice. God's Word could never be authoritative if He overlooked man's transgressions of disobedience. God's promises of reward for obedience would lose all significance if His condemnation for disobedience was not fulfilled. Classic Christian doctrine taught that Justice requires propitiation for man's sin against God, and appeasement of His anger against sinners by some reparation. In the Middle Ages, Anselm of Canterbury taught that sinful man needed to make satisfaction for his offense to God's honor and dignity, because when he scorned God's commands, and relied upon authority inferior to God, he detracted from the glory which God intended for His creation.

Thomas Aquinas explained that sin created a disorder of justice when man unduly indulged his own will. There could be no forgiveness until equilibrium in the order of justice was restored through the sinner suffering something he does not will. Justice could be satisfied only by punishment as a compensation for pleasure wrongfully taken in sin. Punishment for evil committed is deserved strictly on the basis of the wrongdoer's lack of merit. The connecting link between punishment and justice is its being deserved; a retaliation whereby a sinner receives just desserts for his conduct.[3]

We seem to know intuitively that a truly evil man ought to be punished for his unrepented wrongdoing. The sadistic torturer of a death camp who remains impenitent deserves torment and torture for the suffering he has inflicted on others. The child molester who has gratified his own lusts without concern for the damage inflicted upon innocent children, has so disturbed the order of decency that he ought to be denied his own liberty. The terrorist who wantonly inflicts agonies on innocent victims and their families deserves retaliation in kind.

Moreover, fairness and equity are part of God's Justice, since He warns men against prohibited acts, and discloses the consequences of sin. He warned Adam death was the consequence of disobedience if he ate of the tree. Jesus assures us that divine punishment is always fair and rational, that the "servant who knew his master's will, but did not make ready or act according to his will, shall receive a severe beating. But he who did not know, and did what deserved a beating, shall receive a light beating" (Luke 12:47–48; and see Numbers 15:29–30; Deuteronomy 25:2–3).

Jesus' death on the Cross is proof of God's Justice and righteousness. It affirms God's sovereign, implacable decree that sin must be punished and the penalty paid by someone to satisfy God's Justice. Punishment could not be diverted from sinners without the propitiation of a sinless victim who would suffer in the place of sinners. In the death of Christ, God punished and condemned sin through the flesh of His Own Son, in the sight of men, angels, and demons. God's Justice had to be satisfied before His wrath could be turned away from sinners in mercy. Grace was extended to sinners, but only after the full penalty due for sin had been paid by innocent blood, "the righteous for the unrighteous" (I Peter 3:18).

The death of Christ is proof of the holy justice and wrath of God against sin as much as it demonstrates His love and grace in extending mercy. While God is always compassionate toward the repentant sinner, He is unyielding about the sin. He never lets us down when we are mired in sin, but He never lets us off if we are impenitent about it. God reveals that He exercises and delights in "loving kindness, judgment, and righteousness, in the earth" (Jeremiah 9:24). Psalm 62:11–12 affirms God's power, justice, and mercy in perfect combination: "Power belongeth unto God. Also unto thee, O Lord, belongeth mercy: for thou renderest to every man according to his work."

God has tempered His justice with mercy. He has wiped out the sinner's sins and allowed for His reinstatement in Christ. However, if a sinner stubbornly resists God's mercy through Christ, he must pay for his own sins to satisfy God's Justice. God has provided forgiveness, but if sinners choose to reject God's solution, refuse to recognize their own sin or acknowledge their need for the Saviour, then God can only honor their free choice to be left alone, and that is what hell is.[4] Hell is the result of man's free choice and not of God's consignment there, for God has provided full pardon by grace through faith in Christ.

However, mercy spurned leaves a sinner to his own devices to confront inevitable Justice. The sinner who rejects the shelter of cover by the Blood of Christ will ultimately recognize that he must stand in the defectible, sin–stained vestments of his own iniquity. He who pridefully rejects the substitutionary Atonement of Christ has himself chosen to pay the penalty of death for his sins. He must meet God's Justice by himself, by his own choice, and he must fall in the condemnation of his own lack of merit. 2 Corinthians 5:10 says "we must all appear before the judgment seat of Christ; so that each one may receive good or evil, according to what he has done in the body." What one "Has done in the body" refers not to works, but to his response to receive Jesus.

We are doomed to hell without Jesus, and while this is not a popular message, it is communicated out of love. Should not a loved one be spared a terrible fate, and blessed with the greatest gift of the Gospel of salvation in Christ Jesus? If one person knew another was moving toward dire peril, all but the most depraved would warn him of the danger ahead, out of common humanity. Thus, we pass on the warning of Hell for the lost, in a spirit of God's love for sinners.

There is no question God has the power to punish the wicked: "For the wrath of God is revealed from heaven against all ungodliness and wickedness of men who by their wickedness suppress the truth" (Romans 1:18). Jesus warns: "And do not fear those who kill the body but cannot kill the soul; rather fear him who can destroy both soul and body in hell" (Matthew 10:28). Hell should create no discomfort or ambivalence about God's perfect goodness, for He has provided a free gift of salvation in Jesus, and no one proceeds to hell except by his own choice. Satan would deceive sinners to believe there is no hell, in order to dilute their motivation to accept the Gospel, and destroy their incentive to live rightly and accept Jesus as Lord and Savior.

Yet, Jesus says Hell is a real place reserved for rebellious and impenitent sinners (Matthew 3:12, 5:29, 10:28, 13:41–42, 18:9, 23:33; Luke 16:23; and John 15:5–6). Christian eschatology culminates in the destruction of all evil, when the devil, death, and Hades are "thrown into the lake of fire" (Revelation 19:20–21, 20:8–15). Psalm 9:17 forecasts: "The wicked shall be turned into hell, and all the nations that forget God." Isaiah 13:9 warns of the Lord's "wrath and fierce anger" when He lays "the land desolate; and he shall destroy the sinners thereof out of it."

A merciful God may not torture the unsaved in a literal hellfire for eternity, but evil doers will certainly be in conscious torment and aware of separation from God after death, according to Matthew 8:12, 25:30–46; Luke 13:28; and the Parables of the Marriage Feast (Matthew 22:1–4), The Wicked Servant (Matthew 24:51); and of the Rich Man and Lazarus (Luke

16:19). But God must execute the death sentence on every impenitent rebel who has chosen it by disdaining His proffered salvation by grace through faith in Jesus.

Hebrews 10:28–29 asks, if "A man who has violated the law of Moses dies without mercy... How much worse punishment do you think will be deserved by the man who has spurned the Son of God?" The revelation of Hell as the destination of unredeemed sinners is God's persuasion to choose salvation in Christ freely, and not reject God's grace provided at such great cost to Jesus. The penalty of hell, so rightly deserved by sinners can thus be avoided. God has not consigned the impenitent sinner to Hell and His revelations have clearly warned sinners of the consequences of free choice so abused.

GOD'S SUSTAINED GOODNESS DESPITE MAN'S SIN

After the Fall of Adam, human history is a revelation of man's continual sin, and God's patience, forgiveness, forbearance, and goodness despite man's sin. God continued to bless Adam and Eve, and aptly "clothed them" before He expelled them from Eden (Genesis 3:21). Actually, forbidding them access to the tree of life was an act of loving mercy since God did not want them or their progeny to exist eternally in their fallen state. It was necessary that man be made new and holy before he received immortality. God also blessed Adam and Eve with sons, Cain, Abel and Seth, and allowed their offspring to populate the earth.

Similarly, when Cain killed Abel, his brother, God in His Sovereignty punished Cain with exile and deprivations, yet God in His Providence preserved Cain's life in the land of Nod, East of Eden (Genesis 4:16).

In no time at all, mankind, with the exception of Noah, had become so depraved it was beyond redemption, as every father trained his sons in wickedness. Genesis 6:5 explains God's reason for destroying mankind: "God saw that the wickedness of man was great in the earth, and that every imagination of the thoughts of his heart <u>was only evil continually</u>." God gave men 120 years to repent and avoid Judgment but "every" thought was evil "continually." Hearts were so hardened that every man was unredeemable, and every child was doomed, without hope of rehabilitative instruction, to follow the same example of his forebears.

Even when all the world persisted in total and unredeemable evil, God still saved a righteous remnant in Noah and his family from the fate visited upon the AnteDeluvians for their unrepented sin. What might have seemed unjustifiably cruel and appeared evil, extreme, and unloving, was necessary to destroy inveterate corruption, and preserve humanity through Noah, leading to Jesus, the seed of incorruptibility in New Born men. If God was to spend eternity with loving beings, prepared in a livable world, He had to remove unrepentant, rebellious beings from His creation in order to restore its perfection (Genesis 7:5). God then revived the Adamic Covenant of blessing with "Noah and his sons, and said unto them, Be fruitful, and multiply, and replenish the earth" (Genesis 9:1). God's goodness shared the creation He owns, and constituted men as his stewards to reach out and share its abundance with others less fortunate.

Then God proceeded to covenant with Abraham that He would be Protector and God to Abraham and his descendants: "And I will make of thee a great nation... and in thee shall all families of the earth be blessed" (Genesis 12:2, 3; 17:1–18). God made a Blood Covenant, so Abraham and all men would understand it was irrevocable, absolute, and in everlasting remembrance by God (Psalm 112:6; Isaiah 43:26). Then, God established Israel as His nation, so that all peoples might be brought to the knowledge of God through Jesus, The Messiah.

In a brief period of time, man's pattern of sin asserted itself and produced ingratitude, disobedience and infidelity toward God. For this reason, God destroyed Sodom and Gommorah by fire for the wickedness of the inhabitants there (Genesis 19:24), as well as the pagan nations which rejected God, such as Babylon and Assyria. When the Sodomites progressed from ingratitude to foolishness, to darkened hearts rejecting God's loving overtures, God had no choice but to give them up: "for although they knew God they did not honor him as God or give thanks to him, but they became futile in their thinking and their senseless minds were darkened. Claiming to be wise, they became fools" (Romans 1:21–22).

In recounting the lustful sexual perversions of Sodom, St. Paul says: "God gave them up in the lusts of their hearts to impurity.. men committing shameless acts with men and receiving in their own persons the due penalty for their error. And since they did not see fit to acknowledge God, God gave them up to a base mind and to improper conduct. They were filled with all manner of wickedness, evil, covetousness, malice... Though they know God's decree that those who do such things deserve to die" (Romans 1:28–32; see also, Psalm 81:12; Jeremiah 6:19; and Acts 7:42). Significantly, a merciful God revealed to Abraham that He would have saved Sodom, and all its evil inhabitants, despite their total corruption, for the sake of the faithful among them, if as few as ten righteous men could be found there (Genesis 18:32).

At Passover, the Jews were spared, by applying sacrificial blood on their doorposts, from the death angel which destroyed Egypt's firstborn (Exodus 12:12–13). God spared righteous men from the destruction of Jerusalem by instructing His angel to put a mark on the foreheads "of the men that sigh and that cry for all the abominations that be done in the midst thereof," but destroyed all the rest of Jerusalem (Ezekiel 9:4).

God graciously and lovingly vowed to remember his Covenant with man at Genesis 9:15, 16; Leviticus 26:42,45; and Ezekiel 16:60. Moses invoked God's Covenant with Abraham, Isaac, and Jacob when he interceded for the unfaithful Israelites who had worshiped the molten calf, "And the Lord repented of the evil which he thought to do unto his people" (Exodus 32:14). In fact, God went on to extend the Covenant of blessing to David and his seed at 2 Samuel 7:12, which culminated in the new Testament, or New Covenant promises of Jesus Christ.

The disobedience, repeated sin, and unrighteousness of Ancient Israel reflected the deeper rebellion of abandoning or losing faith in God. God spoke of His marriage to Israel and of her harlotry and adultery as she pursued other Gods. Deuteronomy 11:26–28 make it clear that infidelity is the disobedience about which God warns: "Behold, I set before you this day a blessing and a curse: A blessing, if ye obey the commandments of the Lord... And a curse, if ye will not obey the commandments of the Lord your God, but turn aside out of the way which I command you this day, to go after other gods, which ye have not known." When Israel sought these false Gods, the Jewish period of Exile in Egypt resulted.

God still showed mercy to Israel and led them out of Egypt. God personally delivered Israel by parting the Red Sea to allow them to pass through it, and then closing it back upon the pursuing Egyptians. He personally guided the Israelites in a cloud by day and a pillar of fire by night, for forty years in the wilderness. He provided daily manna for food, sweet water for drink, and imparted physical strength for the journey (Deuteronomy 8:3–4). But on the trip from Sinai the people complained about the manna God provided, and faithlessly lusted after the flesh and condiments they had enjoyed in Egypt. So God smote some of them (Numbers 11:5,33).

Nevertheless, a loving God led Israel to the Promised Land where they quickly resumed their infidelity, provoking God to pay "no heed to them" (Jeremiah 31:32; Hebrews 8:8). God declared through Jeremiah: "My people have forgotten me days without number" (Jeremiah 2:32; see also Psalm 81:12). Psalm 78:41–42 says that Israel "limited the Holy One of Israel. They remembered not his hand, nor the day when he delivered them from the enemy." Men's lack of faith in God resulted in restricting God's benevolent operations in their lives as they rejected God's guidance.

Man's perfidy and evil, in contrast to God's faithfulness and goodness, continue to be revealed throughout the Bible, but let us now focus on God's loving kindness. 2 Chronicles 16:9 proclaims God's benevolent intent toward believers: "For the eyes of the Lord run to and fro throughout the whole earth, to shew himself strong in the behalf of those whose heart is perfect toward him." God's promises of abundant, fully satisfying life are also contained in the beloved Psalm 23:1–6: "The Lord is my shepherd; I shall not want. He maketh me to lie down in green pastures... he restoreth my soul.. my cup runneth over. Surely goodness and mercy shall follow me all the days of my life." God promises: "With everlasting kindness will I have mercy on thee.. my kindness shall not depart from thee, neither shall the covenant of my peace be removed" (Isaiah 54:8,10).

God's goodness, reflected in forgiveness, mercy and restoration is summed up in Ezekiel 16:26–62, where God recounts the infidelity and idol worship of Israel: "Thou hast also committed fornication with the Egyptians thy neighbors... Thou hast played the whore also with the Assyrians, because thou wast insatiable... Thou hast moreover multiplied thy fornication in the land of Canaan unto Chaldea... thou givest thy gifts to all thy lovers... Sodom thy sister hath not done... as thou hast done... Neither hath Samaria committed half of thy sins... Nevertheless I will remember my covenant with thee in the days of thy youth, and I will establish unto thee an everlasting covenant... and thou shalt know that I am the Lord."

At 2 Chronicles 7:14 God promises full healing for repentance: "If my people, which are called by my name, shall humble themselves, and pray, and seek my face, and turn from their wicked ways, then will I hear from heaven, and will forgive their sin, and will heal their land." 2 Chronicles 30:9 adds: "For if ye turn again unto the Lord, your brethren and your children shall find compassion... for the Lord your God is gracious and merciful, and will not turn away his face from you, if ye return unto him." Jeremiah 3:12 summons repentance: "Return thou backsliding Israel, saith the Lord, and I will not cause mine anger to fall upon you: for I am merciful, saith the lord." These are not the expressions of a vengeful God, filled with rancor, but of a loving Father who yearns for His prodigal child's return.

Proverbs 28:13 says: "He that covereth his sins shall not prosper: but whosoever confesseth and forsaketh them shall have mercy." See also, Leviticus 4:26; I Kings 8:35; 2 Chronicles 16:9; Psalms 31:19, 32:5, 33:18–19, 37:4, 86:5, 138:8; Isaiah 43:25, 44:22, 55:7; Jeremiah 18:8; Micah 7:19; and Zachariah 3:4,7, 4:6–7.

The threat of punishment was always conditional, and withdrawn from those who returned to God's way in the Old Testament. When the Israelites repented after chastening, God always restored them, and raised up judges to deliver them (Judges 2:16). But when King Manasseh was so wicked that he corrupted all Judah beyond repentance, God was provoked to bring evil against the entire nation (2 Kings 21:11–12). Whenever the wicked were raised up by God as an instrument of His vengeance, they prevailed for only a brief moment in the span of eternity, as long as it suited the providence of God. Then, these instruments of Israel's conquest would be judged for their own iniquity (Isaiah 11:15–16).

Jesus gives us the Parable of the Prodigal Son to assure us that God's reception and restoration of the penitent child is full, and without punishment or revenge. The Parables of the Lost Coin (Luke 15:8–9) and the Lost Sheep (Luke 15:4–6), can be taken as assurances of God's pursuit of the unsaved, and joy over their recovery. A coin is an inanimate object and can represent anything God possesses and seeks to reclaim. Sheep can represent living creatures God possesses, and include the Shepherd's regular flock, as well as those strays from other flocks, which do not yet know the voice of the Shepherd. But a returning son can pertain only to one who knows Jesus as Lord and Savior, for we become sons of God only by adoption through Jesus Christ (Ephesians 1:5; Romans 8:13–15, 8:23; Galatians 4:5,). The Prodigal Son is a Parable of further mercy assured for wayward Christians who sin, repent, and return to God.

GOD'S TENDER MERCIES TO ALL MEN

Because He is good, God is concerned and does care about His children. He intends and provides only good for us; He delivers us from temptation, and empowers victory over the world, the flesh, and the devil. He provides for our material and spiritual needs; comforts us in affliction and grief; and makes Himself available for communion and fellowship. He showers us with blessings of beauty and bounty in nature; with benevolence and order in the universe. He favors us with other beings who love us, and He bestows tailor–made graces in answer to our prayers. If He does not initiate good, He promises at least to work all things "for good with those who love him, who are called according to his purpose" (Romans 8:28).

2 Samuel 22:31–32 declares: "As for God, his way is perfect; the word of the Lord is tried: he is <u>a buckler to all them that trust in him</u>... and who is a rock, save our God?" Isaiah 26:3 promises peace as a reward for faith in God: "Thou wilt keep him in perfect peace, whose mind is stayed on thee: <u>because he trusteth in thee</u>." See also, 2 Samuel 22:2–3; Psalm 139:3,5. Thinking about God, the historically recorded series of His deliverances, and about His goodness, inspires trust and brings peace.

We could not readily believe God's revelation of His goodness, if it was not verified routinely by empirical knowledge about our earthly living conditions. Fortunately, God's goodness is demonstrated in countless graces He extends to all persons. Matthew 5:45 says: "For he makes his sun rise on the evil and on the good, and sends rain on the just and on the unjust." Psalm 145:9 puts it: "The Lord is good to all: and his tender mercies are over all his works." Most of us tend to take for granted the countless prosaic boons God's loving care routinely provides. Consider our planet: located in a balanced solar system, perfectly positioned so that it becomes neither too hot nor cold to sustain life in its journey around the sun. God has fixed earth's size and location in the galaxy to provide gravity exactly suitable to sustain life. For, we do not fly off the surface into space, nor are we crushed ruthlessly to the ground as an inert mass. All this is accomplished amidst a creation of infinite beauty, variety, and congeniality, despite man's corruption of his home.

God has also provided the opportunity to share earth's blessings and abundance in collaboration with Him. He provides the seed; men plant and husband it; and God gives rain, sunshine, and nutrients to the soil to prosper growth and harvest. Likewise, God gives us the blessing of children (Psalm 127:3), but leaves much of their upbringing to parental training and prayer.

We tend to take for granted the wonders of our human body, which pumps blood, and delivers oxygen autonomically. Our mind assimilates and retains sensory impressions in the world about us, and experiences, entertains, enjoys, and savors love, joy, beauty, nobility, aspirations and ideals. God tells us to thank Him in all things and for all things (Ephesians 5:20; I Thessalonians 5:16), because it is so easy to forget the plethora of blessings He provides to everyone.

Every second of the day, the average adult heart faithfully pumps 13 pints of blood through the entire circulatory system, which consists of 60,000 miles of arteries, veins, venules and capillaries. Your wondrous heart, which beats sixty times per minute, or 360 times per hour, will beat 8,000 times today or nearly three million times this year without your even thinking about it.

Your lungs consist of air sacs and membranes, which automatically provide oxygen to the entire body, and especially the brain, where millions of cells would start dying after a few minutes without oxygen. Your autonomic respiratory system, breathes in and out fifteen times per minute, or 750,000 times per year. A person fifty years of age has enjoyed thirty–five million breaths without giving much thought to them, because Jesus upholds all things in the universe by the word of His power (Hebrews 1:3).

The skin is the largest organ of the body, which air–conditions the body efficiently, without producing noise or other pollutants to the environment. It removes waste from the body; and protects it from armies of invading germs. It heals wounds; protects visceral organs, muscles and other systems from exposure, and packages all this within a sensitive, and attractive container.[5]

The Psalmist recalls how God answers our prayers for deliverance: "Hear me when I Call, O God of my righteousness: thou hast enlarged me when I was in distress" (Psalm 4:1). "Thou hast enlarged my steps under me that my feet did not slip" (Psalm 18:36). "He brought me forth into a large place; he delivered me, because he delighted in me" (Psalm 18:19). God responds and enables our ability to cope with worldly afflictions when they visit us, and He lifts us to the next level of service and stewardship.

God has also given us the example of parental protection in all beasts of the animal kingdom, by implanting in all mothers an instinctive desire to protect and nurture their young, with exemplary tenderness and caring. These creatures, like human mothers, have acquired this loving trait from God, Who possesses parental characteristics most perfectly. God uses wonderful imagery to communicate His desire to care for believers, as a mother cares for her young. Isaiah 66:13 says: "As one whom his mother comforteth, so will I comfort you; and ye shall be comforted in Jerusalem." Jesus proclaimed to a scornful Jerusalem: "How often would I have gathered your children together as a hen gathers her brood under her wings, and you would not" (Luke 13:34).

Psalm 61:4 declares: "I will abide in thy tabernacle for ever: I will trust in the covert of thy wings." Psalm 91:4 puts it: "He shall cover thee with his feathers, and under his wings shall thou trust." Deuteronomy 33:27 says: "The eternal God is thy refuge, and underneath are the everlasting arms" (see also, Psalm 91:9). God describes Himself as our Father, and also our tender, loving mother, so we can not doubt His commitment and care for us, His children. And believing it, we must faithfully and expectantly act accordingly. Proverbs 18:10 says we find safety from uncongenial elements in the world by hastening to the sanctuary of the Lord: "The name of the Lord is a strong tower: the righteous runneth into it, <u>and is safe</u>."

Because of His goodness, God cares for, is involved in, and concerned with His children: "for thou, Lord, hast not forsaken them that seek thee" (Psalm 9:10). Psalm 40:1 relates: "I waited patiently for the Lord; and he inclined unto me, and heard my cry." See also, Deuteronomy 4:31, 31:6; I Samuel 12:22; Isaiah 41:17, 49:15–16.

God is benevolently involved during our worldly pilgrimage in regulating the affairs of His children and their environment. God goes before us to smooth our path; accompanies us and guides our way; sustains our journey; then follows behind to heal and restore the blunders and failures of our lives. Psalm 37:23–24 says: "The steps of a good man are ordered by the Lord: and he delighteth in his way. Though he fall, he shall not be utterly cast down: for the Lord upholdeth him with his hand.". Psalm 145:14 declares: "The Lord upholdeth all that fall, and raiseth up all those that be bowed down." Psalm 139:3 acknowledges: "Thou compassest my path and my lying down, and art acquainted with all my ways." "Thou has beset me behind and before, and laid thine hand upon me" (Psalm 139:5). Proverbs 24:16 adds: "For a just man falleth seven times and riseth up again." God prepares our way (Exodus 23:20), sustains us throughout the journey, and tenderly restores us with another chance each time we fail.

God assures us at Psalm 50:15: "Call upon me in the day of trouble: I will deliver thee, and thou shalt glorify me." Psalm 84:11 puts it: "For the Lord God is a sun and shield: the Lord will give grace and glory: no good thing will he withhold from them that walk uprightly."

Psalm 23:4 reminds us of God's comforting presence: "Yea, though I walk through the valley of the shadow of death, I will fear no evil: for thou art with me." Jesus assures believers of His presence at Matthew 28:20: "lo, I am with you always to the close of the age." Regardless of what comes our way, Jesus makes it possible for believers to "continuously offer up a sacrifice of praise to God, that is, the fruit of lips that acknowledge his name" (Hebrews 13:15). Identification with and submission to God is the key to praiseworthy blessings: "And they shall put my name upon the children of Israel; and I will bless them" (Numbers 6:27). Christians are grafted on to the children of Israel, and bear the name of Christ, as they inherit the promises to Israel under the New Testament.

Many Old Testament passages equate God's righteousness with the deliverance of His people; not because they deserved salvation, but because He is gracious. Psalm 143:11 beseeches: "Quicken me, O Lord, for thy name's sake: for thy righteousness' sake bring my soul out of trouble." See also, Psalms 24:5, 31:, 98:2; Isaiah 45:21 and 51:5.

Because God loves you and created you for fellowship with Him, "God in the midst of thee is mighty; he will save, he will rejoice over thee with joy; he will rest in his love, he will joy over thee with singing" (Zephaniah 3:17). God is in love with you even in failure, rebellion and defeat. But He is thrilled in your victory, and joyful over your success to the point He sings because of your holiness. The Hebrew word 'rejoice' means to spin around under the influence of an overwhelming emotion. God is so delighted in His redeemed, and so happy sharing their success in righteousness that he sings for joy[6]. Luke 15:7 speaks of "joy in heaven over one sinner who repents."

GOD'S GOODNESS TOWARD AMERICA

Because America has been ordained, constituted, and existed as a nation under God, we have enjoyed exceptional, manifest blessings. The Continent is vastly wealthy in material resources, beauty, climate, and geographic insularity, which has provided a most agreeable habitat in the earth. Christopher Columbus believed he was divinely guided to discover America. God declares His desire to bless His own, and the American experience proves that a nation serving God will be blessed. Isaiah 65:24 promises: "And it shall come to pass, that before they call, I will answer; and while they are yet speaking, I will hear."

Our Founding Fathers were predominantly Christian, God–fearing men who acknowledged the new nation must exist under God. In 1620 the Pilgrims enacted the Mayflower Compact "for the glory of God and the advancement of the Christian faith." The Declaration of Independence proclaims the "laws of nature, and of nature's God," and that "We hold these truths to be self–evident, that all men are created equal, that they are endowed by their Creator with certain unalienable rights." Spiritual leaders enforced Christian beliefs during our earliest centuries, and recognized that our blessings were not only for our enjoyment, but to bless the entire world. Spiritual principles derived from Godly values have sustained the nation in religious, political, economic and social freedoms and equal rights, which have been a beacon of hope for oppressed people everywhere.

American soil has been insulated from many wars, while blessed with victories abroad, and then endowed with magnanimity so that we extend a helping hand to the vanquished, in the name of God.

Though we have enjoyed God's favor in America for two centuries, there is no guaranty His blessing will continue if we increasingly forsake our anointing as a nation under God. His promises of blessing have always depended upon His people's commitment to obedience. The nations which rebel against God's Commandments are guilty of the sin of infidelity in turning to other gods of wealth, self–reliant pride, or self–gratification. The history of Israel in the Old Testament was always one of mercy on the heels of repentance, following God's clear warning of doom for continued infidelity, voiced through His prophets. The nations which failed to heed the warning always felt God's wrath until they repented or were destroyed, from the time of Noah, unto Israel, Judah, Babylon, Assyria, Chaldea, Greece, Rome, and every other fallen empire throughout history.

God promises that His love will embrace the repentant sinner who returns to His way. Only impenitent rebels are targeted for wrath and punishment. So America needs to ponder how much longer it can presume upon God's mercy without being judged unfaithful. Our national flirtation with abortion, divorce, homosexuality, pornography, and public reluctance to acknowledge God are not consistent with being a nation under God, committed to serve Him as a model for the world.

Faith incorporates a trust in God's goodness: that he remains interested in His children; that He necessarily acts perfectly in every endeavor, even though not always in a manner comprehensible to man; and that in the exercise of sovereign dominion He intercedes in the world on behalf of believers. Hebrews 11:6 declares: "And without faith it is impossible to please him. For whoever would draw near to God must believe that he exists and that he rewards those who seek him." That reward is to find God: "Draw near to God and he will draw near to you." (James 4:8).

God's perfect goodness necessitates that in every instance He must conform to the highest level of goodness which He has revealed. He can do no evil; He is incapable of neglect or unkindness. He cannot be merciless, ungracious, or unworthy, and is incapable of desertion, lying, or duplicity. For, "the will of God (is) what is good and acceptable and perfect" (Romans 12:2). Good is defined by what we recognize has been willed by God. Since God is good and wise, He can give only good gifts to His children, and it violates God's nature to bestow harmful things such as snakes, rocks, or useless objects upon his children, when nurture is appropriate (Matthew 7:11).

God has provided the constant certainty of His Word, contained in Scriptures, which not only reveal and detail His character, but outline His plans and purposes for creation, and prescribe the lifestyle for men which is most pleasing to Him, and most beneficial to us.

The names assigned to God reveal, explicate, and define His nature and benevolence toward believers. The generic names, El and Elohim, when translated El–Shaddai, "Almighty God" (Genesis 17:1), acknowledge the omnipotence, personal force, might, and power of the true God.[7] When God described Himself to Moses as "I am that I am" (Exodus 3:14), He indicated an open–ended provision of power and grace for the needs of His Creation and creatures. God was, is, and will be, whatever is necessary to provide the full and abundant life Jesus proclaimed for believers. This unfinished characterization of God's persona means He is the infinite Deliverer, Comforter, Provider, Lover, Husband, Wisdom, Peace, Rest, Righteousness, and All in All (I Corinthians 15:28, KJV).

Alexander Cruden has traced five names of God which reveal His goodness and expand upon the name Jehovah.[8] Each name is episodic, and revealed a newly discovered characteristic of God as He manifested the nuances of His grace through various crises or events in human history.

Thus, Jehovah–Jirah, literally translated: "it shall be seen and the Lord will provide," was the name assigned by Abraham on the occasion when God supplied a ram for the blood sacrifice, as a substitute for Isaac (Genesis 22:14). The name is a reminder that God always sees our need, and always provides for it.

Jehovah–Nissi, literally "The Lord is my Banner," was the name assigned by Moses to the place where God gave assurance he would utterly destroy evil, personified by Amalek. He promised to erase "the remembrance of Amalek from under heaven," from generation to generation (Exodus 17:14–16). Our military service under God's Banner requires trust in God, alone, for the victory. For the battle is His, as the champion of His people in their struggle against the world, which is exemplified by Amalek.

Jehovah–Shalom, literally "The Lord is peace," was the name applied by Gideon at the place where God gave assurance Gideon would prevail in battle against the Midianites: "Peace be unto thee; fear not: thou shalt not die" (Judges 6:23–24). This name of God reminds us there is nothing to fear with Him on our side, and this constitutes a source of the divine peace which passes all understanding.

Jehovah–Shammah, literally "The Lord is there" was the name the Lord revealed to Ezekiel to declare His presence in Jerusalem, which was to be inhabited by "the tribes of Israel for inheritance" (Ezekiel 48;29, 35). The name reflects God's assurance of His constant presence and comfort in the midst of His people. Jesus is named Immanuel, which means "God with us" (Isaiah 7:14; Matthew 1:23); present within and among believers in the world.

Jehovah–Tsidkenu, literally "The Lord is our Righteousness," was the name ascribed by Jeremiah upon God's revelation that "Judah shall be saved, and Israel shall dwell safely" in their own land (Jeremiah 23:6,8). The name signifies God's assurance that when we surrender our self–righteousness and find our security in God's grace and imputed righteousness, we will dwell safely in the Lord.

To these names we may add Jehovah–Repheka, "the Lord that healeth thee" (Exodus 15:26); Jehovah–Tsebaoth, "the Lord of Hosts" (Isaiah 31:5; I Samuel 17:45–47), Who is a mighty warrior on behalf of the righteous, fighting against evil;[9] and Jehovah–Rohi, "The Lord is my Shepherd" (Psalm 23:11); and as such, my guide, provider, and protector. God's name is also, Jealous, for he does not tolerate worship of any other God, "for the Lord, whose name is Jealous, is a jealous God" (Exodus 34:14; and see also, Exodus 20:5; Deuteronomy 4:24, 32:16; Psalms 78:58, 79:5; Ezekiel 39:25; Nahum 1:2). Having exposed the vulnerability of His love for man, God insists on exclusively occupying the primary place in our hearts.

We are blessed by God in another way we usually take for granted. It is easy to question God's goodness when there are natural catastrophes, mass disasters, or personal pain and suffering, if we assume that God is responsible for everything which occurs in His Providence. Yet, it is easy to overlook God's Providence and forget to thank Him for the countless times we and our loved ones are spared from disaster, tribulation, travail, or pain. We forget how long God has kept us in good health, until we start to lose it. We ignore His ongoing deliverance from collisions and crashes until we encounter a graphic scene of destruction. We take prosperity and comfort for granted until we are beset by financial problems. Then we seek God, and reassurance of His intent to bless us as His children.

If one develops heart trouble because this self–regulating system is failing, that is an appropriate time to thank God for the millions of heartbeats He has already allowed you to enjoy, as well as for years to come. If one develops difficulty breathing as the body deteriorates with age, then that is the time to thank God for the wonderful, respiratory system which has already enjoyed millions of breaths.

If God intends every moment of our personal pain, we can be thankful it reminds us to appreciate all the hours we have been spared pain. We can be thankful we need to be driven back to God as the source of all our blessings; that we need to become less proud, unloving, impatient, unfaithful, or wasteful in our stewardship of God's resources. If God orchestrates everything, including suffering, which befalls every person for benign purposes, then we are forced to recognize that all other things which appear to occur by chance, serendipity, or contingency, are the result of divine intervention to bless, protect and uphold God's children.

Even–handedness requires us to recognize that God's invisible restraints on evil, His interventions, and His goodness are also responsible for withholding affliction from us. If a plane crashes, or a saint dies in agony from cancer, and we attribute it directly to God's intent, we must also thank Him for the greater number of aircraft which do not crash, and countless lives which continue to enjoy good health. We ought not assume God has nothing to do with deliverance from affliction, if we impute all suffering to His invention. We should be grateful not only for the respites from cold and darkness, but for the positive blessings of light and warmth we take for granted from Him, unappreciated and unacknowledged.

We can give thanks in, or while enduring suffering if we believe God will turn it to good, here or Hereafter, or will bless us in some other way for our patient long–suffering. We can endure if we expect eventual deliverance from the suffering as he helps us to evade, mitigate, or escape the consequences of the difficulty which besets us. But we can give thanks <u>for</u> the suffering only if we believe it is authored and intended by God for some benevolent purpose, or that He will convert these terrors to good for all who love Him and walk according to his purposes. If a severed limb or paralyzed spine is not restored in this world, we can be certain of total healing at Christ's Second Coming; that our "spirit and soul and body be kept sound and blameless at the coming of our Lord Jesus Christ. He who calls you is faithful, and <u>he will do it</u>" (I Thessalonians 5:23–24).

Indeed, "no one can receive anything except what is given him from Heaven" (John 3:27). "What have you that you did not receive? If then you received it, why do you boast as if it were not a gift?" (I Corinthians 4:7). "Blessed is the Lord, who daily loadeth us with benefits" (Psalm 68:19). "Every good endowment and every perfect gift is from above, coming down from the Father of lights" (James 1:17). Acts 17:25 reveals that God "himself gives to all men life and breath and everything." (See also, I Corinthians 3:7; 2 Corinthians 10:17: 2 Timothy 2:1; I Peter 4:11; Deuteronomy 8:18; Isaiah 26:12; and I Chronicles 29:12).

God has given enough light by which His total goodness is affirmed and perceived. Indeed, He has revealed His very nature and intent in His Word: "How precious also are thy thoughts unto me, O God! How great is the sum of them" (Psalm 139:17).

Because man's debt to God was caused by the affront to God's dignity by denying Him the obedience and reverence owed to one's Father, a sinner is incapable of vindicating himself, or earning acceptance by works. A sin is measured by the dignity of God, while man's attempt to rectify the insult to God can only be measured by man's own worth.[10] That is why no profuse apology or submissive acts by sinners can restore the balance which sin disturbed, or honor God as much as sin has dishonored Him. If you spit in a man's face you may literally take back exactly what you gave by wiping the spittle away, but you have done nothing to satisfy the injustice or disrespect to another's dignity.

No sinner can be saved without understanding this is why he needs a Saviour, Whom God has ordained as Jesus. We cannot embrace the depths of God's love without first recognizing the extent of our hateful behavior towards Him. We cannot fathom the extent of divine forgiveness without comprehending how far we have departed from His way. We cannot seek the cure of our blessed Savior, until we diagnose the diseases of sin, depravity and iniquity which beset natural man. We are attracted toward the love of our Lord, at the same time we are moved to escape the life of sin which offends and alienates us from our righteous God, and merits a fearful but deserved penalty.

Every sinner must recognize that he needs God's grace and help to bridge the gulf separating man from God. For, man unaided cannot be justified by his own virtue or righteousness; or achieve his own moral reformation. He cannot rise again by his own strength; nor be reconciled with divine friendship. He can no more will a totally changed heart or new spirit than he can create his own physical being. No man is so good he does not need a Saviour, and no man is so bad he cannot be saved by Jesus.

At the convergence of God's Justice and His love, a Saviour was necessary to atone for mankind's sin with his own righteousness; to render obedience; propitiate God's Justice; rescue man from his sin; effectuate God's love; and restore man's right relationship with God. We cannot journey to Easter without first passing through the experience of Good Friday's redemptive sacrifice.

GOD'S GOODNESS IN PROVIDING A SAVIOUR

The "wages of sin is death" (Romans 6:23), but God shows His love for us in Jesus, though we were lost and totally corrupt, because "God so loved the world that he gave his only Son, that whoever believes in him should not perish but have eternal life: For God sent the Son into the world, not to condemn the world, but that the world might be saved through him" (John 3:16–17).

It is difficult to acknowledge Jesus as our Saviour unless we understand from what we are saved. Sin is what necessitates a Saviour from the penalty for our sin; from the wrath of God because of sin; and from the natural inclination of man to sin after the fall. "But God shows his love for us in that while we were yet sinners Christ died for us. Since, therefore, we are now justified by his blood, much more <u>shall we be saved by him</u> from the wrath of God. For if while we were enemies we were reconciled to God by the death of his Son, much more, now that we are reconciled, <u>shall we be saved by his life</u>" (Romans 5:8–10). The verb "be saved" is in the future tense, and the justified believer will be finally saved at the last day, although the effects of salvation are manifested through manifold graces in this world.

Matthew 18:11 relates that "the Son of man came to save that which was lost." Jesus reveals that He is God's only provision for salvation, and the exclusive way to reconciliation with God: "I am the way, and the truth and the life; no one comes to the Father, <u>but by me</u>" (John 14:6). I John 5:11–12 adds: "God gave us eternal life, and this life is in his Son. He who has the Son has life, he who has not the Son has not life." John 3:17 proclaims: "For God sent the Son into the world, not to condemn the world, but that the world might be saved through him." Jesus reveals: "I am the door; if any one enters by me, he will be saved" (John 10:9). Acts 4:12 says of Jesus: "And there is salvation in no one else, for there is no other name under heaven given among men by which we must be saved." I Corinthians 15:22 adds: "For as in Adam all die, so also in Christ shall all be made alive."

God's plan of salvation for mankind was to make over men into the likeness of Christ, because of, and through the righteousness, perfect obedience, and sacrificial, cleansing Blood of Jesus. Jesus reported to God: "I glorified thee on earth, having accomplished the work which thou gavest me to do" (John 17:4). His work was to complete atonement for man's sin; to redeem, rescue, and ransom sinners from the clutches of Satan. Jesus was not removing a burden God had put on men, but the burden of sin and its consequences, which Satan had put on men. Jesus was ransoming and redeeming men from their bondage to sin. He was thereby restoring them to right relationship with God by giving satisfaction to God's justice on behalf of sinners. Jesus accomplished reconciliation of sinners with the Father; vicarious death and sacrifice for man's sins; substituting His righteousness for the sins of the unjust; and right–standing or justification of sinners before God by His precious Blood.

This saving work expresses the love of Jesus for every sinner and overshadows any love we might imagine, for He bore our sins, suffered, and died on the Cross, that we might avoid death and our own just and deserved punishment for sin. He descended to earth and became a man, rejected and despised, that we might ascend to Heaven and become part of His glorious, resurrected body. He gave up His privileges as the Son of God for a time while He walked the earth, so that redeemed sinners might succeed to them in Him for eternity. He removed Himself and departed from God's side, so that throughout eternity we might be as near to God as Jesus, Himself.

Jesus gave up His glory for a time (John 16:5), so believers might be glorified with Him. He gave up His riches "so that by his poverty you might become rich" (2 Corinthians 8:9). He gave up His privileged relationship with God, so that you might share it in the time to come. He surrendered His pre–eminence, "to serve, and to give his life as a ransom for many" (Mark 10:45). He did not relinquish His divine nature, but temporarily abdicated His divine attributes so that we might inherit them in Him.

Jesus was "forsaken" by God when he bore our sins (Mark 15:34), so that God would always be with us. Galatians 3:13 says: "Christ redeemed us from the curse of the law, having become a curse for us." I John 4:9–10 explains: "In this the love of God was made manifest among us, that God sent his only Son into the world, so that we might live through him... He loved us and sent his Son to be the expiation for our sins." See also, Romans 6:3–4, 6:23. God's wrath and Justice met and embraced God's mercy, grace, and love at the Cross.

Jesus accomplished our salvation by taking on all the evil ever perpetrated by man, every one of our sins, and paid our penalty by His death so we could escape it. "For our sake he made him to be sin who knew no sin, so that in him we might become the righteousness of God" (2 Corinthians 5:21). By voluntarily diverting God's wrath from men, Jesus vicariously suffered the retributive penalty of death as though He deserved it Himself. It was not possible for God to "remove this cup from" Jesus (Mark 14:36), since God's justice required a full measure of suffering to cancel man's debt. Ephesians 5:2 says of Christ's atonement: "Christ loved us and gave himself up for us, a fragrant offering and sacrifice to God." Jesus was a mediator "between God and men" and "gave himself as a ransom for all" to God (I Timothy 2:5–6). God, "even when we were dead through our trespasses, made us alive together with Christ (by grace you have been saved)." (Ephesians 2:5).

Nothing "in all creation, will be able to separate us from the love of God in Christ Jesus our lord" (Romans 8:39). We are "the flock under his care," whom He guides and watches over (Psalm 95:7). Jesus confirmed God's will to do us good, when He went about healing the infirmities of all that were sick and oppressed (Matthew 8:16, 9:35, 12:15, 14:36; Acts 10:38). He did so on God's authority, and because it was pleasing to Him (John 8:28–29; Mark 1:41; Psalm 91:3,10).

The essence of New Testament faith, based upon promises in God's Word, is confidence that God will continue to be good and do good (James 1:17). We are blessed through Jesus to be adopted children of a God Who is perfectly loving, caring, kind, and good; the Author of every benevolence, Who intends only good for his children. Jesus proclaims God's intent to bless believers under the new Covenant: "I am come that they might have life, and... have it more abundantly" (John 10:10, KJV). God's New Testament plan of redemption is thus better for man than God's original plan of creation, as corrupted by man.

The essence of divine love is expressed by Jesus: "Greater love has no man than this; that a man lay down his life for his friends" (John 15:13). God continues to love us by desiring our highest good, and he wills to help us enjoy His best. If we would only focus on God's love, rather than our temporary lack, we would never doubt the divine Providence of His blessings.

Christians become heirs of the promises to Abraham through Jesus Christ. Galatians 3:26,29 reveals: "for In Christ Jesus you are all sons of God through faith... And if you are Christ's, then you are Abraham's offspring, heirs according to promise." Romans 8:16–17 teaches: "it is the Spirit himself bearing witness with our spirit that we are children of God, and if children, then heirs, heirs of God and fellow heirs with Christ." Through Christ we are made adopted sons of God (Romans 8:15, 9:4; Galatians 4:5–7; Ephesians 1:5–7; 2:18; 5:2; I John 3:16). Astounding as it may seem, because of Jesus, and because we are in Jesus, God loves us as much as He loves Jesus. Jesus prays for His Church: "that they may all be one; even as thou, Father art in me, and I in thee, that they also may be in us, so that the world may... know that thou has sent me and <u>hast loved them even as thou hast loved me</u>" (John 17:21,23).

Six thousand years of human history have demonstrated that man cannot save himself or be justified without Jesus.[11] We can live only if Jesus is in us and we live through Him. At John 10:9 Jesus declares: "For apart from me you can do nothing. If a man does not abide in me, he is cast forth as a branch and withers, and... thrown into the fire and burned." At John 6:33,35 Jesus reveals: "For the bread of God is that which comes down from heaven, and gives life to the world... I am the bread of life; he who comes to me shall not hunger, and he who believes in me shall never thirst."

Christ's quest was to save the lost sinner, release him from bondage to sin, isolation and loneliness, and give him total victory over the world. Jesus came to destroy the works of the devil and take away sin (I John 3:5,8); to introduce the Father to men; and lead believers to the Father. Luke 19:10 says: "For the Son of man came to seek and to save that which was lost." Thus, when from the Cross Jesus said, "It is finished" (John 19:30), He used the Greek word "tetelestai," which connotes payment in full. The debts of sinners were then and there fully remitted; including every sin ever committed or to be committed, regardless of how heinous the sin, or how corrupt or inveterate the sinner (Colossians 2:13–14; I John 2:2). Jesus' redemptive work on earth was completed on the Cross and fully satisfactory to God (2 Peter 1:17).

Colossians 1:16–20 sums up Christ's significance for mankind: "For in him all things were created... He is the head of the body, the church, he is the beginning, the first–born from the dead... and through him to reconcile to himself all things, whether on earth or in heaven, making peace by the blood of his cross."

Man cannot be saved without Jesus Christ as his Saviour, and he cannot be saved without personal faith in Jesus as that Saviour. The Bible also identifies Jesus as Lord as well as Saviour (2 Peter 1:11, 2:20, 3:2). Romans 10:9–10 explains: "if you confess with your lips that Jesus is Lord and believe in your heart that God raised him from the dead, you will be saved. For man believes with his heart and so is justified, and he confesses with his lips and so is saved." The confession that Jesus is the resurrected Lord is both believed and articulated. His resurrection identifies His uniqueness and distinction from the pantheon of Greek and Roman Gods, as the pre–eminent Lord over all, in unbroken union with God. Faith operates in the heart to produce righteousness, and confession functions in the mouth to receive salvation (Romans 10:10).

Our faith is in the fullness and entirety of Jesus as Lord and Saviour. Both faith and repentance are yoked blessings driven by the grace of God to perfect the New Birth. Repentance acknowledges that God's justice requires penalty for sin and we are guilty of affronting God's holiness by our sin.

Indeed, Jesus is God's proof of His good will and intentions toward man, despite the presence of evil in the world. God does not use affliction to punish the faithful in heart, who penitently strive to do His will and follow Christ. If God sent Jesus to save and deliver you when you were a sinner under condemnation, it would be inconsistent with His justice and loving nature if he tormented or punished a Christian whose total redemption has been accomplished by Jesus. Jesus has already paid the price and cancelled the debt for a believer's sins; past, present and future, and it is inconceivable God intends to punish His faithful on the earth for trespasses he has previously expunged and forgiven in Christ 2,000 years ago (2 Corinthians 5:19; Colossians 2:13).

If God gave us the greatest gift of Christ's loving sacrifice 2,000 years ago, would He inconsistently withdraw the lesser manifestations of that gift now? Romans 8:32 declares not: "He who did not spare his own Son but gave him up for us all, will he not also give us all things with him?"

Since God's perfection is defined by His goodness and loving kindness, He is incapable of inherently evil occurrences, such as the severing of limbs in accidents; or the deaths of passengers aboard a crashed airliner. He could not possibly intend the evil inflicted upon victims of mass murderers, or terrorist bombings; or birth deformities. He could not possibly arrange the death of babies at the hands of drunk drivers or abortions; nor genocidal exterminations of children reared in Christian homes; nor all pointless evils which are irreconcilable with God's goodness. For, what is good is defined and established by what God does and the purposes He proclaims.

Sin, which violates God's Law and very nature, could not have been ordained by a Holy God Who prohibits it. If God fore-ordained everything, it would mean God required Adam and Eve to be disobedient and eat the forbidden fruit, inferred from the fact they did so. Yet, God also decreed they should not eat thereof, placing both decrees at odds, impossible of reconciliation unless we wrongly view God as an evil puppet-master, manipulating His created beings indiscriminately, or rightly acknowledge the reality of free will.

Justice would be a mockery if God instigated human evil, or blinded the unsaved from the light of salvation, and then punished them for eternity for their sins and rejection of Jesus. It does not make sense that God would declare a purpose and then compel men to work against that purpose. God created men for worship and fellowship with God. It is inconceivable He would intend them to go astray in sin, since that conflicts with God's dominant purpose of goodness and benevolent design.

We cannot rationalize, and try to insert inherent good into intrinsic evils by focusing on the good God produces out of them. We cannot escape the fact that the innate quantity of evil far outweighs the good we can perceive in the act, because we want to assume it was intended as God's instrument to accomplish a higher good. How could the source and repository of the fruit of the Holy Spirit: love, joy, peace, patience, goodness, kindness, faithfulness, gentleness, and self-control (Galatians 5:22–23), be the cause of overwhelming evil consequences by His intentional, deliberate decree? Although His Sovereignty might entitle God to do as He pleases, how could the loving Father we know, viciously direct a serial killer to murder families, or set the path of a tidal wave to drown and destroy certain areas and residents, rather than others. We would execute, or at least imprison for life, any earthly father who authored the things which we wrongly ascribe to a perfect, loving Heavenly Father.

We know that God is incapable of evil because we detest evil in our own imperfect way, only because we have received God's revelation about His character and purposes. Destruction and suffering fill even unspiritual men with loathing for the perpetrator, and sympathy for the sufferer. How could God, Who Jesus compared to an ideal earthly Father, do on a large scale, what He has directed us to refrain from doing on a small scale, or for which we would mete out punishment in even the most primitive legal system? If God has transformed believers in such a way that evil is repulsive to us because of the regeneration God has fashioned, how then could He do these evil things, when He reconstitutes our spirits in His image in such a way as to remove them?

God has plainly revealed in His Word that there will be times He trains, chastens, chastises, and leads us through suffering, to elicit spiritual qualities He wishes to develop in us. Nevertheless, the vast majority of our travails are self–inflicted, caused by our own disobedience, or caused by the free acts of other men or satanic demons.

The next two Chapters remind us of the marvelous blessings which God's goodness bestows on repentant sinners who are Born–Again in Christ. One's literal regeneration or transformation into the likeness of Christ is accomplished, as His righteousness is actually imparted to a new heart and spirit. This sanctification is an ongoing process by the Holy Spirit dwelling within a believer. We are blessed with further divine resources to withstand the assaults and temptations of the world: we are given a hedge of protection by God; guardian angels; God's armor to shield us against all the fiery darts of Satan; the name of Jesus and authority to act as His agent; the power of prayer to invoke God's help in our need and by intercession for the needs of others, and many other blessings.

The Bible has more than 7,000 promises for the abundant life Jesus brings to the faithful. We have no need to invent new blessings when we can stand on these explicit promises, because God's Word is trustworthy and always fulfilled. In fact, the fullness of Christian life calls us to expand our faith and bless others through intercessory prayer, by claiming God's promises on their behalf. So it is vital to familiarize ourselves with these precious, providential promises of God for His children. "For all things are yours, whether... the world or life or death or the present or the future, all are yours; and you are Christ's; and Christ is God's" (I Corinthians 3:21–23).

CHAPTER 2

GOD'S GOODNESS IN THE BLESSING OF SALVATION IN CHRIST

"For God so loved the world that he gave his only Son, that whoever believes in him should not perish but have eternal life. For God sent the Son into the world, not to condemn the world, but that the world might be saved through him."

– John 3:16-17.

It is doubtful we can comprehend in this life how much God loves us. His gentle grace deals tenderly with sinners in the world in order to save them from themselves by persuasion and conviction of each sinner's need for a personal Saviour. The Creator of all the universe has abased Himself to pursue us and proclaim His love. He has tolerated disobedience, rebellion, pride, contempt, and irrelevance from men in order to be constant in His grace and love for them. He has extended forgiveness, infinite compassion, and tender mercies, as He ministers to, and provides for our needs and desires. He waits patiently for each man to realize his need for a Saviour from sin and come to the knowledge of the truth.

The wonder of it all is that God could still love men enough to save us in Christ, even though fully aware from before our creation of our repeated rebellion and sin. In the last Chapter we traced mankind's emerging depravity, sinfulness, and unfaithfulness toward God, despite His constancy, loving-kindness, and fidelity. Humanists think man is inherently good, but a look at any child from birth until he is trained reveals the constituent, carnal self-centeredness of all fallen beings. We are unclean, unrighteous sinners, by nature, which alienates every man from God. (Genesis 8:21; I Kings 8:45; Psalms 14:3, 53:3, 51:5, 58:3; Proverbs 20:9; Isaiah 48:8, 64:6; Ecclesiastes 7:20; Jeremiah 17:9; Romans 3:23; I John 1:8).

I John 3:4 declares that "sin is lawlessness," or rebellion against God's revealed will. Hence, even sins against another person are also sins against God (Genesis 20:6; Psalm 51:4). Man's sinfulness has produced alienation and separation from a righteous God. Isaiah 59:2 asserts: "Your sins have hid his face from you, that he will not hear." This separation by sin from divine righteousness and spiritual resources makes it impossible for man to atone for his own sin or work out his own salvation. Only God can restore fallen men, and his great, loving gift to mankind is salvation and spiritual reformation by His grace, and unmerited favor.

In His perfect love, God has overlooked man's sinful nature, and accomplished the restoration of rebellious sinners to fellowship and right relationship with Him by providing Jesus Christ, His Son, as the substitute to redeem men from sin and atone for the sins of all men. God sent Jesus to die for the sake of sinners while carnality was the condition of all men. Jesus rescues, ransoms, and redeems men from their sin nature, compulsion to sin, and its deadly consequences.

We saw in the last Chapter how God's goodness toward men provided Jesus as God's exclusive provision to rescue men from the predicament, consequences and penalty of sin. Man's response is to believe. Jesus is Lord and Saviour, the Messiah by Whom eternal life, reconciliation, justification, restoration, and redemption have come. Jesus was God's instrument, by God's grace, to satisfy God's Justice, through Jesus' suffering and death, which served as substitute, sacrifice and propitiation for mankind's sins. Through Christ, believers are made adopted sons of God, and heirs to the promises made to Abraham (Romans 8:15, 9:4; Galatians 4:5-7; Ephesians 1:5). We are saved by the cross, and quickened through the resurrection, of Christ.

Jesus brings the full and final revelation of God's plan for salvation of sinners in Him. God had commissioned the Prophets of Old to preach repentance to an idolatrous Israel, and He sent Jonah to Nineva to urge conversion. In Jesus, the actual and complete deliverance of sinners has been accomplished by God's grace and love. The sinner who is in New Covenant with God under the New Testament of Jesus can expect to receive full, abundant life and Covenant blessings.

Jesus has declared His unity and oneness with God, and thus shares the same perfect character, nature, attributes and characteristics, such as omnipotence and love. Jesus is "The Word" who "became flesh and dwelt among us" (John 1:14). John 1:1-2 reveals: "In the beginning was the Word, and the Word was with God, and the Word was God." At John 8:57, Jesus refers to Himself by God's characterization, as "I am." He reveals: "I and the Father are one" at John 10:40. "And he who sees me sees him who sent me" (John 12:45). "He who has seen me has seen the Father... Believe me that I am in the Father and the Father in me" (John 14:9,11). Jesus prayed for His followers: "Holy Father, keep them in thy name which thou hast given me, that they may be one, even as we are one... that they may all be one, even as thou, Father, art in me, and I in thee, that they may also be in us" (John 17:11,21).

Colossians 2:9-10 teaches about Jesus: "For in him dwells the whole fullness of deity bodily, and you have come to fullness of life in him, who is the head of all rule and authority." Consequently, Jesus shares the almighty power of God. Jesus reveals at Matthew 28:18: "All authority in heaven and on earth has been given to me." Jesus clearly had power over evil: "whenever the unclean spirits beheld him, they fell down before him" (Mark 3:12). He transmitted this power to the Apostles: "And he appointed twelve to be with him, and to be sent out to preach and have authority to cast out demons" (Mark 3:14-15; and see also, Luke 10:19).

Luke 4:36 affirms Jesus' power over demons: "For with authority and power he commands the unclean spirits, and they come out." At John 17:1-2 Jesus prays: "Father, the hour has come; glorify thy Son... since thou hast given him power over all flesh." Ephesians 1:11 speaks of "the purpose of him who accomplishes all things according to the counsel of his will." Hebrews 1:2-3 reveals that God has not abandoned the universe He created, but has established Jesus as "the heir of all things, through whom also he created the world. He reflects the glory of God and bears the very stamp of his nature, upholding the universe by his word of power."

Without the ongoing dynamism of Christ, all forces, including evil ones, would simply wind down. I Corinthians 15:27 confirms that "God has put all things in subjection under his feet." Therefore, evil is not a function of God's impotence, but is declared to be subordinate to Jesus. Evil is not co-equal with God, and not even a close second in power. Satan was defeated by Jesus Christ on the Cross 2,000 years ago, and his eventual consignment to Hell and destruction is assured with the coming of God's Kingdom (Revelation 20:10).

JESUS REMITS EVERY SIN AND OFFERS SALVATION TO EVERY SINNER

Jesus has brought and made a New Covenant or New Testament, which is superior to the Older Testament or Covenant which God made with Abraham and Moses. "Christ has obtained a ministry which is as much more excellent than the old as the covenant he mediates is better, since it is enacted on better promises" (Hebrews 8:6). The Covenant with Moses promised that an Israelite would be saved as the reward for submitting to, honoring, and trusting God, and by faithfully obeying the Law (Exodus 19:5, 20:1-17; Deuteronomy 5:1-21). In return, God covenanted that he would not turn from man, but keep faith with all future generations which did not depart from His way.[12] A Gentile could embrace the Covenant if he embraced Judaism because he recognized the true God of Israel.

It is true that God's earlier Covenant with Abraham originated in faith, and when Abraham believed God, it was reckoned to him as righteousness (Genesis 15:6; Romans 4:3,9). Jesus' New Covenant is the same: "Therefore, since we are justified by faith, we have peace with God through our Lord Jesus Christ" (Romans 5:1). The words, Abraham's faith "was reckoned to him as righteousness were not written for his sake alone, but for ours also" (Romans 4:23). Nor should we forget the comparable faith and obedience of Isaac, who knowingly and willing submitted himself to be the sacrifice offered by Abraham (Genesis 22:8-9), thus prefiguring Christ's obedient submission to God on the Cross. As we saw in the last Chapter, men under the Old Covenant could not keep faith with God, but turned from his way, sought other idols, and practiced evil constantly. Priestly sacrifices and the shedding of blood were instituted to offer atonement to God.

Jesus' New Covenant is better because He became the sacrificial lamb, Whose shed blood brings remission of sins and the guaranty of salvation to those who believe in Him (Hebrews 9:12-14). Jesus' New Covenant is better because He involves the Holy Spirit in an indwelling, ongoing ministry of transforming a believer and progressively changing him into the likeness of Christ. Man still cannot keep the New Covenant unless enabled by God. Now, however, God accepts you on the basis you have accepted His Son by faith. Salvation is not based on you or your works, but on what God has done for you.

Jesus' New Covenant is better because he extended the Gospel to the Gentiles as well as Israel, to include all nations. Jesus' Great Commission to the Church is a universal mandate: "Go into all the world and preach the gospel to the whole creation. He who believes and is baptized will be saved; but he who does not believe will be condemned" (Mark 16:15-16; Matthew 28:19-20; see also Luke 10:1). At Acts 20:21 St. Paul speaks of expanding the salvation message "both to Jews and to Greeks of repentance to God and of faith in our Lord Jesus Christ." Repentance is an instant turning of the heart away from sin, and toward Christ, trusting Him in faith for salvation and strength to obey Him by the spiritual transformation He works. When we invite an unbeliever to "try Christ and see," we refer to the fuller life He promises, including the full blessings of obedience. Romans 1:16 refers to "the gospel: it is the power of God for salvation to everyone who has faith, to the Jew first and also the Greek." The Gospel is specifically extended to all nations at Acts 13:47-49; Galatians 3:13-14; Ephesians 3:6-7; I Corinthians 15:1-3). But Jesus also applies its effect to all men.

Jesus extended the Gospel to the most wretched and despicable of sinners; to "great crowds" (Matthew 7:28, 8:1), revealing: "For <u>everyone who asks receives</u>, and he who seeks finds" (Matthew 7:8). "<u>Every one</u> then who hears these words of mine and does them will be like a wise man who built his house upon the rock... it did not fall, because it had been founded on the rock" (Matthew 7:24-25). At Matthew 11:28 Jesus invites all: "Come to me, all who labor and are heavy-laden." At Matthew 16:24 Jesus proclaims: "If <u>any man</u> would come after me, let him..." John 3:16 says that God "so loved the world that he gave his only Son, that <u>whoever believes</u> in him may have eternal life." Titus 2:11 proclaims: "For the grace of God has appeared for the <u>salvation of all men</u>." I Timothy 2:4, 6 asserts that God "desires <u>all men</u> to be saved and to come to the knowledge of the truth. For... Jesus, who gave himself as a ransom <u>for all</u>." This general call to faith in Christ and his sacrifice to remit every sin in the world also appears in Luke 2:10-11, 13:3; John 1:12, 1:29, 3:17, 3:18, 12:47, 16:8; Acts 17:30-31; Romans 4:11, 10:13, 11:26; Galatians 3:22; and Revelation 22:17.

Among Born-Again believers there are two basic views about the extent of man's participation in his New Birth. The first view focuses on God's desire that <u>all</u> men be saved. Consequently God graciously gives all men sufficient revelation in nature and in conscience to recognize His existence, power, and benevolence (Psalm 19:1-2; Romans 1:19-20). God routinely works salvation by the Word of the Gospel, by the witness of believing Christians, and the quickening and conviction by the Holy Spirit. The Word, the Spirit, and a child of God are all designated agents of salvation. Man has genuine freedom, ceded lovingly by God to all men to allow their uncoerced choice, willfully given, to accept God's grace of salvation in Christ. The reality of human freedom is reconciled with the Sovereign Providence of Almighty God, Who has relinquished a miniscule part of His power to freedom, so that man's choice for Christ can be genuine when made.

God's grace has given every man the capacity to grasp revelation, discern right from wrong, and to recognize man's personal need to repent sin and confess Jesus as Lord and Saviour. However, there is spiritual warfare waged against God's call and mercy during our time on earth. The world, the flesh and the devil conspire to contest God's call by providing attractive and distracting sinful alternatives to holiness.

Man is free to defer his choice for Christ or even reject completely the revealed truths of the Gospel, because of hardness of heart through not heeding God's revelation of Himself in creation and conscience, and by inveterate attachment to the world and the flesh. Jesus labels these sinners who cannot understand or bear to hear the Word because "You are of your father the devil, and your will is to do your father's desires" (John 8:43-44). Only their pride and response to worldly allures prevent their salvation by allowing Satan to blind their eyes and minds, and harden their hearts against the Gospel truths (Luke 4:18; John 9:39, 12:40; I Corinthians 1:18-24; 2 Corinthians 3:14, 4:4). The Word could convict all who hear It, but Satan steals the Word, and his worldly system contests it so that it bears no fruit (Mark 4:15-19).

God combats Satan's wiles and allures by persistent calls, pursuit, persuasion, reward, punishment, and grace to motivate faith and obedience to win sinners to Christ by free choice. The examples of the thief on the cross, the prodigal son, and the laborers in the Vineyard reveal God's grace and forbearance in waiting until even the last hour to extend His mercy to penitents (Luke 23:43; Luke 15:11-32; Matthew 20:1-16), except where their recalcitrance, rejection, and evil are so fixed that God gives them up (Romans 1:24). When a man persists in resisting God's revelations and persuasions, and hardens his heart, he remains in the darkness of his own choice and excludes himself from the Kingdom of God by persisting to work his own way to salvation, if indeed he gives it any thought at all, rather than rely on grace, faith, and Christ.

We have many examples where God issues a special call of Sovereign election to His chosen servants. As a master chess-player, God can anticipate man's feeble resistance and from His vantage over eternity can over-rule any human obstinacy to God's call. The Greek word for "draw" signifies an irresistible attraction or compulsion, selectively inducing an obedience to the will of Him who calls.

Assuredly, God predetermines, and therefore specially calls some men, as He pleases in His Almighty Sovereignty. He persuaded Saul of Tarsus, who had mercilessly persecuted the early Christians, to come to Jesus when God added physical blindness to his spiritual darkness. God called Jonah to special service by literally excluding every other available alternative, until Jonah finally submitted to God's election. God emboldened Gideon to lead the liberation of Israel by using gentle confirmation of wet and dry fleeces to effectuate His call. However, it does not mean that by selecting some specially in advance, God intends to exclude all others not so uniquely called. For, God can still issue a general call to some or all others, intending to elicit their willing response to salvation by the Gospel, witnessed through the human agency of believers, and quickened by the Holy Spirit.

The second view of salvation focuses on this natural depravity of man, and posits man's total inability to make any response to salvation, or to grasp the Gospel revelation without the special grace of God electing and calling him for the New Birth. All men are lost unless they respond to the Gospel, and only the elect can respond because of God's particular call or election. God's Sovereignty decides who He elects, calls, and enables for reasons we may not presently discern. These chosen can rejoice in the certainty of their election, once they have responded to Jesus by God's grace through faith. All others remain in evil and darkness, sons of the devil, unable to comprehend the Word's revelations.

Thus, there are many devout Christians who believe in a pre-determinism by which God elects, calls, and imparts saving faith only to some men. See John 6:37,39: Acts 2:38-39, 13:48; Romans 8:28-30, 9:20-23.[13] Men who are not elected or called by God remain in their carnal, doomed condition, and do not desire, nor are they able, to receive God's grace through faith in Christ. Advocates of this view focus on God's Sovereignty, demonstration of power, and preference for an elect, by saving only them and scorning the remainder of mankind, who are born with natural, evil predilections, and deserve condemnation.

This limited view of salvation seeks confirmation in the Old Testament, where God chose Israel as His "people, my chosen... formed for myself" (Isaiah 43:20-21), to the exclusion of heathen nations, unless converted by the Jews to belief in God. Hence, in electing Israel for His people, God set the precedent for excluding all others from His choice. By this view, when Acts 20:21 extends salvation "both to Jews and to Greeks", it denotes gathering in some select Gentiles as well as some Jews, but is not an embrace of every individual within the group, and does not dismantle God's pre-destination of individuals within each group.

God certainly has the power to choose whomever He pleases for salvation or destruction, even though the depravity of all men provides no discernible basis for God choosing to pre-destine some rather than others. Romans 9:20-23 asserts: "But who are you, a man to answer back to God?... Has the potter no right over the clay, to make out of the same lump one vessel for beauty and another for menial use? <u>What if God,</u> desiring to show his wrath and to make known his power, has endured with much patience the vessels of wrath made for destruction, in order to make known the riches of his glory for the vessels of mercy, which he has prepared beforehand for glory, even us whom he has called, not from the Jews only but also from the Gentiles?"

Under either approach, God can persuade and urge — without coercing — whomever He pleases to repent and embrace Jesus. He can elect whomever He pleases for salvation, and need do nothing affirmative to exclude the rest, since every unsaved man is naturally inclined toward eternal damnation. Yet, there is nothing in God's character which suggests or reveals arbitrary selection of men to be saved. We would have to believe that God has ordained damnation for all mankind because all are sinners. Then He provided Jesus to atone for sin because of His great love for mankind and then inconsistently He withholds grace from the majority of sinners, under the operation of Sovereign election. While Romans 9:20-23 poses a hypothetical question, recognizing God's unrestrained power, it remains an inquiry, rather than a revelation that God in fact has exercised that power. In the context of a God of perfect love and goodness, it is incomprehensible why God would choose some for salvation and others for eternal damnation, although in His Sovereign will He is unaccountable for any election He chooses to make.

Indeed, God has given us an example of extreme selectivity in the Flood at the time of Noah, when all life on earth, except Noah, his family, and some animals on the Ark were destroyed. And we have no difficulty understanding the moral imperative that unrepentant evil cannot enter eternal bliss. On the other hand, <u>all</u> the evil persons among the Ninevites to whom Jonah preached, were effectively called to repentance and responded to the call.

Alternatively, language of election or pre-destination could be based upon God's foreknowledge of man's free choice to believe. I Peter 1:2, KJV, says that believers are "elect according to the foreknowledge of God." The passage does not say election is based on God's choice, but on His foreknowledge. And those whom He "foreknew he also predestined to be conformed to the image of his Son... he also justified; And those whom he justified he also glorified" (Romans 8:29-30).

It seems far more consistent with God's revealed goodness and perfect love, coupled with Jesus' expiation for the sins of all men, to recognize that God allows all men free choice to receive or reject salvation, because there is some great value in the gift of freedom. Freedom is a supervening, exalted blessing for man, and the right exercise of man's free choices glorifies God. Even though freedom has the inherent potential for wrong choice and consequent suffering, it is tolerated by God's Sovereignty because its blessings provide the highest good for mankind by the gifts of participation, collaboration, and contribution to spirituality and holy acts..

The following verses do indicate that God wills all persons to be saved, provided they freely respond to His proffer of grace through faith in Christ, Whom God has established as the exclusive way of reconciliation and salvation. They confirm that when the New Testament extends grace to "all men", it is not only to the Gentile nations, but to every individual; all of whose sins have been paid for by Christ's Atonement, and all of whom are now called by the Gospel. Indeed, 2 Peter 2:1 verifies that the sins of evil men are covered by the Blood of Christ, and speaks of false prophets who secretly bring destructive heresies, "even denying <u>the Master</u>

who bought them." This indicates their inclusion among those who have been called, and their eligibility for deliverance from sin, if they would only choose to receive salvation in Christ.

In speaking of little children, Jesus discloses: "So it is not the will of my Father who is in heaven that one of these little ones should perish" (Matthew 18:14). John 7:37 invites: "If anyone thirst, let him come to me and drink." Revelation 22:17 affirms: "Let Him who desires take the water of life without price." Acts 17:30 reveals "The times of ignorance God overlooked, but now he commands all men everywhere to repent... and of this he has given assurance to all men by raising him from the dead." Acts 2:21 citing Joel 2:32, says: "And it shall be that whoever calls on the name of the Lord shall be saved."

Romans 11:32 reveals: "For God has consigned all men to disobedience, that he may have mercy upon all." Romans 5:18 also says: "Then as one man's trespass led to condemnation for all men, so one man's act of righteousness leads to acquittal and life for all men." Jesus bore the wrath of God to atone for every sin of all sinners, and did not endure the pain in vain. If all men were not made eligible to be saved, Jesus' expiation for the sins of the whole world would be a futile, superfluous act, and it was not. All men become sinners through Adam's sin, and all men can be saved through the righteousness of one man, Jesus. Indeed, why would Jesus weep over the lost souls of Jerusalem (Luke 19:41), unless some who had been called were so hard-hearted they had squandered salvation by refusing to respond? If God elected only some for salvation selectively, and intended to abandon the rest, Jesus would have known that, and had no occasion to weep over the lost, since He always shared God's will.

Jesus teaches: "I, when I am lifted up from the earth, will draw all men to myself" (John 12:32). Romans 3:22-23 speaks of "The righteousness of God through faith in Jesus Christ for all who believe. For there is no distinction; since all have sinned and fall short of the glory of God." 2 Corinthians 5:14,15 says: "For the love of Christ controls us, because we are convinced that one has died for all;... And he died for all." I Timothy 4:10 says: "we have our hope set on the living God, who is the Savior of all men, especially of those who believe." Hebrews 2:9 says that Jesus died: "so that by the grace of God he might taste death for every one." If all men are not called by the general invitation of the Gospel, then Jesus' payment of the price for their sins would be a work of supererogation. He would have ransomed men by His Blood, yet God would have withheld their opportunity to respond by selectively excluding them from His call.

2 Peter 3:9 adds: "The Lord is... forbearing toward you, not wishing that any should perish, but that all should reach repentance." The terms "any" and "all" are inclusive, and exclude no one from God's grace. If God predestined men He would have no need for patience or forbearance, since he would simply recruit His final class of redeemed men and then bring the End Time. However, if men freely choose to respond to Him, God would be dealing with overlapping generations, and would abide the decision of each new generation, so everyone might have time to respond to God's grace. I John 2:2 says Jesus "is the expiation for our sins, and not for ours only but also for the sins of the whole world."

In the Old Testament God clearly declares His intention toward sinners and the need for some response by them: "I have no pleasure in the death of the wicked; but that the wicked turn from his way and live: turn ye, turn ye from your evil ways; for why will ye die, O house of Israel!" (Ezekiel 33:11, 18:23; Jeremiah 7:23-28). Thus, God's will that all men be saved, as well as the free choice of men to respond, are affirmed. Jesus told the unbelieving Jews: "you refuse to come to me that you may have life" (John 6;40), indicating the choice was ultimately and solely their's despite God's general revelations and specific persuasions. See also Proverbs 1:24-26, 29:1; Isaiah 53:6; Matthew 23:37; John 5:40, 12:32; Acts 7:51; Romans 2:11, 5:18; I John 2:2.

The undiscriminating universality of God's call to grace through Jesus, and the possibility of free choice rejecting that call, are illustrated in the parable of the Marriage Feast at Matthew 22:2-13. There, Jesus relates that the original guests invited by a king to a banquet declined to come, and even killed the messengers bearing the invitation. For this, they were destroyed. The king then sent his servants out to "invite to the marriage feast <u>as many as you find</u>. And those servants went out into the streets and <u>gathered all whom they found</u>, both bad and good, so the wedding hall was filled with guests" (Matthew 22:9-10). Obviously, every invitee did not answer the original call; and the second summons was extended to everyone, indiscriminately.

The Parable makes it clear that even if God's original election and predestination were meant for the remnant of Israel, after the coming of Jesus He chooses to invite all men to salvation. The Jews were first elected and called to salvation, but rejected it. God honored their freedom and modified their pre-destined status to be the first chosen among the elect. Their willful refusal to respond to God was an assertion of human choice against His intent, although allowed only by His permissive granting of this freedom.

Jesus goes on to relate in the parable that when the host looked at the guests, "he saw a man who had no wedding garment," and for that reason had him bound and cast into outer darkness (Matthew 22:11,13). It was the custom in Jesus' time for the host to give his guest a wedding garment to wear,[14] so the invitee's refusal to benefit from what was offered him, is a representation of sinners refusing to "put on Christ" (Romans 13:4). The guest was called and initially participated, but refused to receive the gift of salvation through faith in Christ as Lord and Saviour, and ended in outer darkness.

The parallel Parable of the Great Banquet at Luke 14:16 expresses the universal call to salvation in even more striking terms. Here, those originally favored with an invitation to a banquet declined to come for various unworthy reasons. The host then instructed his servant: "Go out quickly to the streets and lanes of the city, and bring in the poor and maimed and blind and lame." When this was done, and there was still room, the master told his servants: "Go out to the highways and hedges, and <u>compel people to come in</u>, that my house may be filled" (Luke 14:21,23). This clearly reflects God's desire for any and all men to be included in the banquet, using the utmost persuasions, once the original invited guests declined to accept.

In the Parable of the Laborers in the Vineyard, the Householder not only extended his invitation to work for him to latecomers arriving at the eleventh hour, but through His unmerited generosity, his later invitations were extended to <u>every</u> latecomer that he found unoccupied (Matthew 20:3-6). If an employer decides to hire everyone who responds to his advertisement, the applicant must still choose to apply and signify His acceptance before the employer's choice of hiring is complete.[15]

We are reminded that the freedom to choose is initiated by God's grace, and man's desire to choose likewise comes as a gift from God, but any man who does not willingly choose to respond to grace by faith will not be chosen by God. Those men who respond are the ones who are elected for the blessings which God determines to award "whosoever will" in His economy of salvation.

God's call is no longer just for Israel, but is a universal one. However, unless a person responds as God has designated, he cannot be chosen or elected by the King. He is barred by his own abuse of freedom in refusing to answer the call. Even though now invited to enter, a person is still required to enter voluntarily by the narrow gate, which is Christ (Matthew 7:13; Luke 13:24), before he can avail himself of the benefits of Christ's merit.

While Christ suffered and atoned <u>sufficiently</u> to provide enough grace to cover the sins of all men, His grace is <u>efficient</u> in individual instances, only when received by faith, freely exercised by each believer. God's call and offer of salvation is <u>provided</u> for all, but is <u>effective</u> only for those who believe by a personal response of faith. The meaning of life on earth comes from man's opportunity to say yes to Jesus; to recognize one's personal responsibility for sin, and how it has offended God and alienated sinners from Him.

Life is an occasion to reap the rewards of eternity, by recognizing one's need for a personal Saviour; to see that Jesus is God's only provision for salvation through the substitutionary Atonement of Jesus. And to understand that we are saved by grace through faith in Jesus as Lord and Saviour, because of God's and Jesus' love and mercy. Life is an opportunity for believers to "press on toward the goal for the prize of the upward call of God in Christ Jesus" (Philippians 3:14). It is man's chance to pursue what Christ pursued for us, and have one's position in Christ fixed, while He fixes the conditions which need transforming. The goal toward which we press is to be like Christ and to be with Christ here and Hereafter.

In the Old Testament, God called all Israel to salvation and deliverance, but individual members were free to decline His invitation. "But of Israel he says, 'All day long I have held out my hands to a disobedient and contrary people'." (Isaiah 65:2; Romans 10:21). Offering salvation to Israel did not mean that every individual was guaranteed automatic inclusion among the saved, but only those who responded in faithful submission. Nor does the new Testament expand salvation to embrace every sinner automatically, unless each individually expresses a willing desire to receive God's grace. So we hear the question: If God loves everyone, why doesn't He simply save, or arrange for every man to respond to salvation, despite individual recalcitrance? There are several reasons. God has provided Jesus' substitionary, sacrificial atonement as His way for every sinner to be saved. And that requires a voluntary, free response by each person to God's gift of salvation, by grace through faith in Jesus Christ. This is the only way to salvation consistent with God's preference for free choice and an equal opportunity for each to be saved. Forcing a sinner to change would be inconsistent with freedom. Allowing an unredeemed sinner into the assembly of believers would wreak havoc on both the sinner and the saints, if unrepented evil mingled with goodness.

Thus, eternal life in Christ is not applied automatically to everyone, even though it is universally available, to all men. A sinner remains in sin, as a child of Satan (John 8:44; I John 3:10), lost and unsaved, until he willingly chooses to receive God's redemption and salvation. He is unreconciled to God until he responds to grace; receives, appropriates, applies, and accepts personally what God is offering to transform his life and restore fellowship and right relationship. At Revelation 3:20 Jesus teaches: "Behold I stand at the door and knock; if <u>anyone</u> hears my voice and opens the door, I will come in to him and eat with him, and he with me."

Some Christians shy away from the idea of any active saving faith which requires more than passive belief, regarding it as equivalent to a work derogating from God's complete work of grace, independent of any contribution by man. They fear that any initial determination by man to earn or merit salvation; even obediently choosing to follow Jesus as Lord, is more than faith in Him, and violates Galatians 3:2,5 that we receive the Spirit "by hearing with faith," not "by works of the law." Yet, exercising faith in Christ involves the same obedient submission to God's will and word, as determining to follow Jesus as Lord.

We often think of faith as passive thought, and works as active obedience to God's commands. Yet, faith involves an act of submissive obedience in response to God's directives and promised benefits (James 2:18-26). The response of faith is required for salvation, but in no way diminishes the reality that salvation is accomplished exclusively by God's grace. John 1:12 says: "But to all who received him, who believed in his name, he gave power to become children of God; who were born... of God." John 5:24 adds: "he who hears my word and believes him who sent me, has eternal life." God gives the power, but the receiving and believing are free acts of men, in obedient submission. Indeed, the faith necessary to receive the gift of salvation is singularly not a work, but man's admission he cannot merit or work for salvation, but must accept it by God's pure grace.[16]

There is no man-made merit or righteousness in man's exercise of will which acknowledges full reliance on God. In fact, faith is exercised, evidenced, and expressed by obedient acts. Noah had to build and board the Ark to express his faith (Genesis 6:14,18). God gave direction and made promises to Abraham, and Abraham had to show faith by obediently leaving his comfort and following God's leading (Genesis 12:1). Jesus called Levi with the words, "Follow me" (Mark 2:14). At Matthew 4:19 He summoned Peter and Andrew to "Follow me, and I will make you fishers of men." From the beginning, faith's response is not only believing Who Jesus is, but also involves following Jesus as He leads the way. One must exert as much effort to receive Jesus as Lord, as to receive Him as Saviour, by recognizing his sin, his need to change, and his need to entrust his transformation and deliverance to the One Lord and Saviour.

Accordingly, man's response to God's invitation to be saved, is not a work, but God's designated way of exercising faith in Christ. How else could we express faith, but by audibilizing our consent? Romans 10:9 promises: "If you confess with your lips that Jesus is Lord and believe in your heart that God raised Him from the dead, you will be saved." God enables our faith by hearing His Word, but our acceptance of grace by faith becomes an act of man's free will, which does not detract from faith which originates with God, and is enabled by His grace via the Word.

SALVATION DEPENDS UPON GOD'S GRACE THROUGH FAITH

If a person willingly chooses to receive Jesus Christ as Lord and Saviour by grace through faith, it does not matter whether the response to God's call comes by pre-destination or personal determination, in the sense that in either scenario the blessings of conversion, faith, and repentance have originated with God and resulted in salvation. Prevenient grace from God enables one to recognize his personal sin and its offensiveness to God, producing a conversion or change of attitude to seek God's salvation in Jesus Christ. Jesus reveals that "No one can come to me unless the Father who sent me draws him; and I will raise him up at the last day" (John 6:44). "No one can come to me unless it is granted him by the Father" (John 6:65). The recognition that Jesus is the Christ, or Messiah is likewise given by the grace of God (Matthew 16:15-17; I Corinthians 12:3). Man's salvation is entirely God's plan, enablement, and grace.

Both the desire for repentance, and the ability to repent are granted by God's grace. Jeremiah 3:22 promises: "Return, ye backslidden children, and I will heal your backsliding." 2 Timothy 2:25-26 speaks of unsaved sinners: "God may perhaps grant that they will repent and come to know the truth and they may escape from the snare of the devil." See also, Hosea 14:4; Acts 5:31. 11:18; and Romans 2:4. Romans 9:16 concludes that God's salvation and compassion "depends not upon man's will or exertion, but upon God's mercy."

God accomplishes everything, and salvation neither depends upon nor requires human goodness, meritorious works, or previously changed lives. The freedom which results from a new, regenerated, transformed nature, is also the gift of God: "So if the Son makes you free, you will be free indeed" (John 8:36; and see 2 Corinthians 3:17; Galatians 5:1).

God brings about one's regeneration, or change to a new spirit being, contemporaneously with the New Birth. John 1:12-13 tells us concerning Jesus: "But to all who received him, who believed in his name, he gave power to become children of God; who were born, not of blood nor of the will of the flesh nor of the will of man, but of God."

Whether we focus on man's faith and belief; on God's power; the cleansing Blood of Christ; or Spirit Baptism into Christ's death and resurrection, unless man undergoes a New Birth, he can neither see nor enter the Kingdom of God. Jesus teaches at John 3:3-8: "Truly, truly, I say to you, unless one is born anew, he cannot see the kingdom of God... unless one is born of water and the Spirit, he cannot enter the kingdom of God. That which is born of the flesh is flesh, and that which is born of the Spirit is spirit. Do not marvel that I said to you, 'You must be born anew.' The wind blows where it will, and you hear the sound of it, but you do not know whence it comes or whither it goes; so it is with every one who is born of the Spirit."

The New Birth is solely a matter of God's grace. You had no voice in your physical birth, and you have no voice in your spiritual New Birth when God calls you. When Jesus called forth Lazarus from the dead (John 11:43), Lazarus had no participation in his resurrection. It was simply the call of Jesus which brought Lazarus to life. Presumably, Lazarus could have declined to come forth, and remained in his tomb. Likewise, the Word calls hearers to come forth in faith, and creates, provides, and quickens the faith by which those dead in sin can respond to God's call (Romans 10:17). But we remain free to spurn the call, at our own peril.

It is illogical to think that the beneficiary deserves credit for receiving a gift, rather than the donor who gives it. Faith is simply receiving something offered by grace, and is the opposite of doing something meritorious as a work. Is a beggar who reaches out to receive a gift, any less at the complete mercy of the giver, than a blind or armless beggar who receives the free gift in a cup put to his lips? If a man is drowning, and about to sink, and a rescuer extends a hand to pull him to safety, does his response of reaching out mean he has accomplished his own rescue? And if the drowning man struggles or refuses to cooperate and reach out, but pulls away and drowns, has he not frustrated his rescue? You are saved "If you confess that God raised him from the dead" (Romans 10:9). Surely, speaking your confession does not detract from God's grace, since He has designated the manner of acceptance. If a radio station offers a prize to any listener who phones in, the response and minor effort of calling the station to accept in no way detracts from the fact the gift is free, and given by the grace of the station. The beneficiary's effort in receiving is simply the designated affirmation of acceptance, and in no way diminishes the largesse; or makes it any less a free gift.

If a rich king invites the poor to a banquet at his home, neither their willingness to eat, nor their journey to dine, obtains or pays for the feast, which remains the gift of the king, even though both the journey and the eating are necessary to receive the free gift. Without faith and submission we cannot receive salvation by grace, though neither human act merits it. Faith is simply the hand of a beggar reaching out to receive the gift proferred by a King in the manner decreed by Him, and human intention to receive falls far short of a meritorious work.

Jesus healed ten lepers, but sent them first to show the priests, "And as they went they were cleansed" (Luke 17:14). Jesus healed a man who had been blind from his birth, but before the healing was complete, Jesus told the man: "Go, wash in the pool of Siloam (which means Sent). So he went, and washed and came back seeing" (John 9:7). Certainly, the designated obedient responses of the lepers and the blind man in no way diminished Jesus' sole authorship of the miracles.

God's gift of freedom dignifies, and even exalts, man, but it is alright for man to be exalted if it has been granted by God for His glory, and man's proper exercise of free choice redounds to the glory of God. If God intentionally makes a gift to man, allowing him to participate in a process which expresses faith, and enhances worth, we need not deny the gift because it evokes human will or exertion. There is a vast difference between man pridefully arrogating God-like characteristics to himself, and God lovingly bestowing a gift of divine import to His beloved creature. There is ample evidence God has graciously given freedom to man, as a loving gift which also glorifies God as it shares His glory with man through, by, and because of Jesus.

The response and acceptance of God's saving grace which God has designated for sinners is an individual exercise of faith in Jesus Christ as Lord and Saviour, the Messiah and Son of God. John 3:16 puts it simply: "For God so loved the world that he gave his only Son, that whoever believes in him should not perish but have eternal life." Conversely, "he who does not believe is condemned already, because he has not believed in the name of the only Son of God" (John 3:18). John 20:31 says the signs Jesus performed are recorded in the Bible: "that you may believe that Jesus is the Christ, the Son of God, and that believing you may have life in his name."

Hebrews 11:6 says: "without faith it is impossible to please him." Salvation by faith was foretold in the Old Testament. Psalm 34:22 says: "The Lord redeemeth the soul of his servants: and none of them that trust in him shall be desolate." God as Deliverer of Israel from evil in the world was a common theme of salvation in I Samuel 7:8; I Chronicles 16:35; Psalms 55;16, 71:3; Isaiah 25:9, 33:22; and Zechariah 9:16.

God uses His Word in Scripture as the instrument to stimulate faith in believers. James 1:18, 21 reveals: 'Of his own will he brought us forth by the word of truth that we should be a kind of first fruits of his creatures... Therefore... receive with meekness the implanted word, which is able to save your souls." Romans 10:13-17, KJV, agrees: "Every one who calls upon the name of the Lord will be saved. But how are men to call upon him in whom they have not believed? And how are they to believe in him of whom they have never heard?... So faith comes by hearing, and hearing by the word of God." Jesus says: "the words I have spoken to you are spirit and life" (John 6:63). 2 Timothy 3:15 urges us to study the "sacred writings which are able to instruct you for salvation through faith in Christ Jesus."

The heart of the Gospel message which Jesus first delivered to the Jews, is that their long-awaited King, Jesus the Messiah, had come; therefore, "The time is fulfilled, and the kingdom of God is at hand; repent, and believe in the gospel" (Mark 1:15; and see also, Matthew 4:17, 10:7, 12:28; Luke 17:21). When the Jews, His "own people received him not" (John 1:11),

Jesus extended the Gospel to all men who would confess Jesus as Lord and be born-again by faith in Him, as Risen Saviour.

St. Paul defined the Gospel as "the word of the cross (which) is folly to those who are perishing, but to us who are being saved it is the power of God... we preach Christ crucified... to those who are called, both Jews and Greeks, Christ the power of God" (I Corinthians 1:17-24). Romans 1:1,3 speaks of "the gospel of God... concerning his Son Jesus Christ our Lord." I Corinthians 15:1-3 speaks of "the gospel... by which you are saved... that Christ died for our sins."

Jesus gives us a simple reminder that we are saved by looking to him for salvation: "And as Moses lifted up the serpent in the wilderness, so must the Son of man be lifted up, that whoever believes in him may have eternal life" (John 3:14-15). When Moses interceded for the Israelites to deliver them from the fatal bites of a plague of fiery serpents, God commanded him to make a serpent of brass and put it on a pole in sight of all the people, "and it shall come to pass, that every one that is bitten, when he looketh upon it, shall live" (Numbers 21:8). Today, sinners who are 'snake-bitten' by sin must look up to Jesus for healing, as for every thing. When we trustingly fix our gaze on Jesus, He grants the mercy His Word promises: "and I, when I am lifted up from the earth, will draw all men to myself" (John 12:32). Evangelists, missionaries, and witnesses are the modern Moses who lift Jesus up, so He can be seen by all the people.

Ephesians 2:8-9 puts it: "For by grace you have been saved through faith; and this is not your own doing, it is the gift of God — not because of works, lest any man should boast." Romans 9:16 agrees: "So it depends not upon man's will or exertion, but upon God's mercy." Titus 3:5 adds: "he saved us, not because of deeds done by us in righteousness, but in virtue of his own mercy." See also, John 1:12-13, 3:36, 5:24, 6:29, 6:40, 10:28; Acts 2:21, 10:43, 13:48, 16:31, 17:28; Romans 10:13 (citing Joel 2:32); I Timothy 1:16; and I John 5:1, 5:10-13.

THE RIGHTEOUSNESS OF JESUS IS IMPUTED TO BELIEVERS

At the New Birth, the very righteousness, holiness, and faithful obedience of Jesus are imputed to a believer, so that he is justified; covered, and washed clean by the Blood of Christ. Jesus' shed Blood serves as the sacrifice by which Atonement and propitiation for sin were made (Hebrews 9:22). We are justified before God because Jesus offered Himself as our substitute. In the eyes of God, man's faith is counted as righteousness because of the vicarious sacrifice of Jesus. His sins are remitted; and he is established as positionally righteous or sinless before God. I Corinthians 1:30 says that God made Jesus "our wisdom, our righteousness and consecration and redemption." God has forgiven and forgotten our sins because of Jesus, and "made us alive together with Christ (by grace you have been saved)... So then you are no longer strangers and sojourners, but you are fellow workmen with the saints and members of the household of God" (Ephesians 2:1,5,9). Jesus is He who is able to let you stand blameless before God (I Corinthians 1:8).

Jesus "has now reconciled in his body" believers who were formerly sinners (Colossians 1:22). "And you who were dead in trespasses... God made alive together with him, having forgiven us all our trespasses" (Colossians 2:13). I Corinthians 6:11 adds: "you were washed, you were consecrated, you were justified in the name of the Lord Jesus Christ and in the Spirit of our God." See also, 2 Thessalonians 1:11; Hebrews 7:25; I Peter 3:24; and I John 4:9).

The righteousness of Jesus is ascribed or attributed to sinful believers because of their faith, which is reckoned to them as righteousness. Romans 5:8 explains: "God shows his love for us in that while we were yet sinners Christ died for us." Romans 4:3-5 establishes: "Abraham believed God, and it was reckoned to him as righteousness... And to one who does not work but trusts him who justifies the ungodly, his faith is reckoned as righteousness." See also, Galatians 2:15-16, 3:2,5; and 2 Timothy 1:9. Romans 3:22 says believers can receive "the righteousness of God through faith in Jesus Christ for all who believe."

Romans 10:9 reveals: "if you confess with your lips that Jesus is Lord and believe in your hearts that God raised him from the dead, you will be saved. For man believes with his heart and so is justified, and he confesses with his lips and so is saved... For, everyone who calls upon the name of the Lord will be saved." John 1:12-13 puts it: "To all who received him, who believed in his name, he gave power to become children of God; who were born... of God." Titus 2:14 adds that Jesus "gave himself for us to redeem us from all iniquity and to purify for himself a people of his own who are zealous for good deeds."

Forgiveness, which originates as an act of grace and mercy by God, and allows for a sinner's return to right-standing, is pre-figured in the Old Testament. David confessed at Psalm 32:5: "I acknowledged my sin unto thee, and mine iniquity have I not hid. I said, I will confess my transgressions unto the Lord; and thou forgavest the iniquity of my sin." God says at Isaiah 44:22: 'return unto me; for I have redeemed thee... I have blotted out... thy transgressions." As already noted, without submitting to Christ and appropriating His righteousness to one's own account, we cannot be restored to right-standing with God. The Pharisees practiced the minutiae of the law punctiliously, but their hearts were not right. Israel had "a zeal for God," but "being ignorant of the righteousness that comes from God, and seeking to establish their own, they did not submit to God's righteousness" (Romans 10:3).

God has made Jesus our righteousness and consecration (I Corinthians 1:30), "For our sake he made him to be sin who knew no sin, so that in him we might become the righteousness of God" (2 Corinthians 5:21). If only we would abandon our self-righteousness, we would find an inexhaustible supply of holiness in Jesus, from Whom our source of righteousness originates. We need to receive this promise by faith, and boldly draw our righteousness from Jesus, rather than attempt to produce our own, unaided.

In the Gospel, "the righteousness of God is revealed through faith for faith" (Romans 1:17), from start to finish, from Jesus to man; and "the righteousness of God (comes) through faith in Jesus Christ for all who believe" (Romans 3:22). The crown of righteousness is the prize from the Lord "to all who have loved his appearing" (2 Timothy 4:8).

GOD'S BLESSING OF REGENERATION AND RENEWAL

God's love and goodness provide far more than imputed or positional standing of righteousness for believers, through the substituted righteousness of Christ. The essential blessing which precedes all others is the new Birth which occurs by God's grace through man's faith in Jesus Christ as Lord and Saviour (Ephesians 2:5). We need a sovereign cleansing of our sin nature, administered by the Holy Spirit, washed in the water of regeneration, and literally re-made by a New Birth from God. God enters the life of the believer and makes him a regenerated "new creation" (2 Corinthians 5:17) in the image and character of Christ, and gives a believer "newness of life" (Romans 6:4, 8:11; I Corinthians 2:16; 2 Corinthians 4:16; Galatians 3:27; Ephesians 4:12-15, 4:22-24; Colossians 3:9-10; and I Peter 1:2-4, 3:18).

We are not only restored to right-standing with God, but also forgiven our sins; actually sanctified and made righteous; made members of God's household (Ephesians 2:19); and of Christ's Body, His Church of believers (Luke 3:16; I Corinthians 12:13; and Ephesians 4:4-5). It is all accomplished by the obedient faithfulness and shed Blood of Christ.

The Church was purchased by the Blood of Christ (Acts 20:28). Romans 5:9 says "we are now justified by his blood." "In him we have redemption through his blood, the forgiveness of our trespasses" (Ephesians 1:7). We were once far from the covenants of promise, but by Jesus' blood we "have been brought near" (Ephesians 2:13). His precious blood washes, regenerates, and cleanses us from all sin (I John 1:7; I Corinthians 6:11; Revelation 1:5). "You were ransomed from the futile ways inherited from your fathers... with the precious blood of Christ" (I Peter 1:19). "Under the law almost everything is purified with blood, and without the shedding of blood there is no forgiveness of sins" (Hebrews 9:22). Jesus is the culmination of the Old Testament sacrifices, perfect in His offering of Himself, and given once for all. Therefore, "we have confidence to enter the sanctuary by the blood of Jesus" (Hebrews 10:19).

God intends to make us actually or literally righteous, first by a regeneration or literal transformation to a new spirit being in the image of Christ, and then by ongoing, imparted righteousness by the Holy Spirit, until members of the Church "all attain to the unity of the faith... to mature manhood, to the measure of the stature of the fullness of Christ" (Ephesians 4:13).

A believer's conversion, or change of mind leads to and becomes part of, the new Birth when it is coupled with faith in Jesus as Lord and Saviour. I Peter 1:23 explains this, too, is accomplished by God's power through the Word: "You have been born anew, not of perishable seed but of imperishable, through the living and abiding word of God." Indeed, if conversion and the New Birth do not occur, the unsaved person has no choice but to exist in his old nature of rebellious disobedience (John 5:44; Romans 8:6-8). This is precisely why the Gospel calls for a New Birth, in order to transform the old, sinful man into a New Man, re-made in the image of Christ.

Coinciding with the new Birth, God brings about the conversion of a believer's mind by digging the soil of his heart, to break it open and make it receptive to the Word's seeds of faith and repentance. In the Parable of the Barren Fig Tree at Luke 13:8, Jesus, as Vinedresser and Intercessor, assures God He will "dig about" the unfruitful tree, which represents the heart of unsaved man, as well as apply fertilizer to feed and nourish it, to bring about fecundity.

However, before the tree, or human heart, can receive the needed aliment; assimilate and convert it into fruit, the soil in which it is planted must be softened and opened so the gifts can be received. This may involve some suffering for humans as God allows various afflictions to rend the heart, as a hoe tears up the ground, until the elements necessary for divine life have been received.[17]

The Holy Spirit accomplishes the re-creation of the new Man and baptizes a believer into the Body of Christ by a symbolic burial and resurrection shared with Christ (Luke 3:16; I Corinthians 12:13; Ephesians 4:4-5). Romans 6:3-4 queries: "Do you not know that all of us who have been baptized into Christ Jesus were baptized into his death? We were buried therefore with him by baptism into death, so that as Christ was raised from the dead by the glory of the Father, we too might walk in newness of life... So you also must consider yourselves dead to sin and alive to God in Christ Jesus." Romans 8:11 adds: "If the Spirit of him who raised

Jesus from the dead dwells in you, he who raised Christ Jesus from the dead will give life to your mortal bodies also through his Spirit which dwells in you." Galatians 3:27,29 adds: "For as many of you as were baptized into Christ have put on Christ... And if you are Christ's, then you are Abraham's offspring, heirs according to promise."

With the Baptism which raises one a New Man, the Holy Spirit baptizes believers <u>into</u> the Body of Christ, the Ecclesia, or those called out from the world; the Church, comprising all who believe in Jesus Christ as Lord and Saviour (I Corinthians 12:13).

Romans 12:2 puts it: "Do not be conformed to this world, but be transformed by <u>the renewal of your mind</u> that you may prove the will of God, what is good and acceptable and perfect." I Corinthians 1:4-9 says that in Jesus " in every way you were enriched in him with all speech and all knowledge... so that you are not lacking in any spiritual gift, as you wait for the revealing of our Lord, who will sustain you to the end, guiltless in the day of our Lord. God is faithful, by whom you were called into the fellowship of his Son." 2 Corinthians 5:17 adds: "Therefore, if any one is in Christ, he is a new creation, the old has passed away, behold the new has come."

Galatians 3:27 explains: "For as many of you as were baptized into Christ have put on Christ." Ephesians 4:22-23 calls man to renewal: "Put off your old nature which belongs to your former manner of life and is corrupt through deceitful lusts, and be renewed in the spirit of your minds, and put on the new nature, created after the likeness of God in true righteousness and holiness." I Peter 1:3-5 says of Jesus: "we have been born anew to a living hope... and to an inheritance which is imperishable, undefiled, and unfading, kept in heaven for you, who by God's power are guarded through faith for a salvation ready to be revealed in the last time."

I John 5:18 says: "We know that any one born of God does not sin, but He who was born of God keeps him, and the evil one does not touch him." God's power "has granted to us all things that pertain to life and godliness," that through God's promises "you may escape from the corruption that is in the world because of passion, and become partakers of the divine nature" (2 Peter 1:3-4). Again, the Word which reveals God's promises is instrumental in our receiving the divine nature.

The idea that sinful man needs a new, clean heart; restored and regenerated in a right spirit, appears throughout the Old Testament.[18] David prayed for mercy at Psalm 51: 1-10: "Blot out my transgressions. Wash me thoroughly and I shall be clean... Create in me a clean heart, O God; and renew a right spirit within me." God promises a New Covenant to Israel at Jeremiah 31:33: "After those days, saith the Lord, I will put my law in their inward parts, and write it in their hearts; and will be their God, and they shall be my people." See also, Deuteronomy 30:6; I Samuel 10:6,9; and Ezekiel 18:31. At Ezekiel 36:26-27 God says: "A new heart also will I give you... And I will put my spirit within you, and cause you to walk in my statutes, and ye shall keep my judgments, and do them." See also, Psalm 37:6. God is indeed the author and perfecter of a believer's regeneration and literal holiness. Through Jesus, we "have access in one Spirit to the Father" (Ephesians 2:18). God is He, "who by the power at work within us is able to do far more abundantly than all that we ask or think" (Ephesians 3:20).

GOD'S BLESSING OF IMPARTED RIGHTEOUSNESS

The New Birth is also accompanied by and accomplished through the indwelling presence of the Godhead. This indwelling is both the start of regeneration, and the means of ongoing sanctification. At Acts 2:38-39 Peter teaches: "Repent, and be baptized every one of you in the name of Jesus Christ for the forgiveness of your sins; and <u>you shall receive the Holy Spirit</u>. For the promise is to you and to your children and to all that are far off, every one of whom the Lord our God calls to him." I John 4:12,15 proclaims: "if we love one another, God abides in us and his love is perfected in us... Whoever confesses that Jesus is the Son of God, God abides in him, and he in God."

God communicates His divine life to believers in a spectacular way by literally indwelling them. When, at the New Birth, we receive the gift of the Holy Spirit, God personally enters into our lives in the most intimate manner and union to accomplish spiritual change. He is no longer a God "out there," immanent in Creation, or simply "with us," but He has established Himself as an indwelling motivator and enabler of a believer's spiritual life. God is in us, His life empowers us, and He is present with us as a Person. This is God's work in you, for you, and with you, because of Jesus.

Even more, God has accomplished a mutual indwelling with believers, beyond friendship, which permits total merger, absorption, mingling, and the most private discourse and spiritual intercourse possible. There is a synthesis of the divine and human personalities; a shared identity, as God's imparted perfect life shapes us into the image of Christ. Not that we change God in any way, nor lose our own identity, though we are incorporated into, and complete, the Body of Christ, of which Jesus is the Head, with all the interaction, interdependence, and exchange of energy, as cells and nerves in a physical body (Romans 12:5; Galatians 3:28). As we are assimilated into its corporate structure, we draw strength from associating with other members of Christ's Body. We cannot give anything to benefit God directly, but He bids us love him by sharing our strength with weaker members, by supplying comfort, encouragement, edification, example, and sharing our time, treasure, and talent.

God uses imagery of marriage to illustrate spiritual union, when He refers to Himself as Israel's husband (Isaiah 54:5; Jeremiah 31:32). Ephesians 5:31-32 urges husbands and wives to join and become one, as Jesus and the Church do. However, married union is but a pale imitation of the interchange of identities which takes place on a spiritual level in the greater merger between God and believers, which involves an indwelling by the Holy Spirit; a commingling of persons in one another; an infusion of divine life and identity into men; and an imparting of Christ's character. This constitutes and promotes the most cohesive joinder and inherent contact possible between intimates.

Jesus establishes believers as constituent parts of His Body, which is the key to literal union with God. For, He places believers in Him, and He is in God, just as God is in Jesus, which allows us to be in God. We can visualize ourselves as being in Him like a drop of water in the sea, at the same time the sea is in each drop, its constituent part, and <u>is</u> the aggregate of all the individual drops of water and so much more. We retain our own individuality and identity, as a grain of sand is separate from, yet merged with its beach. We are privileged to comprise, and be part of the whole. The body is composed of, in, and the life of, thousands of healthy cells, while each cell is also in the body, part of the body, and shares the life of the body.

Because the Holy Spirit dwells within believers, we are called to live and walk by the Spirit (Galatians 5:25). We are blessed with "the fruit of the Spirit... love, joy, peace, patience, kindness, goodness, faithfulness, gentleness, self-control" (Galatians 5:22-23), which reflect and impart the character of Jesus Christ. Galatians 4:5-7 teaches that Jesus was sent "to redeem those who were under the law, so that we might receive adoption as sons. And because you are sons, God has sent the Spirit of his Son into our hearts... So through God you are no longer a slave, but a son, and if a son then an heir." We are "filled with all the fullness of God" (Ephesians 3:19; see also, Ephesians 1:5).

Jesus makes it clear at John 14:23 that the Godhead indwells believers: "If a man loves me, he will keep my word, and my Father will love him, and we will come to him and make our home with him." At John 17:20-26 Jesus prays for "those who are to believe in me... that they may all be one; even as thou, Father, art in me, and I in thee, that they may also be in us... I in them and thou in me... that the love with which thou hast loved me may be in them, and I in them." See also, Luke 17:21; John 6:56, 10:38, 14:17, 14:20, 15:5, 15:9, 17:11; Acts 17:28; Romans 5:5, 8:10-11; I Corinthians 6:19; 2 Corinthians 4:10; Galatians 2:20, 4:6; Ephesians 3:16-20, 4:6, 5:8; Colossians 1:27; and I John 2:8, 4:12-16).

God helps us to elude sin and its consequences of suffering by re-constituting New-Born Men as transformed and regenerated persons, no longer under the natural compulsion to sin. When we avoid sinning we eliminate whatever painful consequences originate with sin. God accomplishes a new imperviousness to sin by giving His children a new heart, instilled with reverential awe, so we will not wish to depart from His way. Regeneration makes us dead to sin and alive to God in Christ (Romans 6:11). Although we are sill capable of sin like unredeemed or natural men, because of God's enabling we are no longer under that compulsion to sin. We increasingly resist undergoing or responding to the temptations of sin.[19] For, a Christian's new nature frees him from the bondage of sin and enables him to resist sin.

Sin also corrupts the inner man and his very nature. God's grace and mercy provide us with ongoing sanctification or holiness by infusing the holiness of Christ into us, through an ongoing transformation of our new nature into Christ's nature. The holiness of Christ is thus imparted to us. We have been restored to right relationship with God, Law and Justice. Justification has corrected a broken relationship <u>outside</u> of us. And regeneration and sanctification transform our nature <u>within</u> us. We have been restored to a <u>position</u> of rightstanding and to a <u>disposition</u> of holiness.[20]

This spiritual growth with which God blesses believers progresses through three phases, each depending solely upon God's power, yet all involving man's free and willing response by faithful receptivity to God's grace and power for holiness. The first phase, which God accomplishes at the new Birth, is called regeneration, or the literal transformation of the new, inner, spiritual man into the likeness of Christ. The second phase is called sanctification, progressing in the filling of the Spirit during the believer's earthly sojourn, in which God increasingly and continually imparts Christ-like character to believers. The third phase is glorification, or the fulfillment and final deliverance of spiritual perfection in the next world. It is also accomplished solely by God's power, with the believer's fervent concurrence and desire to be re-molded and transformed, by submitting to the Lord.

We can see that regeneration occurs in a moment, when the sinner is converted and made new. Sanctification is a successive process of growing in holiness, ongoing during one's lifetime. And glorification lasts for eternity. Thus, Jesus will not give glorification to sinners still in bondage to sin, but provides for perfecting of our spirituality at His Second Coming. Then, although "What is sown is perishable, what is raised up is imperishable" (I Corinthians 15:42). "Just as we have borne the image of the man of dust, we shall also bear the image of the man of heaven" (I Corinthians 15:49). Philippians 1:10-11 speaks of being "pure and blameless for the day of Christ, filled with the fruits of righteousness which come through Jesus Christ."

Clearly, our salvation is an ongoing process, beginning when God decided, before the foundation of the world, that a fallen mankind would be in need of salvation, and He set the plan of redemption in motion. We were saved 2,000 years ago when Jesus went to the Cross as a substitute for sinners to redeem men from the penalty of sin. We were saved at the New Birth when the Holy Spirit baptized us into the Body of Christ; Christ's righteousness was imputed to us; and our deliverance became fixed in time. We are being saved from the power of sin while in the world, as Christ's righteousness is actually imparted by the indwelling Holy Spirit, and we literally grow holier. Today Jesus continues to bless believers as our High Priest and Intercessor with God by delivering His own from the world, the flesh, and the devil. And we will be saved from the wrath to come, in the Hereafter, when we are removed from sin's presence, glorified, and placed for eternity in a Paradise of perfect love and righteousness, accomplished through "Christ in you, the Hope of Glory" (Colossians 1:27).

At the resurrection of the faithful dead in Christ, Jesus also raises us who are alive, "changed in a moment," unto immortality (I Corinthians 15:51-54). Our sanctification will be completed and we will be freed from pain and sorrow as we are re-united with the Lord when he returns for His Church (I Corinthians 1:8; 2 Corinthians 3:18; Ephesians 4:13. 5:25-27; Philippians 1:6, 3:20-21; Colossians 1:22; I Thessalonians 3:13; Revelation 21:4; Isaiah 25:8, 35:10). I John 3:2-3 speaks of our glorification: "Beloved, we are God's children now; it does not appear what we shall be, but we know that when he appears we shall be like him, for we shall see him as he is. And every one who thus hopes in him purifies himself as he is pure."

Every Christian saved by grace through faith in Jesus as Saviour will be made perfect in Heaven as part of Christ's Church or Body (I Corinthians 15:42; Ephesians 5:27; Colossians 1:22). God uses His Word, the Holy Scriptures, as the instrument of man's regeneration and sanctification. The very faith which a believer exercises at the new Birth "comes by hearing, and hearing by the word of God" (Romans 10:17, KJV). The Gospel "is the power of God for salvation to every one who has faith" (Romans 1:16). James 1:18 explains that the Word accomplishes our spiritual growth: "Of his own will he brought us forth by the word of truth that we should be a kind of first fruits of his creatures." Acts 20:32 says: "And now I commend you to God and to the word of his grace, which is able to build you up and to give you the inheritance among all those who are consecrated." At John 17:17, KJV, Jesus prays: "Sanctify them through thy truth: thy word is truth." I Peter 2:2-3 summons us: "Like newborn babes, long for the pure spiritual milk, that by it you may grow up to salvation; for you have tasted the kindness of the Lord."

Because the New Born man has been regenerated and has the Godhead dwelling with him, he continues to be literally made new as the very character of Jesus is actually and continually imparted to him in increasing measure. I Peter 4:1-2 reveals: "Since therefore Christ suffered in the flesh, arm yourselves with the same thought, for whoever has suffered in the flesh has ceased from sin, so as to live for the rest of the time in the flesh no longer by human passions but by the will of God."

GOD'S BLESSING OF ONGOING SANCTIFICATION

God alone accomplishes man's regeneration in a new spirit being, and God alone is responsible for a believer's fulfilled transformation to spiritual perfection by completing the good work begun in him. Jesus reveals at John 5:21: "For as the Father raises the dead and gives them life, so also the Son gives life to whom he will" through an ongoing process of sanctification.

Jesus establishes the necessity for a Christian's connection to Him for this process of growth in literal holiness: "I am the vine, you are the branches. He who abides in me, and I in him, he it is that bears much fruit, for apart from me you can do nothing" (John 15:5). The fruit of the Spirit, which provides and exemplifies the character of Christ is automatically produced by divine power when we abide as a branch attached to the vine of Christ. Just as our regeneration is connected to the Word by which faith comes, so our consecration or sanctification is sustained by the Word. Jesus says at John 17:14,17: "I have given them thy word... Consecrate them in the truth; thy word is truth."

The Holy Spirit is the Agent through Whom our sanctification flows. Romans 8:11 promises: "If the Spirit of him who raised Jesus from the dead dwells in you, he who raised Christ Jesus from the dead will give life to your mortal bodies also through his Spirit which dwells in you." According to Romans 8:28-30, the good that God works in everything is "with those... called according to his purpose... those whom he foreknew he also predestined to be conformed to the image of his Son... and those whom he called he also justified; and those whom he justified he also glorified."

At I Corinthians 1:4-8, St. Paul speaks of God's grace by which New Born men are: "enriched in him with all speech and all knowledge... so that you are not lacking in any spiritual gift, as you wait for the revealing of our Lord Jesus Christ; who will sustain you to the end, guiltless in the day of our Lord." When we turn to, and behold "the glory of the Lord," we are "being changed into his likeness from one degree of glory to another; for this comes from the Lord who is the Spirit" (2 Corinthians 3:18). Ongoing sanctification is imparted by the Word, in which Christ's character is revealed and detailed, so that we can behold the glory of the Lord, and be transformed as we do.

The life and holiness of Heaven are imparted and infused into a believing soul here on earth to accomplish our sanctification. Regard how often God promises cleansing in the Scriptures! "Though our outer nature is wasting away, our inner nature is being renewed every day" (2 Corinthians 4:16). God has ordained that Christian conversion and regeneration, begun at the New Birth, progress in holiness and sanctification throughout life, to culminate in spiritual perfection at the Coming of Christ.

2 Corinthians 5:17,21 reveals: "if anyone is in Christ, he is a new creation; the old has passed away, behold the new has come... so that in him we might become the righteousness of God." Our spiritual transformation is worked by God, Who "is able to provide you with every blessing in abundance... for every good work... He... will supply and multiply your resources and increase the harvest of your righteousness" (2 Corinthians 9:8-10).

Ephesians 4:13-16 tells us God gives gifts to the Body of Christ: "until we all attain... to mature manhood, to the measure of the stature of the fullness of Christ... we are to grow up in every way into him who is the head, into Christ, from whom the whole body... makes bodily growth and upbuilds itself in love." Colossians 2:19 says Jesus is: "the Head, from whom the whole body, nourished and knit together through its joints and ligaments, grows with a growth that is from God."

Believers can be "confident of this very thing, that he which hath begun a good work in you will perform it until the day of Jesus Christ" (Philippians 1:6, KJV). Philippians 1:9-11 prays that "your love may abound more and more... so that you may... be pure and blameless for the day of Christ, filled with the fruits of righteousness which come through Jesus Christ." Philippians 2:12-13 commands: "as you have always obeyed, so now... work out your own salvation with fear and trembling; for God is at work in you, both to will and to work for his good pleasure" (see also, I Thessalonians 4:1-3). However, you cannot change yourself, but the Holy Spirit will work the necessary transformation. When you slip, keep asking God to cleanse you, and complete your spiritual progression to Christ-likeness, which confirms your New Birth.

Significantly, God alone enables obedience to His commandments, by which human cooperation in holiness is enabled. Consequently, we obey because God works an automatic, progressive transformation, following the New Birth, and man's obedience cooperates with the operations of the Holy Spirit in our faith and holiness. Philippians 3:21 says Jesus "will change our lowly body to be like his glorious body, by the power which enables him even to subject all things to himself."

Colossians 1:21-22 says believers are reconciled in Jesus, "in order to present you holy and blameless and irreproachable before him, provided that you continue in the faith, stable and steadfast." Colossians 3:9-10 explains: "you have put off the old nature with its practices and have put on the new nature, which is being renewed in knowledge after the image of its creator." This knowledge is imparted by, and feeds us by, God's Word.

I Thessalonians 5:23-24 prays: "May the God of peace himself sanctify you wholly; and may your spirit and soul and body be kept sound and blameless at the coming of our Lord Jesus Christ. He who calls you is faithful, and he will do it" (See also, I Thessalonians 3:12). I Timothy 6:11 says we are to aim at, and God wishes to bless us with, spiritual riches of "righteousness, godliness, faith, love, steadfastness, gentleness." According to Titus 2:11-14: "the grace of God has appeared for the salvation of all men, training us to renounce irreligion and worldly passions, and to live sober, upright, and godly lives in this world... To redeem us from all iniquity and to purify for himself a people of his own who are zealous for good deeds." It is Christ's work, "For by a single offering he has perfected for all time those who are consecrated" (Hebrews 10:14). Hebrews 13:21 explains that in this transformation to Christ-likeness, God is "working in you that which is pleasing in his sight."

I Peter 4:1-2 says that because of Jesus' suffering: "whoever has suffered in the flesh has ceased from sin, so as to live for the rest of the time in the flesh no longer by human passions but by the will of God." 2 Peter 1:3-4 exults: "his divine power has granted to us all things that pertain to life and godliness, through the knowledge of him who called us to his own glory and excellence, by which he has granted to us his precious and very great promises, that through these you may escape from the corruption that is in the world because of passion, and become partakers of the divine nature." See also, Colossians 1:10; I Thessalonians 4:1; 2 Thessalonians 1:3,5; and I Peter 3:18).

As we shall see in the next chapter, believers are also invested with blessings of God's protection, comfort, and deliverance; the full armor of God; the name of Jesus; the gifts and fruit of the holy Spirit; authority over Satan; guardian angels; ongoing forgiveness and cleansing; freedom from the guilt, condemnation and punishment of sin; and countless others, to assure our victory over the world, the flesh, and the devil. God blesses us with enlightenment and guidance through His Word to aid our collaboration in acting rightly and fellowshipping with Him. He also sustains us in adversity, and empowers us to endure, elude, and escape travails.

THE NEW BIRTH IS IMMEDIATE AND ASCERTAINABLE

There are major Christian denominations which teach that personal salvation cannot be secured, not determined, until death and the Last Judgment, when each will be judged by constancy in faith and obedience. However, God lovingly gives the comfort of knowing, and Scripture guarantees, that the believer's New Birth occurs instantaneously, verifiably, and certainly in this time and world. John 5:24 says: "he who hears my word and believes him who sent me, has eternal life; he does not come into judgment, but has passed from death to life."

The New Birth incorporates a response to God's call to virtue, and then verifies the effectiveness of this election. 2 Peter 1:10-11 calls us to "be the more zealous to confirm your call and election, for if you do this you will never fall; so there will be richly provided for you an entrance into the eternal kingdom." When Zacchaeus repented of his sins after faithfully welcoming Jesus, Jesus proclaimed: "Today salvation has come to this house... For the Son of man came to seek and to save that which was lost" (Luke 19:9-10). And Zacchaeus' transformation was instantly evidenced as he restored all that he had stolen. I John 5:13 explains: "I write this to you who believe in the name of the Son of God, that you may know that you have eternal life." While we are still mortal and able to sin, we have the assurance of our coming immortality and glorification in Christ.

The occurrence of the New Birth is an ascertainable event, by which the Christian, saved by grace through faith, can subsequently verify his salvation and new, developing spiritual nature. New Born Christians can be sure of their salvation, despite relapses into sin and occasionally yielding to fleshly temptations.

First, we can confirm the New Birth by our possession of spiritual peace derived exclusively from our restored right relationship with God and His comforting presence. The knowledge of Heavenly bliss and restoration to come, surpasses and obliterates any worldly difficulties we may experience. Romans 5:1 puts it: "since we are justified by faith, we have peace with God through our Lord Jesus Christ." Jesus says at John 14:27: "Peace I leave with you; my peace I give to you; not as the world gives do I give to you. Let not your hearts be troubled, neither let them be afraid." The rage of guilt has been stilled; the torment of wretchedness has been vanquished; and the torrent of terror has been dammed by the gentle peace of God, imparted by the Holy Spirit.

God gives us the assurance of security that once we are saved, He will preserve our salvation. Jesus says of His sheep: "My Father, who has given them to me, is greater than all, and no one is able to snatch them out of the Father's hand" (John 10:29; see also, John 6:39-40). "Neither death... nor anything else in all creation, will be able to separate us from the love of God in Christ" (Romans 8:38-39). This certainly is the source of Christian peace, which passes all understanding (Philippians 4:6).

Second, the New Birth is evidenced by a discernible increase in actual righteousness. Occasional sins will persist amidst a believer's desire to avoid them and seek God's Kingdom, as contrasted with practicing evil habitually, which evidences an unsaved condition that has no concern for the Kingdom. The New Man has a desire to submit to God's will and walk the way He prescribes. If you are saved, your deeds will reflect it by persevering in good by God's transforming power.

I John 2:36 teaches that you cannot know the Lord without actual works obeying His commandments: "And by this we may be sure that we know him; if we keep his commandments... He who says he abides in him ought to walk in the same way in which he walked" (See also, John 15:5, 8:31; I John 2:29; and 3 John 11). Indeed, the New Born believer will evidence not only peace in his life, as verification of his new Birth, but also begin to exhibit all the Spirit's fruit of holiness in his life; "love, joy, peace, patience, kindness, goodness, faithful-ness, gentleness, self-control" (Galatians 5:22-23). Romans 1:5 identifies Jesus as He "through whom we have received grace and apostleship to bring about obedience to the faith."

Third, he who possesses these fruits of imparted righteousness will be driven to express and evidence them in good works, which are supernaturally inspired and empowered. Ephesians 2:10 establishes good works as the paradigm of the Christian walk: "For we are his workman-ship, created in Christ Jesus for good works, which God prepared beforehand, that we should walk in them." St. Paul proclaimed at I Corinthians 15:10: "I worked harder than any of them, though it was not I, but the grace of God which is with me." The New Man, re-made in the image of Christ, is "zealous for good deeds" (Titus 2:14).

St. James unequivocally connects faith with one's good works at James 2:14-18: "What does it profit, my brethren, if a man says he has faith, but has not works?... faith by itself, if it has no works, is dead... Show me your faith apart from your works, and I by my works will show you my faith." Good works and the desire to do them are the natural fruit of regeneration and sanctification (Ephesians 1:19, 3:16-20; Philippians 4:13; and Colossians 2:19).

Fourth, a specific fruit of the Spirit's sanctification and the obedient good works which accompany regeneration is reflected in the believer's possession of divine love. I John 3:14 says: "We know that we have passed out of death into life, because we love the brethren." See also, I John 3:18-19, 4:7, 16, and 5:13. Usually, a burning desire to witness the Gospel to the unsaved is triggered by loving concern for the imperiled, immortal souls of the lost.

Fifth, a believer will know spiritually and confidently, by the Holy Spirit's ratification, that Jesus is exactly Who He claims to be — the Son of God, Messiah, our Lord and Saviour. John 20:31 confirms that the Word is God's instrument for transmitting faithful certainty: "these are written that you may believe that Jesus is the Christ, the Son of God, and that believing you may have life in his name." Romans 8:14-16 teaches: "you have received the spirit of sonship... it is the Spirit himself bearing witness with our spirit that we are children of God." When Peter confessed that Jesus was "the Christ, the Son of the living God," Jesus declared: "flesh and blood has not revealed this to you, but my Father who is in heaven" (Matthew 16:16-17). We receive a complete certainty of conviction about Christ's identity, a consciousness wrought in the soul by the Holy Spirit, that a change has been accomplished in us. This impression of truth on our spirit is a real experience of inner awareness. See John 14:26, 15:26; I Corinthians 2:12; Colossians 1:12; 2 Timothy 1:7; I John 3:24, 5:10-11. Recognizing Jesus as Lord is a gift of grace: "No one can say 'Jesus is Lord', except by the Holy Spirit" (I Corinthians 12:3).

GOD'S WORD AT WORK:

God's love is mightily expressed in His blessing of the Word, which is both the instrument that accomplishes multiple blessings, and is itself a magnificent blessing. The Word brings about faith for the New Birth and is involved in accomplishing the New Birth. The Word effects regeneration of the New Man with a new spirit by the Holy Spirit. It guides us by disclosing God's will, as no other repository of wisdom does, so we can obediently cooperate in fulfilling God's plans for us. It teaches believers how to act righteously in deed, as well as how to be righteous in character. Then it enables this very righteousness by feeding and nurturing spiritual growth in the New Man.

The Word provides the portal to know, commune, and fellowship, with God, by revealing and detailing His character, will, and purposes for man. The Word is God's instrument of healing, and is the weapon of choice for resisting the onslaughts of the world, the flesh, and the devil. Scripture gives us pleasure, profit, purification, and protection from sin. It is able to cleanse us from secret and presumptuous sins by revealing them and showing us how to live (Hebrews 4:12).

Jesus says that the Word is our means to spiritual life: "It is the spirit that gives life, the flesh is of no avail; the words that I have spoken to you <u>are spirit and life</u>" (John 6:63). Romans 1:16-17 says the Gospel "is the power of God for salvation to every one who has faith... For in it the righteousness of God is revealed through faith for faith... He who through faith is righteous shall live." 2 Thessalonians 2:13-14 adds: "God chose you from the beginning to be saved, through consecration by the Spirit and belief in the truth. To this he called you through our gospel." James 1:21 urges every man to "receive with meekness the implanted word, which is able to save your soul." I Peter 1:23 reminds us: "You have been born anew, not of perishable seed but of imperishable, through the living and abiding word of God."

The operation of the Word initially brings about regeneration at the New Birth, by the saving grace of God. Jesus says at John 15:3-4: "<u>You are already made clean by the word</u> which I have spoken to you. Abide in me, and I in you." Through the Word's "very great promises,... you may escape from the corruption that is in the world because of passion, and become partakers of the divine nature" (2 Peter 1:4). Since we are saved by grace through faith, it is significant that faith comes from hearing the Word (Ephesians 2:5; Romans 10:17).

Thereafter, by faith in the promises of the Word, we continue to grow in holiness, spirituality, and sanctification. Jesus prays for His disciples at John 17:17 KJV: "Sanctify them through thy truth: thy word is truth." Holiness is found through the Word: as we hear it preached; meditate on its truths; incorporate it into our prayers; desire Christ as His glory unfolds in the Word; and obediently appropriate and obey the truths of the Word, because they reveal God's will.

As in so many blessings, we see that God's Word in Scripture is His instrument to accomplish our transformation to holiness. And, as in other blessings, the pace of our growth in holiness is influenced by the extent we internalize and appropriate the Word as our own. Our soul is the soil in which the Word grows like a seed (Mark 4:14, 26-30). The Holy Spirit uses what we learn and ingest from Scripture to nourish us; reveal God's grace; and provide orientation, deliverance, and transformation into the likeness of Christ. The Word accomplishes our Holiness, the life of Christ in us, by the working of the Holy Spirit, just as our faith also grows as it feeds upon the Word. For example, the Word "is living and active," like a sword, tenderizing our hearts, and "discerning the thoughts and intentions of the heart" (Hebrews 4:12). The Word becomes the instrument of the Holy Spirit, who applies the power of God to convert, convict, regenerate, and transform the believer, whose faith has come by hearing the Word of God.

In the Old Testament, God humbled Israel with hunger, "that he might make thee know that man doth not live by bread only, but by every word that proceedeth out of the mouth of the Lord doth man live" (Deuteronomy 8:3). Psalm 1:1-3 establishes: "Blessed is the man that walketh not in the counsel of the ungodly... But his delight is in the law of the Lord; and <u>in his law doth he meditate day and night</u>. And he shall be like a tree planted by the rivers of water, that bringeth forth his fruit in his season... and whatsoever he doeth shall prosper." Remember that the fruit of the Holy Spirit listed at Galatians 5:22-23; are all reflections and characteristics of divine holiness.

Proverbs 4:13, 20-22 says: "Take fast hold of instruction; let her not go; keep her; for <u>she is thy life.</u>.. My son, <u>attend to my words</u>, incline thine ear unto <u>my sayings</u>... <u>For they are life</u> unto those that find them." When we rely upon God's Word to provide the blessing of holiness, it will be the seed, food, and water to nurture an increase. James 1:18 says God "brought us forth <u>by the word of truth</u> that we should be a kind of first fruits of his creatures." I Peter 2:2 says of the Word: "Like newborn babes, long for the pure spiritual milk, that by it you may grow up to salvation." God has given us the Word as an instrument by which to grow spiritually, so that our actual righteousness increasingly corresponds to the righteousness of Christ. But we must have the intensity of a baby's craving to ingest the spiritual nourishment.

Jesus' Word must become an integral part of your life if it is to take root and bear fruit. Abiding in Jesus is reflected in holy life and obedient works consistent with His character. At John 15:7,8 Jesus says: "If you abide in me, and <u>my words abide in you</u>, ask whatever you will, and it shall be done for you. By this my Father is glorified, <u>that you bear much fruit</u>, and so prove to be my disciples." Matthew 3:8 urges us to "Bear fruit that befits repentance." It is no coincidence that Jesus is the Vine and the Word in Whom we are to abide. In everything, including our holiness and faith, He is the absolute Life from Whom we draw all vitality.

We may not understand how the Word develops holiness in our new spirit man, but we can know that growth in holiness is occurring; that our spirit is equipped to assimilate the divine nurture, as much as our body is equipped to digest nature's products. The Word is God's spiritual food from which growth in holiness comes by routine feeding; as habitually as eating three meals daily. Just as a starving man is not immediately restored to full strength by one morsel of food, but increases in strength as he continue to eat, so holiness is made stronger as more of God's Word is regularly ingested to feed and water the Word already implanted. The Word prunes and cleanses a Christian when wielded and applied by the Holy Spirit (Hebrews 4:12).

The Word, like any seed, is self-generating once it is planted, as long as it is fed and watered. Remarkably, the Word is also the food and water which stimulates continued growth for the seed to produce fruit (Isaiah 55:10-11). St. Paul noted in preaching the Word: "I planted, Appollos watered, but God gave the growth" (I Corinthians 3:6). Paul had originally planted the seed of the Word in Corinth. Appollos had watered it with the Word of God by preaching to the faithful, and God had prospered the Word's fruition. So, when we "have tasted the goodness of the word of God and the powers of the age to come," we are like "land which has drunk the rain that often falls upon it, and brings forth vegetation useful to those for whose sake it is cultivated, (and) receives a blessing from God" (Hebrews 6:5-6; and see also, John 15:3).

2 Peter 1:3-4 confirms that the Word's promises produce growth in holiness: "His divine power has granted to us all things that pertain to life and godliness, through the knowledge of him who called us to his own glory and excellence, by which he has granted to us his precious and very great <u>promises, that through these you may</u> escape from the corruption that is in the world because of passion, and <u>become partakers of the divine nature</u>." Acts 20:32 speaks of God's "word of his grace, which is able to build you up and to give you the inheritance among all those who are consecrated."

Philippians 2:14-16 says believers can "be blameless and innocent, children of God without blemish... <u>holding fast the word of life</u>." Jesus describes faithful disciples as "those who, <u>hearing the word</u>, hold it fast in an honest and good heart, <u>and bring forth fruit</u> with patience" (Luke 8:15). Patience, or constancy in holiness proceeds from a believer keeping his heart open to the food, water, and sunlight of the Word. The unchangeable nature of the Word is what brings constancy to the holiness and faith of believers. The Word bears fruit, according to God's specific promise, by inspiring faith in hearers to seek blessings from the Lord. This faith in turn, sustains the constancy of belief in the Word, and enables a Christian to bear holy fruit faithfully for the Lord. We accelerate fruitfulness by our receptivity to the Word and our faith in it.

Colossians 1:5-6, 10 proclaims: "The word of the truth, the gospel which has come to you, as indeed in the whole world it is bearing <u>fruit and growing</u>... to lead a life worthy of the Lord, fully pleasing to him, <u>bearing fruit in every good work</u> and increasing in the knowledge of God." Colossians 3:16 adds: "Let the word of Christ dwell in you richly." We must put the Word in our hearts and contemplate, reflect, and meditate upon it, then God does the transforming of one's character into holy fruit.

When a man ingests, savors, digests, and is immersed in, and saturated with God's Word, divine life is imparted to, and activated within him. The kingdom of God grows within a man, originating in the Word, which Jesus compares to a seed which sprouts and grows, and "produces of itself" (Mark 4:14, 26-32). James 1:21 speaks of "the implanted word, which is able to save your soul." The inherent power of the Word to work transformation in men by God's power is also proclaimed in I Kings 8:56: Psalm 107:20; Daniel 9:12; Isaiah 55:10-11; Jeremiah 1:12; Ezekiel 12:25; Matthew 24:35; Romans 1:16; Colossians 1:5-6; I Timothy 4:5; Hebrews 4:12; I Peter 1:25, 2:2; and 2 Peter 1:4).

God uses the Word as a seed germinating within a believer to bring forth the Kingdom of God and finish the transformation to actual holiness. (Matthew 13:18-23; Acts 20:32; I Peter 2:2). Jesus teaches: "You are already made clean by the word I have spoken to you" (John 15:3). Christ loves His Church and "cleansed her by the washing of water with the word" (Ephesians 5:26). Luke 8:15 says that the Word, held fast in an honest and good heart, brings "forth fruit with patience."

Philippians 2:13 says that "God is at work in you" to accomplish spiritual transformation, and it is "the word of God, which is at work in you believers" (I Thessalonians 2:13), so that we 'have the mind of Christ' (I Corinthians 2:16). The indwelling Word gives powerful effect to a believer's prayers when it produces one's utterance of God's will: "If... my words abide in you, ask whatever you will, and it shall be done for you" (John 15:7; See also, Psalm 119:11; Philippians 2:16; and Colossians 3:10).

GOD'S WORD GIVES UNDERSTANDING AND GUIDANCE FOR RIGHTEOUSNESS

God has provided His Word by which we grow spiritually, through the Holy Spirit Who empowers, consoles, and enlightens believers by explicating the Word, so that divine life and comfort are imparted and developed for our literal transformation (John 14:26, 16:13-14; Romans 8:4, 14, 16:26; and Ephesians 1:9, 17). God gives us His wisdom to understand, and the power to use the Word, which reveals His forgiveness and deliverance from temptations to sin, and the suffering they produce. He gives us spiritual insight — what we call conscience — to know what is right and wrong, and cooperate in receiving holiness, so we avoid the suffering attached to sin. We can know what is right in God's sight (Luke 8:17; Romans 15:14; I Corinthians 1:5).

The Holy Spirit is the agent of our sanctification, and uses the Word to accomplish our transformation to Christ-likeness. Jesus promises the Holy Spirit "will teach you all things, and bring to your remembrance all that I have said to you," which is contained in the Word (John 14:26). John 16:13 adds: "When the Spirit of truth comes, he will guide you into all the truth... and he will declare to you the things that are to come." "He will take what is mine and declare it to you" (John 16:15). It helps when we have the Word on deposit in our hearts, so it is available for recall.

God's voice becomes more intelligible as the Holy Spirit begins to interpret the Scriptures to us, and we increasingly comprehend divine revelations. More than knowledge, however, the Holy Spirit helps us supernaturally to re-hear the implanted Word, which provides insight and understanding to nurture our spirit. James 1:5 also reveals and gives unalterable assurance of God's promises to bless the faithful with spiritual knowledge: "If any of you lacks wisdom, let him ask God who gives to all men generously and without reproaching, and it will be given him." See also, Luke 11:13; Ephesians 1:17-18.

God's Word is a mirror to induce holiness by showing us our defects in contrast to God's righteousness, revealed, detailed, and prescribed in the Word. It is a hammer to break us down in our pride and self-sufficiency, so we will seek to imitate the holiness of God (Jeremiah 23:29). It is also a light to guide us; a water to wash us; a food to nourish us in the process of spiritual growth; and a medicine to heal our infirmities, both spiritual and physical. The law is like a diagnostic test that reveals a fatal condition. It does not heal, but drives us to the Great Physician for cure of our congenitally defective hearts.

Commands to be holy, as God is holy (Leviticus 20:7) produce a love for God's righteousness, and righteousness promotes the obedience which blesses us. One obeys the reasonable advice and warnings of Scriptures, and benefits from the built-in blessings of right living. Conversely, blessings are withheld when we practice stubborn, prideful disobedience. For, we will reap what we have planted: blessing for obedience, and woe for disobedience. When one focuses on the delights of sin, he will not be heard by God. Hands clutching worldly treasures are not open to be filled with Heavenly blessings, including the much desired divine health and prosperity.

God leads us in the right direction by delivering us from temptations to sin, which forestalls the occurrence of sin and its resultant suffering. He promises to guide, instruct, and enable us in His way, so we avoid sinning, for "the wages of sin is death" (Romans 6:23). For example, His guidance to avoid borrowing (Deuteronomy 15:6; Romans 13:8) will steer us away from falling into debt and its resulting financial suffering, poverty, and destruction of prosperity. Psalm 32:8 assures: "I will instruct thee and teach thee in the way which thou shalt go: I will guide thee with mine eye." "The steps of a good man are ordered by the Lord" (Psalm 37:23). "And the Lord shall guide thee continually, and satisfy thy soul in drought, and make fat thy bones: and thou shall be like a watered garden, and like a spring of water, whose waters fail not."

If we entrust all to God, He will clearly reveal His preferences; He will erect barriers to all paths which do not lead to His will for us. He will turn us in the right direction, and push, draw, persuade, and entice us in the way we should go. Proverbs 3:6 puts it: "In all thy ways acknowledge him, and he shall direct thy paths." Jesus promises at John 8:12: "I am the light of the world; <u>he who follows me</u> will not walk in darkness, but will have the light of life." This light is available and visible when we seek to follow Jesus' way.

If we cannot identify God's will or fathom the reason behind our dearth of blessings, then we should pray for enlightenment, and God will freely illuminate the darkness of our ignorance (John 16:13, 14:26; I Corinthians 2:9-10; I John 2:27). If you wander off the road, away from faith toward doubt and fear, then hearing the Word will revive faith and restore you from the by-way of doubt back to the road of faith (Romans 10:17). God restores us to right relationship by repentance, forgiveness and cleansing (I John 1:9). He enables us to judge ourselves truly, so we should not be judged (I Corinthians 11:31). 2 Corinthians 13:5 calls us to "examine yourselves to see whether you are holding to your faith."

You may be as strong as Sampson, but without God's power, you will be weak. You may be as wise as Solomon, but without God's wisdom you are no match for Satan's cunning, which has been sharpened over the millennia. Without Jesus in you, you are an empty container, easily crushed by the vise of vice.

God's Word is reliable, and inspires our faith, because God Himself guarantees that His Word of promise will be fulfilled: "For I am the Lord... I say the word, and will perform it, saith the Lord God" (Ezekiel 12:25). "Heaven and earth will pass away, but my words will not pass away" (Mark 13:31; and see also Psalm 111:7-8; Isaiah 46;11; 2 Timothy 2:13; and I Peter 1:25). God's Word is contained in Holy Scripture, and "All Scripture is inspired by God" and fulfilled by His power (2 Timothy 3:16). 2 Peter 1:20-21 adds: "no prophecy of scripture is a matter of one's own interpretation, because no prophecy ever came by the impulse of man, but men moved by the Holy Spirit spoke from God." "In many and various ways God spoke of old to our fathers by the prophets; but in these last days he has spoken to us by a Son" (Hebrews 1:1-2). "The Jews were entrusted with the oracles of God" (Romans 3:2). God used men in the process of writing the Scriptures, but the Word is God's; imparted and inspired by the Holy Spirit.

God will move Heaven and earth to fulfill His Word when we invoke and rely upon it, because God has promised to back up His Word fully and forever with His power (Jeremiah 1:12; Ezekiel 12:25). God also enforces His Word of condemnation for rebellious sinners (Daniel 9:12). God sometimes expresses His attributes by speaking directly to specific men in the Scripture: "For the scripture says to Pharaoh, 'I have raised you up for the very purpose of showing my power in you'." (Romans 9:17; see also, Jeremiah 1:4, 2:1-2). We are assured by Scripture that God's promises, including those of blessing, are unalterable and irrevocable, for God is totally good and faithful to His Word (Psalm 89:1-2; Lamentations 3:23). God's Word says exactly what He means: "Every word of God is pure... Add thou not unto his words, lest he reprove thee, and thou be found a liar" (Proverbs 30:5-6; and see also, Revelations 22:18-19).

There are indications the Word is invested by God with self-fulfilling power. Acts 20:32 says God's Word of grace "is able to build you up and to give you the inheritance among all those who are consecrated." I Thessalonians 2:13 speaks of "the word of God, <u>which is at work in you believers.</u>" Hebrews 4:12 says: "For the word of god is living and active." God says of His Word at Isaiah 55:10-11: "it may give seed to the sower and bread to the eater: So shall my word be that goeth forth out my mouth: it shall not return unto me void, but <u>it shall accomplish</u> that which I please, and it shall prosper in the thing whereto I sent it." Once spoken, God's Word continues to exist, just as a being continues to exist once he is conceived.

Nevertheless, it is well to remember that God's power underlies and activates the Word, through the Holy Spirit: "for the written code kills, but the Spirit gives life" (2 Corinthians 3:6); and "we serve not under the old written code but in the new life of the Spirit" (Romans 7:6). We learn of the Spirit and receive Him, in the Word. Galatians 3:2,5 explains we receive the holy Spirit, not by works of law, but "by hearing with faith." We are "saved, through consecration by the Spirit and belief in the truth. To this he called you through our gospel" (2 Thessalonians 2:13).

The sweet language of the Word also reveals the character of God, and instructs us in behavior which fulfills God's will. We don't automatically know God just by being saved. Only the Bible reveals Him in ways we can comprehend. And the more we know Him, the more he can use us to serve Him. Thinking God's thoughts, as we learn them from the Word, helps us to see God's viewpoint about our lives, and conform our actions to His plans and purposes. Psalm 119:9 tells us a believer can "cleanse his way by taking heed thereto according to thy word." Proverbs 2:6 reveals that "the Lord giveth wisdom: "out of his mouth cometh knowledge and understanding," which deliver us "from the way of the evil man" (Proverbs 2:12).

Indeed, Jesus, as the Word, in the human life He lived, is the exegesis of God; the revelation and explanation of God's nature and character, and the fulfillment of all His purposes for man. Jesus says at John 14:9-10: "He who has seen me has seen the Father... Do you not believe that I am in the Father and the Father in me?" Jesus is the exemplification, replication, and representation of God's character for which we are to strive. He also embodies "the truth" (John 14:6), and Titus 1:1 puts it: "knowledge of truth... accords with godliness." Imitation of Christ is the portal to being holy, as God is holy.

Through the connecting channels of God's Word we can commune with Him regularly and constantly; savor His grace; and delight in His blessings. When Martha complained that Mary was enjoying Jesus' company, while Martha grudgingly prepared dinner, Jesus said: "one thing is needful. Mary has chosen the good portion, which shall not be taken away from her" (Luke 10:42). Mary knew that attention to Jesus' Word supersedes any worldly involvement in our faith life. When we depend on God for our blessings, we will not rely on our own works. We will cooperatively strive to obtain and nurture seed from the Word, but depend only on God for the increase.

"The Word of God is living and active, sharper than any two edged sword," for it "discerns the thoughts and intentions of the heart" (Hebrews 4:12). With one edge, it cuts away and shapes our character as it sanctifies and trains the cooperative response of our hearts. The other edge of the "sword of the Spirit, which is the Word of God" (Ephesians 6:17), is part of God's armor to protect us from Satanic attack and preserve our holy character. The Word is also double-edged in that it leads believers to blessings for obedience, but warns impenitent sinners of penalties for disobedience to its commandments. It especially warns of eternal condemnation for those who reject its Gospel of deliverance.

However, we will not succumb to adverse circumstances or persecutions imposed by the world system, which lead to unbelief, if we seek refuge in God's command to pray always and in every place to God the Father, through Jesus the Son, for power to have faith as well as receive blessings and resist Satan. We are then enabled, as a mature, empowered disciple of Christ, to exercise our will to resist Satan, take authority over all his power; and bind him here on earth, as a concrete exercise of our faith in God's promises of deliverance (I Peter 5:8-9). "And after you have suffered a little while, the God of all grace, who has called you to his eternal glory in Christ, will himself restore, establish, and strengthen you" (I Peter 5:10; and see Psalm 23:3). The Word is also one of God's instruments of healing (Psalm 107:20; Isaiah 6:10; Matthew 13:15).

The Word can be used to fight back when Satan attacks you, since we are in a spiritual battle in which Satan assaults our emotions, worldly appetites, and fears, to weaken our resolve and endurance. Keep the Word ready at hand to resist the sneak attacks of Satan. We are freed from sin-consciousness by God's forgiveness and cleansing (I John 1:9), so whenever Satan accuses you of the past, send him away with a reminder of his future, as disclosed in the Word. When Satan sought to tempt Jesus three times, our Lord resisted and overcame Satan each time by quoting Scripture (Luke 4:4-12).

Just as Jesus is God's only provision for salvation by grace through faith, so Jesus is God's only channel to other blessings by faith. His Word must be in us, and He must be in us in the sense we abide in Him and draw nurture from Him. The reward for abiding in the Word is to be blessed with what is promised: bearing spiritual fruit, rendering loving service, witnessing power, and the many facets of abundant life: material needs, prosperity, health in this world, and heavenly rewards in the next.

The Word is God's instrument, when quickened by the Holy Spirit, to bring about growth in holiness and transformation to Christ-likeness. After we have digested the Word, we are called to hide the Word in our hearts; to "meditate therein day and night" (Joshua 1:8), so that what our mind learns, our heart may also know. Just as food eaten must be digested, so the Word taken in must be digested, savored, pondered, reflected upon, questioned, related, internalized, and applied to our daily lives. We are blessed and sustained spiritually by a Word-fed and Spirit-filled soul. The measure of faith we have in God's Word is directly proportional to the measure of fruit produced in us by the Word (Mark 4:24).

It is paradoxical, but when we abide in the Word, the Word is in us, and when the Word abides in us, we are immersed in the Word. This is parallel to the concept we can occupy that which occupies us; we can be in Jesus at the same time He is in us (John 17:21,23).

We need not puzzle over how the Word works. If you drink water you will get wet, because wetness is a property of water. You may not understand how the energy from food nourishes the physical body, but we can recognize that the process occurs as the body grows. Likewise, God's Word will nurture you spiritually and soak you in faith if you ingest it, so we can know that growth is occurring. Just as your body is nourished by food, and is pre-programmed to do that, so the inner spiritual man is adapted to be fed by the Word he digests. We know that words can carry and elicit love, hate, fear, and other emotions, and elate or deflate, as they bombard the hearer. Why should God's Word not also serve to provide growth in faith and spirituality? This is one way faith becomes the substance of things hoped for, when the Word is ingested by man and absorbed by his developing spirit being.

Imagine a world without the Word. We would have no direct revelation of the promises of salvation, resurrection, glory, grace, faith, hope, or love. The Word is indeed God's anchor to hold us to the blessings of more abundant life which Jesus brings to believers. God speaks directly to every believer by His Word to bring the Gospel for salvation; instruction and nurture for righteousness; and our blessed hope for eternity. The Word provides joy through its assurances; delight by its revelation of God's character; strength and guidance to overcome the world; and incomparable satisfactions by our obedience to God's commandments, which pleases and glorifies God.

CHAPTER 3

GOD'S BLESSINGS TO OVERCOME THE WORLD

"And after you have suffered a little while, the God of all grace, who has called you to his eternal glory in Christ, will himself restore, establish and strengthen you."

– I Peter 5:10.

We have seen how God's consummate love and goodness provide for salvation, rescue, redemption and atonement for sinners, called by grace through faith in Christ as Saviour. He promises the triumphant return of Our Lord to usher in an eternity of Heavenly bliss in the glorious presence of God, himself. In the meantime, we are left to sojourn in a world of suffering generated by our own sins; of afflictions imposed by Satan; persecutions caused by other men; and disasters inherent in the operations of nature. There will also be pains which accompany growth in holy character and perfection of our faith in God.

Yet, our Deliverer does not harm us, nor leave us defenseless against the world. As sure as suffering is forecast for believers, we can rely upon God's promises to sustain us in all our tribulations. His great blessing to believers is the certain assurance He will eventually deliver us from suffering in this world. We must be wary, but need not fear the temptations and influences of Satan, the torments of other men, nor the otherwise dire eternal consequences of committing our own sins.

God may not always provide swift extrication from situations, elimination of problems, nor immediately help us elude, escape, or evade peril. Rather, God's rescue is likely to take the form of His comforting presence which empowers and strengthens believers to endure through afflictions, knowing we will ultimately overcome them and have victory in Jesus. In all these, our Father promises to rescue us eventually from any predicament into which we have placed ourselves, and from the evil of the world which assaults us.

Impliedly, there could be no basis for belief in any material or earthly blessings from God, or for divine health and wealth, unless we could be sure of eventually enjoying them free from perpetual suffering. For, we seldom have the fuller, more abundant life Jesus promises, unless we also have substantial freedom from pain and suffering, and ultimate surcease which extricates us from ordeals and difficulties into which we have fallen, or which threaten to engulf us. We must be able to rely on the certainty that the dawn always follows the darkness.

The full scope of God's rescue from suffering is outlined by St. Paul, who spoke of "my persecutions, my sufferings, what befell me at Antioch, at Iconium, and at Lystra, what persecutions I endured, yet <u>from them all the Lord rescued me</u>" (2 Timothy 3:11). Significantly, at

Antioch, Paul was driven out by the Jews who stirred up persecution against him (Acts 13:50), and He regarded this as a rescue from potential harm. At Lystra, Paul was stoned, dragged out of the city, and left for dead (Acts 14:19). Yet, Paul considered Lystra as equally a rescue by a faithful God, since he was delivered after he endured and survived, rather than escaped, the peril. At Iconium, Paul fled before he could be harmed, when he learned of plots against him (Acts 14:6), and deliverance took the form of avoiding encounter with harm. At Malta, Paul's ship and cargo were wrecked during a storm, but all human life was spared (Acts 27:23,44). See also, 2 Corinthians 11:24.

God did not take Paul's thorn in the flesh away from him, but delivered Paul through endurance, saying; "My grace is sufficient for you, for my power is made perfect in weakness"; allowing Paul to endure and be "content with weaknesses, insults, hardships, persecutions, and calamities" (2 Corinthians 12: 9-10).

Paul was delivered in different ways by God, but primarily by grace to bear with his travails. He recognized suffering as a friend to accomplish some divine improvement in him; to test his endurance and faith, and grow spiritually. Paul was able to persist by focusing on the day of deliverance and the promise of Heavenly reward for perseverance. He was so sufficient in the Lord, he learned to be content in all circumstances (Philippians 4:11).

Jesus strengthens the faith of believers with His assurances to "have no fear" of natural phenomena (Mark 6:50); nor of sickness (Luke 8:50); nor of lack or insufficiency of food, clothing and shelter (Luke 12:31-32); nor of other men (Hebrews 13:5-6; Proverbs 29:25); nor of Satan (Hebrews 2:14-15). Nor do the faithful need to fear God because of sin, since He has forgiven our sins through Jesus, including those not yet committed, and allows believers, as His children, to come boldly to His Throne of Grace for repentance, forgiveness, and cleansing, as well as to offer petitions.

We need not fear Satan or other men because we are under God's protection, and if He allows any infliction of suffering to reach us, we can be confident He will enable us to endure it and eventually deliver us from travail. "Weeping may endure for a night, but joy cometh in the morning" (Psalm 30:5).

When we seek deliverance from suffering, we will always find refuge in the Lord. And each experience of His mercy will only confirm His benevolence. Psalm 34:4-8 explains: "I sought the Lord, and he heard me, and delivered me from all my fears... and saved him out of all his troubles... The angel of the Lord encampeth round about them that fear him, and delivereth them. O taste and see that the Lord is good: blessed is the man that trusteth in him." Your confidence and security in God will increase with each deliverance by Him from the struggles and disasters of life, as His reliability is dependably manifested on each occasion of deliverance.

The actual existence of angels arrayed in battle was witnessed by Elisha's servant, after Elisha prayed that his eyes be opened: "and he saw: and behold, the mountain was full of horses and chariots of fire round about Elisha" (2 Kings 6:17). The Lord sent an angel in answer to King Hezekiah's and Isaiah's prayers, to destroy the Assyrians (2 Chronicles 32:21). Hezekiah had observed: "Be strong and courageous, be not afraid nor dismayed... for there be more with us than with him: With him is an arm of flesh; but with us is the Lord our God to help us, and to fight our battles" (2 Chronicles 32:7-8).

Psalm 32:7 rhapsodizes: "Thou art my hiding place; thou shalt preserve me from trouble; thou shalt compass me about with songs of deliverance." "The Lord is my defense; and my God is the rock of my refuge" (Psalm 94:22). Psalm 27:4-5 prays one might "dwell in the house of the Lord all the days of my life... For in the time of trouble he shall hide me in his pavilion: in the secret of his tabernacle shall he hide me; he shall set me up upon a rock." If suffering involves a denial of something for which we have petitioned, God will even soften the deprivation by changing the very desires of one's heart to conform to God's will.[21]

Psalm 34:17-19 says: "The righteous cry, and the Lord heareth, and delivereth them out of all their troubles... many are the afflictions of the righteous: but <u>the Lord delivereth him out of them</u> all." "God is our refuge and strength a very present help in trouble" (Psalm 46:1). God promises at Psalm 50:15: "call upon me in the day of trouble: I will deliver thee, and thou shalt glorify me". God's benevolence permeates Psalm 91:2-15: "He is my refuge and my fortress... he shall cover thee with his feathers, and under his wings shalt thou trust: His truth shall be thy shield and buckler... Thou shalt not be afraid for the terror by night; nor for the arrow that flieth by day... There shall no evil befall thee... For he shall give his angels charge over thee, to keep thee in all thy ways... He shall call upon me, and I will answer him: I will be with him in trouble, I will deliver him, and honour him." He puts a hedge of protection about us, as He did for Job (Job 1:10). See also, Psalm 4:1, 34:4-7, 40:1-2, 46:1-5, 46:9, 55:22: Isaiah 58:11, Jeremiah 29:11; Habakkuk 3:17-19; and Job 36:15.

GOD ENABLES ENDURANCE OF SUFFERING

On those occasions when God does not snatch us, untouched from danger, and we do undergo torment or sorrow, we can be sure of God's unequivocal promise to help us endure our affliction until He delivers us out of it. There seems to be one area in every life where God expects us to endure it, with His help, after which He will deliver us in His own time and pleasure. It is true no trouble touches us which is not common to man (I Corinthians 10:13). But it is wise to remember that Job was a man who, for a time, suffered total loss of property, possessions, family, and health. Only renewed faith in God sustained his endurance, deliverance, and restoration.

Endurance by the reassuring presence of God, and reliance on His promise to protect and sustain His children while they sojourn in a hostile world is a common Old Testament theme. Isaiah 41:10 calls us to have courage: "Fear thou not; for I am with thee... I will uphold thee with the right hand of my righteousness." Isaiah 40:29,31 promises: "He giveth power to the faint; and to them that have no might he increaseth strength... they that wait upon the Lord shall renew their strength; they shall mount up with wings as eagles; they shall run, and not be weary; and they shall walk, and not faint."

Isaiah 43:21 promises protection and help to overcome or vanquish harm: "Fear not: for I have redeemed thee, I have called thee by name; thou art mine. When thou passest through the waters, I will be with thee; and... when thou walkest through the fire thou shalt not be burned." When Shadrach, Meshach, and Abednego were condemned to the fiery furnace for refusing to bow down to an idol of King Nebuchadnezzar, they faithfully entrusted their lives and deliverance to God (Daniel 3:17). Consequently, the King saw Jesus with the three men in the furnace, and observed "the form of the fourth is like the Son of God" (Daniel 3:25). You can't do any better than having Jesus literally present with you in the fiery flames, and none of the three was harmed by the ordeal. Daniel trusted in God, and an angel was sent to "shut the lion's mouth," so he emerged unscathed from the lions' den to which he had been condemned (Daniel 6:22).

God promises to deliver us "from the noisome pestilence" (Psalm 91:3); that "the righteous is taken away from the evil to come" (Isaiah 57:1). God's grace and goodness, manifested in the eventual deliverance of believers from affliction, is confirmed in (2 Samuel 14:14, 22:31; Psalms 18:2,30; 56:9, 103:4,11,119:117, 121:4-8; Proverbs 2:7, 16:9; and Isaiah 54:8,14,17; 43:1-2, 46:4, and 2 Corinthians 2:14.

When we are confronted with worldly travails, I Peter 5:9-10 declares: "If you will resist Satan, firm in you faith... after you have suffered a little while, the God of all grace, who has called you to his eternal glory in Christ, will himself restore, establish, and strengthen you."

God gives us strength not only to resist temptations to sin, and avoid the suffering which flows from yielding to sin, but to endure the sufferings inflicted by others or by our own sin, aided by our awareness of God's concern. God so cares about us that He puts our tears in His bottle (Psalm 56:8), and numbers the very hairs on our heads (Matthew 10:30). He loves us totally (John 3:16; Romans 8:38-39), and guides and protects us as "the flock under his care" (Psalm 95:7).

The Creator of the universe has assumed the care and keeping of each believer, as a Shepherd guides and protects His flock, finds nurture for them, restores and refreshes them, and His rod and staff comfort each one (Psalm 23:4). Jesus adds at John 10:14-15: "I am the good shepherd; I know my own and my own know me... and I lay down my life for the sheep."

Such a Good Shepherd cannot possible abandon us to danger; or run off in the face of peril; leave us to fend for our own needs; neglect to heal our wounds; or fail to restore us to the right paths. If we recognize Him as our Good Shepherd, we will rightly experience fullness of joy, reliance, and comfort. If we doubt He serves as our Good Shepherd, it is the same as denying His self-characterizations and repudiating His care.

"For the eyes of the Lord are upon the righteous, and his ears are open to their prayer" (I Peter 3:12, citing Psalm 34:15). Jesus watched over the disciples from the shore, as they struggled through the night with the wind at sea. Only later did he walk upon the water and still the wind (Mark 6:48,51), although he had them in His sight throughout their ordeal.

If we cannot avoid or escape trials and temptations, we can overcome them by enduring them, because God allows us to commit to Him all our cares and concerns about our eventual rescue. The New Birth brings a peace based on Christ's assurance of salvation and deliverance. Matthew 6:25,34 teaches: "do not be anxious about your life... do not be anxious about tomorrow." Rather, "Cast all your anxieties on him, for he cares about you" (I Peter 5:7). "Have no anxiety about anything, but in everything by prayer and supplication with thanksgiving let your requests be made known to God" (Philippians 4:6), Who answers all prayers offered in the name of Jesus (John 16:23). "And the peace of God... will keep your hearts and minds in Christ Jesus" (Philippians 4:7). 2 Timothy 1:12 concludes: "I know whom I have believed and I am sure that he is able to guard until that Day what has been entrusted to me."

We are freed from the dread of suffering or loss by the assurance that God, Himself, will comfort us in need or sorrow, and also enable other members in the Body to console us. According to 2 Corinthians 1:4-5: "Blessed be the God... who comforts us in all our affliction, so that we may be able to comfort those who are in any affliction... For as we share abundantly in Christ's sufferings, so through Christ we share abundantly in comfort too." The Lord will use you, too, to comfort others with the apt word, regardless of how vulnerable, inadequate, or unappreciated you may feel. At Isaiah 66:13 God promises: "As one whom his mother comforteth, so will I comfort you; and ye shall be comforted in Jerusalem." The word 'comfort' is derived from two Latin words meaning to gain strength or fortitude from being with, or in the presence of, another person. Comfort includes power to withstand troubles or peril, and overcome them to our profit, as ordeals strengthen our character.

The God Who comforts us is the same Father Who so loved the world that He sent His Son to save mankind, not to judge it. He gives us the Holy Spirit as an abiding Comforter, with infinite power to console: "to be with you forever" (John 14:16). We need not go unconsoled for even a moment, because we have an indwelling, caring Paraclete, who pledges to "comfort me on every side" (Psalm 71:21). The Comforter will bring divine peace by bringing to our remembrance all that Jesus has said (John 14:25), as revealed in His Word: "that by steadfastness and by the encouragement of the Scriptures we might have hope" (Romans 15:4). Isaiah 61:1-2 portends the Messiah's anointing: "The Lord hath sent me to bind up the brokenhearted... to comfort all that mourn."

2 Timothy 1:7 KJV puts it: "For God hath not given us the spirit of fear; but of power, and of love, and of a sound mind." Just as God gives us faith, He also gives us the power, love, and light to repel fear. Overcoming is by His power, but we must cooperate in receiving faith, which strengthens us.

God not only refrains from tempting us, but He also promises He will not allow a greater burden of temptation to befall us than we can bear. I Corinthians 10:13 promises: "No temptation has overtaken you that is not common to man. God is faithful, and he will not let you be tempted beyond your strength, but with the temptation will also provide the way of escape, that you may be able to endure it."

The promises of deliverance from temptation is a triple one. First Satan and other men cannot tempt us with any enticements which are not common to man. They must be normal, customary, and ordinary in the world. Nothing unusually sophisticated or attractive can be fashioned against us. Thus, we can draw strength from the example of Jesus, "who in every respect has been tempted as we are, yet without sinning" (Hebrews 4:15). We can look to, and draw strength from, the example of other saints who have resisted sin, knowing we share the same temptations as they, and no more.

Secondly, God literally sorts and sifts any temptation before it reaches you, and lets nothing arrive which you are unable to bear or manage. He "will not let you be tempted beyond your strength." God will not test a spiritual babe in advanced literary composition when he is just learning the alphabet. God limits the intensity, frequency, and duration of our sufferings to keep them manageable according to our personal progress and capacity to tolerate them.

Third, God promises a way of escape from every temptation, by supernaturally empowering believers to endure anything they encounter in the world, by his grace and strength. At the very least, advanced age will eventually come to the rescue of a believer beleaguered by temptation, by diminishing the appetites of the flesh. The fruit of the Holy Spirit, outlined at Galatians 5:22-23 is the divine provision for overcoming temptation. The fruit of love helps us resist the temptation to harm another, For "Love bears all things, believes all things, hopes all things, endures all things" (I Corinthians 13:7).

Whenever God enables us to avoid sin and withstand temptation, then we have escaped or eluded the suffering which results from sin. If we can be insulated from Satan's temptations to sin, then we can avoid the consequences, "For the wages of sin is death" (Romans 6:23). Slavery to sin "leads to death" (Romans 6:16), and suffering which results from sin is a most virulent, protracted foretaste of death.

In this sense, the imparted righteousness, regeneration or transformation which God works at the New Birth becomes a believer's primary insulation against suffering which proceeds from sinning. For, a new heart which hates sin because God hates sin, is less susceptible to temptation and commission of sin. Believers need not succumb to temptation because: "We know that any one born of God does not sin, but He who was born of God keeps him, and the evil one does not touch him" (I John 5:18). And if we do not sow the wind of sin, we will not reap the whirlwind of suffering which sin produces.

The writer of Hebrews 13:21 prays that we are enabled to resist sin, and that God may "equip you with everything good that you may do his will, working in you that which is pleasing in his sight, through Jesus who strengthens me." The Blood of the Lamb which washes us clean frees us from our sins (Revelation 1:5), and frees us from guilt. Because believers are occupied and filled with the indwelling Holy Spirit, there is no room for Satan or his demons. "You are of God, and have overcome them; for he who is in you is greater than he who is in the world" (I John 4:4). It is God Who accomplishes our holiness (John 15:5; I Corinthians 15:10; 2 Corinthians 3:5, 12:9; Philippians 2:12,13).

Carnal men obey the laws and drive within the speed limits because they fear punishment for violating them. Dread of divine wrath and impending judgment for wrongdoing is a great stimulus to doing right. Fear of the Lord includes elements of terror, fright, and consternation that one's despising or disdaining God will lead to dreadful loss. The sinner who scoffs at God's salvation must fear the consequences of his own choice, for he must pay his own penalty for sin if he refuses to claim God's grace by faith in Jesus as Lord and Saviour.

Jesus warns at Matthew 10:28: "And do not fear those who kill the body but cannot kill the soul; rather fear him who can destroy both soul and body in hell." God does not hesitate to warn us of the reality of hell and damnation to deter us from evil and motivate us toward holiness and salvation as an adjunct of drawing us to Him by His love. Ecclesiastes 3:14 says: "I know that whatever God doeth, it shall be for ever: Nothing can be put to it, nor any thing taken from it; and God doeth it, that men should fear before him."

Spiritual men living in the world obey the law because it is inherently right, and ordained by God for their well-being. Their reverence for God is to please Him because of the excellence of His character. If obedience is based on any fear, it is not so much a dread of God ever doing anything to harm us, but of the inevitable natural consequences ordained for unrepented sin. Reason directs us to avoid anguish, loss, and alienation, should God honor our free choice to reject His call. Christian fear is not of damnation, because "perfect love casts out fear" (I John 4:18), and Christians have experienced the perfect love of God, unmistakable in his salvation.

The sovereignty, magnificence and grandeur of God's power inspires a Christian to develop the fear of God in the more mature spiritual sense of reverential devotion, awe, and honor for one's Father, as the glorious, majestic, and holy Creator of the universe. This sense of wonder includes respect and deference that a child has for his Father. It involves veneration, honor, and esteem for the God of the universe and Saviour of the world, who allows us to hear His Word and communicate with Him in prayer.

Believers need not fear the wrath of God which is leveled against unredeemed sinners, but we need to respect His discipline against sinful conduct. If He is truly Lord, one will obey Him to avoid any affront to His honor and dignity. We will obey Him because we love Him; are thankful for His pardon and forgiveness; and wish to please Him. Reverential fear of offending

God should deter every Christian from sinning, as much as God's love motivates obedient holiness to glorify Him.

A Christian is not likely to sin if he remembers that he is never free from divine scrutiny; that his temple and vessel of grace are desecrated by his embrace of sin; that each sin is a rebuke to Jesus' Atonement and a repulse to the indwelling Spirit. More importantly, we have God's assurance that His grace is more than equal to the task of overcoming commission of, and temptation to sin. Romans 5:20 declares: "but where sin increased, grace abounded all the more." If imperfect earthly fathers know how to give good gifts to their children, "how much more will the heavenly Father give the Holy Spirit to those who ask him?" (Luke 11:13). And it is the Spirit through Whom our actual righteousness is increased. We are rewarded: "If ye will fear the Lord, and serve him, and obey his voice, and not rebel against the commandment of the Lord, then shall both ye and also the king that reigneth over you continue following the Lord your God" (I Samuel 12:14).

Psalm 111:10 teaches that "The fear of the Lord is the beginning of wisdom. A good understanding have all they that do His commandments." It reminds us we are creatures and totally dependent on our Creator. Ecclesiastes 8:12 affirms: "it shall be well with them that fear God." For, fear of God's sovereign power moves us to submission, and can even motivate unbelievers to benefit God's people. Rahab heard how the enemies of Israel had been destroyed at the Red Sea, and recognized that God was in control of all events which impacted His chosen People. Consequently, she did not betray the two Israelite spies, but assisted them in conquering Jericho (Joshua 2:9-10). Blessings of knowledge, deliverance, mercy, sufficiency, salvation, and reward are promised him who fears the Lord at Psalms 25:14, 33:18, 34:7, 34:9, 85:9, 103:11,13,17; 111:5, 145:19, and 147:11; Jeremiah 39: and Luke 1:50.

God further accomplishes our resistance to sin by focusing our attention on Him, for we will have no room to contemplate sin when we are thinking about God's lovely character. A principal way of escape from the worldly thoughts, wrongs, and slights which penetrate your consciousness is to hasten to the haven of fellowship with God on the transport of God's Word. When your focus is on God; to thank Him, enjoy Him, please Him with obedience; or receive with jubilation His blessings and protection, you will not be overwhelmed by worldly circumstances. Be aware of God, love his presence and his eternal, enduring values, and today's worldly fears will dissolve. Above all, recognize your weakness, and pray to Him for strength to overcome the temptation, or otherwise remove it before it reaches you. Even an unsaved alcoholic sees the wisdom of finding a new route to avoid passing his favorite bar, rather than risk being tempted by it.

There is a special awareness of God's presence when we think of His triple promises to control and limit our suffering to what is common to man; what we can endure; and that He will provide a way of escape (I Corinthians 10:13). If God is regulating our suffering in these ways, the implications are awesome. For, if God is always aware of, and present in, the suffering we experience, then his constancy makes anything bearable. If Jesus shared the same temptations, and endured the suffering on the cross to demonstrate his love for us, then we can be strengthened by the same power of God which enabled Christ's example.

St. Paul's advice at Philippians 4:8-9 is: "whatever is true... honorable... just... pure... lovely... gracious, if there is any excellence, if there is anything worthy of praise, think about these things. What you have learned... and seen in me, do; and the God of peace will be with you." Hebrews 12:4 summons us to be encouraged by Jesus' example of committing no sin: "In your struggle against sin you have not yet resisted to the point of shedding your blood."

Those living in closest communion with God will be most aware of their privileges of God's favor, blessings, and companionship. They will maintain a healthy fear of losing them by acts, through weakness or stupidity, which grieve the Holy Spirit. We know that God uses chastisement to keep His children from harm and trained in righteousness, love, and witness. The simple awareness of that penalty can also serve effectively to create a reverential fear which deters any conduct in conflict with that training.

OVERCOMING BY LOOKING TO JESUS

God also helps us withstand suffering by providing Jesus as our example of how to endure suffering to the glory of God. Hebrews 12:1-3 calls believers to "run with perseverance the race that is set before us, looking to Jesus the pioneer and perfecter of our faith, who... endured the cross... Consider him who endured from sinners such hostility against himself, so that you may not grow weary or fainthearted." When we look to Jesus in the midst of our suffering, we will be helped to persevere by knowing that Jesus went through and overcame His suffering by the power of God He now shares with us.

We will also remember all that Jesus endured for us, and gain courage and inspiration from His gift, lest we squander it by ingratitude. Even our greatest suffering must pale by comparison to His, and the example of His endurance must give us fresh strength to persevere. St. Paul said, "For this slight momentary affliction is preparing for us an eternal weight of glory beyond all comparison" (2 Corinthians 4:17). It is 'slight' in comparison with what Jesus suffered on the Cross, and it is 'momentary' compared with the glory of Heaven for which it is preparing us. Affliction drove Paul to the point he "despaired of life itself" (2 Corinthians 1:8). Yet, he could occupy for Christ by looking to Jesus, the pioneer and Author of our faith, whose example teaches loving grace and mercy, despite the sin and injustice in the world.

The sacrifice of Jesus' life for us must also give fresh purpose to our lives. A child who has been snatched from peril at the cost of another's life is not likely to waste his gift of survival. If we protest that God has made a world in which sin and suffering are possible, we need to remember that the cost was far greater to Him than to us. For, He accepted the need to suffer for us because of His love, and took on that responsibility at the Cross. We have a God Who not only limits our suffering, but Who endured greater suffering and temptation than we ever will. He has dignified our suffering by joining us, feeling and sharing man's pain, anguish, grief, and death.

We respond in faith to God's sacrificial love because redemption from our corrupted freedom to sin cost Him personally far more than worldly suffering could ever cost us. We learn from Jesus that true love and joy involve suffering voluntarily for other's well-being, despite the cost or sacrifice to oneself. God is so sensitive to human suffering from sins that He made them His very own at the Cross, and shared them lovingly with man, rather than blindly or mechanically as the Old Testament sacrifices. Jesus is the vital, sustaining Head of an incomplete, suffering Body until we are raised imperishable. And He knows and intercedes for all that His Body undergoes in the world.

Jesus can still use us for His purposes in whatever condition we may be, despite our pain. We can emerge courageously from our trials with a greater perception of the needs of others, and a greater strength to minister to those needs, because of Christ's example. Thus, we can give thanks in all things and for all things, even though there may be no inherent good in suffering. What can become good is our reaction to God working change in us, as He works all things for good for those who love Him. We can respond in a positive, creative way which develops character and serves others according to Christ's example to the glory of God. What is evil about suffering occurs when we let it destroy us or separate us from God.[22]

Surely, the example of Jesus' total love for sinful men is a guarantee that He will also give Born-Again believers the victory over affliction. We may not know why our suffering is prolonged, but we can have no doubt He will eventually deliver us in the divine Providence of His sovereignty, even if it must be left to Heaven. Jesus' example on the Cross teaches that tragedy and darkness will always be followed by deliverance and the light of victory.

Jesus is our example that all suffering is not for punishment or deterrence of sin. Some is beyond our understanding. Jesus was perfectly in the will of God, perfectly obedient and holy, and perfectly anointed as God's ministering redeemer. Yet, He suffered more than any man, and is our example to follow to glory. God does call us to suffer, as Jesus did, at I Peter 3:19-21: "For one is approved if, <u>mindful of God </u>he endures pain <u>while suffering unjustly</u>... But if when you do right and suffer from it you take it patiently, you have God's approval. For to this you have been called, because Christ also suffered for you <u>leaving you an example,</u> that you should follow in his steps." When you suffer unjustly in reliance on the complete love and sovereignty of God, you are necessarily "mindful of God."[23] If we are persecuted, we are to follow Christ's example (Philippians 2:7), and not revile or threaten in return.[24]

We are to bear with suffering, but it is not because we are required to undergo the same suffering Jesus did. God's purpose is to conform us to the character of Jesus, not His sufferings, which were unique to Him as Saviour of all mankind. God is not transforming us into another Saviour, but into a cloned Christ-like character. To that end, we will accept and endure suffering, and draw near to Jesus and share with Him as our character is being re-worked by God, through pain, into His image. We will accept suffering, as Jesus did, comforted and emboldened by His example, which teaches us to be obedient and submissive to God's direction for our lives.

Just as we will have no room for thoughts of sin when our minds are occupied with thoughts of Jesus, so we will not feel pain inflicted upon us, when our thoughts are focused on Him. Many soldiers injured in the midst of combat have attested that they never felt the pain of their wounds until their attention to the battle ended. As warriors in the Church Militant, we should be so occupied with the battle against Satan that we cannot notice the spiritual wounds he inflicts, because we are intent on following our Commander, Jesus. We can conquer the world because "The law of the Spirit of life in Christ Jesus has set me free from sin and death" (Romans 8:2). My transformed inner man is no longer under compulsion to sin, though still able to do so. Jesus is "the resurrection and the life," raising new life in dead spirits, and sustaining that life continually after the Resurrection.

Isaiah 53:5, reprised in Matthew 8:17, says: "he was wounded for our transgressions, he was bruised for our iniquities." Isaiah 53:12 continues: "he bare the sin of many, and made intercession for the transgressors." Isaiah 63:9 adds: "In all their affliction he was afflicted." When He walked the earth, Jesus had enormous compassion for every suffering person. On the Cross, Jesus literally felt our suffering for sin.

We, imperfect beings, have all experienced the sheer unbearable weight of the suffering of others around us. Can you imagine, then, the exquisite, empathetic, suffering of our perfect, all-loving Father, as He views the griefs of His children? At the same time, He is sure His plan and system for human collaboration will produce maximum joy for all concerned throughout eternity. He knows that the child who falls while learning to walk, will soon expand his horizons through running, playing, and locomotion. He knows that the child who is disciplined and chastened will develop a transformed, Christ-like character, and eventually enjoy the mature fellowship of his Father, as a blessing superior to irresponsible freedom.

The suffering servant draws comfort from looking to Jesus and recalling that God, Himself, bears our suffering. This makes bearing our sorrows easier, because misery needs company, and what better companion than God. Also, knowing that God empathizes with us, yet allows the suffering to continue, somehow validates the essential rightness of God's sovereignty and operations which allow the potential for suffering. Indeed, God overcame evil through Jesus' suffering love, to fulfill His plan of man's salvation. Suffering motivated by love was the Divine weapon by which Jesus conquered Satan for eternity. God is so much a part of our suffering, because He is in us, and we are in Him. There is a correspondence between our travails and the Atonement, in which Jesus suffered for our sins by vicariously suffering for us. 2 Corinthians 5:21 reminds us: "For our sake he made him to be sin, who knew no sin."

We ought not glorify our own importance in suffering and loss, when it is so trivial in comparison to the quantity and intensity of suffering experience by the Lord! We ought not squander so precious a deliverance of blessings and fullness of life by the Saviour, by focusing on our temporal and material lack. We ought not ignore the love elicited by the Saviour's own love for all men, by neglecting to minister to the desperate needs of others because we are engulfed in our own trivial pursuits. Jesus has compassion for human helplessness, and calls us to relieve suffering in the mankind He loves so much. He confides His continuing involvement in the needs of the downtrodden: "as you did it to one of the least of these my brethren, you did it to me" (Matthew 25:40).

In addition to Christ's example of faithful endurance, we can also look to the lives of martyrs and saints for incentive to persevere in faith and obedience to overcome persecution and suffering. After recounting their ordeals of torture, mocking, scourging, chains, imprisonment, stoning, dismemberment, destitution, affliction, and ill-treatment, Hebrews 12:1 challenges: "Therefore, since we are surrounded by so great a cloud of witnesses, let us also lay aside every weight and sin.. and let us run with perseverance the race that is set before us, looking to Jesus."

After Paul received his thorn in the flesh, his faith was fortified by God's assured deliverance, either by elimination of, or enablement to tolerate, any affliction. Paul attested: "For the sake of Christ, then I am content with weaknesses, insults, hardships, persecutions, and calamities; for when I am weak, then I am strong" (2 Corinthians 12:10). Paul understood, as we can because of his example, that God's strength is perfected and expressed in full measure, when one's own weakness steps aside and enables the Lord to take over and work his wondrous ways.

When Paul understood that God was re-working affliction to provide a superior blessing, Paul could prefer the fruits of God's ways even at the loss of freedom from pain. His peace was based on total reliance in God's gracious workings. Future problems became instruments of Christ's sufficiency, for just as He is adequate for today, He will be the same for tomorrow. By

God's grace we can accept our travails, and by His power to endure we will overcome them. By His presence we can find peace and contentment.

Paul's words, "For the sake of Christ" give us assurance of divine resources as long as affliction involves, or results from, our doing the work of Christ. Or, if we have incurred suffering in our own folly, we can depend on supernatural power to endure if we turn it to divine purposes, such as correction and training in holiness "for the sake of Christ." For, we are then re-focused on eternal values rather than our suffering. Paul was aware, as a redeemed child of God, that he was too loved ever to be ignored or forgotten in danger, scorn, or peril. Because Paul was in God's service, there was no doubt that God would take the responsibility, and care for him in the performance of God's work. Even if God leads us through dark valleys, they are still God's, and He makes no mistake in the path He chooses for His beloved.

We can also advert to the example of Stephen, and other Christian martyrs for assurance God provides endurance for any suffering He allows to reach us. Stephen, when about to be stoned to death, retained the peace of the Lord, because he was: "full of the Holy Spirit, gazed into heaven and saw the glory of God, and Jesus standing at the right hand of God" (Acts 7:55). God filled Stephen with the Holy Spirit, and God sustained Stephen with a vision of a concerned Christ "standing," perhaps to view better the events which affected Stephen. When we focus on Jesus, we will know that He is with us, especially in adversity (John 14:26-28; Acts 2:25; Colossians 3:1-2; Hebrews 12:2).

Paul and Silas were freed by an earthquake from their chains and cells in a Philippian prison (Acts 16:26), yet they felt no compulsion to seize their opportunity to flee. Paul said he was content in any circumstance, "for I have learned in whatever state I am, to be content... I can do all things in him who strengthens me" (Philippians 4:11,13).

We are helped to endure suffering, by focusing on all the eternal blessings which God has bestowed upon us. God freed Job from concentrating on the enormity of his suffering, by recounting the marvels of His creation (Job 38:1, ff). Job was given humility in the knowledge he had no claim upon God for anything. Job's suffering was infinitesimal and insignificant in comparison to God's universe, and God would eventually restore him without the suffering. The vantage of eternity can quickly put these fleeting moments of suffering here on earth in proper perspective. The return of Christ for His Church is a believer's blessed hope. For, God's ultimate rescue from worldly affliction is a glorious Heaven, free from all travails.

Knowing that a caring God answers the prayers offered by His children can be so comforting a thought that it helps us bear any suffering. The actuality of deliverance in response to prayer is itself a cardinal blessing, yet the anticipation of God's relief is no less a reality. Even when we pray wrongly, we can be assured God will provide proper blessings, as he heeds the intercessions of Jesus, the Holy Spirit, and other believers, on our behalf. The prayers of a believer interceding on our behalf is a great blessing permitted by God, since "The prayer of a righteous man has great power in its effects" (James 5:16). Psalm 34:15 says: "The eyes of the Lord are upon the righteous, and His ears are open unto their cry."

Intercessions on behalf of believers by Jesus and the holy Spirit constitute great blessings provided by God's grace for the deliverance of His faithful. Jesus is constituted as our High Priest (Hebrews 2:17; 3:1), to assure our forgiveness and enable believers to draw near to God, and "with confidence draw near to the throne of grace, that we may receive mercy and find grace to help in time of need" (Hebrews 4:16). He makes intercession for our sins, according to Hebrews 7:18-25: "A better hope is introduced, through which we draw near to God... This makes Jesus the surety of a better covenant... he holds his priesthood permanently, because he continues forever. Consequently, he is able for all time to save those who draw near to God through him, since he always lives to make intercessions for them." See also, I John 2:1-2; Romans 8:34; and Hebrews 4:15.

Jesus' intercessions with God include insulating us from the temptations of Satan, so we will not sin. Jesus told Peter: "Satan demanded to have you, that he might sift you like wheat, but I have prayed for you that your faith may not fail; and when you have turned again, strengthen your brethren" (Luke 22:31-32). Jesus knew that Peter would renounce Him three times before dawn, but that he could still be trusted, when he "turned again," to tend the Lord's sheep (John 18:25-27, 21:15-17). And for this, Jesus prayed to God in intercession, so Satan's temptations could not overcome Peter, though he would falter for a night. Peter's faith, which ultimately did not fail, was faithfulness to Jesus; faith in His reliability to keep His promises. Though his faith failed for a night, it was later strengthened by Jesus. Peter not only kept his salvation, despite denying Jesus, but was restored to eminently faithful service.

The blessing of confidence in our salvation is secured in the knowledge that our sins are remitted because of our High Priest's perpetual intercessions on our behalf, so that we escape our deserved punishment for sin of eternal destruction. Jesus says: "whoever lives and believes in me shall never die" (John 11:26; see also, John 3:36, 5:24, 10:28).

God has also provided divine intercession by the Holy Spirit as a further control on worldly suffering, so that we will succeed in overcoming temptation or enduring suffering. Romans 8:26-27 says: "Likewise the Spirit helps us in our weakness: for we do not know how to pray as we ought, but the Spirit himself intercedes for us with sighs too deep for words... because the Spirit intercedes for the saints according to the will of God." Even when we fail to pray, or our prayers depart from God's will, the Holy Spirit lovingly transforms both our desires and our petitions, so they conform to God's will and interpret our true needs, which pleases God; coincides with what is best for us; and maximizes our blessings.

GOD'S BLESSING OF DIGNITY THROUGH PRAYER

God dignifies believers by allowing their participation in prayer to petition for one's needs, or intercede for the needs of others. Prayer is technically communicating a request to God, but common usage refers to any communion with God as prayer. The privilege of prayer allows us to communicate with God to express our praise, worship, thanksgiving, and enjoy the pure pleasure of dialogue with the wisest, most loving Father in existence. Prayer is God's gracious provision for direct access to the mind, ear, voice, and might of God.

A believer cannot offer effective prayers which seek a specific answer, without first believing that God listens to our petitionary prayers because of Jesus; always answers them, and chooses to respond by granting what is best for the one who prays, according to God's perfect wisdom and will. God accommodates our wholesome desires and allows prayer to affect outcomes by inviting His interventions in our affairs and the concerns of others. Jesus authorizes believers to "ask and ye shall receive, that your joy may be full" (John 16:24).

Prayer is ineffective unless we believe that God has promised in His Word to intervene supernaturally in worldly affairs in answer to individual prayers; that He has unlimited Sovereign power to effectuate His will; and His answers will always be providential, benevolent, and conducive to our highest good as the result of His perfect love and goodness toward man.

Man's part is to pray for God's moving in such manner. St. Augustine knew that without God, we cannot, but without us, God will not. Man is free, God is personal to each of us, and the world is a sphere for their creative collaboration.[25] When God commands us what to do, He tells us to do what we can, and to ask for what we cannot do. He helps us so we can obediently do what He has directed.[26] Thus, prayer denies both chance and fate. Chance would mean whatever happens does so without any power regulating it. Fate would mean that everything is foreordained by rigid laws which are unyielding and beyond man's control to effect change by prayer.

God's grace not only allows us to pray to him, but promises to hear, consider, and respond to our prayers. Hebrews 4:16 invites believers to approach God in prayer: "Let us then with confidence draw near to the throne of grace, that we may receive mercy and find grace to help in time of need." Psalm 55:17 expresses this confidence in God: "Evening, and morning, and at noon, will I pray, and cry aloud: and he shall hear my voice." Psalm 22:24 tells us that "he hath not despised nor abhorred the affliction of the afflicted; neither hath he hid his face from him; but when he cried unto him, he heard." When Jesus prayed for Lazarus, He affirmed: "Father, I thank thee that thou hast heard me. I know that thou hearest me always (John 11:42). God heeds our prayers, too, according to Exodus 8:12, 22:27; Judges 10:12; I Kings 7:9; Joshua 10:14; 2 Chronicles 7:12-15; Isaiah 45:11, 58:9; Jeremiah 29:12, 33:3; Psalms 3:5, 16:6, 50:15, 55:16-17, 90:15, 107:28, 138:3, 144:19; and Hosea 14:2.

When we pray, we are expressing our belief that God has promised to respond, and has the power to effectuate our requests, along with the millions of other prayers offered to Him. We cannot pray effectually unless we believe God rules the universe and is ultimately in charge of worldly affairs, exercising sovereignty and dominion over His Creation. Prayer confirms we believe God intends good for us; has supreme authority over Satan, evil, and wrong; and can be trusted to fulfill His revealed assurances to bless us; deliver us from evil; and transform us to the spiritual likeness of Christ.

Thus, prayer seeks a result which must depend upon God's power and providence. Since God's power is made perfect in weakness (2 Corinthians 12:9), recognizing our feebleness becomes our greatest strength, since man's insufficiency precedes God's enabling. And the greater our weakness, the greater the potential for God's power and intervention in our lives. We do not replace our strength with an equal power, but with the omnipotence of Almighty God — an exchange exclusively for our advantage, as limited human power is surrendered to divine plenary power.

Scripture reveals the reality of God's response to prayer. God had shared with Abraham His intent to destroy Sodom and Gomorrah "because their sin is very grievous" (Genesis 18:20). Abraham was privileged to intercede on behalf of the righteous living there, and obtained God's response and promise not to destroy the cities if as few as ten righteous men could be found there (Genesis 18:24-32). Unfortunately, Sodom was destroyed because that many could not be found. Yet, a gracious Lord permitted Moses to intercede for the wilderness Israelites who worshipped a golden calf (Deuteronomy 9:16-29; Exodus 32:32, 33:17). Jesus guarantees that God will answer prayers offered in Jesus' name. 2 Corinthians 1:20 says that in Jesus "all the promises of God find their Yes in him. That is why we utter the Amen through him to the glory of God".

As a general rule, we can expect the things for which we pray to be answered by God, because His Word reveals His will to bless us with more abundant life in Christ (John 10:10).

Romans 8:32 challenges: "He who did not spare his own Son but gave him up for us all, will he not also <u>give us all things with him</u>?" Since God already has a predisposition to bless His children, we can believe He will answer our prayers which seem to be according to his will, unless they are wrong or hurtful.

Justification for such reliance on God's blessing in answer to prayer is expressed at I John 5:14: "if we ask anything <u>according to his will</u> he hears us. And if we know that he hears us in whatever we ask, <u>we know that we have obtained the requests made of him</u>." Faith is the key to answered prayer, for we must have faith God will grant our requests. Jesus says at Matthew 21:21: "If you have faith and never doubt... even if you say to this mountain, 'Be taken up and cast into the sea,' it will be done. And whatever you ask in prayer, you will receive if you have faith." See also, Matthew 6:6, 7:7, 9:29. 17:20; Mark 9:23, 11:23-24; Luke 17:19; and Philippians 4:6.

We can be certain that any promises explicitly expressed in God's Word are indicative of His will, and our prayers will be answered. Thus, we can expect comfort in mourning; mercy if we are merciful, (Matthew 5:4,7); healing (Exodus 15:26, Psalms 31:24, 41:3, 103:2-3); success (Psalms 1:1-3, 20:4; Proverbs 16:3); wisdom (Psalm 32:8; James 1:5); and hundreds of other specific blessings promised in Scripture. God wants us to pray for what He wills, expressed in the Word. Such prayers facilitate God accomplishing what is for our benefit, because they express our welcome, receptivity, and submission to His purposes. They evidence our faith, because they are based on specific Bible promises by which faith comes, and are within the parameters of God's will.

You are entitled to pray for a Cadillac, under the authority of requesting those things for which you hope, in the name of Jesus, but if you pray for the power or comfort of the Holy Spirit, or any specific promise, you can be certain it will be granted, because God's Word has revealed that is His will (Luke 11:13).

Jesus teaches at John 14:13: "whatever you <u>ask in my name,</u> I will do it, that the Father may be glorified in the Son." See also John 15:16 and 16:23-24. Praying in Jesus' name does not mean we invoke some mystical power by using His name. It means we pray as His agent, by His authority, guidance, and expressed purposes, making our request for His sake and honor. We can be sure of answered prayer when we act under our Power of Attorney, as his representative for His purposes revealed in the Word; not to exploit our association with Him selfishly. We pray in His memory, for His sake, and for the progress and accomplishment of the work He began when He was here, and still continues by His Holy Spirit and through His disciples.[27] Since Jesus wants it, we have a right to expect an answer and have faith in his Word.

A thirst for righteousness is also conducive to answered prayer. At Matthew 6:33 Jesus promises God will provide our needs, if we seek first the Kingdom of God. At John 15:7 Jesus adds: "If you abide in me, and my words abide in you, ask whatever you will, and it shall be done for you." And let us remember that God's Word promises at James 5:15-18: "confess your sins to one another, and pray for one another, that you may be healed. <u>The prayer of a righteous man has great power in its effects</u>. Elijah was a man of like nature with ourselves and he prayed fervently that it might not rain, and for three years and six month it did not rain on the earth. Then he prayed again, and the heaven gave rain, and the earth brought forth its fruit." We are still privileged to ask for many things, including satisfaction of our desires, even if not expressly authorized by God's Word, but a specific Word promise gives greater assurance of God's affirmative answer.

God answers our prayers from the perspective of promoting our eternal welfare. He will deny unwise temporal and material requests which are not conducive to salvation. So it is always appropriate to pray in resignation and submission to God's will that our petition be granted only if it is in accord with His will. Such surrender expresses love and adoration for God. You will not desire anything except what He wills. You will not object to anything if He permits it. You will follow whatever He has planned for you because your best interests are inseparable from His will for you.[28]

Since God has promised to act in response to our prayers, a corollary assumption is that God may not confer the blessing we desire if we do not trouble to pray for it. James 4:2-3 specifies: "You do not have because you do not ask. You ask and do not receive, because you ask wrongly, to spend it on your passions." This extends to our prayers on behalf of others. An unsaved person who hears our witness to the Gospel may not be receptive to the Word we communicate, because we have failed to ask God to prepare his heart and bestow prevenient grace. Of course, God innovates, initiates, or withholds action solely as He wills, without the help of any man, but the function of prayer has been designed by God to play an integral part in transacting human affairs.

Negative prayer may also reflect the spiritual law of sowing and reaping, so that our negative, faithless declarations to God may produce only negative results of prayer. If we dwell on doubt, sinfulness, and unworthiness — all of which have a proper place in prayer if we intend to entrust them to the Lord — then negative thought predominates our prayers, and such lack of faith in God's transforming power in answer to prayer, invites only negative results.[29]

While the prayers of a righteous man have efficacy, conversely, unrighteousness and sin left unrepented, can hinder our prayers (Proverbs 1:28, 28:13; Isaiah 59:2; Romans 1:28). Prayers of the unrighteous are not heard by God (I Peter 3:12; Psalm 66:18; Isaiah 59:2). Being unreconciled to a brother thwarts our prayers (Matthew 5:23-24). Husbands should be considerate of, and bestow honor on, their wives, "in order that your prayers may not be hindered" (I Peter 3:7). Pride is a bar to effective prayer (Luke 18:14; James 4:6). However, praying to God for help in overcoming inconsideration, unforgiveness, and unrighteousness will reveal sin, and lead to self–judging, confessing, and forsaking sin, which is the key to healing your condition and correcting hindrances to prayer.[30]

There are times God may not grant good health, because it may turn one's attention away from God and salvation, resulting in the loss of a soul. No parent would give a sharp knife to a child because its glitter is attractive. Some of our petitions are denied because we cannot see the harmful consequences if they were granted. But God can, and even in denial, always acts in our best interests because He loves us.

At Matthew 18:19 Jesus promises: "if two of you agree on earth about anything they ask, it will be done for them by my Father in heaven." This does not impose an added condition or restraint on prayer, requiring a minimum of two persons praying together to be effective. We have countless examples of Moses, Abraham, Jeremiah and others effectively offering solitary prayers, which God granted. God had decreed that King Hezekiah was to die, but when Hezekiah prayed alone for mercy, the Lord gave him an additional fifteen years of reign (Isaiah 35:1-5). When two or more believers pray for the same thing, faith is fortified by the agreement of united believers. Agreement, though not infallible, provides confirmation that a prayer is consistent with the Word and the leading of the Holy Spirit.

We are called to pray constantly, and everywhere. Jesus provides our example of when and how to pray. He prayed incessantly, both privately and in public (Luke 6:12). He prayed at any and every time of day, and He always prayed according to, and for the fulfillment of, God's will (Matthew 26:42). Jesus directs us: "always to pray and not lose heart" (Luke 18:1); to "pray at all times in the Spirit" (Ephesians 6:18); and to "be constant in prayer" (Romans 12:12 and see Psalm 55:17). I Thessalonians 5:16 says: "Pray constantly... for this is the will of God in Christ Jesus for you," while I Timothy 2:8 says "that in every place the men should pray." Jesus says at Matthew 6:6: "When you pray, go into your room and shut the door and pray to your Father who is in secret; and your Father who sees in secret will reward you." Matthew 7:7 adds: "Ask, and it will be given you... For everyone who asks receives, and he who seeks finds, and to him who knocks it will be opened."

We are called to persevere in prayer (Luke 11:8, 18:1-8, 21:36; Colossians 4:2); not to change God's mind, but to confirm the constancy of our desires, and position ourselves to receive all the blessings God is preparing and waiting to give us. For, God has promised: "Call unto me, and I will answer thee, and shew thee great and mighty things, which thou knowest not" (Jeremiah 33:3). God does not resist persevering prayer. The Roman Catholic idea of a novena is to offer devotions for nine days, with the repetition reflecting the faith and perseverance encouraged by the Lord. Indeed, one of the reasons our prayers are not answered is because we abandon them too soon. We shrink from prayer at the first sign of inattention, distraction, disappointment, or apparent denial, when we should persevere by seeking God's enablement of our prayers.[31] We are called to wait upon the Lord, patiently, and patience is a fruit of the Holy Spirit, bestowed by God's grace.

The Stoic, Seneca, observed that what we purchase by prayer is most costly to us. No lawyer would think of addressing a judge or jury unprepared, and wasting their time with disorganized, thoughtless prattle. Yet, how many of us presume that the Judge of all the earth is readily available and receptive to impulsive, banal, or inane chatter. Prayer demands a cost of time in our devotions: time to meditate and prepare for our visit with Almighty God. Prayer exacts effort to sustain our concentration in discourse with our heavenly Father, and resist the intrusions of worldly clamor. Prayer costs obedient submission to God, as we say: "Not my will, but Thine be done." Prayer costs humility as we confess our sins to God, in our quest for forgiveness and cleansing. And then true repentance will cost the surrender and sacrifice of slothful, and self-indulgent habits.[32]

Furthermore, simply because God is available to, and solicits the worship of, His faithful (John 4:23-24), it does not follow He is at our beck and call, or that we cannot estrange ourselves from God.[33] Isaiah 55:6 warns: "Seek ye the Lord while he may be found," and Isaiah 45:15 notes: "Thou art a God that hidest thyself," implying there can be times God shuts out indifferent suitors, impenitent sinners and defiant rebels.

Your supplications should be as specific as possible, which reflects your deliberate evaluation of needs, but God is equally receptive to inarticulate, disjointed, and unspecific communications which seek His peace and comfort, rather than some specific boon. Audible prayers are always appropriate (Psalms 27:7, 28:2, 142:1). Spontaneity can be as effective as thoughtful, skillful preparation. However, God is entitled to reverential awe, and thoughtful worship. Routine prayers can be stale and brittle, if they become rote recitations and lack any practical significance to the utterer.[34] Persevere in prayers, and pray frequently. God takes your prayers as seriously as you take them, and responds according to the fervor of your requests.

Repetition, by bombarding the gates of Heaven with prayer, need not be a contradiction of faith, but an avowal of your sincere need and total dependence upon God for your answer. Start out modestly in your petitions, asking God first to improve you. Then, as answered prayer strengthens your faith, make progressively bigger requests of God.

Yet, be compliant, obedient, and accepting of God's answer. His intelligence beggars yours, and a denial of your prayers is invariably for your own good. Submit by relinquishing the solution to God's decision. If nothing else, you will be greatly relieved of responsibility for the outcome if you entrust it to God and cast all the care on Him.[35]

Philippians 4:6 teaches: "Have no anxiety about anything, but in everything by prayer and supplication with thanksgiving let your requests be made known to God. And the peace of God, which passes all understanding, will keep your hearts and your minds in Christ Jesus." We can be free of anxiety because God gives us the assurance we are kept in Christ Jesus. When we offer thanksgiving, it is implied our supplications and requests will be answered when they coincide with His will; that we can know, rely upon, and expect God to keep His Word. Thus, peace follows these faithful prayers of thanksgiving.

Isaiah 26:3 confirms peace is derived from trust in God: "Thou wilt keep him in perfect peace, whose mind is stayed on thee: because he trusted in thee." Faith in God's promises of blessing brings peace while in the world, because we trust in His integrity to perform the assurances of His Word. Prayer which is faithfully turned over to God, gives believers an opportunity to see Him at work on that which has been entrusted to Him.

It is not what a man does for God which counts, but what God accomplishes through human agency. If God works through a yielded believer who draws power to act from God, there is no limit to the possibilities of human performance through prayer.[36] But we must first relinquish our own power and seek to gain God's enablement, fulfilled in human weakness, when pledged to His purposes. There is intrinsic good in prayer because it reminds us of our total dependency on God and preserves this right relationship between Giver and beneficiary. Prayer reminds us of His Providence, and is pleasing to God because we show our obedient dependence upon Him as we share in His process of blessing, and reap the benefits from answered prayer. Prayers which incorporate God's will and desire what God wants, are God's way to get Heaven's will on earth; not earth's will into Heaven.

The privilege of prayer blesses believers by reminding us of our total dependency on God for "every good and perfect gift" which comes from above (James 1:17). Faith and prayer go hand in hand. Praying without faith God will answer is ineffective because "without faith it is impossible to please God" (Hebrews 11:6). Faith that God will deliver what we desire is more effective with prayer, because it highlights and acknowledges that faith accomplishes results only by God's power.

Since God wishes to establish our total reliance upon Him for everything, he calls us to pray to him for everything. We are to thank Him in prayer for every blessing, and this obedient submission to His will is a source of great joy as He blesses us. God's love intends to stimulate our reciprocal love as He blesses us. It is difficult for unsaved, natural man to think in terms of accepting any gifts from God, because receiving implies inferiority, indebtedness, and obligation to the Giver. And this is inconsistent with natural man's self-image of power and importance. On the other hand, a Christian's delight soars whenever God blesses him, and that is precisely God's intent in having us realize that blessings originate in His love, so that we love and appreciate Him "because he first loved us" (I John 4:19), and continues to bless His children as a loving Father.

In this limited partnership between faith and divine power, a believer is directed by God to participate in a process, but always aware that any delegation of power comes only from God, based on prayer. For example, a believer is authorized to turn Satan away by willfully opposing him: "Resist the devil and he will flee from you" (James 4:7); provided, however, we first "Submit yourselves, therefore, to God... Draw nigh to God and he will draw nigh to you" (James 4:7-8).

Likewise, we believers are permitted to clothe ourselves in the "full armor of God," with which we can withstand "all the fiery darts of the evil one" (Ephesians 6:11-16); yet with a caveat: we contend against evil only as God's empowered servant: "Pray at all times in the Spirit, with all prayer and supplication. To that end keep alert with perseverance, making supplication for all the saints" (Ephesians 6:18). Jesus promises that God will provide our needs, and knows them before we ask for them (Matthew 6:8). But He still instructs us to pray daily for these needs (Matthew 6:11), so we will not forget that God alone supplies them, and so we can recognize our total dependence upon Him for every gift, and to remind us of His grace and love.

God has decreed that believers will be transformed to the image of Christ and raised perfect at his Second Coming (Ephesians 4:13). Yet man is privileged to be charged with the collaborative duty to "Be Holy," and to pray for that transformation. God allows us to have a say in our progress toward holiness; not by willing to be better by our own power, but by willing to seek God's enablement and acceleration of holiness and spiritual growth in our lives. I am to pray always for that transformation which is worked only by the Holy Spirit, and to the extent I fail to collaborate by praying, I frustrate and retard the operations of the Spirit. The more I pray for change and become receptive to the Spirit's workings, the speedier and more effective will be my growth in righteousness. God delights in our holiness, so we may be sure He will respond to such entreaties.

THE BLESSING OF COMMUNION WITH GOD

The privilege of prayer is not only a blessing which allows us to seek the desires of our hearts, but also because it permits us to commune and fellowship with God. Prayer rises to the level of discourse which exchanges the intimacy of friendship with our Heavenly Father, and is inherently joyful. Our prayer life is revelatory of our true relationship with God. When two people love one another, each cannot wait to be with the other. He desires to spend all his time with her, and share all he plans, thinks, and does with her. When we are hungry, we are driven to eat; when we are thirsty we must have drink; when we are tired we must sleep.

Likewise, the hungrier we are for God, the more we must pray! The more we enjoy His presence, the more we would seek Him! The deeper our love for God, the deeper our involvement with Him in prayer! Conversely, if we do not pray, we may not be comfortable with God; may not enjoy His presence; nor delight in the comfort of His fellowship. Logically, if we truly enjoyed praying more than we enjoyed the time-consuming trivia which occupies life, we would pray more so we could spend more time in the presence of our greatest lover. Prayerlessness is proof that other things are more important than God in our lives.

Since prayer is basically conversation with God, you will always have something to say if you incorporate traditional forms of prayer into your dialogue with God. Prayer warriors identify some of these basic avenues for communion as praise, worship, adoration, thanksgiving, gratitude, repentance; petitions to grant one's desires for blessing; for help in overcoming our shortcomings; for mercy in remission of punishment; intercession, directions for guidance, and daily marching orders.

The Lord's Prayer involves most of these elements. It starts with acknowledgement of paternal love: "Our Father." It recognizes God's transcendence: "Who art in Heaven," and worships His sanctity: "hallowed be thy name." It expresses the Christian's blessed hope of Christ's return: "Thy Kingdom come," and offers submissive obedience to God: "Thy will be done." It then petitions for one's daily needs, and forgiveness of sins. It affirms our duty to forgive others, and praises God's goodness in not tempting us, but delivering us from evil (Matthew 6:9-13). The Lord's Prayer says eloquently what we might say clumsily. Its repetition should make a deepening impression as we meditate upon the depths of its expression, provided we do not repeat it thoughtlessly by rote.

Prayer necessarily involves listening for God's replies, since all conversation alternates between listening and speaking. God has given us one mouth and two ears, perhaps so we may listen more than we speak, and He specifically instructs: "Be still and know that I am God" (Psalm 46:10). If we do not listen for an answer, it indicates we have asked a rhetorical question, and do not really expect an answer. Not waiting for God's response is arrogant, discourteous, insincere, and unintelligent.[37]

Petitioning, or asking for our own needs and desires is the form of prayer with which most of us are familiar. We must not stop communicating our needs to God, even though He has promised to provide them (Matthew 6:8,11). This helps us to remember that every good and perfect gift comes from above (James 1:17). Indeed, it might be false pride and independence to assume self-sufficiency by refusing to ask God for our daily needs. Certainly, God is strong enough to deny your unwise petitions, and wise enough to train you in appropriate perception and assertion of true needs, so your desires eventually coincide perfectly with His will.

Praying for worldly, material needs is an honorable form of petition, and the exemplary prayer Our Lord gave the disciples involves undiluted petitioning for our daily bread (Matthew 6:11). But praying for spiritual needs seeks fulfillment of eternal values. We come submissively to God, seeking His guidance in our lives; praying that He substitute His life for ours and transform us into the likeness of Christ; and entreating that we might be fitted for witnessing the Gospel to the unsaved, or ministering to the needs of the Church. Intercessory prayers for the needs of others is noble because it coincides with love, care, and concern for immediate family, loved ones, friends, neighbors, suppliers of our needs, governmental leaders, missionaries, clergy, oppressed Christians, widows, prisoners, the poor, the downtrodden, their families, and the unsaved. God will increasingly use our stewardship, as we grow in our awareness of the needs of others, and in our readiness and willingness to minister to them.

Jesus has given us a model for intercessory prayer at Luke 11:5-6: "Which of you who has a friend will go to him at midnight and say to him, 'Friend, lend me three loaves; for a friend of mine has arrived on a journey, and I have nothing to set before him'." Christians are permitted, indeed they are called to intercede, in the name of Jesus for the needs of the unsaved, the poor, the afflicted, ministries, and revival for the spiritual needs of their nation. First, we must acknowledge the responsibility to intervene on behalf of those God sends our way; for our 'friend' who "has arrived on a journey" and needs provision. We must acknowledge our total reliance on God's resources to supply those needs for which we pray, and our requests should be limited only by the limitless resources of our Father. Even the rich man in hell recognized the needs of his brothers to be warned by someone of the consequences of sin (Luke 16:27-28).

God will respond to our importunities, and provide the means to meet the needs for which we pray (Luke 11:8). But first we need sustained begging to overcome our reluctance, and evidence our serious commitment, stewardship, selflessness; and dependence upon the loving grace of God. He never betrays our confidence, but we may need the fruit of patience while we persist in prayer for others, and undergo our own spiritual transformation.

Praise and worship are among the Bible's prescriptions for legitimate conversation with God, as they bring joy, rejoicing, and enjoyment of God. Praise is intertwined with joy in the Scriptures (Psalms 5:11, 22:3, 27:6, 28:7, 32:11, 33:1. 35:9, 42:1, 43:4, and 47:7). Thus, as we recount all His glory and blessings to us, God replies with remarkable grace, and imparts joy, the second fruit of the Holy Spirit (Galatians 5:22). Psalm 22:3 says God "inhabitest the praises of Israel." Once we recollect and appreciate every good and perfect gift God has provided from above, we cannot help but rejoice, because God is present through our praises.

We may start with thanksgiving for our five senses, and express gratitude we are not blind, but enjoy the wonderful gift of sight, which enhances reading the Word, delighting in beauty, and effectively serving others. Our hearts and lungs function autonomically, year after year, without any thought on our part. Psalm 50:23 says offering praise glorifies God. So we can thank Him for what has been bestowed in love: His Creation; loving family members, the Body of Christ, and daily blessings. We have the benefit of His holiness, moral excellence, perfection, and infinite purity, which He graciously shares with believers. Above all, we have the blessed hope and secure promise of future glory in His presence for eternity, made possible because of God's grace through faith in Jesus as Lord and Saviour.

Prayers of praise fill you with joy; appreciation of what you might otherwise take for granted; which prompts intercessory prayer and selfless concern for others who are blind, deaf, lame, or somehow less fortunate than you; all while allowing you to enjoy fellowship with God as you communicate these sentiments in praise and worship to Him. Celebrate your relationship with God; the fullness of life, forgiveness, blessings, and Heaven which God's grace has provided. Rejoice in His unswerving love for you; the comforting reassurance of His presence; his availability; His constancy; and His uncritical acceptance of you. Appreciate that he freed you from bondage to sin and guilt; delivered you from the world, the flesh and the devil; and enabled your submission to His loving care and guidance.

Praise is valued, not so much by what we give God, as by how it benefits us, and focuses the creature's attention on the Creator's grace. Prayer allows us to share our enjoyment with the Giver of all things, as praise glorifies Him for the grandeur of His Creation, while worship honors Him for the beauty of His character. Philippians 4:8 calls us to think about whatever is true, honorable, just, pure, lovely, gracious, excellent, and worthy of praise; and God alone "is altogether lovely" (Song of Solomon 5:16). Is it any wonder the angels and elders around God will be occupied and satisfied for eternity, singing the praises of our wonderful, awesome God (Revelation 4:8-11, 5:9, 7:11-12)?

Praise God that every encounter with him can be an experience in the depths of His love; the height of His power; the width of His mercy; and the breadth of His grace in fulfilling your needs. In the enduring fidelity of His love, he has pledged to grow His life in you until, as part of the Body of Christ, you attain "the measure of the stature of the fullness of Christ" (Ephesians 4:13).

GOD WORKS ALL THINGS FOR GOOD

Undeniably, there is comfort in the thought that God controls everything in creation and, if we must endure suffering and calamity, at least they are actively meted out or regulated as part of God's grand, benevolent plan for mankind and the individual. God's Providence benefits us eventually, even though we might not fathom the ultimate good in the series of events which seem evil and hurtful to us. Moreover, even as to those afflictions which are neither intended nor sent by God, but are incidental to the freedom originated by Him, we are assured that he will divert their evil potential to the benefit of His suffering child.

There is just as much comfort in knowing that suffering is an unintended consequence of God's intent to bless man with freedom, as in believing God benignly intends every affliction befalling men. In either case, God reserves the right to intervene in history whenever He pleases, including in answer to human prayers to limit and alleviate suffering.

Because God is sovereign, any evil worked by Satan and other men will always be transformed to promote some larger, undisclosed aspect of God's beneficial plan for creation and His children. God manipulates and re-directs human and demonic evil for the ultimate good of His own. God lovingly uses human sin, and the pride and rebellion reflected in sin, to glorify God ultimately, by establishing a plan of redemption, despite human sin, when man is willing to be changed with God's help.

Job ended up blessed by God with long life, and more wealth, lands, and family than he had before his travails (Job 42:12-16). Joseph revealed to his brothers: "ye thought evil against me; but God meant it unto good, to bring it to pass, as it is this day, to save much people alive" (Genesis 50:20). The slavery into which Joseph was sold by his brothers, and even the unjust suffering in jail at the hands of Potiphar's wife, led to his circumstances in Egypt from which he could save his nation and his family. God delayed Joseph's blessing, and re-directed his life to achieve a place of eminence, in God's good time and purpose.

If we believe God initiates and plans every misfortune, there can be no evil, but only ultimate good God intends for us, and we can give thanks <u>for</u> all things, because they are inherently good if sent by a loving God. If evil originates in the wrongful acts of free beings, then we can give thanks <u>in</u> all things because God will work them into good for us and our over-all benefit. Either approach affirms God's goodness and His Sovereignty. As to those afflictions and trials which God does send to train and develop character, we accept them submissively and with obedience to God, perhaps even passively, because they originate in His will for us, and promote our spiritual good. If afflictions and trials originate in the mangled freedom or carelessness of other beings, then we can reasonably attempt to escape them, because they are not intended by God, even though He will transform them ultimately to good.

Acceptance of <u>apparent</u> evil which befalls us, but is actually intended for a transcendent good, was practiced by Jesus, Who did nothing to confound or frustrate God's will (John 5:30). Jesus counseled non-resistance to the seizure of one's worldly goods, because disciples are not to covet them: "Do not resist one who is evil... and if any one would sue you and take your coat, let him have your cloak as well" (Matthew 5:39-40). In the Garden of Gethsemane Jesus voluntarily surrendered to the ultimate suffering through Crucifixion, because it was God's will that He bear, propitiate, and atone for, all the sins of man (Luke 22:51; John 18:12).

When Peter attempted to dissuade Jesus from submitting to the Crucifixion, Jesus reproached Peter: "Get behind me, Satan! You are a hindrance to me: for you are not on the side of God, but of men" (Matthew 16:23). Obviously, Peter lacked discernment of God's plan, even though Jesus had just revealed he would be killed and be raised up on the third day (Matthew 16:21). Certainly, Jesus was aware of the intrinsic good in this most despicable of all human acts, crucifying the Son of God, which was integral to accomplish the salvation of mankind.

When Jesus suffered and died upon the Cross, God transformed the evil of the crucifixion "by the hands of lawless men," into a vehicle to serve His own "definite plan and foreknowledge" (Acts 2:23). God intended to lay all the evil of mankind upon Jesus, in order to save penitent sinners eternally. Who could have suspected at the time that the evil of Jesus' shed blood and death would become a substitutionary Atonement in actuality, relieving sinners of their justly deserved punishment? Thus, "it pleased the Lord to bruise him; he hath put him to grief" (Isaiah 53:10), yet, only for the higher good of saving all men who faithfully receive Jesus as Lord and Saviour.

Consequently, believers can have faith that what originates or appears as evil in the world will be ultimately determined and revealed as spiritually good, as God exercises sovereign dominion over everything in all of creation. Romans 8:28-30 assures us: "We know that in everything God works for good with those who love him who are called according to his purpose. For those whom he foreknew he also predestined to be conformed to the image of his Son... And those whom he predestined he also called; and... also justified; and... he also glorified." Our deliverance may not be revealed until Heaven, but we can be certain that suffering will end in perfect good by God's hand. For, if we are foreknown, predestined, called, and justified, we will be glorified.

Saul of Tarsus "laid waste the church, and... dragged off men and women and committed them to prison" (Acts 8:3),with egregious evil intent to destroy Christianity. Stephen was stoned to death and martyred for Christ, even as he asked forgiveness for his murderers (Acts 7:60), leaving a courageous example of faith, which emboldened many Christian martyrs. Yet, these persecutions also provoked flight, and scattered escaping Christians to outlying regions throughout the existing world, where they were in place to preach the Gospel and turn the world upside down (Acts 8:3-4). No doubt the exiles of the dispersion felt like scattered sheep, yet their faith would confirm that seed can be scattered with positive, fruitful results when worked out by God as a strategic planting to propagate the Gospel.[38] However, that does not mean He initiated or provoked the human evils of persecution or murder.

Paul, in his own wisdom, thought it would be highly profitable to preach in Asia, but was "forbidden by the Holy Spirit" from going there (Acts 16:6). He then thought evangelism in Bithynia would be successful, "but the Spirit of Jesus did not allow them" (Acts 16:7). Paul subsequently received a divine vision of a man from Macedonia saying: "Come over to Macedonia and help us" (Acts 16:9), and he obediently proceeded to evangelize Europe; a result which may not have occurred had he prevailed in his desire to go to Asia, which clashed with God's plan, although it had seemed right to Paul. God had thwarted Paul's intent, because He was preparing and presenting superior opportunities, by opening the door to Europe.

It does not follow that God fore-ordains circumstances, simply because His sovereignty is able to change human history. God turned Joseph's captivity and betrayal by his brothers to advantage, but that does not mean God moved the brothers to act out of jealousy. Rather, it means that their free, evil acts were diverted to good purposes by an omnipotent God.

Yet, the good God works does not always translate into worldly happiness, health or prosperity. Instead of material, immediate, temporal values, God may be working our good on a spiritual, eternal level. The good God wills and works may not always conform to our conception of good, but it will always produce God's transcendent best. Of course, God's good always corresponds to man's good, but we may not always recognize what good is being worked by God, or how it contributes to our gain. Our spiritual goals of Christ-like character, and fellowship with God are being produced by suffering, to bring us to know God better and to be more like Him.[39] We are conformed to the image of Christ through suffering as much as by blessing.

The good which God works out of our suffering is often spiritual riches rather than worldly gain. When we divest ourselves of self, we gain Christ. When we sacrifice and disdain everything temporal, we gain the Kingdom of God. Philippians 3:7-8 says: "But whatever gain I had, I counted as loss for the sake of Christ. Indeed I count everything as loss because of the surpassing worth of knowing Christ Jesus my Lord." Jesus says at Matthew 16:25: "For whoever would save his life will lose it, and whoever loses his life for my sake will find it," and "Sell all that you have and distribute it to the poor, and you will have treasure in heaven; and come, follow me" (Luke 18:22). Even death, which is accounted as the worst thing that could happen in worldly terms, is the best thing that could happen spiritually, when it is the corridor to eternal bliss.

Does Jesus promise the riches of God's grace and glory in more abundant life? Such abundance refers to spiritual growth and capacity to enjoy eternity as well as joy in the world (James 1:12). Does Jesus promise healing? It is first and foremost the healing of men's souls by overcoming sin which is God's eternal concern, as well as healthy mortal bodies. Does Jesus promise prosperity? He refers to the prospering of spirituality, as well as material wealth. Does Jesus promise joy? Certainly our joy in Godly and spiritual things is His primary concern, taking precedence over happiness in worldly material things. All these divine blessings are compatible with eternal, spiritual life, as much as physical or worldly rewards.

Jesus has made it clear that he accomplishes our spiritual and eternal healing, prosperity, joy, and abundant life through tribulation, torment, trials, testing, and training. In all of these there inheres a level of discomfort approaching or incorporating pain and suffering. This is often inconsistent with, or opposed to, the immediate, temporal and worldly blessings we identify as health, wealth, and happiness.

For example, perseverance, or patience is required to develop eternal, spiritual values, and our perfection and crowns are necessarily deferred to Heaven, even as we are called to pursue and hunger for them, seeking the Kingdom in this world (Matthew 6:19-20; Luke 12:33; Philippians 3:8; I Timothy 6:19; I Peter 4:7; James 1:4). Impatience, on the other hand, is compatible with worldly blessings and enjoying them fully now, or in the immediate future.

It is possible to be humble in the midst of profusion of God's blessings. But it may not be possible to learn humility without humbling circumstances. Paul's thorn in the flesh was to suppress pride in his elation at the spiritual revelations disclosed to him. We can only build muscles by resistance to forces. We can only learn obedience by exposure to trials and temptations enticing us to abandon the way of righteousness (Hebrews 5:8). We can only exercise and develop faith through absences, deprivations and denials, which provide occasions for faith.

We need also to recognize, according to Matthew 6:33, that spiritual blessings which exact momentary pain are not incompatible with worldly blessings which produce temporal happiness. These blessings exist side by side in varying proportions from time to time. A believer may be blessed with beauty, status, good health, wealth, and all the fullness of life they bring. Yet, he may still be in spiritual training to develop friendship with God, or a character devoid of pride or impatience. He may know sorrow through disrespectful children, loss of loved ones, or any of the myriad misfortunes common to men. Yet, he may prosper in spiritual, eternal blessings through trials, at the same time he enjoys or lacks material, transient blessings.

AUTHORITY OVER SATAN

God's great blessing of love is to give believers power, as legates of Christ, over the world, the flesh, and the devil; to be conquerors in, through, and because of Christ. Jesus warns that Satan is the thief and murderer who would extinguish your life and steal your prosperity (John 10:10; Hebrews 2:14). Therefore, when beset by suffering, it is appropriate to focus your anger on Satan, and use the weapon of faith God has provided to overcome his temptations and persecutions. James 4:7 says believers can be confident that when they "submit to God" and "resist the devil... he will flee from you." I Peter 5:9-10 assures us that we can resist temptation and Satan's incitations to suffering: "Resist him, firm in your faith" and God will "restore, establish, and strengthen you."

Significantly, God provides all the strength and power to overcome Satan, but in conjunction with a believer's act of will to resist Satan while submitting to God. In this way, Jesus has given believers, collectively, authority in His name to overcome "all the power of the enemy" (Luke 10:19), by binding him here on earth, knowing he will be bound in heaven (Matthew 16:19). The victory is yours through Jesus Christ, and the intensity of your faith in God's power is the key to overcoming.

I John 5:4 confirms that: "Whatever is born of God overcomes the world; and this is the victory that overcomes the world, our faith." When we are equipped with the armor of God, our shield of faith, we are "able to withstand in the evil day, and having done all, to stand" (Ephesians 6:13). The Master's charge to His servants is "Occupy till I come" (Luke 19:13, KJV). It should be no surprise that the Word upon which we are to rely, and by which faith comes, contains the very promises of God's dependable rescue and deliverance which have been outlined here.

Our Great Commission calls for initiatory action, not only defensive passivity. We are given divine power for "tearing down of strongholds" (2 Corinthians 10:5). Christians must contend against evil spiritual principalities which contest our holiness, commitment to God, faith in Jesus, evangelistic witnessing for Jesus, and any attempts to serve God in our stewardship of love for others. The Christian commitment has never been passive, but a militant execution of our Lord's charge to serve as warriors for God. 2 Timothy 2:3-4 exhorts: "Take your share of suffering as a good soldier of Christ Jesus... (whose) aim is to satisfy the one who enlisted him." Psalm 18:34-35 notes: "He teacheth my hands to war, so that a bow of steel is broken by mine arms. Thou hast also given me the shield of thy salvation: and thy right hand hath holden me up." Psalm 144:1-2 concurs: "Blessed is the Lord my strength, which teacheth my hands to war, and my fingers to fight: My goodness, and my fortress; my high tower, and my deliverer; my shield, and he in whom I trust."

Christians are trained for fighting, pursuing, and subduing enemies of the Lord. Our very bodies serve as the Temple of the Lord, and must be defended against worldly tendencies toward dissipation of the flesh and destruction of spiritual possessions.

When Jesus sent seventy disciples into the towns, He told them to "heal the sick in it and say to them, 'The kingdom of God has come near to you'" (Luke 10:9). When the disciples discovered Jesus' power in them, they returned with joy and exulted: "Lord, even the demons are subject to us in your name! (Luke 10:17). Jesus replied: "I saw Satan fall like lightning from heaven. Behold, I have given you authority... over all the power of the enemy" (Luke 10:18-19). Jesus was not reminiscing, out of context, about Satan's initial fall from Heaven, nor disconnecting from the subject of the disciples' authority. He was confirming His awareness that, on this first occasion when men exercised Jesus' power in His name and subjected evil spirits to divine authority, the impact was so startling it had caused Satan, who still had access to God to accuse men, to fall from heaven. When men went out as agents of Jesus, their deputed authority "over all the power of the enemy" was enough to stagger and knock Satan out of Heaven.[40]

God has given us His armor, "that you may be able to stand against the wiles of the devil" (Ephesians 6:11), both in temptations to sin, and in persecutions and afflictions instigated by the devil, which result in suffering and cast doubt on God's reliability and protection. Satan seeks to weaken our belief in God's Word, and incites us to follow our own way, rather than God's. The armor is God's, but we are responsible to "put on" the armor, since we must contend "against the principalities, against the powers, against the world rulers of this present darkness, against the spiritual hosts of wickedness in the heavenly places" (Ephesians 6:11, 12).

All the armor fortifies us for witnessing to the Gospel of Christ; serving God; living righteously, or avoiding temptations to sin, which are Satan's major weapon. However, if we do not exercise authority by putting on God's armor, we will be subject to the world's and satanic incitations to sin, and lack spiritual offensive weapons.

It should not be surprising that every part of "the whole armor of God" originates in faith, which comes by hearing the Word. All faith begins with Jesus, Who is the Word, and the Author and Pioneer of our faith, including faith to overcome the world: "Who is it that overcomes the world but he who believes that Jesus is the Son of God?" (I John 5:5).

In donning God's armor, you are to "gird your loins with truth" (Ephesians 6:14), and in Christ we "have heard the word of truth" (Ephesians 1:13), by hearing the Word, from which faith comes (Romans 10:17). Truth is based on God's Word, and anchors us to our security in God's deliverance. Satan's lies cannot make us doubt God when we depend upon His promises as true. "God is not a man, that he should lie" (Numbers 23:19). Jesus is the truth (John 14:6). Alliance with truth gives us an attitude of being right. We can be dedicated and committed to God's plan for battle and for progress.

We are to "put on the breastplate of righteousness" (Ephesians 6:14), and our "faith is reckoned as righteousness" (Romans 4:15). God is "The Lord Our Righteousness" (Jeremiah 23:6), and "the source of your life in Christ Jesus, whom God made our wisdom, our righteousness and consecration and redemption" (I Corinthians 1:30). We should strive to be actually holy, but when we sin, we must hasten to God for forgiveness and cleansing of all unrighteousness (I John 1:9). Thus restored, we are impervious to Satan's accusations of unworthiness, and incitations to doubt. Our armor will defend us against Satan by faith through the Word's gracious assurances.

Our feet are to be shod "with the equipment of the gospel of peace" (Ephesians 6:15), and the Gospel comes by the Word which brings faith (2 Thessalonians 2:13,14; 2 Timothy 3:15). The Gospel of peace thus comes from security in the promises of God to secure our future, and bring our salvation and deliverance to completion (Philippians 1:6); of acceptance and reconciliation with Him, free from condemnation (Romans 8:1); and assurance of His forgiveness of confessed sin (I John 1:9). When we are at peace with God, we can faithfully turn over every problem to Him.

We are to "strive for the faith of the gospel" (Philippians 1:27). We are to take "the shield of faith, with which you can quench all the flaming darts of the evil one" (Ephesians 6:16). Satan tempts us to disbelieve God, but our faith reaffirms God is in control, and we will have no doubt if we believe God's promises.

We are to put on the "helmet of salvation" (Ephesians 6:17), and salvation also comes through the operations of faith (Ephesians 2:8). We are to take "the sword of the Spirit, which is the word of God" (Ephesians 6:17), and by the Word we refute Satan's logic, just as Jesus did three times on the Mount of Temptation (Matthew 4:4-10). All the armor is to be accompanied by prayer, as an expression of our faith, and as man's acknowledgement that everything is accomplished by God's power, not ours. Ephesians 6:18 says we are to "Pray at all times in the Spirit, with all prayer and supplications."

ANGELS

One of the earliest classifications of angels appears in THE CELESTIAL HIERARCHY, written by Dionysius the Areopagite about 400 B.C., which lists nine choirs of angels gathered into three divisions. The highest-ranking choirs of angels are the Seraphim, Cherubim, and Thrones, who surround God in perpetual worship (Isaiah 6:2; Revelation 4:6-8). Seraphim introduce the end of the world. Cherubim serve God and Christ in heaven (2 Samuel 22:11; Psalm 18:10), and destroy the wicked (Ezekiel 9:2-8, 10:2-7); while Thrones hold up the thrones of God and Christ (see also Exodus 25:18-22; Numbers 7:89; I Samuel 4:4; Ezekiel 1:6, 10:1).

The second division of angelic choirs consists of Dominations, Virtues and Powers. Dominations are leaders of angels; Powers wear armor and engage in battle (Ephesians 1:21; Colossians 1:16, 2:15); while Virtues represent good. Dionysius' third division consisted of Archangels, who carry messages to earth. Next, were Princedoms or Principalities, who identify with a geographic location. The lowest rank are Guardian Angels, who are with men for our protection, and therefore removed from heaven.

The number of angels is incalculable. Daniel estimated one hundred million "stood before" God, and one million angels "ministered unto him" (Daniel 7:10; see also, Genesis 32:1-2; Psalms 68:17, 103:21). Angels were present when the world was created and "shouted for joy" (Job 38:4,7). After the Fall of Adam, God placed Cherubims to guard Eden and the tree of life (Genesis 3:24).

Three angels are identified by name in the Scriptures: "Lucifer, whose pride corrupted his freedom and who degenerated into Satan (Isaiah 14:12); Michael, named as "one of the chief princes" (Daniel 10;13,21; Jude 9: Revelation 12:7); and Gabriel (Daniel 8:16; Luke 1:18,26). The Apocryphal and pseudepigraphical books, which are of doubtful authenticity, name eight archangels: Michael, Gabriel, Raphael, Uriel, Sariel, Raguel, Jeremiel, and Phanuel (Enoch

9:1, 20:1, ff, 40:9, 54:6, 71:8,13; 4 Esdras 4:36; Tobit 3:8,17, 12:15), and two angels, Ananias and Azarias, identified as forebears of Raphael (Tobit 5:13).

From the earliest times, angels have enjoyed a special function in God's relationship with men, most notably as God's messengers and agents of protection over His people. Angels accompanied God when He appeared to Abraham in the plains of Mamra (Genesis 18:2). When Hagar, Sarah's maid, was driven from Abraham's camp because she was pregnant with the illegitimate Ishmael, it was the angel of the Lord who directed her to return and submit to Sarah, and promised: "I will multiply thy seed exceedingly, that it shall not be numbered for multitude" (Genesis 16:10). Fourteen years later, when Ishmael scorned Isaac, the legitimate son of Abraham and Sarah, resulting in Hagar being again driven from Abraham's camp, it was the angel of God who reaffirmed to Hagar that Ishmael will be made "a great nation" (Genesis 21:18). Abraham affirmed that God had covenanted to "send his angel before" Abraham to prepare his way and minister to Abraham (Genesis 24:7).

Two angels were sent to Sodom to guide and deliver Lot and his family from the sinful city before its destruction (Genesis 19:1, 15-16). Jacob saw the angels of God in a dream, ascending and descending a ladder to Heaven (Genesis 28:12). He was met by a host of angels at Mahanaim (Genesis 32:1-2), and wrestled with an angel to win its blessing (Genesis 32:24-29). The angel of the Lord killed Herod when he accepted the worship of his subjects, and did not give the glory to God (Acts 12:23).

At Exodus 3:2-4, the angel of the Lord appeared to Moses in a burning bush, without being consumed, and when Moses' attention was attracted, God spoke to him from the midst of the bush. (See also, Acts 7:30). Afterwards, the death angel which God sent to destroy the Egyptians, was stayed from entering the houses or smiting any of the Israelites (Exodus 12:23). Later, when Israel was fleeing from the Egyptians toward the Red Sea, the angel of the Lord "went before the camp of Israel, removed and went behind them," to protect their rear from the pursuing Egyptians (Exodus 14:19). While Israel was encamped at Sinai, God promised them an angel to keep them in the way and bring them into the Promised land; he was an angel to whom God had delegated much authority: "Beware of him, and obey his voice, provoke him not; for he will not pardon your transgressions: for my name is in him. But if thou shalt indeed obey his voice, and do all that I speak; then I will be an enemy unto thine enemies" (Exodus 23:21-22; and see Exodus 23:23; I Chronicles 22:15).

When the Israelites dwelt among the Canaanites and worshipped Baal at their pagan altars, an angel of the Lord re-affirmed the Covenant with Israel, but chastened them for their disobedience, and foretold that the pagans "shall be as thorns in your sides and their gods shall be a snare unto you" (Judges 2:3). The angel of the Lord was sent by God as a sign to encourage Gideon and confirm the he would conquer the Midianites (Judges 6:11-22).

Before Samson was conceived, the angel of the Lord appeared to his mother and informed her she would bear a son who would "deliver Israel out of the hand of the Philistines" (Judges 13:3). However, she was not to have strong drink, and the child was not to cut his hair, but to be a Nazarite unto God (Judges 13:4-5). When Samson's father, Manoah, prayed to God for confirmation he would have a son, the angel of God came again to Samson's mother, and repeated the same directions (Judges 13:8-14). However, the angel refused to divulge his name, when requested to do so, and ascended in the flames which went toward heaven from Manoah's sacrificial altar (Judges 13:18-20).

When Balaam sought to curse Israel, contrary to God's will, the progress of his donkey was prevented by an angel visible only to the animal, until the Lord opened the eyes of Balaam. The angel advised Balaam that he would have killed him, had not the donkey stopped, and then instructed him according to God's will in how to deal with those wishing to curse Israel (Numbers 22:5-35).

An angel, who identified himself as Gabriel, advised Zachariah that he and his wife, Elizabeth would give birth to John the Baptist, in answer to their prayers, and he would "turn many of the sons of Israel to the Lord their God" (Luke 1:11-16). When Zachariah questioned the possibility of an old man siring a child, the angel struck him dumb until the child was born (Luke 1:20), so that Zachariah could not speak doubt. Ecclesiastes 5:6 confirms that we should not speak unbelief to angels: "Suffer not thy mouth to cause thy flesh to sin; neither say thou before the angel, that it was an error; wherefore should God be angry at thy voice, and destroy the work of thine hands?"

In the New Testament, an angel occasionally stirred the waters at Bethesda to heal the first person who entered the pool (John 5:29). When the beggar, Lazarus, died, he was carried by angels to Abraham's bosom, but when the rich man died, he apparently went to Hades unaccompanied (Luke 16:22). At Acts 12:7-11 an angel of the Lord freed Peter from prison by removing his chains and opening the iron gate leading out. At Acts 27:23 an angel assured Paul that though his ship would be lost, he and his companions would all be saved from a violent storm and not be destroyed.

God also provides angels to aid disciples in resisting sin by their exhortation and encouragement in escaping temptation, or in enduring suffering. We know that the angels who worship Jesus (Hebrews 1:6), and serve the Lord: "excel in strength, that do his commandments, hearkening unto the voice of his word" (Psalm 103:20). Jesus has "more than twelve legions of angels" attending Him (Matthew 26:53). Two angels were present at His tomb (John 20:12). Jesus told Nathanael: "Hereafter ye shall see heaven open, and the angels of God ascending and descending upon the Son of man" (John 1:51, KJV). Angels ministered to Jesus and strengthened Him when He was beset by the world (Matthew 4:11; Luke 22:43).

Jesus reveals "And I tell you, everyone who acknowledges me before men, the Son of man will also acknowledge before the angels of God; but he who denies me before men will be denied before the angels of God" (Luke 12:8-9; and Revelation 3:5). The angels of God rejoice "over one sinner who repents" (Luke 15:10). They are the reapers of the "sons of the kingdom" at "the close of the age" (Matthew 13:38-39).

We know that angels observe the Church and its activities (I Corinthians 4:9, 11:10; I Timothy 5:21; Hebrews 13:2), and learn from the Church: "that through the church the manifold wisdom of God might now be made known to the principalities and powers in the heavenly places" (Ephesians 3:10). "Angels long to look" into the secrets of grace and salvation (I Peter 1:12).

Angels are constituted by God as "all ministering spirits sent forth to serve, for the sake of those who are to obtain salvation" (Hebrews 1:14; and see Matthew 18:10 and Luke 16:22). God gives us His angels to keep us from harm, and ease our way in the world (2 Kings 6:16; Psalms 34:7, 91:11, 103:20; Isaiah 63:9; Daniel 6:22, 3:28; Acts 12:11, 12:15, 27:23-34; Matthew 4:6; Luke 4:11; and Hebrews 12:1). God used an angel to bring God's wisdom to Daniel, and reveal God's love for him (Daniel 10:11). Angels advised Mary and Joseph about the virgin birth of Jesus, and explained how He was to be reared (Matthew 1:20,24; Luke 1:26-34).

We will see that the operations of natural law may result in harm to people, but as an inherent and incidental property of the elements, rather than intention by God. We cannot attribute such harm to God's purpose or intent, nor can we infer He is disinterested in the potential for harm. He has furnished the angels to minister to and assist the needs of believers, and credible stories of rescues by angels from natural disasters and potential accidents are legion, and well documented.[41]

When Jesus sent forth the seventy disciples to witness, and they returned exulting, "Lord, even the demons are subject to us in your name!" (Luke 10:17), Jesus responded, "do not rejoice in this, that the spirits are subject to you; but rejoice that your names are written in heaven" (Luke 10:20). Angels are holy spirit beings, the counterpart to unholy demons, and might be expected to respond similarly to the name of Jesus invoked by believers. Some believe God has provided by grace the means and empowerment for believers to activate and dispatch angels in the name of Jesus to help and minister to our needs, by encouraging and persuading those with whom we deal to act rightly and refrain from harming us. Some believe, with God's blessing, we can even borrow other guardian angels to assist us when they are not employed by unbelievers to whom they have been assigned by God. I Corinthians 6:2-3 reveals: "Do you not know that the saints will judge the world?... Do you not know that we are to judge angels? How much more, matters pertaining to this life!"

It should also be comforting that there are always twice as many angels available to aid believers than there are fallen angels assigned to attack them. Remember that a third of the angels fell with Lucifer (Revelation 12:4,9), while the remaining two-thirds remain faithful to God, and obey His Word, including instructions to aid and protect believers. We are reminded to pray always (Luke 18:1), so we never lose sight of the fact that God's power undergirds our enlisting the help of angels in Jesus' name.

HEAVEN AS THE REWARD OF FAITHFULNESS

One of the great paradoxes of Christianity is that our suffering here on earth fits us for reward in heaven. The more we are fashioned by sorrow in this world, the greater will be our joy in the next. The less we invest in this world, the more treasure we will store up in Heaven. The greater our material poverty here, the greater our spiritual prosperity Hereafter. The greater our abasement on earth, the nobler our glory in Heaven. The humbler we are now, the more exalted we will be then.

Indeed, our endurance of affliction here is often sustained by our blessed hope of deliverance Hereafter. The prospect of Heaven is both the first and final consolation of suffering. For 1900 years after Christ, the more abundant life which He promised could only be understood in terms of a Heavenly deliverance from the present nasty, brutish, and short earthly life. Not until the industrial revolution brought about systems of economic productivity, rapid transportation, communications, and longer life through medicine and nutrition, could men envision an earthly utopia in fulfillment of the Christian life. Before that, Christians derived God's peace primarily from the blessed hope of Christ's return, and the assurance that despite whatever this world inflicts upon us, we will realize freedom from pain in the Hereafter.

Even when we are most blessed by God, we detect there is still something wrong with this world; some tragedy just around the corner; always the impending gloom of past and future disappointments, grief, pain and suffering. The hope of Heaven does not obliterate suffering, but makes it bearable. The blessings we receive and the miracles God bestows are primarily indications of the future which we anticipate; our true blessed hope. Without that hope, there is no hope at all. Psalm 9:12,18 indicates God will rectify unjust suffering: "When he maketh inquisition for blood, he remembereth them: he forgetteth not the cry of the humble... For the needy shall not always be forgotten: the expectation of the poor shall not perish for ever". I Corinthians 15:17,19 says: "If Christ has not been raised, your faith is futile and you are still in your sins... If in this life we who are in Christ have only hope, we are of all men most to be pitied"

Our purpose in life is to know God, and our end in life is to join Him at death. Ecclesiastes 12:7 notes: "Then shall the dust return to the earth as it was: and the spirit shall return unto God who gave it." Jesus promises at John 14:2-3: "In my Father's house are many rooms; if it were not so, would I have told you that I go to prepare a place for you? And when I go and prepare a place for you, I will come again and will take you to myself, that where I am you may be also."

God has ordained an eschatology or final ending to history, in which evil is vanquished, the righteous prevail, and Jesus reigns as Lord forever. Suffering intensifies at the hands of Satan just before the return of Our Lord for His Church. Jesus outlines various woes which will make men faint with fear and foreboding, "And then they will see the Son of man coming in a cloud with power and great glory... raise your heads, because your redemption is drawing near" (Luke 21:27-28). Indeed, in any generation, the proliferation of woe in the world is not an evidence of God's absence or unconcern with our suffering, but a present reminder of Christ's imminent return.

Our great and blessed hope for deliverance is in trusting God for final rescue through Jesus Christ at His Second Coming. "For the grace of God has appeared for the salvation of all men... awaiting our blessed hope, the appearing of the glory of our great God and Savior Jesus Christ" (Titus 2:11-12 and see John 14:3). The Second Coming of the Lord will bring an end to Satan's reign over the world, and deliver mankind from bondage to sin forever (Psalm 110:1; I Corinthians 15:25; and Philippians 3:21).

2 Thessalonians 1:7 says God will "repay with affliction those who afflict you" and "grant rest with us to you who are afflicted, when the Lord Jesus is revealed from heaven with his mighty angels." "For if we have been united with him in a death like his, we shall <u>certainly</u> be united with him in a resurrection like his" (Romans 6:5). If we are now in Christ, we are alive in Him, and are assured it is forever. Then, after the Second Coming, we go to a Heavenly home of joy and peace in the eternal presence of the Lord; reunited with our saved loved ones; where there is no more pain or suffering (John 11:24; I Corinthians 2:9, 15:51; 2 Corinthians 4:17-18; Romans 8:18; Revelation 7:16, 21:3-4, 27).

In Heaven, there is no more death, and Hosea 13:14 promises: "I will ransom them from the power of the grave; I will redeem them from death." "Death is swallowed up in victory... O death, where is thy sting?" (I Corinthians 15:54-55). "For as in Adam all die, so also in Christ shall all be made alive" (I Corinthians 15:22 and see also 2 Timothy 1:12). Revelation 21:3-4 says about heaven: "God himself will be with them, he will wipe away every tear from their eyes, and death shall be no more, neither shall there be mourning nor crying nor pain any more, for the former things have passed away." Pain and death are real, but they are present reminders of a future reunion when there will be no more pain or sorrow.

Heaven will be such a wonderful place, beyond our wildest imaginations, that believers will praise God for what He is doing and Who He is, for all eternity. We may not know what Heaven is like, now, but we know the presence of God will be so awesomely wonderful, that in appreciation of his character and creativity we will be content to join the elders and angels who constantly and forever sing His praises, as he creates all things by the power of His will (Revelation 4:8-11, 7:11-12, 11:13, 14:3, 15:3-4, 41, 19:4-7; and Job 38:4-7).

The presence of God and His works will satisfy us in so many ways that we will genuinely delight in worshipping and glorifying Him for the joy of inexpressible wonders. Psalm 17:15 says: "As for me, I will behold thy face in righteousness; I shall be satisfied, when I awake, with thy likeness." We will be with Jesus where he is, and behold His God-given glory (John 18:24).

Here on earth, we are blessed with a foretaste of that heavenly joy in God's communion: "in thy presence is fullness of joy" (Psalm 16:11); "thou wilt make me full of gladness with thy presence" (Acts 2:25); "Rejoice in the Lord always" (Philippians 4:4). The fact we will be inspired to praise and worship God because of His glorious presence, suggests that His creativity is marvelous, ongoing, and eternal (Isaiah 65:17), manifesting His goodness and love for creation. God's character will inspire true, acceptable worship of God with reverence and awe. He continually gives of himself so that the wonders of heaven are beyond imagination for those who love God (Isaiah 64:4).

Mainly, however, the joys that await us in Heaven are ineffable, indescribable beyond expression in worldly terms. I Corinthians 2:9 characterizes them as: "What no eye has seen nor ear heard, nor the heart of man conceived, what God has prepared for those who love him." 2 Corinthians 4:17 refers to heaven as "an eternal weight of glory beyond all comparison," for which we are being prepared by "slight momentary affliction." St. Paul says: "Thanks be to God for his inexpressible gift," and 2 Peter 3:13 foretells: "new heavens and a new earth in which righteousness dwells."

Even when the faithful do not receive the promises in this world, "God is not ashamed to be called their God, for he has prepared for them a city" (Hebrews 11;16). When we are reviled and persecuted for the sake of Christ, "Rejoice and be glad, for your reward is great in heaven" (Matthew 5:11-12). When we serve Christ as his agent or instrument and find affliction or contempt in the world, our blessings will be specially rewarded for eternity by God. He uses persecution and affliction to turn us to Him, or to remind others of their blessings in being spared such suffering or persecution. The rewards are simply deferred for the afflicted to a far better time and place.

To the extent suffering builds character and sanctifies us in holiness, we are being built toward glorification and being fitted for the society of Heaven. We are perfected as part of Christ's Church or Body in Heaven, when Jesus returns for His Church (I Corinthians 15:42; Ephesians 4:13. 5:25-27; Philippians 1:6, 3:20-21). Jesus points out that when we suffer, we are fashioning new treasures, replacing worldly and temporal joys and gifts with the eternal, spiritual blessings of Heaven.

Jesus teaches that actions which demonstrate obedient devotion to Him will be persecuted in the world, and otherwise involve struggle, but will be ultimately rewarded: "Blessed are you when men revile you and persecute you and utter all kinds of evil against you falsely <u>on my account</u>. Rejoice and be glad, for your reward is great in heaven" (Matthew 5:11-12; and see also, Luke 6:22-23). Jesus then exhorts believers to give alms, loans, forgiveness, and love to other men; to practice piety and charity in secret; and pray privately; by all of which believers will "lay up for yourselves treasure in heaven" (Matthew 6:20). Jesus adds at Matthew 19:21: "Sell what you possess and give it to the poor, and you will have treasure in heaven." See also, Luke 12:31,33; and I Timothy 6:18-19.

At Luke 22:28-30 Jesus tells the Apostles: "You are those who have continued with me in my trials; as my Father appointed a kingdom for me, so do I appoint for you that you may eat and drink at my table in my kingdom, and sit on thrones judging the twelve tribes of Israel." (See also, Matthew 19:28 and Mark 10:30) Leaving our surroundings to follow Jesus will result in reward and inheriting "eternal life" (Matthew 19:29). At John 16:22 Jesus gives this comfort: "So you have sorrow now, but I will see you again and your hearts will rejoice, and no one will take your joy from you." Jesus also tells of a rich man who selfishly feasted and enjoyed his possessions in life, and went to Hades in torment, while Lazarus, a beggar who faithfully suffered privation and evil things in life, went to Paradise (Luke 16:19-25). Believers, who are persecuted and martyred during the Great Tribulation of the End Times, will be blessed, "that they may rest from their labors, for their deeds follow them" (Revelation 14:12-13).

For centuries, Christians have endured suffering in the knowledge that Heaven sets all things right: "that the sufferings of this present time are not worth comparing with the glory that is to be revealed to us... For in this hope we were saved" (Romans 8:18,24). 2 Corinthians 4:16-18 confirms: "So we do not lose heart. Though our outer nature is wasting away, our inner nature is being renewed every day. For this slight momentary affliction is preparing for us an eternal weight of glory beyond all comparison, because we look not to the things that are seen but to the things that are unseen; for the... things that are unseen are eternal."

2 Corinthians 5:1-5 promises: "For we know that if the earthly tent we live in is destroyed, we have a building from God, a house not made with hands, eternal in the heavens. Here indeed we groan, and long to put on our heavenly dwelling... For while we are still in this tent, we sigh with anxiety... so that what is mortal may be swallowed up by life. He who has prepared us for this very thing is God, who has given us the Spirit as a guarantee." 2 Thessalonians 1:5 says God's righteous judgment will be evidenced when believers are: "made worthy of the kingdom of God, for which you are suffering."

Our suffering here builds a storehouse of blessings Hereafter, according to Scriptures which teach Heavenly reward is connected to, or commensurate with, experiencing earthly suffering: "If we suffer, we shall also reign with him" (2 Timothy 2:12, KJV). Unless we are willing to experience the humiliation of Jesus we will not participate in His exaltation. But because we suffer with Him, we shall also be raised with Him.[42]

We can bear suffering, "for you know that the testing of your faith produces steadfastness. And let steadfastness have its full effect, that you may be perfect and complete, lacking in nothing" (James 1:4). I Peter 1:4-7 reminds us to rejoice despite suffering, because we have the promise in Christ of "an inheritance which is imperishable, undefiled, and unfading, kept in heaven for you, who by God's power are guarded through faith for a salvation ready to be revealed in the last time. In this you rejoice, though now for a little while you may have to suffer various trials, so that the genuineness of your faith... may redound to praise and glory and honor at the revelation of Jesus Christ." I Peter 3:14 adds: "But even if you do suffer for righteousness' sake, you will be blessed."

I Peter 4:13-14 says: "rejoice in so far as you share Christ's sufferings, that you may also rejoice and be glad when his glory is revealed. If you are reproached for the name of Christ, you are blessed, because the spirit of glory and of God rests upon you." "And after you have suffered a little while, the God of all grace, who has called you to his eternal glory in Christ, will himself restore, establish, and strengthen you" (I Peter 5:10). See also, Psalm 58:10-11; 2 Corinthians 1:5, 3:18; Ephesians 3:19, 4:13, 4:22; Colossians 3:10; and 2 Peter 5:1.

While an abundance of blessings is promised faithful obedient servants in this life, the more abundant life promised by Jesus primarily pertains to the quality and quantity of blessings in the Afterlife. When Jesus finally delivers His Church from the world, the Bible promises a number of crowns rewarded to believers. The Greek word for 'crown' indicates that these crowns resemble the wreath awarded the victor of a contest or race, rather than the diadem worn by a king. The crown of life is promised to one who endures trials because he loves the Lord: "Blessed is the man who endures trial, for when he has stood the test he will receive the crown of life which God has promised to those who love him" (James 1:12). Revelation 2:10 likewise promises to those who are tested, thrown into prison, or undergo tribulation: "Be faithful unto death, and I will give you the crown of life." God has ordained that the way to your crowns is the way of the Cross. There are no short-cuts.

If I have kept the faith, fought the good fight, and finished the race, I have "laid up for me the crown of righteousness... to all who have loved his appearing" (2 Timothy 4:8). When we run our race to the end and "exercise self-control in all things," then we receive an imperishable crown (I Corinthians 9:25). Wisdom earns a "crown of glory" (Proverbs 4:7,9, 14:24).

There is also a crown of rejoicing for those who have gathered fruit for the Lord by witnessing to the Gospel. I Thessalonians 2:19 says: "For what is our hope or joy or crown of boasting before our Lord Jesus at his coming? Is it not you? For you are our glory and joy." (See also, Philippians 4:1). Our crown of joy will be based on, and flourish in, reunion with those who have received Christ through our ministry of witnessing. For the elders who willingly tend the congregation or flock by loving example, "when the chief Shepherd is manifested you will obtain the unfading crown of glory" (I Peter 5:4).

The crown may be literal adornments, worn as a symbol of recognition and honor, which will intrinsically constitute our reward, or they may translate into special experiences, joys, blessedness, or service in eternity.[43] They will be glorious, imperishable and unfading in Heaven, but your claim is not fixed while in the world, and you must "hold fast what you have, so that no one may seize your crown" (Revelation 3:11). In other words, salvation may be secure, but rewards may be forfeited by conduct which abandons the works leading to reward.

Significantly, these crowns are not the source of individual pride, for we shall join the elders in acknowledging Christ's glory, honor, and power as truly deserving our crowns. Revelation 4:10 explains that in Heaven we gladly give them to Christ: "the twenty-four elders fall down before him who is seated on the throne and worship him who lives for ever and ever; they cast their crowns before the throne, singing..."

We are being prepared by our afflictions for the consolation of our blessed hope of Heaven in Christ's return. For, if we endure and persevere in overcoming — both in obedience and in bearing our suffering — we are assured by the revelation of Jesus that we are being fitted for eternal blessings: "the tree of life"; "the crown of life"; not to "be hurt by the second death"; "the hidden manna"; "power over the nations" to "rule them with a rod of iron"; "the morning star"; to "be clad thus in white garments"; to be enrolled in "the book of life"; to be made "a pillar in the temple of my God"; and to sit with Jesus on His throne (Revelation 2:7, 10,11,17,26,27; 3:5,12,21).

Even though believers will be raised imperishable, Matthew 8:11 assures us that the personalities of Abraham, Isaac and Jacob are preserved in the kingdom of Heaven, for we shall sit down with them. Indeed, the rich man who died and went to hell retained memory of his family, awareness of his brothers still on earth, and recognized Abraham and the beggar Lazarus in Paradise (Luke 16:23-24). Moses and Elijah, though dead for centuries, were recognizable when they appeared at the Transfiguration of Jesus (Luke 9:28).

The names of the redeemed are written in the Book of Life (Luke 10:20; Philippians 4:3; Revelation 13:8, 20:12-15), and receive their reward in the Hereafter. St. Paul looked forward to reunion in Heaven with those who had heard the Gospel through his ministry (I Thessalonians 2:19). The retention of memory at the Judgment is confirmed by Romans 14:12: "So each of us shall give account of himself to God." (See also, I Peter 4:5). Likewise, the martyred saints in Heaven know they have been redeemed, and seek vindication for their martyrdom (Revelation 6:9-11).

We will be made perfect in knowledge according to I Corinthians 13:10-12: "when the perfect comes, the imperfect will pass away... For now we see in a mirror dimly, but then face to face. Now I know in part; then I shall understand fully." We shall "be like" Jesus (I John 3:2), and we shall be with Jesus (Luke 23:43; 2 Corinthians 5:8; Matthew 25:21,23). That is Heaven!

Let us rejoice in these glimpses of Heaven and the wonders revealed in the Scriptures. "And I saw the holy city, new Jerusalem, coming down out of heaven from God, prepared as a bride adorned for her husband; and I heard a great voice from the throne saying, 'Behold the dwelling of God is with men. He will dwell with them, and they shall be his people" (Revelation 21:1-3).

"For, behold, I create new heavens and a new earth; and the former shall not be remembered, nor come into mind. But be ye glad and rejoice for ever in that which I create; for behold, I create Jerusalem a rejoicing, and her people a joy. And I will rejoice in Jerusalem, and joy in my people; and the voice of weeping shall be no more heard in her, nor the voice of crying" (Isaiah 65:17-19).

"Eye hath not seen, nor ear heard, neither have entered into the heart of man, the things which God hath prepared for them that love him" (I Corinthians 2:9, KJV).

"But according to his promise we wait for new heavens and a new earth in which righteousness dwells" (2 Peter 3:13).

"For the Lord himself will descend from Heaven with a cry of command... And the dead in Christ will rise first; then we who are alive, who are left, shall be caught up together with them in the clouds to meet the Lord in the air; and so we shall always be with the Lord. Therefore comfort one another with these words" (I Thessalonians 4:16-18).

CHAPTER 4

A CELEBRATION OF GOD'S SOVEREIGNTY

"I am God, and there is none else; I am God, and there is none like me, declaring the end from the beginning... my counsel shall stand, and I will do all my pleasure."

- Isaiah 46:9–10

God's Sovereignty is coterminous with His goodness and love: as wide, expansive, enduring, vast, and deep as His being. Just as God *is* love, He *is* omnipotent or all-powerful. His love is permeated and effectuated by his power, and His power is fused with, and motivated by, His love. He is One, and the attributes of His being are co-extensive, eternal, intertwined, and immutable. His omniscience and perfect wisdom assure the perfect, complete, best application of His power and love to Creation.

His Word reveals that in Christ all that is God, or possessed by God, will be shared for eternity with believers who come to God through Christ by grace through faith. God's perfect goodness and loving kindness depict His Sovereignty as Divine Providence, revealed in His blessing, benevolence, care and concern for His children. He deflects harm from them; delivers them from evil, and provides a profusion of blessings, worldly, temporal, spiritual and eternal (Acts 14:17, 17:25). He promises the certainty of eternal bliss in His presence for those who accept salvation by faith in Jesus as Lord and Saviour in a Heaven devoid of evil, sickness, suffering, or tears (Revelation 21:4).

Who God is defines what he does, and what He does defines what is good. Nothing God does can be intrinsically evil because He *is* good. Genesis 18:25 inquires: "Shall not the Judge of all the earth do right?" What God declares is what is right: "I the Lord speak righteousness. I declare things that are right" (Isaiah 45:19). What man may regard as right is irrelevant if it contradicts God's Word, and can be attributed to man's limited comprehension of God's ways, Whose judgments are far above, out of man's sight (Psalm 10:5). His thoughts are not man's thoughts and His ways are not man's ways (Isaiah 55:8).

Omnipotence means God has plenary power to accomplish whatever He pleases. Starting at Genesis 17:1 and in scores of subsequent passages, God declares: "I am the Almighty God," He Whose power is totally mighty and unlimited by anything, including evil. God summons men to "Lift up your eyes on high, and behold who hath created these things... by the greatness of his might, for that he is strong in power; not one faileth" (Isaiah 40:26). The created universe proclaims the Sovereignty of God: "Ever since the creation of the world his invisible nature, namely, his eternal power and deity, has been clearly perceived in the things that have been made" (Romans 1:20). Psalm 19:1 affirms: "The heavens declare the glory of God; and the firmament sheweth his handy-work." "He ruleth by his power forever" (Psalm 66:7).

When God cursed the earth because of Adam's sin (Genesis 3:17), He subjected what He had created to His wrath and mercy in the exercise of His Sovereign dominion: "for the creation was subjected to futility, not of its own will but by the will of him who subjected it in hope; because the creation itself will be set free from its bondage" (Romans 8:20).

God reveals that He is in absolute control of creation, and uses His immense power without restraint to originate, regulate, manipulate, orchestrate, direct, and intervene in the affairs of creation as He pleases. God declares His absolute sovereignty and dominion at Isaiah 14:24, 27: "Surely as I have thought, so shall it come to pass; and as I have purposed, so shall it stand... For the Lord of hosts hath purposed, and who shall disannul it? And his hand is stretched out, and who shall turn it back?"

Isaiah 46:9–10 adds: "I am God, and there is none like me. Declaring the end from the beginning, and from ancient times the things that are not yet done, saying, My counsel shall stand, and I will do all my pleasure." Psalm 115:3 says: "our God is in the heavens: He hath done whatsoever he hath pleased." Psalm 46:8–9 says: "Behold the works of the Lord, what desolation he has made in the earth. He maketh wars to cease unto the end of the earth; he breaketh the bow, and cutteth the spear in sunder." Psalm 103:19 says that the Lord's "kingdom ruleth over all."

God notes at Job 41:11: "Who hath prevented me, and I should repay him? Whatsoever is under the whole heaven is mine." Job 42:2 attests: "I know that thou canst do everything, and that no thought can be withheld from thee." Ecclesiastes 3:14 challenges: "I know that, whatever God doeth, it shall be forever; nothing can be put to it, nor anything taken from it; and God doeth it, that men should fear before him."

Daniel 4:34–35 affirms that God's Providence orders worldly events and watches and cares over every detail to work His will, intent, plan, and purpose in us. He uses both sweet and bitter, blessing and adversity: "whose dominion is an everlasting dominion, and his kingdom is from generation to generation... and he doeth according to his will in the army of heaven, and among the inhabitants of the earth: and none can stay his hand, or say unto him, What doest thou?" Even when Daniel mourned for 21 days because it seemed his prayers for understanding had been ignored, God had already dispatched an angel with Daniel's answer (Daniel 9:23; 10:2, 14).

God's Sovereignty is proclaimed at Isaiah 40:13,15: "Who hath directed the spirit of the Lord, or being his counselor hath taught him?... Behold, the nations are as a drop of a bucket, and are counted as the small dust of the balance: behold, he taketh up the isles as a very little thing."

At Jeremiah 18:6 God asserts: "O house of Israel, cannot I do with you as this potter?... Behold as the clay is in the potter's hand, so are ye in mine hand." He declares: "I am the Lord: that is my name: and my glory will I not give to another" (Isaiah 42:8). When King Nebuchadnezzar became proud and attributed the greatness of Babylon to his own power and majesty (Daniel 4:30), he was deposed by God from his throne and lost his glory. He lived like a madman among the wild animals "till he knew that the most high ruled in the kingdom of men, and that he appointeth over it whomsoever he will" (Daniel 5:21). See also, Daniel 4:17; Proverbs 21:1; Revelation 19:16.

God has made Jesus heir to all power and dominion on earth and in heaven. Jesus is in control of the door to salvation, as well as all doors to opportunity, "who has the key of David, who opens and no one shall shut, who shuts and no one opens... Behold, I have set before you an open door which no one is able to shut" (Revelation 3:7–8). Jesus alone opens doors of advantage and second chances, and shuts them, all in furtherance of his Sovereign will for each of us. Jesus reveals: "All authority in heaven and earth has been given to me" (Matthew 28:18). "For from him and through him and to him are all things. To him be glory forever" (Romans 11:36). See also Acts 17:24; I Corinthians 15:22–27; Ephesians 1:9–11; and Hebrews 1:2–3.

2 Corinthians 5:2–5 observes: "Here indeed we groan... we sigh with anxiety... so that what is mortal may be swallowed up by life. He who has prepared us for this very thing is God." And according to Born-Again theology, he who is saved by grace through faith in Jesus is secure in his salvation, despite the temptations and persecutions of the world, and our sinful responses to them. Jesus says at John 10:28–29: "I give them eternal life, and they shall never perish, and no one shall snatch them out of my hand. My Father who has given them to me, is greater than all, and no one is able to snatch them out of the Father's hand." See also, John 6:39; 17:12; 18:9.

Romans 9:19 queries: "For who can resist his will?" and the answer is impliedly, 'No-one!' Romans 11:29 declares: "For the gifts and the call of God are irrevocable," and Romans 11:36 puts it: "For from him and through him and to him are all things."

Ephesians 1:11 explains the scope of God's Sovereignty which operates in Jesus "According to His purpose which he set forth in Christ as a plan for the fullness of time, to unite all things in him, things in heaven and things on earth. In him, according to the purpose of him who accomplishes all things according to the counsel of his will." Colossians 1:17 notes the scope and duration of Jesus' power: "before all things, and in him all things hold together." Hebrews 1:2–3 affirms that God created the world through Jesus, Who is "upholding the universe by his word of power." Revelation 19:6 celebrates: "Hallelujah! For the Lord our God the Almighty reigns." See also, Romans 2:5–11; I Corinthians 8:6; and Revelation 4:11; 20:11–15.

Perhaps God's Sovereignty is best demonstrated by fulfillment of His Word "that goeth forth out of my mouth: it shall not return to me void, but it shall accomplish that which I please, and it shall prosper in the thing whereto I sent it" (Isaiah 55:11). Isaiah 46:11 agrees: 'I have spoken it, I will also bring it to pass. I have purposed it, I will also do it."

Ezekiel 12:25 declares God's omnipotence: "For I am the Lord: I will speak and the word that I shall speak shall come to pass." Joshua 23:14 reminds Israel: "that not one thing hath failed of all the good things which the Lord your God spake concerning you; all are come to pass unto you and not one thing hath failed thereof."

Numbers 23:19 says: "God is not a man, that he should lie... hath he said, and shall he not do it? Or hath he spoken, and shall he not make it good?" I Kings 8:56 confirms: "there hath not failed one word of all his good promise." God promises at Psalm 89:34: "My covenant will I not break, nor alter the thing that is gone out of my lips." Isaiah 40:8 adds: "the word of our God shall stand for ever."

The New Testament also attests to God's Sovereignty in the fulfillment of His purposes: "heaven and earth will pass away, but my words will not pass away" (Mark 13:31); "scripture cannot be broken" (John 10:35); "till heaven and earth pass away, not an iota, not a dot, will pass from the law until all is accomplished" (Matthew 5:18).

God also acknowledges that He is the creator of evil, in the sense He is the Author of everything in Creation, including processes intended for good, which are incidentally capable of producing evil if the being to whom the process is entrusted perverts his freedom. God cannot do evil, for what He does defines what is good (Romans 12:2).

God's Sovereignty declares He is the First Cause of evil, only in the sense He created the circumstances which allow, but do not necessitate, evil choices by man. God's permission of an act is not the same as God's commission of the act. He has instituted certain good processes which permit participation by created beings with free will. These carry the incidental, inherent potential for wrong choices made by free beings to whom God has consigned the power of choice. Such delegation of power is consistent with God's omnipotence and Sovereignty, since He chooses to assign some portion of determination by the gift of freedom. Man has not usurped such power, but is vested with it by God for His benevolent purposes. If man misuses his free choice so that evil results, harmful consequences are not specifically intended or necessarily willed by God in those circumstances or occurrences. The same constituent properties of fire which warm us against the cold, illuminate the darkness, and cook our food, can also burn and scar us, because of their intrinsic nature, without any intent of the Creator to harm anyone.

Thus, Isaiah 45:7 says: "I form the light, and create darkness: I make peace, and create evil: I the Lord do all these things." Amos 3:6 says: "shall there be evil in a city, and the Lord has not done it?" Proverbs 16:4 adds: "The Lord hath made all things for himself: Yea, even the wicked for the day of evil." God refers to the original impress of His hand on all Creation: "Who hath made man's mouth? Or who maketh the dumb, or deaf, or the seeing, or the blind? Have not I the Lord?" (Exodus 4:11). I Samuel 18:10 relates that "the evil spirit from God came upon Saul", and he tried to kill David. At Isaiah 54:16 God declares: "I have created the waster to destroy." (See also, Deuteronomy 32:39,41: I Samuel 2:6–7; Job 9:22; Psalms 51:8; 66:11–12; and Ecclesiastes 7:14).

There is a sense in which God's Sovereignty is reflected in His use of instruction, chastening, and chastisement which produce suffering in a man's life. Job knew every thing that reached him was ultimately controlled by God: "shall we receive good at the hand of God, and shall we not receive evil?" (Job 2:10). Hosea 6:1 acknowledges that some suffering originates with God: "Come and let us return unto the Lord; for he hath torn, and he will heal us; he hath smitten and he will bind us up." God authors instructional reproofs for our good, always with merciful intent.

Jesus declares He is the vine to Whom we must be attached if we are to be vital in holiness, and that God will cut us, even if that is painful, so we may become what He intends. God "is the vinedresser … every branch that does bear fruit he prunes, that it may bear more fruit" (John 15:2). The Heidelberg Catechism attributes suffering to God: "All things, even health and sickness, come to us, not by chance, but by God's hand."

God's Sovereignty is also expressed when He establishes legitimate authorities to rule over nations and men, to promote the peace and order of the righteous, and punish lawbreakers. Law does not restrain freedom but expands the freedom of all by protecting the equal freedom of everyone. The criminal may be restrained, but the integrity of the righteous is preserved by his incarceration, and its deterrence of other wrongdoers from harming them. Psalm 22:28 affirms: "For the kingdom is the Lord's; and he is the governor among the nations." God rules over every kingdom and in His "hand are power and might, so that none is able to withstand" Him (2 Chronicles 20:6). Proverbs 21:1 notes: "The king's heart is in the hand of the Lord, as the rivers of water: he turneth it whithersoever he will."

Romans 13:1–4 directs: "Let every person be subject to the governing authorities. For there is no authority except from God, and those that exist have been instituted by God. For rulers are not a terror to good conduct, but to bad … he is the servant of God, to execute his wrath on the wrongdoer."

Jesus confirms the legitimacy of secular government at Matthew 22:21 when He directs: "Render therefore to Caesar the things that are Caesar's." Jesus acknowledged Pilate's authority to pronounce judgment to crucify or free Him, but pointed out: "You would have no power over me unless it had been given you from above" (John 19:11). Pilate was definitely accountable to God, and the Crucifixion was arranged as part of God's benevolent plan to redeem mankind by Christ's voluntary submission and sacrifice.

Moreover, God intervenes in history by responding to our prayers that those in authority will be righteous for our good (I Timothy 2:1–2). When we take God at His Word and pray His revealed Word back to Him, we can be confident He will honor our prayers, as He honors His own established Word.[44] Indeed, if we did not trust God's Sovereignty there would be no purpose in praying to Him in full, faithful reliance that He intends to, and can be absolutely depended upon, to perform and deliver according to his revealed promises.

The very fact that believers pray for anything is an acknowledgement of God's sovereign power, and a response to His promise that the "prayer of a righteous man has great power in its effects" (James 5:16). God's sovereignty is expressed in His intervention in the world in response to prayer; in His manipulation of human acts to accomplish His purposes according to prayers; and in intercessions which reflect His will. His power is ubiquitous and He can respond to billions of requests simultaneously.

Since God authors every good and perfect gift from above (James 1:7), and "The Lord is good to all: and his tender mercies are over all his works" (Psalm 145:9), we can pray "Thy will be done" (Matthew 6:10) in absolute confidence His power is available and His will is perfectly good for us, even though we may not always comprehend it. In time, we can recognize and verify empirically every instance God discernibly answers prayers by the special impress of His hand. You can know God is in Sovereign control of all creation when other Christians feel moved by the Spirit to provide your needs, without any request or suggestion by you.

GOD'S SOVEREIGN CONTROL OVER INDIVIDUAL LIVES

God not only regulates the epic sweep of nations and events, but is also involved in individual activities. He alone determines the time of our coming and going on earth; when every human is born or dies, in conjunction with the free acts of our parents in pro-creation, and with the possible acceleration of death by our own hand or that of another free agent. We have no choice in our parents, nationality, color, or genetic origins, according to Psalm 47:4: "He shall choose our inheritance for us." God assigns our portion and lot in life; fills our cup; determines the limits of who we are, what we are able to do, and what circumstances reach us, according to Psalms 16:5, 142:5; and Lamentations 3:24. Acts 17:26 says: "He himself gives to all men life and breath and everything. And he made from one every nation of men to live on all the face of the earth, having determined allotted periods and the boundaries of their habitation."

Throughout life, God continues to be involved with the individual. Psalm 37:5, 23 says: "Commit thy way unto the Lord; trust also in him; and he shall bring it to pass … The steps of a good man are ordered by the Lord." Proverbs 16:1 attests to God's Sovereign direction over man's affairs: "The preparations of the heart in man, and the answer of the tongue, is from the Lord." "The lot is cast into the lap; but the whole disposing thereof is of the Lord" (Proverbs 16:33). Proverbs 16:9 agrees: "A man's heart deviseth his way: but the Lord directeth his steps." Proverbs 20:24 explains: "Man's goings are of the Lord; how can a man then understand his own way?" See also, Deuteronomy 4:39; I Samuel 2:6–7; 14:6; I Chronicles 29:11–12; Psalms 10:16, 66:7, 83:18, 90:2, 135:6; Proverbs 21:1; Daniel 2:20–22, 4:17, 4:35; Isaiah 25:1, 37:26, 40:17, 43:13; and Lamentations 3:37.

Job perceived God's hand controlling or directing his suffering: "when he hath tried me, I shall come forth as gold ... But he is in one mind, and who can turn him? and what his soul desireth, even that he doeth. For he performeth the thing that is appointed for me .... Therefore am I troubled at his presence: when I consider, I am afraid of him ... and the Almighty troubleth me" (Job 23:10–16). God certainly controlled Satan's trials of Job, forbidding both harm to Job's person or the taking of Job's life (Job 1:11; 2:6). Satan's access to Job was limited by God in this cosmic test of human faith, even when Job felt he had been forsaken by God.

In the New Testament, Jesus reveals God's concerned involvement with a single sparrow, and thus with the smallest detail in Creation at Matthew 10:29–31, KJV: "Are not two sparrows sold for a farthing? And one of them shall not fall on the ground without your Father. But the very hairs on your head are all numbered. Fear ye not therefore, ye are of more value than many sparrows." In this context, Jesus is affirming God's loving care and concern for each of us, rather than stressing intent or will to regulate us. God sees us, knows us, and delivers us, but He does not manipulate every incident of our lives.

Acts 17:25–28 affirms that God made the world, and is not "served by human hands, as though he needed anything, since he himself gives to all men life and breath and everything ... for in him we live and move and are." No man can count on completing his plans for tomorrow, for his days are numbered by the Lord (Daniel 5:26). Jesus told the rich man who dreamed of storing his wealth in barns forever, that he would keep them for a brief lifetime: "Fool! This night your soul is required of you; and the things you have prepared, whose will they be?" (Luke 12:20). Certainly, the future is not in our control, and the circumstances of life cause us to react as much as regulate. Death inevitably extinguishes the bonfire of life's vanities. James 4:14–15 puts it: "you do not know about tomorrow. What is your life? For you are a mist that appears for a little time and then vanishes. Instead you ought to say, 'If the Lord wills, we shall live and we shall do this or that'."

St. Paul recognized God's involvement in the persecutions and sufferings of his life, and attributed his imprisonment to the will of God: "Do not be ashamed then of testifying to our Lord, nor of me his prisoner" (2 Timothy 1:8). Even though Paul was imprisoned by the Romans, he referred to himself as "Paul, the prisoner of Jesus Christ for you" (Ephesians 3:1, 4:1, KJV; Philemon 9).

In the Christian life, God assumes control over our lives, based on individual consent to be changed and developed, which occurs at our New Birth in Christ. At the outset, God gives the grace of saving or prevenient faith, so that man can respond to Jesus as Lord and Saviour (John 6:44, 6:65; Matthew 16:15–17; I Corinthians 12:3). He imparts the grace of repentance to man so conversion is possible (Acts 11:18; 2 Timothy 2:25–26). Philippians 2:13 assures Christians that God engineers transformation from within, and "is at work in you, both to will and to work for his good pleasure." God not only insinuates His character into believers, but also imposes His will so that our desires and actions progressively conform to His. We are "chosen and destined by God the Father and sanctified by the Spirit for obedience to Jesus Christ" (I Peter 1:2). All these improvements are the exclusive work of God.

Even though we are privileged to seek a specific spiritual gift of the Holy Spirit (I Corinthians 12:31; James 1:5), God metes out the gifts according to His will and intent, and "apportions to each one individually as he wills" (I Corinthians 12:11). Still, the Holy Spirit gives at least one of the spiritual gifts, or charismata, to every Christian: "To each is given the manifestation of the Spirit for the common good" (I Corinthians 12:7; see also I Corinthians 7:7).

God created everything in all the universe to subserve His wise and benevolent design and plan for redemption.[45] God has a general plan for every human life: that you worship and glorify him; that you be saved from your deserved penalty of sin; that you be blessed and prosper in your choices; that you enjoy the more abundant life, coming to know and fellowship with God; and be glorified, conforming to the image of Christ in His Body, to be with God for eternity (Romans 8:29). When a Christian accepts that God has redeemed his life to generate, evidence, and express love, service, stewardship, witnessing, and growth in holiness, he appreciates God's intimate involvement in pre-destining these general purposes for every saved life.

It is comforting to believe that God has ordained everything for good: what one's occupation or calling shall be, whom he shall marry, the number of children with which one is blessed, and other major events and accomplishments of the more abundant life. Yet, the mere fact God's Sovereign will can accomplish anything He chooses, and no-one can resist His will, does not mean that He predetermines every act of men. Consistently with human freedom, God has not ordained, intended, orchestrated, or irresistibly willed the vast number of actions decided by each one of us.

There are also times God expresses His Sovereignty by bestowing His grace upon whom He wills, and hardening the heart of whom He wills. He chose to rescue only Noah and his family from the flood. He chose Abraham to bless him with heirs beyond number, and through his lineage the Messiah would be born (Genesis 12:3; 15:5; Matthew 1:1). God then preferred Abraham's second son, Isaac, over the first-born Ishmael, for the line of succession to Christ (Genesis 21:12–13; Galatians 4:22–28).

When Pharaoh refused to release the children of Israel, God declared: "For now I will stretch out my hand, that I may smite thee and thy people with pestilence; and thou shalt be cut off from the earth. And in very <u>deed for this cause have I raised thee up, for to shew in thee my power</u>; and that my name may be declared throughout all the earth" (Exodus 9:15–16). Of this event, Romans 9:17–19 quotes the Exodus passage and adds: "So then he has mercy upon whomever he wills, and he hardens the heart of whomever he wills ... why does he (man) still find fault? For who can resist his will?"

While not quite the level of a divine decree, God's bestowal of grace on one person rather than another, will greatly influence the accomplishment and outcome of their lives and situations. God chose to bestow His grace upon Jacob, rather than Esau, "though they were not yet born and had done nothing either good or bad, in order that God's purpose of election might continue, not because of works but because of his call" (Romans 9:11; see also, Malachi 1:2–4) which suggests God foresaw the wickedness of Edom, (which proceeded from Esau). Romans 9:19–23 then inquires: "But, who are you, a man, to answer back to God? Will what is molded say to its molder, 'Why have you made me thus?' Has the potter no right over the clay, to make out of the same lump one vessel for beauty and another for menial use? What if God, desiring to show his wrath and to make known his power, has endured with much patience the vessels of wrath made for destruction, in order to make known the riches of his glory for the vessels of mercy, <u>which he has prepared beforehand for glory</u>?"

GOD'S IRRESISTIBLE WILL EXPRESSES ABSOLUTE SOVEREIGNTY

God may cede some authority to make pedestrian decisions to men, who have genuine freedom of choice, through His <u>preceptive will</u>, which expresses what pleases Him, e.g. we are to pray His will be done on earth. Yet God allows man to flaunt this type of God's will, even though He wishes it. Yet, only this <u>desired</u> will of God affords such latitude to men. The <u>determined</u> will of God is certain to be fulfilled, for He does not relinquish control of ultimate things, in which His irresistible will, plan, and eternal purpose have been ordained before the beginning of time. This is God's <u>decretive</u> or determining will, which will be accomplished, and cannot be contradicted by any man. There will be establishment of His Kingdom in a Heaven from which all pain, sorrow, sin and evil have been banished. He brooks no interference as far as the eschatological or final things, when death and Satan are destroyed in eternal flames, and a new Heaven and earth are provided for man's eternal reconciliation with God. Revelation 19:20 predicts that the Beast and False Prophet will be "thrown alive into the lake of fire", along with the devil, "and they will be tormented day and night for ever" (Revelation 20:10). God wills that Satan and his fallen angels be excluded from Heaven, as outlined in the Book of Revelation, and no angelic or human choice can override His will on that point (Revelation 20:10, 13–14). Nothing will prevent the consignment and torment of Satan and his demons to the lake of fire for eternity.

Redemptive history through Christ, the Messiah, is irrevocable, and redemption of the saved by God's grace through faith in Christ is inevitable and irreversible. Jesus was "delivered up according to the definite plan and foreknowledge of God" for crucifixion (Acts 2:23). Acts 3:18 characterizes the Atonement as: "what God foretold by the mouth of all the prophets, that his Christ should suffer, he thus fulfilled." God's irresistible will worked in harmony with Jesus' free consent to obey God at the Cross, and with human free choice to murder Jesus, exercised by the Romans and Jews.

God alone determined to offer salvation to sinners; to make salvation available by His grace through faith in Jesus and His redemptive work on the Cross. God alone determined that he who freely put his faith in Christ would be forgiven, reconciled, and have eternal life by responding to God's grace. God will not permit freedom to subvert God's plans for final deliverance of creation and eternal salvation for believers.

Once human faith in Christ is exercised, nothing can prevent God's process of individual salvation, regeneration, sanctification, deliverance, and glorification of the redeemed in and through Jesus Christ. Ephesians 1:4–11 concludes: "he chose us in him before the foundation of the world, that we should be holy and blameless before him. He destined us in love to be his sons through Jesus Christ, according to the purpose...of him who <u>accomplishes all things according to the counsel of his will</u>."

2 Thessalonians 2:13 promises believers: "God chose you from the beginning to be saved, through consecration by the Spirit and belief in the truth", and God's plan to redeem fallen

mankind existed before time. It makes sense that God would fulfill His prophecies to validate His Word and accomplish His eternal purposes.

Nothing can prevent the fullness of God's Church, which will be composed of all believers in Christ. Jesus designates the Body of Christ, His Church consisting of all believers, as unconquerable, and declares: "I will build my church, and the powers of death shall not prevail against it. I will give you the keys of the kingdom of heaven, and whatever you bind on earth shall be bound in heaven, and whatever you loose on earth shall be loosed in heaven" (Matthew 16:18–19). Jesus declares to His Church: "Behold, I have given you authority to tread upon serpents and scorpions, and over all the power of the enemy; and nothing shall hurt you" (Luke 10:19).

In the eternal plan of redemptive history the Church will be able to defend itself in the power of the indwelling Holy Spirit, against the assaults of Satan. And the Church-militant will inexorably triumph over Satan and Hell, itself, in the battle for men's souls. I John 4:4 declares that we are "over-comers", because "He who is within you is greater than he who is in the world." Regarding "tribulation, or distress, or persecution, or famine, or nakedness, or peril, or sword … in all these things we are more than conquerors through him who loved us", because we cannot be separated from the love of God in Christ (Romans 8:35,37).

God has decreed in His Sovereignty that when believers "resist the devil … he will flee from you" (James 4:7). 2 Corinthians 10:4 says: "the weapons of our warfare are not worldly but have Divine power to destroy strongholds." Romans 8:2 says: "the law of the Spirit of life in Christ Jesus has set me free from the law of sin and death," according to God's perfect plan of redemption for mankind.

In the eschatology of final things, God has ordained the return, or Second Coming of Christ for His Church, after which Jesus promises we will spend all eternity with the Lord: "And when I go and prepare a place for you, I will come again and will take you to myself, that where I am you may be also" (John 14:2–3). Nothing can forestall the Second Coming of Christ for His Church at the end time. Our blessed hope is Christ's return and the Rapture of the Church described at I Thessalonians 4:16–17: "For the Lord himself will descend from heaven with a cry of command, with the archangel's call, and with the sound of the trumpet of God. And the dead in Christ will rise first; then we who are alive, who are left, shall be caught up together with them in the clouds to meet the Lord in the air; and so we shall always be with the Lord."

God promises to complete the regeneration of New Born men to the likeness of Christ: "He who began a good work in you will bring it to completion" (Philippians 1:6), despite Satan's contesting or any demonic activity to the contrary. God has revealed He initiates, supplies, and accomplishes all spiritual operations on behalf of willing believers: salvation, repentance, conversion, faith, love, endurance, good works, and holiness (2 Peter 1:3; Ephesians 4:11–13).

Romans 8:30 puts it: "For those whom he foreknew he also predestined to be conformed to the image of his Son... And those whom he predestined he also called; and those whom he called he also justified; and those whom he justified he also glorified." This means that God's Sovereignty determined our salvation "before the foundation of the world" (Ephesians 1:4); assures our Heavenly glorification to fulfill His will; accomplishes our transformation by His power; and confirms His will that Jesus finish the redemption and salvation of mankind assured at the Cross two thousand years ago.

To effect His irresistible will, God intervenes in history to offset human misuse of freedom which would otherwise affect the full salvation of His faithful children. As He wills, He intercedes in human affairs on His own initiative or in answer to prayers. He will direct every process; control every affair; and order every event to fulfill His plan of redemption, even if it neutralizes and overrides free choice. We will see that He seldom controls how free decisions are made, but instead indirectly manipulates the outcome of myriad, unrelated choices of men, to work good in the lives of those who love Him, who are impacted by others' free decisions and actions. Romans 8:28 explains: "We know that in everything God works for good with those who love him, who are called according to his purpose." Freedom is possible because God meliorates any harm, by using His Sovereign interventions to correct and adjust man's doings to accomplish His unalterable, eternal purposes.

In short, He will determine His purposes and accomplish the fulfillment of His will, despite the careless or evil machinations of men to resist and frustrate God's intentions.

GOD'S PERMISSIVE WILL CEDES SOME SOVEREIGNTY TO FREE BEINGS

God, as Sovereign, controls and retains ultimate authority over all things. We have just seen that God's Sovereignty is inviolate, as long as God so chooses. Whatever God wants to happen will happen. Whatever God allows to happen, will be turned to good by Him. If God has brought a trial, there is never any reason to fear it, because He intends it only for our good. As long as we have faith God corrects evil originating with others, and turns it to good, there is no need to insist He intended or sent evil initially, when it can be traced to the brutal reality of human free choice.

Paradoxically, I Timothy 2:4 proclaims God "desires all men to be saved and to come to the knowledge of the truth." 2 Peter 3:9 affirms: "The Lord is... longsuffering to us-ward, not willing that any should perish, but that all should come to repentance." Yet, God's Word also reveals He allows His will to be spurned by disobedient, rebellious human choices. All men are not saved, and God does not compel unbelieving rebels to embrace salvation in Christ, but permits them freely to pursue error unto their own destruction, without desiring that result.

God's forbearance with sinners confirms He has yielded some Sovereignty to men to fulfill His gift of free choice, which He honors, despite the possibility of error when man wrongly exercises that choice in opposition to God's expressed will. Yet, God still tolerates potential abuse of freedom, capable of producing results not desired by God, because the gifts which prompt His yielding of power accomplish overwhelming blessings and transcendent good for the benefit of the creatures so blessed. That He chooses not to force rebels and sinners to turn to Him for salvation is a verification of the freedom God has invested in every human.

Freedom resolves any apparent inconsistency between God as King, Who controls and orders all acts, and God as Judge holding men responsible for their actions.[46] Man is left free to challenge God's Sovereignty, and is responsible for consequences of evil actions, disobedience, and wrong choices. The nature of sin is still sin, and is not excused by God's Sovereignty. All of sin's evil originates with man; and remains separate from God. Every prophetic warning of doom is conditional on man refusing to repent, change his ways, and obey God. When Ninevah heard the preaching of Jonah and repented its evil, God reversed His decree of doom for the City (Jonah 3:4,10). When Sodom would not repent its perversion, it was destroyed, together with all its inhabitants, except for Lot and his family (Genesis 18:21, 19:24–29).

The Great White Throne Judgment of Revelation 20:12 relates: "Also another book was opened, which is the book of life. And the dead were judged by what was written in the books, by what they had done." One might argue that God pre-determined who was elected for salvation, but Revelation 20:12 bases Judgment on "what they had done." And there is no way God's Justice in condemning evil-doers could be based on anything other than their willing, free choice to be rebelliously disobedient, in defiance of God's will they be saved by obedient compliance with God's revelations about Jesus.

It has been said that God initiates and controls the direction of human history, but gives man wide latitude and freedom along the course taken, much as a liner headed for Europe will arrive at its destination, regardless of, and despite passengers exercising almost total freedom to act aboard the ship. The Captain oversees the integrity and joy of the passengers, but intervenes in their affairs in direct response to a petition for aid, or for the restoration of order aboard ship. The Captain allows every passenger great liberty of choice to act as he pleases, unless the welfare and safety of other passengers are threatened, or there is attempted interference with the ship's prescribed course. Unwilling passengers are free to "jump ship" if they refuse to reach the destination, but such abandonment is wholly man's part, and the captain does his part in arriving as scheduled.

Such a plan of direction by God gives us security without rigidity, and allows for mature self-realization, to His glory. Along the journey, God can fellowship with believers and delight us with learning, entertainment, joyful interludes, revelation, and astonishments aboard ship, as we are carried toward our scheduled destination.

God wants us to choose freely among right alternatives. He leads us to graze in designated pasture, but not in a particular spot. He offers samples from among a smorgasbord of many choices that please us, but expects us to eat at His table. The owner who walks his dog expects him to stay near along the route and not pull too far ahead. The pet may enjoy exploring where he pleases, and pausing along the way, but will be restrained if he turns into harm's way.

From the beginning, God shared dominion over Creation with Adam and Eve: "And God blessed them, and God said unto them, be fruitful, and multiply, and replenish the earth and subdue it: and have dominion over the fish of the sea, and over the fowl of the air, and over every living thing that moveth upon the earth" (Genesis 1:28). When Adam surrendered dominion and assigned it to Satan by believing his lies, God's perfect integrity honored the dominion He had entrusted to Adam, even though it allowed sin to enter the world (Romans 5:12–18).

Yet, consistently with human freedom, God has not ordained, intended, orchestrated or irresistibly willed the vast number of actions decided by each of us. Human decision involves God's permissive will, by which He has voluntarily ceded a part of His Sovereign will to free beings. God has given us broad mandates, such as not to marry or be unequally yoked to, an unbeliever (2 Corinthians 6:14). He will counsel us about the wisdom of our choice, and bless it, but He probably entrusts the choice of partner to individual preference, drawn from the hundreds of compatible believers we may encounter.

God has vested man's freedom with capacity to apprehend the rightness of a choice or action, based upon God's general revealed will. We can use our intelligence to ask God for direction, and pray for specific guidance. He promises to provide wisdom in His Word; in the inner assurance of the Holy Spirit; and in the wise counsel of other believers.

God's irrevocable plan of redemption for mankind, predestined, guaranteed and ordained by the Crucifixion of Jesus, illustrates the interaction of God's Sovereignty using and incorporating the free acts of men. God's Sovereign plan to save a fallen mankind is affirmed at Acts 2:23–24: "This Jesus, delivered up according to the definite plan and foreknowledge of God, you crucified and killed by the hands of lawless men, but God raised him up, having loosed the pangs of death." At the same time, the human actors were willingly involved, freely participating and personally responsible as the lethal instruments of God's purposes: "For the Son of man goes as it has been determined: but woe to that man by whom he is betrayed!" (Luke 22:22).

God ordained the death of Jesus by using unbelievers to accomplish the divinely ordained plan of redemption: "there were gathered together ... Herod and Pontius Pilate, with the Gentiles and the peoples of Israel, to do whatever thy hand and thy plan had predestined to take place" (Acts 4:27–28). We cannot know whether God motivated Jewish leaders and Roman pagans to act in definite ways to execute God's plan exactly as prophesied. We know that God has the intelligence and power to persuade men to act in any way God wishes. He can influence natural events and human agents to affect every aspect of our existence if He so chooses. Jonah and Balaam may resist God's call and direction for a time, but He has infinite means at His command to induce and even coerce compliance with His will.

We cannot know whether God, in His wisdom, anticipated that some men would freely respond to events according to their carnal predispositions, and their motives would coincide with and fulfill His plan of redemption. Nor can we know whether God, in His omniscience, simply foresaw and recorded how evil man freely acted at the historical moment of crucifixion. All we can know is that the truly free acts of unbelievers verified the accuracy of Biblical prophecy for believers (Acts 3:17–18).

What we can also know is that God has provided a clear example of relinquishing His power to promote the good of men. Philippians 2:6–8 relates that Jesus "Though He was in the form of God emptied himself, taking the form of a servant, being born in the likeness of men. And being found in human form he humbled himself and became obedient unto death." This example of self-limitation was God's way of lifting man up, redeeming and restoring him to share God for all eternity by grace through faith in Jesus. For man's sake, Jesus forsook His equality with God; renounced the prerogatives of divine majesty, and suppressed His glory, privileges, and supernatural attributes so He could be truly human in sinless obedience, sacrifice, and atonement.

THE OMNISCIENCE OF GOD

God's Sovereignty rests on a tripod of omnipotence, omniscience, and omnipresence; He is all-powerful, all-wise, and everywhere. He controls, orchestrates, initiates, and regulates billions of random human acts to accomplish His comprehensive plan for redemption, and His purposes for individual Christians. He is capable of hearing, assimilating, and responding to billions of prayers offered up to Him simultaneously. From His vantage in eternity He can foresee events before they transpire in historical time. He has centuries to arrange human events to achieve imperceptibly the result He desires in answer to prayer at the exact, appropriate moment in historical time. He is capable of providing fellowship, comfort, guidance, spiritual transformation, and chastening to hundreds of millions of His children, steadily motivating believers to love, serve, encourage, edify, educate, or evangelize others.

It is well to remember at the outset that we cannot put God into predictable categories, nor presume to explain His ways, which are so far above ours. Isaiah 40:28 explains: "the everlasting God, the Lord, the Creator of the ends of the earth, fainteth not, neither is weary; there is no searching of his understanding." In His omniscience, God has access to facts and considerations we can neither perceive nor fathom. Psalm 139:2–4 recognizes: "Thou knowest my downsitting and mine uprising, thou understandest my thought afar off. Thou compassest my path and my lying down, and art acquainted with all my ways. For there is not a word in my tongue, but lo, O Lord, thou knowest it all together." Romans 11:33 declares: "O the depth of the riches and wisdom and knowledge of God! How unsearchable are his judgments and how inscrutable his ways." God's unknowable ways are also noted at Isaiah 45:15, 55:9; Deuteronomy 29:29; Psalm 77:19, 147:5; Proverbs 25:2; Ecclesiastes 11:5; Daniel 2:22; and Romans 9:19–23.

Psalm 37:18 teaches: "The Lord knoweth the days of the upright." Psalm 44:21 asks: "Shall not God search this out? For he knoweth the secrets of the heart." Isaiah 46:10 says God declares "the end from the beginning and from ancient times the things that are not yet done." Jeremiah 32:19 attests to God's greatness and wisdom: "Great in counsel, and mighty in work: for thine eyes are open upon all the ways of the sons of men: to give every one according to his ways, and according to the fruit of his doings" (see also, Psalm 139:1–2). Jesus tells the Pharisees at Luke 16:15: "God knows your hearts: for what is exalted among men is an abomination in the sight of God." I John 3:20 adds: "God is greater than our hearts, and he knows everything." See also, Matthew 9:4; 10:29–20; Acts 15:8; I Corinthians 2:11, 8:2; Hebrews 4:13.

However, there are also prophecies that are fulfilled because God has orchestrated, arranged, predetermined, or directed the events, exercising Sovereign control to make sure they happen. God's foreknowledge of who will be saved and going to heaven seems to be based on His choice, as suggested at Ephesians 1:4: "he chose us in him before the foundation of the world, that we should be holy and blameless before him." Acts 13:48 speaks of the Gentiles who received the Gospel: "they were glad and glorified the word of God; and as many as were ordained to eternal life believed." Jesus says at John 6:44: "No one can come to me unless the Father who sent me draws him." This is interpreted to mean that God foreordains some men for salvation, and they respond by exercising faith in Christ. I Peter 2:8 observes, in speaking of the Jews' rejection of Christ: "for they stumble because they disobey the word, as they were destined to do." God's Word reveals pre-destination as well as human freedom, and only God can reconcile the reality and co-existence of apparent antinomies.

We encounter difficulty whenever we conclude that God's omniscience results only from His predeterminations, originating in His will, independently of man's free acts in history. The difficulty with identifying absolute Sovereignty as the sole explanation of God's foreknowledge is its implication that God ordained Adam's fall, Cain's murder of Abel, and all other evil acts of men, which are patently contradictory to God's perfect goodness, which intends only good in Creation.

On the other hand, we know God wills all men to be saved, "But they have not all heeded the gospel" (Romans 10:16). Acts 13:46 also reveals human free choice, since God first offered salvation in Christ to the Jews, but "you thrust it from you, and judge yourselves unworthy of eternal life." One might reasonably infer that God would not ordain or predetermine their rejection of Christ, and then engage in the futile act of offering salvation to the Jews, knowing He had compelled their rejection of it. If men act wrongly, but choose freely in rejecting Christ, then God's omniscience is not based on His choice, but on what He can foresee as the choices of men through the corridor of time from His vantage point above history.

Once we recognize that God has given freedom to man, His foresight sees what man's will freely determines as man's acts. Man must still exercise choice, but God foresees it from His position in eternity. Once God sees man's decision, as influenced by the persuasions of God insinuated into history, it is determined in the sense it will come to pass. If God has an infallible knowledge of future free acts, then the future is completely determined in the sense God absolutely knows what man's free act will be. But the act was genuinely free when chosen by man at that moment in history which God foresaw.

This pre-determinism does not mean that man has been coerced or compelled to act in a certain way. It means only that once God has seen man's free act, it is determined as accurately noted by God, and must transpire in time, because an omniscient God cannot be wrong in His foreknowledge. God's control is not based on compulsion of events, but on the knowledge of what free choice will do in response to God's persuasions, not coercions. The fact of God's foreknowledge means He is certain of His clear knowledge of all that will take place, but His foreknowledge does not determine, in the sense of dictating, what will take place.[47] The inevitability of the event is fixed in advance when God knows infallibly that it will occur in history by man's free choice. When a man freely accepts Christ as his Lord and Saviour, it has been pre-determined in the sense God observed that choice from eternity, and after that, it had to occur. Whatever God knows, He determines, and whatever He determines, He knows.

If you could somehow watch a race a day in advance, you would know the result, although you did not control or cause it. However, the event would be fixed because your foreknowledge is based on a future truth. So it is with God's vantage from eternity, as He infallibly foreknows all earthly events, based on observing human free choices exercised in time. Our actions are free when performed, but determined from God's position over all history. God's election is then based on God's omniscience about man's free choice to believe or not.

Romans 8:29–30 says of believers: "For those whom he <u>foreknew</u> he also predestined to be … called … justified … glorified," as if these events are already completed in the knowledge of God. I Peter 1:2, KJV characterizes believers as the "elect according to the foreknowledge of God." To a New-Born believer, these events are not complete in our experience, for we have not yet been glorified. God sets the reward of glorification upon His perception of man's future act. The future for us is present knowledge to God, though yet to be experienced by us. Foreknowledge could also signify that God is so intelligent He can predict historic consequences because He understands the minds of men so well that their conduct is foreseeable to Him. Thus, the involvement of men clamoring for the death of Christ was not ordained or coerced by God as necessary evil to accomplish good. Rather, God foresaw that evil men would conspire freely to harm Jesus, and their involvement was pre-destined based on God's inerrant foreknowledge. These are bewildering possibilities, and who can presume to know which alternative explains God's omniscience?

In any event, the inescapable conclusion of prophecies fulfilled is that the Forecaster has perfect knowledge and power to guarantee the happening of the event in advance of its occurrence in time. God gave Daniel a correct, prophetic interpretation of the handwriting on the wall — that God was about to take King Belshazzar's life. And when the king died that very evening, it revealed God foreknows, and therefore determines, — or in this case initiates — prophetic events (Daniel 5:4–30).

The Old Testament prophecies corroborated by subsequent events, and consequently confirmed as God's revelation, dealt with the destruction of Solomon's Temple and of Jerusalem; the exile of the Jews from Israel; their return to the promised land; the extension of belief in the God of Israel to the Gentile world, and the rise and fall of cities and world empires, as well as the specific manner of their destruction. All the Biblical prophecies predicting the downfall of cities and nations which have been fulfilled, are irrefutable proof of God's total control over creation, as well as His power to foresee, ordain, and fulfill historical events. For example, God pronounced judgment on Tyre, predicting its total destruction as punishment for its enmity toward Israel: "Behold, I am against thee, O Tyrus, and will cause many nations to come up against thee … And they shall destroy the walls of Tyrus … It shall be a place for the spreading of nets in the midst of the sea; for I have spoken it, saith the Lord God" (Ezekiel 26:3–5).

The prophecy about Tyre is remarkable because it was originally landlocked. After Nebuchadnezzar first besieged the city, it was moved to an island to insulate it from another attack, by surrounding it with water. 200 years later, Alexander the Great used the ruins of the first city to build a causeway of rocks to the relocated island-city and totally despoiled it. As predicted, Tyre has never been rebuilt: "And I will cause the noise of thy songs to cease; and the sound of thy harps shall no more be heard … Thou shalt be built no more" (Ezekiel 27:13–14).

As related in the New Testament, God sent an angel to assure Paul that he and his shipmates would not lose their lives in the loss of their ship during a storm (Acts 27:23), but Paul had to exhort the men not to jump ship, lest they be lost (Acts 27:31). God had both the power to guarantee, and foreknowledge that none of the men would drown, but they had free choice to depart or be persuaded by Paul to remain on the ship to preserve lives. Who can say God merely foreknew in advance the free acts of the men, rather than determined to motivate them to stay by Paul's persuasions, to demonstrate His power by guaranteeing their safety?

The Atonement of Christ on the Cross reflects God's predetermination that a blood sacrifice by a sinless man was necessary to redeem fallen sinners. Yet, Jesus revealed He freely laid down His life: "No one takes it from me, but I lay it down of my own accord" (John 10:18).

Judaism preserved the prophecies about the Messiah in the Old Testament, and even modern Jews retain, honor, and acknowledge them as authentic. Consequently, these prophecies have special cogency because they could not have been manufactured by Christians, but repose in the lore and religious oracles of the Jews, most of whom do not accept Jesus Christ as the Messiah. Nor is there any likelihood that the Messianic prophecies were altered, since the hostility which existed from the outset would not permit either Jew or Christian to make any alteration favorable to the other's position. Thus, if the recorded life of Jesus fulfilled the Old Testament prophecies about the Messiah, His authenticity is established by Scripture. The odds of even ten separate prophecies occurring by chance or coincidence, rather than design, have been estimated to be one in billions. Following are more than ten of the fulfilled Scriptural prophecies about Jesus, the Christ, which confirm God's foreknowledge and omnipotence.

The Old Testament forecast the Messiah's coming by a convergence of time and place, uniquely applicable to, and exactly coincident with the Advent of Jesus Christ.[48] As prophesied by Jacob, after the Messiah appeared, Judah lost its independence and Jerusalem and the temple were destroyed (Genesis 49:10). The Messiah was to come, as Jesus did, within 483 years of the Persian command to restore Solomon's temple, as prophesied by Daniel (Daniel 9:25–27). Jesus entered the Second Temple and filled it with glory, as predicted for the Messiah in the Old Testament, when He received the blessings of Simeon, sat among the teachers, and drove out the moneychangers and merchants (Luke 2:27, 46; Matthew 21:12).

The ancestral lineage of Jesus through both Mary and Joseph fulfilled the genealogy required of the Messiah destined to rule God's Kingdom as the designated descendant of Abraham, Isaac and David (Matthew 1:1; John 7:42). Micah 5:2 said that the Messiah would be born in Bethlehem, yet be co-eternal with God from the beginning. And this coincides with Jesus' human birth and existence with God from the beginning (John 1:14; Revelation 1:8). Jesus' birth also fulfilled the Old Testament prophecies that Wise Men would come from the East to worship the Messiah, and that His coming would be immediately preceded by a messenger (John the Baptist), to prepare the way of the Lord.

Exactly as forecast for the Messiah in the Old Testament, Jesus preached in Parables; entered into Jerusalem "riding upon an ass", and was anointed with wisdom through the Spirit of God. He turned His wrath upon corruption in the House of God, opened the eyes of the blind, unstopped the ears of the deaf, and serves as "a priest forever according to the order of Melchizedek", all as forecast in the Old Testament. Isaiah 53:4–6 predicted that the Messiah would bear our sorrows and sins, and heal us by His stripes, and Jesus accomplished this "to fulfill what was spoken by the Prophet Isaiah", according to Matthew 8:17 and I Peter 2:24. Jesus fulfilled the prophecies that the Messiah would be rejected by His friends and family; betrayed and denied by His disciples; and refuse to defend Himself against unjust accusations.

God promised that he would raise up another Prophet, "like unto" Moses (Deuteronomy 18:15, 18), and even the Jews recognize that this prophecy pertains to the Messiah. Only Jesus qualifies as "like unto" Moses in scores of ways. Both saw God face to face. Each was a lawgiver communicating the commandments of God to His people. They both were deliverer, intercessor, priest and miracle worker, living exemplary lives.

Both Moses and Jesus escaped the decreed destruction of male infants by fleeing from their homeland. Divine notification was given when it was safe to return. Moses declined to become the son of Pharaoh's daughter, and Jesus refused the rulership of this world, each motivated by a desire to serve only God. In their youth, both had exceptional wisdom beyond their years, and magicians and demons respectively acknowledged Divine power working in each of them. Both were noted for their meekness and subservience to others. Both performed healings, signs and wonders, and both lost the support of their brethren and own people. Both fasted forty days.

Moses' face shone when he descended from the mount, and Jesus' face shone in the Transfiguration. Moses parted the Red Sea and was God's agent to feed the Israelites in the wilderness. Jesus walked on the water and fed five thousand with loaves and fishes. Moses worked with twelve spies and seventy elders who inherited the power to prophesy. Jesus sent twelve Apostles to preach His Gospel, and sent forth seventy disciples who possessed miraculous powers through Him.

A skeptic of prophecy may say that after Jesus learned how the accident of His birth coincided with some of the Messianic prophecies, He manipulated events in His life to correspond with other forecasts. Yet, many of the predicted incidents were beyond His control, and in no way could have been orchestrated by Jesus. Such prophecies are especially compelling when they are fulfilled by instrumentalities ignorant of the occasion foretold, or even hostile to the Divine purpose motivating it. Many of the events qualifying Jesus as the Messiah according to prophecy were not authored by His hands, but were accomplished through independent acts by enemies beyond His control.

Thus, the Jews tormenting Christ were unintentionally fulfilling Old Testament prophecies that they would persecute the Messiah. The predicted treachery by Judas in Psalm 41:9 and Zechariah 11:23–13 was not initiated by Jesus. John 17:12 refers to Judas as the "Lost ... son of perdition." The prophesied price of thirty pieces of silver (Zechariah 11:12, Matthew 26:15) paid for betrayal was not set by Jesus. Judas' repudiation of the silver; and the purchase of the potter's field were all predicted, but transpired independently of Jesus (Matthew 26:14–27:10). The suffering and contempt which the condemned Messiah would endure, predicted in Psalms 22:14–16, 22:18, 34:20, 69:21; Isaiah 50:6, 52:14; and Micah 5:1, were fulfilled by Christ's suffering inflicted by scorners, as related in Matthew 27:30–48; Mark 15:16–32; Luke 23:11–39; and John 19:28–37.

The crown of thorns; the spear that pierced His side; the crucifixion itself, and Christ's Resurrection (John 2:19; I Corinthians 15:4), were all prophesied and were all the result of intervening, independent causes. Nor did the Jews living at the time of Christ deny that these external events occurred. Therefore, since these things happened and took place independently of Jesus' initiative, they truly confirm the validity and divine origin of the Hebrew Messianic prophecies of the Old Testament. In a sense, because the <u>means</u> were as impossible for human wisdom to foretell, as the event predicted, the instrumentalities inimical to God are equally prophetic and reveal that Jesus is the Messiah proclaimed in the old Testament and guaranteed by God to be the Saviour of His people. Prophecy fulfilled confirms that Jesus was delivered as a willing sacrifice by the determined counsel, sovereignty and foreknowledge of God.

WHEN GOD'S SOVEREIGNTY INFLICTS SUFFERING

A traditional view of God's Sovereignty as absolute and perfectly benign, holds that He is absolutely unrestrained in the exercise and application of His power. He acts as He wills, when He wills, and where He wills.[49] And because God is perfectly good, what he does and thinks establishes the standard for man of what is good and proper. Absolute Sovereignty denotes that God plans, designs, purposes, intends, initiates, instigates, originates, orchestrates, controls, calculates, micromanages, and manipulates everything that happens in the universe.

Absolute Sovereignty embraces the idea that since everything God does is good, there can be no genuine evil in the world; a view lampooned by Voltaire in <u>Candide</u>, an 18th century tale of an unbridled optimist, who believed that everything happens for the best in this best of all possible worlds. Carried to its extreme, the idea of an all-powerful, totally good, but micro-managing God posits that every detail of every person's life is intended and manipulated by God to accomplish some transcendent good at some point in God's creation. God's Sovereignty thus implies the exercise of total control and dominion over creation, and admits no ceding or assignment of any part of His power. He elects those who will be saved, and abandons the rest of sinners to their deserved destruction.

The implications of absolute sovereignty for a theodicy of evil are significant. Any suffering which reaches us could not be accidental or initiated by other beings, but is purposefully designed, planned, and sent by God and therefore good. Because of the conjunction of God's unlimited power and perfect goodness, we must take comfort and assurance that suffering serves a good purpose in accordance with God's righteous plans and determination, which we are seldom wise enough to perceive.

If God originates, intends, and plans every detail of one's life, then we must believe that God purposes this ordeal as a current means to accomplish an eventual benefit. Then, what appears as evil is actually good, although we simply cannot discern, nor yet appreciate how, when, and what good God is working in our lives. God is in control and intends everything as happening for your benefit, as the sharp edge of misfortune prunes your fruitless inclinations and chisels away at your sinful nature, to transform you into the image of Christ. We need only recognize that suffering produces something of value as it transforms us by God's power. God is not only working good in or through the circumstances, but in the transformed believer.

Since God exercises absolute Sovereignty for the good of believers, what is evil from the imperfect, relative vantage point of one afflicted, is always congenial and absolute good from God's faultless perspective. What we perceive to be evil, in reality promotes eternally good, transcendent, supervening, and spiritual objectives. Affliction is God's medicine to cure our sin or faithlessness, even though suffering may bring its own kind of pain. We would thank the physician who amputated a gangrenous limb if we were certain it was necessary to save life. We would know enough to thank the pharmacist who dispensed ill-tasting medicine, if we were sure it would cure a deadly malady. Likewise, we are to have confidence in God's goodness and wisdom when He initiates or applies painful measures, which promote and produce our spiritual healing.

In the economy of salvation, the principle of sacrificing a part, in anticipation of saving the whole, is endorsed by Jesus: "If your right eye causes you to sin, pluck it out and throw it away; it is better that you lose one of your members than that your whole body be thrown into hell" (Matthew 5:29; and see also Matthew 18:8). It is better for an individual or mankind to lose a part, figuratively, than for one or all men to degenerate into a Godless condition, deservedly destined for destruction.

We must be like the little child who has just been vaccinated to reduce vulnerability to disease. He will cry out in pain, and doubt the trustworthiness of the father who coaxed him to receive the needle for his own good. He cannot understand how the benefits of vaccination far outweigh the momentary prick of pain. He can only cling to his father, and depend upon his goodness until the pain subsides, and the incident is forgotten.[50]

To put suffering in perspective, the purpose of life is not to have a good time, but to attain to one's highest good: to achieve the righteousness of Christ by growing in holiness in conformity to His character. God cares more about our holiness than our temporary happiness. You must embrace what is good for you, rather than what may be momentarily sweet and pleasant, or to your liking. Health and wealth are truly blessings from God in this life, but they may be temporarily suspended while God fashions some paramount blessing for eternity.

God may temporarily postpone some earthly, transient benefit while He advances some higher, eternal, spiritual blessing of freedom; development of holy character; training in spiritual warfare; or heavenly reward. Since God is perfectly good and the source of loving kindness, Genesis 18:25 queries: "Shall not the Judge of all the earth do right?" His power is inextricably linked to, and used for good, and can never be tied to evil. Only the highest good and grace can originate and emerge from our ordeals. God devises a plan for one's life, reveals it, and guides us according to it. If we wander too far He will draw us back and block the false paths and frivolous detours we have chosen. If we disobey and do not repent, He will chasten and chastise us until we submit to His direction.

God's exercise of absolute Sovereignty, dominion, and control does not design chaos and evil, but authorizes the occasional and temporary application of suffering and destruction to promote the total order and good He has ordained. For example, we all recognize the need to punish evil, including imprisoning a sadistic mass murderer, even though it may also result in depriving his children of their father.

Because God is in control, a believer need have no fear or doubt about any pain, suffering, or tribulation; not because they are unreal or illusory, for they are genuine; but because their temporary visitations are avenues to far superior blessings provided and directed by God. Trials require utmost trust and confidence in God's Providence, based upon God's promises that suffering serves some salubrious purpose known to God, even though not always perceptible to man. We may not be able to understand or appreciate how Providence blessed us until we view it from the perspective of eternity, but God's goodness is always trustworthy and will always be vindicated. We should offer praise and thanksgiving for every travail or apparent evil God provides to produce good for us.

An example frequently used to illustrate our inability to visualize what God is accomplishing, involves the weaving of an oriental rug by knotting various colored threads together. From the underside of the rug, one can see only a disarray of unconnected knots. But on the smooth surface of the rug, a harmonious, coordinated, pattern is emerging.

There are examples of God withdrawing one blessing because He intends a better one to develop. The sacrifice or suspension of some immediate, transient or earthly advantage, in order to achieve a superior, prospective benefit, is chronicled in the Talmud, the authoritative body of Jewish tradition, concerning a journey of Rabbi Akiba. The tale illustrates God's regnancy in arranging maximum benefit during our difficulties. Rabbi Akiba took his lamp, rooster and donkey to a foreign village, whose inhospitable residents refused him shelter for the night. He then gave thanks to God and retired to the forest, where the wind blew his lamp out, his rooster was devoured by wild animals, and his donkey was stolen by thieves. Being a devout man, the Rabbi offered thanks and praise to God as each of these incidents occurred.

In the morning, he learned that the inhospitality of the village and the hostility of the forest had really spared him from harm by brigands who pillaged the unfriendly village and killed all its inhabitants. Moreover, on their way to the village they had marched close to where he was encamped in the forest. Had he been in the village, or his presence in the forest betrayed by his lamp, rooster, or donkey, he too would have been murdered. Indeed, he truly had every occasion to offer thanks and praise to God throughout his ordeal. He initially did not fathom the true benevolence and working out of his apparent travails to accomplish the greater earthly benefit of survival for him.

When the Turks occupied much of the Middle East in the early 20th century they conscripted young men from the conquered nations for military service in the Turkish army. One teenager fell from a tree, suffered a broken arm, and grumbled about the restrictions imposed by his injury. However, when the Turks came to conscript recruits, he was rejected as disabled. His apparent misfortune was transformed into superior good for him as he avoided military impressment by the enemy.

We can see God's Providence in a third story involving a shipwrecked seaman stranded for years on a desert island. Though he prayed for rescue, it was not forthcoming, and he believed himself abandoned by God. His faith in God almost dissolved when his hut burned down, and all his accumulated treasures were destroyed. Yet, the day following the fire a rescue ship appeared on the horizon in response to the 'smoke signals' which had ascended the day before and attracted the rescuers' attention. The castaway's deliverance was accomplished by what had seemed an unbearable loss the previous day.

PRAYERS OF THANKSGIVING

God calls us to give thanks in all things and for all things. I Thessalonians 5:17–18 tells believers to 'pray constantly, give thanks in all circumstances; for this is the will of God in Christ Jesus for you." Ephesians 5:20 directs believers: "always and for everything giving thanks in the name of our Lord Jesus Christ to God the Father." Faith requires us to trust in God's working a good result, and therefore to give thanks at the outset; together with praise for His doings. For, every occurrence in our lives presents some reason for offering thanks and praise to God for its unseen blessings. It may mean we are thankful for the affliction itself, because it is intrinsically good. Or, if God has not sent it but simply allowed it to reach us and transform us by God's power, it becomes His instrument to promote our spiritual blessing.

If the pain is inherently good, we can focus on giving thanks for it, and treasure the painful event, itself, because God has initiated or controlled it; He has sent it or allowed it to reach us because of its effective working of good in us. Giving thanks for all things forces a sufferer to focus attention on the value inherent in the very tribulation he would shun, because it may be intended to promote the highest blessing of Christ-like character in us. Or it may be a blessing for the Body of Christ by calling attention to God's work in empowering sufferers to overcome affliction. It may be good because an affliction which besets another may involve God's chastening and remind others of the need for each to return to God's way.

If God has originated, directed, or utilized a particular suffering for good purposes, then believers ought to accept it by faith in God's benevolence. I Peter 4:19 says: "let those who suffer, according to God's will do right and entrust their souls to a faithful creator." I Peter 3:14 confirms: "if you do suffer for righteousness' sake, you will be blessed." God assures the believer who resides in the Lord that He will shield him from real evils of snares, pestilence, terror, arrows, or destruction; that "There shall no evil befall thee" (Psalm 91:10). Consequently if God the Deliverer permits suffering to reach or "befall" believers, then it cannot be intrinsically evil, but must be good in ways we cannot yet apprehend. Or, we have temporarily slipped out of our residence in the Lord, and He uses suffering as our 'wake up' call to return to Him.

Our prayers can also signify that we are giving thanks despite the genuinely evil activity which afflicts us, although it has not been initiated by God, but arose independently by the free act of a lesser being, and we trust God to relieve or compensate for it here or Hereafter. It is God's will that we give thanks in, or during all things, not necessarily for the painful circumstances, themselves, but for the blessed result of future, spiritual, eternal values God will work through this adversity. At the very least, remembering to thank God in all circumstances expresses one's gratitude for all God's blessings, especially His gift of eternal salvation, against which all suffering pales and dissolves by comparison.

We can thankfully tolerate all circumstances and afflictions because we know God will sustain us to endure, elude, or escape them all. He redresses our grievances for evil, pain, or persecution; and promotes ultimate deliverance and good, on earth and in Heaven. We can endure all suffering because our blessed hope lies in the return of Jesus, when we will be reunited with our departed loved ones, and we will spend eternity in the presence of the Lord, content to sing His praises as He unfolds ineffable wonders and joys forever. We can trust God and express confidence He will make it all come out right in the end, even if we have to wait until the next life. Jesus is our example of patient suffering, enabled because "he trusted to him who judges justly" (I Peter 2:23) and "who for the joy that was set before Him endured the cross" (Hebrews 12:2).

Since we have the assurance of salvation, and can also trust in God, we too can rejoice in "an inheritance which is imperishable, undefiled, and unfading, kept in heaven for you ... In this you rejoice, though now for a little while you may have to suffer various trials" (I Peter 1:4,6). "But rejoice in so far as you share Christ's sufferings, that you may also rejoice and be glad when his glory is revealed" (I Peter 4:13; see also, Philippians 3:10).

When we pray, we can thank God for any response He makes, because it will be whatever is best for our over-all good. Philippians 4:6–7 urges: "Have no anxiety about anything, but in everything by prayer and supplication with thanksgiving let your requests be made known to God. And the peace of God, which passes all understanding, will keep your hearts and minds in Christ Jesus." Thanksgiving, which anticipates God's blessing expresses faith God will dependably answer our prayers by sending only what is truly good when we entrust the care to Him. Colossians 4:2 says: "Continue steadfastly in prayer, being watchful in it with thanksgiving," and see also, Ephesians 6:19, and Psalm 100:4. We must be watchful, for thanksgiving is to be a part of, and incorporated into our prayers, in implicit recognition that God's answer, whatever it may be, is praiseworthy because it accomplishes our highest good. We do not focus on what or how we would like God to answer, but only upon God's will, reflected in His choice of answer, as He forges our character and directs our future.

We become thankful for the privilege of being able to depend completely upon God's Sovereign control and benevolence, and yield to His perfect love, trusting His all-knowing wisdom. I Chronicles 29:11–13 observes: "Thine, O Lord, is the greatness, and the power, and the glory ... for all that is in the heaven and in the earth is thine ... and thou reignest over all ... now therefore our God, we thank thee, and praise thy glorious name." Prayer, with thanksgiving, is our submissive acknowledgement that whatever God answers is right, because He is in control, and all-wise. God has His reasons for delay or denial in answering prayer, and whatever worldly thing has been sacrificed in the quest for God will eventually be revealed as valueless in comparison to gaining Him.

The Bible says that our prayers of thanksgiving consecrate, by God's word, anything which is in Creation, including marriage and eating meat offered to idols: "For everything created by God is good, and nothing is to be rejected if it is received with thanksgiving; for then it is consecrated by the word of God and prayer" (I Timothy 4:4–5). Consistently, Colossians 3:17 teaches us to "do everything in the name of the Lord Jesus, giving thanks to God the Father through him."

If God has made His Sovereignty vulnerable by choosing to limit His power and cede some self-determination to man's free will, it can only be regarded as His expression of confidence in His ultimate power. Only because He is omnipotent would God venture to give man freedom, and tolerate man enjoying the dignity of collaboration by accepting salvation in Christ, or participating in evangelism, stewardship, intercessory prayer, and spiritual growth. God depends on believers to exercise freedom responsibly as part of His plan to redeem mankind and reveal His omnipotence. If God were not absolutely confident He could work the change in man with man's voluntary cooperation, then he would not have self-limited His awesome and plenary power, and risk men defeating His purposes by their freedom to act thoughtlessly, foolishly, or sinfully.

The good God sponsors may be independent of the suffering we experience, or may reside intrinsically within it. In any case, whatever God allows to reach us is praiseworthy either because He has intended and initiated it, or because He promises to use it to work good for us. Whether God originates our pain or transforms evil inflicted by another free being to a good result, we can give thanks because a Providential Father is diverting suffering to good, and will sustain us in overcoming it, either here or Hereafter.

GOD'S POWER AS SELF-LIMITED

God may intentionally afflict man for a variety or reasons, which we shall shortly examine. But we ought not proceed from God's occasional use of suffering to train or correct men, to a universal principal of divine involvement in the minutiae of life. Just because God is able to schedule and coordinate billions of contingent and random acts; to direct and divert nature to accomplish His objectives; to motivate and persuade voluntary acts by men; and even to use Satan's demons to serve His benevolent purposes, it does not follow that God has done so in a particular instance.

Because God is all-powerful it does not mean He has actively exercised complete control, sovereignty, and domination over every operation of creation, or over every detail of one's life. Quite often, God takes what Satan and men have woven for evil into the human tapestry, and ultimately re-weaves it into the beauty of His loving purposes. The initiation may not have been the will of God, but by the time its effects reach us, His Sovereign power has transformed evil and suffering into a benevolent instrument impacting our lives. Any incident which God permits in our lives is assimilated into His plans, adapted to His good purposes; adopted as His own arrangement, whether He initiated it or not, and is perfected by God's use of ordinary occurrences and natural processes.

God may appear to use evil as His agent to accomplish good purposes, but what He does defines what is good; and He transforms the evil intentions perpetrated by free agents into good results for those who love Him. He does not necessarily calculate, intend, or orchestrate every suffering that transpires in the world, but simply re-directs the evil caused by other free beings to good purposes and results. In this process, His Sovereignty is absolute, because He continues to guard His children and limit the severity of what reaches us, commensurate with our resources to endure it. He always provides a way of escape from our travails (I Corinthians 10:13).

It is certainly comforting in the midst of pain to believe that God's Sovereignty involves Him in every particular of a believer's life, and He has visited misfortune for some benign purpose. However, faith in God's Providence to modify evil originating with others into good for His children can contribute to our consolation, peace and assurance as much as supposing every evil which befalls us is intended, planned and authored by God for our ultimate and supervening good.

God need not cause suffering in order to re-work it for good. Because He is Sovereign, He can work good out of what is intrinsically evil and independently caused. Because God transforms evil into good, we ought not conclude that God <u>contrives and initiates</u> what can only be genuine evil to accomplish good purposes. All the comforts and accomplishments of God's Sovereignty and Providence are equally evident, plenary and enjoyable, whether we regard our suffering as initiated and intended by God, or recognize that God allows and tolerates suffering which originates with free beings in His creation, but which He always transforms to ultimate good for His faithful.

We will shortly examine the reasons why God allows freedom, and conclude that freedom necessitates the opportunity to choose wrongly, if freedom is to have any meaning. And it is the wrongful or corrupt exercise of freedom by men and demons, which produces much of the evil and suffering in Creation. God's Sovereignty remains absolute, yet self-limited in that God has ceded, yielded or assigned some of His power and authority to other free beings by giving men genuine freedom of choice, which is capable of inflicting harm on oneself or others.

As developed in the next Chapter, it is impossible to ignore the blessing of freedom, and the reality that God allows man to defy and frustrate God's intent for man's highest good. When God withdraws His direct control in the interest of freedom, evil can result. God is light, and we define darkness as the absence of light. God is good, and evil is the absence of good. God is life, and death is the absence of life. Still, freedom is such a blessing for man, that God absents His control over human free choice. Evil exists independently of God when perpetrated by other free beings. For, in creating beings with free will, God submits His omnipotence to the possibility of defeat by man's disobedient resistance to his legitimate empowerment in free choice.

Because God allows evil to exist in His Creation, we ought not conclude that His tolerance is equivalent to His intention to work evil. His permission of suffering is not tantamount to His creation or infliction of it. In fact, several reasons argue against God being the author of evil, or of every transaction, including directing Satan to provoke men to evil. There are some acts so inherently evil, venal, or corrupt that it is impossible to conceive they originated with God, the repository of love and goodness. Consider the perverted clergyman who, with reckless indifference sexually violates or tortures young children. What of the vicious serial rapist who then blinds and disfigures his victims permanently by wantonly throwing acid in their eyes so they cannot identify him? Is there the slightest possibility that God could have inspired such heinous wickedness for any good purpose? How can we attribute these objectively contemptible acts to a perfect, good God who hates sin and commissioned His only begotten Son to die for that sin, so that sinners might be saved? God finds sin so repulsive that He turned away even from Jesus when He was laden with mankind's sin on the Cross (Mark 15:34). There are genuine evils resulting from free acts apart from God.

How can we impute to God those deplorable atrocities for which we would condemn ordinary humans to prison and death? We know how scandalous and contemptible sin is because God has identified it for us in His Word, and called us to shun iniquity and pursue holiness because He is holy (Leviticus 11:44). We sojourn in an alien land where we are tempted, not by God, but by the world, the flesh, and the devil, and we sin against God when we freely succumb to temptation. There are authentically evil things, and if they originated with a perfectly Holy God, it would constitute a house divided, which could not stand (Matthew 12:25).

Attributing absolute Sovereignty to God, in which we assume He intends and designs every event in creation, down to the smallest detail, in order to deny free will, leads to ridiculous conclusions about God's endorsement of evil. Why would God call you to holiness through avoiding evil, and transform you into a new spirit being capable of resisting evil, and then visit what can only be regarded as nefarious evil upon you? It is difficult enough to understand why God tolerates evil in His universe for freedom's sake, but it is preposterous to argue that He designs evil for his children. The real problem with defending a concept of total Sovereignty which admits of no freedom to creatures, but insists on God intending every event and occurrence, is that it forces us to attribute really evil acts to God.

Yet, because God is perfectly good, He can have nothing to do with actual evil, which is a reality in creation, and has existed conceptually since God identified the tree of knowledge of good and evil in the Garden of Eden (Genesis 2:17). God told Adam to dress and "to keep" the Garden of Eden (Genesis 2:15), which meant to guard it. In the same sense, after the fall of Adam, the Cherubim and flaming sword were placed by God at the Garden to protect or "keep the way of the tree of life" (Genesis 3:24), by guarding it. Evil was a threat to Edenic bliss from the outset, and Adam failed to guard his charge against the evil temptation of Satan. Scripture relates that evil emerged and actualized in Creation by the Fall of Adam, which brought sin and death into the world to all men and creation (Genesis 3:15; Romans 5:12,19; 8:20–22). God then verifies His intent to restore total good to Creation by abolishing the devil, sin, death, pain, and mourning in the new, eternal heaven and earth (Revelation 20:10; 21:4). Thus, it is inconceivable God could have <u>intended</u> to introduce or establish evil in His Creation.

If God's Sovereignty requires Him to calculate every incident intentionally, and free choice is eliminated, we are left with the illogism that He created Lucifer nearly perfect, while simultaneously intending him to evolve into an evil Satan. He would have created the angelic host with an initial purpose to have one-third of them fall with Satan, so they can burn in flames for all eternity; an odd reward for instruments appointed to execute God's ordained purposes. Indeed, unless freedom was a reality, there could be no just punishment imposed for disobedient evil, since it was all performed at a Sovereign God's behest. If God allows no free acts of rebellion in derogation of His absolute Sovereignty, then all things Satan does — his lies, thefts, and murders — are directed by God, divinely appointed and apportioned as He allows, to accomplish evil objectives. All this smacks of some whimsical cosmic diversion of a god amused by his creature's perverseness, rather than the acts of our righteous God Who changes not, and calls us to holiness.

Likewise, if we regard absolute sovereignty as meaning God alone decides and intimately controls even the smallest detail of every incident in history, then it must mean God planned the Fall of man intentionally. If God originates everything purposely, then He has also sanctioned and adopted as His own act and purpose all suffering inflicted by one man against another. The idea of God intending man to perform evil is contrary to God's good and loving nature, and violates God's declared plan for harmony in His Creation, and obedience in His children. It violates God's revealed character to think that He planned the Fall of man by imposing conditions for obedience which He had to know would not be realized or fulfilled by Adam.

An absolute sovereignty which denies free choice to men confounds the freedom we all know experientially. I am not free to do all things, such as lifting a large truck off the ground by my own strength, but I can decide whether I will stand or sit, stroll or race, play baseball or basketball. It is preposterous to think that God is involved in whether I wear a brown or blue suit on Tuesday, or would occupy His mighty intellect with hundreds of other daily, inconsequential acts. These are decisions He can and has entrusted to the free choice of man. As we shall see in the next Chapter, he values freedom so much that he even entrusts the decision about personal salvation to human choice and response.

We have seen God's concern and benevolence toward Creation, and especially toward faithful men; for He numbers the hairs on every head, and knows or wills when even a sparrow falls to earth (Matthew 10:29–39). He knew us before we were formed in our mother's womb, and His foreknowledge encompasses every incident in creation throughout time. He intervenes in answer to prayer and on His own initiative, to guide our steps and deliver us from worldly perils. Yet, we cannot infer from His control over life or death, as He measures our days (Psalm 39:4), that He is concerned with whether a sparrow flies north or south on any given day, or whether a man enjoys swimming or jogging as a diversion.

Certainly, God calls men to priestly vocations, and anoints them with spiritual gifts for ministry (2 Timothy 1:11, 14). He persuades an Ananias to seek out Saul of Tarsus to facilitate his becoming St. Paul (Acts 9:10–17). Assuredly, God directed Philip to seek out and assist the Ethiopian Eunuch in his conversion (Acts 8:26–32). But it does not follow that God directed random, insignificant actions by Ananias or Philip on the other days of their lives.

Even if God exercised direct control over Moses', Joseph's, and Esther's lives, it does not follow He is concerned with every event in the lives of those multitudes who will never rule Israel, Egypt, or Persia. Moses, Noah, Abraham, Joseph, David, Jonah and Job were chosen for significant positions of responsibility, requiring God's detailed attention and regulation of events in lives He used to accomplish significant purposes. St. Paul may have needed a messenger of Satan to keep him from becoming proud about the abundance of revelations he received (2 Corinthians 12:7), but most of us, though we are privy to Bible knowledge, will not receive such full revelations, and may have no need for comparable regulation by satanic agency to preserve us from devilish pride.

Freedom means that God instructs His children about broad principles which are pleasing to Him, but entrusts discretion to them about when or how to act, what to do, or how best to serve Him within these guidelines. He provides a general rule of love, and furnishes examples of love in action, but leaves the execution and performance to us. He will answer specific inquiries for enlightenment, and is pleased when we totally rely upon Him for guidance, but he does not compel us to seek intricate instructions about trivial details. He gives us judgment, supernatural counsel, and direction for the asking. He speaks to us in His Word, our conscience, and in wise counsel from many holy advisors.

When we tell an unsaved person that God has a wonderful plan for His life, we should understand it applies to God's plan of redemption and salvation for sinners by grace through faith in Jesus, and not that God has ordained who is to be a waiter rather than a plumber in life; or precisely who must be your marriage partner. God may respond to prayerful invitation to make one's marriage in heaven, but choice is still left to the individual. Not everyone will be a physics professor or surgeon when limited in intelligence, aptitude or ability. But this does not mean God has rewarded one with skill but withheld it from another in every instance. These disparities are also likely to result from fortuitous genetic circumstances run rampant in an imperfect world. Does Jesus really have less love for one who is born with a paucity of brains or beauty than a more gifted individual whose good fortune inclines to pride and arrogance?

SOMETIMES SOVEREIGN INTENT: SOMETIMES HUMAN FREEDOM

God has revealed there are specific occasions He has used pain to accomplish His good purposes; or punished human evil, aware of the attendant suffering it involves; or trained and chastened His child to deter sin and foster obedient righteousness. The very fact God has revealed multiple explanations for His use of, or involvement in, pain and suffering indicates no single reason accounts for the suffering which originates with Him. At the same time, irresponsible satanic or human freedom also explains and is responsible for all of the evil and most of the suffering in the world.

God has revealed there are occasions He punishes men, cities, or nations for their unrepented evil. He declares He visits vengeance unto the third and fourth generation of those who hate Him (Exodus 20:5; 2 Kings 10:30). He destroyed all mankind because of its sin, except for Noah and his family, at the time of the Flood. He destroyed the Tower of Babel and scattered the nations, and He destroyed Sodom and Gomorrah for their evil. He directed King Saul to "utterly destroy" the Amelekites, and then deposed Saul from reign when he disobeyed the command. The Old Testament assaults of Assyria, Babylon, Chaldea and Egypt upon Israel were instituted by God to chasten the nation in its sin and turn its attention back toward God for mercy and reconciliation.

Nevertheless, the fact that God sometimes punishes nations and men for their sins does not mean that every catastrophe, pain, or suffering is intended by God. Jesus said the Galileans whose blood Pilate had mingled with their sacrifices were not "worse sinners than all the other Galileans, because they suffered thus" (Luke 13:2). And the eighteen persons who died when a tower in Siloam fell on them, were not "worse offenders than all the others who dwelt in Jerusalem" (Luke 13:4). Jesus explains that God did not visit birth defects upon a baby born blind to punish him or his parents (John 9:3), but to glorify God upon his deliverance by Jesus.

Soldiers in a platoon wiped out by enemy fire may be random victims of war, rather than sinners deserving punishment and targeted by God for annihilation at that moment. Cancer and AIDS are more likely to be accidents of a creation wounded by sin, transmitted by human acts, than be punishments meted out by God to the truly evil and rebellious. The winter storm which suddenly descends upon the high Alps and annihilates a party of mountain climbers does not necessarily originate in God's intent to punish evil-doers, but may be a blind or casual accident of nature, rather than a causal 'act of God', literally orchestrated by Him.

There are times the collapse of a bridge or building, or the mechanical failure of a jet plane carrying hundreds of people is attributable to human negligence, rather than God's intent to assemble precise victims for the moment of catastrophe. Terrorist attacks on innocent civilians arise out of human hate, envy, and vengeance, and are not necessarily planned by God as a wake-up call to repent and faithfully return to Him. The bravery of passengers disarming a hijacker at the risk of their own lives, or the selflessness of rescuers rushing into a burning building may glorify God by example, but are not likely to have been orchestrated by God initially for that purpose.

A crazed sniper haphazardly shooting strangers from afar cannot be deemed God's messenger. In fact, if his defense was "God told me to do it," we would automatically argue his insanity if he believed it. For, we know God does not provoke such things.

If every misfortune were sent by God, then because every person in affliction deserves his punishment and has done something to incur God's displeasure, we may as well trip a blind man, or shove a lame man to the ground, to help God's teaching along. It would be wisdom to thus side with God in reprisal for the misdeeds of sinners, for to help such a one contradicts and inhibits God's administration of correction. Likewise, a baby's crying should never be indulged by any show of concern, since God has begun to teach her righteousness through distress. No matter how much we might wish to intervene to assist our child in a predicament, we ought not. For, these difficult circumstances must be from God, Who is using them providentially to supplement our child's training, necessitated by our deficient methods and efforts.

The Scriptures teach that God sometimes uses Satan and demons to act as His agents under His direction. St. Paul's thorn in the flesh was a messenger of Satan sent to temper any exultation in the abundance of revelations divinely imparted to him (2 Corinthians 12:7). The early Church used Satan as an agent to chasten sinners and drive them back toward God and the safety of the Church (I Corinthians 5:5; I Timothy 1:19–20). It is possible, as suggested by philosophers, that God sometimes uses Satan to expose man to temptation, since there is no real choice in obedience without temptation to sin; or so that man's perception of evil can be usefully contrasted with righteousness.

God sometimes looses Satan as His instrument to test or challenge believers, so we can discover how reliable or weak our faith is, and strengthen our faithfulness by divine power, where necessary. Yet, whether Satan has initiated evil or God has employed him as an agent, Satan's eternal torment will be to understand that the evil by which he meant to destroy a believer's faith was in fact fitting man with Godly character for eternity, fashioned by a Sovereign God's loving and transforming hand.

We know there are times God contrives measures to chasten and train us for our benefit and good, which will produce suffering as part of the instructive process. Discipline, which originates with God, can be embraced with joy because it orders our steps (Psalm 37:23), and transforms us to the image of Christ, "changed into his likeness from one degree of glory to another" (2 Corinthians 3:18). When God actually guides and trains us, resistance or resentment is futile and until we respond, we will continue to feel the pain, as Jesus pointed out to Paul: "it is hard for thee to kick against the pricks" (Acts 9:5, KJV).

Yet, most suffering does not originate with God. If we will but recall our own contemptible, natural inclinations, there will be no question that unsaved and backslidden men also have the power by their own free act to inflict suffering and persecution upon others. Moreover, Jesus has revealed that Satan is the true author of sickness and disease (Luke 11:14–18; Acts 10:38), and is a thief and murderer who "comes only to steal and kill and destroy" (John 10:10; see also, Matthew 12:26–28; Mark 3:23–26; and John 8:44). A mathematician might say that Satan divides and subtracts, while Jesus adds and multiplies.

Yet, if we deny that God has allowed freedom to men and Satan, we will wrongly attribute satanic and human inflictions of pain to the will of God. Then, carried to its extreme we will regard suffering fatalistically, as the Moslems do, and become resigned to accept it because we believe it is God's will and must be borne with patience, apathy, and submission. We will do nothing to alleviate its severity or inequity. "Islam" literally signifies submission to God's will, doing nothing to frustrate, avoid, resist, or overcome it. We would think we are staying in God's will by stoically accepting, entering into, and fully experiencing every pain and deprivation because we believe God has graciously sent it.

What is required is discernment, gained by prayers of inquiry into what is God's will. We ought not confuse God's grace in transforming evil into good; with belief God has intended evil. We can be truly blessed when we are persecuted for Jesus' and righteousness' sake, for then "our reward is great in heaven" (Matthew 5:10–12). But we ought not confuse God's corrective grace with attributing evil to Him, nor believe He authors every temptation simply because He provides with the temptation: "the way of escape that you may be able to endure it" (I Corinthians 10:13).

God's character prevents Him from using Satan as His agent to tempt men to evil and sin, although God allows Satan liberty to test or try men's faith in the world, even though Satan intends to turn tests and trials into temptations. Sin is defined as doing what God has commanded man not to do (Romans 7:7). The fact that God will test a believer's faith, as He did with Abraham, who was called to sacrifice Isaac, does not mean God tempts men to sin. James 1:13–15 is emphatic on the point: "Let no one say when he is tempted, 'I am tempted by God'; for God cannot be tempted with evil and he himself tempts no one; but each person is tempted when he is lured and enticed by his own desire. Then desire when it has conceived gives birth to sin; and sin when it is full-grown brings forth death." Desire is indulged by a free will, choosing to yield to temptation to evil; rebelliously doing that which God forbids.

Certainly, there are times God has used affliction to guide events in the life of an anointed person to accomplish some designated objective and purpose of God. Suffering and exposure to evil forces accompanied the journey of every prophet and New Testament Apostle. Esther was in danger when she interceded with King Ahaseurus on behalf of her people, the Jews, yet Mordecai told her: "who knoweth whether thou art come to the kingdom for such a time as this?" (Esther 4:14)

It is conceivable that in God's Providence He determined in advance that Moses be rescued from the river; that his sister would be present when the basket was recovered by Pharaoh's daughter; that his mother would be summoned to act as nurse, all to protect and prepare Moses for his anointed role in God's plan for Israel (Exodus 2:4–9, 12–15). But by what stretch of logic can we argue that Moses' killing of an Egyptian was ordained by God? To provoke his flight from Egypt? Surely God had means at His disposal to transplant Moses, other than instigating a murder, in absolute contravention of His Commandment not to kill. It is far more likely the sins of Old Testament saints have been disclosed to confirm God's gracious forgiveness of the sins to which all humans in every age succumb.

It is possible God orchestrated the betrayal of Joseph into slavery by his jealous brothers to send him to Egypt, but it is also possible the brothers were not prompted by God, but chose to harm Joseph on their own initiative, out of envy. Joseph recognized: "God sent me before you to preserve you a posterity in the earth, and to save your lives by a great deliverance. So now it was not you that sent me hither, but God … ye thought evil against me; but God meant it unto good" (Genesis 45:7,8,20). God's actions in "sending" and "meaning it" for good are as consistent with transforming evil originating with others into good, after the fact, as with God initiating or orchestrating the brothers' wrongdoing.

It is possible that God contrived to imprison Joseph in order to strip him of all pride and self-reliance in preparation for his eventual responsibilities and service in Egypt. But He may also have converted the evil treacheries initiated by Potiphar's wife by re-working them into good. If we assert that God's Sovereignty requires Him to author every human activity, then God would have driven Potiphar's wife to lust, adulterous impulses, and lying about Joseph.

Not only are these sinful acts despised by God, and therefore inconsistent with His nature, but if God manipulated everything she did, God would have relieved her of responsibility for her illicit passion, whims and every evil she did (Genesis 27:24–26; 39:7–20). In fact, even Satan would be exonerated from responsibility for the evil he incites, if God has orchestrated it.

To what end would God have inspired David's adulterous lust for Bathsheba and the murder of Uriah, her husband, when God immediately condemned David's conduct through the prophet, Nathan (2 Samuel 12:1–7), and punished David with the loss of his son (2 Samuel 12:18)?

Must we conclude that St. Paul's imprisonment and confinement of his ministry was intended by God to teach him some lesson at the end of his anointed service, or were they more likely evils perpetrated by wicked men, chronicled and preserved as an illustration for us of St. Paul's faithful endurance under the worst circumstances, by God's grace? Whether God originated it, or evil men victimized Paul in the corrupt exercise of their freedom, God was able to transform imprisonment into an encouraging example for us. It is not necessary, simply to preserve intact the power of God, to assume that Sovereignty overrules every free choice of evil men.

It is not reasonable to conclude that God orchestrated all the suffering inflicted upon them, or sins which occurred in the lives of Moses, Joseph, and David to prepare them for their unique position in history. Neither is it reasonable to conclude that sin exists so God can demonstrate the exercise of His grace in the sweet forgiveness and merciful release of sinners from guilt. St. Paul repudiated this view at Romans 6:1–2: "Are we to continue in sin that grace may abound? By no means! How can we who died to sin still live in it?" It is far more reasonable to assume that God's love turns man's iniquity to good despite sin, when sin is repented. We can trust in the Lord's goodness and power that He will restore our righteousness and rectify all wrongs committed by us (I John 1:9), or inflicted by others. We need not assume that evil originates with Him, so He can transform it into good, simply to deny independent human freedom.

We must recognize there are many times God uses adversity and affliction as mechanisms to create Godly, spiritual character in believers. Pain is lovingly applied by a caring Father so we can grow in faith and love through these liberating and strengthening travails, as they cleanse us of all self-centeredness and develop the spiritual fruit of love for fellow sufferers.

Suffering which originates because of our faith in Christ, or which we consecrate to Christ, becomes a blessing when it helps us to know Him (Philippians 3:10), and become aware of what agonies Christ bore as our substitute out of infinite love for us. Sharing suffering as He did, gives us not only insight into the depths of His love for us, but also His faithfulness and obedience to God on our behalf. God is honored and glorified when our faith, love, and obedience is thus inspired. Moreover, Jesus is one with His Church (Matthew 25:40; Luke 10:10; John 15:18–21), and He equates persecution of His Church with persecution of Him (Acts 9:1, 4–5). Hence, we not only comprehend what He suffered on the Cross, but also His ongoing compassion for affliction in His Body, the Church, because He feels what His Church endures in every generation when it is persecuted.

In turn, this understanding of what Jesus feels over the suffering of Christians makes us more compassionate for the healing and salvation of other men. We can "complete what remains of Christ's afflictions for the sake of His body, that is the Church" (Colossians 1:24), and make our suffering more efficacious as we translate it to intercessory prayer and comfort for others (2 Corinthians 1:5–7).

We can regard suffering as a blessing because the Bible promises reward for such faithfulness by glorification in the next life (Romans 8:17; 2 Timothy 2:12). Finally, we can rejoice in suffering as it refines, strengthens, and proves our faith (I Peter 1:6–7), and purifies and disciplines the family of God (I Peter 4:17–18), all of which manifest God's great love and concern for us.

God chastens, chastises, and trains us in His way of spirituality by abrasive measures to purify our transformation to gold, and by blows of hammer on chisel to shape our features into the character of Jesus (Hebrews 12:6,10). In time, with a little irritation, God makes a pearl out of a sand particle in an oyster, and muscles are strengthened by their resistance to force. God may impose delays in receiving blessings to advance the virtues of patience, hope and perseverance, which are the result of trials (Romans 5:3–5). Steadfastness will develop you to "be perfect and complete, lacking in nothing" (James 1:4). God may use humiliation and crushed pride to cultivate a truly humble spirit of submission to the Lord. God may withdraw prosperity to remind us that blessing is not found in the abundance of possessions, but in the regulating of one's desires by temperance. We may learn that heightened anticipation of a single blessing temporarily withheld can exceed the aggregate pleasures of many gifts received indifferently.

We do not deny the reality of pain, nor rejoice as masochists in every trial, but in the fact God works eternal, spiritual good to produce what He wills through the pain of suffering. We do not celebrate the fact of pain, but the opportunity for growth introduced by pain.[51] If pain alerts us to some malfunction which needs treatment, then suffering gives us occasion to respond and transform an unpleasant situation into a positive experience — to work beneficial change in our attitudes and relationships with God and men.

When God uses pain to chasten a believer, He means to produce joy over one's progressive transformation to the image of Christ. We rejoice because God cares enough to force our spiritual growth by the infliction of pain, while investing us with the dignity of participation in the process. Stress and arduous effort are intrinsic to the learning process, and growing pains can accompany spiritual as well as physical maturing and proficiency. More, innate qualities in a process with a potential for harm may have been created or caused by God, without His intending misfortune to befall man. God created the law of gravity for benevolent purposes, and the law can operate to cause a man to fall to his death, but God does not necessarily intend an accidental fall and its harmful consequences from the blind functioning of the law.

Scripture reveals that God institutes certain occurrences which cause pain and suffering, so that He might be glorified by demonstrating His love and mercy in healing and deliverance. The man blind from birth was born that way, not to punish him or his parents, but that the healing "works of God might be made manifest in him" (John 9:3). When Jesus delayed in healing Lazarus, his death was allowed so that his resurrection by Jesus might cause beholders to believe Jesus was sent by God (John 11:42).

There are times God plans or uses the misfortune we see in another to prompt our appreciation of our own good fortune in having been spared bearing such a cross. God can turn another's suffering into a boon for us when we become appreciative and thankful for our own blessings previously received but taken for granted. Another's pain may be intended to strengthen our resolve of faith because we witness affliction nobly endured by another's unwavering faith in God, despite his pain.

Yet, God's occasional planning of such suffering does not mean He plans every such occurrence every time. Deformed babies are still produced by random, genetic distortions, and not specifically manufactured by God so He can infuse His strength into parents who must endure the hardships of rearing a dependent child. Every catastrophe has not been plotted by God to make us appreciate the urgency of making a decision for Jesus, or witnessing that need to others. God can use dreadful events, which occurred without His intent or design, to remind all survivors of man's need for God to deliver them from evil, but He can accomplish this same result when evil occurs independently, without instigating it.

God has also revealed He uses suffering to stifle self-sufficiency and elicit trust, reliance and dependence upon His goodness and benevolence. Once He has captured our attention, we can be blessed by renewed righteousness and fellowship with Him. However, His quondam use of misfortune for this purpose, does not mean he always authors misfortune, or has sanctioned the evil independently worked by free beings. It is true that faith is not fully tested until we have been thrust into totally helpless circumstances, where our only resource for deliverance is total reliance on God's mercy by divine intervention. Sometimes, God can inflict grief or anguish to remind you of your need for Him and His longing for you. God can also use dire circumstances beyond our control, created by others, to compel our turning to Him for help in our desperate need. There are no atheists on the battlefield, but that does not mean God has orchestrated wars or authored every misfortune to turn our attention to him and crystallize our faith under pressure.

A panic-stricken parent, who has just lost his toddler in a crowded mall, will quickly turn to God for help. The anguished wife will beseech the Lord for assistance when advised that her husband is en route to the hospital following a horrible accident. Such occasions give God a unique opportunity to show He is our Deliverer in these trying circumstances, but he can use these incidents to attract our attention when they occur through human carelessness, without designing them to provoke our return to Him.

It is comforting to know that we can rejoice when a dead saint in Christ has graduated to his blessed reward of eternal bliss in the presence of the Lord, and that we will be re-united with him in Christ for all eternity. However, taking comfort in the fact our saved ones are with God does not necessarily mean He has killed a busload of children in a highway accident because He yearns for their immediate presence in heaven; not when a thousand years are as a day to the Lord (2 Peter 3:8).

If a tornado or volcano wipes out a town or sinks an ocean liner, God may use the incident as a reminder of life's transience and man's total need to depend on God. Worldly annihilations pale in significance when compared to the consequences of eternal destruction for unbelieving rebels. Tragedy may inspire survivors to give immediate heed to the Gospel of Christ, by recognizing eternal damnation in hell is worse than any earthly catastrophe or worldly privation. But this does not mean God initially prepared every misfortune to bless survivors with fresh insights and revelations of the penalty for sin.

Personal suffering is intentionally sent for the therapeutic purpose of letting us know Jesus better by experiencing, reacting, and developing appreciation for the limitless depths of His sacrificial love, comfort, and deliverance. Suffering is benevolent when it helps us learn that having Jesus in this world is to have everything. One of the most precious blessings we receive through suffering is to appreciate that Jesus' friendship and salvation are all that matter, even when one has lost all earthly honors and possessions. We can be thankful He works good out of every experience He allows to reach us, and that He cares enough to pursue us by any means.

God can transform tragedy into good by driving survivors back to Him for comfort, strength, and wisdom. However, we need not embrace the extreme view that God instigated nazi death camps for the benign purpose of reminding survivors of their terrible need for God to transform and deliver them from evil. Nor need we believe God initiated suicide bombings to remind us that unsaved, rebel destroyers abound in the world, and believers must redouble their efforts to carry out the Great Commission, and witness to those so desperately in need of conversion, redemption, and newness in Christ.

God has far gentler methods of instruction to push the redeemed closer to God in appreciation, gratitude, and thanksgiving for His abundant grace, especially by promising to provide an eternity free from pain or sorrow. There are no doubt times God can arrest the attention of sinners only by the persuasions of fear, but that does not mean every misfortune is lovingly bestowed by a didactic Creator who has no softer way to train us in love, humility, patience, and selflessness.

A God wise enough and powerful enough to create the universe is wise and powerful enough to deliver His creatures from worldly concerns. If we are perplexed by affliction, it may not be so much a matter of God keeping us in darkness, as our inability to receive the light, even as Moses could not look directly upon the Shekinah glory of the Lord (Exodus 34:20). Job is an example of how we should respond to afflictions which beset us, with total trust in God, since man's ignorance of God's operations both commands and commends total reliance upon His goodness, knowledge, love, and power. Job recognized he came into the world with nothing, and would leave the same way. Anything in between was a gift from God. What God gives will always return to Him, sooner or later. Our focus ought not be on the source or reason for suffering, but upon God's re-fashioning of it, and man's proper response to it. How God does it, how He adjusts, re-constructs, and orchestrates each need and tolerance, is His work. Man's part is unwavering faith in God's ability to make things right eventually. Our gratitude is for constraints, by and through the love of Christ, and the transforming power of the Holy Spirit, unto obedience.

CHAPTER 5

BLESSINGS HAVE INHERENT POTENTIAL FOR HARM

"For freedom Christ has set us free: stand fast therefore, and do not submit again to a yoke of slavery."

- Galatians 5:1.

Often, God's blessings themselves, such as exercising freedom of choice, intrinsically bear the seeds of adversity when wrong choices are made. If man's joy lies in submission to God in order to know Him, then man must choose to respond to God's call, or refuse to do so at his peril. With freedom, the man who refuses to accept conviction of his sin, to acknowledge his guilt for sin, or embrace God's grace, remains incapable of accepting forgiveness, turning to repentance, seeing his need for a Saviour, or seeking salvation freely offered by God in Christ.

Because man has free will, every blessing is two-edged. God exalts us by giving all men freedom to choose, even if wrong choices work harm contrary to God's intent or man's best interests. There must be something very special about freedom which explains why God tolerates and honors His gift to man, even when an individual employs freedom of choice to his own destruction, by perversion of God's purposes. You know the purpose of a car is to provide safe transport to one's destination, and the car's function can foolishly be wasted by using it as a battering ram, which results in the car's destruction by its own motion. Likewise, life's principal purpose and opportunity are not collision, but transport to God's presence, to know God, and find salvation in Christ — not to rebel by disobedience that puts us out of God's way and collides with His will. The purpose of human life can also be foolishly corrupted by man's use in sinful pursuits which result in human destruction.

Every spiritual process carries its own, inherent potential to cause suffering if man chooses wrongly, and perpetrates hurtful consequences. Yet, God has established and allowed voluntary human collaboration in divine endeavors, despite the potential for harm to self or others, because of the transcendent value in preserving man's participation in the process. While we are unsaved, we are unregenerate and free to perpetrate evil by our constituent nature, and wrong choices carry inherent, hurtful consequences of suffering in the world. Because of His perfect goodness, God does not, and indeed He could not, desire us to do evil in our natural condition, so only human freedom which chooses wrongly can account for evil and its painful consequences before we are saved. Otherwise, we must attempt all sorts of intellectual contortions to attribute to God what is patently evil.

If God doesn't intend to cause suffering as part of the blessing of freedom, it is legitimate to ask why he doesn't eliminate or remove suffering from the operations of free choice. After we are saved, the very gifts of participation in divine processes vest us with freedom to obey God's will, or we can yield to temptations of the flesh and disobey Him. If we fail to do what He has entrusted to us, then consequences can be evil, and this is inherent in the very gifts of participation God bestows upon us, although originally designed only for good. For, God has expressed His love by according believers great responsibility for what we sow in His Kingdom.

For example, a saved Christian is called to cooperate in his own holiness, which is being developed in us by God. If we disobediently choose not to cooperate, we will not lose our sanctification or ultimate glorification, but our holiness can be retarded; our fellowship with God impeded; and our heavenly reward diminished while on earth. Grace spares us from having any responsibility for initiating or accomplishing our salvation in Christ, but it does require us, once saved, to collaborate in our progressive holiness unto glorification by remaining receptive to the Holy Spirit's transforming work: "For we are laborers together with God" (I Corinthians 3:9, KJV). We are saved solely by Christ, but once saved, we are to collaborate in actually conforming to our saved condition: "work out your own salvation with fear and trembling; for God is at work in you, both to will and to work for his good pleasure" (Philippians 2:12-13; and see I Corinthians 15:10).

Likewise a disciple of Christ is called to be a good steward and minister to the needs of others. Galatians 5:13 says: "For you were called to freedom, brethren; only do not use your freedom as an opportunity for the flesh, but through love <u>be servants of one another</u>." If we disobediently fail to do so, then the Body of Christ, as well as the unsaved, will be poorer for our idleness, passivity, and neglect.

We are also called to offer intercessory prayers for the needs of others, and our failure to obey may inhibit blessing which God has intended to be funneled through, or triggered by our petitions on behalf of others.

Too, we are called to bring the Good News of salvation in Christ to the unsaved, but if we faithlessly neglect to witness to others, then they remain in their natural condition, predisposed to sin and capable only of evil. Their incorporation into the Body of Christ may be delayed, or possibly forfeited by our failure to fulfill the obligations of the Great Commission. For, only by hearing the Word can a sinner be convicted, converted, and respond to God's grace (John 5:24; Romans 10:17; 2 Timothy 1:10; James 1:21).

Freedom also means that man is able to disregard God's guidance, and disobey God's commands, when his attention is captured by worldly allures, even if this results in evil consequences for himself and others. Still, God's purpose of freedom is to bless and allow a believer to cooperate and receive blessings based upon his obedience and submission to God.

GOD'S BLESSING OF DIGNITY THROUGH FREEDOM

Since God's gift of freedom carries with it the potential for suffering whenever a man chooses wrongly and acts to the harm of himself or another, it is proper to ask why God tolerates this aberrant sacrifice of earthly blessings and spiritual fullness of life. When God allows one blessing to be diminished in the interests of preserving some other value, such as freedom, we can only conclude that a loving God is promoting a higher purpose as more valuable and important. If freedom has the potential for suffering when abused by man, then God presumably regards freedom as a superior value. For, a good and perfect God intends only to bless His faithful children.

Since God never desires our harm, then His tolerance for man's imperfect use of freedom can only mean that He has some dominant purpose to promote and sustain the aggregation of individual dignity, which is expressed through freedom of choice. God so values human freedom and dignity of participation that he will not override their exercise, even at the risk of harm befalling one person at the hands of another. God's voluntary relinquishment of some control in the world to human and demonic freedom has allowed and tolerated the free acts of other beings to inflict persecution and suffering on believers in the world. So important is freedom that God even allows man's transfer to Satan of dominion over the earth, and tolerates the malfunctions which that produces, including birth defects, in a world groaning in travail under man's sin (Romans 8:22).

To preserve freedom God subordinates His desire that no individual suffer harm or loss, in order to achieve the higher collective good from maximum freedom under which all men can flourish. In God's economy of salvation a man is genuinely free to reject God's love; to renounce Jesus' salvation; to embrace stubborn rebellion and disobedience; and to pursue sin rather than holiness. The inquiry of this chapter asks what could make freedom such a supervening good that it even sacrifices lesser goods of self-preservation or individual salvation.

Because the reality of freedom is questioned from many sources, and because its authenticity is essential to an explanation of suffering, we take a moment to establish that freedom is a genuine blessing from God. At one extreme, some psychologists and environmentalists argue that man's actions are predetermined by the orientation imposed by one's environment, compelling him to act involuntarily in certain ways. Consequently, he ought not be held responsible for his actions.

Some geneticists argue that predispositions inherited from one's ancestors deny man freedom to resist inherent tendencies. They argue that if God fashioned our genetic structures or programmed our minds so that we have literally irresistible impulses or predispositions to act in certain ways, we could not be held responsible for acting as we do, any more than we can control our height or the color of our skin. As genetic tendencies and DNA constructs are uncovered, these have been asserted as a defense of irresistible impulse by kleptomaniacs, alcoholics, and homosexuals to justify their behavior on the ground, "God made me that way." If God pre-determined everything, and compelled every outcome, men would be truly pawns, lacking freedom against pre-destined propensities. Hereditary defects are not instituted by God, but are the effect of sin corrupting God's perfect creation. Consequently, they may contribute to man's propensity to sin, but do not overcome his free will to resist sin.

St. Paul says at Romans 7:23: "I see in my members another law at war with the law of my mind and making me captive to the law of sin which dwells in my members." Yet, even if there are genetic predilections to act in certain ways, God was always aware of these fleshly tendencies to sin, and still labeled stealing, drunkenness, and homosexuality as sins to be avoided by men. God confirmed human freedom by commanding men to refrain from sin, even though fleshly allures of which God was aware, would regularly tempt us to sin. God did not intend fallen man's natural proclivity to sin in the flesh, although freedom made man susceptible to sin, and Adam's original sin corrupted our flesh and introduced tendencies to sin into the world (Romans 5:12, 7:18).

There is another sense in which we commonly say that man is not free to act. Most men are not free, no matter how much they may desire it, to lift a truck off the ground, run a mile in less than a minute, be an Olympic Gold Medallist, or even to afford a year-long tour of the world. Thus, we say we are not 'free' to do these things when we mean we are not <u>able</u> to do them. However, we ought to avoid confusing lack of power or ability to do physical acts with the ability freely to make moral choices. Even natural man is free to desire to do what is right. The freedom to will or desire an act is different from the power or ability to do it. I can will to be saved for eternity, but lack the power to author my own salvation. I can will or desire, as St. Paul, to be righteous but lack the ability <u>to do </u>what is right, without supernatural intervention. I can lack the power to save myself from sin, but have the will power to choose freely to resist or respond to God's offer of salvation by grace through faith, by personal belief.

When we are saved, Jesus frees us from the penalty of sin (Hebrews 2:15), and from the power of sin. He has delivered us from slavery or subservience to sin by supernaturally enabling and empowering us to resist sin. Without Jesus, natural man lacks power or ability to be righteous, and lacks freedom to behave as God wills, because he is a slave of sin (John 8:34). This freedom which Jesus gives by deliverance from natural proclivities to sin in our fleshly nature, is as much a real investiture of freedom, as freedom to choose God willingly is enabled by the prevenient grace of God.

Jesus invests His disciples with genuine freedom in yet another way. Because God forgives and forgets the sins of believers, and cleanses the penitent of all unrighteousness because Jesus paid the penalty for us, we are freed from bondage to guilt and self-reproach for our sins. God's faithfulness in His promise to forgive and forget frees us to cooperate confidently and reliantly in our transformation to Christ-like holiness. We are free to accept slavery to righteousness; to be what God wants us to be; and act responsibly in obedience to God, for our own good.

Moreover, simply because God is omniscient, it is not necessarily because He has predetermined every act at the expense of freedom. He has the capacity to know the end from the beginning because He is all-knowing. It does not follow that He is all-knowing because He has willed, ordained, and pre-determined each and every occurrence in advance. His knowledge may well be because He can see down the corridor of time from His vantage, and observe future free acts of creatures to whom He has delegated true freedom.

Put another way, God's knowledge of the future is tied to His intent only if God actually ordains, controls, initiates, and orchestrates every condition and action involving man and Creation. However, if man is truly free, as strongly implied by God holding him responsible for his actions, then God may foresee the future from His vantage point in eternity. Yet, the event must still take place in time so that man's free choice has genuine opportunity and occasion to occur.

This means, for example, that God's test of Abraham's willingness to sacrifice Isaac was a real event, with Abraham's decision based upon his genuine free choice to submit. God's omniscience could foresee the result and know in advance that Abraham would proceed in faithful obedience, but the human decision still had to occur in time. Otherwise, such a test would have no significance if God orchestrated human response and manipulated man's choice in some meaningless charade.

Likewise, God had foreknowledge of Israel's reaction to the test of faithfulness in the wilderness, but Israel still had to reach the moment when the nation chose to respond and turn to God in obedience, or not. If Israel's response was not free, then the test would have been meaningless, and the punishment of wandering forty years as a consequence of choosing wrongly would not have been just. If God had controlled or directed their response, they could not have expressed a volitional act, nor justly been held responsible for grumbling and turning from God. God's perfect, advance knowledge of the event pre-destines its certain occurrence in the sense it will happen. But it does not pre-determine it in the sense God intends or coerces it, contrary to human freedom.

Romans 8:29-30 says of God that "those whom he <u>fore</u>knew he also pre-destined to be conformed to the image of his Son... And those whom he predestined he also called; and those whom he called he also justified; and those whom he justified he also glorified." However, the basic premise is based upon God's <u>fore</u>knowledge of a person's choice, upon which God then pre-destined them to be called, justified, and glorified. Consider. God has declared that every soul was already <u>known</u> to Him before it was created (Jeremiah 1:5, 29:11; Psalm 22:9, 139:13, 16; Job 31:15, 33:4, Isaiah 44:2). The Romans passage does not say God knew the elect, but <u>fore</u>knew their responsive decision which became predetermined in God's perfect knowledge, and led to salvation.

Predestinationists attach significance to the fact that in the passage, God's pre-destining precedes God's calling of an individual. However, this is also consistent with man's free response to God which predetermines the event in God's perfect foreknowledge. God's Word lifts up, informs, invites response, and empowers faith, enabling <u>all</u> men to be saved in Christ. When a man responds by faith, God enables, by calling or drawing him to, eternal salvation (John 1:12).

Some advocates of total sovereignty allow for no yielding of authority or relinquishment of power by God to any creature. They conclude that every occurrence in the universe is orchestrated, intended and ordained specifically by God, and that every act a man commits is planned and pre-determined by an all-wise and all-powerful God, so that man is not free to choose otherwise.

This view denying freedom of choice is not consistent with the Biblical revelation that God holds man responsible for his disobedience; that sin resides in the flesh and draws man to disobedience, but he is still free to resist or obey God. No doubt God looks down with compassion when human failure to behave as He has taught us, results in suffering for his children. Evil must be at least as much of an offense to God's moral order as it is to man's.[52] He must side with victims of evil, rather than the perpetrators, but our conclusion is that He does not always overrule human choices for evil, lest He destroy the very essence of freedom — choice. God has limited Himself, except in His fixed purposes involving redemption, and has chosen not to intervene in the world to take away our freedom, even though this leaves us free to harm one another. He has relinquished a part of His Sovereignty temporarily, to enrich human experience by freedom of choice.

SOVEREIGNTY ASSIGNS LIMITED POWER TO HUMAN FREEDOM

There are four aspects of freedom which God chooses to invest in men. The first freedom is the opportunity accorded every natural man to discern and desire what is right, and thereby choose God. God has revealed His existence in Nature. He has revealed in the law what He ordains as right. He has given every unredeemed man a conscience to discern right from wrong;

to apprehend the revelations of the Bible; and to recognize sin as violation of God's Law. The delusions which blind natural man to the revealed truths of God's Word (Matthew 13:13-15; Romans 11:7-10; and 2 Thessalonians 2:10-11), are imposed only after man has inveterately rejected these natural persuasions.

Without Jesus, no natural man can fulfill his will to do right because of his bondage to sin and Satan, but he is still free to desire what is right, even though he is incapable of always doing what he wills. God motivates and enables right choice by revealing His will; by convicting man of sin; by empowering repentance over sin; and providing faith to choose rightly (2 Timothy 2:25-26; Acts 11:18). God does not withdraw freedom, but persuades right choice by imposing accountability for wrong choices; by conviction of sin; and by revealing His loving kindness, which inspires attempts to obey and please God in gratitude and appreciation for His grace.

The second freedom accompanies the New Birth, when man is liberated from death, the eternal penalty of sin, which brings death and separation from God. The significance of our salvation and spiritual blessings Hereafter, as well as here, puts earthly concerns in proper perspective. Like Christian martyrs through the centuries, we can be fearless in the face of death because of our eternal security in Christ. "Thou wilt keep him in perfect peace, whose mind is stayed on thee: Because he trusteth in thee" (Isaiah 26:3).

This aspect of freedom given by God is derived from the certain knowledge that He has forgiven all our sins, because of the actual righteousness of Christ vicariously imputed to us, when we receive by faith His Atonement on the Cross for our sins. Micah 7:19 notes: "He will have compassion upon us;... and thou wilt cast all their sins into the depths of the sea." Psalm 103:3-12 gives assurance that God "forgiveth all thine iniquities... He hath not dealt with us after our sins... as far as the east is from the west, so far hath he removed our transgressions from us." It is a curious thing, but because of polarity or the axis of rotation, if you go far enough north on the globe, you will eventually start heading south. But if you head east, you go round and around, and in relation to North, you will never head west without reversing direction. (See also, Isaiah 38:17, and 44:22).

The third freedom God bestows on believers is from the compulsion to sin, by transformed character regenerated at one's New Birth by grace through faith in Christ. We may have entered the world with a sin-nature, but God transforms believers into New Men, able to resist sin, and possessing the very mind of Christ (I Corinthians 2:16). We can know, desire, and attain righteousness, and escape the worldly consequences of sin.

Our new, changed nature has given us freedom from sin, not to sin in reckless disregard of God's desires. For, we are free only when we reside in God's will, abiding in His Word and in a holy Christ, the Vine in Whom we are branches. The holiness of God's Law remains that to which we willingly aspire. But we are no longer in spiritual jeopardy if we fail to attain that objective, because God has forgiven us in Christ and empowered us to succeed if we keep striving obediently. A New Born man in Christ is transformed to the nature of Christ and freed from bondage to the law of sin in His flesh (Romans 7:23). He is still able to sin, but no longer under compulsion to sin as his life style. Thus, freedom intends you to fulfill your God-ordained purpose; rather than claim a license to do whatever strikes your fancy.

When we focus on faith, rather than works for salvation; and on God's love, rather than punishment to satisfy God's Justice, we find God's forgiveness flowing from God's grace and love. This forgiveness has freed believers from anxiety, sin-consciousness, and ongoing guilt for sin. Christ's sacrifice on the Cross was the perfect expression of God's perfect and total love for mankind. "There is no fear in love, but perfect love casts out fear. For fear has to do with punishment, and he who fears is not perfected in love" (I John 4:18). God's Justice prevents exacting the punishment for sin twice, when Jesus has already paid the penalty for our sins, and we have accepted Him by grace through faith.

God forgives and forgets our repented sins because of Jesus, and cleanses the penitent of all unrighteousness in the Blood of Jesus. We can be totally certain that God will not hold any sins: past, present, or future, against us when we are Born-Again followers of Jesus. Jesus atoned for every sin we would ever commit, and we had not yet perpetrated any of them when He redeemed us from sin 2,000 years ago. God rescues believers from even their self-inflicted suffering from sin, because the sin which creates your predicament now was forgiven long ago, and your faith in Christ can now embrace that reality.

God's deliverance by forgiving our transgressions is absolute and unqualified. His forgiveness is mirrored by His instruction to imperfect mortals to forgive others seven times seventy times (Matthew 18:22). How much greater and constant will be His perfect, infinite forgiveness? Yet, God's forgiveness comes with a condition, for it is predicated on our truly forgiving the trespasses of others against us (Mark 11:26; Luke 6:37).

A fourth aspect of freedom from guilt and sin-consciousness is derived from the ongoing forgiveness which God extends to believers on earth who continue to sin. If we backslide, despite our new nature and intent not to sin, we are assured of forgiveness and cleansing in the Blood of Christ — restored to righteousness; and this rids us of the millstone weight of sin-consciousness and guilt (I John 1:9). Isaiah 55:7 adjures believers: "Let the wicked forsake his way, and the unrighteous man his thoughts: and let him return unto the Lord, and he will have mercy upon him; and to our God, for he will abundantly pardon." God summons His people at Jeremiah 3:1,12: "yet return again to me, saith the Lord... Return, thou backsliding Israel, saith the Lord, and I will not cause mine anger to fall upon you; for I am merciful... and I will not keep anger for ever." Hosea 14:4 adds: "I will heal their backsliding, I will love them freely: for mine anger is turned away from him."

Peter denied Jesus three times, and yet was fully restored when he wept tears of repentance (John 21:19). Just as the father of the Prodigal Son restored him to full status, including material comforts, so God through Jesus will restore us to right relationship with Him, and every blessing and privilege as His children. We have a right to expect God, based on His own promises, to rescue us from our own folly, just as the Prodigal Son was fully reinstated after he repented and returned to his father.

We are freed from all earthly anxiety and concern because we are assured that God provides all our material needs of food, shelter and clothing when we "seek first the Kingdom of God" (Matthew 6:33). We need have no other earthly worries because a caring Christ lovingly shares and bears our burdens and you can "cast all your cares on him, for he cares about you" (I Peter 5:7). If we focus our thoughts on the Lord and trust His promises: "Thou wilt keep him in perfect peace, whose mind is stayed on thee; because he trusteth in thee" (Isaiah 26:3). This is so, especially if we focus on seeking righteousness: "And the work of righteousness shall be peace; and the effect of righteousness quietness and assurance for ever" (Isaiah 32:17).

Yet, forgiveness and relief from guilt have several caveats. The certainty of forgiveness is meant to reveal and celebrate the dependability of God's loving constancy, not to incite sinful presumption to take advantage of God's kindness by more sin (Romans 6:1). Nor can we be unforgiving toward others and expect our hard-heartedness to deserve God's forgiveness toward us. And confession implies genuine repentance and intent to turn from sin and toward God; to be obedient, do better, and be righteous, aided by His grace.

Unfortunately, the Scriptures do not directly explain why God continues to tolerate freedom when it can produce evil resulting from man's wrong choices. We must draw reasonable inferences about God's preferences from the passages which speak of and confirm the free choice men have to obey God. Secondly, a dire penalty is imposed for man's failure to obey God. This would accord with God's loving-kindness, goodness and Justice, only if man is truly free to choose right from wrong, and deserves the penalty of wrong choice. Third, as sentient beings, we are experientially aware of free choice. I can go back in or out of the door as often as I please, or not. If God were to dictate all my choices and compel my return and departure simply to amuse Himself, this would be inconsistent with His goodness and intelligence. To paraphrase Descartes' famous syllogism: "I choose willfully, therefore I am free."

Lastly, because the purpose of man is to glorify God, we should be able to verify and measure freedom by the extent it fulfills that purpose. If we can demonstrate that freely choosing God over evil constitutes man's loving recognition, appreciation, expression, and glorification of God's excellence, creativity, and glory, then we may apprehend one reason God tolerates freedom.

SCRIPTURE CONFIRMS THE REALITY OF FREEDOM

The reality of freedom was first confirmed when God allowed one-third of His angelic congregation to defect when they freely chose to follow Lucifer in rebellion (Revelation 12:3-9). God left them free to depart the heavenly sanctuary and proceed irretrievably toward destruction (2 Peter 2:4; Jude 6). God gives man the same freedom to disobey and rebel, even to his own harm, since such rebellion embraces and prefers sin, and initiates and deserves eternal damnation.

In the Garden of Eden God expressly vested freedom in man, "saying, Of every tree of the garden thou mayest freely eat" (Genesis 2:16). He intimated Adam's and Eve's genuine freedom to choose when He instructed them not to eat of the tree of knowledge of good and evil, lest they die (Genesis 2:17). God created man with freedom and was pleased, and pronounced that it was very good. Yet, in this perfect Creation, the potential for evil was intrinsic to this very good; and resident in the free will which God had given created beings. For, freedom of choice to obey allowed for wrong decisions, resulting from pride and aspiration to be like God: first in Lucifer, and then in Adam, which conflicted with, and overrode the creature's submissive obedience to God, the Creator (Isaiah 14:14; Genesis 3:5-6).

Adam's failure to choose rightly would constitute an irresponsible abuse of freedom, causing the Fall of man, and the entry of sin and death into Creation. The Fall is proof of man's freedom of choice, and this choice becomes the basis for God's Justice that any mis-use of freedom by departing from God's will, produces consequences which bring suffering and punishment. None of this was planned or intended by God; only tolerated as a possible, but intrinsic consequence, contingent upon man's wrong use of freedom.

It is illogical to believe that a God Who is love and loved His creature, Adam, and blessed him with His fellowship and dominion over all the earth, would have manipulated or intended Adam to sin and lose those blessings. Indeed, the existence of sin verifies free choice, since a holy God would not command or direct men to commit sin, "for God cannot be tempted with evil and he himself tempts no one; but each person is tempted when he is lured and enticed by his own desire" (James 1:13-14). Each of us confirms freedom every time we exercise our will and choose to sin, despite God urging us by His Word and the conviction of the Holy Spirit not to sin. This is not to ignore the reality of hereditary limitations, nor of environmental coercions and influences. But a believer in the Old Testament was always free to resist sin; confident of being sustained by God's power in righteousness, when it was sought by man.

The explanation why an all-wise, Sovereign God, foreknowing the consequences, might permit Adam to sin, is that God preferred and allowed Adam to have the blessing of freedom of choice, and with that genuine freedom came the inherent, unrestrained power to choose wrongly.

Nor is there any suggestion in Scripture that God provoked Cain to murder Abel, intending to accomplish some higher divine purpose, such as drawing Adam closer to Him to seek comfort in his grief. No, the first murder was the product of one man's frustration, jealousy and resentment of his brother, perpetrated by his own impulsive, free act of will.

God's call to faithfulness was ignored throughout the Old Testament. God gave the Antedeluvians 120 years to repent (Genesis 6:3), and during that time Noah probably preached repentance and faith, but won only seven converts, while the rest of mankind freely, but faithlessly, chose to reject God and pursue evil (Genesis 7:7). Man's freedom to reject God was also proved during the time of Elijah, when he could find only 7,000 men in all Israel who did not bow the knee to Baal (I Kings 19:8; Romans 11:4). John the Baptist attracted some followers, but Daniel, Isaiah, Jeremiah, and all the prophets who called men to righteousness, had insignificant impact upon their contemporaries. Jonah was able to convert all of Nineveh, and ironically he resented God's forgiveness and mercy upon the sinful Ninevites who freely repented and returned to God (Jonah 4:1).

The very fact that God repeatedly called the Israelites, our spiritual predecessors, to repentance, obedience, and holiness verifies human will and ability to choose rightly. For God does not tempt us with vain pursuits, or empty disciplines. Despite the enormity of any sin, man's change of mind, freely exercised, can claim God's offer to change His heart, and to "have mercy on whom He will have mercy" (Exodus 33:19; Romans 9:15). God reveals that if the wicked will freely choose to forsake his way, and the unrighteous man his thoughts, then "let him return unto the Lord, and he will have mercy upon him; and to our God, for he will abundantly pardon" (Isaiah 55:7). Likewise, Proverbs 28:13 says: "He that covereth his sins shall not prosper: but whoso confesseth <u>and forsaketh them</u> shall have mercy." "Whoso walketh uprightly shall be saved" (Proverbs 28:18).

Deuteronomy 30:19 also affirms free choice given by God: "I call heaven and earth to record this day against you, that I have set before you life and death, blessing and cursing; therefore <u>choose life,</u> that both thou and thy seed may live." Joshua 24:15 declares: "choose you this day whom ye will serve... but as for me and my house, we will serve the Lord." God accuses the wicked of corrupting their free choice at Isaiah 65:12: "when I called, ye did not answer; when I spake, ye did not hear; but did evil before mine eyes, and <u>did choose</u> that wherein I delighted not."

The history of Israel is a constant reflection of God's punishment imposed for the wrongful, but freely chosen, acts of the Jews. Clearly, God would not require an obedient response from man if God had denied man the power of choice.[53] On one occasion, after David disobeyed God by taking a census of Israel, and sought to repent, God even gave him a choice of three punishments for his penance (2 Samuel 24:12). So, on this occasion, at least, God did not pre-plan a specific penance for David, but entrusted it to human choice.

Jesus promises His disciples "will know the truth, and the truth will make you free... So if the Son makes you free, you will be free indeed" (John 8:32, 36). Galatians 5:1 adds: "For freedom Christ has set us free: Stand fast therefore, and do not submit again to a yoke of slavery" to sin. The New Testament speaks of human free choice, rewarded with salvation, or punished for rebellion by willful rejection of Jesus. Believers are called to "remember the predictions of the holy prophets and the commandment of the Lord", but scoffers "deliberately ignore this fact" (2 Peter 3:2, 5). Acts 7:51 refers to "stiff-necked people, uncircumcised in heart and ears, you always resist the Holy Spirit."

At Matthew 23:37-38 Jesus bemoans the infidelity of Jerusalem: "How often would I have gathered your children together as a hen gathers her brood under her wings, and you would not! Behold, your house is forsaken and desolate." 2 Peter 2:1 warns "of false prophets denying the Master who bought them." Luke 7:30 notes: "the Pharisees and lawyers who rejected the purpose of God for themselves." See also, John 3:18, 5:40, 12:37; Romans 1:18, 21, 10:21; 2 Peter 3:5; and Isaiah 65:2. These acts could not have occurred, nor been justly condemned without genuine human freedom to choose wrongly.

Jesus declares that He was anointed "to proclaim liberty to the captives" (Isaiah 61:1), and "where the Spirit of the Lord is, there is freedom" (2 Corinthians 3:17). It is hard to believe in the necessity of the Crucifixion and the substitutionary sacrifice of Christ, unless God had given free choice to man, and imposed responsibility for each personal decision. John 8:44 affirms man "wills" to do evil, because of his nature as a child of Satan.

God demonstrates the reality of human freedom by declaring that He has "no pleasure in the death of the wicked; but that the wicked turn from his way and live" (Ezekiel 33:11), and that it is His will all men be saved (I Timothy 2:4). Jesus asserts: "and I, when I am lifted up from the earth will draw all men to myself" (John 12:32). Yet, it is clear, although Jesus is attractive to most men, they are free to resist Him, reject God, and frustrate His intent they be saved. It started when God gave true freedom of choice to Adam in the Garden, with the simple direction to eat freely of every tree, "But of the tree of the knowledge of good and evil, thou shalt not eat of it" (Genesis 2:17). Free choice continued when God called Adam to Him in the Garden, immediately after Adam had sinned, but Adam freely chose to withdraw and hide from God (Genesis 3:8).

Men are free even to reject the faith which could save them. Jesus gathered only a "little flock" (Luke 12:32), and was rejected by most of the Jews He was sent to save. He forecast that only a few would find the narrow way of life in Him (Matthew 7:14). Even disciples who shared some knowledge of Jesus, were still free and able to depart the faith (John 6:66; I Timothy 4:1). Jesus also willed to do healing and good for His own townspeople, but their lack of faith impeded His intent: "And he did not do many mighty works there, because of their unbelief" (Matthew 13:58; and see also Mark 6:6 and Matthew 17:20).

All around us we see unbelievers who hear the Gospel, by which faith comes (Romans 10:17), and yet they choose freely to scoff and reject available faith, which is authored and offered by Jesus. Scripture reveals that rejecters of Christ are not saved, but lost for eternity (John 3:18). John 1:11-12 stresses the free act of receiving Jesus as Lord: "he came to his own home, and his own people received him not. But to all who received him, who believed in his name, he gave power to become children of God." See also, Luke 7:30; John 5:40, 7:17; Acts 7:51; and Romans 1:21-23.

The fact that a just God passes Judgment on the deeds and decisions of rebellious sinners who reject Jesus (Revelation 20:11-15), and honors their free choice to serve Satan, speaks volumes about the reality of human freedom. The Judgment of damnation would be unjust if it were not based upon man's genuine opportunity to exercise free choice and responsibility. For, freedom is synonymous with choice between alternatives. The sinner deserves the Judgment of damnation because he has chosen to resist and reject God's freely given, but exclusive way of salvation in Christ. Thus, each recalcitrant must bear the consequence of his choice as determined by the fairness of God's justice.

No matter how we might wish it were otherwise, we must accept this as the fate of stubbornly unrepentant sinners, on the authority of our loving Saviour. His sacrifice has made it all possible for men to avert destruction and enter the narrow door through faith in Him. If rebels continue to reject the way of Christ, the Lord, they have chosen to be judged harshly by their own insufficient works, and share the fate of ungodly multitudes in the time of Noah.[54]

The sinner deserves the Judgment of damnation because he has chosen to resist and reject God's freely given, but exclusive way of salvation in Christ. Free will must include the ability to respond in a different way from that prescribed by God. Freedom can avoid doing a particular act, even if it resists and frustrates God's will and desire. God's moral laws prescribe conduct which we should or should not do, and if we <u>ought to act</u> in a certain way, we should at least desire to act in that way. Jesus serves as our substitute for obedient response to God, and He is free for the taking by grace through faith. An unrepentant sinner is thus guilty of two acts of rebellion. First, he willfully chooses not to repent after he has disobeyed God by sinning contrary to God's commands. Second, he willfully spurns Jesus, Who is God's only provision for personally escaping the penalty of that sin. If God holds us accountable for how we act, then we must have a choice in acting rightly as God prescribes, "For he will render to every man according to his works" (Romans 2:6).

Jesus gives yet another indication that God has given men freedom, even if it frustrates God's will by their disobedience. Jesus teaches us to pray to the Father like this: "Thy kingdom come, Thy will be done, On earth as it is in heaven" (Matthew 6:9). There is no evidence that Jesus ever prescribes a futile or inane prayer. If God willed and orchestrated everything that happened and over-rode human choices, it would be futile and inane to pray that His will be done on earth and in one's own life. If God destined certain men for destruction, their resulting disobedience would confirm and conform to His will, regardless of anyone's prayer to save them. Conversely, those He predestined to be saved would inevitably conform to His will, regardless of any lack of prayer.

The only way it makes any sense to pray that God's will be done on earth is when men are truly free to contest God's will for their salvation and holiness. Then, the power of prayer would serve some purpose to collaborate in accomplishing God's will by invoking supernatural power to change. Even if we petition for God's intervention to save us, the object of prayer is to enable and fulfill our desire by making it coincide with God's will through collaboration rather than coercion.

Fortunately, awareness of alternatives, clear warning from God, and personal choice always precede any human incorrigibility. Men are given discernment to judge right from wrong, as well as the Law, to identify specifically what is wrong, and outline how man responds to do right. God gives wisdom freely for the asking, and endorsed Solomon's request for wisdom. James 1:5 assures believers: "If any of you lack wisdom, let him ask God who gives to all men generously and without reproaching, and it will be given him."

Two Parables told by Jesus confirm that God's invitation to salvation can be freely rejected by the invitees. In the Parable of the Marriage Feast, Jesus compares the kingdom of Heaven to a banquet a King planned for his son. He "sent his servants to call those who were invited to the marriage feast; but they would not come" (Matthew 22:2-3). More servants were sent, but the guests "made light of it and went off, one to his farm, another to his business, while the rest seized his servants, treated them shamefully, and killed them" (Matthew 22:4-5), all to avoid accepting the invitation.

In the parable of the Great Banquet, Jesus confirms freedom to decline the grace of salvation by men who are unwilling, and intently occupied with their own affairs. The attraction of the feast is not strong enough to draw them from the engrossment of the world. Here, the invitees "all alike began to make excuses" to view a field just acquired; to examine a yoke of oxen just bought; and to tend to a new wife (Luke 14:18-20). Declining to attend the King's banquet is a willful act, comparable to refusing God's invitation to receive the free gift of grace for salvation in Christ. It is an act moving God to anger, and producing consequences for which one is responsible, because free choice was exercised in the decision Fortunately, God pursues other invitees, using persuasion to "compel" their attendance (Luke 14:23)..

The rich young man asked Jesus how to inherit eternal life, and Mark 10:21 says: "Jesus looking upon him loved him, and said to him,... 'go, sell what you have... and come, follow me'"; but he was not able to follow Jesus because he had great wealth, and loved it more than he loved Jesus. It is inconceivable that a loving Jesus would invite someone He loved to follow Him, and then disable him from complying. Jesus wanted the rich young man to be saved, but honored his freedom to walk away and prefer his worldly attachment to wealth.

God gives faith to men through hearing His Word (Romans 10:17); John 1:12 relates of Jesus: "But to all who received him, who believed in his name, he gave power to become children of God." The acts of receiving and believing in Jesus precede the empowerment by God. The passage does not say, (although it easily could have, if so intended), that God first empowers men to receive Jesus and then they believe in his name and become children of God. It says that those who freely respond to Jesus by believing, are then empowered by God to become His children. Belief, though initiated by God's grace, is also man's responsibility, and is based upon his free choice to respond or not.

Acts 13:46 affirms that God spoke the Word first to the Jews, but "Since you thrust it from you, and judge yourselves unworthy of eternal life, behold we turn to the Gentiles." The offer of salvation in Christ given first to the Jews, which they rejected, indicates that God did not pre-determine their condemnation. For He would never engage in a futile act of offering what He ordained would be rejected. It was a matter of their own free choice.

Freedom, evidenced by man's rebellion against God, is documented in Romans 1:21-28: "men who by their wickedness suppress the truth... for although they knew God they did not honor him as God... but they became futile in their thinking... they exchanged the truth about God for a lie and worshiped and served the creature rather than the Creator... they did not see fit to acknowledge God... they were filled with all manner of wickedness, evil... they not only do them but approve those who practice them."

The unbeliever who rejects the Gospel bears the consequences for his free, but faithless choice: "he who does not believe is condemned already, because he has not believed in the name of the only Son of God" (John 3:18). 2 Thessalonians 1:8-9 promises punishment for rebels who reject God: "inflicting vengeance upon those who do not know God and upon those who do not obey the Gospel of our Lord Jesus. They shall suffer the punishment of eternal destruction and exclusion from the presence of the Lord." 2 Thessalonians 2:11-12 also identifies condemned sinners as men who "refused to love the truth and so be saved" and "who did not believe the truth but had pleasure in unrighteousness." Matthew 25:41 bases condemnation of the Lost Goats who sinned by not feeding the hungry or ministering to the needy, as caused by their own acts.

God does not compel salvation, and Jesus does not force Himself on unbelievers, but seeks to persuade voluntary consent by men to reign over their lives. At some point, an individual's persistent rebellion in pursuit of evil will provoke God to give that sinner up to his hardness of heart (Genesis 6:5-7; Hosea 4:17, 5:15; Psalm 81:11, 12; Romans 1:24, 28). Still, despite the enormity of any sin, a man's change of mind in repentance can lead to embrace of God's grace at any time before death.

Revelation 3:20 is Jesus' invitation to the Church, those already saved by grace through faith, to respond freely to His indwelling presence: "Behold, I stand at the door and knock; if any one hears my voice and opens the door, I will come in to him and eat with him, and he with me." Perhaps such freedom is only available to those who are already saved, made free, and transformed, but this volitional act of man to open the door or not is clearly required. Jesus affirms genuine freedom of choice originating in personal desire, to accept salvation at Revelation 22:17: "let him who desires take the water of life without price." Man chooses, and then God regenerates and transforms him spiritually.

The Parable of the Talents (Matthew 25:14, ff.) and the Parable of the Pounds (Luke 19:12, ff.) teach that man is responsible for his use of God's gifts, and enjoys reward or suffers loss according to his response. Romans 1:29-31 outlines the myriad sins of men, and then challenges: "We know that the judgment of God rightly falls upon those who do such things... For he will render to every man according to his works... for those who are factious and do not obey the truth, but obey wickedness, there will be wrath and fury. There will be tribulation and distress for every human being who does evil" (Romans 2:2-9).

HUMAN FREEDOM ENABLES MAN TO GLORIFY GOD

The Bible proclaims that man's purpose in life is to glorify God. Freedom can be God-given only to the extent it is consistent with, and fulfills that purpose. At Isaiah 43:7 God declares of every believer: "I have created him for my glory, I have formed him; yea, I have made him." Man's pre-eminent purpose is to glorify God; not in the sense of making Him glorious, for man cannot add anything to God's essential glory; but in the sense we acknowledge Him to be glorious and the originator of every glory in creation. We glorify God because of His integrity, character and the beauty and order with which he infuses Creation; not because He lavishes gifts upon us, or simply because He is Providential in giving.

Satan's challenge to God concerning Job implied that God was only worth worshipping as long as He showered blessings upon Job, but if God withdrew His grace, Job would quickly renounce God (Job 1:11, 2:5). Indeed, when Job was under siege, and Satan had stripped him of all he possessed, including his wealth, children, and health, Job's wife counseled him to "curse God, and die" (Job 2:9). In this cosmic test of human faithfulness, Job's response proved he was not conditioned to love God simply because God rewarded him with profuse blessings. Instead, Job proved that man can freely love God for the integrity and beauty of His character and creativity, even after losing personal blessings, and regardless of circumstances or environment.

Pain and loss gave Job, as us, a chance to offer God an unbribed worship; an opportunity to glorify God for His excellence and holiness, rather than for His gifts. Job affirmed that saving faith does not depend on the promise or possession of worldly things: "Though He slay me, yet will I trust in Him" (Job 13:15). Love for God is not based on circumstances, but on pure devotion to God; not expectation of blessings. Through tribulation, Job learned about God's excellence. As a redeemed soul, truly converted, Job did not abandon God. Then Job was rewarded for his faith with replenished wealth, children, and health. Pain had enabled Job to appreciate God's Sovereignty in a way the comfort of his original hedge of protection could not.

Results which glorify God through submission and obedience are a legitimate measure of rightness, since man is made for God's glory (Leviticus 10:3; John 21:14, Romans 15:6; I Corinthians 6:20; and I Peter 2:12, 4:16). Joshua advised Achan that he could give glory to God even by submitting to His Justice, acknowledging God's right to chastise sinners; and confessing his sin to God (Joshua 7:19).

Psalm 50:23 says: "Whoso offereth praise glorifieth me." See also, 2 Corinthians 1:20. Psalm 22:23 teaches: "Ye that fear the Lord, praise him; all ye the seed of Jacob, Glorify him," and this is done by praising his attributes and works, with thanksgiving. Jesus commands that we set an example by our lives: "Let your light so shine before men, that they may see your good works and give glory to your Father who is in heaven (Matthew 5:16; and see I Peter 2:12). God was glorified by the obedience of Jesus (John 13:31-32, 21:19); "that the Gentiles might glorify God for his mercy" (Romans 15:9).

Jesus prayed, "Father... glorify the Son that the Son may glorify thee" (John 17:1), and was glorified by God "and in him God is glorified" (John 13:31). Believers will be glorified in the Hereafter, but until then God does not share or impart His glory directly to them, declaring: "my glory will I not give to another, neither my praise to graven images" (Isaiah 42:8). The best we can do is reflect His glory by acting on His behalf; being holy as He is holy; and by witnessing to His praiseworthiness (Isaiah 44:8).

Likewise, man is to glorify Jesus by reflecting His glory, mirroring His character and being organically attached to Jesus, the Vine. Jesus says at John 15:8: "By this my Father is glorified, that you bear much fruit, and so prove to be my disciples." At John 17:10 Jesus prays for "those whom thou hast given me, for they are thine; all mine are thine, and thine are mine, and I am glorified in them."

St. Paul calls Christians to live in harmony: "that together you may with one voice glorify the God and Father of our Lord" (Romans 15:6). Romans 4:20 tells us that Abraham glorified God by unfailing trust in His promises, and that "he grew strong in his faith as he gave glory to God." As we express belief in Him and His Word, we glorify God at the same time we strengthen and grow in our faith. For Christians, the epitome of faithfully glorifying God is to believe His revelation that Jesus Christ is Lord, and our faithful confession of Lordship is "to the glory of God the Father" (Philippians 2:11). Conversely, the wrath of God is called down upon idolaters, who "exchanged the glory of God for images resembling mortal man or birds or animals or reptiles" (Romans 1:22). After we are saved we glorify God by offering submissive obedience freely, willingly, and with intent to glorify God thereby.

I Corinthians 6:20 says: "You were bought with a price. So glorify God in your body." I Corinthians 10:31 adds: "So, whether you eat or drink, or whatever you do, do all to the glory of God." "Glorify God by your obedience in acknowledging the gospel of Christ, and by the generosity of your contributions for... others" (2 Corinthians 9:13). Our obedient good works in caring for others, rather than oneself, glorify God. Our visible works help us to glorify God (Matthew 5:16). 2 Corinthians 4:15 notes than when we are quickened in the flesh and resurrected with Jesus: "it is all for your sake, so that as grace extends to more and more people it may increase thanksgiving, to the glory of God." I Peter 4:11 exhorts believers to render "service as one who renders it by the strength which God supplies; in order that in everything God may be glorified through Jesus Christ." We are to glorify God by shunning immorality which sins against one's own body, which is "a temple of the Holy Spirit within you" (I Corinthians 6:18-19).

And herein lies the connection between man having free choice and the quality of worship and glory he gives to God. Jesus told the Pharisees that if His disciples did not worship and exalt Him: "if these were silent, the very stones would cry out" (Luke 19:40). Yet, it is self-evident that a human freely appreciating and glorifying the Lord is vastly superior to inanimate worshipers such as stones. We can infer that God wants a love like Job's, willingly given despite the withdrawal and lack of God's gifts. But Job had to be free to do so, or his travails would have been in vain in this exemplary test of man's love for God. Free choice is essential to genuine glorifying, which is based on appreciative and intelligent worship.

A believer's free choice glorifies God when it is rightly exercised by rational men freely and obediently choosing between equally attractive moral alternatives. God is glorified by the willing response of man to His love, a freely given requital embracing God's will by a reciprocal expression of love for Him. We glorify God by recognizing and applying His saving grace to our lives; in choosing to receive Jesus as Lord and Saviour; in freely choosing to submit obediently to God; in seeking to accelerate the pace of one's own holiness by collaborating in the transforming work of the Holy Spirit; and facilitating God's gift to Jesus of a redeemed Church attaining the "measure of the stature of the fullness of Christ" (Ephesians 4:13).

God is glorified when a man is attracted by God's glory, and freely and lovingly exercises choice by electing to be like Him in holy character; in choosing to witness in obedience to the Great Commission, all in response to God's expressed will and directives. We glorify God by reflecting His glory in obedient submission. We glorify God, as well as share His glory, by obediently fulfilling His perfect will for us, as much as by worshipping Him because of His glory. Similarly, when we pray to God according to His will, we give God opportunity to display or manifest His goodness and power through His gracious response and answer to our petitions, to His glory.

Yet, there is a second way man has been made for God's glory. We are not only to give glory to God, but Scripture reveals we are also endowed with God's very own glory in, through, and because of Jesus Christ. The more dignity man receives as a gift from God, such as in the faculty of free choice, the more meaningful is the glory he offers to God. In other words, the more glory a worshipper has received from God, the more God is exalted or glorified as His glory is reflected in, and dispersed among believers.

Jesus says that we are given the same glory He has; that is, we are glorified by God's gifts of freedom, fellowship, salvation, holiness, and the Kingdom, with the same glory as Jesus, Himself. David exulted at Psalm 21:5; "The king shall joy in thy strength, O Lord; and in thy salvation how greatly shall he rejoice!... His glory is great in thy salvation; honour and majesty hast thou laid upon him. For thou hast made him most blessed for ever." Jesus connects love to glory, as He reports to God: "The glory which thou hast given me I have given to them, that they may be one even as we are one... so that the world may know that thou has sent me and hast loved them even as thou hast loved me... that the love with which thou hast loved me may be in them, and I in them" (John 17:22-23, 26); and see also, I John 3:1. This means that believers are given God's glory, of which freedom is a part, as proof of His love for us, and because He loves us right now as much as He loves Jesus, because of Jesus, and because we are in Jesus. He has given us the gift of salvation, as He did to David, and knows our need and will supply it. He knows our well-being and will arrange it, as a loving Father, including the glory of free choice. Jesus reveals at Luke 12:32: "It is your Father's good pleasure to give you the Kingdom." We will even have some part in judging the world and fallen angels (I Corinthians 6:2-3).

Indeed, Christians advance from glory to glory, proceeding from regeneration to sanctification to glorification, as we, "beholding the glory of the Lord, are being changed into his likeness from one degree of glory to another; for this comes from the Lord who is the Spirit" (2 Corinthians 3:18). Romans 8:30 asserts: "and those whom he called he also justified; and those whom he justified he also glorified." We are "heirs of God and fellow heirs with Christ, provided we suffer with him in order that we may also be glorified with him" (Romans 8:17).

Because God is love, we can infer that one reason He blesses us with the glorious gift of freedom is because He wishes to impart a highly valuable gift to His beloved, despite the fact it has the intrinsic potential for harm when mis-used. The same freedom God gives man, which glorifies the Creator by making man the best he can be, also exalts man, the creature. The privilege of freedom by which man participates and makes a choice to obey God and believe in Jesus, vests man with the utmost dignity and virtue because it dignifies, exalts, and glorifies man by enhancing his stature and responsibility.

Clearly, God regards man's dignity from genuine freedom of choice as a pre-eminent good in creation's hierarchy of values. We have already seen that God's gifts to man reveal His love and grace, to His glory. Yet, there is another superlative aspect of freedom which God apparently cherishes, even at the risk of man's defection from God's purposes.

VOLUNTARY CHOICE IS SUPERIOR TO COERCED OR PRE-PROGRAMMED RESPONSE

The requital of God's perfect love by the reciprocal love a human freely and willingly offers to Him is far superior to subservience motivated by fear. A response voluntarily from within is superior to conquest from without, or a reaction imposed by the compulsions of implanted character. Even an animal can be made to submit by fear, intimidation, or pain, but it is better to train and persuade a pet by reward and praise, and thereby enjoy reciprocal love and care afterwards.

Freedom which chooses rightly is superior to pre-programmed good, even though freedom has a potential for abuse, or the possibility of self-destruction because of wrong choices which reject God. Even with its inherent possibility for fatal error or the infliction of suffering upon others, freedom is still preferable to life without free choice. God allows the risk of harm or suffering bad consequences from wrong choices in order to preserve the integrity of freedom, even though a potential evil of suffering intrinsically accompanies the mis-use or corruption of free choice.

Any freedom of human participation makes God vulnerable to failure because of man's inadequacy. Yet, He continues to tolerate and champion our sharing in His work. Man's willing freedom of choice to stand with God necessarily carries with it the abuse of freedom to fall in rebellious opposition to Him. There can be no freedom without the risk of error in choice which produces evil consequences for violating God's spiritual law. The perversion of free choice can possibly or potentially occur, and sometimes does, but God does not necessitate nor mandate its actuality.

Loving God because one is controlled, programmed, manipulated, or designed to love gives no honor to the beloved. Only love based on free choice to love or not is authentic, sincere, and esteeming for both parties. Love is one thing not even God can coerce. It is genuine only if it is freely given. Love cannot be forced. God coerces no-one to love Him, for unless love is freely offered, it would not be love. God cannot give man the freedom to reject Him, and at the same time compel a man to embrace Him. God apparently deems man's uncoerced love as preferable to compulsions of implanted instinct. There is significance in choosing good only so long as we are also free to choose evil. This ability to choose morally is what distinguishes man from the animals, and loss of freedom to choose would reduce man to the level of a beast.

God chooses not to compel our obedience, nor prohibit our freedom to sin. He most certainly has identified sin; warned us of its consequences; set up strong punitive deterrents to sin; persuaded our obedience; empowered our compliance with His will, and delivered us from our failures. But He never forces obedience, other than by persuasions which appeal to His love and our self-interest. Consequently, some intercessory prayers may be denied, even though in accord with God's will. God desires all men to be saved, and a woman may fervently pray for the salvation of her husband. God surely responds to such prayers with divine persuasions and inducements to heed God's call. Yet, He has ceded part of His power to man's freedom, and God voluntarily chooses not to force any one to respond, because it is also God's will to leave man with genuine freedom, even if it allows his self-destruction.

In an attempt to preserve free choice and abolish suffering; it is sometimes suggested that God could create beings so that they must always freely choose the good. They would still make choices, but their nature or character would be so constituted that they willingly choose only good. However, any automatic response which is pre-determined by one's nature is precisely the robotic reply which denies freedom. A genuine choice is what defines freedom. Pre-determining nature in any way — unless to allow choice — is a denial of freedom.[55] One might say that God has pre-determined human nature with a <u>potential</u> for imperfection, by allowing man freely to choose between good or evil. But beyond this, God has not set constraints on human freedom.

Freedom is an integral part of human personality, as it develops reciprocal love, appreciation, glorification, and worship, inspired by God's love, grace, and revealed excellence. Without free choice, we would not have independent human personality. A robot programmed to act only in pre-set ways would be a most boring companion. Man would be reduced to an automaton unless he had power to make his own choices, freely choosing to love God.

He might have been created more morally complete and spiritually advanced, but his lack of free choice would have left him with less dignity and worth. Without free choice, we would not have independent human personality, which God pronounced as "very good" at Creation (Genesis 1:31).

A perfectly created man, constituently incapable of making a wrong choice, would also be unable to make a personal decision of his own, Every choice would be based on information programmed into him by God. He would be perfect, sinless, guiltless, and error-less, but he could not fashion or develop ideas, make decisions, or form opinions. He could regurgitate the expressions of love, but he would lack capacity to offer love out of free choice. Apparently, God chose to create man with ability to discern, evaluate, judge, choose, and decide, even at the risk of disobedient, wrong determinations being made by man.

A virtue which results from free choice in real situations requiring moral decision transmits and bestows far greater value than the same virtue imposed by divine fiat. A free man who is able to think and will for himself is superior to an android or automaton who is so constituted that his nature automatically determines what his response must be.[56] There is always the risk of abusing freedom, but the potential for expanded freedom and dignity makes the risk tolerable.

Some familiar examples may explain how transcendent good integrated into a system justifies retaining the advantages, despite an inherent potential for harm. This is so, when intrinsic characteristics articulate, constitute, and define the entity's very character, and remedies for abuses can be provided. Consider the game of football, where the actuality of injury is not necessary to make the game what it is meant to be, but the risk or possibility of injury while playing is essential to the integrity of any game involving physical contact. Whatever we might call it, the game would not be enjoyed as football without the elements of bodily contact, or running at full speed. If someone is hurt, but not disabled, he does not withdraw from participation, but thrives on continued contact. Indeed, for many players, the very contact is what defines and makes the sport most enjoyable. Injury or setbacks are inherent risks of the game we willingly accept because the aggregate pleasures and advantages from participation exceed temporary injury.

Likewise, a free man who drives his car recklessly can maim or kill innocent bystanders, and the same vehicle which transports and speeds us to our destination is capable of maiming the human flesh it carries. Still, we do not abandon or destroy the highway system because speed causes occasional accidents. Rather, we try to educate all drivers in a responsible use of driving privileges, because of the vast and collective benefits to all users of the roadways.

Similarly, the possibility of suffering, rather than its actuality, is acceptable as necessary for the development of a free man's personality and spirituality. God chooses to train men in the proper use of freedom, rather than discard the blessing because it carries the potential for harm. Properly used and responsibly enjoyed, freedom is pain-free, and the blessing God intended. God has not created evil amidst freedom, nor decreed the occurrence of suffering as a condition, agent, or instrumentality of Christian salvation or sanctification. Only the possibility or risk of suffering is necessary for free choice, not the actuality or fact of suffering.

We can conceive of a world in which God constantly and routinely corrected the abuse of free will by His creatures, by preventing the consequences which produce suffering. He could make a hard object temporarily soft so it was incapable of harm when used as a weapon or involved in a man's fall. He could stifle any sound waves that carried hurtful language, or make the speaker mute during hurtful utterances. However, taking the possibility of such suffering out of the order of nature or human free will would destroy both order and freedom. If wrong actions were impossible at the moment of utterance or doing because of God's intervention, then freedom would be void.[57] Instead, God allows the utterance or action, but chooses to work all things for good, including evil produced by freedom, while preserving freedom.

God could not remove the incidental suffering inherent in the essential process of free choice without withdrawing the very character of freedom — even freedom to reject God or to harm others. If God withdrew the potentially disastrous consequences of freedom flowing from choice, He would be removing the very nature of freedom, just as removing contact to avoid injuries would destroy the very nature of football games. It is not possible for God to give men freedom to choose Jesus, and at the same time predestinate or compel, as distinct from persuade, them to act in a certain way.

Genuine human freedom to choose or resist God would be negated if God somehow disallowed or prevented the consequences which flow from man's irresponsible exercise of free choice or action. God gave freedom to men to establish and promote their dignity. Men were created free, but not created exclusively nor constituently good. If God did not allow the potential to sin, there could be no free will, and men would be mere puppets, at the sacrifice of their dignity and the value of their choice in freely responding to the call of God. If God made a universe from which all possibility of suffering were eliminated, by destroying free will, He would also remove man's participation in choosing to embrace the higher purposes of spiritual transformation. Rather, God wills to overcome sin by replacing man's ignorance with wisdom; sinfulness with holiness; and indifference with responsibility.

Since God chose to create this precise world, it is logically impossible for Him to create, at the same moment in time, any other kind of world, including a 'perfect' one. St. Thomas Aquinas observed that even God's omnipotence does not permit a contradiction of God's own logic, or make logical inconsistencies possible. So, He cannot give us genuine freedom, and at the same time withdraw choice or the harmful consequences of wrong direction or decision which define choice, without destroying the very nature and character of freedom. Even God cannot create a weight so heavy that He cannot lift it. He cannot create at the same moment or in the same space, both an immovable object and an irresistible force, although He can alternate them infinitely. One or the other must prevail; they cannot co-exist simultaneously, for they are logical contradictions. Nor can God make the same person a natural blond, redhead and brunette at the same instant. He cannot make the world simultaneously round and flat, or a man both short and tall, clean-shaven and bearded.

THE BLESSING AND RISK OF DIGNITY BY PARTICIPATION

Perhaps the blessing of participation is so important because the privilege of sonship is enhanced by appreciation and fuller understanding of something in which we have invested time and effort, and for which we have strived and contended. Indeed, the very hallmark of maturity is responsibility and accountability: learning to do one's duty without being monitored or supervised. When we are motivated by a desire to please, honor, and glorify God, we freely accept the responsibility to obey Him willingly and consistently. God has willed to entrust to believers on earth the completion of parts of God's work, by a believer's free decision and choice to collaborate.

Perhaps God intends to bless His children by letting them share in the intrinsic joy and achievement of overcoming one's shortcomings and developing one's skills in the advancement of holiness. God enables and enhances the creation of human personality in the image of Christ, and also establishes the best conditions for the emergence and development of humanness. Cooperative participation by man, despite the risks of failure, becomes God's instrument for the supernatural opportunity to grow spiritually.

Without challenges in the world, we could never develop spiritual sinews or mature muscles. We might never progress in holiness in a world without suffering. Growth is accelerated by challenge. If we stumble and fall, that is part of the only way we can develop proficiency in walking, or strong spiritual muscles to grow in holiness. Did not Job develop patience and an appreciation for God through his trials? A truly loving Father allows arduous challenges to reach us so we can build and strengthen spiritual muscle and rejoice in overcoming adversity. Human personalities, with the capacity for love, goodness, and joy, can only develop amidst their attendant potential for error, pain, and suffering.[58]

God's goals for man in this world include choosing Him willingly, and desiring to become like Him. Man's happiness in this world is only incidental to an eternal, spiritual joy with God in Heaven, for which a cruelly provocative world prepares us. A parent prepares his child for independence, and this means forcing the child to leave the crib, walk, and continue to gain proficiency. The parent lovingly teaches a child to walk, knowing she must someday walk away. A parent lovingly encourages a child to speak, knowing she will someday declare her independence to do the work and live the life for which parental training has prepared her, consciously using parental resources and guidance. Christians learn to empty themselves so they can be filled with the Spirit, but they are not excused from contributing all their effort to joint spiritual enterprises. There is mutual pride in genuine growth and development, produced by parent and child in cultivating and exercising sound judgment, relying upon accepted parental principles.

God graciously offers a loving partnership, advancing hand-in-hand and step-by-step along the road to holiness, as we choose to be holy like God, and "being changed from one degree of glory to another" (2 Corinthians 3:18). There is a joy which accompanies accomplishment and creativity; a jubilation from application, staying the course, and graduating, especially with high honors. Certainly, a father can color within the lines better than his child; and fashion a model racer, or kick a soccer ball better than his small son. But a wise parent allows free expression by his child in all these areas, because growth, proficiency, and personality proceed only by practice, experience, and personal involvement. Children take pride in growing by experience, and the wise parent lets his children develop their own drawing, invention, constructing, and creating, with materials provided by the parent. Thus, God constitutes believers as "Fellow workmen for God; you are God's field, God's building" (I Corinthians 3:9).

Certainly, God is loving and generous enough to bestow the joy of creativity and fulfillment in our own spirituality, using his resources, power, and wise counsel. God lets us grow, develop skills and character by practice and doing, because it gives us dignity and joy. If God always intervened to prevent any harm or hurt to His children, they would never improve their personal Christ-like character by a process of learning from mistakes, trials and error. The exercise of freedom contributes to growth, and continues to exalt both the Giver and the user of free choice. To reassert God's dominion by intervention would return our weakness and create our helplessness. Withholding God's power lets man use and enlarge his spiritual acumen and resources of prayer and faith, in response to God's urging, inspiring, and leading.

Parents soon learn that a child does not attain desired maturity or responsibility without first being entrusted with obligation and accountability. The power and wisdom definitely comes from God, and man must empty himself of self-centeredness and self-sufficiency to make room for the Holy Spirit in his life. True maturity means we willingly trade independence, and choose to depend on God to work out His Kingdom through transformation of human minds and hearts. God chooses to advance holiness in collaboration with each believer, sometimes by the prodding of affliction, and the use of God's strength in yielded human weakness.

Participation in spiritual processes entrusts a New-Born believer with freedom to respond, and imposes a responsibility to exercise rightly the free choice of collaboration which God has bestowed. Thus, we are directed to ask of the Lord so we may receive: to seek so we shall find: to knock so it may be opened to us (Matthew 7:7; Luke 1:9). We are to abide in the Lord, by holding the Word of salvation fast and abiding in it (I Corinthians 15:1-2; I John 2:25), which is accomplished by frequent recourse to, and refreshing in, the Word. We are to come boldly to the throne of grace "to receive mercy and grace to help in time of need" (Hebrews 4:16). God empowers and God responds, but man is privileged to collaborate in, and is responsible to initiate and sustain his longing for and receipt of the Kingdom and its treasures. Man is charged to be obedient; to be holy; to pray; and to witness, in order to invite God's blessings, which are promised the obedient and holy believer.

We participate in expressing our desire for the Kingdom by hungering and thirsting after righteousness, with such ardor it might be compared to seizing the kingdom by force or violence. We must desire God's blessing with such zeal that we would wrestle with an angel throughout the night, and even bear the wound of the encounter, as Jacob did (Genesis 32:24-26). We must exercise faith and turn to God alone, to be saved (Isaiah 45:22). Once saved, God will carry the spiritual infant until he is ready to walk, as well as the mature believer who is disabled from walking, but only on condition we have first desired to walk according to His way.

We must determine to have an attitude of disdain for the things of the world, and seek only Christ: to suffer "the loss of all things, and count them as refuse, in order that I may gain Christ... that I may know him and the power of his resurrection, and may share his sufferings, becoming like him in his death" (Philippians 3:8-10).

THE BLESSING AND RISK OF PREDICTABLE NATURAL LAWS

When God had completed His creation of the universe, including man, He pronounced the result "very good" (Genesis 1:31). Something then set nature askew, and less than the idyllic Garden in which God placed Adam. St. Augustine conjectured that Satan's fall had cosmic consequences which corrupted earth's suitability for man, and imposed a savage struggle for existence. Satan's access to Adam and Eve in the Garden was a contributing factor to the Fall of man, and its consequences for the world. Creation shared God's condemnation of Adam's sin of infidelity, as God pronounced a curse on the earth to make man's life more difficult (Genesis 3:17).

As a result, "the creation was subjected to futility, not of its own will but by the will of him who subjected it in hope; because the creation itself will be set free from its bondage to decay... We know that the whole creation has been groaning in travail together until now." See also, Jeremiah 12:4, 11; Acts 3:21; 2 Peter 3:13. Nature is presently not as balanced or benign as God originally designed it, but will be restored by God when believers are resurrected at the return of Christ. Romans 8:23 concludes: "not only creation, but we ourselves, who have the first fruits of the Spirit, groan inwardly as we wait for the adoption as sons, the redemption of our bodies."

Thus, Adam's original Fall consigned the world to disorder and degeneration, and nature was set amok by God and diverted from its perfect harmony with man. God has honored the consequences of Adam's abuse of freedom in wrongly choosing to believe Satan, and allowed Satan to remain the assignee of man exercising dominion over the world. Changing corrupted, sinful hearts by transforming the New-Born man to the image of Christ, does not alter the reality of spiritual evil in control of the rest of the world. Believers are empowered to cope with the world and overcome it, and eventually be free of evil in the Hereafter, but we are not able to eliminate evil in the world.

Nature; like man, must also await its full redemption, when Jesus restores Creation and establishes a new earth, finally freed of Satan (Isaiah 11:6-9, 41:17-20; Revelation 20:10, 21:1). God has rescued Creation through Jesus, but both man and nature must share a new Birth through a process of travail originating in regeneration, and proceeding to eventual glorification in new spirit bodies and a new heaven and earth. In the meantime, we exist in an interim state of imperfection triggered by man's original sin.

Man will encounter instances of nature run rampant, as disasters of flood, earthquake, and hurricane occur, and afflict believers as well as evil men. As a consequence of man's ongoing disobedience, his effectiveness in exercising dominion over Creation has been affected, and his relationship with his Creator has been marred.[59] When men abandon God and ignore His instructions, they commit sin, which simply invites responsive, reciprocal, or retaliatory sin from others. Human rebellion against God generates and proliferates most of man's suffering.

Nature is in disharmony because man is in disharmony with God. Germs and viruses, the venom of snakes and scorpions are indications of something wrong in the system. Gonorrhea, diabetes and birth defects can cause blindness, but not by the intent of God. AIDS can attack our marvelous immune systems, but not according to any plan of God. Because Satan now exercises dominion in the world, it bears the seeds of his corruption as well as of God's bounty. Consequently, innocent children can succumb to viruses, bacteria, or mutant chromosomes causing birth defects or deformities.

Unsaved men add to the world's brutality by relinquishing God-given dominion and control of the world to Satan. The unsaved man's plight of alienation from God, and of slavery to powers of darkness, suffuses, and is shared by, all creation. Mankind's destruction of his environment has ancient roots, which impact every member of society. When mankind abuses natural law by poisoning the planet's soil, air and water with toxic substances and nuclear wastes, then individual members must suffer the same injurious consequences as the active polluters. As a victim of this exposure, the fate of the individual is irreversibly tied to the fate of all men inhabiting the planet. The collective miseries of national wars, famine, economic cataclysm, or contagious disease, will afflict believers and atheists alike.

Isaiah 24:5-6 explains how modern creation is in travail: "The earth also is defiled under the inhabitants thereof; because they have transgressed the laws, changed the ordinance, broken the everlasting covenant. Therefore hath the curse devoured the earth, and they that dwell therein are desolate." The Apocryphal Book of Enoch links man's sin to natural phenomena, recognizing that human iniquity can corrupt nature's powers, shorten the years, curtail rain and fertility, and alter the course of the sun and stars.

Voltaire pondered how an earthquake which killed thousands of people could be used by God as punishment for sin. He wondered if God selected the least virtuous segment of the populace to be destroyed, or whether the selection was random so as to include good persons along with the evil ones deserving destruction, even New-Born Christians and babies. Of course, Voltaire was asking the wrong question because God does not intend mass natural disasters for punishment, simply because He allows these possible consequences of nature's modified, but now normal operation, law and order.

Natural processes, events and elements have inherent in them a risk of harm, which God tolerates because of the phenomena's value. In nature the order which proceeds from natural physical laws brings the blessings of certainty and predictability to our world. We can depend on water boiling or freezing at fixed temperatures as a general rule. We know if we jump up, gravity will usually bring us down to earth. The routine operations of a world still preponderantly congenial to man are reminders of how benevolent God's provisions are. Sowing and reaping, night and day, gravity, and eclipses are proofs of systematic regularity in creation which give stability, predictability, law and order to daily existence.

Most natural disasters are simply the operations of neutral, natural laws, unintended by God for harm, but part of a functional world. We continue to welcome their benefits because of the greater good they also provide. For example, the nature of fire accounts for its warming, illuminating and cooking. Yet, its intrinsic properties allow fire to burn human flesh or reduce its user to ashes. Electricity is man's benevolent servant when it provides light and heat, but it can also shock, burn, and electrocute its beneficiary.

The same water which bathes an infant can also drown her in a moment of parental inattention. The potential to destroy life by drowning is an inherent property of water, essential to its liquidity which occupies empty space, including lungs submerged underwater. Drowning, however, is not an occurrence or actuality necessary to enjoy water's benefits as a thirst quencher, cleansing agent, universal solvent, or recreational facility. The boiling water which cooks food and sterilizes surgical instruments can also scald and burn its users, but no-one suggests outlawing water.

In its frozen state water can provide refrigeration and recreational surfaces, but ice can also cause slips, falls, and fractures. Yet, God cannot exclude the possibility of people slipping on icy surfaces without dismantling the orderly operations of temperature, or withdrawing the enjoyment of figure skating, curling or hockey.

Likewise, if a man falls to his death off a high cliff, it is simply the operation of a natural principle of gravity, rather than God's intent. If God intervened capriciously in the order established by His natural law, we would truly have chaos. If God suspended or repealed the law of gravity so that no one could fall while slipping on an icy surface or from the roof of a high building, turmoil would result. Weightlessness would bring a slew of new problems, as bodies rose into the air, and rain no longer fell to the earth. The planet, which is held in place by gravity, would rotate out of its orbit and either become too hot or too cold for comfortable human life, as it approached or receded from the sun. Changing the physical laws to avoid risk of occasional harm would not necessarily eliminate suffering, nor produce an increase in blessings.

The warm air so welcome in a tropical paradise, can cause a raging tornado when it collides with cooler air which has just relieved oppressive heat in another part of the world. The wind which powers sailboats for recreation, can devastate seacoast towns when it attains hurricane proportions. Soil supports life and buildings, but its properties of occupying space can also smother and suffocate someone buried beneath it. If a group of mountain climbers have enjoyed scaling the heights of the Alps, we cannot attribute their deaths to God's intent if they are exposed and freeze in a sudden, high altitude blizzard.

We cannot separate the possible harm, or remove the potential harmful consequences from these natural processes and phenomena without destroying their very nature. Yet, few abandon or reject the benevolent uses of fire, water, wind, soil, or electricity because of their inherent properties which occasionally cause harm. We know that some functions of nature are innate in the character of the elements and cannot be altered without altering their operations. We know that a natural order which attains the highest good of man through a predictable, congenial, environment also has the potential for harm in its operations, although not specifically intended or necessarily willed by God for infliction on disobedient children. To call these "acts of God" is a misnomer; these are acts of nature in a basically orderly creation, which tilts toward disorder until Jesus return (Romans 8:22-23).

THE BLESSING AND RISK OF CERTAINTY IN SPIRITUAL LAWS

Just as He establishes predictability in natural laws, so God ordains spiritual laws which have inevitable consequences following certain actions. Spiritual law is a blessing to man, because it provides assurance and predictability of results if obeyed by man. God's laws are revealed in His Word, and obedience always produces reward as we see in the next Chapter. We do not live in a universe of spiritual anarchy, for the conduct which conforms to God's will is clearly spelled out in Scripture. The consequences of disobedience are clearly identified as loss and misery, while obedience produces joy and blessings. Certainty of reward for obedience is a blessing and comfort to him who is obedient, but a dread to him who disobeys and deserves the woeful harvest of what he has sown in sin.

The burden of proper, obedient use and care of freedom has been entrusted to men for their development and enjoyment by their loving Father. When freedom is mis-used by sowing sin, then man harvests the harmful consequences of suffering, unintended by God in the sense of punishment, because it proceeds exactly from what man has sown: "For the wages of sin is death" (Romans 6:23). When man acts rightly and sows faithful obedience, he can depend on reaping only good, and none of the suffering he encounters will be produced by his own hand.

That we are responsible for the consequences of our conduct, is an underlying principle in contact sports and games where we devise and abide by rules which promote fullest enjoyment of the activity. If a rule is violated because of our unsportsmanlike conduct, a penalty is imposed, and the certainty of discipline or punishment assures the best conditions for fairly playing and enjoying the game. If we are penalized rightly and fairly, we do not decide to withdraw from participation, because the same rules also serve to protect us by leveling the playing field in our relations with others.

In the following Chapters, we will see that suffering is an integral part of human existence, even for believers. We will also see that much suffering is connected to the blessing of freedom given to men. Even if we act rightly, the freedom of others can still cause harm by corrupt use. Obedience is God's principal mechanism for assuring the proper and responsible use of freedom. If we will only do what God directs, and be what He intends us to be, a great deal of suffering would be avoided or alleviated. Responsible freedom imposes accountability for our actions: accountability in meeting God's standards of holiness; in rendering loving service to God and others as good stewards of His blessings; in offering intercessory prayers for one another; and in witnessing the Gospel to the unsaved according to our Great Commission from Christ.

There is a connection between suffering and the responsible exercise of freedom. God does not ignore suffering, nor spurn those in distress, need, or illness. He has created and constituted New Born Christians, the Church, the Body of Christ, as His hands, feet and voice to represent Him and impart His love in the world. When we do not heed His call to obedience to God's Law we become major contributors to the suffering of self and others in the world. If we fail to share God's blessings with others, there will be privation. If we fail to pray in intercession for others, their needs may not be timely met. If we fail to witness, the unsaved soul remains a sinner without hearing of God's transforming power. If we resist spiritual growth, our access to the Kingdom in this world will be retarded. Consequently, our failure to participate responsibly in God's work will result in suffering for others; expand the horizons of our own sinfulness; and contribute to evil in the world.

The constituent tragedy of freedom amidst finite human existence is that the value of blessing must struggle with the possibility of error. The spiritual value of morality must struggle with the possibility of choosing to do evil. The human privilege of appreciating freedom, beauty, love, and friendship must struggle with the possibility of experiencing heightened sensitivity to pain.[60]

Yet, freedom is not a situation or condition where unknown peril awaits choice. God has provided that freedom's responsibility is modulated by the intelligence to appreciate the consequences attached to one's free will. God has given full warning and disclosure of the dangers of wrong choice. Man does not make an ignorant choice, but makes his selection with informed consent and appreciation of the revealed consequences for choosing wrongly. God gave man freedom with the potential for corrupting choice. But He also gave us Jesus, Who can be embraced by man's right exercise of free choice, as the guaranty and empowerment of redeemed, transformed lives, freely choosing to be made obedient, holy, loving, and spiritually fruitful.

God commands all men to be holy and avoid evil. He gives all men freedom to obey or not. Obedience produces man's highest good designed by God. And disobedience in pursuit of sin by yielding to evil impulses will produce suffering for both the wrongdoer and his victims. When God created man with freedom; with the capacity to make decisions and determine his own course of action, God also obligated man to obey his Creator. God imposed a responsible use of this freedom, for which man was accountable.

Freedom which disobeys God is mis-used and irresponsible. It evidences man's prideful intent to direct his own life independently of God, and to usurp God's delegated authority under freedom. Pride is at the root of disobedience. When we assert independence and claim we are as good or great as God, we reject all reasons to submit to Him and defiantly choose not to obey Him. Slavery to sin may free us from obedience and righteousness, but the only result is enslavery to death (Romans 7:20-21). When man escapes from submission to God, he enters a terrible subservience to worldly domination, in a world cursed by God and still ruled by Satan.

Fortunately, once we yield to our Creator, we have greatest freedom, and are spiritually empowered to live and love within the intent and plan of our God-given blessings. "For the law of the spirit of life in Christ Jesus has set me free from the law of sin and death" (Romans 8:2). Genuine freedom, in the Christian view, does not defy God, but intelligently adjusts to His purposes revealed in the Word and individual conscience. God is transcendent, unchangeable, in charge, and will not adjust to man's way of thinking. The New Birth in Christ suppresses the degeneracy of pride and degradation of rebellion and replaces them with respect for God's proper law and order, and full spiritual benefits resulting from compliance.

While the natural man may be free to make decisions and do what he wants to do, he is not naturally free or able to do what he ought to do. He ought to obey God and avoid sin, but carnal man wants to sin, and even "the plowing of the wicked is sin" (Proverbs 21:4). Romans 7:22 explains the transformation wrought by Jesus: "But now that you have been set free from sin and have become slaves of God, the return you get is sanctification and its end, eternal life." Romans 6:16-18 adds: "you are slaves of the one whom you obey, either of sin, which leads to death, or of obedience, which leads to righteousness. But thanks be to God, that you who were once slaves of sin have become obedient from the heart... and having been set free from sin, have become slaves of righteousness."

Instead of being a "servant of sin" (John 8:34), when a believer follows God's benevolent direction, the obedient servant of the Lord is exalted. Giving honor to God honors us before God: "Them that honor me I will honor" (I Samuel 2:30), and "if any one serves me, the Father will honor him" (John 12:26). When God is exalted and glorified by His creatures' obedience, Daniel 9:4 notes that God gives "mercy to them that love him, and to them that keep his commandments." Jesus teaches at John 14:23: "If a man loves me, he will keep my word."

God wills that no harm come to another in the exercise of one's personal freedom. He clearly teaches that freedom is intended to be responsibly exercised by following God's directions for its use in love. Jesus also connects loving Him with the obedient service of feeding His lambs and tending His sheep (John 21:15-17). The gift of freedom loses no integrity when God curtails it by a rule of obedience which expresses love, to intensify its enjoyment by all beneficiaries and maximize its collective value.

When we choose to obey God we accept this benevolent servitude to Him for our highest good. Jesus frees a Christian from bondage to sin, and purchases our freedom in Him. Christian freedom requires wise acceptance of God's rule for our own benefit and that of other men. It is a servitude of responsibility for the use of our freedom, gratefully accepted, because the burden of serving Christ is carried and enabled by Him, and is a light one (Matthew 11:30), producing infinite blessings to the faithful. God delegates specific activities to believers, but accords maximum freedom or latitude in how and when we perform them. In this collaboration, God retains dominion over final things, and orchestrates whatever he wishes, using other resources to replace our failed performances. We rightly remain free within the limits of God's plan and purposes, with renewed opportunities for spiritual growth and compliance.

Obedience is not optional, but God's mercy and grace are patient and forgiving toward our derelictions of duty. God ordains, directs, and administers His will, and man is obligated to respond obediently, or suffer the consequences of his misguided free choice. This reality of choice imposes what has been called "the dreadful burden" of freedom, because of responsibility for, and consequences from, one's own actions. Sin always hauls its own aftermath; a sorrowful cortege drawn by the operation of neutral natural laws and absolute spiritual laws.

God has ordained these laws to benefit men, but their abuse by man can harm him, making him responsible for his own actions. Suffering is always dependable and prominent in the retinue of sin, unless mitigated by confession and forgiveness.

In the natural world there are many examples of loss to one who flaunts natural laws. Those who use their freedom to swim against the tide will soon exhaust their energies and resources by futile resistance to fixed forces already set in motion. They would travel much farther and faster if they harness the observable forces of nature and ride the current's crest to their own advantage, as sail boaters learn to harness the winds. One is also free to venture out into a blizzard without protective clothing, but he will eventually succumb to the raging elements outside. We have already noted that the abuse of an automobile for an undesigned purpose as a battering ram, will soon result in forfeiting one's means of transportation, mobility, and the freedom it afforded. Likewise, if we devastate the use of our moral freedom by pursuing carnality, rather than serving God obediently, we will diminish freedom's usefulness. We may even end up destroying the earthly vehicle which must carry us to salvation.

Further, food sustains man, but gluttony brings obesity and physical ailments. Sex procreates mankind, but illicit sex brings disease and unwanted pregnancy. The physical law of gravity holds objects in their proper place, but leaping from a great height foolishly flaunts the law, and will collide with harm at ground level. Violating the proper use of freedom can terminate all one's freedoms in death. God institutes the law and its benefits, and provides instructions for its proper use. Man abuses the spiritual law and suffers the consequences of its normal operations when applied abnormally.

Freedom is given to avoid sin, not to sanction sinning (Romans 6:1-2). Freedom is for willingly and lovingly serving others, and is not "an opportunity for the flesh" (Galatians 5:13). Grace is not a license to sin, but a stimulus to be responsive and responsible in obedience to God. Without Jesus, natural man has moral limitations on his will, just as he has physical limitations preventing him from leaping over a tall building or lifting a car. But Jesus can transform our nature, enable our desire to obey God, and free us to do what we ought by the New Birth.[61]

OBEDIENCE IS PART OF FREEDOM UNDER GOD'S SOVEREIGNTY

Christians believe that an individual's best interests are promoted by obediently following God's directives, because a perfectly good God can intend only good for us. We must cooperate and persevere in self-fulfillment in harmony with divine purposes; responsibly, and according to God's instructions. Man is obligated by reason to follow the directives of God for his own good, and exercise his freedom toward that end. When we reject the moral law of God under the guise of freedom to determine our own destiny, we have subjugated the free will to nonrational forces and passions. The alcoholic who insists on 'freedom' to drink, becomes slave to an inanimate bottle, and to the uncontrolled appetite which he has whetted under the pretense of liberty.

Freedom recognizes and accepts the necessary restraints of correction in order to develop mature qualities of character and judgment. The exuberant puppy whose tail demolishes fragile ornaments, or who dashes into dangerous street traffic to greet its master, must be trained to temper or restrain its expressions of love until it learns to avoid harm's way. A puppy who is left 'free' to chew furniture, jump on toddlers, or wet the living room rug, may not be destroyed, but his undisciplined nature is not fit for admission to the inner sanctums of his master's society. A child who has not learned to curb his selfish desires and aggressions is not yet fit for the society of others. The children of God are similarly unfit for the intimacy of God's society until they have learned to subordinate their passions and ambitions to His wishes.

God, as a parent responsible for training His children, has ordained certain spiritual laws which are as fixed and immutable in their effects as physical laws, and when flaunted, imperil a Christian's spiritual safety. If we are to become holy, as our Heavenly Father is holy, then obedient conformance to His instructive Word accomplishes our benefit, since the Word reveals and details the true character of God which we are called to emulate. We can appreciate that the holiness, abundant life, blessings, and deliverance God promises are developed by obedience in submission to God's laws. Our complete submission becomes our complete fulfillment.

The spiritually mature Christian understands that obedience is inherently rewarding, and prays with the Psalmist: "Make me to go in the path of thy commandments; for therein do I delight" (Psalm 119:35). Jeremiah 6:16 puts it: "ask for the old paths, where is the good way, and walk therein, and ye shall find rest for your souls."

What belongs to God cannot be appropriated to ungodly purposes without damaging the vessel, itself. For, God has revealed that we are to use our freedom to choose life in Him, by faith in Jesus Christ, Whose holiness is our wholeness. If we pervert the purpose of our freedom which is to choose God, we will ultimately lose both the exercise and enjoyment of freedom. If we abuse our freedom by choosing to sin, we harm others, as well as ourselves.

Squandering of energies under the guise of freedom to do what one wishes is self-defeating and produces only conflict, wasted effort, and eventual destruction. We have not been freed to live in sin, while others are still in bondage. We have been freed from sin, not to sin. I Peter 2:16 puts it: "Live as free men, yet without using your freedom as a pretext for evil; but live as servants of God." Paul asked, "Do we then overthrow the law by this faith? By no means! On the contrary, we uphold the law" (Romans 3:31). So we are to relinquish voluntarily our self-interest because of our love for God. We are to surrender the freedom to pursue selfishness in order to express our love for God in obedient, loving service to Him and others. Galatians 5:13 explains: "For you were called to freedom, brethren; only do not use your freedom as an opportunity for the flesh, but through love be servants of one another." See also, James 1:25.

The maximizing of freedom under a system of law and order exposes the wrongness of license, or undisciplined freedom. To have unfettered freedom of action, one could dwell in isolation on a desert island and have no restraints whatever. However, few men choose to live as a recluse, because the quality of life, leisure, and creative activity would be diminished. For, man is challenged to his utmost only in society which provides developmental opportunities.

Clearly, if an individual is to live among others, each must responsibly and voluntarily limit his freedom to act, commensurate with the same freedom for, and limitation upon, others. A homely legal maxim declares that any right to swing my fist ends where your nose begins. By accepting equal and reciprocal limitations on individual freedom every person in a society increases his freedom. By expanding freedom of movement, his total leisure or freedom is increased because of the advantages of specialization and organization, as well as by the protection afforded under laws which restrain others from harming him, or restricting his freedom.

Obedience to law produces order and gives each the maximum amount of freedom without harm to oneself or others. Men loosed unto unrestrained license will collide with one another, curtail one another's freedom, destroy the order of their system, and extinguish their own excellence. Order discourages and restricts only irresponsible freedom. Law does not restrain him who rightly obeys it, but only him who wrongly breaks it. Railroad tracks do not restrict a train's operation, but make it possible for the train to function for the purpose intended. God's rules do likewise, by keeping us on the straight and narrow.

An orderly system of traffic lights illustrates how law and order free us from making hazardous decisions at every intersection. True, we are not free to disobey traffic regulations, and our freedom to proceed is momentarily restricted whenever we encounter a red light. However, we are free to move confidently whenever we have a green light, because others are dependably restrained from proceeding when they have a red light. Since we can rely upon this system of lawful order and universally obligatory regulations, we all avoid becoming hopelessly entangled in collisions and traffic jams. We are free to go farther and faster than we could without the organization, safety, and security of the law, which governs all men alike.

Although we sacrifice some freedom to act as we please when we obey all traffic regulations, we are free to follow any number of routes we choose within the system. Total freedom of choice and movement is expanded, rather than curtailed, when we accept minimal restraints of an integrated system of law. Regulatory limitations impose no denial of liberty as long as total freedom and expression is expanded in this way. The power to ignore traffic laws is not the start of freedom to drive, but the death of it, for if one expects reciprocal obedience to the laws from others, he must himself obey them.[62] In short, by having some restraints mutually applied to every person's freedom, God arranges maximum total freedom for everyone. There is a risk of collision when one person abuses his freedom, but the potential for expanded freedom to travel makes the potential risks tolerable.

In nature, compliance with law produces harmony and order, not restriction of movement. The laws of gravity and motion in the heavens keep the planets moving in their place and proper course. Obedience to their ordered route is essential to free movement and their very existence. Without obedience to their proper course, the heavenly bodies would stagger into one another, and destroy their movement, harmony and being. What keeps them freely moving is obedience to the forces of their constitution and non-departure from their appointed orbits.[63]

The spiritual man finds that slavery to God's will also produces maximum individual dignity and personal freedom. Self-fulfillment for everyone thrives under an orderly system of law, because it affords equal protection and opportunity to all others. When we freely and responsibly accept God's Sovereign rule, we ally ourselves with supernatural forces and divine purposes which already exist for our benefit and growth.

By submitting to a system of order in society, I further develop, maximize, and expand the quantity and quality of freedom, since I do not have to spend hours weaving a suit of clothes, because others, more adept at it choose to do so, and I am freed to devote my liberated time to pursuits I find most agreeable. I, too, can specialize and increase in productive proficiency, and gain more leisure time. The benefit of freedom is using time to do what I choose and ought to do. Specialization in an orderly society produces efficiencies which benefit every individual beyond what he could realize in isolation.

An operative system of law in society also frees me from the task of self-defense by furnishing this necessary protection and security. I need not maintain an overnight vigil to safeguard my life and home against intruders or invading hordes. The greater leisure which law thus frees and expands, provides freedom to do what one prefers to do. It frees every man to develop his highest faculties and pursue quality goals and self-realization.

Similarly, in the spiritual realm, if we accept the security and comfort of God's order by submission to His rule, we are protected from harmful spiritual forces and baser pursuits, which frees us for true spirituality. Jesus' tether or yoke is not a cruel restraint on the individual will, but a guide to keep one headed in the right direction, and away from wandering into danger. The yoke of Christ which is light and easy is made for two (Matthew 11:29), and when you walk beside Him, He not only shows the way, but lovingly bears all the weight of your burdens. We sacrifice no freedom in harness with Christ, but gain purpose, endurance, and fulfillment. His strength is made perfect in our weakness (2 Corinthians 12:9).

God's spiritual laws are like walls, necessitating some limitations, but primarily shielding Christian freedom of action from oneself, as well as assaults by others. A prisoner in jail views the only purpose of walls as confinement and the harsh imposition of authority. But a free man under siege appreciates that the walls of a fortress provide valuable protection and security for his total liberty by keeping out those who seek to enslave or destroy him. Law preserves and enlarges freedom by insulating its beneficiaries from the violence and transgressions of assailants. The shepherd's staff with which God gently prods the sheep back to safety, does not constrict liberty. It establishes protective boundaries in which maximum quality freedom and fulfillment can be experienced, exercised, expanded, enjoyed, and prolonged.

Freedom <u>from</u> external dangers is often as important as freedom <u>to</u> express oneself. The hedge of protection which God sets around His righteous one (Job 1:10), not only excludes and protects against evil, but also limits unspiritual activities by those surrounded by the protective wall. God warned unfaithful Israel: "I will hedge up thy way with thorns, and make a wall, that she shall not find her paths. And she shall follow after her lovers, but she shall not overtake them... then shall she say, I will go and return to my first husband; for then was it better with me than now." Thus, God's restrictions on freedom emerge from God's protection and concern for our safety and best interests. He does not restrain us to withhold joy, but to avoid our loss of blessings. God's restraints express divine, paternal love, care and devotion for His children.

CHAPTER 6

GOD'S BLESSINGS OF PARTICIPATION BY FAITH

"And without faith it is impossible to please him. For whoever would draw near to God must believe that he exists and that he rewards those who seek him."

– Hebrews 11:6.

God bestows a special dignity upon man by the blessing of faith. By man's exercise of faith, God permits him to receive and personally appropriate blessings which God intends and promises for His children. Romans 10:17 says: "So faith comes from what is heard, and what is heard comes by the preaching of Christ." If Jesus has said it in the Bible, the Word of God, then it is true and reflects God's will. We rely upon God's will and Sovereign power to do what He says in order to perform and fulfill His purpose, as expressed in His Word. If we pray according to a promise in the Word, we pray for what God intends, and our will coincides with the revealed intent and perfect will of God, so we can depend upon constancy and fulfillment of His promise.

Hebrews 11:1, KJV says: "Now faith is the substance of things hoped for, the evidence of things not seen." Thus, faith is not concerned with what presently exists and is visible, or what we can perceive by sensory impressions of sight or sound. Faith is concerned with what is invisible in the present, or what is yet to come, "things not seen," and "things hoped for."

Faith comes by the grace of God, through the Word, which gives evidence or proof which produces personal conviction of its truth. God, in His omnipotence, can inspire faith in any way He pleases. He has revealed a dependable way to acquire faith in the promises of His Word. The blessing of faith comes by learning the Word which is our responsibility, so we can receive what God has provided by His Word. We are sure, or certain, because God's Word says so. We accept, and are convinced by the Word's proof that unseen hopes have, or will, become realities. A believer must read, hear, and know the Word, for faith to germinate. Otherwise, there is nothing deposited in your heart for the Holy Spirit to call up and bring to your remembrance what Jesus says in the Word.

The Bible relates instances where belief in God's promises and averments was engendered by an epiphany or encounter with God. Adam, Abraham, and Moses, had personal encounters with God and received His Word directly. St. Paul, the Apostles and disciples of the early Church experienced directly the Word uttered by Christ. Thomas believed in the Resurrection when he felt the wounds in Christ's hands and side. Gideon believed God's assurance of victory when a fleece was made moist while all else was dry. For the rest of us, faith comes by hearing the Lord's Word contained in Scripture.

There is a special cogency about the Old Testament records because the Jews had so many personal experiences with God; His miracles, holiness, and deliverance, such as the parting of the Red Sea, that they could sustain belief in Him and in the promises of His Word. The remembrance of these occurrences, when recorded and maintained intact, together with genealogical records in the Scriptures, verify all revelations imparted, including the Genesis account of Creation. Likewise, the New Testament reports personal recollections about Jesus, His ministry, benevolence and resurrection. These have been preserved intact, and stimulate belief in all revelations, including Christ's authentication of the Old Testament truths.

Faith is man's conviction, based upon and responding to God's assurance, that man's reliance personally appropriates, activates, or sets in operation a supernatural process of fulfilling God's promise for him. God's Word reveals He will do what He says. He instructs and expects us to believe it, and make a direct connection with His Sovereign Providence. If we fail to exercise faith, we may not receive the promised blessing. If we hoard our faith and fail to exercise it in intercessory prayer to promote blessings for others from God, we may retard or defer their blessings, and contribute directly to their privation and suffering.

All faith of believers comes by the grace of God. Romans 12:3 exhorts us "to think with sober judgment, each according to the measure of faith which God has assigned him." Galatians 5:22 lists faith among the fruit of the Holy Spirit, which, you will recall is available as God's gift for the asking (Luke 11:13). I Corinthians 12:8 lists faith as a gift of the Holy Spirit given to individual members of the Body of Christ "for the common good," growth, and edification of the Body (I Corinthians 12:7). Ephesians 2:8 affirms: "For by grace you have been saved through faith; and this is not your own doing, it is the gift of God" (see also, 2 Peter 1:1). While God provides our faith, He does not believe for us. That is man's part, by exercising free choice to believe.

One's salvation, including the faith to embrace Christ as Lord and Saviour, is the gift of God's grace. It is essential that salvation be received by faith which comes by hearing the Scripture's Good News (Galatians 4:5; Ephesians 1:5, 2:9). Salvation begins with the revelation and conviction that when you deserved to die as a sinner, God saved you from eternal damnation by grace through faith in Jesus as Lord and Saviour. Saving grace is offered to all men, but it extends to and is effective for, only those who faithfully believe in God's promise. God intends every man to be redeemed in Christ, when he receives salvation by grace through faith (Acts 2:21; I Timothy 2:4,6; I John 2:2; 2 Peter 3:9). Unbelief chooses to reject the truth of God's Word of promise, and accounts for not receiving the blessing of God's promised, saving grace.

The New Birth occurs through faith which apprehends and appropriates the truth of God's promise of salvation, with the conviction that salvation's reality has become one's personal blessing. Faith in such case does not need to occur more than once to receive, secure, and respond to the event. The act of faith simply confirms, makes certain, and convicts of belief that the event has occurred. We may reaffirm our belief many times throughout life, but our faith in the occurrence has made, evidenced, and affirmed the reality of salvation the first time we exercised faith. Faith will be strengthened as our love and holiness develop and evidence the New Birth, and the Holy Spirit confirms the event has occurred and is sealed.

Saving faith is unique, because once you have received it by grace from God, He sustains it, and sees that it is never lost. He may even use trials to strengthen, increase, and sharpen our faith, so that our overcoming proves the authenticity of faith, and gives cause for rejoicing and confidence in the perseverance and endurance of divine faith from God.

There are other events, often concerning eschatology, or final things, in which we believe and have firm conviction, because God has revealed these events in His Word. However, our faith does not accelerate or bring the occurrence about. We believe our sins have been forgiven; that the Holy Spirit will sanctify and transform us into the image of Christ, and we will be glorified; that we have been baptized into the Body of Christ. We believe and have hope that the resurrection of our bodies will occur; we will be part of the Rapture of the Saints; that Christ will return a Second time and completely vanquish evil; and that Heaven is our eternal habitat. Faith in such events perceives the truth of their occurrence, apprehends such truth, and gratefully receives its promise by God's grace, because we have embraced Christ as Lord and Saviour by faith. However, no amount of fervent belief, intense reliance, or serial conviction can trigger, facilitate, or make these events more of a reality or actuality, because they have been ordained by God and pre-determined to occur. All we can do is embrace, and confidently expect, that we are personal beneficiaries of the blessing because God has said so. Faith simply evidences, confirms, and makes certain our conviction of belief that events have, or will, occur. Lack of personal faith will not cancel or deter the event ordained by God.

There are indications unbelievers can invoke the power of the Word by believing it, to prophesy, cast out demons, and do mighty works in the name of Jesus (Matthew 7:22). However, although rebellious sinners may do such things, Jesus clearly says that evildoers will not enter the Kingdom of Heaven, because they did not do God's will (Matthew 7:21, 23). Consequently, the blessings promised by the Word are intended for, and depend upon one being a disciple of Christ, and embracing salvation in Him.

A Sovereign God who wishes all men to be saved, can provide salvation to whomever and however He pleases. God may save a sinner who is ignorant of the Gospel, because he has sought God and lived righteously according to the knowledge revealed to all men in conscience, nature and the heavens (Deuteronomy 4:29; Psalm 19:1-2; Romans 1:18-21). God may also provide special illumination apart from the Word. The Philistines who desecrated the ark of the Lord, recognized the need to seek propitiation for their wrongdoing after the Lord punished them with tumors and a plague (I Samuel 6:3), yet they did not repent or turn toward the Lord, despite the special revelation communicated by God's remonstrances.

The Great Commission to the Church to witness the Gospel to all the world remains God's principal method of evangelism for the salvation of sinners, whom the Holy Spirit convicts by quickening or vitalizing the Word we share. It is a Commission no believer may take lightly. I Corinthians 2:14 discloses that a sinner who has not been saved by grace through faith in the Gospel is an "unspiritual man" who "does not receive the gifts of the Spirit of God... and he is not able to understand them because they are spiritually discerned" see John 3:3. While no-one is barred from hearing the Good News, one's attachment to sin or hardness of heart may make him incapable of perceiving its truths or responding to Christ.

In our daily lives, the faith with which we are most familiar is the reliance which invites or elicits God's promised blessings for more abundant life. Such faith can facilitate or enhance the operations of reward by the intensification or fervency of our reliance on the Word of promise. God intends personal faith to be the foundation or basis for fulfillment of hope; the very essence or substance of the thing hoped for. Somehow, faith supernaturally triggers divine power, and transforms or solidifies it into substance, actuality, or existence of the thing promised by God. Where faith exists, it is a substance which is transmuted into blessing, much as energy translates into matter in the physical world.

The greater our faith, trust, and reliance in God's Word, the greater our assurance and certainty of the promise's realization, actuality, and fulfillment. Faith for the abundant life starts with conviction of a promise's truth. It then uses personal, ongoing, appropriation and internalization of the Word to activate or accelerate present reality. This is the basis of the health and wealth doctrine: that by faith a believer can realize health, prosperity, or any blessing promised in the Word. We are privileged to participate in the blessings of obedience, prayer, stewardship, witness, and holiness through faith which brings about the more abundant life in this world by one's intensity of application, continual exercise of faith, and dependence on the Word.

The Holy Spirit's power transforms a believer's holiness to the likeness of Christ, but man's faithful cooperation can accelerate and facilitate the process. A New-Born believer is privileged to participate in the blessing of receiving God's promises for more abundant life by exercising faith that God will perform and fulfill His promises. God's grace, alone, promises and provides rewards, and apportions them in any manner, as and to whom He chooses. But He has designated faith as a disciple's part to trigger personal receipt and embrace of supernatural blessings, and faith becomes the substance of such things hoped for.

Hebrews 11:3 affirms that God creates actual things out of the unseen; out of nothing: "By faith we understand that the world was created by the word of God, so that what is seen was made out of things which do not appear." And God's principal plan to bless man is through the exercise or prayer of faith. Prayer, motivated by faith, is man's channel to accept God's grace, based on assurance that God's blessing is meant for you; that God controls all creation, including your life; and that He is able to deliver on His promises declared in His Word.

Ongoing faith is possible by ongoing recourse to the Word, by which faith comes, and when we possess and have the Word deposited and resident in our hearts, we can draw upon it for courage and conviction to endure when tempted, afflicted or persecuted. We can share faith with others whose faith is flagging, by exhorting and encouraging belief that the Word's promises can be personally appropriated and fulfilled. The Holy Spirit can always call up the Word we have on deposit, to remind us of what Christ has said in His Word to bolster our conviction and assurance.

THE ELEMENTS AND EXERCISE OF SAVING FAITH

The core of saving faith is believing that Christ's death paid for all your sins; and that by believing in Him as Lord and Saviour, you can receive forgiveness and eternal life. First, faith perceives the truth intelligently or intellectually, that Jesus paid for your sins to satisfy God's Justice, and make your reconciliation with God possible. Second, faith assents to that truth; is persuaded by, convinced of; gives credence to; and receives the proposition emotionally. Third, faith relies upon or trusts in that truth volitionally, choosing to accept it by and as an act of will. Specifically, saving faith recognizes Jesus is Saviour; personally appropriates that truth for one's circumstances or situation; and depends upon, commits to, and trusts Jesus as the way to forgiveness and reconciliation with God.[64]

Romans 10:9-10 strongly implies that faith is in a total person, Jesus Christ, Who must be trusted as both Saviour and Lord: "if you confess with your lips that Jesus is Lord and believe in your heart that God raised him from the dead, you will be saved. For man believes with his heart and so is justified, and he confesses with his lips and so is saved." If we are to trust Jesus as Lord, (as well as Saviour), then we must be willing to obey His rule and submit to His Sovereignty over our lives.[65] This need to receive Jesus as Lord is confirmed by Luke 14:27,33 where Jesus tells the multitude accompanying Him: "Whoever does not bear his own cross and come after me, cannot be my disciple... whoever of you does not renounce all that he has cannot be my disciple." Faith in the Lord requires submission to His Way in order to forsake the wretched life of sin which explains man's need for a Saviour. The concept of receiving Jesus in His total person — as Lord and Saviour — is not unique. God's wholeness is inseparable, and we cannot separate His love and mercy from His justice. Every aspect of God's personality was integrated and accommodated in His relationship with man, as mercy met justice at the Cross.

A dispute arises over whether the faith needed for salvation is simply recognition that Jesus is the one way to forgiveness and life, or also concurrently requires repentance for sin and submission to His Lordship. References to His Lordship, it is argued, require only belief and trust in His divinity and sovereignty. They are not concerned with literal or subjective submission to his rule in order to be saved. Saving repentance means changing one's mind to acknowledge Jesus is God, and more than mere man. But others believe repentance involves sorrow over sin. Such fine distinctions are unnecessary.

True, it can be seriously argued that saving faith necessarily involves confession and repentance of sin. One cannot believe in Jesus as the Saviour from sin and its penalty, without also acknowledging the need to abandon the sinful life from which he must be saved. This implies one's awareness of the need to submit obediently to Jesus as the Lord, and follow His superior way. Jesus died for our sins in order to save us from them and their penalty. Accordingly, He must want us not to sin, but to obey and follow His way, to be consistent with His Atonement. By seeking Jesus as Saviour, you necessarily seek Jesus as Lord by declaring your intent to renounce your sinful way, and turn toward the Lord's way, which is the completion of repentance. This intent to turn from sin and toward God, although no affirming works have happened yet, is sufficient for conversion and the new Birth by grace through faith.

If one needs only faith in Jesus as Saviour to be saved, he will shortly be transformed by his regeneration to a condition of holiness, where he must submit to Jesus as Lord and desire to follow His way in renunciation of sinful life. This increased holiness as enabled by the Holy Spirit, will increase righteous works. As our knowledge of God increases, we will learn what pleases Him, and our obedient works will increasingly reflect our growing holiness and knowledge. Without this submissive obedience to the Saviour who reigns and rules over willing subjects with their advance consent, we could not be fitted for the society of God.

Anyone who professes faith in Jesus as Saviour, but is not transformed by the New Birth to penitence, and driven to trust in Jesus as Lord, has demonstrably not been saved. Salvation will always involve trust in Jesus as Saviour, plus submission to Jesus as Lord, either simultaneously, or ensuing almost immediately after faith in Jesus as Saviour. You cannot know Jesus until you have acknowledged your sin, and appreciate the wretchedness and peril of your sinful condition, which necessitates your need for the Saviour. When you despair of your own desperate wickedness; and conviction of sin finally leads you to tears of remorse and repentance, then Jesus comes with gracious forgiveness. He lovingly lifts you up, and imparts new spiritual life and regeneration, the balm of Gilead which cleanses you of unrighteousness.

The distinction is of no practical value to anyone other than someone making a 'deathbed' confession of faith, like the thief on the cross, who had no time in life to be transformed and become a disciple. Let us leave that question to God, Who allowed the thief to steal Paradise at the last hour. After all, saving faith in Jesus, which triggers the New Birth, inherently reflects and involves some fruit of the Holy Spirit in the love, joy, peace and faith which accompany the New Birth and indwelling Spirit.

That is why it is useless to debate whether the New Birth can be embraced simply by acknowledging the need for Jesus as Saviour, or must be preceded or accompanied by repentance and obedient submission to Jesus as Lord. Indeed, this distinction is lost on Roman Catholic and Eastern Orthodox Christians who believe that salvation can begin, but before it is completed, one's desire to be saved by faith in Jesus must be routinely evidenced and continually expressed in obedient works submitting to His Lordship.

What matters is that there must be a faith-filled acceptance of Jesus as Saviour, which must be accompanied by a faith-filled confession that Jesus is Lord, either contemporaneously or immediately following the belief in Jesus' Resurrection (Romans 10:9-10). Even if a believer only hears about and receives Jesus as Saviour, he is far better than without Jesus at all, and his conviction of the need to confess Christ's Lordship will occur as soon as the avowal of submissive obedience to the Lord is communicated. If conviction of sin and repentance are not concurrent events, they will immediately ensue by the indwelling of the Holy Spirit, Who undertakes our sanctification "for obedience to Jesus and for sprinkling with His Blood" (I Peter 1:2). "And I am sure that he who began a good work in you will bring it to completion at the day of Jesus Christ" (Philippians 1:6).

Faith in Jesus as Saviour, must necessarily be accompanied by obedient submission to Jesus as Lord, because God has commanded it (John 3:16; Romans 10:9). He has arranged for regeneration of a new spirit in a believer, implanting a new desire to be righteous, and He has ordained the Holy Spirit to accomplish holiness by an ongoing process of sanctification. One who has received Jesus as Saviour, yet stubbornly seeks to live a worldly life, will be led to holiness and obedience because of his new nature. This is done with his implied consent, because he cannot seek salvation from sin without intent to forsake it and obediently submit to the Lord. God will enable whatever is necessary to fit him for eternity.

We cannot be rescued from the penalty of sin by our Saviour without also submitting to His Lordship, and turning from our sinful ways by following Him (Luke 14:27). Jesus warns that not everyone who calls Him Lord, prophesies, or casts out demons in His name shall enter the Kingdom of Heaven, "but he that doeth the will of my Father" (Matthew 7:21-23; see also, Matthew 7:14; Luke 6:40, 13:23). The foolish maidens who had no oil for their lamps were likewise denied entrance to the Lord's marriage feast (Matthew 25:1-13). They desired to be with the Lord, but had never committed to His rule and way, and were thus unprepared at His Second Coming, since they had no good works, which would have evidenced the true faith by which obedient works come.

Let us be clear. God's grace alone provides saving faith, perseverance in faith, repentance, and our obedience. We do not assure retaining our salvation by persevering in faith, or doing good works. Perseverance and works result from, and evidence true faith, which includes submission to the Lord's way. God completes our salvation, and gives us the power, and reveals the keys to success: and salvation is evident because we have submitted and turned from sin. We have started cooperating in changing our lives, and God is bringing it to completion, as evidenced by our perseverance and good works (Philippians 1:6).

There are possibly some men who have never connected salvation with sin, but were motivated to embrace Jesus as some benefactor to rescue them from the meanness of the world and improve their earthly existence. God forbid, they may even have been invited by well-meaning Christians to try Jesus as a passport to Heaven, or as an experiment in receiving the more abundant life here on earth. However, there is no true saving faith without perceiving and detesting the personal sinfulness which is offensive to God. The sinner turning to Jesus must appreciate the need for rescue from the penalty for sin, and hence his need for a Saviour.

When we trust Christ as both Lord and Saviour, we surrender the soul as guilty and defiled, and receive Christ as the source of forgiveness and eternal life.[66] We cannot recognize the need for a Saviour as our passage to Heaven, without recognizing our need to abandon sin, and admitting there is something preventing our doing it on our own. And that inability to submit and obey is what compels us to turn, submit to Jesus and follow Him as Lord, for cleansing and enablement. Unless you have been convicted of sin by the Holy Spirit, and want to be saved from the penalty for sin, which is an implicit confession of a sinful life, there is no New Birth or salvation. A sinner cannot recognize why he needs a Saviour, or turn to Jesus as that Saviour, without first understanding the wretchedness of sin which necessitates his salvation. Obedience to the Lord then actualizes repentance as the fulfillment of submission to the Lord's way.

BY FAITH MAN CLAIMS GOD'S BLESSINGS

Once you are God's saved, Born-Again child, regenerated and sanctified, He promises He will continue to bless you according to His riches in glory in, through, and because of Christ Jesus (Philippians 4:19), despite the sins you have committed. Romans 5:8 puts it: "But God shows his love for us in that while we were yet sinners Christ died for us. Since, therefore, we are now justified by his blood, much more shall we be saved by him from the wrath of God. For if, while we were enemies we were reconciled to God by the death of his Son, much more, now that we are reconciled, shall we be saved by his life."

Jesus says we must look to Him for salvation, in recognition that He is a saving God. He must be seen and visualized through the Word, and ever be the object of our attention and affection. Faith is as easy as looking at Jesus, any time and any place, with comprehension He is our Lord, Saviour, Deliverer, and Perfector of our faith. 2 Corinthians 1:20 says of Jesus: "all the promises of God find their yes in him. That is why we utter the Amen through him, to the glory of God." Our faith is expanded to rely on God's Word promising He will guide and enlighten us; make us holy; and continue to save and deliver believers. These are the bases for our faith that God will provide more abundant life, full of His peace, expanding in love, and growing in faith and holiness.

God answers any prayer He chooses in any manner He chooses, but the Bible prescribes prayers filled with faith as His way to elicit the promised blessings from God. Prayer is the vessel which carries our petitions upward to God, but effective prayer must be faith-filled, and believe that God will honor our requests because He promises to do so. We must believe God will deliver what He has promised, and it will inevitably result because God declares its fulfillment in His Word.

Faith is an ongoing prerequisite to claiming the blessings which God promises the faithful: "Whatever you ask in prayer, believe that you receive it, and you will" (Mark 11:24; see also, Luke 18:1,7; and I John 5:14-15). Jesus commands faith at Mark 5:36: "Do not fear, only believe." Romans 14:23 adds: "for whatever does not proceed from faith is sin," including the prayers we offer. Hebrews 11:6 puts it: "Without faith it is impossible to please him, for whoever would draw near to God must believe that He exists and that He rewards those who seek Him," and James 4:2 teaches: "You do not have, because you do not ask." God's all-pervasive plan, as our loving Father, is to bless believers by grace through their prayers of faith.

Romans 1:17 imposes a new life-style for believers: "The righteous shall live by faith." We are to "think with sober judgment, each according to the measure of faith which God has assigned him" (Romans 12:3). 2 Peter 1:1 says all believers have the same measure of faith or ability to believe as the Apostles and: "have obtained a faith of equal standing with ours in the righteousness of our God and Saviour Jesus Christ." 2 Corinthians 4:13 says we share "the same spirit of faith" as David, when he wrote: "I believed, therefore I have spoken" (Psalm 116:10).

In the Old Testament, which is a precursor and shadow of the New, a believer is charged to fix the Word in his heart and trust it, before he can benefit: "keep thy soul diligently, lest thou forget the things which thine eyes have seen, and lest they depart from thy heart all the days of thy life: but teach them thy sons" (Deuteronomy 4:9). The prescription for a believer's success is set forth at Joshua 1:8: "This book of the law shall not depart out of thy mouth; but thou shalt meditate therein day and night, that thou mayest observe to do according to all that is written therein: for then thou shalt make thy way prosperous, and then thou shalt have good success."

The Word, when quickened and explicated by the Holy Spirit, has supernatural effect to work changes in man, and its effectiveness reflects its identity with Christ, Who was with God from the beginning (John 1:1). It is the instrument through which the Holy Spirit works spiritual transformation, empowers works, and shapes the conscience in men. "For the word of the cross is folly to those who are perishing, but to us who are being saved it is the power of God" (I Corinthians 1:18; and see also, John 1:12; Acts 1:8; Romans 15:13, 19; Ephesians 3:20; and 2 Peter 1:3-4). We are to receive and embrace the Word with the same zeal as the Beroeans (Acts 17:11).

Jesus' Atonement is sufficient for the whole world, but it is efficient only for those who receive and confess Him as Lord and Saviour. God's grace uses the Word to transmit the doctrine of sin and the Gospel of Salvation to all men. However, some men have developed such hardness of heart they cannot respond to conviction of sin or fear of Hell. Yet, God can impart prevenient or saving grace to whomever He pleases or elects, enabling them to respond to conviction of sin and the Good News of the Gospel.

Psalm 1:1-3 puts it: "Blessed is the man that... his delight is in the law of the Lord; and in his law doth he meditate day and night... and whatsoever he doeth shall prosper." Meditation requires repeating, speaking, and thinking about the Word, until its varied meanings have been revealed to you by the Holy Spirit. Proverbs 4:21-22 tells us to heed God's Word: "incline thine ear unto my sayings. Let them not depart from thine eyes; keep them in the midst of thine heart. For they are life unto those that find them, and health to all their flesh."

The hallmark of Abraham's faith was that "no distrust made him waver concerning the promise of God," despite its apparent impossibility, that he would become the father of many nations, even though he was "about a hundred years old" and Sarah, his wife, was barren

(Romans 4:20). If you, too, would not falter or stumble in your Christian walk of faith, then you should share this conviction that God is "able to do what he had promised" (Romans 4:21).

Jesus asked two blind men who sought healing: "Do you believe that I am able to do this?" and when they said 'yes', He established the rule for receiving blessings by grace: "According to your faith be it done to you" (Matthew 9:28-29). On the other hand, faith allowed Peter to walk on the water only as long as he trusted in the presence and power of Jesus. When the sea's turmoil caused him to lose confidence, Peter started sinking, and Jesus said: "O Man of little faith, why did you doubt?" (Matthew 14:28-31). Neither could the disciples work a cure because of their "little faith" (Matthew 17:20), on which occasion Jesus said: "if you have faith as a grain of mustard seed, you will say to this mountain, 'Move hence to yonder place,' and it will move; and <u>nothing will be impossible to you</u>."

At Matthew 21:21, Jesus teaches: "If you have faith and never doubt... it will be done. And <u>whatever</u> you ask in prayer, you will receive, if you have faith." Mark 9:23 adds: "<u>All things</u> are possible to him who believes." Unlimited blessings are also indicated at John 14:13-14: "<u>Whatever you ask</u> in my name, I will do it, that the Father may be glorified in the Son; if you <u>ask anything</u> in my name, I will do it." (See also, John 15:16, 16:23-24).

Jesus affirms at Mark 11:23-24: "whoever says to this mountain, 'Be taken up and cast into the sea,' and does not doubt in his heart, but <u>believes that what he says will come to pass</u>, it will be done for him. Therefore, I tell you, whatever you ask in prayer, believe that you receive it, and you will" (See also, Luke 18:1,7). I John 5:14-15 explains: "This is the confidence which we have in him, that if we ask anything according to his will he hears us. And if we know that he hears us in whatever we ask, we know that we have obtained the requests made of him."

At Mark 9:23 Jesus teaches: "All things are possible to him who believes," just before He cast out an unclean spirit in response to a father's profession of belief. Jesus healed a leper with the direction: "Rise and go your way; your faith has made you well" (Luke 17:18). In the Parable of the Sower, Jesus tells of seed sown, which He identifies as the Word, some of which falls by the wayside, "and the birds came and devoured it" (Mark 4:4). Jesus teaches that Satan "immediately" steals the Word from hearers when they fail to cherish the Word (Mark 4:15; Luke 8:12). The birds dispatched by Satan to devour the Word represent the world's temptations, tribulations, persecutions, cares, and desires which distract and prevent a hearer from embracing the truth.

Jesus also explains in the Parable why other seed in rocky soil fails to yield grain, when it springs up briefly without root, and withers away (Mark 4:4-6). Seed also fails because of thorns "which choke the word, and it proves unfruitful," and these thorns are "the cares of the world, and the delight in riches, and the desire for other things" (Mark 4:18-19). Worldly involvements and preoccupations are thorns capable of choking the Word which would otherwise bear fruit. The delight in riches can entice your attention away from the Word by filling your consciousness with thoughts of worldly wealth. The desires for prestige, power, popularity, achievement, or celebrity status similarly serve to drive out the Word because they reflect preference for worldly rewards.

Jesus then assures believers that it is possible to bear fruit according to our faithful reliance on, and reception of, the Word's promise. He explains: "And these are they which are sown on good ground: such as hear the word, and receive it, and bring forth fruit, some thirty-fold, some sixty, and some a hundred" (Mark 4:20; Matthew 13:23). Fruitfulness comes in varying degrees. Who would not want to claim a hundred-fold production of fruit, if possible? Who would not prefer the thirty-fold or sixty-fold harvest of fruit over total lack of it, when the seed is stolen, rootless, or choked by the weeds of worldliness?

Jesus reveals God's principle of increase via faith in the Word: "Take heed what you hear; the measure you give will be the measure you get, and still more will be given you. For to him who has will more be given" (Mark 4:23-24; see also, Luke 6:38). The extent to which we believe the Word, trust in it, respect, and rely upon it to work in our own lives, determines the extent of fruit the Word produces in us and for us. The key to the Word bearing fruit of the Holy Spirit is the measure of respect and reliance with which any promise of the Word is received and appropriated as God's assurance of blessing, intended to benefit you, personally. The Spirit recalls to us what Jesus has said, and the greater our familiarity with the Word, and the more we have studied and digested it, the greater will be our remembrance and fruit-bearing.

If you do not trust the Word, or if you regard it with impersonal detachment, it will bear no fruit. When Jesus returned to His hometown and taught there, His Word was not received because the people's familiarity with His family bred contempt for Him: "And they took offense at Him... And He did not do many mighty works there, because of their unbelief" (Matthew 13:53-58). They did not trust the Word and consequently bore no fruit.

If you trust the Word with a measure of only thirty-fold, believing or recalling the Word's promise only partly or infrequently, then the fruitfulness you yield as a disciple will be thirty-fold. If your faithful dependence on the Word is a steady 60%, your increase will be a comparable sixty-fold. When Peter walked on the water in response to Jesus bidding him to come, he placed full faith in Jesus' Word. "But when he saw the wind, he was afraid," and began to sink (Matthew 14:28-31), giving us an example of faith in Christ's Word somewhere between thirty-fold and sixty-fold, because it was distracted by worldly conditions.

If service to the Lord fully occupies your spirit, and you would utilize God's blessings, wisdom and power to the fullest one hundred-fold, then seize the particular Word of precious promise with every resource at your command, every moment of your existence. Embrace it with all your might and concentration; digest it, meditate upon, apply, and live it, if you would enjoy full fruition.

Do you want the full one hundred-fold measure of God's love, protection, rest, peace, holiness, and power? Then fill yourself with the particular Word of promise concerning these blessings, and totally savor, cherish, consider, and delight in it. Devour and absorb its promise, as you appropriate it to your own advantage. Bring yourself to the point you think, speak, and act according to the Word, which coincides perfectly with God's will. One who is sinful should seek divine holiness and obedience by a total immersion and burgeoning of faith in the Word's many promises. One should daily don the full armor of God, which is fashioned by the Word, for ongoing protection against the assaults and fiery darts of the evil one (Ephesians 6:13-18).

The Parable of the Sower is so fundamental to a disciple's understanding and application of faith in the Word to secure blessings, that Jesus says: "Do you not understand this parable? How then will you understand all the parables?" (Mark 4:13). The principle of embracing the Word to produce fruit applies universally, whether your reliance upon God's promise is for holiness, overcoming suffering, fellowship with God, or good stewardship in His service. The principle of growing and bearing fruit by hearing, measuring, faithfully receiving, and personally appropriating the Word, applies to every promise of blessing and enduement contained in the Scriptures: both to being and to having; to what we are becoming in Christ-likeness, and what we are receiving in spiritual and material blessings.

If we sow money into a ministry to reap material gain, we are acting on the Word's principle of growth that an increase in our own prosperity and abundance of blessings will be produced, according to our exercise of faith in God's Word (Luke 6:38; 2 Corinthians 9:6-11).

If you would develop Christ-like character and nurture the growth of the Kingdom within, then "think about... whatever is true... honorable... just... pure... lovely... gracious... and the God of peace will be with you" (Philippians 4:8-9). When you are filled with the Word, you cannot be occupied with the world. For, what is more lovely and pure than God's own character and thoughts revealed, detailed, and expressed in the Word? Our faithful obedience to its precepts will open our hearts to the Holy Spirit's transforming bestowal of God's nature, mercy, love, and justice in us.

If you would grow in the specific fruit of the Spirit: "love, joy, peace, patience, kindness, goodness, faithfulness, gentleness, self-control (Galatians 5:22-23), then seize the assurance of Luke 11:13, which promises: "If you then, who are evil, know how to give good gifts to your children, how much more will the heavenly Father give the Holy Spirit to those that ask him." If you believe and trust in that promise, the Word teaches that all disciples receive the Spirit "by hearing with faith" (Galatians 3:2, 5, 14). Receiving the Spirit can only signify having the fullness of the Spirit — to enjoy His fruit, which increases your holiness, spirituality, and Christ-like character. To bear these fruits of the Spirit, claim the Word's promises for your personal benefit. Yearn for the Spirit with 100% of your desire and attention, and you will enjoy 100-fold increase in fruit of the Spirit; a return Jesus promises is possible for fervent believers.

If you would reap the Spiritual fruit of love, then absorb Romans 5:5: "hope does not disappoint us, because God's love has been poured into our hearts through the Holy Spirit which has been given to us." If you would reap the spiritual fruit of joy, then "Be glad in the Lord," "Rejoice in the Lord," and "sing praises unto the Lord" (Psalms 32:11, 33:1, and 27:6). Embrace these Scriptures which teach that concentrating on the blessings God promises or bestows, impels us to praise Him, and praise reminds us of our blessings and brings joy.

If you would reap the Spiritual fruit of peace, then seize the Word which invites you to cast all your cares on the Lord because He cares for you (I Peter 5:7), and enjoy safe haven and deliverance in Him. Your complete trust in the Lord is evidenced by submitting all your concerns to His care and governance. We rely on God's Providence, which guarantees the safety, security and well-being of a believer's affairs.

The promise of bringing forth fruit, "some thirty-fold, some sixty, and some a hundred" of Mark 4:20 cannot be talking about salvation, because a Christian is either Born-Again and saved, or he remains unsaved and lost. It is not, therefore, possible to be saved by degrees, but it is possible to increase in fruit-bearing by degrees of faith in a Bible promise.

Remember, that not every belief in Christ is equivalent to saving faith in Him. James 2:19 notes: "You believe that God is one; you do well. Even the demons believe —and shudder," but clearly they are not endowed with divine faith. "At the Passover feast, many believed in his name when they saw his signs which he did; but Jesus did not trust himself to them, because he knew all men" (John 2:23-24). Belief becomes saving faith only when it comes by the Word, and is sustained by the Word.[67] Luke 8:15 says that those in good soil, who are fruitful: "are those who, <u>hearing the word, hold it fast</u> in an honest and good heart, and bring forth fruit <u>with patience</u>," that is with diligent application and perseverance.

At John 8:51 Jesus says: "Truly, truly, I say to you, if any one <u>keeps my word</u>, he will never see death." "If what you heard from the beginning abides in you, then you will abide in the Son and in the Father" (I John 2:25). St. Paul reminds the Corinthians of "the gospel, which you received, in which you stand, by which you are saved, <u>if you hold it fast</u> — unless you believed in vain" (I Corinthians 15:1-2). I Timothy 4:16 agrees: "Take heed to yourself and to your teaching; <u>hold to that</u>, for by so doing you will save both yourself and your hearers." According to Colossians 1:23 we are reconciled and will become holy, "<u>provided</u> that you continue in the faith, stable and steadfast, not shifting from the hope of the gospel which you have heard."

Since faith comes by hearing the Word, it follows that faith will be strengthened by constant recourse to the Word's promises in the areas where we seek to bolster our faith. Much of our faith has to do with using it as an instrument of receiving the blessings promised by God in His Word; of using it to produce fruit in our lives. Jesus compares the Word to a seed planted in the human heart, which grows when watered, nurtured, and fed by our faith. Man's great privilege is to tend the Word faithfully and responsibly in order to realize the fruitfulness or fulfillment of God's promises. As we prayerfully feed and water the initial Word/seed of God's promise, with sustained faith generated by steady access to the Word, our faith becomes "the substance of things hoped for, the evidence of things not seen" (Hebrews 11:1).

Fruitfulness has a direct connection with the extent of one's immersion in the Word. It has to do with how diligently and sincerely you measure or adopt the Word; your constancy in attendance upon, appropriation of, and merger of it into your very character and service to the Lord. The place and honor you give the Word, and the extent of your commitment to keep it fast in your heart is the measure of fruit you will receive.

The intensity with which you pay attention, mark, internalize, perform, and live consistently with the Word's directives, determines the depth of your faith; the extent of your fruit, and the volume of your blessing harvested in return. Indeed, the blessings you enjoy usually reflect the measure of your constancy in receiving, believing, and applying the promise and power of God in His Word.

Jesus teaches that the effectiveness of faith is in direct proportion to how the hearer becomes a believer by measuring or embracing God's promised Word of blessing. The key to the Word bearing fruit is constant attention to, and unwavering attendance upon, the Word in one's life. Internalize, learn, memorize, and repeat the Word until it becomes a familiar, inherent, and integral part of your spirit, recalled and spoken with the same ease as reciting your name or recounting personal experiences. You need to be covered, surrounded, and drenched with the Word on the outside, and thoroughly saturated and absorbed with the Word on the inside. You must make it totally the guide and light of your life.

You need to build the Word of God firmly into consciousness, so you can expectantly, trustingly, and triumphantly recall, relate, relay, and rely upon the Word's assurances. Make it the motivating power of your life! Give yourself to the Word and become addicted to it, intoxicated by its full-bodied joy, and totally dependent upon God's power, not yours. You will find that increase in fruit follows the thought, study, reverence, attention, and importance with which you measure the Word, and incorporate it into your being and doing.

For optimum growth, the Word must be ingested daily, and you must assimilate the Word into your spirit, before it can do you any good, just as food must be digested by the physical body after it is seen and tasted. God freely provided manna from heaven to sustain the Israelites in the wilderness, but it had to be gathered and eaten fresh daily, and stale manna would putrefy (Exodus 16:20-21). Likewise, the living water and bread of life which we had yesterday will not sustain us days hence. We must replenish them regularly or we will hunger and thirst anew. No matter how vividly we remember the taste of breakfasts past, it is not the same as eating a real meal for sustenance today.

Faith, too, is a testament to free choice, because faith is an act of volition as well as a gift. Belief is based on what I receive by sensory perception. If I see a man cross Niagara Falls on a high wire with another man on his back I can believe he performed the feat because I saw it. Faith that he can carry me on his back is an act of will based on belief, so that I elect to entrust my safety to him. Faith is a matter of choice, because I can choose to entrust my life to him, or not.

In salvation, the grace of faith comes from God, but I must elect to use it. "For God so loved the world that he gave his only Son, that whoever believes in him should not perish but have eternal life" (John 3:16). Demons believe Jesus is God, because they have personal knowledge of that fact, but choose not to submit obediently to Him as Lord. Men must choose to believe in Jesus as Lord and Saviour because such faith comes by hearing the Word (Romans 10:17), and receives the promise. Sensory impressions and worldly experience cannot yet validate the truth of such belief, and one can only entrust the matter to God in reliance on His integrity to perform what He promises. Eventually, the experience of its fulfillment will confirm the authenticity of God's promise. Faithlessness is choosing not to believe, but it is still a matter of free choice. Faith is not based upon feeling something is believable, but upon willfully choosing to believe because God has said so.

FAILING FAITH IMPEDES BLESSING

Even though God promises blessings and freedom from pain and poverty to the faithful, we see all about us evidence of Christians who are unblessed, unsanctified, fearful, sick, bound, impoverished, and spiritually forsaken. In the midst of national abundance we can find Christians in abject poverty, although their Heavenly Father owns all the wealth in the world, and can create infinitely more with a single word of command. How can such lack be consistent with our Father's loving character when He clearly expresses His intent to shower blessings upon His children and to free them from want and pain?

Certainly, there are times when suffering can be a blessing in disguise, initially intended and sent by God, or subsequently transformed by Him into good for believers. But we are speaking here of denial of blessings so severe it actually produces suffering — the worldly antithesis of blessings as exemption from suffering; because blessings are absent, not by God's plan, but as a result of being effectively delayed or barred by some conduct on the part of a Christian.

The most obvious explanation is that the professor of faith is not truly Born-Again and saved. Kingdom blessings are for those who have entered the Kingdom by grace through faith in Jesus as Lord and Saviour. It is self-evident that one who is not saved in Christ remains unattached to the source of blessings promised God's children. A branch severed from the vine will never bear spiritual fruit. It must first be grafted on by the Divine Husbandman. We should be careful not to judge the efficacy of another's salvation, but we can and ought to judge the sincerity of our own commitment to salvation. Many believed or claimed that they prophesied in Jesus' name, cast out demons, and did many mighty works in His name, yet He declared to them: "I never knew you; depart from me, you evil-doers" (Matthew 24:22-23; Luke 13:25-27; and see also, Acts 19:13-16).

The unsaved man will share generally in God's blessings of sun and rain, "for he makes his sun rise on the evil and on the good, and sends rain on the just and unjust" (Matthew 5:45). However, "The unspiritual man does not receive the gifts of the Spirit of God, for they are folly to him, and he is not able to understand them because they are spiritually discerned" (I Corinthians 2:14; and see also, I Corinthians 2:12; James 3:14-17). Thus, "the word of the cross is folly to those who are perishing, but to us who are being saved it is the power of God" (I Corinthians 1:18).

The second area of self-examination, prompted when blessings are not forthcoming, is to see if our faith is based on the Word's promises, rather than on a hope for un-scriptural, personal desires. Faith is not a leap in the dark, but an enlightened reliance upon God's Word in the Scriptures. We do not have to know how electricity works to know that when we turn a switch on, electricity provides power to activate and illuminate. We may not know how faith works, but we can know when we switch on God's Word, He provides power to illuminate, grow, and bless.

Thank God, the Word is readily accessible to most of the world through the marvels of printing, radio, television and computer networks transmitted and maintained by missionaries and evangelists. We cannot be saved without faith in Jesus' promise of salvation, and we cannot be blessed without faith in Jesus' promises of blessing. It is stubborn, rebellious disobedience to reject God's Word of salvation by grace through faith. It is just as rebellious to disdain God's Word of promise for blessings. We receive and claim both promises by faith in the Word.

Faith must always focus on the promise of God's Word, and not any contradictory evidence from the senses or worldly stimuli. Faith remembers that God's power "calls into existence the things that do not exist" (Romans 4:17) to conform the natural world to His will. "Seeing is believing" is the world's way, but "believing is seeing" is God's way through faith in His Word. God does not change, but He alters the material, sensory world. Ecclesiastes 11:4 summons believers to plant the Word in faith, and sustain it in total disregard of worldly conditions or human perceptions, for: "He that observeth the wind shall not sow: and he that regardeth the clouds shall not reap." The dark storm will eventually and always be followed by sunshine, and midnight will yield to dawn.

God always delivers believers from the world, the flesh, and the devil, but faith requires our collaborative participation in prayer and trust. God entrusts believers as co-workers to express faith in the Word. Reaping a harvest must be preceded by sowing the seeds of faith. Romans 8:6 reminds believers to look only to Jesus: "To set the mind on the flesh is death, but to set the mind on the Spirit is life and peace." Christians may confidently expect, by reliance upon God's Word, to overcome the world and be delivered from its allures and assaults, "for we walk by faith, not by sight" (2 Corinthians 5:7). Faith knows better than to seek confirmation in the visible or sensory realm, but only in God's Word of promise. Confidence does not come only when the sensory world shows results confirming that your prayers were answered. Faith in the Word brings immediate conviction that your constancy will bear fruit if you patiently give God's seed of promise time to grow.

Even though the promised blessing is not instantly manifested as a physical fact, God's Word evokes faith, or unshaken belief God will deliver you from the world, and change worldly conditions. We need to walk by faith in the Word of God, already ordained and constituted in the Heavenly, spiritual realm for our benefit; we ought not walk by sight or evidence of deprivations in the world about us. It is not necessary to deny actual symptoms or the sensory realities which objectively demonstrate deficiencies in the world. You must purpose to resist worldly doubts in the reality, provision, and delivery of your promised blessings, confident God will intervene and eliminate or modify worldly conditions because His Word so promises.

The key to faithful pursuit of blessings is prayer, rather than some independent assertion of rights or claim of privilege as a child of God. God gives us the blessings, but He wants us to ask for them and to rely on Him. Persistent prayer verifies that it is really our heart's desire and not some transient whim of which we will soon weary. So we are called to persevere in our petitions (Luke 11:8, 18:4; Ephesians 6:18). Prayer helps us remember that blessings are provided by God's grace, and not something we can demand simply because God has revealed His pleasure in blessing us.

It is true that no parent delights in having to dress a child who has already learned to dress himself, and God has invested and enabled believers with rights and privileges to act in many areas. But it is very important when petitioning for benefits, to remember they originate with and through God, and not by faith as some independent substance or mechanism we control. When we use the term 'faith-healing', we refer to Divine healing by God through faith. Faith is not the healer, but the link to God's deploying divine resources which heal our physical and spiritual sickness.

It may be too obvious for discussion, but a principal reason Christians do not receive God's blessings is because they do not exercise faith, based on the objective guaranty of God's Word. Faith should always be specific, and based on a particular Word of promise from God which is heard by a disciple (Romans 10:17), and then personally received and claimed. Faith is specific whenever it is based on specific Word promises. He who does not know the Word cannot ask in faith, and he who does not ask, will not receive (James 4:2).

The believer who is ignorant of a Scriptural promise is no different from an unbeliever, since in either case no faith can be generated or exercised. The Born-Again Christian who neglects to study his Bible, and is therefore ignorant of the Word's promises, may be as distant and estranged from the blessings of faith as the outright skeptic or doubter. He cannot know God's disposition to bless, and lacks the basis on which to respond in faith to God. God's grace will continue to bless believers generally, but only God knows what specific blessings He reserves for faithful prayer.

Third, a believer may be aware of a Bible promise of blessings, and plant or appropriate the seed of the Word initially, but then fail to nurture and cultivate its growth by faith unto fruition. Often, there is no depth to our faith because we have not digested, internalized, and assimilated the Word. Bearing fruit may not reach perfection in this lifetime, but mature growth ought to be the direction of our lives. Faith will do a disciple no good if it is lacking in him, or he fails to exercise it, and it will do little good if it is lukewarm. The measure of attention we give the Word, is the measure of spiritual harvest we will get back.

It might seem unfair to the carnal mind, when Jesus proclaims the result of failure to embrace the Word: "For to him who has, will more be given; and from him who has not, even what he has will be taken away" (Mark 4:25). Yet, Jesus is simply stating the spiritual principle of growth, which operates fairly and impartially. If a man cherishes the Word, it will multiply. If he disdains the Word/seed he has received, then that Word will not bear fruit, but will itself wither and die of neglect, or be stolen away by Satan, the thief in the world. So, he who neglects the Word will lose it, as well as any increase. It is possible to lose patience and extirpate the Word in anxiety, frustration, or doubt provoked by the sufferings and enticements of the world. Then, without seed, it is impossible to grow a harvest for reaping.

Our constancy in faith invites God to supply His power of growth for the Kingdom within believers. We are called to "pray always" to affirm our true desires, and as an expression of our collaboration to be made more like Jesus. Meditation in the Word produces faith, which waters the seed already planted within a believer's heart. God's Word is our sustenance by which we persevere in faith by hearing the Word. The seed inspires faith, which is nurtured by regular recourse to the Word. In God's economy of faith, He has regulated or limited Himself and the amount of His power released on our behalf, and responds to prayer based upon the extent of our faith. Prayer, energized by faith, activates God's divine power, which resides in every believer. God's power is fully in us, and enables us "To think with sober judgment, each according to the measure of faith which God has assigned Him" (Romans 12:3). Faith, in abundant measure equal to that given the Apostles (2 Peter 1:1), has been given each believer by Christ, the author of our faith. The faith He has given us is sufficient for all things: we need only develop its prayerful use and fuller application.

A Born-Again Christian does not need to increase his faith, but increase his effective use of what he has. When the Apostles asked Jesus to "Increase our faith" (Luke 17:5), He indicated that the faith they already possessed could accomplish anything they believed: "If you had faith as a grain of mustard seed, you could say to this sycamine tree, 'Be rooted up, and be planted in the sea', and it would obey you" (Luke 17:6).

Ephesians 3:20, KJV, reveals that God "is able to do exceeding abundantly above all that we ask or think, according to the power that worketh in us." The power may be dormant until we activate it. We evoke this power by dwelling on the Word and nurturing our faith, by inviting the indwelling Holy Spirit's fruit of faith to operate. Prayer, energized by faith, activates or facilitates God's divine power, which resides in every believer. If we have little faith, reflected in little prayer, we do not enlist God's ability to do all that we ask. The more faith and prayer we offer, the more God is able to do in accordance with, and in proportion to, the measure of His power activated and working in us.[68] Prayers which ask, but are not fashioned with faithful reliance upon God's ability to answer, are effete. Faith without prayer, forgets that God's power, alone, quickens faith. Through Jesus we "have confidence in God, who raised him from the dead and gave him glory, so that your faith and hope are in God" (I Peter 1:21).

When we do not receive the fullness and abundance which God intends, it may be because of unbelief in God's love, power, and the reality of His promises. Faith works only when we put it to work and invoke it, which is our responsibility. If we focus on our own lack of worth and unfitness to be blessed, and lose faith in God's all-sufficient grace, then our own self-centeredness can erect a wall against God's gifts. We need to recognize, acknowledge, and be convicted of such unbelief in our hearts. We need the power and faith of God's Word of promise to tear down our barriers of unbelief. God's sun will always shine through our windows unless we board them up with doubt and block out the light. God's illumination and blessing remain constant, but faithlessness may have put us in utter darkness.

FAITH STOLEN BY SATAN

We have seen that Satan is a prime cause of human suffering. One of His techniques to cause suffering and impair Christian effectiveness is to attack our faith by taking away the Word. In the Parable of the Sower, Jesus says that "the evil one comes and snatches away what is sown" in one's heart (Matthew 13:18). He can provoke his followers to inflict "tribulation or persecution... on account of the word" (Matthew 13:21), or stir up "cares of the world and the delight in riches" to "choke the word, and it proves unfruitful" (Matthew 13:22).

Jesus also identifies Satan as an enemy who "while men were sleeping... came and sowed weeds among the wheat, and went away. So when the plants came up and bore grain, then the weeds appeared also" (Matthew 13:25-26). It is significant that Satan "went away" after planting evil thoughts, impulses and tendencies, "while men were sleeping"; hence we would be unaware of his secret activity without this warning from Christ.

The embrace of faith is partly a matter of one's will. Faith is a determination to reject doubt and wavering, and to trust God's promises because He has given them. We reject any possibility of God's deceit in the authenticity of His promises or in His goodness, love, and power. God never sends doubt about Himself in these matters; but Satan does, and it is Satan's fiery darts which we must resist by the shield of faith (Ephesians 6:16). God's Word is absolutely reliable, because He has said it; whereas our feelings can be untrustworthy, and our doubts inspired by Satan.

James 3:5-6 reminds us of the consequences of careless words: "How great a forest is set ablaze by a small fire! And the tongue is a fire. The tongue is an unrighteous world among our members, staining the whole body, setting on fire the cycle of nature, and set on fire by hell." Since the kindling used to start a conflagration is consumed quickly by the raging fire, it is easy to forget what and who started the flames of doubting words which consume our faith.

We need to remember it is Satan who seeks to provoke one's pronouncement of evil or doubting thoughts and words. Satan is the one who seeks to murder our faith and steal our blessings (John 10:10), by planting tares of doubt, and magnifying our fears and uncertainties (Ephesians 6:12; and 2 Corinthians 10:3-5). Satan will use other men, even professing Christian leaders, to assault our faith, persecute our beliefs, and create doubts that Bible promises are intended for us or for our times. We need to examine whether we have been drawn into doubt by Satan or even other Christians who misguidedly teach that faith in God's promises cannot effectively claim God's blessings for believers.

Two things are certain: Satan will attack us, and God will deliver us, according to I Peter 5:8,10: "Your adversary the devil prowls around like a roaring lion, seeking someone to devour. Resist him, firm in your faith... And after you have suffered a little while, the God of all grace... will himself restore, establish, and strengthen you." David declares at 2 Samuel 22:2-3: "The Lord is my rock, and my fortress, and my deliverer... he is my shield, and the horn of my salvation, my high tower, and my refuge, my Saviour; thou savest me from violence" (See also, Job 5:19; Psalms 18:2, 31:20, 27:5, 91:1). Thus are described the details of our spiritual sanctuary in God: "Lord, thou hast been our dwelling place in all generations" (Psalm 90:1). We will still be assaulted by the world's persecutions and temptations, but we will be secure and inviolate in the Lord, our Dwelling Place.

Despite God's faithfulness, doubt becomes your declaration that the name of Jesus and the promises of God are not enough to overcome Satan and the world. If you contradict the promise of God's Word by doubting it, your doubt constitutes the same type of transfer of allegiance to Satan as Adam's, based on what Satan says in the natural world, rather than what God has said in His Word. That is embracing the darkness of the world, rather than the spiritual enlightenment of the Word. When the Word is thus stolen by Satan and darkness descends, the darkened heart, emptied of the Word, ingests the world's evil and poison, and will speak evil and doubt. Doubt and unbelief will grow out of your disdain for God's Word, and the substitution of your own ideas and careless words, once you begin to doubt the integrity of God's promises.

While faith comes from hearing the Word, fear comes from experiencing and responding to Satan's deceits in the sensory world. Fear becomes the substance of things undesired, and feeds on itself. Fear negates faith and produces oppression (Isaiah 54:14), and Satan can turn oppression into sickness, which only Jesus can heal (Acts 10:38). The only instances where healing did not occur in Jesus' ministry were because of the disciples' lack of faith (Matthew 17:19), or because of the afflicted person's own unbelief (Matthew 13:58; Mark 6:5-6; see also Matthew 14:29-31 where Peter's fear and doubt started his sinking in the water).

In all things, we are to endure, persevere, stand fast, and resist the devil, so that we may overcome and stand as conquerors in Christ's victory. When the benefits of God's love are blocked, we ought to examine and judge ourselves to make sure our faith is based on explicit promises in God's Word, and we have truly eliminated all doubt.

Jesus warns us that faith, which comes by hearing the Word, can fail. He told Peter He would pray that he stay steadfast in faith because Satan "demanded to have" him. (Luke 22:31; John 17:17-20; see also, I Corinthians 13:2). Being forewarned, our duty is to resist Satan knowing he must flee (James 4:7; I Peter 5:9), repelling him by invoking an appropriate Word of God, as Jesus did, constantly and faithfully (Luke 4:3-12).

We must also cooperate to prevent doubt entering in by taking responsibility to "destroy arguments and every proud obstacle to the knowledge of God, and take every thought captive to obey Christ" (2 Corinthians 10:5). We must immerse ourselves in the Word, for the heart occupied by the Word will have no room for the world, The heart filled with Jesus will have no room for Satan. The heart which bears spiritual fruit in loving thought, deed, and service will have no room for sin. The best confession of the Word is by living it in obedient actions which mirror your decision to believe the Word for your benefit and God's glory.

It is best to anticipate and think through the situations in which Satan will tempt us, and defend ourselves with the Word, expecting to receive the blessing of God's promises. Your foundation of faith must be solidly built in advance to withstand worldly assaults, for it is difficult to build a dependable fortification during a hurricane, or in the midst of assault by enemy troops in combat. While the Word is always effective, it is far better to stand and build on the Word when you have no problems, and be prepared for their approach. Hosea 4:6 warns: "my people are destroyed for lack of knowledge." Proverbs 29:18 agrees: "Where there is no vision, the people perish." God has provided knowledge and vision in His Word, where His purposes and weapons are reliably and clearly communicated. It seems prudent that one would faithfully establish himself in the Scriptures on healing, and appropriate them while in good health, to deter the occurrence of illness, rather that wait until assailed by it.

MEANDERING FROM FAITH TO FAITH

There is a Scriptural sense in which our faith grows in spurts, which can be measured periodically to show growth, just as a child's physical growth can be demonstrated. Romans 1:17, KJV says that the Gospel is the power of God which brings salvation to believers, "For therein is the righteousness of God revealed from faith to faith: as it is written, The just shall live by faith." Yet, the transitional period between these spurts of growth is often punctuated by dry spells, where seeds of faith whither in the arid soil of one's doubt, and bear no fruit. Spiritual growth is a process from one degree of faith to another; from one period of faith to another. We begin with the faith imparted by the Holy Spirit, with which we embrace Christ for salvation, and that gives birth to and enables actual righteousness by which we daily live through Christ.

God may provide faith to believers, but each must cooperate in sustaining faith in God's power and enablement by which to live by faith. God does not believe for us. Each must affirm by his conduct that he still believes in Christ's effectiveness as Lord and Saviour.

Whenever we are beset by doubt, and offer up petitions devoid of confident trust, it is essential to restore our faith. Whenever obedience or blessings are not forthcoming, the first thing we must check is our faith. Thus, 2 Corinthians 13:5 cautions: "Examine yourselves, to see whether you are holding to your faith. Test yourselves. Do you not realize that Jesus Christ is in you? — unless you indeed fail to meet the test!" I Corinthians 11:31 says: "if we judged ourselves truly, we should not be judged." Thus, in all the deserts of unblessing, we must determine the cause, starting with our exercise of faith, and ask: "Are blessings being withheld or delayed because my faith is halfhearted, as expressed and evidenced in unrighteous works?" The Holy Spirit's fruit of faith is encouraged by abiding in Christ through consistent obedience to His Word (John 15:2-7; I John 2:6, 10, 17; 3:6, 24; 4-12, 16; 2 John 9). Remaining in the Word, and obediently living according to its precepts is the key to enduring in faith.

God exhorts believers to wait for Him, to be patient, persistent, prayerful, tenacious, persevering, run the race, and endure. Yet, with the passage of time, our constancy may waver, and our confidence flag. If we must wait for God to deliver on His promised blessings, believers can succumb to the poison of doubt. The longer promises go unfilled and prayers go unanswered, the more faith can wane and unbelief flourish. There is no reward for occasional, intermittent, or double-minded faith, which will not "receive anything from the Lord" (James 1:8).

The ten scouts who brought back a negative report after reconnaissance in the land of Canaan made an 'evil report' because it was filled with fear and doubt (Numbers 13:32). Joshua and Caleb, the two reconnoiterers who returned a 'good report', spoke in faith and, because they relied on God's favor, believed the land could be taken.[69]

A believer can fall if he neglects to sustain faith and confirm his trust in the Lord (I Corinthians 10:12, 9:27; Ephesians 6:13; 2 Peter 1:10). He can allow unbelief to topple his stand of faith. Indeed, the Word of Good News was of no benefit to the Jews, "because it did not meet with faith in the hearers" (Hebrews 4:2). Unbelievers are "broken off" from the root which supports them and from their faith and the power of God. Unbelief leads to a "fall away from God" (Hebrews 3:12). We cannot claim Christ's blessings if we fail to sustain our faith. Hebrews 3:6 puts it: "And we are his house <u>if we hold fast our confidence</u> and pride in our hope."

James 1:6-8 says that the seeker of divine wisdom is to "ask in faith, with no doubting, for he who doubts is like a wave of the sea that is driven and tossed by the wind. For that person must not suppose that a double-minded man, unstable in all his ways, <u>will receive</u> anything from the Lord." You are literally blocked from the light if you are unstable in commitment or "double-minded" about the Word. Just as "no city or house divided against itself will stand" (Matthew 12:25), so the divided mind will lack strength to sustain faith. I Timothy 2:8, KJV, urges "that men pray every where, lifting up holy hands, <u>without wrath and doubting</u>."

One form of defective, double-minded faith is claiming a Bible promise tentatively, without really believing God intends to deliver on His Word to an unworthy sinner. The New Born believer who is not convinced he is fully pardoned in Christ, or is incredulous about God's benevolence toward him, may disregard the Word's assurances, and assume, faithlessly, that God will not squander blessings on a worm such as he. His expectations that he will receive nothing will not be disappointed. Proverbs 27:3 says: "For as he thinketh in his heart, so is he." Doubt may focus on negative circumstances where God's blessings have been withdrawn or denied in the past, and cause him to doubt his present usefulness as a servant of the Lord.

A second form of double-mindedness may occur when the conscious mind perceives the truth of the Word's promises and seeks to believe them. However, the unconscious mind may create a "double-mindedness" if it has learned and retained traditions contrary to what the Word teaches. Jesus notes this possible result of doubting by corrupting the Word, at Mark 7:13: "thus making void the word of God through your tradition, which you hand on." Jesus was criticizing the Scribes and Pharisees for disbelieving God's Commandment, "Honor thy father and thy mother," by their tradition which condoned shirking the support of one's parents, with the excuse that the funds were already designated as corban, or a gift to God.

Other men may influence us to doubt that God's blessings apply to this present time. Matthew 15:14 says of false teachers, including those who reject faith: "Let them alone; they are blind guides. And if a blind man leads a blind man, both will fall into a pit."

Another form of double-minded faith may be to accept the Word's promises while we read them, and later forsake them as we live moment to moment. We declare our faith by the words of our mouth (Romans 10:10), and if our actions speak a confession contrary to the faith inspired by the Word, what we say and do will contradict what we initially professed, and retard fruitfulness.

James reveals that the same tongue which pronounces a believer's confession of the Word, is also capable of confessing evil. It is a "restless evil, full of deadly poison... From the same mouth come blessing and cursing" (James 3:8,10). Evil can enter our lives through the evil utterances of our mouths. "Thou art snared with the words of thy mouth, thou art taken with the words of thy mouth" (Proverbs 6:2). "The wicked is snared by the transgression of his lips" (Proverbs 12:13). "A fool's mouth is his destruction, and his lips are the snare of his soul" (Proverbs 18:7). A wind-tossed ship will go aground unless its rudder is used to guide it toward safe shores, and, like a rudder, man's tongue is the guide of his whole body and life (James 3:4).

We can accept that suffering and deprivation will temper blessings, as Satan, the world, and we, ourselves cause separation from God. However, when God promises health, prosperity, and other earthly blessings, it follows He must deliver them sometime in this world, or faith would not be demonstrably fulfilled. Faith will sustain us for a while in most things, and for great lengths of time in some things, such as belief in the Afterlife. But in other promises verifiable in this world, if God never delivered on His promises, after a time they would no longer be trustworthy.

If I have faith in a bridge, airplane, building, or person, it is not my faith which makes or creates reliability. It is the inherent trustworthiness of the person or instrument which provides justification for faith. As we grow in knowledge of the Lord's delivery on the promises of His Word, our confidence will be bolstered by growing acquaintance with Him.

The confirmation of God's promised blessings occurs when He fulfills His promise. Indeed, every believer can attest to many faith expectations which were not disappointed, but were fulfilled and thus confirmed faithful reliance on God's promises. It is comforting to be fortified by recollections of having faithfully withstood affliction of all kinds, by the indisputable power of God. Remember how God has brought you through painful times before, and you can depend that God will do it again. Remember how God has intervened in answer to your desperate prayers, and take hope.[70] Remember every good and perfect gift which God has bestowed upon you from above, in the recollected affirmance of His Providence.

FAITH IN WEALTH RATHER THAN IN GOD

Succumbing to the worldly temptations of wealth and possessions seeks material and worldly advantages according to our own desires and timetable, in disregard of God's schedule and bestowal of gifts. Avarice substitutes one's own decisions in place of God's guidance, and relies on personal power to achieve the desired result, rather than total dependency on God's Providence.

This preoccupation with wealth and present possessions may explain why the blessing of resources is denied a believer who misappropriates blessings exclusively and wrongly to his own advantage. The danger of wealth lies in exalting oneself rather than God (Deuteronomy 8:17), and in succumbing to idolatry by worshipping money more than God. Hence, Jesus warns: "No servant can serve two masters; for either he will hate the one and love the other, or he will be devoted to the one and despise the other. You cannot serve God and mammon" (Luke 16:13). Paul condemned greed and idolatry and identified covetousness as idolatry (I Corinthians 5:11; Ephesians 5:5).

Know this before you are enticed to fall into love with wealth, and you become enslaved to mammon. Whether you scratch and claw to acquire wealth quickly, or struggle slowly to accumulate comforts, be assured that your new god has turned you into a servant bound to acquisitions. The love of wealth will be the master you hate for what it has done to you, but when a Christian serves two masters it will always be at the expense of serving God.

Jesus warns: "Take heed, and beware of all covetousness, for a man's life does not consist in the abundance of his possessions" (Luke 12:15). If anything, true spirituality calls for detachment from worldly things. It is God's pleasure to give believers the Kingdom, but Jesus counsels: "Sell your possessions, and give alms; provide yourselves with... a treasure in the heavens that does not fail... For where your treasure is, there will your heart be also: (Luke 12:33-34; Matthew 6:19-21).

Jesus explained to the rich young man who sought eternal life: "go, sell what you possess and give it to the poor, and you will have treasure in heaven; and come, follow me" (Matthew 19:21). This rich young ruler could boast that he kept six of the Commandments, but Jesus saw his heart and knew that he violated the Commandment, 'Thou shalt have no other Gods before me'. The man loved wealth more than he valued having Jesus, and he departed "sorrowful" rather than give up his possessions (Matthew 19:22).

Jesus warns against attachment to worldly wealth, and cautions that the Word may be choked and made unfruitful when the hearer takes "delight in riches"(Matthew 13:22). Jesus singles out rich men as seriously hampered in their ability to reach the Kingdom, declaring at Matthew 19:24: "it is easier for a camel to go through the eye of a needle than for a rich man to enter the kingdom of God." The greedy rich man who contemplated enjoying his wealth in new barns was called a fool for his attachment to worldly goods: "So is he who lays up treasure for himself, and is not rich toward God" (Luke 12:21). Psalm 62:10 puts it: "if riches increase, set not your heart upon them." Indeed, "He that trusteth in his riches shall fall" (Proverbs 11:28).

I Timothy 6:17-18 summons the rich to hope on God, "who richly furnishes us with everything to enjoy," so we can share prosperity with others: "They are to do good, to be rich in good deeds, liberal and generous... so that they may take hold of the life which is life indeed." Wealth does not inherently disqualify one from becoming saved, or staying saved. In fact, the promise that the rich should do good deeds in order to "take hold of life," constitutes an endorsement or tolerance of wealth by Jesus. It is the love of money, not the money itself, which is the root of all evil (I Timothy 6:10).

I Timothy 6:5 warns of potential dangers in love of wealth, by condemning base motives for piety, and depraved men who imagine "that godliness is a means of gain... But those who desire to be rich fall into temptation, into a snare... But as for you, man of God, shun all this; aim at righteousness." Hebrews 13:5 cautions: "Keep your life free from <u>love of money</u>, and be content with what you have, for he has said, 'I will never fail you nor forsake you'."

However, wealth can become incompatible with serving Jesus if it seduces its owner into self-reliance, avarice, and oppression; which are major deterrents to sustaining faith and walking with the Lord. Wealth renders the rich uniquely susceptible to temptations and vanities, immersing them in worldliness and unreceptivity to the Word of salvation. Wealth can destroy a believer's reliance on God, and instead place his confidence in worldly goods, human ability, and power. A believer may be too spiritually immature at a given moment to cope with the potential pride and temptation sired by opulence or power. Their absence then becomes a blessing from the Lord.

Wealth can offer even the poor man overwhelming opportunities to sin, if it consumes him with envy and lust for wealth. I Timothy 6:8-10 warns that: "those who <u>desire to be rich</u> fall into temptation, into a snare, into many senseless and hurtful <u>desires that plunge men into ruin and destruction</u>. For the love of money is the root of all evils; it is through this craving that <u>some have wandered away from the faith</u> and pierced their hearts with many pangs." A penniless man who is obsessed with acquiring wealth is in greater jeopardy than an obedient rich man who both enjoys and shares his wealth as a steward of God's gift, but is not pre-occupied with its gain. Proverbs 30:8-9 petitions: "give me neither poverty nor riches... Lest I be full, and deny thee, and say, Who is the Lord? or lest I be poor, and steal, and take the name of my God in vain."

Sinful disobedience leads to loss and deprivation, when one fails to do what he knows is right. James 4:17, 5:1,3 speaks of the rich man who "knows what is right to do and fails to do it, for him it is sin. Come now, you rich, weep and howl for the miseries that are coming upon you... Your gold and silver have rusted, and their rust will be evidence against you and will <u>eat your flesh like fire</u>." Obviously, the rich man must take painstaking care to follow Jesus' way and be obediently loving and a good steward of God's wealth in charity toward others, and for God's purposes. A saved rich man will do right, and serve God with his resources, but an unsaved person, whether rich or poor, has little desire to do right.

This is not to say that God declines to shower blessings upon whom He will in His pleasure, without any apparent connection to their righteousness, faith, or good stewardship. Nor is Christianity incompatible with wealth, for many of the Church's patriarchs, such as Abraham, David, Solomon, and Job have enjoyed great wealth, and the Church's functions must be sustained by the availability of the Lord's bounty. Nevertheless, God's promise is to meet a believer's need (Philippians 4:19), not his greed.

What is sinful is the bondage of desire for wealth which corrupts a Christian's desire for spiritual blessings. A Christian should be uncomfortable with wealth because his spiritual character discerns that sustained luxury is incompatible with love for others; and as long as there is even one person still in need, God's law of love demands sharing. Prosperity is having enough for one's own needs. It is being satisfied with, and accepting whatever blessings the Lord bestows as one's portion. Christians are not called to grovel in poverty, nor to revel in opulence, but to expect and enjoy sufficiency. True prosperity is sharing in a vital, growing, healthy Body of Christ, which has been nurtured by the shared and loving blessings which each one has received from the Lord.

IMMATURITY AND WORLDLINESS AS BARS TO BLESSINGS

Our spiritual immaturity often impedes access to God's grace and blessings, and initiates or self-inflicts suffering. How could God entrust the higher gifts or stronger spiritual powers to irresponsible spiritual babes? A teenager will shortly operate the family car, but his toddler sister is far from ready to be entrusted with driving. Children must behave maturely before they can receive mature blessings. Jesus puts it: "If then you have not been faithful in the unrighteous mammon, who will entrust to you the true riches? And If you have not been faithful in that which is another's, who will give you that which is your own?" (Luke 16:11-12; and see also, Jeremiah 12:5).

Before we can discern the Word of righteousness, we may need to mature spiritually by having our "faculties trained by practice to distinguish good from evil" (Hebrews 5:14). God imposes personal obedience, maturity, and training in righteousness as preconditions to receiving spiritual blessings and powers by grace. Faith must mature through knowledge of the Word and practical training in applying it, before awesome power is entrusted to a spiritual tyro. No parent would let an inexperienced toddler cross a busy intersection alone, to encounter perils he is not ready to appreciate or avoid. Neither will God allow a spiritual babe with little substance in his faith, and little familiarity with the Word, to be exposed to anything destructive, or beyond his capacity to enjoy or endure (I Corinthians 10:13).

Generally, God's wisdom denies our unwise prayers, because of His love for us. There are exceptions which prove the rule, and teach us to be careful what we pray for, lest we receive it. There are instances when God answers unwise prayers, after warning His people of their mistaken judgment, and he allows them to suffer the consequences of their choice. When the children of Israel demanded a king to rule them to imitate what was done in neighboring countries, God advised against their request, but granted it, and Israel immediately regretted their choice (I Samuel 8:7-19).

If we seek only self-gratification from the blessings of Our Father, it is not surprising if He denies us, because He is training us in His higher purpose of mature, unselfish, and loving spirituality. What parent would give a child a third or fourth helping of cake or ice cream, no matter how much the child's appetite cried for more, but his judgment was too immature to appreciate the discomfort which follows gluttony? Surfeit, like over-exposed film, turns black.

No parent would give a child everything he seeks, but will protect him from the hazards of excess and immature exuberance. Most parents have learned to withhold more than is actually needed for their children's comforts, lest sated children become spoiled, ungrateful and selfish. Nor will our Heavenly Father bestow prosperity upon an immature unbeliever, who has not yet attained wisdom, but would squander blessings on his worldly passions.

James 4:2 explains why God withholds some promises, in a passage which seems, when taken out of context, to promise unlimited blessings: "you desire and do not have... You do not have, because you do not ask." However, the passage continues: "you ask and do not receive, because <u>you ask wrongly to spend it on your passions</u>. Unfaithful creatures! Do you not know that friendship with the world is enmity with God?"

Our motives may be unworthy worldly ones behind our prayers: such as fame, power, pride, covetousness, vindication, gratification, revenge, or self-glorification. Certainly God will not bless us with the desires of our hearts based upon such unworthy sinful desires. If we pray for a ministry of healing for our own glory, rather than God's, it is not likely the gifts of healing will ever be expressed through us. People who pray in public "that they may be seen by men," crave the reward of man's adulation, but are not likely to have their prayers rewarded (Matthew 6:5).

A wrong motive destroys what might otherwise be a worthy prayer. We should seek holiness to please God, and better know, serve, and glorify Him — not to enhance our status with men. We should seek resources for better stewardship in sharing with others — not for our own advantage. So it is possible to pray for what is promised, but not according to the promise, because we do not pray according to God's will, and in conformance to His intent in extending the promise. We must ask God to perform His promise for the same reason God gave the promise, and not to waste it on our passions, but to devote it to our stewardship.

A child cannot appreciate why his headstrong impulses were frustrated, because he lacks the wisdom developed by experience, maturity, insight, and hindsight. Yet, the Father had His reasons for withholding or denying wishes, and did not allow harm to afflict His child.

OUT OF SYNC WITH GOD'S TIMING

In the sense unanswered prayer produces suffering, caused by denial of blessings, it may be that the timeliness of one's prayers is out of synchronization with God's timing, which is as important as His purposes in one's life. God's answer may be "later," as well as "no." Parents have often refused a child's request for some cherished object, and declined to give any reason. The parents have already obtained the gift, but are saving it for the child's birthday or Christmas. The child is given no explanation for the refusal, until he receives the gift at the appropriate time, according to his parent's timetable. Likewise, we must be committed to trusting God's judgment, and submitting to His will, because it is loving, perfect, and perfectly good for us. Deferral is not refusal, and delay is not denial.

It may be that our petitions seek something transiently good, when we are intended to receive something infinitely better. Acts 3:4 tells of a lame beggar, who, "Seeing Peter and John about to go into the temple, he asked for alms." Had he received the coin which he requested, its value would have soon been spent. But Peter had no silver or gold to give. Instead, he gave what he had, and said: "in the name of Jesus Christ of Nazareth, walk," and the lame man received healing (Acts 3:7-8); something infinitely superior to the coin he originally solicited.

Paul begged three times to have the thorn in his flesh removed by God (2 Corinthians 12:8). Paul must have wondered why his pleas for deliverance had not been answered, especially when the pains interrupted his work for the Lord. If ever we are denied our prayers, we should remember that the Apostle Paul did not receive the answer to his prayers that he expected. What he learned was that the Lord's strength was powerful enough to see him through every difficulty.[71] The Lord's answer is: "My grace is sufficient for you, for my power is made perfect in weakness," and Paul came to understand "when I am weak, then I am strong" (2 Corinthians 12:9-10). St. Augustine observed that God may impose impossible burdens so we will learn to turn to Him for enablement.

In the midst of any affliction, Jesus is sufficient for everything, and His strength becomes ours. His goodness supplies every need and withholds every harmful thing. One reason God compares His Kingdom to a growing seed, is to admonish believers to be patient, for God's response to prayer is not always instantaneous, even though it is guaranteed eventually (Psalm 37:7-9; Isaiah 40:31). God may provide immediate results in answer to prayer, as He pleases in His Sovereign will. Healing often accompanies evangelism to confirm a believer's witness to the Gospel (Mark 16:15-18), but we have no right to expect instant gratification of our desire for healing.

Usually, God denies unwise prayers that immerse us in self-indulgence, foster the idea we are self-sufficient, draw us away from God in the enticements of pleasure, or lead us into temptation. He will say 'no' to second best, if he plans something infinitely better for us in another direction. Only God knows how many times He has denied a daughter's prayers to unite with the "man of her dreams," later to present her with the mate who will truly bring contentment and joy for a lifetime. God answers enough prayers to keep us in the faith and undiscouraged, and he refuses enough prayers to keep us from evil ways and characters.

If a believer is not yet mature enough to cope with the worldly distractions which accompany status or success, we would expect a loving Father to withhold such blessings until He has nurtured maturity and holiness in His child. Ecclesiastes 3:1 declares: "To every thing there is a season, and a time to every purpose under the heaven... a time to plant, and a time to pluck up that which is planted." Isaiah 30:18 explains: "And therefore will the Lord wait, that he may be gracious unto you, and therefore will he be exalted, that he may have mercy upon you." How much more will we appreciate God's answer to our prayers, after we have waited for His grace. Perhaps our gratitude would be short-lived, shallow, and scant if God immediately responded to fulfill our desires.

Jesus was aware that events were deferred until appropriate within God's plan and timing. He delayed two days before going to raise Lazarus from the dead. He also waited for the appointed hour of the Atonement, saying: "My hour has not yet come," "My time has not yet come," and "his hour had not yet come" (John 2:4, 7:6,30, 8:20).

And of course, Jesus' prayer to be spared the Cup of Atonement, was never granted, because His death on the Cross was necessary according to God's will, to save all sinners in God's economy of salvation (Mark 14:36,42). God's answer to Daniel's prayers for wisdom was delayed three weeks while His angel messenger contended with a demon, identified as "the prince of Persia" (Daniel 10:13).

We need to pray for the Spiritual fruit of patient endurance by God's grace and power, whenever God delays blessings which are not consonant with His plan or purpose for our lives, and we are languishing in the desert of fruitlessness. There is no Scriptural promise of immediate gratification, ready blessing, or deliverance on demand. Rather, God teaches most blessings involve developmental processes, and we have need of patience and endurance (Luke 8:15, 21:19; Romans 5:3-4, 8:25; Hebrews 6:12, 10:36, 12:1; James 1:3-4; Revelation 3:10).

We need to believe God's assurances of freedom from the negative forces of worry, fear, oppression and terror, for He has promised: "it shall not come near thee" (Isaiah 54:14). We must learn that Jesus instructs us to parry the thrusts of sensory impressions of the world when He says: "Do not fear, only believe" (Mark 5:36), preparatory to raising the dead daughter of the synagogue ruler.

Above all, we need to re-immerse ourselves in the Word of promise by which faith comes. We need to draw edification and encouragement from other members of the Body of Christ who testify that faith works and is God's principal avenue of blessing. We need to recall God's faithful deliverances throughout our lives and theirs, and confirm the general course and flow of His blessings for believers. We don't go by feelings, but by absolute confidence and reliance in what God's Word says has transpired. If this is the quantum of faith for salvation by grace through faith, the same principle would apply for healing, prosperity, or any other promised blessings of God. Increased faith may come by asking, "Lord increase our faith," but it assuredly comes as we increase our hearing of and familiarity with the Word. Likewise, love may come by praying for it, but it surely proceeds from closer fellowship with the Divine Lover through His Word.

Some ancillary laws of the harvest of reaping what we have sown, necessitate patience. In nature, we reap in a different season from when we plant. Genesis 8:22 forecasts: "While the earth remaineth, seedtime and harvest... summer and winter... shall not cease." Thus there will always be an interval between planting and harvesting, and patience is necessary. Ecclesiastes 3:1 puts it: "To every thing there is a season, and a time to every purpose under heaven." Galatians 6:9 asserts: "And let us not grow weary in well-doing, for in due season we shall reap, if we do not lose heart."

A second corollary is that we cannot undo last season's planting, but we inexorably reap in kind according to what we have sown. We may regret what we have sown, but we cannot undo it. We can only change this year's planting to raise a different crop next season. In nature, God does not intervene to alter these laws, and in the spiritual laws of planting and reaping we ought not expect God's intercession to alter His spiritual law. This is the consequential explanation of suffering. If we plant rejection of God's ways, we will harvest the dire consequences of failing to obey what is ordained for our good. God's usual deliverance is to comfort and help us endure the consequences of what we must reap, to see it through, rather than escape it by a miracle. God does not send the affliction, and often does not eliminate or remove it from a believer's life. What He will do is give us the courage, strength and hope to work our way through; to endure, and thereby overcome, the problem. We can be comforted in the knowledge that God is as outraged as we by the suffering men cause one another.

Faith is trusting God when He is not answering your prayers, and seems to be ignoring your needs. Yet, Jesus did not necessarily promise health or wealth for this world. He promised trouble, struggle, and persecution here (I Peter 4:12-13). But He promised you would never be alone, and that you would always have His peace. Hence, we can infer that the abundant life Jesus promises believers is in part intended for a later time and place; Hereafter, rather than here in the world.

This is confirmed by the hall of faith, the suffering believers enumerated in Hebrews Chapter 11: "These all died in faith, not having received what was promised, but having seen it and greeted it from afar, and having acknowledged that they were strangers and exiles on the earth... But as it is, they desire a better country, that is, a heavenly one. Therefore God is not ashamed to be called their God, for he has prepared for them a city... And all these, though well attested by their faith, did not receive what was promised, since God had foreseen something better for us, that apart from us they should not be made perfect" (Hebrews 11:13-16, 39). God retains all your prayers, and stores all your tears until the appointed time when they are eventually answered. Remember how long God waited to send Jesus to save a sinful world. Remember that "with the Lord one day is as a thousand years, and a thousand years as one day" (2 Peter 3:8).

Intense faith is evoked and follows God in the dark, not in the light; in times of denial, rather than prosperity; not in clement weather, but through storms; in time of pain and abandonment, for there is less need for faith when we have the certain reality of God's presence and blessing. Your faith is more precious in bad times of testing, than in good times of ease, as long as you don't doubt in the dark what God has taught you in the light.

The abundant life Jesus promises His disciples is sampled here on earth, but feasted upon sumptuously Hereafter. Here, we see through a glass darkly, but then face to face, as He greets us at the end of our earthly walk. Jesus has conquered death on our behalf; still it is appointed unto each to die here, but we shall know immortality there. Likewise, we are ransomed, healed, restored, and made new, in part, here; but fully Hereafter.

When God delays a favorable answer to our prayer, we must have faith that He is busy on our behalf, and delay is the means which God uses to prepare us for something better. Our confidence in His goodness must be the basis for our quiet patience, to which He calls us, even when we would prefer to see some immediate results. Hebrews 6:11-12 encourages: "show the same earnestness in realizing the full assurance of hope until the end... imitators of those who through faith and patience inherit the promises." "For you have need of endurance, so that you may do the will of God and receive what is promised" (Hebrews 10:36). God was present, though not visible, even when Jesus was killed, and He is present during our travails, too.

God's call to patient endurance is directed toward our impulsiveness and impatience in wanting the desires of our heart. Moses was prepared for service during decades of inactivity. Joseph waited for years languishing in prison to be prepared for a responsible position in Egypt. David eluded Saul in wilderness, wood, cave, and mountain for years before he was ready to assume the leadership of Israel. Jesus waited thirty years before beginning His three years of public ministry.

God opens and shuts doors when the time is right for us to enter, or depart from a certain way. Paul and Timothy were "forbidden by the Holy Spirit to speak the word in Asia. And when they had come opposite Mysia, they attempted to go into Bithynia, but the Spirit of Jesus did not allow them" (Acts 16:6-7). Asia was barred, but a vision invited Paul to Macedonia, to establish the Church at Philippi, Thessalonica, Beroea, Athens, and Corinth, leading to the greater witness throughout Europe.

God may close a door we wish to enter, to test our faith in Him; or to build strength of character by developing patience and perseverance. We may be delayed in our progress until God's timing is right for our useful participation. God may have reserved what we desire for someone else, better suited or qualified to serve Him.

Even past disobedience may prevent our advance, as past rebellion forfeits the opportunity God presented. You may have deprived yourself of the opportunity when it was first offered, and God honored your choice and closed the door, so that now it is too late. The Israelites who lacked faith to enter the promised land, but later sought to trust God, obey Him, and go fight the Amorites, were denied God's anointing because their response of faith was expressed too late (Deuteronomy 1:41-42). God intended their victory originally, but they professed patience when they were really faithless and afraid, and they lost the opportunity.

Leviticus 26:31 also forecasts that a disobedient Israel would try to revive sacrificial worship, but it would be too late, as God warns: "And I will make your cities waste... and I will not smell the savour of your sweet odors."

God's route is the only way to go. What driver has not taken an unfamiliar shortcut and lived to regret it? Most shortcuts are poorly surfaced, unsafe, dangerous, and destructive of the vehicle which transports us. They are usually bumpy, rutted, and highly stressful; uncomfortable, and in the end, take longer than the right way. Being transformed into the likeness of Christ simply takes time for one to mature, just as growing from adolescence to adulthood cannot happen overnight. God's schedule is correct and precise, and we need faith not to hasten it. Good public relations can build an image in a brief period, but building character and fellowship with Him takes time to develop. Proving your reliability could occur in a spectacular instant, but it may also progress through many small incidents of consistent dependability. Spiritual maturity comes by patience, and exacts a price, which may be sacrificing some lesser blessing we sought from God.

God usually denies petitions which reflect immature judgment, and are simply too outrageous, irresponsible, frivolous, destructive of our true good, or logically inconsistent. Because God is good, He will not make true what is false, or make right what is inherently wrong, simply to cater to the vanity of a disciple. Nor will God honor the misbegotten prayers of the witless student who seeks to revise history and install Lincoln as the first President, to ratify his wrong answer on a test paper. Could God violate His own righteousness by granting the misguided, selfish prayers of a burglar or cocaine dealer for success in his criminal ventures? There are clearly limits on a faith doctrine of name it and claim it!

You cannot expect God to rewrite the past if you have wrongly maligned another with hate-filled words. What you have freely done will run its course and bear its consequences unless God intervenes in answer to prayer to ease the effects, and helps restore the shattered relationship. God will not bless you in the misappropriation of your neighbor's property or wife, as David learned after his adulterous lust for Bathsheba culminated in the death of their child (2 Samuel 12:14-15). Because God is just, one would not expect Him to engineer and misappropriate a job promotion which rightfully belongs to someone more qualified, or for which the believer is unprepared. God may withhold job advancement and its prosperity from a believer to turn him toward service in another aspect of ministry for which he is better suited.

Faith and piety are no assurance of wisdom. Praying sincerely for a dry day so one can enjoy a picnic or ballgame, may not coincide with the paramount interests and petitions of gardeners or farmers who need rain for their crops. If one child of an elderly, comatose parent prays for immediate, painless death, while a second child prays for speedy restoration of consciousness, then someone's prayer, though well-intentioned, must be denied, for God cannot say 'yes' simultaneously to contradictory prayers. He will do what He deems in the best interests of all concerned.

Even God cannot do logically contradictory things. For example, there cannot be an immovable object and an irresistible force existing at the same moment in time. What is immovable can resist any force, and what is irresistible can move any object. God can alternately advance one or the other, at any moment He pleases, but He will not violate the logical constraints of His own reason. Nor will He make a man both bearded and clean-shaven at the same moment, although He is free to do anything He wishes at any time; but He chooses not to contradict His own laws of logic.

God cannot do anything inconsistent with His nature. It is impossible for him to lie (Titus 1:2; Hebrews 6:18). He has always existed, and nothing created Him, yet it is impossible for Him to produce another uncreated God. He cannot carry out both of two mutually exclusive alternatives, not because His power meets an obstacle, but because logical, intrinsic contradictions are impossible to reconcile.

What is God to do when a desperately ill patient awaits an organ transplant, but his operation must be delayed until another person dies to make the organ available? We can be sure that God will bring about the greatest good for both persons and balance the anguish of the waiting patient with the enjoyment of life by the prospective donor, as each prays in his own interest. We would not expect God to displace one child from fulfilling God's plans for him, simply because of the prayers of another. We can only be sure that the Lord and Creator of all things will do right, and be thankful we are not burdened with such decisions.

While you, as a disciple, have access to potential power to move mountains by faith (Matthew 17:20), you would not really expect God to release His awesome power if your purpose was carnal, frivolous, prideful; if it was not considerate of others, or did not promote His Kingdom's purposes. The spiritually immature Christian who wants blessings only for himself, does not yet appreciate that God's grace is meant to be shared with others. He is denied his immature prayers and premature desires because he cannot appreciate the devastating consequences caused to inhabitants of the valley from haphazard dislocations, when by faith he seeks to move mountains for frivolous or selfish purposes, only.

God cannot commit the full volume and extent of His supernatural power to a believer who has uncontrolled anger or immature speech, whose hostile or careless words would harm or visit destruction upon others. A believer must walk with God constantly, and habitually have His Word ready to communicate every moment, as Jesus did, before he can expect increasing participation in divine power. Only then, can our prayers, thoughts, and labors fulfill God's Sovereign purposes in weaving a divinely planned, but humanly spontaneous and distinctive tapestry.

A young child lacks the ability to recognize and enjoy the full range of his father's intellect, wit, love, fellowship, possessions, or glory. Even perfect love can be stultifying and repugnant to one too immature to comprehend or appreciate what God is offering. Growth is a process, and in God's ordinance, only time and experience can produce that maturity.

We cannot expect God to give us the full measure of righteous fruit until we have first grown up into the light, spread our branches, fed on the Word, and blossomed in spiritual strength and capacity. No parent would give a large sum of money to a small child, who lacks discernment to appreciate and utilize the gift. He must first be trained to comprehend its value and limitations. God may withhold granting the immature desires of our hearts, until we learn the undistracted, responsible application of our blessings to His purposes and glory.

God's general will is for health and healing of His people, which most believers do enjoy most of the time, through the body's natural healing mechanisms and the God-given skills of physicians and pharmacists. Yet, a sexual disease naturally incurred in the course of physical sins, will not always be arrested in its development, nor will the natural consequences of physical laws be suspended. God may choose to use that disease as a means to some superior blessing, such as learning to obey or routinely trust in God.

Nor would a Sovereign, loving God spontaneously abort an unwanted pregnancy, nor condone the murder of an unborn baby, despite the great anguish an out-of-wedlock birth may bring to carelessly indifferent lovers. The natural consequences of disrupting one's life to support an unwanted family, or to live with an unloved spouse, may be borne as the result of sinful lust. God may not cancel worldly debts incurred unwisely by believers, but He may enable repayment by the penitent borrower, after time, struggle, and chastening.

God's response to prayers may be self-limited where the freedom of another person is involved and honored by God. For example, no matter how zealous or pure the intercessory prayers for a lost loved one, God does not compel a choice for salvation which violates another's freedom, even to save the lost soul. Nor will God, Who has proclaimed His hatred of divorce, force a wayward spouse to return to his home, despite the fervent prayers of an abandoned wife. For, such would interfere with the genuine freedom of choice God has accorded each person. One would hope that God is so persuasive He always prevails in drawing a sinner voluntarily to God's way. But experience encounters many spouses who corrupt their freedom, and stubbornly rush to divorce and re-marriage, as well as many unsaved, lost souls who persist in rebelliousness even unto their death.

Suffering can be borne if we sustain implicit trust in God's grace and power, and have patience until they are revealed. God's plan will have its way, and in His time. What God ordains will be fulfilled, and "though it tarry, wait for it; because it will surely come, it will not tarry" (Habakkuk 2:3). Jesus told Martha at the grave of Lazarus: "Did I not tell you that if you would believe you would see the glory of God?" (John 11:40). God's delays are often a means of developing faith. If He wants you to wait, the Holy Spirit will always sustain and encourage you by reminding you of God's promises in His Word, to strengthen your trust and endurance in Him. Jesus appeared to Martha to rekindle her faith at the grave of Lazarus (John 11:27). God reassured Abraham and Sarah they would have the promised child, Isaac, even though they had waited 25 years for fulfillment of the promise (Genesis 18:10, 12:4, 17:1, 6:19).

It is possible for a believer's faith to be intact, and his reliance properly placed in the Word's promise, and blessings will still be withheld. When God uses chastening in the process of transforming a believer, the granting of blessings may be too great a distraction, and interrupt God's purposes for the individual. In such case, they may be withheld until the Christian is mature enough to cope with them, or spiritual enough to apply blessings for God's higher purposes.

God's perfect rightness, goodness, and justice assure that in His exercise of sovereign dominion over Creation, He will providentially accomplish His purposes for the individual. If we seek blessings contrary to God's intent at a given moment, our desires will be frustrated, even though we may lack maturity to discern the wisdom behind God's denial, which always seeks to accomplish our highest good.

When a faithful Christian believes that certain blessings are the unconditional right of every believer, but they are not, then faith can be destroyed when the apparent promises are not fulfilled. Out of ignorance about what Scripture actually says, the unblessed disciple may wrongly infer that he lacks faith, whereas his knowledge is defective. The confusion may lead to self-condemnation and further deterioration of faith, when in reality it is his understanding of Scripture which is faulty.[72] For example, a believer may understand that he has a power to heal in the name of Jesus, whereas gifts of healing are not meted out to every believer, but the Holy Spirit "apportions to each one individually as he wills" (I Corinthians 12:11).

One cannot regard every general promise of blessing as absolute and applicable in every situation and time. There are blessings from God which are directed toward the total Body of believers, but may not necessarily filter down to every member. God prospered Ancient Israel, and yet poor individuals continued to beg at the temple gates. Many of God's blessings are intended for the world to come, and early Christians suffered privations and persecution, just as today, Christians in unbelieving nations suffer persecution for their faith while in this world.

Victory is assured and power and blessings are intensified and multiplied when sought by the concerted action of believers. However, one soldier does not possess all the might of the entire army, even when clothed in the authority or protective armor supplied to him. It would not be wise to attack an enemy battalion single-handedly, simply because your leader has declared your troops superior to the enemy, and forecast ultimate victory over them. The unarmed flag-bearer will enjoy the spectacle of the enemy retreating before him, only as long as the full army is behind him. Likewise, the believer removed from the warmth, nurture, prayers, and protection of the Body of Christ has removed himself from the multiplied Spirit-power which resides in the Church of Christ.

The Christian whose blessings have dried up, should never yield to passivity, nor let his faith waver. Jesus has already paid for every sin committed, and deliverance by way of forgiveness and cleansing continues to follow confession of sin. There is no reason for suffering to be connected to sin, since there is ongoing forgiveness for ongoing sins which are repented. We need to invite God's revealing of the sins in our life which sever us from fellowship with Him and block our blessings. We need to confess and repent these sins so that they can be forgiven and forgotten, and we can be fully restored to communion with God. God is faithful and does not abandon the penitent believer, simply because he authored his own misfortune. If there is a lesson to be learned, learn it quickly by judging yourself. Then move on to the next level of glory, as you advance in virtue away from the vices of pride, profligacy, hatred, or envy. And do it with joyful heart because Jesus has given you His joy and peace (John 15:11, 14:27).

Remember that under the New Covenant, obedience is empowered through the New Birth. Born-Again Christians have been regenerated and literally transformed to the character of Christ. The New Birth inevitably produces willing and cooperative compliance with God's persuasions to obey, as the Holy Spirit continues to work sanctification in the life of a believer. The New Testament assures ever better promises of blessings for obedience because God's grace through faith brings about a conversion and truly transformed life of loving obedience, as God conforms our desires to His will. Obedience to God's Word of instruction thus blesses and delivers us from worldly trials and privation.

As we see in the next Chapter, faith necessitates, and is often coupled with corresponding works as the precise fulfillment, expression and evidence of faith. Obedience can be the faithful response which God designates and requires as a condition for the operation of blessings. When we fail to exercise faith properly by obedience which activates God's Word, we may deprive ourselves and others for whom blessing, and God's Providence are intended. Without faith it is impossible to please God, and works, as prayer, are often the vessels in which our faith is transported.

Faith is knowing that even when we can't see God or detect His hand in the affairs of life, we can be assured that He is with us. He sees us and His hand is guiding, controlling, and orchestrating His benevolent purposes for our lives, despite adversity, or perhaps by means of it.

CHAPTER 7

GOD'S BLESSINGS OF PARTICIPATION BY OBEDIENCE

"Do not be deceived; God is not mocked, for whatever a man sows, that he will also reap. For he who sows to his own flesh will from the flesh reap corruption; but he who sows to the Spirit will from the Spirit reap eternal life. And let us not grow weary in well-doing, for in due season we shall reap, if we do not lose heart."

– Galatians 6:7-9.

Obedience to the Lord is a Scriptural pillar of the Christian faith. Certainly, salvation is based solely on God's grace through faith as far as Born-Again Christians are concerned. Obedience in good works has nothing to do with meriting salvation or saving faith in Jesus as Lord and Saviour. Yet, a believer, once saved by grace through faith, is summoned to dutiful obedience. This is necessitated by Christ's Lordship, for faith which saves is faith in a complete Christ: He Who is both Lord and Saviour. Just as we must recognize that our personal sin and its penalty is that from which we must be rescued, and for which we need a Saviour, so we must recognize His Lordship which entitles Him to faithful obedience by which we henceforth flee from sin and approach beatitude.

Safe in the security and assurance of salvation in the New Birth, we tend to overlook the legitimate functions of obedience for one who is saved by grace. For, God has mandated and blessed us with work to do and fruit to bear as co-workers with Him: to share, participate in, and advance His objectives, to His glory. Obedience is God's blessing to man to participate in His purposes, especially holiness, witnessing, stewardship, and intercessory prayer. God has chosen to bless His children by allowing them to receive and enhance every blessing of salvation by the operation of obedience to the Word. Consistent with God's principle of increase; of reaping what we sow; of receiving in proportion to our input, man cooperates in his own blessings by obedience to the Word. He can reap what he desires by abiding in the Word and doing what the Word instructs, by planting obedient works as well as sowing faith. For, then his desires conform to God's as revealed in the Word.

In a way, obedient works are simply an expression, evidence, extension, and result of one's faith in the Word. Internalizing and appropriating the Word involves more than simply thinking and dwelling on it. Faith also involves following the Word's precepts and actively rendering obedience to the Lord, consistent with the Word which shapes one's belief. Remember that God has covenanted to perform according to our faith, based upon the measure of our reliance upon His Word of promise. If we do not believe the promise applies to us initially, we will never invoke it.

If we persist in unbelief, we will wander from our corridors of blessing. For, we sin when we disobey the Word, according to I John 3:4: "Sin is lawlessness." Romans 7:7 observes: "if it had not been for the law, I should not have known sin... Apart from the law sin lies dead." Sin reveals lack of faith and constitutes disbelief in what God's Word says about the commission, consequences, and penalty of sin. Disobedience stifles promised blessings by revealing lack of trust in God's goodness and power to bless us abundantly according to our faith. Disobedience specifically expresses lack of faith in God's promise to dwell in us and strengthen us, allowing us to be both changed and enabled to obey.

The Biblical model for freedom is a life regulated by God's guidance, according to God's Word, as enabled by God to render voluntary obedience for our own good and the good of others. Jesus did not free us to continue sinning, but to recognize the ultimate good for oneself and others, by submissive, faithful obedience. We have been freed from bondage to the flesh to serve God in enlightened, responsible liberty, patterned by the Word, and fashioned by God's enablement. We must cooperate in achieving God's highest purposes for man: Godly character, loving ministry to other men; witnessing for Jesus, all offered in loving and willing obedience by believers. Submission to God thus produces maximum individual freedom and fulfillment. We must actually grow into the positional, imputed righteousness God has given us in Jesus. He imparts ongoing holiness, and accomplishes the transition, but we must remain open and receptive to our transformation to Christ-likeness.

Jesus explained that "I have not come to abolish the law and the prophets... but to fulfill them." Jesus obeyed the law by a perfectly sinless life and, as the only man ever to do so, could satisfy God's justice by a perfect, substitutionary atonement sufficient for the sins of all men. Jesus also fulfilled the law by revealing the Old Testament was fully contained or perfected in a new law of love. Jesus further enables believers to share His righteousness under the law by imputing His righteousness to believers, as well as by enabling increasing obedience to the law by actually imparting righteousness to believers. Old Testament law thus remains authoritative for us under the New Covenant.

The obedience which Jesus supernaturally endows is vastly superior to man's feeble efforts to obey in his own power. If you are tempted to sin, or to vacillate before beginning any project, let Jesus speak to you from the Cross. There, He suffered unspeakable agonies to free you from sin and disobedience, so you could be delivered for eternity, and for usefulness now. Imagine what He endured for love of you, and now He waits for your invitation to empower you in your gift of freedom from sin and procrastination. You must never again presume to embrace indifference, when it cost Him so much to free you for meaningful existence and effort. So always ask Jesus to enable you to do His will, whenever you are about to succumb to the habit of sin, and he will deliver you. Paradoxically, obedience occurs by God's sovereign, enabling grace, yet our willing concurrence is also essential.

Man's corruption of freedom is perhaps most glaring when we disobey God's Word of instruction. Our freedom is intended to bless us mightily, but when we willfully disobey God's directions, we produce sin and its aftermath of loss. When we deliberately forsake God's help and strength to resist sin, our disobedience plants seeds of eventual harm and destruction, which can be reversed only by God's grace, if we repent and seek cleansing.

Faith is expressed in obedience and evidenced by our works. Faith necessarily coincides with, and corresponds to, obedience to God's Word. Obedience, as a reflection of faith, can help us embrace the blessings of more abundant life Jesus promises. Because of the marvelous transformation wrought in a believer's spirit at the New Birth, he is empowered to obey by the infinite love and power of God. God identifies good works as the hallmark of believers, and He empowers them to desire and perform holy deeds. Ephesians 2:10 reveals: "For we are his workmanship, created in Christ Jesus for good works, which God prepared beforehand, that we should walk in them."

James 2:18-26 explains that faith and works are really obverse sides of the same coin: "Show me your faith apart from your works, and I by my works will show you my faith... faith apart from works is barren. Was not Abraham our father justified by works, when he offered his son Isaac upon the altar? You see that faith was active along with his works, and faith was completed by works... You see that a man is justified by works and not by faith alone... For as the body apart from the spirit is dead, so faith apart from works is dead." Obedience is simply sowing the Word in trusting faith and reliance it will bear the promised fruit, which we will reap in time.

Our obedience to the Lord is motivated by the clear requirements of Scripture. It is necessarily implied by Christ's Lordship; it is confirmed by the revealed need for repentance. It is generated by our self-interest in receiving spiritual prosperity by following God's prescribed way: by receiving blessings promised for obedience. Obedience arises out of love, gratitude, and thanksgiving for our Father, Whom we wish to please as dutiful children.

Throughout this Chapter, we will identify many Scriptures demanding obedience by believers. We begin with the Bible's clear call to repentance, as evidence of faith and obedience to our Lord and Saviour. Without repentance, there is no personal appropriation or appreciation of Christ's sacrifice on behalf of sinners, and no forgiveness of sins. Harsh as it may seem, one cannot walk the narrow way leading to life, and perhaps cannot even enter the narrow gate of the New Birth, without repentance which expresses submissive faith.

Matthew 7:13-14 demands: "Enter by the narrow gate; for the gate is wide and the way is easy, that leads to destruction, and those who enter by it are many. For the gate is narrow and the way is hard, that leads to life, and those who find it are few." Luke 14:26-33 spells out the cost of true discipleship, which Jesus says must be undertaken before starting the journey: "If anyone comes to me and does not hate his own father... and even his own life, he cannot be my disciple. Whoever does not bear his own cross and come after me, cannot be my disciple... So therefore, whoever of you does not renounce all that he has cannot be my disciple."

CHRIST'S LORDSHIP REQUIRES REPENTANT OBEDIENCE

There is nothing very hard about embracing a loving Saviour Who has borne all our sins, but it is difficult to recognize personal sin and choose to forsake it to please that same Saviour and submit to that same Lord. You may focus on repentance as the initial submission of human will to the Lord, or focus upon God's enabling of repentance as part of saving grace, but repent you must if you are to be a Christian. And repentance must include a sorrow for the sin which offends God, and an intent to reform life and follow God's way obediently. You will either know Jesus as Saviour of the repentant, or as Judge of impenitent, lost rebels.

Under the Old Testament there was no forgiveness without repentance, and the same is true under the New Birth. Repentance is not a work of man, but a part of the sinner's understanding of his need for a Saviour. It comes by conviction of the Holy Spirit that one's sin must be abandoned in light of this new understanding. You cannot accept grace without acknowledging your need for it as a sinner in the past, and recognizing the need for God's enabling to purge sin from your life in the future.

Repentance unto salvation is sufficient when a believer detests the sin which has alienated him from God's fellowship and he resolves to turn from sin.[73] An <u>intent</u> to avoid sin, renounce ungodly ways, and reform one's life in obedience to God is sufficient for one to enter life by the narrow gate. Actual reformation by good works is not necessary to receive God's saving grace. Even the worst sinner, totally devoid of personal merit, can embrace forgiveness of sins and eternal salvation, merely by intending to forsake and reverse his sinful way of life.

It is clear that faith and repentance are two aspects of the same transaction. Faith is turning toward Jesus and repentance is turning from sin. Faith and repentance go together, for you cannot turn toward Christ without turning from sin, which is diametrically opposite from Jesus. Both are necessary for the New Birth, and both result, and are developed inexorably, from the Spirit-filled life. Only the penitent can understand he needs Jesus as Lord as well as Saviour. There is no need to dispute whether a sinner must repent sin before, at, or after conversion and New Birth. Repentance invariably accompanies and evidences the New Birth. Habitual absence of obedience to Christ is convincing proof one has not submitted to His Lordship, and therefore not been Born-Again. God calls every man to repent, and enables it, so awareness of lack of obedient submission to the Lord should trigger immediate repentance to confirm and secure one's New Birth. Jesus died to acquit you of sins; not to sanction their continuation, but to follow Him in righteousness.

The call to repentance is such a vital part of each Christian's faith, that it was the first utterance of Christ's public ministry (Matthew 4:17; Mark 1:14; Luke 13:3, 24:46-47). It was the first exhortation of John the Baptist (Matthew 3:2; Luke 3:3,8; Acts 13:24, 19:4). Repentance was the first sermon preached by the Apostles who were sent out by Jesus (Mark 6:12). It was the first instruction to believers on the Day of Pentecost, given by Peter to the unsaved men of Israel (Acts 2:38, 3:19); and among the final end-time revelations of Jesus (Luke 24:47; Revelation 2:5,16,21, and 3:3,19).

At Luke 5:31-32 Jesus says: "Those who are well have no need of a physician, but those who are sick; I have not come to call the righteous, but sinners to repentance" (Paralleled in Mark 2:17; and see also, Matthew 10:22). A sinner who procrastinates and does not rush in repentance to Jesus for forgiveness and cleansing is like a patient who says he is too sick to go for examination and treatment by his physician. He cannot receive the cure without first acknowledging the symptoms of illness, and presenting himself for healing in a receptive posture of submission.

Acts 17:30 warns: "The times of ignorance God overlooked, but now he commands all men everywhere to repent." Romans 2:4 queries: "Do you not know that God's kindness is meant to lead you to repentance?"

2 Timothy 2:25-26 equates repentance with escaping the devil in order freely to embrace immortal life: "God may perhaps grant that they will repent and come to know the truth, and they may escape from the snare of the devil, after being captured by him to do his will."

Hebrews 6:1 identifies repentance and faith as elementary doctrines of Christ by which to enter the narrow gate of discipleship.

It is so important that all men have an opportunity to repent that 2 Peter 3:9 reveals about Jesus' Second Coming: "The Lord is not slow about his promise as some count slowness, but is forbearing toward you, not wishing that any should perish, but that all should reach repentance." What appears to be a worthless weed will not be rooted up prematurely, but will be granted a full opportunity to be transformed into fruitful service (Matthew 13:29-30).

The Bible identifies three phases of repentance which must accompany, or immediately follow, saving faith in Jesus. The first of these is appreciation of sin: both the intellectual comprehension of personal wrongdoing, and the emotional conviction of that truth. It is an affirmation which involves appreciating the need for personal regret for offending God.

The second phase of repentance is confession of one's personal sin, which incorporates making apology to God for the affront to His holiness. Genuine repentance involves remorse for the offense to God's dignity by sin. Worldly repentance involves regret or fear for loss of status or benefit. Thus, Esau and Judas Iscariot 'repented' their wrongs, but were motivated by worldly grief over what they had lost, rather than horror over their loathsome repudiation of Godly values (Genesis 27:38; Matthew 27:3; 2 Corinthians 7:10).

The third phase of repentance is a volitional determination of the will to obey God's Commandment to be holy and sinless. It includes an affirmation and resolve to turn toward God and away from sin, by declaring a desire to commit one's life to the Lordship of Christ. 2 Chronicles 7:14 says: "If my people, which are called by my name, shall humble themselves, and pray, and seek my face and turn from their wicked ways: then will I hear from heaven, and will forgive their sin, and will heal their land." Repentance can only be proved genuine by fruit worthy of repentance in a transformed life. Intent to change may be enough for salvation, but fruitful obedience evidencing repentance is an essential part of the Christian life and walk enabled by the New Birth.

In fact, obedience is the principal objective proof of Christian conversion, for the test of service to the Lord is fruitfulness and productive use of one's time, talent, and treasure for the Lord. The servant who failed to invest and earn profit with his Master's talent was called "worthless" and cast into the outer darkness (Matthew 25:30). "Moreover it is required of stewards that they be found trustworthy" (I Corinthians 4:2). Reward is based on what we have accomplished with what the Master has given us. The test is faithfulness in serving the Master.

OBEDIENCE MOTIVATED BY REWARD

Scripture teaches that after the New Birth, rewards and blessings are meted out for believers' obedient intentions and works. Believers stand before Christ at the Bema seat of Judgment, where one's works are "revealed with fire, and the fire will test what sort of work each one has done" (I Corinthians 3:13). Good works for Jesus will be rewarded, but frivolous acts which did not serve God's purposes, will "be burned up, he will suffer loss, though he himself will be saved." Obedience evidences, expresses, and demonstrates faith in God's Word of promise that there are earthly blessings and Heavenly rewards for those who obey after they are saved by grace through faith. Our faith and conversion cannot be sterile, but are always demonstrated by how we act in accord with them by bearing spiritual fruit. It is what Galatians 5:6 refers to as "Faith working through love." Our faith and salvation will always be reflected in our works.

As we mature in our Christian walk, our motivation for obedience will be pure, unadulterated love for God, and a desire to reciprocate His love: to please and glorify Him by doing what He asks of us. Obedience will feel right and joyful in the knowledge we are doing what God has designated as good for us, and because our every thought, word and deed is permeated with love, which is a Spiritual fruit provided by God in inexhaustible supply. Love is God's marvelous gift to us because it includes and expresses the very nature of God, Who is love (I John 4:8). When you do a loving act, you are intimately experiencing and involved with the Lord.

We should all aspire to the mature faith of Job, who proved it was possible for a man to love God for Himself, even when deprived of every gift previously received from God. Yet, at the start of every human relation with God, obedience is encouraged by a promise of reward, coupled with a corresponding warning of loss for disobedience. Thus, Adam was blessed with freedom to eat and enjoy every tree of the Garden of Eden, "But of the tree of knowledge of good and evil, thou shalt not eat of it: for in the day that thou eatest thereof thou shalt surely die" (Genesis 2:17).

God began His relationship with Israel as His chosen people with promises of blessing in the world for faithful obedience and loyalty to Him, coupled with admonition of punishment and grave loss in the event of Israel's infidelity and disobedience to God. The fear of loss for disobedience was a necessary adjunct to God's promise of reward for obedience. Even in loving desire to please God, we should remind ourselves that whom you obey is your master (Romans 6:16). If you yield to a demon's temptations, he becomes your master: a consequence to be dreaded by any believer. The habit of obedience was initially cultivated and encouraged by God's promises of reward in the Old Testament because the Israelites did not have God's Spirit indwelling them, and their sinful natures made it difficult to obey God out of love, without the extraneous prodding of reward for obedience.

Under Christ's New and Better Covenant, believers receive the indwelling of the Holy Spirit; regeneration; imparted righteousness; transformation to Christ-likeness; and enablement to obey because of their new nature. God's love in a believer makes it possible to respond in obedience out of love, without the bribery of reward. And so we find the New Testament speaks of suffering, privation, persecution, and travail in the world because we live a Christ-like life. Reward and blessings are still promised under Christ's New Covenant, but we are content, in the peace of the Lord, to expect and await the realization of most of them in the Hereafter.

At the start of one's Christian walk, self-interest is appealed to by the promise of blessings, often expressed in terms of sowing a prescribed obedience to reap a predictable consequence of rewards. In fact, sowing faith in the Gospel of salvation by grace is the first act of sowing obedience to believe and trust God's promise of salvation by grace through faith. Self-interest underlies our initial response to most promises of God to bless His children. It is only after spiritual maturity that we avoid the modern tendency to use the Word to promote our advantage, and stress obeying the Word because of our gratitude and love which seeks to please God.

The genius of blessing in allowing believers to participate in God's plans through obedience, coincides with the foreseeable law of sowing and reaping set forth in Scripture: If we plant sin, we will irrevocably reap suffering or privation; if not here, then in the Hereafter. If we plant righteousness in obedience to God's laws, we will inevitably reap a harvest of spiritual prosperity, health and answered prayers; if not here, then Hereafter. If we submit obediently, it accomplishes our highest good, as we prosper spiritually. As we grow in holiness through obedience to the Word, we are better equipped to fellowship and walk with God. We are fitted to know Him by complying with His will, as reflected in His Word. As we copy His character by obeying His will for us, we are increasingly fitted for obedience in stewardship, prayer, and witnessing to minister in love to others.

Obedience originates with blind faith that God prescribes what is best for His children, and His dictates both deserve to, and can profitably, be followed. Often, the commands which God imposes to test obedience are irrational from man's point of view. Surely, Noah could not justify building an ark in the middle of dry ground, and Joshua must have wondered about God's command to circle Jericho thirteen times to bring about its defeat (Joshua 6:3-4). Yet, it was how God chose to prove each man's faithful submission, so that he might occupy the world for God.

SOWING OBEDIENCE TO REAP BLESSINGS

Every Christian is familiar with the law of sowing and reaping in the context of faith. We know that "faith comes from what is heard, and what is heard comes by the preaching of Christ" (Romans 10:17). Faith must originate with, and be based on God's Word, otherwise it is nothing more than a wish something will happen. A lukewarm confession of faith can be expected to produce a meager harvest of blessings. But a strong confession of faith in the Word, which is literally lived, articulated in every thing we say, and drenches, pervades and inhabits our every thought, utterance, and act, can be expected to produce a plentiful harvest. For there is a fixed law that the measure of faith we give or sow, has fixed consequences, and determines the measure of blessing we reap or receive. When you follow the principles of God, He blesses you and prospers you; He becomes involved in what you do because obedience evidences your reliant faith in Him.

In all spiritual and earthly things, except as meliorated by God's grace and intervention, there is a fixed law of harvesting what we plant. "God is not mocked, for whatever a man sows, that he will also reap" (Galatians 6:7). God has ordained a spiritual law of receiving in kind according to what we have first given. A righteous man wins a reward commensurate with his obedient submission to the Law of God's Covenant or Testament. Man is blessed for obedience and cursed for disobedience to God's Word.

As in all things, even our ability to sow and harvest seed obediently comes from God. 2 Corinthians 9:10 says: "He who supplies seed to the sower and bread for food will supply and multiply your resources, and increase the harvest of your righteousness." One of the purposes of receiving seed is to share it by good works: "And God is able to provide you with every blessing in abundance, so that you may always have enough of everything and may provide in abundance for every good work" (2 Corinthians 9:8). 2 Timothy 3:16, 17 adds: "All Scripture is inspired by God... that the man of God may be complete, equipped for every good work."

Titus 2:14 says Jesus "gave himself for us to redeem us from all iniquity and to purify for himself a people of his own who are zealous for good deeds." Titus 2:8 teaches that we are to be regenerated and renewed in the Holy Spirit "so that those who have believed in God may be careful to apply themselves to good deeds." See also, 2 Thessalonians 2:17; Hebrews 10:24;

and I Peter 2:12). The reward for sowing God's seed by giving to others is your own blessing: "You will be enriched in every way for great generosity... for the rendering of this service not only supplies the wants of the saints but also overflows in many thanksgivings to God" (2 Corinthians 9:11-12; and see Ecclesiastes 11:1). You are called to bless even those who wrong you, "that you may obtain a blessing" (I Peter 3:9).

We can consume God's seed and appropriate it exclusively to our own purposes. But sufficiency and abundance, as well as growth in holiness, are related to the extent of our giving to others, or sowing the seed to harvest and share it: "The point is this: he who sows sparingly will also reap sparingly, and he who sows bountifully will also reap bountifully. Each one must do as he has made up his mind, not reluctantly or under compulsion, for God loves a cheerful giver" (2 Corinthians 9:6-7). Likewise, St. Paul told the Philippians that because of their loving obedience in charity: "my God will supply every need of yours according to his riches in glory in Christ Jesus" (Philippians 4:19).

Mark 4:24 confirms that man's cooperative intent is necessary to sow and nurture the seed from God obediently and faithfully. As in all matters of faith, the measure we reap is dependent upon the amount we sow; and reward is related to personal effort: "the measure you give will be the measure you get, and still more will be given you. For to him who has will more be given; and from him who has not, even what he has will be taken away" (paralleled at Matthew 13:12 and Luke 8:18). Luke 6:38 puts it: "give, and it will be given to you; good measure, pressed down, shaken together, running over, will be put into your lap. For the measure you give will be the measure you get back."

Obedience based on the Word is pure faith in expectation and reliance on God's promise. In the natural world, giving as directed by God depletes our wealth. But in the spiritual realm, it increases our blessing, even as much as a hundredfold, over and beyond that which we have planted, given, or invested (Mark 10:29; Luke 18:29-30; and Matthew 19:29). Through obedience, we expect to reap more than we plant.

We will reap in kind according to what we have sown. We cannot undo last season's planting. You cannot sow corn seed and reap roses. In the spiritual realm of consequences you cannot sow evil and reap good. Galatians 6:4,8 says: "But let each one test his own work, for each man will have to bear his own load... For he who sows to his own flesh will from the flesh reap corruption; but he who sows to the Spirit will from the Spirit reap eternal life." Thus, God's grace blesses us with the privilege of following and deploying the dependable, fixed law of sowing and reaping, so that we can faithfully plant what God directs, confident we will harvest God's promised blessing in his good time and pleasure.

Obedience by planting seed to share God's blessings with others will determine the various blessings we receive from God here and Hereafter. Deuteronomy 26:13,18 links giving with receiving blessings: "I have... given them unto the Levite, and unto the stranger, to the fatherless, and to the widow, according to all thy commandments... I have not transgressed thy commandments... And the Lord hath avouched thee this day to be his peculiar people... And to make thee high above all nations which he hath made, in praise, and in name, and in honour; and that thou mayest be an holy people unto the Lord thy God."

Believers may obediently sow or invest their resource into the Lord's work and ministry, and pay in the coin of faith, service, or wealth; of time, talent, or treasure, with faithful expectations of reaping a specific reward, such as an increase in wealth, and a harvest of good health, prosperity, or any spiritual blessing. One may pray for the healing of others in anticipation of being blessed with his own healing. A believer may do this according to laws of tithing, charity, stewardship, or sowing and reaping. They may give tithes, a part of their income, or invest the talent God has given them, in order to receive prosperity or some other blessing for their obedience (Malachi 3:10). Believers will obediently share their blessing with others, in loving charity, or ministering to the needs of both saved and unsaved by praying for the needs of others, or by witnessing to the Gospel, or supporting evangelistic ministries to harvest souls. Sowing obedient compliance by giving to others reaps the promised blessings of receiving from the Lord in multiplied measure (Luke 6:38; 2 Corinthians 9:10-11). But if we are meager in giving, our reaping will be scant at harvest.

The Beatitudes of Matthew 5:3-11 promise specific rewards for sowing specific human intentions and conditions. The poor in spirit will be blessed with the kingdom of Heaven. Mourners, or those who grieve over their paucity of spiritual attainment, will be blessed with comfort.[74] The meek will inherit the earth. The merciful shall be blessed with mercy. The pure in heart will be rewarded with seeing God. Peacemakers will be blessed as sons of God. Those who are persecuted for righteousness' sake will be blessed with the kingdom of Heaven. If we obediently and collaboratively adopt these right attitudes and intentions, then we will be blessed as promised.

Conversely, if we are disobedient and faithless, we will reap no divine reward, but only suffering and privation. A few seeds at planting will provide a profusion of fruit at harvest time, whether we have sown evil or good. Hosea 8:7 puts it: "For they have sown the wind, and they shall reap the whirlwind." "A little yeast leavens the whole lump" (Galatians 5:9; I Corinthians 5:6).

If we do not heed God's revelations and calls to obey Him to accomplish His spiritual objectives of holiness, loving service, witnessing, and intercessory prayer, He may use suffering to motivate and achieve these ends in us. He wishes us to prosper spiritually and become like Jesus, by training and learning, rather than painful experience brought about by disobedience. But we will acquire and develop these character traits either quickly by obedience in response to instruction, or gradually by the rigors of suffering.

As for basic needs of food, clothing, and shelter, "your heavenly Father knows that you need them all. But seek first his kingdom and his righteousness, and all these things shall be yours as well" (Matthew 6:32-33). We will be rewarded with all our fundamental needs as long as we are faithful in seeking the righteousness of God, in obedience to the command to be holy, as God is holy. Our prayers may start out seeking carnal things, but they will eventually mature to the point of asking for God's righteousness, which is the free gift by grace from the Holy Spirit. We are promised sufficiency for our needs if we obediently "present your bodies as a living sacrifice, holy and acceptable to God, which is your spiritual worship. Do not be conformed to this world but be transformed by the renewal of your mind, that you may prove what is the will of God, what is good and acceptable and perfect" (Romans 12:1-2).

The focus of our obedience is multi-dimensional. We must look back in joy to recall our ransom of deliverance in Christ. We must look upward to recall who we are in Christ. We must look inward to see our heart's growing conformance to God's holiness. We must look outward to serve in a ministry of loving stewardship. And we must look ahead to heaven and the promise of our blessed hope in Christ. But we are responsible for seeking the Lord and His Kingdom, if we are to be rewarded. Just as a barber can service only those who come to him and sit still while he works, so God promises to help those who seek Him, and patiently abide His spiritual tonsure.

It will become abundantly clear, as we progress through these pages, that the blessings of abundant life which appear to be absolute and unconditional for the faithful, are in actuality, laced with pre-conditions and modifications. Our faith requires, and is expressed and evidenced by obedience (James 2:18-24). Submissive obedience which leads to a harvest of blessings, by implication requires the sowing of active obedience before there can be any reaping. We are called to "hunger and thirst for righteousness" before we can be satisfied (Matthew 5:6), and this goes beyond mere passive desire. It requires active seeking and pursuit of God. We can come boldly before His throne of grace, but we must always do so in a spirit of repentance, worship, and teachableness, ready to submit obediently to His will for our good.

If we are to seek the kingdom of God to receive blessings (Luke 12:29-31), then know that seeking involves aiming at, striving continually, and actively pursuing the spiritual character exemplified by the Kingdom.

If we are to abide in Christ (John 15:5-10), or abide in the Word (John 15:3-8), we can do so only by submissive obedience to God's will, for sin and rebellion cannot abide in a holy Lord; nor can we, without obedience, abide in His Word, which counsels holiness, goodness, kindness, and departure from sin.

Many of the promises of blessing are made to the collective Body of believers, first the nation Israel, and then to the Church comprising the Body of Christ. We can understand this principle when we consider that the gifts of the Holy Spirit are assigned to the aggregate Body of Christ, and no single believer possesses all the gifts of the Spirit. Yet, as a member of Christ's Body, we are individually entitled to benefit from, and share in, the Spiritual gifts which have been apportioned among the members "for the common good" (I Corinthians 12:7).

Likewise, the Body of Christ enjoys previously unknown spiritual prosperity and health collectively, as Spiritual gifts accomplish the "building up the body of Christ, until we all attain to the unity of the faith and of the knowledge of the Son of God, to... the measure of the stature of the fullness of Christ" (Ephesians 4:12-13). Christian nations in the twentieth and twenty-first centuries have enjoyed more economic prosperity, public health, and advantages than at any time since the Garden of Eden. Admittedly, within American society, there are individuals who experience pain, privation, and poor health. Yet, as a member of a prosperous society, even the poorest have access to knowledge, roads, indoor plumbing, shelter, food, raiment, and longer lives on a scale unknown to all but the wealthiest in ages past.

This leads us to the final condition which must be met before blessings can be harvested and enjoyed. Many blessings are promised for enjoyment here on earth, but many are also intended for the Hereafter. "The measure of the stature of the fullness of Christ" promised in Ephesians 4:13 is obviously something we do not fully attain until glorification after the Second Coming of Christ (Romans 8:17). A feature of sowing and reaping is that reward must necessarily be deferred until the seed has ripened: "And let us not grow weary in well-doing, for in due season we shall reap, if we do not lose heart" (Galatians 6:9). The faithful examples acclaimed in Hebrews Chapter 11 for their obedient faithfulness, "though well attested by their faith, did not receive what was promised, since God had foreseen something better for us, that apart from us they should not be made perfect" (Hebrews 11:39-40).

Chapter 12 is devoted to the new Testament warnings of Christ that believers can expect suffering, privation, persecution, torment, and death in this world. The New Testament which empowers and encourages obedience, and then promises reward Hereafter, also affirms trials: "Blessed is the man who <u>endures</u> trial, for when he has stood the test he will receive the crown of life which God has promised to those who love him" (James 1:12).

Obedience is a wonderful blessing when we do what God directs in His Word, which coincidentally and directly furthers our own interests. For, we can depend upon the promise of God's Word to reward us when we obey. Conversely, disobedience dependably produces loss or despair, if not here, then Hereafter.

Believers may obediently plant Christ-like character: sowing goodness, kindness, gentleness, and holiness in order to reap an increase in righteousness and grow in likeness to Christ. God alone bring about this transformation of character, but man has a part in collaborating: "Blessed are those who <u>hunger and thirst</u> for righteousness, for they shall be satisfied" (Matthew 5:6). When we hunger and thirst for righteousness, we search for God where He is, and He is always situated diametrically opposite from sin. Psalm 42:1 says: "As the deer pants for streams of water, so my soul pants for you, O God." We cannot slake our thirst unless we go to the source of living water. We cannot thirst for righteousness without living according to God's righteousness, and seeking Him where He will be found. It is when you think about whatever is true, honorable, just, pure, lovely, gracious, excellent that "the God of peace will be with you" (Philippians 4:8-9). Conversely, he who sows sin, and hungers for worldliness rather than righteousness, will reap evil and not find God. Ephesians 5:9 explains that "the fruit of light is found in all that is good and right and true."

Hence, Luke 12:29-31 cautions: "do not seek what you are to eat and what you are to drink, nor be of anxious mind. For... your Father knows that you need them. Instead, seek his kingdom, and these things shall be yours as well."

Hebrews 11:6 speaks plainly that a pre-condition to receiving rewards is first seeking God: "For whoever would draw near to God must believe that he exists and that he rewards those who seek him." We are rewarded with drawing near to God, when we believe we receive our reward because we seek Him. Searching for God involves a quest for His fellowship, but also His guidance, deliverance, and strength for our Christian journey. We are to seek and find, not only material reward, but the Giver's fellowship as our reward. Jeremiah 29:13 explains: "And ye shall seek me, and find me, when ye shall search for me with all your heart." See also, Deuteronomy 4:7; Job 14:15; Psalm 145:19, and Joel 2:32.

Even if the only reward we receive involves drawing near to God, there is a pre-condition of first seeking Him. And seeking Him involves our turning and <u>walking His way</u> of righteousness in order to draw near to Him. A selfish motivation to seek God is prescribed by Scripture, in order to receive the blessings of finding Him and obtaining the promised reward. Even salvation is in part selfishly based on our eternal reward for responding to grace as prescribed in Scripture. However, as we grow spiritually we will offer obedience voluntarily because it is the principal way of requiting God's love by obedience to please Him.

Moreover, the great satisfaction of expressing our love through obedience becomes the highlight of its blessing. Our dominant motive is not to receive rewards, but to enjoy fellowship with the Lord, here and Hereafter. God is found in His Word, which expresses His character, His will for believers, and His desire for what we are to be and do. In our disdain for worldly possessions, our zest for the Kingdom must be like the merchant "who, on finding one pearl of great value, went and sold all that he had and bought it" (Matthew 13:45). Our disdain for the world activates our response to Christ's directive: "Give to every one who begs from you;

and of him who takes away your goods, do not ask them again... and lend, expecting nothing in return" (Luke 6:30,35).

Obedience conducts believers to the portals of God's peace. Knowing that we are in harmony with God's spiritual forces and processes frees us from anguish and bondage to this world. We can then entrust all details to God, Who promises to shape the conditions of life into what is best for us. When a Christian's vision is focused on the world to come, he is detached from the cares and temptations of this world. He can gratefully enjoy the gifts he receives as God's will, without rebelling against what he cannot control, or coveting what is not his. He can relinquish worldly concerns with disdain, for he knows that undue attachment to them interferes with his spirituality. His obedience insulates him from the influence of hostile worldly forces, and denies them any dominion over him.

Psalm 24:3-5 asks: "Who shall ascend into the hill of the Lord?... He that hath clean hands, and a pure heart... He shall receive the blessing from the Lord, and righteousness." Psalm 34:12-16, reprised at I Peter 3:10-12 reveals: "he that would love life and see good days, let him keep his tongue from evil and his lips from speaking guile. Let him turn from evil and do right. For the eyes of the Lord are upon the righteous, and <u>his ears are open to their prayer</u>. But the face of the Lord is against those that do evil to cut off the remembrance of them from the earth."

Psalm 18:20-22 teaches: "The Lord rewarded me according to my righteousness; according to the cleanness of my hands hath he recompensed me. For I have kept the ways of the Lord, and have not wickedly departed from my God... and I did not put away his statutes from me." Psalm 37:25 observes: "I have been young, and now am old; yet I have <u>not seen the righteous forsaken</u>, nor his seed begging bread." Psalm 84:11 puts it: "The Lord God is a sun and a shield: the Lord will give grace and glory: No good thing will be withhold from them that walk uprightly." Psalm 37:3-5 promises God will bring to pass the desires of our hearts if we will have faith, obey, and "Trust in the Lord, and do good... Delight thyself also in the Lord; and... Commit thy way unto the Lord." Psalm 91:1 promises refuge, deliverance, courage, and protection for him: "that dwelleth in the secret place of the most High." The promise is not made to all believers, but only those who are willing to reside in the Lord's secret place. A commitment to abide by the 'rules of the house' is strongly implied if one is to dwell in God's presence, not just during tribulation, but on a constant and continual basis.

Proverbs 11:18 puts it: "To him that soweth righteousness shall be a sure reward," and Proverbs 11:31 reveals: "the righteous shall be recompensed in the earth." The Apocryphal Ecclesiasticus 16:13-15 says of God: "as his mercy is, so his correction judgeth a man according to his works. The sinner shall not escape in his rapines... All mercy shall make a place for every man according to the merit of his works."

When we sow righteous acts in obedience to God's call, God works our sanctification, saying: "Sanctify yourselves therefore, and be ye holy; for I am the Lord your God. And ye shall keep my statutes, and do them: I am the Lord which sanctify you" (Leviticus 20:7-8). Jesus gives further insight into how obedience to God's Word puts us in conformity with God's will and purposes, brings answered prayers, and blesses us with spiritual fruitfulness: "He who abides in me, and I in him, he it is that bears much fruit, for apart from me you can do nothing... If you abide in me, and <u>my words abide in you</u>, ask whatever you will, and it shall be done for you. By this my Father is glorified, that you bear much fruit, and so prove to be my disciples...

If you keep my commandments, you will abide in my love" (John 15:5-10). We abide in Christ and His love by obeying Him!

When a believer cooperates in acts which express God's Word abiding in him, his growth in character and holiness is supernaturally accomplished. Our new nature is no longer under compulsion to sin: "No one who abides in him sins... He who does right is righteous, as he is righteous... No one born of God commits sin; for God's nature abides in him, and he cannot sin because he is born of God" (I John 3:6-9). As Samuel Smiles observed: "Sow a thought, and you reap an act; Sow an act, and you reap a habit; Sow a habit, and you reap a character; Sow a character, and you reap a destiny."[75]

However, if we sow sin, we reap wickedness, not blessing. In the Old Testament, Proverbs 22:8 teaches: "He that soweth iniquity shall reap vanity: and the rod of his anger shall fail." Proverbs 28:9 confirms: "He that turneth away his ear from hearing the law, even his prayer shall be abomination." Job 4:8 says: "they that plow iniquity, and sow wickedness, reap the same." Evil is seldom planted with an intent to reap evil consequences, but involves acting to gratify some immediate desire, in disregard of the consequences forecast for such sinful acts. Evil actions breed evil consequences in the world. Obadiah 15 puts it: "As thou hast done, it shall be done unto thee: thy reward shall return upon thine own head." Hosea 10:12 affirms: "Sow to yourselves in righteousness, reap in mercy."

The New Testament propounds the same inflexible law that if we sow obedience we will reap blessings of spiritual growth, prosperity, and be rewarded with good, but if we sow sin, we must reap sinful fruit. Ephesians 6:8 calls Christians to render "service with a good will as to the Lord and not to men, knowing that whatever good any one does, he will receive the same again from the Lord." Impliedly, failure to render obedient service merits no recompense, but fathers dire consequences. Colossians 3:25 puts it starkly: "For the wrongdoer will be paid back for the wrong he has done, and there is no partiality."

Jesus further connects one's obedient conduct to earthly reward, and identifies the measure of one's giving as determining what he receives, applied to a broad spectrum of conduct: "love your enemies, and do good, and lend, expecting nothing in return; and your reward will be great... Judge not, and you will not be judged; condemn not, and you will not be condemned; Forgive, and you will be forgiven; give, and it will be given to you" (Luke 6:35-37; paralleled at Matthew 7:1-2).

On the other hand, he who does not pass on God's mercy to his fellow men, will lose his blessings. The Parable of the Unforgiving Servant teaches that failure to forgive the debt someone owes you will revoke the forgiveness previously extended to you by the Lord (Matthew 18:23-25). Through obedience, we are summoned and empowered to enrich the lives of others.

Jesus declares: "It is more blessed to give than to receive" (Acts 20:35). It is the giver who receives the greater blessing from the Lord, so that giving is its own reward, because every loving deed carries intimate involvement with God, Who is love. At Genesis 27:29 Isaac pronounced: "cursed be every one that curseth thee, and blessed be he that blesseth thee."

Luke 9:24 enunciates the basic rule of giving all of oneself to the Lord to gain everything: "For whoever would save his life will lose it; and whoever loses his life for my sake, he will save it." Ephesians 6:6-8 calls us to act "as servants of Christ, doing the will of God from the heart, rendering service with a good will as to the Lord and not to men, knowing that whatever good any one does, he will receive again from the Lord." Ephesians 2:10 notes we are:

"created in Christ Jesus for good works, which God prepared beforehand, that we should walk in them."

The fruit and blessing proceeding from faithful obedience to the Word also includes an abundance of offspring (Genesis 1:22,28; 8:17, 9:7, 35:11; Leviticus 26:9; Deuteronomy 28:4; and Jeremiah 23:3).

The blessing of peace, a fruit of the Holy Spirit, is promised him whose obedience pleases the Lord: "When a man's ways please the Lord, he maketh even his enemies to be at peace with him" (Proverbs 16:7).

OBEDIENCE AND BLESSINGS IN THE NEW TESTAMENT

The promise of a hundred-fold return to him who exercises his faith, in the Parable of the Sower at Mark 4:20, alludes to the extent and depth of our trust, reliance, and belief in a specific Word of blessing. It has its counterpart in connection with a hundred-fold return based on unswerving obedience in following Jesus' way, which also verifies our faith. Jesus explains at Mark 10:29-30: "Truly, I say to you, there is no one who has left house or brothers or sisters or mother or father or children or lands, for my sake and for the gospel, who will not receive a hundred-fold now in this time, houses, and brothers and sisters and mothers and children and lands, with persecutions, and in the age to come eternal life." The blessings are for "now in this time," as well as for "the age to come," when we experience the blessing of eternal life.

The reward of an hundred-fold in houses, relatives, and lands is contingent upon forsaking the world for the sake of Jesus and the Gospel, which means living for Jesus in total obedience and commitment to His way. In addition to full faith in the Word, blessings are also conditioned upon the extent of obedience to the Word, in which the Lord's purposes and direction are revealed, outlined, and recounted. Ephesians 6:8 says: "whatever good any one does, he will receive the same again from the Lord." We will receive from the Lord after we have first given to Him and other men by tithing and good stewardship. As a general rule, we first sow obedience with faith, and then we reap the promised blessings.

We must seek the imputed righteousness of Christ in and through the New Birth before we can be heirs of the New Covenant and its promised blessings. After we are Born-Again we must also obediently seek the actual, imparted, practical righteousness of God by obeying His will. We are to strive for the Kingdom of God and His righteousness, which is the repository of all spiritual, eternal blessings. If we will seek God's kingdom by emulating His holiness, Jesus says there is no need to be anxious about food, drink, or clothing (Matthew 6:32-33; Colossians 3:1-4). God blesses us through faith by His grace, if we follow and obey Him, by seeking to understand His will and purposes, and submitting to them under His governance.

We cooperate in seeking the Kingdom of God by seeking the glory of God through the Lordship of Christ over our lives.[76] In this endeavor we are enabled by grace through faith at the new Birth, because we are "chosen and destined by God the Father and sanctified by the Spirit for obedience to Jesus Christ and for sprinkling with his blood" (I Peter 1:2). The sprinkling of believers with Christ's blood seals His covenant at the New Birth, even as it spiritually transforms and regenerates the New Man. The Holy Spirit then provides ongoing sanctification and enables us to be actually obedient to the Lord, as the Blood of Christ continues to cleanse the repentant sinner. We can be obedient because we are actually made righteous.

Jesus says that those who are meek, that is, submissive to God's will, are those who will "inherit the earth" as their reward (Matthew 5:5). When we follow Jesus' way obediently, and renounce the world in search of holiness, for the sake of the Kingdom of God, we "receive manifold more in this time" (Luke 18:30). When we collaborate with God by obediently seeking the holiness which He works in us and act conformably, we are blessed with righteousness. Matthew 5:6 promises: 'Blessed are those who hunger and thirst for righteousness, for they shall be satisfied." Jesus adds at Luke 6:35-36: "love your enemies, and do good, and lend, expecting nothing in return, and your reward will be great, and you will be sons of the Most High... Be merciful, even as your Father is merciful."

It is inevitable that we will be assailed by the storms and torments of life. If we hear the words of Jesus and do them, we will have built our lives on the strong foundation of obedience and righteousness (Matthew 7:24-25; Luke 6:46-49). However, without a foundation built on obedience to the Word, our resistance to worldly assaults is enervated and lacks endurance, leading to ruin.

Bearing fruit which reflects the holiness and character of God is another reward of obedience to God's will. Isaiah 3:10 directs: "Say ye to the righteous, that it shall be well with him: for they shall eat the fruit of their doings." Jeremiah 17:10 likewise says: "I the Lord search the heart. I try the reins, even to give every man according to his ways, and according to the fruit of his doings." Matthew 3:8 summons us to "Bear fruit that befits repentance," and repentance requires an intent to turn from evil and toward God's way. Jesus says that our character is reflected in the fruit we bear and will lead to reward or punishment: "every sound tree bears good fruit, but the bad tree bears evil fruit. A sound tree cannot bear evil fruit... Every tree that does not bear good fruit is cut down and thrown into the fire. Not everyone... shall enter the kingdom of Heaven, but he who does the will of my Father who is in heaven" (Matthew 7:15-21).

Colossians 1:9-10 defines fruit as good works which please God because they obediently conform to His will: "that you may be filled with the knowledge of his will... to lead a life worthy of the Lord, fully pleasing to him, bearing fruit in every good work and increasing in the knowledge of God." Acts 5:32 speaks of the gift of "the Holy Spirit whom God has given to those who obey him." Jesus connects membership in His family to evidence of one's obedience: "whoever does the will of God is my brother, and sister, and mother" (Mark 3:53).

Our obedience in witnessing to the Gospel of salvation pursuant to the Great Commission of Mark 16:15 will also be judged and rewarded here and Hereafter according to our works. Our zeal in witnessing blesses us with gathering in a harvest of fruit, as unsaved souls are transformed into Born-Again men. There is reward for obediently preaching the Gospel. St. Paul notes: "For if I do this of my own will, I have a reward... I do it all for the sake of the gospel, that I may share in its blessings" by sharing them with others (I Corinthians 9:17,23). Evangelism is one of the loving, fruitful works endorsed by Jesus at John 4:36: "He who reaps receives wages, and gathers fruit for eternal life, so that sower and reaper may rejoice together."

St. Paul speaks of his planting the seed of the Word, while Apollos watered it, and God gave the growth. Paul concludes at I Corinthians 3:8-13: "He who plants and he who waters are equal, and underline each shall receive his wages according to his labor. For we are fellow workmen for God... each man's work will become manifest: for the Day will disclose it, because it will be revealed with fire, and the fire will test what sort of work each one has done."

Jesus confirms at Luke 11:28 that God rewards obedience, and intends submissive servants to enjoy earthly and heavenly joy. "Blessed rather are those who hear the word of God and keep it." A servant who is faithful and wise will be set over all the master's possessions (Luke 12:44), and have growing spiritual capacity to enjoy his God-given blessings.

Jesus teaches that although believers are given different talents or wealth, men will receive disparate rewards on the basis of how they discharge their duty to promote the Master's purposes. The man with many talents who produces an increase in them will be rewarded according to his fidelity and zeal. In the Parable of the Talents at Matthew 25:21 Jesus speaks of rewarding a fruitful servant: "Well done, good and faithful servant; you have been faithful over a little, I will set you over much; enter into the joy of your master." However, another servant who had been given only one talent, hid it, and failed to put it to use, thereby demonstrating his contempt for the need to develop his talent. Consequently, his talent was taken away from him and given to the servant who had effectively used his talent.

Diligent effort which produces fruit on earth, and reflects faithful reliance on the Word, will be rewarded with even greater gain in God's Kingdom to come. The same result was accomplished in the Parable of the Pounds at Luke 19:11-27 where the servant who wisely invested his pounds was rewarded with greater authority, while the slothful servant who did nothing with his pound had it taken away and was endowed with no further authority. Our obedient, faithful service determines the blessings we are given by the Lord.

Jesus, Whose life always sets the example for our lives, explains that He enjoyed the anointing from God because he always acted in compliance with His will: "And he who sent me is with me; he has not left me alone, for I always do what is pleasing to him" (John 8:29). "I seek not my own will but the will of him who sent me" (John 5:30). "I do nothing on my own authority but speak thus as the Father taught me" (John 8:28). Even in the face of death on the Cross, Jesus expressed His submission to God's will: "Father, if thou art willing, remove this cup from me; nevertheless not my will, but thine, be done" (Luke 22:42). John 9:31 says we have God's ear in prayer when we are obedient; "We know that God does not listen to sinners, but if any one is a worshiper of God and does his will, God listens to him." Jesus reveals the lesson for believers at John 12:26: "if any one serves me, the Father will honor him." Our objectives must reflect God's purposes before our acts are given divine effect.

Luke 14:27 calls for a disciple's active, continuing commitment to follow Christ's way, and bear his own burden, by severing worldly ties and pursuing the course outlined in the Word: "Whoever does not bear his own cross and come after me, cannot be my disciple." Matthew 11:29 uses imagery which shifts the burden to Jesus, when we submissively walk His way onto paths of righteousness: "Take my yoke upon you, and learn from me; for I am gentle and lowly in heart, and you will find rest for your souls." When yoked to Jesus, He bears the weight of all our cares and burdens. His presence brings precious rest and security, and His wisdom provides comfort, inspiration, and safety. His example leads to righteousness, rest, and peace. Indeed, He supernaturally empowers the accomplishment of our obedience.

The Epistles agree that believers are rewarded for their obedience to God, but suffer loss for disobedience, both here and Hereafter. Acts 5:32 speaks of "the Holy Spirit whom God has given to those who obey Him." Romans 2:5-8 explains: "For he will render to every man according to his works: to those who by patience in well-doing seek for glory and honor and immortality, he will give eternal life; but for those who are factious and do not obey the truth, but obey wickedness, there will be wrath and fury. There will be tribulation and distress for every human being who does evil."

Romans 16:19-20 confirms that victory is the reward of obedience in overcoming Satan's opposition and frustration of blessings: "For while your obedience is known... I would have you wise as to what is good and guileless as to what is evil; then the God of peace will soon crush Satan under your feet." In the Old Testament, God promises to "rebuke" Satan for the sake of the tither's obedience, "and he shall not destroy the fruit of your ground" (Malachi 3:11).

Ephesians 6:6-8 calls us to act "as servants of Christ, doing the will of God from the heart... knowing that whatever good any one does, he will receive the same again from the Lord." Romans 8:28 connects blessings with obediently honoring God's purposes: 'We know that in everything God works for good with those who love him, who are called according to his purpose." See also, I Corinthians 6:9-10; Galatians 6:5; Colossians 3:5-9, 23-24; and Hebrews 2:1-2).

I Timothy 6:11-12 summons the "man of God" to "aim at righteousness, godliness, faith, love," by which he will "Fight the good fight of the faith; take hold of the eternal life to which you were called when you made the good confession." I Timothy 6:18-19 cautions against devotion to wealth, and identifies obedient good deeds as the wealthy man's evidence of saving faith. The rich "are to do good, to be rich in good deeds, liberal and generous, thus laying up for themselves a good foundation for the future, so that they may take hold of the life which is life indeed." Hebrews 6:9-10 recognizes "better things that belong to salvation. For God is not so unjust as to overlook your work and the love which you showed for his sake in serving the saints."

Hebrews 10:35-36 KJV puts it: "Cast not away therefore your confidence, which hath great recompense of reward. For ye have need of patience, that, after ye have done the will of God, ye might receive the reward." Hebrews 12:15-16 adds that unrepented sin can frustrate grace: "see to it that no one fail to obtain the grace of God; that no 'root of bitterness' spring up and cause trouble, and by it the many become defiled; that no one be immoral or irreligious." James 1:22-25 teaches: "But be doers of the Word, and not hearers only... he who... perseveres, being no hearer that forgets but a doer that acts, he shall be blessed in his doing."

I Peter 3:7 says that failure to be considerate of one's wife and give honor to her produces loss of blessings: "husbands, live considerately with your wives bestowing honor on the woman... in order that your prayers may not be hindered." I John 2:3-6 connects fellowship with God to obedience: "by this we may be sure that we know him, if we keep his commandments... he who says he abides in him ought to walk in the same way in which he walked." I John 2:17 promises: "he who does the will of God abides forever." I John 5:14 says: "And this is the confidence which we have in him, that if we ask anything according to his will he hears us... and we know that we have obtained the requests make of him." Indeed, we "stand mature" when "fully assured in all the will of God" (Colossians 4:12).

Revelation 1:3 issues a summons to repentance and changed lives in response to revelation of end-time events: "Blessed is he who reads aloud the words of the prophecy, and blessed are those who hear, and who keep what is written therein." At Revelation 2:23-26 Jesus calls for constancy in faithful obedience, revealing that he "will give to each of you as your works deserve... only hold fast what you have until I come. He who conquers and keeps my works until the end, I will give him power over the nations." See also, Revelation 2:28; 2:7, 10; 3:5; 3:12, 21; 20:12, and James 1:12.

OBEDIENCE AND ABIDING IN THE LORD

Jesus promises at John 15:3-8 that a believer receives blessings when Jesus' words abide in him: "As the branch cannot bear fruit by itself, unless it abides in the vine, neither can you, unless you abide in me. I am the vine, you are the branches. He who abides in me, and I in him, he it is that bears much fruit, for apart from me you can do nothing... If you abide in me, and my words abide in you, ask whatever you will, and it shall be done for you. By this my Father is glorified, that you bear much fruit, and so prove to be my disciples." When we abide in Jesus, the transformation of our character is facilitated. When Jesus' Word abides in us, we bear fruit, and we share Christ's holiness and service, so we can expect our prayers to be answered.

Abiding in Jesus necessarily requires observing how Jesus talked, walked, and acted, and appropriating these examples as one's own. Having Jesus' Word abide in you, necessarily implies submission to His rule, and obedience to His commands. We cannot draw upon Jesus' strength and blessing if we reject His teaching. We must be attached, connected, and incorporated into Jesus' Body, so that His Word and Spirit flow through us, as a precondition to prayer power and receiving God's answers to our petitions.

Christians are called to abide in Christ and let His Word abide in them. Abiding in Christ begins with intent to increase our faithful reliance upon the promises of His Word. Abiding in the Word involves doing what the Word instructs, so we may grow in character and increase in spiritual blessings because of our increased capacity to enjoy them. Conversely, when we are not abiding in the Word, nor it in us, then we will receive nothing. For we have seen that the measure of blessings is in direct proportion to the measure by which we receive and apply the Word to our lives (Mark 4:20). The measure of your obedience to God's purposes determines the measure by which He promises to respond to the desires of your heart.

In fact, Jesus tells us that obedience is the way we abide in His love, and when we obediently love Him, we receive the love and indwelling of God. John 14:21-23 reveals: "He who has my commandments and keeps them, he it is who loves me; and... will be loved by my Father, and I will love him and manifest myself to him. If a man loves me, he will keep my word, and my Father will love him, and we will come to him and make our home with him." Jesus adds at John 15:10: "If you keep my commandments, you will abide in my love, just as I have kept my Father's commandments and abide in his love, These things have I spoken to you that my joy may be in you, and that your joy may be full. This is my commandment, that you love one another as I have loved you." Friendship with Jesus is also promised for obedience at John 15:14.

Ephesians 3:16-19 says that when a believer practices love in obedience to the commandment, he receives power "to know the love of Christ" and "be filled with all the fullness of God." When you obey, "the peace of God... will keep your hearts and minds in Christ Jesus" (Philippians 4:7; see also Amos 5:14). Obedience to the Word is the door to abiding in the Lord according to I John 2:24: "If what you heard from the beginning abides in you, then you will abide in the Son and in the Father." Likewise, I John 3:24 affirms: "All who keep his commandments abide in him, and he in them. And by this we know that he abides in us, by the

Spirit which he has given us." I John 4:16 puts it: "he who abides in love abides in God, and God abides in him."

Love from God, with all the security, well-being, intrinsic joy, and fellowship implied by love, is specially promised as a reward for the obedience of loving others.[77] Because God is love, when we obediently love others, we receive the blessing of actually knowing God, as he embodies and pervades the love we express. More, when love is reciprocal, and each person recognizes an obligation or duty to love others for the sake of Christ, he also is entitled to expect that he will likewise be loved by others in obedience to Christ.

When Jesus told His Mother, "Woman, behold your son," and then told John "Behold your mother" (John 19:26-27), He was constituting humans as His agents to administer love and comfort to one another on His behalf in His absence. Jesus gave Mary a duty to be a mother to John, but He also gave her a benefit to receive John's love as a son. These reciprocal acts were tantamount to giving them to the Lord (Matthew 25:40), and He in turn, passes them on to the other,[78] much as if deflected off a satellite in the sky, or passing through a funnel.

Obedience is necessary to abide in Christ, and the fruit of the Holy Spirit, of which love is the first named, will be manifest in our lives, to the glory of God, by His power in response to our prayers for the fruit of the Spirit.

Obedience is the operation that evidences one's abiding in the vine, Who is Christ, and makes a believer fruitful and productive. We can ask whatever we want and receive it, <u>if</u> we abide in Jesus, because then <u>what we will want is the Spiritual fruit</u> which grows by abiding in the Lord, from Whom all sustenance and growth proceeds. The word 'if' in I John 2:24 requires the process of abiding to be operative, in order for the promise of fruit to occur. The vine's vitality must abide in the branch for it to bear fruit of Christ-like character, so that His will becomes our will. If we seek something contrary to Christ's character, then we are not abiding in Him, and not obedient. If we pray for something contrary to Christ's character it will not be given, because we are obviously not then abiding in the vine.

It is no coincidence that Jesus is the Vine and the Word in Whom we are to abide. In everything, He is the absolute life from Whom we draw all vitality. Christ's "word of power" upholds us, as it upholds everything (Hebrews 1:3), but if we do not build the Word of Godly living into our spirit and invoke its protection, we lack the structural frame-work for utilizing blessings in obedient, holy living. We are not prepared for, dependent upon, nor receptive to, that Word. We will reap exactly as we have sown. Consequently, we should train ourselves always to determine what God's Word says concerning any matter, and then seek to follow it obediently.

God's wishes are revealed in His Word, and to the same degree you honor and obey God's will, He will honor and fulfill your wishes. When God's Word abides in you, it produces your obedience and faithfulness to the Word. We receive what we want from God because our desires now coincide with His will.

Obedience requires us to walk Christ's way, follow His footsteps, and imitate His life and character. After Jesus tells the rich young man to follow Him, he proclaims that the hundred-fold blessings of Mark 10:30 are for those who have "left" worldly attachments <u>for His "sake and for the gospel"</u> (Mark 10:21,29). Leaving the world to follow Jesus necessitates obedient submission and conformance to His way. He who leaves his surroundings to follow Jesus will also inherit "eternal life" (Matthew 19:29).

Holy conduct makes it easier to see God because obedience demonstrates and proves our receptivity to the will and purposes of God for us, and makes us holy as He is holy. This is not because we have grown by our own strength or determination, but because our submission to God's purposes, desiring to serve as a vessel of grace, facilitates, accelerates and cooperates with the operations of the Holy Spirit. Lordship expects submissive obedience when we seek favor from our Saviour and Deliverer. Jesus establishes a pre-condition of obedience before pouring out blessings, material needs, and abundant life for believers on earth.

Loving, righteous obedience signifies a believer's faith and desire for blessings, and makes him receptive to the proffered grace of more abundant life in quantity, quality, and duration. God's resources are a gift from God and a demonstration of His love for us. The rationale of obedience is agreement in the rightness of God's will by striving and acting so as to be in accord with it. Penitence and confession of sin arise out of agreeing with God about His assessment of our sins as evil. When we adopt God's position, we can expect our healing and restoration to be accomplished by Him. Trust and confidence in God's promises underlie a vital and active faith which lives in obedience to God's word, free from sin and rebellion.

Jesus does not replace faith with works as the basis of Christian identity. He simply asserts that works necessarily and inexorably evidence, express, and result from faith. Good deeds and righteousness are consequences of faith. Unless you are saved by faith, you cannot be righteous, for we remain carnal without saving faith. But if you are positionally righteous by grace, you will act righteously in practice, by God's enablement.

Obedience invites reward, not because we have earned it, but because it positions us to receive the blessings God intends and provides at that time and place. Alignment with the Word positions us for blessings. Obedient works provide access to God's Kingdom on earth by expressing our faithful, voluntary submission to God's rule and receptivity to God's grace. If God leads us through a door and down a path it is for our own good. Refusal to be where God calls us jeopardizes access to His best promises, and substitutes some lesser value for what God intends as His blessing. Obedience determines the highest blessing of our lives, for it fulfills God's benevolent purposes for us.

God's Word reflects and reveals God's will, so obedience to the Word necessarily brings conformance to God's will, and places us where He would have us. Obedience necessarily involves abiding in the Word. So faith-filled, obedient works become the habitual way to experience, evidence, express, be filled with, grow spiritually in, and be girded in the truth of, the Word; all by the power of God. When we obey God's Word and submissively yield to His will, then blessings are meted out, programmed, scheduled as the product of obedience which expresses faith.

Works which are obedient to the Word will sustain faith by providing a congenial environment conducive to faith and hostile to Satan. Obedience to the Word resists the world when we are persecuted for the Word's sake, or tempted by riches or worldly trappings. Our faith is nurtured by encapsulating it in acts of obedience to the Word, by which faith comes.

The Christian walk and exercise of faith seeks to conform, and act according to God's will, consistently with His purposes. If we obey His Word, align our desires with God's wishes, and imitate the life of Christ described there, we will be in conformity with God's plans. Our obedience thereby glorifies God by expressing His perfect love, goodness, and holy wishes.

Your God-given mind is far more wondrous than the most sophisticated computer, and it, too, operates on the principle of program-input. If you feed gibberish into a computer, you will derive only nonsense out of it. If you put carnal, mundane thoughts into your mind, you will draw out only worldly ideas. But when you put the Word in faithfully, then the Word will come out in your every thought, speech, and deed. Jesus teaches that "out of the abundance of the heart the mouth speaks" (Matthew 12:34).

Obedience to the Word puts us in a position to be transformed spiritually by the supernatural power of God. I John 1:7 says when we obediently follow the Word, "if we walk in the light, as he is in the light... the blood of Jesus his Son cleanses us from all sin." The Blood of Christ literally cleanses us of sin when we confess and repent sin, (I John 1:9), which necessarily includes intending to return to God's way. This accelerates our continued walk in the light of God's way. Ruminating, or intellectual cogitation on the Word is one thing, but immersion in the Word by regular obedience to it, increases our fellowship, knowledge, and contemplation of God, as we habitually and increasingly act like Him.

As we behold and focus on the revealed glory of the Lord, we become more like Him. As in a mirror, we begin to imitate His thoughts, Words, and deeds. As we individually behold the Lord, as reflected in the Word, and exemplified in our obedience, we are "changed into his likeness from one degree of glory to another; for this comes from the Lord who is Spirit" (2 Corinthians 3:17).

The Holy Spirit helps us to see and learn about God, and blesses us to become like Him to the extent we cooperate by focusing on the glory of the Lord revealed in the Word (John 14:26; James 1:5-6). For, "His divine power has granted to us all things that pertain to life and godliness, through the knowledge of him who called us to his own glory and excellence" (2 Peter 1:3). Our obedience to the Word helps develop the blessing of Godly character, as we follow the Lord's example related in the Word.

2 Corinthians 4:6 confirms that God "has shone in our hearts to give the light of the knowledge of the glory of God in the face of Christ." In the Gospel "the righteousness of God is revealed through faith for faith" (Romans 1:17). The faithfulness of Jesus, which reveals God's righteousness, is what makes our faith possible. Through our faith in the Gospel, God faithfully reveals and expresses in us His righteousness. See also, Acts 5:32; Romans 6:17,19; 2 Peter 1:3-4; I John 2:24, 3:24, and 4:16-17. There is a connection between obedience and reaching glory, since Jesus "learned obedience through what he suffered" (Hebrews 5:8), as an antecedent 'to enter into his glory" (Luke 24:26). Our obedience in the face of adversity is likewise what prepares and enlarges us for the expanded opportunities and significant occasions to serve and glorify God.

As we gain enlightenment in the Word and practice it, we learn more about the character of God, so that spiritual growth is stimulated as the Word grows within us. God works the change simply by the Word, but our obedient acts facilitate, intensify and mature our holiness. St. Paul told backslid Hebrews that he had much to teach them about Jesus, but this knowledge was "hard to explain, since you have become dull of hearing... but solid food is for the mature, for those who have their faculties trained by practice to distinguish good from evil" (Hebrews 5:11,14). There is a didactic connection between our practice of holiness and the increase of our knowledge of God. Obediently walking in the light of the Word makes it possible for the Holy Spirit to reveal more of the things of God to us.

When we know the will of God and "lead a life worthy of the Lord, fully pleasing to him," we will be blessed with bearing fruit and increasing in the knowledge of God (Colossians 1:9-10). I John 1:6 says: "If we say we have fellowship with him while we walk in darkness, we lie." Hebrews 12:14 teaches that impure hearts will not receive the blessing of fellowship with God, for we are to: "Follow peace with all men, and holiness, without which no man shall see the Lord." The connection between being and doing is this. The more we strive to <u>be</u> holy, the better equipped we are to <u>do</u> works with God and for other men.

OBEDIENCE BASED ON DESIRE TO PLEASE GOD

The primary reason we obey is out of a reciprocal love for God; out of a desire to glorify and please a loving Father, by using the freedom of sonship to obey His commandments. Jesus explains: "If you love me, <u>you will keep my commandments</u>" (John 14:15). A police motto is: "To protect and serve." A Christian's motto ought to be: "To serve and please." In time, reward or fear are replaced by motivations of love; to please God by obedience. His love transforms us, so increasingly we choose to obey to requite His love, as we grow in spiritual maturity.

Obeying the Word stimulates our spiritual development by allowing our involvement in all its prescribed activities.[79] God does not coerce, nor compel, but He calls us to exercise freedom, grow spiritually, and serve lovingly for our own good. He inspires and enables our response to the needs of other men, and in so doing, allows us freely to collaborate in the accomplishment of His plans and purposes. Nothing God produces in believers by-passes human will. God works joy and faith, but my will must cooperate in receiving, rather than resisting them.

We obey because the example of Jesus, Who is always our model, teaches us to obey. If Jesus, being "in the form of God" could empty himself, "taking the form of a servant" (Philippians 2:6-7), then we can submit to Him in the interests of developing our stature, toward the end of perfecting our holiness. We submit because the love of Jesus from the Cross persuades us that He has purchased and redeemed us by His sacrifice, and we can requite His love only by our love expressed in surrender to His will. Jesus' submission in weakness constitutes the ultimate power in effecting God's will, as His selfless agony expresses the love of God, touches and changes the hearts of sinners, and brings remorse. God's way is the persuasion of love rather than the compulsion of power. The sacrificial love of Christ from the Cross, which pricks men's consciences, opens men's hearts, and draws them to God, is more powerful than the parallel fear of eternity in Hell.

I Corinthians 1:23-34 calls the "preaching of Christ crucified, a... folly to Gentiles, but to those who are called... Christ the power of God and the wisdom of God." When we witness to communicate the merciful, forgiving Christ on the Cross, He promises: "and I, when I am lifted up from the earth will draw all men to myself" (John 12:32). Freedom is God's method of achieving His purpose, and no other method could so perfectly express his omnipotence, because God chose it infallibly. Violence, force, and coercion would not change men's hearts. If God chose force to implement His purpose of Christ-like character in men, He would defeat His higher purpose of voluntary, willing desire for Christ.

It would be far easier for God to do things for man than let man do them for himself. We would have no need for physicians since God could heal every person directly. We would have no need for intercessory prayers, since God could comfort and deliver the afflicted directly. We would have no need to witness since God could coerce any response He pleased from those men called to be saved. Yet, God enhances our dignity by anointing our collaboration in all these endeavors.

When we reverentially trust God, our desire is to please Him, so that our wishes coincide with, and reflect His will. When we delight in Him, we wish only to please the object of our love. The desires of our heart will mirror His desires, so the harmony of our wills always produces realization of our desires. Keep in mind that God inspires and enables this identity of holy desires between us and Him, "for God is at work in you, both <u>to will and to work</u> for his good pleasure" (Philippians 2:13). Likewise, Jesus proclaims: "When he has brought out all his own, he goes before them, and the sheep follow him, for they know his voice" (John 10:4; see also, John 7:17; and James 1:5).

Obedience helps us to delight in the intrinsic joy of encountering God's perfect character and intention, as revealed in His Word. We obey the Word because it brings our thoughts, speech and deeds into conformity with the Lord's, and creates a special bond of fellowship. Since God <u>is</u> love (I John 4:8), obedience helps us to experience Him when we are loving toward others. We obey to please our Father, express our faithfulness, and eventually hear the commendation: "Well done, good and faithful servant... enter into the joy of your Master" (Matthew 25:21).

God's reward for patient obedience is the blessing from consciously rejoicing in the awareness of conformance to God's will. Delighting in doing the Lord's will cooperates in executing His purposes and working His pleasure in and through the obedience of believers. Thus, Psalm 1:1-3 can say: 'Blessed is the man that... his delight is in the law of the Lord... and whatsoever he doeth shall prosper." Psalm 40:8 expresses: "I delight to do thy will, O my God; yea, thy law is within my heart." Psalm 112:1 proclaims: 'Blessed is the man that feareth the Lord, that delighteth greatly in his commandments." For, delighting in the Lord expresses acceptance and appreciation of the Lord's character and intentions, which are intrinsically satisfying and blessed.

When we are teachable and submissive, with malleable, softened hearts, we can put our will in harmony with God's and conform our desires to His purposes. When our wishes coincide in this compliant way, we have the special blessing of being immediately satisfied with whatever portion the Lord gives us. We have found the blessing of contentment and rest in the Lord, because we can delight in Him, based on harmony with His will. God accomplishes this by changing our desires to conform to His, as we are obediently willing to accept His work in us. God may not be able to trust you now, but he will, once He has transformed your sinful character in answer to your prayerful invitation to be changed.

Psalm 37:3-9 teaches: 'Trust in the Lord, <u>and do good</u>; so shalt thou dwell in the land, and verily thou shalt be fed. Delight thyself also in the Lord; and he shall give thee the desires of thine heart. Commit thy way unto the Lord; trust also in him; and he shall bring it to pass. <u>And he shall bring forth thy righteousness as the light</u>... those that wait upon the Lord, they shall inherit the earth." The blessing comes when we trustingly commit to God's way, so His way now becomes ours as well. God fulfills and gratifies our desires, because they now exactly coincide with His. Only a stubborn fool would insist on swimming against the current, when he can be propelled and carried to his ordained destination by the divine tide.

As we mature spiritually, with a heart satisfied with what God intends for us, delighting oneself in the Lord focuses on enjoying His fellowship, and better appreciating the winsomeness and excellence of His character. We are also prompted to obey the Lord because we appreciate obedience is for our own good, if we will only follow the guidance of our Father Who loves us, and seeks to insulate us from the destructiveness of worldly influences. Obedience thus involves a healthy fear of the dire consequences of disobedience. Deuteronomy 5:29 says: "O... that they would fear me, and keep all my commandments always, that it might be well with them, and with their children for ever!" Psalm 145:19 declares: "He will fulfill the desire of them that fear him." God often balances the promise of blessing for obedience with the fearsome threat of loss for disobedience: "Behold, I set before you this day a blessing and a curse; a blessing, if ye obey the commandments of the Lord your God, which I command you this day: And a curse, if ye will not obey... but turn aside out of the way which I command you this day" (Deuteronomy 11:26-28).

Deuteronomy 28:1-11 promises that blessings will literally pursue obedient believers: "And all these blessings shall come on thee, and overtake thee, if thou shalt hearken diligently unto the voice of the Lord, thy God, to observe and to do all his commandments... Blessed shall be the fruit of thy body, and the fruit of thy ground... The Lord shall command the blessing upon thee in thy storehouses, and in all that thou settest thine hand unto... the Lord shall make thee plenteous in goods... and... shall open unto thee his good treasure." Deuteronomy 7:9 teaches that God is faithful and "keepeth covenant and mercy with them that love him and keep his commandments."

Joshua 1:8 directly connects success with obedience to the Word: "This book of the law shall not depart out of thy mouth; but thou shalt meditate therein day and night, that thou mayest <u>observe to do according to all that is written</u> therein: for then thou shalt make thy way prosperous, and then thou shalt have good success." See also, Leviticus 26:18; Numbers 15:31; Deuteronomy 4:40, 5:33, 29:9; I Kings 2:3; 2 Chronicles 7:14; Psalm 1:1-3; and Jeremiah 5:25, 7:23, 11:4-5.

One way every believer is called to obedience is by collaboration in labor, effort, and expended energy in response to God's commandment to work. The Ten Commandments direct believers to observe a day of rest to promote our efficiency the other six days of work: "the seventh day is the Sabbath of the lord thy God: in it thou shalt not do any work" (Exodus 20:9-10). St Paul continued to work as a tentmaker and paid his own way, even while he witnessed throughout the world, although he was entitled to receive an offering from the assembled faithful (Acts 18:3; I Corinthians 9:11; Romans 15:27). I Corinthians 3:8 teaches: "each shall receive his wages according to his labor."

The Puritan work ethic which prevailed in America for three centuries honored the Fourth Commandment which affirmatively obligates us to work: "Six days shalt thou labor and do all thy work" (Exodus 20:9). Ecclesiastes 9:10 directs: "Whatsoever thy hand findeth to do, do it with thy might." We are to rely on prayer, not to relieve us of effort, but prayer that asks God to provide opportunity and power to work at our collaborative tasks.

The Old Testament calls men to honest labor, specifically to avoid poverty. Proverbs 20:13 says: "Love not sleep, lest thou come to poverty." "Yet a little sleep, a little slumber, a little folding of the hands to sleep. So shall thy poverty come as one that travelleth, and thy want as an armed man" (Proverbs 6:10-11; see also, Proverbs 10:5, 19:15, 24:33-34; and Ecclesiastes 11:4). Failure to work will result in financial ruin, no matter how much we entrust our prosperity to God, or believe in His promise to bless us financially.

St. Paul cautioned against idleness: "keep away from any brother who is living in idleness and not in accord with the tradition that you received from us... If any one will not work, let him not eat" (2 Thessalonians 3:6,10). "If any one does not provide for his relatives, and especially for his own family, he has disowned the faith and is worse than an unbeliever" (I

Timothy 5:8). 2 Timothy 2:5-6 says: "An athlete is not crowned unless he competes according to the rules. It is the <u>hard-working</u> farmer who ought to have the first share of the crops."

How true the old adage, "God helps those who help themselves." When we disobey His commandment to work diligently, we may be foreclosed from the blessings of prosperity by our own sloth, no matter how much faith we have in God's promise to bless us.

Deuteronomy 8:18 affirms that God "is he that giveth thee power to get wealth, that he may <u>establish his covenant</u> which he sware unto thy fathers." This Covenant promises Abraham and his heirs an inheritance of vast land (Genesis 15:7, 17:8), and tithing sets up the mechanism by which wealth is meted out to obedient givers. God promised the nation Israel it would be blessed in every way with divine prosperity if it simply observed God's Commandments (Exodus 19:5-6; Deuteronomy 28:1-13, 29:9; Joshua 1:5-9; Psalms 1:3, 84:11, 111:5; and Proverbs 19:17).

If we disobey God's laws of industry and thrift we will lose prosperity. We cannot expect God to provide prosperity for us by winning a lottery. Time and again, God's answer will be, "Complete the work I have already given you." God blesses your effort, not inactivity or indolence, and commends to us the diligence of the ant: "Go to the ant, thou sluggard; consider her ways, and be wise; Which having no guide, overseer, or ruler, provideth her meat in the summer, and gathereth her food in the harvest" (Proverbs 6:6-8).

A. W. Tozer has said that miracles follow the plow. If we are hopeless and inert, we have given up any expectations for a harvest in the future. We need to plow for God now, before we can hope on God blessing us with a miracle of growth in the future. If we plant sloth and indifference, we can expect to reap only the wild vegetation which results when God's rain pours down to bless all men. Each must ask; 'Am I failing to reap God's promises because I failed to sow at planting time?'

PROSPERITY AS THE BLESSING OF OBEDIENCE

There is no question that in the beginning, God intended the blessing of prosperity for mankind to be enjoyed in the earth. However, God's promise of blessing was always conditional on man not only believing the Word of promise, but also obeying God's commandments. In the Garden of Eden, man enjoyed every advantage and earthly benefit of dominion over the earth, (Genesis 1:28). However, the blessing was conditioned upon man's obedience to God's command not to eat of the tree of knowledge of good and evil (Genesis 2:17). Disobedience by Adam and Eve led to the Fall of man and introduction of flaws, death and deprivation into Creation (Genesis 2:17).

Afterwards, God repeatedly covenanted with Abraham that "in thee shall all families of the earth be blessed" (Genesis 12:3, 12:7, 13:15, and 15:18). Genesis 28:3-4 declares that the fruitfulness of Abraham's blessing includes material wealth for his heirs. Yet, these promises were conditioned on Abraham's obedience to leave Ur and depart for Canaan (Genesis 12:1), and to "believe in the Lord," which God counted as righteousness (Genesis 15:6). Even as God affirmed His Covenant, he forecast 400 years of servitude and affliction for Abraham's seed because of their idolatry and iniquity (Genesis 15:13).

God's intent to bless man with good fortune, flourishing and prosperity was initially meant for this world, as the Jews have always understood, and was not deferred to the perfect Afterlife. Abraham and Solomon enjoyed great wealth, as did Joseph after his imprisonment. After Job faithfully withstood Satan's attempts to make him curse God, he was rewarded by God with double what he had possessed before his trials. Faithful submission to the Lord as servant to Master, was then, and is now, required to receive the blessing. Psalm 35:27 says the Lord "hath pleasure in the prosperity of <u>his servant</u>." Isaiah promises 'everlasting kindness', 'mercy', and great wealth, and peace as "the heritage of the <u>servants of the Lord</u>" (Isaiah 54:7-17).

Yet, history reveals that God's intended prosperity for Israel was repeatedly frustrated by infidelity and disobedience, resulting in vanquishment and enslavement. It is strange that the Gospel of wealth focuses on faith in God's promises for prosperity, while often ignoring the need for faithful obedience to God's commands. Israel has endured persecution and privation throughout the Diaspora, and suffering at the hands of Nazis and Arab terrorists in recent times. Despite the promises, the Ashkenazim, or European Jews, understood that education was more valuable than material wealth, because it could be carried in flight from the pogroms, while an emigrant was easily dispossessed of lands and treasures.

If we say that Christians are successors to the Old Testament promises to Israel then it can be argued that in modern times Christian nations have enjoyed a standard of comfort which measures up to what would have been considered as opulent throughout history. Even the poorest have access to society's conveniences and improved standards of health, unknown until modern times. Yet, all Christians are not wealthy by the world's standards, and native evangelists in the third world do not have prosperity by any stretch of the imagination; nor did Christian martyrs throughout history. It may be that Israel forfeited its promised blessings because of its disobedient infidelity to the Lord. So we must seriously consider the Old Testament teachings which connect prosperity in this world with obedience to the Lord.

Surrounded by abundance, it is difficult for Americans to remember that God's blessings of prosperity in the world are inextricably connected to human obedience. According to Leviticus 26:2-5: "<u>If ye walk in my statutes, and keep my commandments, and do them;</u> Then I will give you rain in due season, and the land shall yield her increase, and the trees of the field shall yield their fruit. And your threshing shall reach unto the vintage, and the vintage shall reach unto the sowing time: and ye shall eat your bread to the full."

Deuteronomy 8:1,9 connects plenitude with obedience: "all the commandments which I command thee this day shall ye observe to do, that ye may live, and multiply, and go in and possess the land which the Lord sware unto your fathers... A land wherein thou shalt eat bread without scarceness, thou shalt not lack any thing in it." (See also, Deuteronomy 8:11, 18-19). Even as God affirms to Israel: "I have brought him, and he shall make his way prosperous... I am the Lord thy God which teacheth thee to profit" (Isaiah 48:15,17), He forecasts Israel's obstinacy, treachery, transgression from the womb, and failure to obey God's commandments, which produce affliction and lack of peace (Isaiah 48:4,8,10,18).

God repeats His Covenant of blessing at Jeremiah 32:15,41: "Houses and fields and vineyards shall be possessed again in this land... I will not turn away from them, to do them good... Yes, I will rejoice over them to do them good." Yet, at the same time, God reproves Judah's evil from their youth, which provokes God to anger; their disobedience to instructions; impenitence; idolatry, abomination, and defilement (Jeremiah 32:30-35) which will lead to the Babylonian captivity (Jeremiah 25:11).

Job 36:11 speaks of prosperity and pleasure conditioned on obedience: "If they obey and serve him, they shall spend their days in prosperity, and their years in pleasure" (see also, Deuteronomy 30:16; Joshua 1:8; Psalm 128:1,6). Psalm 41:1-2 promises: "Blessed is he that considereth the poor: the Lord will deliver him in time of trouble, The Lord will preserve him and keep him alive; and he shall be blessed upon the earth." Psalm 112:1-6 promises wealth and blessedness to righteous persons, "The man that feareth the Lord, that delighteth greatly in his commandments... the generation of the upright shall be blessed, wealth and riches shall be in his house... the righteous shall be in everlasting remembrance."

Sharing one's treasure with others is an obedience which assures continued prosperity. Proverbs 11:24-25 puts it: "There is that scattereth, and yet increaseth... The liberal soul shall be made fat; and he that watereth shall be watered himself." Ecclesiastes 11:1 says: "Cast thy bread upon the waters: for thou shalt find it after many days." Believers must distribute their substance in order to increase it. They must water others' soil in order to be hydrated themselves. Proverbs 19:17 adds: "He that hath pity upon the poor lendeth unto the Lord; and that which he hath given will he pay him again." Conversely, to be miserly and withhold "more than is meet... tendeth to poverty" (Proverbs 11:24).

When we lack generosity our prayers will be ineffective, for Proverbs 21:13 teaches: "Whoso stoppeth his ears at the cry of the poor, he also shall cry himself, but shall not be heard." Conversely, Proverbs 22:9 promises: "He that hath a bountiful eye shall be blessed; for he giveth of his bread to the poor." Other Old Testament passages connecting obedience to reward are Deuteronomy 24:19; Psalms 1:1-3, 2:11-12, 32:2, 41:1, 65:4, 119:1, 128:1; Proverbs 10:22, 11:24, 21:13, 22:9, 28:8, and 29:7. See also, Mark 4:19 and James 5:1-3.

Clearly these are blessings which have not occurred in this world for the Jews, but relate to eternity with the Lord. Isaiah 57:1 confirms this view: "The righteous perisheth... and merciful men are taken away, none considering that the righteous is taken away from the <u>evil to come</u>," implying present evil must continually be contended against by the righteous. Since the Fall, in the world we are in an ongoing battle with evil, but we shall finally be delivered from evil in Heaven.

GOD'S BLESSING OF TITHING AND GIVING

Tithing is the earliest example of obediently sowing one's wealth in order to reap the blessing of prosperity, and is an antecedent to the modern Gospel of Wealth that prosperity is awarded the faithful sower of treasure into God's provision for His purposes. A believer's giving expresses and evidences faith in the Word of promise. By obedience in giving we strive to be a good steward and share God's wealth lovingly with others. We tithe with expectation our deeds will influence our blessings. The obedient servant plants tithes and offerings for the Lord; gathers the fruit of converted souls for him; reaps spiritual fruit and holy character from him; and is blessed with material and spiritual reward by Him. We expect the wealth we give back to God's service, by obediently sharing his largesse with others, will determine the prosperity we receive on earth.

Tithing is basically a Covenant between God and man, under which God promises to bless the tither who obediently returns the first part of God's wealth to Him. Tithing also incorporates and prefigures, the New Testament concept of good stewardship: of doing what God directs us to do with his resources. It incorporates and anticipates New Testament ideas of charity: of sharing one's bounty with others, and ministering with one's time and talent to any need of others. Tithing also coincides with the directives to obey God's commands, and develop holy character in order better to obey all the commandments of God.

God's Covenant for tithing was with the nation, Israel, and was earmarked for certain specific human needs. It promised blessings for lovingly and obediently sharing with others the firstfruits one received from God. Malachi 3:10-12 expresses God's Covenant with tithers to bless them with wealth to fulfill His Covenant, when they tithe and return or sow part of God's wealth to Him for sharing with others in need: "Bring ye all the tithes into the storehouse, that there may be meat in mine house, and prove me now herewith, saith the Lord of hosts, if I will not open you the windows of heaven and pour you out a blessing, that there shall not be room enough to receive it. And I will rebuke the devourer for your sakes, and he shall not destroy the fruits of your ground... And all nations shall call you blessed; for ye shall be a delightsome land." God is not only benevolent in multiplying the seed invested, but also generous in letting us keep ninety percent of what He gives us.

Giving originates with God, Who bestows blessings upon us, from which we may tithe. Tithing is especially congenial to the principle of sowing and reaping. For the genius of tithing is giving to God to benefit others, with expectations of again reaping or receiving divine blessings and prosperity in multiplied measure. Tithing serves the giver's self-interest by incidentally blessing him according to God's Covenant with givers. But it primarily expresses God's love for all His children, by conditioning givers for the habit, and triggering the practice, of lovingly giving to God for distribution to others. God abounds toward us, that we may abound toward Him in good works which share the grace of abundance. God establishes and encourages a system of giving, as good stewards of the gifts one possesses from God, by a mandate to share what one has with others, so that those in need of material goods may receive them from God through the responsive love of other believers. In exchange, God's blessings are returned to the tither. Tithing establishes a fixed regularity, amount, and pattern of giving to facilitate obedience.

God was blessing even those whose words had been stout or rebellious against Him (Malachi 3:13). Since He was willing to bless disobedient men who did not tithe, it was reasonable to infer He would bless the obedient tither with His love, to a far greater extent. God lets tithers lay hold spiritually on what they have stored up by their past giving, to invite reward and secure present blessings. We need to grasp the truth that God does not ask a tither to give God anything which has not originally been given by God. Then, God rejoices first when His child willingly offers to share with God what he has been given by God; and rejoices again when another needy child enjoys the gift.

God calls for the firstfruits of man's increase: for the very best of the first returns on man's harvest, herds, labor, and sons (Exodus 22:29-30, 23:19). The presentation of firstfruits was practiced by Abel, Noah, Abraham, Moses, Aaron, and the children of Israel (Genesis 4:3-4, 8:20, 14:20, 22:9-14; Leviticus 22:13-21; Numbers 18:21; and 2 Chronicles 31:5). Proverbs 3:9-10 issues a command connected with a promise of incidental reward: "Honour the Lord with thy substance, and with the firstfruits of all thine increase; So shall thy barns be filled with plenty, and thy presses shall burst out with new wine."

God expressly calls for tithing of the increase of one's field to benefit the Levite (priest), the stranger, the fatherless, and the widow, "that the Lord thy God may bless thee in all the work of thine hand which thou doest" (Deuteronomy 14:22, 29; See also, Deuteronomy 16:11,14, 24:19-21, 26:11-13; 2 Chronicles 31:4; Nehemiah 12:44). I Corinthians 9:11 authorizes pastors to share in what is reaped by their flock: "If we have sown spiritual good among you, is it too much if we reap your material benefits?" (See also, Romans 15:27). By kingly custom, a portion is also set aside "for the singers" of the house of God (Nehemiah 11:23, 13:10). The tithe should not be given "for any unclean use" or "for the dead" (Deuteronomy 26:14).

The tithe "is the Lord's; it is holy unto the Lord" (Leviticus 27:30,32), not because it is too sacred to touch, but because God has separated it for His purposes. The tithe is fixed at one-tenth of one's wealth, which is the Lord's; separated for God (Leviticus 27:32; Numbers 18:21; Genesis 28:22; Hebrews 7:4). If a believer neglects or fails to tithe, then he is to redeem his tithe with 20% interest to the Lord on the amount due (Leviticus 27:13,27,31). Every third year is ordained as "the year of tithing" (Deuteronomy 14:28-29, 26:12; Amos 4:4), which was a second tithe set aside for the Levites, alien residents, and widows. The regular tithe was annual and an opportunity to revere the Lord as the source of Israel's blessing, based on the increase "that the field bringeth forth year by year" (Deuteronomy 14:22).

The New Testament also promises to reward believers with blessings for their participation by obedience, especially in loving others. Admittedly, there are verses which promise wealth for believers here on earth, and God freely apportions his beneficence, as and when He pleases. Prayer and faith are identified in Scripture as the keys to the supernatural blessings for which a believer yearns, and Jesus gives apparently unconditional promises of blessings for those who have faith they will receive them. The health and wealth Gospel seizes on these apparently unlimited promises and applies them to blessings of prosperity and healing. See, for example, Matthew 21:21; Mark 11:23-34, 9:23; John 14:13-14, 15:16, 16:23-24.

In the Epistles, Romans 8:32 continues the promise of unlimited blessings for the asking: "He who did not spare his own Son but gave him up for us all, will he not also give us all things with him?" Material blessings seem to be included, since God has given Jesus "the uttermost parts of the earth for thy possession" (Psalm 2:8), and "All authority in heaven and on earth" (Matthew 28:18). Consequently, in modern America Christians have enjoyed unprecedented standards of wealth, as God abundantly provides for our needs. In faith, we have come to expect that our Father will eagerly and lovingly supply our need; for as a perfect Father, he could not do anything else.[80]

Yet, many of the New Testament promises are dependent upon a faith demonstrated by submissive obedience as a pre-requisite to blessing. Others are speaking of some spiritual blessings here, but with most spiritual and material fulfillment Hereafter. Thus, even so basic a promise of sufficiency in food, drink and clothing, frees believers from anxiety over their supply, on condition we cooperate in righteousness; "your heavenly Father knows that you need them all. But seek first his kingdom and his righteousness, and all these things shall be yours as well' (Matthew 6:32-33).

2 Corinthians 9:10 promises to fill our material and spiritual needs: "He who supplies seed to the sower and bread for food will supply and multiply your resources and increase the harvest of your righteousness." I Timothy 6:17 calls the rich to set their hope on God: "who richly furnishes us with everything to enjoy." Philippians 4:19 agrees: "And my God will supply every need of yours according to his riches in glory in Christ Jesus." James 1:17 says: "Every good endowment and every perfect gift is from above, coming down from the Father of lights." See also, Ephesians 3:7.

At Matthew 7:7-11, Jesus promises: "Ask and it will be given you; seek and you will find; knock, and it will be opened to you. For every one who asks receives... If you then, who are evil, know how to give good gifts to your children, how much more will your Father who is in heaven give good things to those who ask him?" The key to blessing is found in the instructions to seek and knock, in search of spiritual benefits.

The parallel passage in Luke 11, explains that our petitions are not granted for material or temporal benefits, but for the Holy Spirit and His fruit: "Ask, and it will be given you; seek, and you will find; knock, and it will be opened... If you then, who are evil, know how to give good gifts to your children, how much more will the heavenly Father <u>give the Holy Spirit</u> to those who ask Him?" (Luke 11:9,13). We are to seek God's righteousness, and we will find it. The good things we receive are spiritual, not material. When we are instructed to knock, it can only mean we are seeking admission to God's presence, but we can come only with an attitude of reverence and repentance. Even after we are Born-Again, we cannot knock for entry into the Kingdom here on earth, while we remain encumbered with unrepented sin or unforgiving heart. The door which we seek to have opened is incompatible with sin, and an attitude of penitent, submissive obedience must accompany our knocking.

Jesus says "The meek shall inherit the earth" (Matthew 5:5), but meekness always signifies submission to God; being teachable, and lovingly considerate of others; the characteristics of Jesus, Who describes Himself as "I am meek" (Matthew 11:29).

If a believer obediently renounces family ties and follows after Jesus, for His sake, for the Gospel, and for the sake of the kingdom of God, he will "receive a hundred-fold now in this time, houses and brothers and sisters and mothers and children and lands, with persecutions, and in the age to come eternal life' (Mark 10:29,30; paralleled in Matthew 19:29 and Luke 18:30). The blessing is connected to following Jesus, which necessitates walking His way, faithfully and obediently. It is accompanied by persecutions, which may detract from the blessing's appeal, but are provoked only because of obvious, obedient Christ-like character. This is also suggested by Ephesians 1:3, which notes God "has blessed us in Christ with every spiritual blessing <u>in the heavenly places</u>," which may relate both to the source, and to the venue in which the blessings are received.

The blessing for obedience is not necessarily immediate. I Peter 5:6 instructs: "Humble yourselves therefore under the mighty hand of God, that <u>in due time</u> he may exalt you." Jesus proclaims at Revelation 22:12: "Behold, I am coming soon, bringing my recompense, to repay every one for what he has done;" focusing on rewards and fulfillment of eternal life in the Hereafter.

2 Corinthians 9:6-11 promises sufficiency for liberality in giving, with material blessings for sharing, and spiritual righteousness: "he who sows sparingly will also reap sparingly, and he who sows bountifully will also reap bountifully... And God is able to provide you with every blessing in abundance, so that you may always have enough of everything and may provide in abundance <u>for every good work</u>... He who supplies seed to the sower and bread for food will supply and multiply your resources and increase the harvest of your righteousness. You will be enriched in every way for great generosity." As we will see in the next Chapter, the very reason for receiving blessings is for sharing with others, as good stewards of God's grace.

We cannot help but be aware of the Biblical promises of sowing and reaping, giving and getting, when we share generously with others (Matthew 25:34-36; Mark 4:24; Luke 6:35; Galatians 6;7; Ephesians 6:8; James 5:1-3; and Philippians 1:5, 4:9, 4:15-19). Yet, our dominant motive in obedient charity must always be out of love for God and righteousness; not for any selfish motive of receiving the special anointing of prosperity God pours out on givers.

God is, and must be, the Sovereign to Whom our wealth is lovingly devoted, rather than simply the means or instrument whereby the end of prosperity is attained.[81]

While it is permissible to be motivated by self-interest in submissively obeying God, since He has revealed His intent to bless obedience, God will also bless you when you faithfully and obediently put yourself in a position to be blessed with a pure motive of pleasing God because you love Him.

Blessings are also promised for obedience in mourning over sin; practicing humility; acting with gentleness; hungering for righteousness; seeking peace; and giving comfort (Matthew 5:4-7), but especially for obedience in love, as we see in the next chapter.

HEALING AS GOD'S BLESSING FOR OBEDIENCE

The vast majority of Americans have enjoyed the grace of good health, in a milieu of good medical care, pharmaceutics, and nutritional advances. There is reason to believe that God's Old Testament promises of health and deliverance from pestilence are intended for this world. Psalm 91:3,6,10,16 promises God "shall deliver thee... from the noisome pestilence... there shall no evil befall thee, neither shall any plague come nigh thy dwelling... With long life will I satisfy him, and shew him my salvation." Psalm 107:19-20 reminds God's people: "Then they cry unto the Lord in their trouble, and he saveth them out of their distresses. He sent his word, and healed them, and delivered them from their destructions." Psalm 30:2 concurs: "O Lord my God, I cried unto thee, and thou hast healed me." (See also I Kings 3:14; and Malachi 4:2).

Yet, even in the 21st Century, much of the world exists amidst high rates of infant mortality, starvation, malnutrition, pandemics, SARS, AIDS, rat infestation, self-inflicted obesity, smoking, drug abuse, pesticides, smog, and scores of recurring and emerging diseases. Even in America, the healthiest among us lives in a progressive condition of deterioration, which proceeds inexorably to old age and death of the physical body. This suggests that the promises of the health and wealth doctrine may actually be intended and reserved for the Hereafter, as was the understanding and expectation for most of the first two millennia of Christianity.

However, there is no denying Jesus clearly reveals that when He bore our sins upon the Cross, He also paid for our sickness and disease, so that the Blood flowing from His wounds cleansed us both spiritually and physically. Isaiah 53:4-5, repeated in I Peter 2:24 reveals: "Surely he hath borne our griefs, and carried our sorrows... But he was wounded for our transgressions, he was bruised for our iniquities... and with his stripes we are healed." To remove any doubt that Jesus' stripes healed us physically as well as spiritually, Matthew 8:17 asserts: "he took our infirmities and bore our diseases." Psalm 103:3 unites and connects physical and spiritual healing, for it is the Lord: 'Who forgiveth all thine iniquities; who healeth all thy diseases."

Jesus' healing ministry on earth revealed it was God's intention to cure all who turned to Jesus for healing. Acts 10:38 relates "how God anointed Jesus of Nazareth with the Holy Spirit and with power; how he went about doing good and healing all that were oppressed by the devil, for God was with him." Repeatedly, and everywhere, Jesus "healed all who were sick' (Matthew 8:16); "Jesus went about all the cities and villages... healing every disease and every infirmity" (Matthew 9:35); "many followed him, and he healed them all" (Matthew 12:15).

They "besought him that they might only touch the fringe of his garment; and as many as touched it were made well' (Matthew 14:36).

Jesus confirmed He did only God's will (John 5:36, 6:38, 8:28-29), and that it was also His will to heal a leper (Mark 1:41). He told one woman He healed: "Daughter your faith has made you well; go in peace, and be healed of your disease" (Mark 5:34). Jesus healed the demon-possessed and the afflicted (Matthew 9:32, 12:22, 17:18; Luke 4:40, 6:19, 8:29, 9:11, 9:42, 13:12; Mark 5:3, 6:56, 9:25; and John 9:7).

Jesus identifies Satan as the author of sickness, who "comes only to steal and kill and destroy' (John 10:10), by stealing our health, and killing us physically. Yet, Jesus reveals: "The Son of man came not to destroy men's lives but to save them" (Luke 9:56). I John 3:8 reveals: "the reason the Son of God appeared was to destroy the works of the devil." Thus, Jesus "went about doing good and healing all that were oppressed by the devil" (Acts 10:38). He repeatedly cast out evil spirits in the course of such deliverance (Mark 5:8, 13, 9:25; Luke 13:12).

Disease, and "every sickness, and every plague" was the curse of the Law under the Old Covenant (Deuteronomy 28:58,61). However, "Christ redeemed us from the curse of the law, having become a curse for us" (Galatians 3:13). This deliverance means that Jesus has vicariously redeemed us from every sickness and every plague, and they are no more our burden than the sins from which He redeemed us. Hence, we can appreciate the full significance of Jesus' assurance to the Church: "Behold, I have given you authority to tread upon serpents and scorpions, and over all the power of the enemy; and nothing shall hurt you" (Luke 10:19).

Starting with the Apostles and disciples, Jesus has vested this ongoing healing power in His Church, and with His evangelists of the Gospel. Jesus imparted to His disciples the same power to "heal the sick, raise the dead, cleanse lepers, cast out demons" (Matthew 10:7-8). He sent seventy disciples out with instructions to enter a town: "heal the sick in it and say to them, 'The kingdom of God has come near to you'." (Luke 10:9). When He earlier sent the twelve Apostles out to preach, He likewise: "gave them authority over unclean spirits, to cast them out, and to heal every disease and every infirmity" (Matthew 10:1; see also, Luke 9:2; and Mark 3:15). In the early Church, when the sick and afflicted were brought to Peter, "They were all healed" (Acts 5:16), and Peter and John healed a lame man (Acts 3:6). See also Acts 9:34, 19:11, and 28:8-9.

There are some who believe that the gifts of healing are not meant for modern times; that they were given only to the early Church to assist its growth by marvelous signs of healing. However, the Great Commission of Mark 16:15-18 is handed down through the Apostles to all believers; not only then, but in every successive age. For, Jesus commands: "Go into all the world and preach the gospel to the whole creation... And these signs will accompany those who believe: in my name they will cast out demons... they will lay their hands on the sick, and they will recover." Matthew 28:19-20 issues the same Great Commission, and specifically instructs the Apostles to "make disciples of all nations... teaching them to observe all that I have commanded you." The complete Great Commission is hereby issued fully to every generation of believers, who have the same need as the early Church for authenticating the Gospel through healing marvels.

The possession of gifts of healing within the developing Body of Christ is confirmed at I Corinthians 12:7-9, which explains: "To each is given the manifestation of the Spirit for the common good. To one is given through the Spirit the utterance of wisdom... to another gifts of healing by the one Spirit." Hebrews 2:4 declares that God validates the Gospel of Salvation "by signs and wonders and various miracles and by gifts of the Holy Spirit." But these gifts of healing necessitate lovingly sharing them with others, since they are given by God to bless others!

James 5:13-16 confirms that healing resides in the Body of Christ, for the common good, and it exists today: "Is any among you sick? Let him call for the elders of the church, and let them pray over him, anointing him with oil in the name of the Lord; and the prayer of faith will save the sick man, and the Lord will raise him up; and if he has committed sins, he will be forgiven. Therefore confess your sins to one another, and pray for one another, that you may be healed." The Holy Spirit has been given to believers, as a guaranty that all Jesus has said will be called to our remembrance, including what He said about healing (John 14:26).

Still, there are many faithful Christians who believe that miracles of healing were confined to Jesus' time, and do not exist today, or were declared for eternal reward, and not this world. They point out that Jesus declared He was sent by God to proclaim release to captives, to set at liberty those who are oppressed, to preach recovering of sight to the blind, and good news to the poor (Luke 4:18, citing Isaiah 61:1-2). Yet, Jesus did not free slaves from their worldly bondage, nor provide prosperity for the poor, nor freedom for most people in the world then, or since His advent. At the pool of Bethesda in Bethlehem, just as the visiting angel before him had healed only one person per visit, Jesus healed only one man who had been invalid for thirty-eight years (John 5:5-9), and apparently left unhealed all the others at the pool (John 5:13). At Nazareth, Jesus "did not do many mighty works there, because of their unbelief" (Matthew 13:58). Thus, even when Jesus was present, and despite the healings He worked, Jesus teaches that some infirmities remain unhealed in the world.

Indeed, Revelation 21:4 clearly implies that pain and suffering are in the world until God restores the new Jerusalem, and only then God "will wipe away every tear from their eyes, and death shall be no more, neither shall there be mourning nor crying nor pain any more, for the former things have passed away." Ezekiel 47:12 speaks of trees in the new world to come, "whose leaf shall not fade... and the fruit thereof shall be for meat, and the leaf thereof for medicine." Revelation 22:2 also speaks of the New Jerusalem, with "the tree of life... and the leaves of the tree were for the healing of the nations."

Nevertheless, there is divine healing in our time, and two things are necessary; faith and obedience, before we can claim it. We must trust God's promises of healing, and put our faith in God, not earthly instrumentalities of physicians or medicines which God provides. King Asa died of disease when "he sought not to the Lord, but to the physicians" (Chronicles 16:12-13). Proverbs 118:8-9 says: "It is better to trust in the Lord than to put confidence in man."

The blessings of Health are indeed promised believers in Scripture, but often in connection with reward for obedience. Exodus 15:25-26 says: "If thou wilt... do that which is right in his sight... and keep all his statutes, I will put none of these diseases upon thee, which I have brought upon the Egyptians: for I am the Lord that healeth thee" (See also, Deuteronomy 7:11,15). I Kings 3:14 teaches: "if thou wilt walk in my ways, to keep my statutes... then I will lengthen thy days." Malachi 4:2 adds: "Unto you that fear my name shall the Sun of righteousness arise with healing in his wings; and ye shall go forth, and grow up."

Because Israel would not return in submission to God, he chastised them with famine, and "I have sent among you the pestilence after the manner of Egypt; and your young men have I slain with the sword... yet have ye not returned unto me, saith the Lord" (Amos 4:10). Psalm 41:1-3 declares: "Blessed is he that considereth the poor: the Lord will deliver him in time of trouble, The Lord will preserve him, and keep him alive; and he shall be blessed upon the earth... The Lord will strengthen him upon the bed of languishing; thou wilt make all his bed in his sickness." When we obey the Lord and cling to Him; if we "dwelleth in the secret place of the most High," then we are delivered "from the noisome pestilence... that walketh in darkness... there shall no evil befall thee, neither shall any plague come nigh thy dwelling" (Psalm 91:1-10). Proverbs 10:27 says: "The fear of the Lord prolongeth days: but the years of the wicked shall be shortened."

Proverbs 3:2 promises to one who lives in obedience to God's Word, "length of days, and long life, and peace." Proverbs 3:7-8 calls you to "fear the Lord, and depart from evil. It shall be health to thy navel, and marrow to thy bones." Obedience to God's Words brings many "years of life" (Proverbs 4;10), and brings "life to those that find them, and health to all their flesh" (Proverbs 4:22), and "the tongue of the wise is health" (Proverbs 12:18).

Death, the ultimate expression of failed health, is forecast as the result of sin at Ezekiel 18:4, 20; Romans 6:23; James 1:15; Deuteronomy 24:16; 2 Kings 14:6; and 2 Chronicles 25:4, and remains the operative principle in our time. Proverbs 10:27, 29 connects enlightened obedience to strength and long life: "The fear of the Lord prolongeth days: but the years of the wicked shall be shortened... The way of the Lord is strength to the upright."

Blessings of healing are specifically promised believers who faithfully obey God and do right. The Fifth Commandment directs: "Honour thy father and thy mother; that thy days may be long upon the land" (Deuteronomy 5:16; Exodus 20:12; and Ephesians 6:3, which adds: "that it may be well with you and that you may live long on the earth. Exodus 23:25 summons believers to "serve the Lord your God, and he shall bless thy bread, and thy water; and I will take sickness away from the midst of thee." Hebrews 12:12-13 concurs that resolutely walking God's way produces healing; "lift your drooping hands and strengthen your weak knees, and make straight paths for your feet, so that what is lame may not be put out of joint but rather be healed."

Do not despair when you realize the disobedience in your life which betrays your vile servitude to sin. God's abiding love and infinite mercy existed long before you or your sins, and the fact God blessed you before you disobeyed, even while foreseeing your faithlessness, is proof your present sins have been forgiven. He knew you were going to sin before you did any of it: Before you were born; Before Jesus died on the Cross, knowing and on account of, that sin; Before the world was created and God forsaw every man's need for a Saviour. Yet, God began blessing you with the precious gifts of life, love, salvation, deliverance, and forgiveness. He continually has conferred all these blessings both before you committed your first sin, and despite the ones you commit today, or will commit tomorrow. Above all, He repeatedly provides forgiveness, cleansing, and a supernatural transformation which enables you to overcome sin, through the simple mechanism of faith, repentance, and fresh willingness to submit obediently.

CHAPTER 8

GOD'S BLESSINGS OF PARTICIPATION IN STEWARDSHIP

"Above all hold unfailing your love for one another... As each has received a gift; employ it for one another, as good stewards of God's varied grace."

– I Peter 4:8, 10.

There are many strands woven into the tapestry of good stewardship. Certainly the concept of reward for obedience to God's commands: especially to love one another, is carried over to the blessing of good stewardship over every resource received from God. Indeed, the distinctive theme of stewardship taught by Jesus is to apply all the gifts we receive to benefit others, both saved, and unsaved, by lovingly sharing and ministering to their needs. We hold God's blessings in trust for their distribution to others as they have need. When we question God's inaction in responding to some condition, God is entitled to say He has already sent us to minister to that need.

A major idea of stewardship involves work to do in service to the Master's best interests; obediently administering the Lord's directives, in furtherance of His wishes. Good stewardship also requires an increase, development, or fructification of the Lord's resources, which we hold in trust during our period of service, whether the gift be time, wealth, talent, or children. What we receive from God must be invested for His purposes and His increase.

Thus, in the Parable of the Pounds, the Master gives ten of his servants ten pounds each, with the instruction: "Occupy till I come" (Luke 19:13, KJV). These servants are in a position of authority in a period immediately preceding their Lord's return, and they are to be occupied in using that authority for the Lord's purposes. Obedience is rewarded, while slothfulness suffers loss, and he who fails to increase the Lord's capital is condemned.

The imposition of good stewardship upon the blessings received from God is a bestowal of a further wonderful blessing of participation in God's purposes for Christians. As in all obedience, we are privileged to experience the intrinsic joy of handling God's gifts as He directs, toward the end of pleasing and glorifying Him by conforming to His will. In a stewardship which bears fruit in obedience, we are privileged to participate in the inherent joy of pleasing our Lord by willingly furthering His purposes. The "true riches" to which Jesus refers at Luke 16:11 result from God allowing His faithful to share, collaborate, and participate as stewards in executing divine purposes and dispensing divine love.

When we participate in God's love by sharing it with others, we enjoy a special, close experience of God, in the joyous envelopment of divine love which accompanies giving. When we act lovingly, we share God with others, and He seems palpably closer because His love is being expressed in loving actions. Jesus incorporated all of God's Commandments in His joint directives to love first God and then other men. We love God by loving men, and we give to God by giving to men. Love allows us positively and actively to share in God's nature, for God is love. In such stewardship of love, we are privileged to participate in experiencing the joy of giving to another, as we share the blessings we received from God specifically to bless others.

Our loving service may also be based upon the imperative of stewardship that, since everything belongs to God, it is right to obey Him in the rendering of our service. Our motive may be that of a mature child's desire simply to please his Father because he knows that compliance is the will and wish of his Father. Our loving service may also be based upon gratitude for all the blessings bestowed upon us, and a desire to share God's gifts with others, so they too may know and acknowledge His grace and love.

In this system of other-directed love, we also receive reciprocal love from others because of the loving environment to which we have contributed. Others requite our love in the name of God in response to our initiative, or because they are similarly obligated to bless us in obedience to God's stewardship of love.

Lastly, as in all obedience, Scripture promises specific spiritual and material rewards, both here and Hereafter, for loving acts toward others in obedience to God. When God lavishes His love upon us in inexhaustible supply for sharing with others, He establishes us as co-workers to participate in His purposes, for His glory. When we fail to do the work assigned, people who have never experienced love become the disaffected and estranged of the world. They suffer in their alienation from God's love, and they inflict suffering on others out of privation and frustration.

As in all blessings from God, failure to exercise our stewardship obediently will result in loss of the blessing, not only for ourselves but for those whom God has intended to benefit from our giving. If I fail to give to the poor out of God's wealth temporarily entrusted to my hands, the poor will suffer because I aborted God's plan for sharing with them. In the world they may register protest of economic injustice with varying degrees of force and stridence, because the faithful have failed to be faithful and share with them what God has given us.

If we disobey the Great Commission and fail to share the Good News of salvation in Christ with them, they may never be saved or transformed, for God has designated us as His messengers of the Gospel. In the world, in their unredeemed state, men will continue to act with hostility and selfishness, for these traits of the natural man can be removed only by a New Birth which regenerates and transforms one spiritually.

If we fail to render mercy and compassion to those in hospitals and prisons, or respond to any lack of the needy in the world, we have failed God's assignment of Good Stewardship. And if we presume to point an accusing finger at God, wondering why He has not relieved the plight of the destitute, afflicted, and spiritually blind, we point three fingers toward ourselves, since He has constituted and empowered us as His agents to facilitate their relief and release from want and sin.

Love for others, as an extension of God's love for us and our love for God, becomes the motive behind stewardship, bolstered by the promise of reward for obedience.

THE COMMANDMENT TO LOVE OTHERS

Our participation in the gift of love begins with Jesus' joint commandments on which "depends all the law and the prophets... You shall love the Lord your God with all your heart, and with all your soul, and with all your mind. This is the great and first commandment. And a second is like it, You shall love your neighbor as yourself" (Matthew 22:37-40). All love in inspired by, and originates with God, and we do love Him "because he first loved us" (I John 4:19). God reveals at Jeremiah 31:3: "Yea, I have loved thee with an everlasting love: therefore with loving kindness have I drawn thee." So the first blessing of God's love is to draw us to His presence, so we may appreciate, worship, enjoy, and glorify Him. God's love is what motivates us to love him for this first and greatest blessing from God. Imagine what the world would be like under a Creator who disdained, or even despised his creatures. It is God's love, also, which inspires our obedience to Him out of gratitude, thankfulness, and a desire to please Him.

While God lavishes His love upon mankind, he has also entrusted to believers its dispensing toward other men. We are certainly called to offer intercessory prayers for the needs and suffering of others, but praying for a poor man's deliverance from want is not all we are called to do as stewards. We are to release him from his poverty to the extent we are able, using and sharing the resources God has entrusted to our stewardship. If Spiritual gifts are for the edification of the Body of Christ, then material gifts are equally intended for sharing.

We are not only to pray for the salvation of the unsaved, but we are to fulfill the Great Commission entrusted to us and witness the Gospel of salvation in Jesus Christ to them. We are not only to love them from afar in the comfort of our homes or churches, but in the daily ministration of washing the grime from their feet.

God imparts the gift of love to believers in inexhaustible supply, so we may prodigiously and profusely share it with all those we encounter. "Every one who loves the parent loves the child" (I John 5:1). Real love for God enables love for others, which gives the gift of God, Himself, to others through our transmitting agency. Jesus tells us how to express our love for others: "You shall love your neighbor as yourself" (Matthew 22:39). Love for others was an Old Testament directive at Leviticus 19:18; Deuteronomy 10:19; and see also, I Corinthians 13:1-3; Galatians 5:14; and James 2:8. Luke 6:31 puts it: "as you wish that men would do to you, do so to them." The natural man loves himself more than anything, and Jesus recognizes this tendency, thereby setting the measure of love for others at a high level. Self-love in a Christian is healthy, not vain, because one recognizes his dignity and value as a child of God, and is considerate of all other men who share that worth actually or potentially.

So important is this duty to love other men, that Christ gives us a second mensuration of love — to treat others as considerately as if they were He. Jesus equates loving kindness toward others: feeding the hungry, giving drink to the thirsty; welcoming the stranger; clothing the naked; and visiting the infirm and imprisoned; as identical with conduct toward Him. "Truly, I say to you, as you did it to one of the least of these my brethren, you did it to me" (Matthew 25:40).

Three times Jesus asked for assurance from Peter that he loved Jesus, and after each assurance, Jesus directed that Peter's profession of love for Jesus be translated into love for others. He instructed Peter: "Feed my lambs... Tend my sheep... Feed my sheep" (John 21:16-17). Here, Jesus did not establish faith, repentance, or obedience, but only love, as the primary sign of discipleship. Colossians 3:23 teaches: "Whatever your task, work heartily, as serving the Lord and not men."

Since we are to love God with all our heart, soul, and mind, the equivalent love for others, as for Jesus, commands total commitment. The best way to evidence our love for God is to love other men. I John 4:20-21 puts it: "he who does not love his brother whom he has seen, cannot love God whom he has not seen. And this commandment we have from him, that he who loves God should love his brother also." See also, Romans 12:10-11; I John 4:11-12.

The third, and deepest dimension of love which Jesus commands is that "you love one another as I have loved you" (John 15:12). Jesus' immeasurable love for man was total, sacrificial, selfless, and greater than any other love. It challenges us to the highest level of giving as the standard for measuring a disciple's love for others. I John 3:16 says: "By this we know love, that he laid down his life for us; and we ought to lay down our lives for the brethren," and see also, John 15:13; 17:23,26.

Jesus' love was so selfless that He "made himself of no reputation, and took upon himself the form of a servant" (Philippians 2:7, KJV). Jesus washed the feet of the disciples to provide an example of how we should serve others (John 13:5). He teaches: "whoever would be great among you must be your servant, and whoever would be first among you must be slave of all" (Mark 10:43-44), and adds: "I am among you as one who serves" (Luke 22:27).

Like faith, love without works is empty and meaningless, for love is more than an attitude of affection or compassion (James 2:15). It is action which benefits the loved one. In a world of privation, avowals of love or concern for the starving millions abroad are empty professions and not love, if they never materialize into sharing what one has received from God with those less fortunate. We can give without loving (I Corinthians 13:3), but it is impossible to love long and truly without giving. I John 3:18 queries: "But if anyone has the world's goods and sees his brother in need, yet closes his heart against him, how does God's love abide in him?"

Jesus commissions believers in an active ministry to others of positive good toward them. Jesus is the only religious leader who imposed this affirmative duty upon believers to do good out of love. Our love is to be active, caring and concerned for the needs of others: "Bear one another's burdens, and so fulfill the law of Christ" (Galatians 6:2).

LOVE NECESSITATES GIVING

Love is outgoing because it is other-oriented, and a love which is never expressed will never be fulfilled, but soon whither and die. A love for the starving masses of India or China is incomplete unless we translate our love and concern into actions which comfort the beloved. James 2:15-17 asks: "If a brother or sister is ill-clad and in lack of daily food, and one of you says to them, 'Go in peace, be warmed and filled,' without giving them the things needed for the body, what does it profit? So faith by itself, if it has no works, is dead."

Compassion for the family grieving over the loss of a loved one offers no consolation if we fail to communicate our sympathy and help to bear their burden. Persistence is necessary, for sharing another's cares must be sustained since it may take time for rejection or bereavement to be healed by the Lord. Comfort is a process, more than an event.

That God's blessings are meant for sharing is confirmed by 2 Corinthians 1:3-4, which speaks of "the God of all comfort, who comforts us in all our affliction, so that we may be able to comfort those who are in any affliction, with the comfort with which we ourselves are comforted by God." Certainly, we benefit personally from God's consolations, but they are also given us as God's designated agent to provide insight and strength as we comfort others. Knowing that the circumstances which require comfort from God are fitting us to minister comfort to the needs of others, is a real source of comfort and endurance in itself, as we confront our trials. Jesus confirmed this when He warned Peter that Satan would attempt to sift him like wheat, "but I have prayed for you that your faith may not fail; and when you have turned again, strengthen your brethren" (Luke 22:32).

As in every endeavor of believers, God stands ready to advise, guide, and empower according to His will. His business is to make you over like Him, with your ongoing consent; to have you love other men through your active service; and to spread the Gospel to others by your witness. In all these endeavors, you can expect God to give you the spiritual and worldly resources to succeed in accomplishing His business, if you will only consult and obey His wishes in all things.

The connection between answered prayer and the commandment to love others, strongly suggests that when a disciple is bearing fruit demonstrated by his love, he opens the channels to receiving whatever he asks in the name of Jesus, to further His ministry of loving service. With the obedience of your unselfish love, faith is irresistible in embracing the Kingdom, and claiming the blessings promised in God's Word. To love is to obey the commandment, and the object of love is always to edify others. Loving acts coincide exactly with Jesus' character and purpose of selflessly loving others. Divine blessings in answer to prayer are connected with the petitioner's intent to "bear fruit" for God's purposes, through loving, shared use with and for others.

Obviously, we have all experienced blessings when God answers our selfish or isolated prayers. God granted Israel's wish for a king, appointing Saul and then David, contrary to God's purpose to lead the nation, Himself (I Samuel 8:7-20), but the departure from God's will always harmed the nation when such prayers were granted. James 4:3 explains: "You ask and do not receive, because you ask wrongly, to spend it on your passions." This is the problem of 'name it and claim it" faith, when we do not sow to share, but seek to reap only to meet our own desires, often beyond what we truly need, and not based on or claiming any Scriptural promise. Such prayers may be the basis for hope, but only God's Word can be the basis of true faith in a divine promise (Romans 10:17). If one does not sow to share, he will not reap beyond what he actually needs.

This concept of prayers of faith is not very satisfying to generations of Americans spoiled by a surfeit of worldly provision. But in every era of history; indeed, throughout most of the modern world, faith looks to future, eternal benefits, and embraces one's actual needs to be met, according to God's promises. Faith is not for every trifling thing we might desire to have, and Americans need to return to the faith of our fathers. Certainly the Apostles and early Christian martyrs had no doubt where their first loyalty and priority lay. It was with God, and not the things of the world, which could be easily forsaken for the sake of having God. James 4:4 goes on to say: "Unfaithful creatures! Do you not know that friendship with the world is enmity with God?"

It is ironic that Moslem terrorists can willingly sacrifice themselves, and the little they have in the world, because privation and poverty have severed them from attachment to any material allures, and focused on the rewards promised martyrs in their afterlife. Christian Americans, conversely, by enjoying prosperity have grown attached to the world and its possessions, and have more fear of losing material advantages, all at the expense of their blessed hope in Heaven's eternal bliss.

Of the three great works to which Christians are called — growth in holiness; loving ministry to the needs of others; and witnessing for Jesus to the unsaved — two of them are intertwined with the needs of others and wholly involve devoted service to others. The blessings God promises are designed and designated to be shared with others, by God's empowering. The blessings may even be contingent upon sharing them with others by liberality in feeding the physically impoverished, nurturing the spiritually deprived, and supporting missions to propagate the Gospel, including our own personal sharing of the Good News.

As with all gifts, the felicity of God's commandment to love constitutes you as His instrument to pass along His comfort, and channel loving blessings to others. Sharing generously is the system ordained by God for disbursing His wealth and wisdom among all believers in the Church, and non-believers in the world. Giving in love imposes a stewardship upon believers to serve as God's hands on earth, and as conduits through which other men may share His material and spiritual blessings. True stewardship coincides perfectly with Christian love for others as one's active charity shares God's gifts of love, comfort, peace, time, talent, and treasure with those less fortunate.

Jesus clarifies the attitude of all disciples toward giving at Matthew 10:8: "You received without pay, give without pay." He tells the rich young man: "If you would be perfect, go, sell what you possess and give it to the poor, and you will have treasure in heaven; and come, follow me" (Matthew 19:21). He tells His followers at Luke 12:33: "Sell your possessions, and give alms; provide yourselves with... a treasure in the Heavens that does not fail." God, the Owner of all wealth, intends to give Christians the Kingdom, and promises sufficiency to all who seek the Kingdom (Luke 12:31).

Galatians 6;2 directs believers to "Bear one another's burdens, and so fulfill the law of Christ." The general rule of Christian giving is propounded at 2 Corinthians 8:11-12: "Your readiness in desiring it may be matched by your completing it out of what you have. For if the readiness is there, it is acceptable according to what a man has, not according to what he has not." The widow's mite was notable because she gave all she had and was not hampered by her lack (Mark 12:42-44).

Jesus' own example of sacrificial giving is reviewed at 2 Corinthians 8:9: "though he was rich, yet for your sake he became poor, so that by his poverty you might become rich." I Corinthians 16:1,2 teaches you are to give as God has prospered you: "concerning the contribution for the saints... On the first day of every week, each of you is to put something aside and save, as he may prosper," so that contributions are accumulated.

We can rejoice unconcerned in the gracious provision from the hand of God, when we acknowledge that what we have is not the result of our labor, but of God's providential care. We can trust God to provide and to preserve what He has supplied. Consequently, we can freely share with others because we are confident of God's sustained and loving provision.[82] There will be times of abasement and abounding, of "facing plenty and hunger, abundance and want," but "I can do all things in him who strengthens me" (Philippians 4:12-13). What we give others is the same gift we received as a blessing, and our giving to others extends the blessing by passing on the original grace of God.

As we see in the following Chapter, the Holy Spirit gives every believer a spiritual gift for the common good (I Corinthians 12:7). If we have received spiritual blessings which are to be spread to all believers, we ought also share our material blessings which have likewise come by the grace of God (Romans 15:27) for distribution to others. Remember that our supply of love from God is inexhaustible, and free for the asking as a fruit of the Holy Spirit (Luke 11:13; Galatians 5:22), as are gifts of grace to enrich the Church, of liberality, mercy, and love (Romans 12:8-10). Our giving should be done with the same fervor as Jesus when He shared His greatest love by giving the greatest gift (salvation) to the greatest number (all men) to be received with the greatest ease (faith). Like Jesus, we can endure our cross if only we will focus on the joy that is set before us (Hebrews 12:2).

Like the Magi, who lavished extravagant gifts upon the Lord, we must focus on the love in our heart for Him, as we give to others. We will not flag in our loving devotion if we keep the joy of serving and pleasing the Lord before us. We must respond with the Israelites' zeal to please God with such generosity that more than enough wealth was amassed to build the Temple, and their gifts of gold and silver eventually were declined (Exodus 36:6-7).

Ephesians 2:10 teaches that believers are God's "workmanship, created in Christ Jesus for good works, which God prepared beforehand, that we should walk in them." Ephesians 4:28 calls us to share the product of our labor: "Let the thief no longer steal, but rather let him labor, doing honest work with his hands, so that he may be able to give to those in need." Hebrews 13:16 concurs: "Do not neglect to do good and to share what you have, for such sacrifices are pleasing to God." I Peter 4:10 affirms: "As each has received a gift, employ it for one another as good stewards of God's varied grace." See also, Proverbs 14:31, 19:17; Psalm 41:1-2; Matthew 25:36-45; and Colossians 1:10.

Indeed, the early Christians diligently practiced the call to interdependence; to sustain one another materially, as well as spiritually, so the weak and poor might be cared for as directed at 2 Corinthians 8:14: "As a matter of equality your abundance at the present time should supply their want, so that their abundance may supply your want, that there may be equality." 2 Corinthians 8:15 cites Exodus 16:18 in commending generosity to the early Church: "He who gathered much had nothing over, and he who gathered little had no lack." Zacchaeus, in response to Jesus' call, gave half of his goods to the poor and penitently made restitution four times over, to those whom he had cheated as a tax-collector (Luke 19:8).

While the tithe had been fixed at ten percent of one's income, the New Testament estab-lishes a standard of giving inspired by the Holy Spirit; spontaneous and voluntary, according to the promptings of one's heart. Acts 2:44-45 relates: "all who believed were together and had all things in common; and they sold their possessions and goods and distributed them to all, as any had need." Acts 4:34-35 explains: "There was not a needy person among them, for as many as were possessors of lands or houses sold them, and brought the proceeds of what was sold and laid it at the apostles' feet; and distribution was made to each as any had need."

The same commitment to giving is expressed at Acts 11:29: "And the disciples determined, every one according to his ability, to send relief to the brethren who lived in Judea." Likewise, the churches of Macedonia "in a severe test of affliction, their abundance of joy and their extreme poverty have overflowed in a wealth of liberality on their part. For they gave according to their means... and beyond their means, of their own free will... But first they gave themselves to the Lord and to us by the will of God" (2 Corinthians 8:2-5; see also, 2 Corinthians 9:1-2).

The early Church which shared all things in common, obviously understood how immer-sion in God's love is marvelously intertwined with sharing the blessings of unity to obey and glorify God in other areas. We are given God's love, power and authority to do God's will;

not to promote our own selfish ends, and therein lies the true blessing. Awareness of steward-ship frees a Christian from the burdens of ownership and accumulation, and is other-oriented. Failure to devote blessings to God's purposes, by failing to share them with others, may account for our blessings drying up.

LOVE AS THE MOTIVE OF GIVING

It is possible for unsaved persons to give to charity without any investment of love. Indeed, in the time of Jesus there were donors who sounded trumpets when they gave alms, amidst much fanfare, to draw attention to their charities and bask in the fawning and acclaim they received. Christians young in their faith may be prompted by the many Scriptural promises of reward to the giver, and others may give for the spiritual reward of simply feeling good which accompanies giving. If our giving is not out of love for others because of love for Jesus, it is of no avail since our giving has the misplaced motive of self-gratification. For, just as we advance from prayers which are petitionary, and progress to intercessory prayers, then prayers of fellowship and communion, and finally prayers of praise and worship, we will find that mature giving progresses to a desire to bear fruit; not for one's own use, but for the Lord's purposes, which He has identified as sharing with, and serving others.

Much obedience is motivated by self-interest, and is used by Jesus. However, the motive of love is not increase to our own gain, but to serve, please, and glorify God by transmitting His love and blessings to others. While we may be privileged to share God's rewards as we transfer them to others, our motive should never be sowing in order to reap self-advantage. Our gratification is to please, and be right with, the Lord, mindful of the inculcation of Hebrews 13:16: "Do not neglect to do good and to share what you have, for such sacrifices are pleasing to God." Our giving must always originate with God, and be for God. Giving may have inci-dental benefits of personal gain, but ideally it should always intend to glorify God and further His purposes by serving the Body of Christ and equipping the needs of others, because we are recipients, sharers, and stewards of God's love and grace.[83]

The Health and Wealth doctrine has been built on the promise that if we sow seeds of giving to bless others, we will reap a profusion of more blessings, usually for our own advan-tage. Luke 6:38 puts it: "give and it will be given to you; good measure, pressed down, shaken together, running over, will be put into your lap. For the measure you give will be the measure you get back." But the law of sowing and reaping is inextricably tied up with a motive of love; so that any increase may better serve others.

2 Corinthians 9:6-12 establishes this principle: "he who sows sparingly will also reap spar-ingly, and he who sows bountifully will also reap bountifully. Each one must do as he has made up his mind, not reluctantly or under compulsion, <u>for God loves a cheerful giver</u>... And God is able to provide you with every blessing in abundance, so that you may always have enough for everything and may provide in abundance for every good work... enriched in every way for great generosity."

Tithing without the motive of love is enervated and purposeless. Jesus approved of the tithing of the scribes and Pharisees, but remonstrated with them for their mechanical applica-tion and wrong motive: "you tithe mint and dill and cumin, and have neglected the weightier matters of the law, justice and mercy and faith; <u>these you ought to have done</u>, without neglecting the others" (Matthew 23:23). Faith and obedient works of charity will not invite divine gifts, power, or Spiritual fruit, unless they express an inner motive of genuine love for others.

If we give according to the law of reaping what we sow, with expectations of receiving in proportion to how we have given, our motive of love is essential, with expectations of receiving more so we can share more. Our giving must be done cheerfully, out of gratitude and thanksgiving for all God has given us. We give back to Him because of His love, which wells up within us so that we willingly wish to share with others out of that love, Then, when you sow bountifully to demonstrate this devotion to the Lord's service, you will reap bountifully from the Lord so you may increase your giving to others and share prosperity with those less fortunate.

There is no meaningful prosperity without serving God in this way. There is none of God's grace, power or wealth without commitment to His principle of love. God has provided all things for His children, but a believer's decision of love in commitment to God's purposes is the only response to God's largesse. I Corinthians 13:2-3 says: "if I have all faith, so as to remove mountains, but have not love, I am nothing. If I give away all I have, and if I deliver my body to be burned, but have not love, I gain nothing." Galatians 5:6 puts it: "For in Christ Jesus neither circumcision nor uncircumcision is of any avail, but faith working through love." Our faith must be active and 'working,' and it must also be motivated by love in obedience to the Word.

For many men, daily work affords no direct, valuable service to God or others, and has no intrinsic value in promoting God's purposes. One's expenditures of time, thought and effort simply produce wealth to be employed and applied in the manner most important to him. How one uses the resulting wealth is the translation of his vital life and time into an expression of what is valuable to him. The Bible says: "For where your treasure is, there will your heart be" (Matthew 6:21; Luke 12:34).

God has commanded His children to demonstrate their belief in His work and the importance of loving service, by entrusting part of their assets to Him. Money represents one's life, time, and energy, and investing it in God's work proves our faith and love for Him.[84] The things with which we surround ourselves are the expression and evidence of where we have invested our time and what we regard as important. Every useless bit of rummage we possess is an indictment against our squandered time and misspent wealth. But when we return the first portion of God's gifts to Him, our collaborative response sets in motion the divine law of abundance and blessings for those who are obedient.

That is why I Peter 4:10-11 directs: "As each has received a gift, employ it for one another, as good stewards of God's varied grace... in order that in everything God may be glorified through Jesus Christ." See also, 2 Corinthians 8:3-7.

More, God's grace which empowers giving does not glorify us, but confirms the goodness of God, thus prompting "many thanksgivings to God" by the beneficiaries whose needs were met (2 Corinthians 9:12). We too, offer thanksgiving for the privilege of serving God in such a gratifying way, as well as for that part of His blessings retained for our own enjoyment. Jesus confirms this at Matthew 5:15: "Let your light so shine before men that they may see your good works and give glory to your Father who is in heaven." We are not to trumpet our good works to attract attention to us, but we are to practice the loving works we preach, even to the unsaved, so that through the works they may come to see Jesus in us and find God. For, one purpose of our life on earth is to glorify God by expressing God's character, which is love, toward men. Because we are thankful to God for His grace, we give willingly to God for His purposes. God has loved us into obedience.

THE REWARDS OF LOVING CHARITY

Scripture promises express rewards for the good stewardship of loving obedience. The principle blessing is the intrinsic joy of pleasing God by dutifully doing what pleases, and has been commanded by, our loving Father. We experience ineffable joy when we know we have compliantly glorified God through our obedient, loving acts which bear fruit. The fruit we bear is Christ-like character, expressed in love and faithful obedience as exemplified by Jesus, our model. Just note how the Scriptures which seem to promise unlimited blessing when we pray in the name of Jesus, are actually calling us to glorify God by our loving obedience which bears fruit.

John 15:7-8 connects the blessing of answered prayer when we use the name of Jesus with obedient love for others which glorifies God by bearing the fruit of the Holy Spirit, reflective of Jesus' character: "If you abide in me, and my words abide in you, ask whatever you will, and it shall be done for you. By this my Father is glorified, that you bear much fruit, and so prove to be my disciples." John 15:16-17 continues to connect Jesus' name with obedient love for others, which calls for this closest identity with the Lord's character: "I chose you and appointed you that you should go and bear fruit and that your fruit should abide; so that whatever you ask the Father in my name, he may give it to you, This I command you, to love one another."

Jesus also promises rewards for prayer in His name, sandwiched between two calls to loving obedience to Him, at John 14:12-15: "he who believes in me will also <u>do the works that I do</u>... whatever you ask in my name, I will do it, <u>that the Father may be glorified</u> in the Son; if you ask anything in my name, I will do it. If you love me, you will keep my commandments." Again, the objective of loving obedience is to rejoice in the knowledge that we have pleased God by glorifying Him in the name of Jesus. Hebrews 13:16 affirms: "Do not neglect to do good and to share what you have, for such sacrifices are pleasing to God."

We are to pray in the name of Jesus for everything, and we will bear the fruit of the Holy Spirit, love, faith and the character of Jesus, so that we may impart fruit to others as an expression of our love for God and them. By the same token Jesus' prime commandment to love is connected with the fruitfulness of loving obedience and glorifying God, through which we receive answers to our prayers. (See also, John 16:23-24 and 16:26-27). Loving obedience in conformity to God's purposes as a condition of blessing is intimated at Romans 8:28: "We know that in everything God works for good with those who love him, who are called according to his purpose."

Stewardship, as subordination to God's will is confirmed by the intercessory prayers of the Holy Spirit, which God intends for our blessing. Romans 8:26-27 reveals: "Likewise the Spirit helps us in our weakness; for we do not know how to pray as we ought, but the Spirit himself intercedes for us with sighs too deep for words. And he who searches the hearts of men knows what is the mind of the Spirit, because the Spirit intercedes for the saints according to the will of God." Christians should be delighted to think the Holy Spirit edits their prayers to communicate them most effectively. What we tend to ignore is that He prays for us "as we ought," and that is coinciding with, and "according to the will of God." "For what person knows a man's thoughts except the spirit of the man which is in him? So also no one comprehends the thoughts of God except the Spirit of God. Now we have received... the Spirit which is from God, that we might understand the gifts bestowed on us by God" (I Corinthians 2:11-12).

If our original prayers are selfish, or ill-advised, the Spirit intercedes on our behalf and transforms our prayers into proper petitions conforming to God's will. With such a powerful ally re-stating our prayers, our selfish and improper ones may never reach God, and will not be answered. But we can expect prayers emended by the Holy Spirit in accord with God's will to be honored because they are in total, submissive compliance to God's purposes. Since we have consented to the Holy Spirit re-making us in the image of Christ, we have impliedly authorized His intercessory prayer to accomplish that for us.

At the same time, the Spirit works transformation in our will to conform our desires to God's perfect will. When we offer prayers and the Spirit conforms them "according to the will of God," He also conforms our will to God's will: "that we might understand the gifts bestowed on us by God." It follows that our prayers will be answered when they conform rightly to God's will because they are offered out of a changed heart in accord with His purposes.

Likewise, when we pray "in the name of Jesus," it connotes far more than an expression of faith that Jesus will use His influence and authority to secure the object of one's prayers invoking His name. Rather, the name of Jesus imposes an incorporation of His purposes by His servants, that God may be glorified. Acting in the name of Jesus implies a loving, extremely deep, intimate self-identification with the purposes and character of Christ, as a part of one's faith.

How can the Father be "glorified," which is the objective of answered prayers, by the unloving or disobedient acts of a natural man, which promote selfish wishes? Any prayer for our own glory, rather than God's, would be ineffective, despite the general language of favorable disposition when we pray in the name of Jesus.

When we were having our own way as transgressors, God redeemed us, and transformed us into the image of Christ, to advance, enhance, and promote His purposes of evangelism, loving service and holy character; not to promote our former carnal objectives which led to destruction. Therefore, would God not be better served by our obedient, loving submission, which reflects His glory, rather than our worldly desires? We glorify God by dispensing His love to others. 2 Corinthians 9:13 says: "you will glorify God by your obedience in acknowledging the gospel of Christ, and by the generosity of your contribution for them and for all others." We are privileged to participate in completing the work of Christ by sharing and relieving the pain and burdens of the afflicted, as He did. We are to witness to His Lordship by sharing His Gospel of Salvation with the unsaved. We are called to share His love by ministering to the needs of others. We are to share His Holiness by seeking it for ourselves and encouraging it in others. We are to promote His purposes by petitionary and intercessory prayer.

When we ask for whatever Jesus would, we receive the blessings of Spiritual fruit and holiness, because we are sharing identity of will with Him. If we bring our lives into alignment with His intent and purposes, we are entitled to pray for anything Jesus would pray for. Our faith empowers us to be ambassadors, doing the will of God instead of our will. The panorama of His will expands and intensifies the power and scope of our acts on His behalf. We receive anything for which we ask, because we ask only what is God's will to give us.[85]

Being authorized to pray in Jesus' name does not entitle us to charge anything we please to His account. Rather, it imposes a fiduciary duty to apply His name only for His purposes and according to His declared intentions. Anything else would be misappropriation of His resources to our own benefit; an embezzlement which would cancel any earthly power of attorney.

In fact, when we speak as Jesus' agent, and in His behalf, He has delegated His authority to promote His purposes, not ours. Our authority is to ask for what He would seek, intend, or direct. Henceforth, our prayers should seek Jesus' purposes, as well as His power to accomplish supernatural change in the world, to promote His agenda. Acting in the name of Jesus is analogous to receiving a Power of Attorney, under which we are identified with, and exercise the authority and power of, His name. As long as we use that authority only for His purposes, we act legitimately. If we misappropriate the Power of Attorney to our own advantage, we are a thief, mis-using our principal's power and wealth to our own account. If we mis-used our agency and did that in the world, we would expect to be summarily discharged from our position of trust and stewardship, and prosecuted criminally. Why should His spiritual authority and empowerment be any different?

The following promises of blessing given for loving obedience must be construed in terms of motive and reward for pleasing God by glorifying Him. Luke 6:35 connects loving works with reward: "love your enemies and do good, and lend, expecting nothing in return, and your reward will be great, and you will be sons of the Most High." So entwined is our love for God with loving acts toward others, that Colossians 3;17, 23-24 instructs: "whatever you do, in word or deed, do everything in the name of the Lord Jesus, giving thanks to God the Father through him... Whatever your task, work heartily, as serving the Lord and not men, knowing that from the Lord you will receive the inheritance as your reward; you are serving the Lord Christ."

Hebrews 6:10 connects one's loving works with reward: "God is not so unjust as to overlook your work and the love which you showed for his sake in serving the saints." I Peter 4:8 advises: "Above all hold unfailing your love for one another, since love covers a multitude of sins." One way love covers a multitude of sins is when we obey the mandate to forgive others, so that while we may notice the sins of others, our love will disregard, overlook and thereby cover, their faults (I Corinthians 13:7).

When we obey in loving acts of charity, we will establish our credit now for reward in the Hereafter. When our faith is evidenced in loving kindness by consoling the afflicted; feeding the hungry and thirsty; and aiding the needy, infirm, stranger, naked, sick and imprisoned of the world, we will hear the invitation: "Come, O blessed of my Father, inherit the kingdom prepared for you from the foundation of the world" (Matthew 25:34). Those who fail to minister to the Lord by ministering to these needy ones, "will go away into eternal punishment, but the righteous into eternal life" (Matthew 25:46).

Again, at Matthew 10:41-42 Jesus equates loving kindness toward others with divine blessing: "He who receives a righteous man because he is a righteous man shall receive a righteous man's reward. And whoever gives to one of these little ones even a cup of cold water because he is a disciple, truly, I say to you he shall not lose his reward" (paralleled at Mark 9:41).

Faithful reliance in the Word, evidenced by obedient conformance to the Word, also reaps heavenly blessings for believers. At Luke 14:13 Jesus urges charitable acts toward the "poor, the maimed, the lame, the blind," such as inviting them to a banquet. For, the benefactor will then "be blessed because they cannot repay you. You will be repaid at the resurrection of the just." Likewise, at Matthew 19:28 Jesus tells the rich young man to "sell what you possess and give it to the poor, and you will have treasure in heaven."

I John 3:18-23 says we are not to "love in word or speech but in deed... and reassure our hearts before him... If our hearts do not condemn us, we have confidence before God; and <u>we receive from him whatever we ask, because we keep his commandments and do what pleases him</u>. And this is his commandment that we should... love one another." See also, Ephesians 6:8; Colossians 3:12-14; and James 1:25.

2 Corinthians 9:10-12 says: "He who supplies seed to the sower and bread for food will supply and multiply your resources and increase the harvest of your righteousness. You will be enriched in every way for great generosity, which through us will produce thanksgiving to God; for the rendering of this service not only supplies the wants of the saints but also overflows in many thanksgivings to God." St. Paul refers to this as God's "inexpressible gift." See also, Ecclesiastes 11:1. The more we give to others, the more God will use our generosity to increase our resources. Because we labor with God, serve His purposes, trust Him constantly for everything, and commune with him in these ways, God uses our giving to increase our righteousness.

Giving allows you to activate the Covenant between God and you and reap abundantly, for the right reasons of sharing with others, increasing the fruits of actual righteousness, and bringing the Gospel to the world. Giving puts you in a position to receive the special anointing and blessings God pours out on loving givers. When you do God's business, then His resources provide prospering, enabling, and anointing so you can thrive in, and maintain, your service to God.

Another reward of a believer's acts of loving charity is the joy of experiencing God, Who is love. Jesus affirms the Old Testament idea that obedience to the commandment to love God and others draws us closer to the Kingdom of God and the blessings of God's love and communion, because God is love and our loving is an intimacy with, and expression of love from, God (I John 4:8). When a scribe avowed that loving God and one's neighbor was the first commandment, and "much more than all whole burnt offerings and sacrifices," Jesus pronounced his answer as "wise" and "he said to him, 'You are not far from the kingdom of God'" (Mark 12:32-34). Jesus praised the man's wisdom in equating love, rather than ritual sacrifice, as the true worship which brought men along the hard way and nearer the blessings of the Kingdom.

We know that mature faith becomes more than mental or spoken assent to the Word, and the works help us to express and persevere in the Word. We become holy by practicing the holiness God works in us. We become loving by the practice of loving acts. Indeed, Ephesians 3:17-19 spells out this connection between the blessing of God's love and our obedience in loving: "that Christ may <u>dwell in your hearts through faith;</u> that you, <u>being rooted and grounded in love</u>, may have power to comprehend... and <u>to know the love of Christ</u> which surpasses knowledge, that you may be filled with all the fullness of God." When by faith we experience the indwelling of Christ, we are rooted in love, and can know His love, and thereby be filled with the blessing of "all the fullness of God."

2 Peter 1:5-8 teaches that faith should be supplemented by virtue, knowledge, self-control, steadfastness, godliness, brotherly affection, and love. "For if these things are yours and abound, they keep you from being ineffective or unfruitful <u>in the knowledge of our Lord Jesus Christ</u>." I John 4:7 puts it: "let us love one another; for love is of God; and he who loves is born

of God, and <u>knows God</u>." Loving obedience brings us spiritually into the presence of Kingdom blessings: to know God and his infusive indwelling of divine life.

It would seem that God calls us to love Him, not because of any need by God to be loved, but because of man's need to find true fulfillment in God, Who is love. In fact, the Trinity is a self-contained, eternal, totally adequate exchange of love between Father, Son, and Holy Spirit. We are privileged to tap into that love by being in Jesus, Who is in God, and the Godhead is in us (John 17:21-23; see also, Colossians 3:3).

Yet another blessing which flows from our acts of loving ministry is the intrinsic joy of sharing God, Who is love, by giving his love to others. There is something about doing a kindness to another which simply feels good, and that is because we have given God's greatest gift of love to another. He who is blessed with a magnificent voice will enjoy singing in private, but his gift is better shared with an audience, and will be even more enjoyed by the singer because of the added joy imparted to others. We enjoy the intrinsic happiness of acting while swept by love, by feeling and being in love.

If stewardship bids us to share our treasure with those in need, then witnessing for Jesus is a key element of stewardship. For, we are called to share our treasure with others, and Jesus is the main treasure of believers. Hence, stewardship coincides with the Great Commission's imperative to share the Gospel with the unsaved.

The final blessing of loving acts stems from the reciprocal giving established by God's law of love, which takes on a special meaning in the Body of Christ. Just as we are to give to others when we are able, so we are entitled to receive from other believers when they are able and we are lacking. The delight of sharing our blessings, which produces fulfillment and pure joy from giving and loving, is confirmed by God positioning believers in the Body of Christ by the baptism of the Holy Spirit. Each of us has a duty of active charity in giving one's talent, time, and treasure to others in the Body of Christ. We may then be rewarded for our obedient loving relationships with others when they reciprocate our love.

Believers are united by mutual need and dependency as One Body, with Christ as our head. Other members have a corresponding duty to share their blessings with you, just as you are obligated to share with them. Each is designated as God's conduit in passing blessings from God, the source of every good and perfect gift from above, to other men. We benefit when others obey God's mandate of love, and their encouragement enables us to fulfill our obligation to love others in reciprocal fashion. Every member of the Body is expected to obey the commandment to love in order to affirm that the system ordained by God is working with the full cooperation of willing, individual members. However, neglecting to act as a good steward and share one's blessings, will result in depriving others of the blessings God intended to impart through His Church.

Our involvement with members of the Body of Christ is a condition of our blessings, so that each may selflessly minister to the needs, edification, and comfort of others, and reciprocally receive the same from them. Each gives and draws strength from sharing one another's burdens. Luke 6:38, KJV explains: "Give, and it shall be given unto you; good measure, pressed down, and shaken together, and running over, <u>shall men give into your bosom</u>. For with the same measure that ye mete withal it shall be measured to you again." (See also, Matthew 7:1-2).

Certainly, God can bless materially without using other men as intermediaries, but these verses establish some circumstances where we can expect other men to be God's instruments for our blessings, and we for them. For God dispenses blessings to His children through the obedient acts of other believers. His system of tithing was ordained to re-distribute His wealth for charitable and ministry purposes. His commands to give, love, and witness are intended to bless other members of the Kingdom, so that all share in the blessings of any one, as was practiced in the early Church.

Our obedience must always be motivated by love for God. Self-benefit should be merely an incidental consequence of God's plan of blessing. Clearly, the thrust of promised blessings is not simply to establish one's personal comfort, but to enable sharing of spiritual values and gifts with others. The believer who seeks blessings only for self-gratification may soon find his faith disappointed since it is not based on God's Word. Praying or operating in solitude may produce denial or frustration of the blessing we seek. Shared blessings express the principal attribute of Christ-like holiness, love, and consideration toward others.

Every believer is intended to represent God's hands in transmitting wealth and restoring blessings to others. Others have an opportunity to give to God for your benefit, just as you should give to God to benefit others. The genius of loving charity commended by God is that all believers both receive and dispense His gifts. The Body of Christ is so constituted that the strong share with the weak, and the weak draw from the strong, and each member will experience weakness and strength in different tasks and times. If we are to share with others, it implies that others are also to share with us, and we should expect, and are meant to be, the beneficiaries of their giving, as God's instruments to bless us.

Others may occasionally need gentle prodding or reminder that they are to supply your needs. An anonymous Arabic proverb says in part: "He who knows and knows not he knows, he is asleep, wake him." When we are in need we become the 'others' who are the object of giving, and to whom gifts are lovingly delivered according to God's direction. We are to reach out to one another so no-one's burden becomes too heavy. "Bear one another's burdens, and so fulfill the law of Christ" (Galatians 6:2).

When God uses the ministry of other believers to heal you, it is not so you can become a healthy, isolated recluse, but to empower and sustain your obedient, loving service for others. When you are strong you should share your strength with others. When you are weak you may draw from others' strength. The healing you are instrumental in bringing to another today, is the same healing you will seek tomorrow through the help and intercession of other believers. Each of us is both a giver and receiver of health in the divine plan of interdependency among the parts of the Body of Christ. Indeed, this manifestation of love by one brother for another in the Lord is a strong witness which attracts an unsaved person to the Christian life style.

In modern times, a king's children are given certain advantages and allowances, not so much because they deserve privileges, but because they have duties to perform and obligations to fulfill by their position as a child of the king. Not only must they comport themselves with propriety, to avoid embarrassing the king, they must also be selflessly available in the service of his people. So it is with children of God, who are called to use their gifts as members of a royal priesthood, primarily for God's purposes, and glory, and only incidentally for their own advantage.

BLESSED WITH STEWARDSHIP TO SHARE IN GOD'S PLAN
OF GIVING

The Christian call to good stewardship is a blessing which allows us to participate in God's plan of lovingly sharing His gifts with others. The heart of stewardship is love. Trust and confidence is placed in a steward and this creates responsibility and performance on his part to do the Lord's will. He must heed the admonition of Paul: "guard what has been entrusted to you" (I Timothy 6:20; 2 Timothy 1:14).

God's Sovereignty and ownership of every resource requires that a steward represent his Master when the latter is absent (Luke 12:43, 19:12). A steward is entrusted by the master to administer the affairs of His house and he holds the Lord's resources for exclusive devotion to the Lord's purposes, exercised according to the Lord's wisdom. His independent activity signifies that his agency is not for the steward's personal use or own ends. His service reflects the disciple's prayer that God's will may "be done on earth as it is in Heaven" (Matthew 6:10).

The concept of stewardship depends on the knowledge that God is the titled owner of every resource in the universe, and entitled to have it applied to His purposes. Nothing man creates or gives can exist without using materials first supplied by God. I Chronicles 29:14 acknowledges: "for all things come of thee, and of thine own we have given thee." Scripture reveals that God twice gave mankind dominion over the earth, first in pristine form to Adam, and then in corrupted condition to Noah, directing each to "Be fruitful, and multiply, and replenish the earth" (Genesis 1;28, 9:1).

The directive to tithe reaffirmed God's ownership of wealth, and designated man's failure to devote wealth to God's purposes as literally stealing from Him. Malachi 3:8 chastises those who fail to return the prescribed portion of wealth given by God: "Will a man rob God? Yet ye have robbed me. But ye say, Wherein have we robbed thee? In tithes and offerings, ye are cursed with a curse; for ye have robbed me, even this whole nation." Thus, Ephesians 4:28 urges: "Let the thief no longer steal, but rather let him labor... so that he may be able to give to those in need." Stealing from God coincides with failing to "give to those in need" under God's system of giving.

Every resource we have comes from God. Without Jesus, we possess nothing of value. Christ's redemption of our souls, and Atonement for sins on our behalf, entitles him to our undivided loyalty. "You are not your own; you were bought with a price, So glorify God in your body" (I Corinthians 6:20; and see also I Corinthians 7:23; Acts 20:28). As the Creator, Owner, Giver and Redeemer of all things in the world, God is entitled to direct our use and disposition of every resource He provides us.

To remind Israel of God's total dominion over their stewardship God directed: "Thou shalt not delay to offer the first of thy ripe fruits, and of thy liquors: the firstborn of thy sons shalt thou give unto me. Likewise shalt thou do with thine oxen, and with thy sheep" (Exodus 22:29-30). God further explains at numbers 3:13: "all the firstborn are mine; for on the day that I smote all the firstborn in the land of Egypt I hallowed unto me all the firstborn in Israel, both man and beast: mine shall they be." See also, Deuteronomy 26:10.

God also ordained a sabbatical year in which one's crops were to be left for the poor, as a testimony to stewardship which shares with, and cares for, others: "and six years thou shalt sow thy land, and shalt gather in the fruits thereof: But the seventh year thou shalt let it rest and lie still; that the poor of thy people may eat... In like manner thou shalt deal with thy vineyard, and with thy oliveyard" (Exodus 23:10-11). God promised abundance for one who responded generously, since in the sixth year he would "bring forth fruit for three years" (Leviticus 25:21).

Likewise, God forbade sale of land "forever" because it belongs to Him and human occupants are but sojourners for a time (Leviticus 25:24).

God also directed Israel to release debtors every seventh year: "At the end of every seven years thou shalt make a release... Every creditor that lendeth ought unto his neighbour shall release it" (Deuteronomy 15:1-2). God required during the annual harvest that the corners not be gathered nor gleaned, but "thou shalt leave them unto the poor, and to the stranger" (Leviticus 23:22). God ordained the Jubilee year every fiftieth year, when all land was to be abandoned by the possessor, and revert back to its original owner for re-distribution to others. This reminds us we have the use of God's wealth in trust, as stewards to share it with others and employ it for God's purposes (Leviticus 25:13,28).

In imposing this responsibility of good stewardship and loving service, God cautions those who receive his bounty to remember that it comes from God, and to guard against the error of thinking falsely that "my power and the might of mine hand hath gotten me this wealth" (Deuteronomy 8:17; and see I Chronicles 29:14; and 2 Corinthians 3:5). Christians must "remember the Lord thy God: For it is He that giveth thee power to get wealth, that he may establish his covenant" (Deuteronomy 8:18).

God proclaims himself the true owner of all wealth, and directs his servants to manage it according to His will. God says: "For every beast of the forest is mine, and the cattle upon a thousand hills... The silver is mine and the gold is mine... all the earth is mine... the land is mine" (Psalm 50:10; Haggai 2:8; Exodus 19:5; Leviticus 25:23). John 3:27 affirms: "No one can receive anything except what is given him from Heaven." "Every good endowment and every perfect gift is from above, coming down from the Father of lights" (James 1:17).

We enter and leave the world with nothing; not wealth, nor position, nor loved ones. Even our spouse, children, and family are God's loved ones, entrusted to us for a brief period in time. Marriage does not continue in Heaven (Matthew 22:30), and children leave parents for their own marriage, spouse, and children while in this world (Genesis 2:24).

David acknowledged that when we give to God, we are simply returning that which He has given us: "Both riches and honour come of thee, and thou reignest over all... for all things come of thee, and of thine own have we given thee... (and) cometh of thine hand, and is all thine own" (I Chronicles 29:12-16).

In turn, God has given Jesus "the uttermost parts of the earth for thy possession" (Psalm 2:8), and Jesus confirms: "All authority in heaven and earth has been given to me" (Matthew 28:18). God, in Jesus, has chosen to share everything with His children: "all that is mine is yours" (Luke 15:31), and made us "heirs according to promise' (Galatians 3:29).

There is another facet of stewardship which stresses productivity and increase. When God blesses us with resources, it is important that we put them to good use. We must increase and grow in the righteousness we are given at the start of our Christian walk. We must increase the prosperity God entrusts to us, so it can be returned to Him for His purposes of sharing with others. Jesus teaches that a wasteful steward will be discharged from his duties (Luke 16:1-2). He who demonstrates poor stewardship by squandering his resources or failing to increase the wealth entrusted to him, will no longer be trusted by the Lord, and will forfeit even the blessings or "true riches" he has. Jesus speaks of bearing fruit in the Parable of the Sower, and warns: "For to him who has will more be given; and from him who has not, even what he has will be taken away" (Mark 4;25).

Good stewardship incorporates the idea that when we fail to increase God's wealth entrusted to us, then we have broken the cycle, and the consequence is failure to prosper, as well as loss of even that which we have. In the Parable of the Talents and the Parable of the Pounds, the steward who failed to invest his resource so it would return an increase to his Master, was called unfaithful by Jesus. Because he sought security, took no risks, and made no effort to serve faithfully, he was divested even of what he had, while those whose assets produced an increase were "set over much" (Matthew 25:21-28; Luke 19:16-24).

Servants are charged with the duty of investing the master's resources to his purposes according to his will, and are rewarded or punished on the basis of the return obtained for his account. Luke 16:10-11 says: "He who is faithful in a very little is faithful also in much: and he who is dishonest in a very little is dishonest also in much. If then, you have not been faithful in the unrighteous mammon, who will entrust to you the true riches?" I Corinthians 3:21, 4:2 teaches: "For all things are yours... and you are Christ's; and Christ is God's. This is how others should regard us, as servants of Christ and stewards of the mysteries of God. Moreover it is required of stewards that they be found trustworthy."

A number of Jesus' Parables confirm the principle of sowing and reaping, as individuals are entrusted with stewardship by their master and directed to act responsibly and produce fruit via a return on the wealth entrusted.[86] The Master has created circumstances which invite mature and responsible use of the steward's freedom, choices, and resources entrusted to Him. One Parable involves a man who goes away, instructing his servants to fend for themselves in administering his wealth in his absence, and the stewards' performances determine their rewards (Matthew 25:14-20). See also, Matthew 25:14-20; Luke 12:45, 16:1-13; 19:11-27; and Matthew 21:33. In the Parable of the Ten Virgins, wedding guests are given the responsibility of alertly awaiting the return of the bridegroom, though none of them knows when the feast will start. Failure to greet the bridegroom results in exclusion from the wedding banquet (Matthew 25:1-12).

Invariably, poor performance through irresponsibility results in loss, as God enforces the motivation of reward for obedience, with the threat of punishment for disobedience.

The Parable of the Sower illustrates that seeds which fall upon good soil "are the ones who hear the word and accept it and bear fruit, thirty-fold, and sixty-fold and a hundred-fold" (Mark 4:20); they will produce in increasing measure. The seed of faith is self-germinating and denotes an organic process of growth which occurs without human effort. However, the soil has to do with a believer's faithfulness, not only in terms of believing for a return, but in actions which nurture and cultivate our seeds, and conform to that belief to produce a harvest. Mark 4:24 says "the measure you give will be the measure you get, and still more will be given you."

The measure of stewardship is faithful discharge of one's duties on behalf of the Master. It is a matter of intent to serve the interests of the Lord, as much as it is actual productivity. Jesus says: "Blessed are those servants whom the master finds awake when he comes... be like servants waiting for their master to come home... Blessed is that servant whom his master when he comes will find so doing" (Luke 12:37, 43). We are to sow the seeds God gives us, and He will produce the increase in a harvest we are privileged to reap.

Good stewardship requires increase and development of whatever God has entrusted to you, whether it be talent, time, or treasure. It involves sharing and distribution of all God's resources to others, as agents of God's love, and ministers in His service to those in need. Increase and sharing are equally important parts of good stewardship in administering God's resources. In fact, sharing is the mechanism for increase in fruitbearing. Even if we pass on all the love which God has given us, returning it to Him and imparting it to others, we could never exhaust God's unlimited supply of His love. If we give away our faith, time, and knowledge in witnessing the Gospel to the unsaved, then the Body of believers increases and grows in fruit. If we cultivate our own holiness, we facilitate our transformation to the likeness of Christ. If we distribute the bounty which God has given us by doing as little as sharing some bread (which we might only marginally enjoy), with those who are starving, we have increased the aggregate enjoyment of all mankind.

The parables of Good Stewardship are concerned with acquisition, accumulation, production, and increase of resources by one's efforts and contributions, more than designating the objects of its blessings. But they establish and commend the idea of sharing in love, as well. Jesus reveals in other Scriptures that we hold our gifts in trust for the express purpose of sharing them with those in need, both the faithful and the unsaved. Clearly, stewardship must evolve into, and include giving of our time, talent and treasure to others. Our giving is an obedient way of evidencing faith in order to reap reward and establish good stewardship by love for others. He who is thankful returns his gifts to the Giver, while the ingrate regards them as his own, and appropriates them exclusively to his own use.

Consider the system of tithing which commands the return to God of a part of His blessings to us, to assure a continuous stream of blessings to share with others and sustain our giving to God. Tithing affirms that God blesses you with the means to finance the spreading and sharing of His prosperity to fulfill His Covenant with others. Giving to God is identical to, identified with, and expressed by, our giving to others.

We should remember that tithing has a double purpose. First, tithing assures the giver will receive blessings under God's Covenant when we give back part of what God has given us. We do not have difficulty believing God's Covenant promise to bless the tither, but we may overlook the first objective or operation of tithing, which is giving to and blessing others, <u>before</u> our blessing as a tither is released. The tither is meant to share in God's blessings, but they are also received from God for sharing with others. Tithing is God's mechanism to devolve blessings on the tither who sows in order to reap (Deuteronomy 8:18; Malachi 3:10), but God's equal, and possibly primary intent, is to bestow blessings on others through our tithing. Tithing assures the re-distribution or sharing of wealth which God has given a believer, with others in need, through our giving back to God.

Those in need are blessed by God through the responsive love of others for God, who share and re-distribute God's love and blessings throughout the Kingdom. The seed of tithing will grow into love-offerings willingly given to share all things with the Body of Christ. A Christian does not regard the gifts he possesses as his own, but employs them to love his neighbor as himself. He comes to rejoice in another believer's success and prosperity as if it were his own, because every good gift comes from above primarily to bless others. This stewardship applies not only to wealth, but to every resource we have. 2 Corinthians 8:14 puts it: "as a matter of equality your abundance at the present time should supply their want, so that their abundance may supply your want, that there may be equality."

STEWARDSHIP ENCOURAGED BY THE UNITY OF CHRIST'S BODY

Our interconnection as members of one Body of Christ mandates cooperation, care, and interdependence with other members of the Body. The New Birth of a believer by grace through faith includes baptism into the Body of Christ by the Holy Spirit: "For by one Spirit we were all baptized into one body... and all were made to drink of one Spirit" (I Corinthians 12:13; see also, John 3:5,8, 6:63; Colossians 1:13). Disciples are adopted into the family of God by this Baptism, and designated by Jesus as his family, "For whoever does the will of my Father in heaven is my brother, and sister and mother" (Matthew 12:49-50).

While God is the builder of His Church, or Temple, we are constituted as co-maintainers with him, as His agents to minister to the needs of others in His house, as good stewards of the house, responsible for the other members in it. One's house and family are to be cared for: "If any one does not provide for his relatives, and especially for his own family, he has disowned the faith" (I Timothy 5:8). Deacons were to "manage their children and their households well," and a bishop was to "manage his own household well, keeping his children submissive and respectful in every way" (I Timothy 3:12, 3:2).

In the definition of stewardship as loving service, perhaps no vehicle has been as useful as the idea of ministering to or edifying other members of the Body of Christ because they are parts of the spiritual Temple of God. A steward is rewarded for his efforts by his Master, but a steward's occupation is to serve the Master's Household. In this respect, Jesus is the consummate example of selfless human activity as a good steward Who dispenses God's graces to and for others.

The steward is a servant in God's house, which has been constructed, and is being built, by God, Himself (Acts 15:16; reprising Amos 9:11). The individual is constituted as one of the building stones in this spiritual structure; "Do you not know that you are God's temple and that God's Spirit dwells in you?" (I Corinthians 3:16; see also, I Corinthians 6:19; and 2 Corinthians 6;16).

Christians are "members of the household of God, built upon the foundation of the apostles and prophets, Christ Jesus himself being the chief cornerstone, in whom the whole structure is joined together and grows into a holy temple in the Lord; in whom you also are built into it for a dwelling place of God in the Spirit" (Ephesians 2:19-22). I Peter 2:5 calls us to Christ, the cornerstone, "and like living stones be yourselves built into a spiritual house, to be a holy priesthood."

In love, we are to edify the members of the Body of Christ, "speaking the truth in love, we are to grow up in every way into him who is the head, into Christ, from whom the whole body... when each part is working properly, makes bodily growth and upbuilds itself in love" (Ephesians 4:15-16; and see Colossians 2:19, 3:16,23; I Thessalonians 5:11,14; I Peter 1:22). When we speak the truth of the Word to a brother who needs to hear it, we edify and build him up. Then he will be at full power when we, in turn, need to be built up and edified by him (2 Corinthians 8:14). Each Christian must nourish others, just as the cells of the physical body transfer blood and nutriments to one another from the source of nature.

"Being rooted and grounded in love" enables disciples to receive God's light and comprehend the love of Christ (Ephesians 3:17-19; I John 2:10); and we must then share it with others in loving fashion. For, "if we love one another, God abides in us and his love is perfected in us" (I John 4:12).

There are many Scriptures which teach that the purpose of blessings, including health, prosperity, and deliverance from demonic assault, is not primarily for self-gratifying purposes, personal comfort, or intrinsic joy in our blessed condition, but rather to empower obedience and service to the glory of the Lord. We are equipped with spiritual weapons and God's armor with which to combat, overcome, and resist Satan here on earth (Ephesians 6:13-18), to minister to others and to promote God's objectives of obedience, holiness, loving service, and witnessing to the Gospel. Miracles, including healings, still occur in our day, as they did in the time of Jesus and the early Church. But they are primarily to demonstrate the divinity and authority of Jesus, and should be sought and received mainly in that light.

Because there is effectiveness in unity and power in concert, a sharing of collective blessings is implied among members of the Body. Many Bible passages emphatically call for action in cooperation with others. Spiritual blessings and gifts are connected to shared and concerted endeavors with other members of the Church. In the Old Testament, the power of believers is magnified by collaborative prayer and effort empowered by the Lord: "five of you shall chase an hundred, and an hundred of you shall put ten thousand to flight" (Leviticus 26:8; and see also, Deuteronomy 32:30; and Joshua 23:10).

God's Covenant of blessings for all mankind was made with an individual, Abraham, through whom "all the families of the earth be blessed" (Genesis 12:2-3). Abraham's blessings were not solely for his enjoyment, but were to be passed on as a blessing for all the families of the earth. Jesus' New and better Covenant is offered to every believer, but resides in His Church. God's offer of salvation is to the individual, but incorporates his entire family in the invitation: "Believe in the Lord Jesus, and you will be saved, you and your household" (Acts 16;31; see also, Acts 16:15; I Corinthians 1:16). Where a believer is wed to an unbeliever, the unbelieving spouse is sanctified through the believer: "Otherwise, your children would be unclean, but as it is they are holy" (I Corinthians 7:14).

Blessings are intended to be enjoyed in a collective sense, in conjunction with other members of the Body of Christ. The Body is intended to enjoy total interconnection, interdependence, and reciprocity as a believer shares in collective blessings in concert with other members. God's original Covenant was with Abraham and his heirs (Galatians 3:29), but His promise of blessings for obedience and a curse for disobedience was made to the nation Israel, rather than to separate members (Malachi 3:12). The individual stood or fell according to the fortunes of his nation.

When God established the nation Israel as His wife (Isaiah 54:5-6), the individual retained his personality, but derived identity and status as a member of the nation, Israel. The evil done by kings sometimes visited evil consequences upon the entire nation. National calamity then struck the nation as a whole and filtered down to every member. Israel was in captivity and exile in Egypt and Babylon as a nation, and each individual also shared in the national exodus from Egypt, and shared in Israel's victories, prosperity, and entry into the promised Land, Each suffered in the collective punishment of wandering in the desert for forty years because of the collective sinfulness of the nation.

When one member, Achan, sinned by disobeying God and personally appropriating some of the spoils of war, God's anger was kindled against all of Israel, even to the point of inflicting defeat in a battle at Ai (Joshua 7:1, 12, 21). Achan's sin was attributed to the entire nation:

"Israel hath sinned, and they have also transgressed my covenant which I have commanded them: for they have even taken of the accursed thing, and have also stolen... neither will I be with you any more, except ye destroy the accursed from among you" (Joshua 7:11-12), which prompted Achan's summary execution.

The New Testament likewise calls for involvement by other members of the Body of Christ in seeking, invoking, and distributing promised blessings. Matthew 18:19-20 promises that the impact of truly effective prayer is enhanced and strengthened by two or more members of the Body seeking the same result in prayer: "if two or more of you agree on earth about anything they ask, it will be done for them by my Father in heaven. For where two or three are gathered in my name, there am I in the midst of them."

It is no coincidence that God's power at Pentecost responded to the unity of believers in one mind and purpose devoted to God in unselfish concurrence in prayer. Acts 4:24,31 relates that when the disciples "lifted their voices together to God... And when they had prayed, the place in which they were gathered together was shaken; and they were all filled with the Holy Spirit and spoke the word of God with boldness." It is no accident that the Lord's Prayer is a corporate one, expressed in plural pronouns of "our Father," "give us," "forgive us," "our debtors," "lead us," and "deliver us" (Matthew 6:9-13).

This collective unity of believers is reprised at I Corinthians 3:16: "Do you not know that you are God's temple and that God's Spirit dwells in you?" The "you" is plural and encompasses the entire Body as the dwelling, or Holy Temple, of God on earth, resident in each believer. Jesus prayed for, and thereby established, the unity of His Church: "I do not pray for these only, but also for those who are to believe in me through their word, that they may all be one; even as thou, Father, art in me, and I in thee, that they also may be in us" (John 17:20-21; see also, Colossians 3:3).

The hundred-fold return of brothers and houses which Jesus promises His disciples (Matthew 19:29; Mark 10:29) is obviously not to be taken literally, even though true. It does illustrate how personal benefits are derived in connection with, and from our relation to the Body. When we follow Jesus we do not receive a hundred new genetically related, blood brothers. Nor do we receive title to a hundred more houses to replace the one we left. What we do receive is a status within the Christian community, which establishes a relationship with other Christians who are also washed in the Blood of Christ, and are adopted sons of God in the family of Christ's Church.

If we make our own self, home, and Spiritual resources available to others, we will have access to a hundred homes and blessings of Christian bothers and sisters we might never enjoy, otherwise. We will receive a hundred-fold return in sharing communal Christian wealth, love, and charity, plus access to the real, spiritual wealth of the Holy Spirit.

Because Jesus is the Head of His Body, the Church, we can share in advantages redounding to the whole Body through His presence, power, and wisdom, but only in relation to, and transmitted by other members of the Body.

Jesus calls us to copy the dishonest steward whose singular zeal for worldly survival was declared by Jesus to be worthy of emulation by Christians seeking to discharge spiritual duties and ensure spiritual well-being (Luke 16:8). Our objective is "to lead a life worthy of the Lord, fully pleasing to him, bearing fruit in every good work and increasing in the knowledge of God" (Colossians 1:10). If we are to honor God by serving others, we must first seek to submit to the Lord, and then receive His power to act according to His will.

As in all grace, you must seek the Kingdom of God, His righteousness, power, and fruit, as a prelude to divine blessings. If God promises food, clothing, and resources to assist others, the responsibility for their provision is all His. And we can cast all the care on Him, in total reliance He will provide whatever resources are needed to do His will, but only if we seek first His righteousness, which is our responsibility (Matthew 6:33). God accomplishes all the transformation and empowerment, but our desire for, and receptivity to His work both invites the promised blessings and facilitates their receipt.

CHAPTER 9

GOD'S BLESSING OF PARTICIPATION IN CHRIST'S CHURCH

"For just as the body is one and has many members, and all the members of the body, though many, are one body, so it is with Christ."

– I Corinthians 12:12.

St. Paul says that the individual members of the Body of Christ are like cells adapted to specific functions of a physical body, in harmony and interdependent with all other parts of the body. Each part of the Body has its own unique function, and every part is not a hand, eye, or heart (I Corinthians 12:14-21). The Body is designed so there are always some members able to impart strength to others who have become weak. In the Church, an interdependence is intended, so that any weaker, grieving, or infected parts are able to draw strength, encouragement, edification, education, or exhortation from the stronger or healthier parts of the Body. In turn, when the strong become weak, as eventually happens, they can draw strength from the other parts of the Body which have grown strong.

The Body of Christ is like an army engaged in spiritual warfare. Every member of the army is not a general, nor a frontline combatant. Some members must be trained and suited to care for the wounded behind the lines. The best fighters are eventually brought to the rear to teach superior techniques to others. Some must be assigned to administration to assure that supplies are transported to, and arrive at, the front lines. Others will be engaged in manufacturing munitions, or providing rest and recreation for battle-weary troops. Every member is not able to do every required task, yet the army, as a whole, performs every necessary function to achieve its objective.

God's plan is for the Body of Christ to be knit together and integrated. The Body exists to further God's purposes for every individual, just as each person must use his gifts to further God's purposes for the Body. All disciples must pray for one another; must help to heal one another; must give to one another in loving charity. Each must be a preacher, evangelist, witness, and messenger; always concerned about the unsaved; always caring for the New-Born spiritual babes of the Kingdom. If a believer is ignorant of these requirements obligating him to use his stature as a member of the Body <u>for God's purposes</u>, then his prayers will be immature, misguided, and possibly unanswered.

Membership of believers in the Church, the Body of Christ, provides strength and encouragement both to grow in Christ-likeness to resist sin, and to sustain the individual during the sufferings of this world. At the new Birth we are incorporated into and established within

Christ's Church, the Body of Christ, over which Jesus is the head: "For by one Spirit we were all baptized into one body" (I Corinthians 12:13).

God cares about the suffering of others, and has constituted believers in the Body as His agents to give consolation, sympathy, succor, support, and love to the afflicted. If we are to share the suffering of Jesus in His compassion for others and complete it for Him in His Body, we must have genuine compassion for others' needs and live to do something for them.

Jesus is intimately connected to His Body, and told Saul that his persecutions of believers was equivalent to attacking Him: "Saul, Saul why do you persecute me... I am Jesus, whom you are persecuting" (Acts 9:4-5). After Saul encountered Jesus, he could then wish: "that I may share his sufferings" (Philippians 3:10). Paul was ready to identify with the sufferings in the Church, which Jesus had revealed were His, also. Paul was equipped to "weep with those who weep" (Romans 12:15), and extend the same comfort to others with which he had been comforted by God.

While the fruit of the Holy Spirit, "love, joy, peace, patience, kindness, goodness, faithfulness, gentleness, self-control" (Galatians 5:22), are intended to transform the individual believer to the character of Christ, they also are meant to be imparted and shared with others to enrich their lives. By way of contrast, the spiritual gifts of the Holy Spirit are given for the common good, and only incidentally for personal enrichment. They do not necessarily work an immediate or direct change in the individual.[87]

The Church is destined for eternal glory shared with Christ, for "He is the head of the body, the church" (Colossians 1:18). God "has put all things under his feet and has made him the head over all things for the church, which is his body, the fullness of him who fills all in all" (Ephesians 1:22-23). Jesus is head over all things for the church, and our identity as believers is inextricably intertwined with Christ, Himself. I Corinthians 3:21,23 puts it: "For all things are yours... the present or the future, all are yours; and you are Christ's and Christ is God's."

With the prospect of such an exalted position for eternity, it is understandable that God will use any means necessary, even chastening, to prepare and qualify the Body, and each individual believer in the Body, for the Christ-like character necessary to receive, fulfill and enjoy eternity in Christ.

THE GIFTS OF THE HOLY SPIRIT

Expansion, equipment, education, and encouragement of the Body of Christ are established as the principal objects of Spiritual blessings, through the dutiful and obligatory use of one's individual gifts for the benefit of others, both saved and unsaved. To this end, God has provided spiritual gifts of the Holy Spirit to make perfect disciples: "for the equipment of the saints, for the work of ministry, for building up the Body of Christ, until we all attain to the unity of the faith and of the knowledge of the Son of God, to mature manhood, to the measure of the stature of the fullness of Christ" (Ephesians 4:11-13). Christians are charged to "encourage one another and build one another up (I Thessalonians 5:11,14).

To this end Jesus apportions gifts to individual members of the Body for the edification of the entire Body (Romans 12:5-8; I Corinthians 10:17, 12:12-27; Ephesians 1:22-23, 2:14-16, 3:6, 4:4, 4:12-16, 5:23, 5:29; Colossians 1:18, 1:24, 3:14). Jesus consecrates the Church, that it "might be presented before him in splendor, without spot or wrinkle or any such things, that she might be holy and without blemish" (Ephesians 5:25-27).

Even "the creation waits with eager longing for the revealing of the sons of God" (Romans 8:19). For, in our growth, "we have become a spectacle to the world, to angels and to men" (I Corinthians 4:9), as we open the door to restoration of all Creation, "because the creation itself will be set free from its bondage to decay and obtain the glorious liberty of the children of God" (Romans 8:21).

I Corinthians 12:7,11 says: "To each is given the manifestation of the Spirit for the common good... All these are inspired by one and the same Spirit, who apportions to each one individually as he wills." These gifts of holy grace are identified as "the utterance of wisdom... the utterance of knowledge... faith... gifts of healing... working of miracles... prophecy... the ability to discern between spirits... various kinds of tongues... and the interpretation of tongues" (I Corinthians 12:8-10).

Ephesians 4:11-12 enumerates five ministry gifts from Christ to His Church: "that some should be apostles, some prophets, some evangelists, some pastors and teachers." See also, I Corinthians 12: 28-31. I Peter 4:10 explicitly connects serving others to one's agency for the Lord: "As each has received a gift, employ it for one another, as good stewards of God's varied grace... in order that in everything God may be glorified" (See also, Romans 12:6-8; I Corinthians 1:7; and Hebrews 10:24-25). Romans 15:12 asserts: "We who are strong ought to bear with the failing of the weak... let each of us please his neighbor for his good, to edify him."

While the gifts of the Holy Spirit are provided to the whole Body of Christ, not every member is possessed of every gift. Thus, each must share the gift he has with others, and depend upon others, as agents of the Spirit's gifts, to share with him those which he lacks. Paul makes this clear as he asks: "Do all possess gifts of healing?" (I Corinthians 12:30), in a context which clearly implies all believers do not possess every gift, although every gift is to be found within the Body of Christ.

Though I may not have a particular gift at this moment, I am authorized to "desire the higher gifts" earnestly (I Corinthians 12:31). And I am assured that such a gift exists somewhere within the Body of Christ. It is important to remember this interconnection among members of the Body of Christ, to avoid becoming disheartened and faithless, when a gift or blessing is withheld from a particular believer.

At I Corinthians 12:12-26 St. Paul observes: "For just as the body is one and has many members, and all the members of the body, though many, are one body, so it is with Christ... The eye cannot say to the hand, 'I have no need of you'... On the contrary, the parts of the body which are weaker are indispensable... But God has so adjusted the body, giving the greater honor to the inferior part, that there may be no discord in the body, but that the members may have the same care for one another. If one member suffers, all suffer together; if one member is honored, all rejoice together." We benefit from revival, heal, and grow spiritually, together.

We learn primarily by the example of Christ, but we can also profit from the examples of others. St. Paul says: "What you have learned and received and heard and seen in me, do; and the God of peace will be with you" (Philippians 4:9). But we can also learn separately from God, and still show amazing similarity. A dozen cookies cut by the same Cutter will automatically share the identity received from their shaper. A dozen members of the Body shaped by Christ, will share the unity of the Holy Spirit in their devotions together.

We can draw strength, comfort, and endurance from the example of other members of the Body of Christ, who were empowered to serve, despite persecutions and sufferings which persisted throughout their ministry. St. Paul suffered from his thorn "in the flesh" at the hands of Satan; it was a prickly, distracting, annoying, physical nuisance; not a spiritual attack. He asked the Lord to take it away three times, and the Lord answered: "My grace is sufficient for you, for my power is made perfect in weakness" (2 Corinthians 12:8-9). The Lord's strength is likewise available to assuage our thorns in the flesh.

The Bible shows that a member in the Body of Christ is meant to be a partner in answering others' prayers for health, as well as be the beneficiary of healing through the intercessions of other believers. The "gifts of healing" are given by the Holy Spirit to some members of the Church "for the common good," expressly for sharing with other members of the Body of Christ (I Corinthians 12:7,9). This idea that a believer must derive and receive his blessings through the Church, the Body of Christ is supported by the method of healing prescribed in Scripture. Jesus says at Mark 16:18 that believers "will lay their hands on the sick, and they will recover."

Physical healing within the Church is promised a believer at James 5:15: "Is any among you sick? Let him call for the elders of the church, and let them pray over him, anointing him with oil in the name of the Lord; and the prayer of faith will save the sick man, and the Lord will raise him up." James 5:16 calls disciples to "confess your sins to one another, and pray for one another, that you may be healed." Health originates in the prayers of others for us, as they fulfill their correlative duty to administer the Spirit's gifts of healing to us who are saved. When the family of God prays together, there is a magnificent visitation of the Holy Spirit in their midst, as God responds to intercessory prayers for the benefit of others.

Clearly, corporate activity by the Body of Christ is deeply significant as the designated method for administering the blessing of healing. This does not mean that we are to turn to ritualism instead of faith, nor does it mean that prayers will be answered only if intercession by others is involved. It suggests believers should adhere to the specific provisions for healing and deliverance prescribed in Scripture, primarily, and whenever possible.

The gifts of the Holy Spirit are distributed among the entire Body of Christ so that each may draw upon and from others. Not everyone will enjoy the same gift: "For as in one body we have many members, and all the members do not have the same function, so we, though many, are one body in Christ, and individually members one of another. Having gifts that differ according to the grace given to us" (Romans 12:4-6). There is unity, but with diversity and differentiation, rather than uniformity among the members.

The gifts of the Spirit, though individually apportioned, are clearly for the collective benefit, unity, and fullness of the Body. No one should be tempted to exalt himself, since He receives and possesses a gift for the use and benefit of others in the Body. We are to "pursue what makes for peace and for mutual upbuilding" (Romans 14:19), and "strive to excel in building up the church" (I Corinthians 14:12,26).

The unity of Christ's Body, of which He is the head, necessitates interdependence and equality. Each member of the Body of Christ shares a reciprocal obligation to share lovingly with others who are less fortunate, so all members benefit from the blessings one has received from God. The entire Body is diminished when one member is deprived of nutrients. The entire body is sick and threatened when one part is feverish, infected, or gangrenous. Interdependence of the members of Christ's Body is assured, because no one member has all the gifts, and we need one another to complete the Body's growth to perfection as an organic unity (I Corinthians 12:7-10).

St. Paul encouraged prophesying as one of the better Spiritual gifts, because it upbuilds, encourages, and consoles the entire Body of believers, whereas speaking in tongues edifies only oneself (I Corinthians 14:2-4). We have a duty not only to grow, ourselves, but to build up the whole Body of Christ (Ephesians 2:19-22. 4:15-16). The Apostles were anointed to build up the Church in the power of Christ (I Corinthians 3:10; Colossians 1:25; 2 Corinthians 10:8, 12:19, 13:10). Each member of the Church, as a good steward, contributes to the well-being and consolation of the House of God in his generation (2 Corinthians 1:5). "Therefore encourage one another and build one another up, just as you are doing... admonish the idle, encourage the fainthearted, help the weak" (I Thessalonians 5:11,14).

Paul refers to "the stewardship of God's grace that was given to me for you" (Ephesians 3:2), and to "servants of Christ and stewards of the mysteries of God" (I Corinthians 4:1). Galatians 6:2 proclaims: "Bear one another's burdens, and so fulfill the law of Christ." I Corinthians 10:24 says: "Let no one seek his own good, but the good of his neighbor," and the Parable of the Good Samaritan expands the duty of care to one's unsaved neighbors outside the household of God. Even the Old Testament prophets who foretold the coming of Christ, were aware they served the future Church, and it had "revealed to them that they were serving not themselves but you, in the things which have now been announced to you" (I Peter 1:12, see also, Romans 6:13, 12:1, 12:4-5).

Clearly, stewardship requires avoiding the temptation to keep God's spiritual gifts strictly for oneself, as if the faith life were a private affair. At the other extreme, we should base our service on God's grace received, rather than our own will or power.[88] Stewardship begins with being entrusted by God with His graces, and proceeds to hold and distribute them lovingly for the benefit of other believers and the unsaved, at the direction of God.

St. Paul said he always sought to "impart some spiritual gift to strengthen you, that is, that we may be mutually encouraged by each other's faith, both yours and mine" (Romans 1:11-12). And all we do must be done with a fervor to edify others lovingly. For, the derivation of 'compassion' is 'with passion.'

We are invited to cast all our cares on Christ because He cares for us, and he, in turn has delegated believers as His representatives to care for one another and reach out in His name to one another so no one's load becomes too heavy. Christ is the Good Shepherd and our High Priest, but He has constituted the Church as deputy pastors to minister to the needs of all others, spiritually and materially, in dispensing God's blessings. We are all constituted as a royal priesthood, charged with the duty of this ministry. Or, to borrow a homely analogy, he calls each of us to be sheepdogs to tend the flock and protect them on behalf of the Shepherd, keeping them on the straight and narrow path toward good pasture.

The Church, the Body of Christ, is not an organization, but an organism, which grows through its connection to Jesus Christ, its head; just as branches are designed to draw strength and vitality from their attachment to the vine (John 15:1-6).[89] If one is supplied by Christ with worldly goods, intellect, physical prowess, or Spiritual gifts, it cannot be a source of pride, because it does not indicate any special favor or entitlement on man's part. God used even Balaam's ass to serve His purposes when it pleased Him (Numbers 22:23-28). We are privileged by grace to serve as God's conduit in funneling His gifts and abundance to others who need food, clothing, comfort, dignity, and assistance in their affliction or immaturity. We are nurtured by our elders in infancy, and after we mature we must reciprocally care for them in their advanced age, even as we tend our children.

If God has entrusted one with physical advantage, such as a gift of strength or sight, it must be used to support those who are weak or blind. For, God's gifts are not exclusively for personal use, but to sustain, benefit, "and have the same care for one another" in ministering to and building up the Body of Christ (I Corinthians 12:25). "Knowledge puffs up, but love builds up" (I Corinthians 8:1).

THE BLESSING OF PARTICIPATION IN WITNESSING

God also enhances human dignity and personality by constituting believers as His agents to communicate the Good News of salvation to the unsaved in all the world. Jesus bestows the Great Commission upon His disciples of every age: "All authority in heaven and on earth has been given to me. Go therefore and make disciples of all nations, baptizing them in the name of the Father and of the Son and of the Holy Spirit, teaching them to observe all that I have commanded you" (Matthew 28:18-20). Mark 16:15-16 continues this successively transferred command: "Go into all the world and preach the gospel to the whole creation. He who believes and is baptized will be saved; but he who does not believe will be condemned." We are made disciples in order to make disciples.

This transference of the Great Commission from Jesus to the disciples to believers of all ages is confirmed at John 15:16: "You did not choose me, but I chose you and appointed you that you should go and bear fruit and that your fruit should abide." We bear fruit by sharing the Good News of the Gospel with the unsaved, out of a loving concern for the salvation of others. When we choose to follow Jesus, then He chooses us to be His witnesses to the unsaved.

The Great Commission allows believers to collaborate and rejoice in the modern miracle of the New Birth in unsaved sinners who repent and receive Jesus Christ as Lord and Saviour by grace through faith. We are blessed with the role of gathering fruit by witnessing in obedience to God's call. When we share God's Word of salvation, the Holy Spirit produces faith in hearers of the Word, and God's enabling grace replaces the old, natural man with a new, transformed spiritual being recreated in the image of Christ.

Natural man is capable of knowing that God exists, based upon the evidence of Creation. Psalm 19:1-2 proclaims: "The Heavens declare the glory of God; and the firmament showeth his handywork. Day unto day uttereth speech, and night unto night sheweth knowledge" (See also Romans 1:19-21). However, without the empowering faith of the Word, communicated by the Holy Spirit in the Gospel of salvation, natural man cannot bridge the gap created by his sin, and cannot earn his salvation by obedience. Unaided by the Holy Spirit, natural man cannot exercise his will to respond to the Gospel. He needs divine intervention to quicken his will so he can receive the grace of God by faith in God's Word. The task of redeemed men since the beginning of Christ's Church, has been to fulfill the Great Commission, and this is one of the reasons we remain in the world after we are saved.

In addition, we know that during the Great Tribulation, which many believe closely follows the Rapture of the Church (Matthew 24:40; I Thessalonians 4:16), God extends new mercy to unbelievers then living. Revelations 6:9, and 7:3-14 speak of new believers who have responded to God's final visitation of mercy: 144,000 Israelites, and innumerable Gentiles who are martyred for their faith. See also, Malachi 4:5-6; Revelation 11:3, 13.

If this be so, and we believers previously lived among these final recipients of God's fresh mercy, who knows if recollections of our faithful witness, confirmed by the Church's sudden departure from earth, might not be factors eliciting their Great Tribulation visitations and responses to salvation. After all, Luke 19:44 says we are to witness by the example of our lives so that the unsaved may respond and glorify God at the time of their visitation.

God calls us to be his voice, hands, and feet in winning sinners to Jesus so they may also discover and glorify God for his mercy in redeeming, ransoming, and reconciling sinners with God. By our witnessing, evangelism and missionary work, God is glorified by the willing actions of submissively obedient sinners who respond to the Gospel's call, as well as by the obedience of believers to whom the responsibility of witnessing has been given. God has honored us by accomplishing the realization of His eternal purpose — the growth of the Body of Christ — through the efforts, responses, and decisions of believers.

Jesus has vanquished Satan and invested His Church with "authority... over all the power of the enemy; and nothing shall hurt you" (Luke 10:19). Jesus has given His Church "the keys of the kingdom of heaven, and whatever you bind on earth shall be bound in heaven, and whatever you loose on earth shall be loosed in heaven" (Matthew 16:19, 18:18). Souls in bondage to Satan are loosed and freed by the Gospel's Word of salvation, when it is witnessed or communicated by the Body to the unsaved. The power of Satan is likewise bound, when the Body is instrumental in evangelizing the unsaved.

Jesus set the example for this unloosing of men bound by sin, death, and Satan, when He raised Lazarus from the dead. As a dead being, Lazarus had no part in his resurrection, since he was called forth by Jesus. But then Jesus gave His disciples a part in the restoration of his life by instructing them to "Unbind him, and let him go" (John 11:44). Everything was accomplished by the power of God, but the Church was invited to be instrumental in freeing those who are bound in the world by administering His love and deliverance to the unsaved and infirm, so they can experience the more abundant life promised by Jesus. Among His miracles, Jesus had raised the dead, yet He promised believers: "he who believes in me will also do the works that I do; and greater works than these will he do, because I go to the Father" (John 14:12). Participating in God's miracle of bringing a dead soul to life may be one of the works Jesus mentions, as we present God's promise of eternal spiritual life to spiritually dead souls, so the Holy Spirit can quicken those dead in trespasses.

Jesus has the power of new life, and we are delegated to lead the spiritually impoverished to Jesus, to unbind them and loose them from the world by transmitting God's unconditional love and care, as ambassadors of God's comfort and encouragement. Joy is also other-oriented and directed outwardly, in service to others to the glory of God. Jesus died that "he might destroy him who has the power of death, that is, the devil, and deliver all those who through fear of death were subject to lifelong bondage" (Hebrews 2:14-15).

Because witnessing involves the struggle for souls of the unsaved, and the liberation of those in bondage to Satan, we can expect this activity to be hotly contested by the evil realm. Ephesians 6:12 reminds us: "For we are not contending against flesh and blood, but against the principalities, against the powers, against the world rulers of this present darkness, against the spiritual hosts of wickedness in the heavenly places." We can expect Satan to accuse us of our unworthiness to speak for Christ; to threaten us with the worldly contempt or disdain we will encounter if we expose our own beliefs to scrutiny by others. He may use the very men in his bondage to discourage our efforts and reject us as Christ's emissary. Yet, the battle is the Lord's, and we are given "the whole armor of God" for these battles of the Church-militant (Ephesians 6:13).

We must never forget that our witnessing is merely communicating the Gospel message, and that we are to entrust the persuasion and conviction of others to the Holy Spirit, for this is God's enterprise and we are but messengers. Hence, we must "Pray at all times in the Spirit, with all prayer and supplication" (Ephesians 6:18). We are insinuated into spiritual warfare, and our enemy is Satan, not the unbeliever captured in his power, whom God loves. Hence, "The law and the prophets were until John; since then the good news of the kingdom of God is preached, and every one enters it violently" (Luke 16:16). "From the days of John the Baptist until now the kingdom of heaven has suffered violence, and men of violence take it by force" (Matthew 11:12).

We must never forget that we are in the midst of violent spiritual warfare, but "the battle is the Lord's" (I Samuel 17:47), and "the weapons of our warfare are not worldly but have divine power to destroy strongholds" (2 Corinthians 10:4). We have the Word of truth, the power of prayer, the Great Commission, and the blessing of the Lord in these endeavors.

God intends the New Birth to originate through communication of the Good News to the unsaved by a believer, a member of the Church, the Body of Christ. You likely received the light of the Gospel through the instrumentality of another person (Romans 10:14), and you in turn must be the means by which the Gospel is witnessed to others. Believers are constituted as "servants of Christ and stewards of the mysteries of God" (I Corinthians 4:1). It is "through the church" that "the manifold wisdom of God might now be made known to the principalities and powers in the heavenly places" (Ephesians 3:10). Believers are God's agents for sharing the Gospel of salvation, which brings about the new Birth by grace through faith.

This corresponds with our greatest expression of deepest love and concern toward others, because it communicates the gift of life, itself. When the joy of the Lord and the fullness of the Holy Spirit are realities in a Christian's life, they shout for release into the world so they can be shared with all others who desperately need salvation. The unsaved are doomed without Jesus, and the knowledge of their destruction should motivate us to present the Gospel of God's love, which also inspires our love for the lost in need of salvation. If they will not respond to God's love through Christ, then they should hear the Gospel's warning of their eternal damnation through Satan.

Compassion for the plight of the unsaved accounts for the scroll, which John was commanded to eat, being "bitter to your stomach, but sweet as honey in your mouth" (Revelation 10:9). John was called to prophesy both the sweet redemption of believers and the bitter destruction of unsaved men at God's great white throne Judgment of the dead (Revelation 20:12). God loves the sinner, but His Judgment must be executed against inveterate, unrepentant rebels who will not accept the free gift of salvation and forgiveness in Christ. God respects a sinner's free and final choice to bear his own sins and their consequences of destruction, rather than be covered by the Blood of Christ.

God has commissioned and allowed believers to help prepare men and Creation for the Kingdom of God by "entrusting to us the message of reconciliation. So we are ambassadors for Christ, God making his appeal through us" (2 Corinthians 5:19-20). The process is arduous because God uses imperfect men as agents to facilitate the perfection of other men by the New Birth, and entrusts the completion of Christ's Body to them. He has delegated the success of the enterprise, the growth of the Body of Christ, to us. Jesus says: "you shall receive power when the Holy Spirit has come upon you: and you shall be my witnesses to the end of the earth" (Acts 1:8; see also, Psalm 51:12-13).

The growth of the Church, by adding new Born-Again men to the Body of believers is accomplished by God, according to Acts 2:47: "And the Lord added to their number day by day those who were being saved" (see also, Isaiah 9:7; I Corinthians 1:9, 3:6-7). In Old Testament times God delivered the Israelites from Egypt, using Moses as His deputy, and required the people to respond to Moses' leadership by faith. Yet, the call was from God to His people, and His power "drew them with cords of a man, with bonds of love" (Hosea 11:1,4).

Just as sinners are free to reject the message of salvation, so believers are free to shirk their responsibility to witness for Jesus. If we do, we will reap the whirlwind of unregenerate men continuing to work evil in our world, because we did not share the transforming power of Jesus with them. More importantly, we are given personal responsibility as watchmen for the immortal souls of the unsaved persons within the zone of our witness (Ezekiel 3:17-19). No doubt our zeal and concern for saving souls would increase if we seriously considered the consequences of a damned soul separated from God and lost for eternity because of our indifference and inaction.

God is sovereign and all-powerful, and He will accomplish the salvation of whom He wills. However, the possibility that God may make special provision, and still deliver those ignorant of Christ's salvation, because they recognize God in the natural universe around them (Romans 1:19-20), does not excuse us from our duty to share the light of the Gospel with all the world. If we fail to preach the truth, we are condemned for our inaction, which contributes to sinners remaining lost. Ezekiel 3:18 warns the watchman over Israel: "When I say unto the wicked, Thou shalt surely die; and thou givest him not warning, nor speakest to warn the wicked from his wicked way, to save his life; the same wicked man shall die in his iniquity; but his blood will I require at thine hand." St. Paul acknowledged the continuing New Testament responsibility to preach the Word to the unsaved: "For necessity is laid upon me. Woe to me if I do not preach the gospel!" (I Corinthians 9:16).

Believers are also privileged instruments chosen by God to overcome evil in the world by the creation of new spiritual beings who respond to the Gospel. If we fail to perform our duty, we risk suffering the consequences of continued evil and death in this world, perpetrated by unregenerate men we did not seek to evangelize. We will encounter and wrestle against evil men who know nothing of God and reject His Word and authority as they pursue evil purposes against believers. Yet, if we never took the time or effort to introduce them to Jesus Christ, their only possible Redeemer and Perfecter, our silence is a contributing cause to their ongoing rejection of Christianity.

The heart of the problem is the problem of the heart in unsaved men, and Jesus is the only solution. Men can be reformed only by the complete spiritual transformation of the New Birth, which comes by grace through faith in Christ. If, in our lethargy we offer no hand to lift them up spiritually; fail to pray for their deliverance; raise no voice of protest; marshal no defense against drug-dealers, crime lords, and terrorists, how can we expect to change, or at least neutralize them? Meaningful social change is accomplished only through individuals transformed by the saving power of the new Life of Christ in them. Their spiritual regeneration and transformation is the guarantee of less sin from them, thereafter.

We may also be privileged to accelerate the Second Coming of Christ by our witness to the Gospel. Matthew 24:14 commands: "And this gospel of the kingdom will be preached throughout the whole world, as a testimony to all nations; and then the end will come." 2 Peter 3:10-12 clarifies the connection: "But the day of the Lord will come like a thief... and the earth and the works that are upon it will be burned up. Since all these things are thus to be dissolved, what sort of persons ought you to be in lives of holiness and godliness, waiting for and <u>hastening the coming of the day of God</u>." Our prayer for, and witnessing to, the unsaved can have an impact on the fullness of Christ's Body, which in turn facilitates when "the end will come." The Church cannot bring heaven on earth, but it can contribute to the fuller individual life Jesus brings to sinners.

Parenthetically, cooperating in the Holy Spirit's transforming power to accomplish our Christ-likeness, can also hasten the Coming of the Lord by accelerating individual progress toward glorification. More, we can pray regularly and fervently for the Coming of the Lord, knowing God answers prayer, and can hasten the Second Coming.

The witness of our lives reflects God's transforming power to perfect faith and holiness. We incarnate Jesus in the world, so He shares, perhaps even experiences, whatever happens to us. And if we fail, through sinning, His reputation is tarnished in the world, and His saving power is misrepresented to skeptical sinners. Our obedient lives contribute to effective witnessing by the example of a submissive, righteous life, empowered by God. I Peter 2:12,15 inculcates: "Maintain good conduct among the Gentiles, so that in case they speak against you as wrong-doers, they may see your good deeds and glorify God on the day of visitation... For it is God's will that by doing right you should put to silence the ignorance of foolish men." See also, Matthew 5:16 and I Peter 3:1-2. Was it not St. Francis who urged: "By all means witness — and speak if you must." A discernibly transformed life is what makes our witness believable, For, we are not only witnesses, but constitute the evidence, if our lives prove the transforming power of the Gospel, as the love of God flows from our lives.

The dire fate befalling the unsaved should inspire gratitude both for one's own salvation and for the privilege of participating in the New Birth of another. Angels may proclaim the Gospel during the great tribulation (Revelation 14:6), but until then, God has chosen saved men as His instruments to witness to lost sinners. The angel of God did not declare the Gospel to Cornelius, but sent him to find Peter, who did (Acts 10:4-39).

Every disciple is charged with the Great Commission, and has the opportunity this very day, to witness to, and pray for unsaved loved ones before their destruction is determined. You also have the privilege to "Love your enemies and pray for those who persecute you" (Matthew 5:44), lest they be eternally lost in the silence and absence of your loving witness and intercession. The Word is the seed planted in the hearts of hearers of the Gospel. Prayer is essential before planting, to prepare the soil of the soul to be broken and receptive.

We are also given the privilege of financing evangelism and missions by supporting their expense, so that the Gospel may be preached to all the world. In this way, we can express our love for other men by sharing and sending them our most precious treasure — the Good News of salvation in Jesus Christ. When we fail to tithe and give to missions, we imperil the Great Commission. For, poverty severely limits the Church's outreach ministry of witness and evangelism.

Romans 10:14-15 recognizes the need to support preachers sent to reach the unsaved: "And how are they to hear without a preacher? And how can men preach unless they are sent?" (See also, I Corinthians 9:11-14; 2 Corinthians 2:14-16). From our abundance we are called to finance the Gospel message to the world, and God will provide sufficient financing and necessary healing to sustain this advancement of the Kingdom. However, if the tithe is withheld, the house of God is forsaken, and the ministry scatters (Nehemiah 13:10).

Christ's Great Commission to witness the Gospel to all the world is ongoing, because we each have to reach our own generation, which has the same desperate need for salvation.[90] Jesus told the disciples: "As the Father has sent me, even so I send you... Receive the Holy Spirit. If you forgive the sins of any, they are forgiven; if you retain the sins of any, they are retained" (John 20:23). Even if the passage refers to some priestly authority to forgive sins, all believers are endowed because Jesus has made all his disciples a royal priesthood of believers (I Peter 2:9). Matthew 16:19 likewise assures: "whatever you loose on earth shall be loosed in heaven," which applies to the unsaved beings freed from bondage to sin when they receive the Gospel, and put their faith in Jesus.

If the unsaved hear the Gospel of salvation, learn about Gods grace, forgiveness and remission of sins, and respond to them, then you have been instrumental in your call to facilitate God's mercy and forgiveness of their sins. If they spurn the Gospel, they remain bound by their sins. If a believer does not spread the light of the Gospel to the unsaved, then their sins are retained in darkness; hence our obligation to witness for Jesus. If believers fail to witness for Jesus, they have betrayed God's trust in them as messengers under the Great Commission, and momentarily frustrated God's desire that all men be saved through the Gospel entrusted to the Body of believers.

THE GIFTS OF HEALING TO CONFIRM WITNESS

A believer is blessed with wealth, partly to confirm God's benevolence toward those in covenant with him. Wealth is also meant to be shared to evidence and express the principal attributes of Christian holiness, love, and consideration toward others. Likewise, a believer is blessed with good health, partly to provide a means for enjoying the more abundant life Jesus promises, but also to enable and sustain his loving witness for others. He may also be blessed with the Holy Spirit's "gifts of healing" for others (I Corinthians 12:9,30) to spread the Gospel and support this loving evangelism to others. Healings may confirm a believer's authority and the Word's authenticity whenever the Gospel of Jesus Christ is witnessed to others. God uses believers to deliver the Kingdom of God to the unsaved through the Word, and he still confirms their witness by supernatural events, such as the sign or blessing of healing (Matthew 28:19-20; Mark 6:15-18).

Clearly, every gift of healing is not restricted to confirming the Gospel message communicated by believers to the unsaved, but there is Scriptural authority to the effect there are <u>some</u> occasions when the gifts of healing are intended for God's purpose of evangelism.

Scripture reveals that health is not always an end in itself, simply to be selfishly enjoyed by a believer. Rather, it is a tool by which a healthy, vital servant may lovingly minister to the unsaved, and draw them to Jesus, better to serve and build the Body of Christ. St. Paul said that his preaching was not by persuasive words of wisdom, but by "demonstration of the Spirit and power, that your faith might not rest in the wisdom of men but in the power of God" (I Corinthians 2:4-5). The Gospel's effectiveness is not in the persuasions of witnesses, but in the Word, confirmed by the Holy Spirit applying the miraculous power of God in healing and forgiveness.

Jesus coupled evangelism with healing signs and wonders when He sent the twelve Apostles out: "he called the twelve together and gave them power and authority over all demons and <u>to cure diseases,</u> and he sent them out to preach the kingdom of God and <u>to heal</u>" (Luke 9:1-2).

Jesus then appointed seventy disciples as laborers in the Lord's harvest, whose witness would be corroborated by supernatural signs of healing: "Carry no purse, no bag, no sandals... And remain in the same house... eat what is set before you; <u>heal the sick in it</u> and say to them, 'The kingdom of God has come near to you' (Luke 10:4-9).

Jesus ordained the Spirit's power to fortify the witness of His early disciples, saying: "you shall receive power when the Holy Spirit has come upon you; and you shall be my witnesses in Jerusalem... and to the end of the earth" (Acts 1:8). Jesus intends us to witness to His Gospel when we have received supernatural power, sometimes manifested in power to heal, cast out demons, and do miracles, all to His glory. The purpose of these gifts is to verify and promote our loving service of witness to others. When supernatural power is manifested, then the unsaved will ask, "what must I do to be saved?", as the Roman Jailer at Acts 16:30.

THE PRIVILEGE OF INTERCESSORY PRAYER

Most of the petitions offered up by inexperienced prayers seek personal benefit, first materially, and then for personal growth spiritually. We may then progress to seeking personal empowerment by God to serve Him better as we minister to the needs of others in loving stewardship. Intercessory prayer may develop concurrently, in which we petition God to minister directly to the needs and wants of others. Our intercessions may begin with the needs of those closest to us as family or friends, and then expand to the needs of sufferers in hospitals and prisons, mourners, fellow Christians, and the unsaved.

We are privileged to pray for all those in any kind of distress. We must especially pray for the conviction and conversion by God's enabling, of the unsaved souls to whom the Gospel will be witnessed. We are to pray that believers are motivated to go and witness to the lost, for "The harvest is plentiful, but the laborers are few; pray therefore the Lord of the harvest to send out laborers into his harvest" (Matthew 9:37-38).

When we pray for the gifts and fruit of the Holy Spirit, the joinder and benefit of other believers gives effect to one's prayers. Indeed, the whole concept of intercessory prayer necessitates involvement of the Church in the welfare of each individual member. Such prayers offered for the benefit of others are the ultimate expressions of love, since their selfless intercessions are totally other-oriented.

Intercessory prayer works because it articulates selfless love for others in action. The motive is not personal gain, but love. Similarly, tithing works when it lovingly seeks to share God's wealth with those less fortunate, rather than appropriate more for oneself. God's formula for making the Church interdependent and One Body requires Christians to pray for one another, and act in concert with one another unselfishly, to be most effective. Likewise, the dominant motive in prayer should be for guidance to devote wealth which one receives from God for God's purposes of sharing it with others. Thus, Acts 20:35 recognizes and establishes the ordinance of love: "It is <u>more blessed</u> to give than to receive." Receiving God's gifts is a blessing, but sharing them with others is an even greater blessing. It is naïve to say God gives wealth only for that purpose, for we know that He promises to reward faithful obedience with prosperity. However, an unselfish prayer, motivated by gratitude, thanksgiving, and love from, of, and for God, seeking to serve as God's agent to meet the needs of others, often seems to invite God's favorable response to our prayers.

Prayer is a conferral of dignity upon man in this special way. When we offer intercessory prayers, man becomes freely involved on behalf of another to influence affairs by seeking God's intervention in the world. We are entrusted with promoting the welfare of the Body of Christ by intercessory petitions on behalf of our brothers and sisters in the Lord, as well as the unsaved. We offer intercessory prayers that loved ones may be saved, depending on God to work or persuade the transformation of hardened hearts, and effect the conversion of lost souls. When we pray, God promises to use His power to draw men to Himself and open their understanding that they may respond to His light. Jesus says at John 12:32 that if He is lifted up, not only literally to Heaven, but also figuratively by our witness, he will draw all men to Himself. The Church can initiate national revival by praying for it. "If my people, which are called by my name, shall humble themselves, and pray, and seek my face, and turn from their wicked ways, then will I hear from Heaven, and will forgive their sin, and will <u>heal their land</u>" (2 Chronicles 7:14).

Abraham's faith was counted as righteousness (Romans 4:3), and he was able to intercede for Sodom by asking God to withhold punishment of the city for the sake of tem righteous men in it (Genesis 18:32). Moses interceded for the Israelites when they had worshipped the molten calf, by reminding God of His promises to bless them, "And the Lord repented of the evil which he thought to do unto his people" (Genesis 32:14).

God directs intercessory prayer as a means to keep us interested and concerned in the needs of others. It was only after Job interceded for his friends to gain a blessing for them that they were forgiven, and God "restored Job's losses" and "gave Job twice as much as he had before" (Job 42:10).

Jesus interceded in prayer for Peter and the Apostles, that Satan would be denied his demands to have them and sift them like wheat (Luke 22:31). Even though Peter had already been chosen by God to witness for the Gospel, Jesus prayed to preserve Peter intact so he could fulfill his calling. I Timothy 2:2 exhorts us to pray for our leaders, that they may be "godly and respectful in every way," so our lives may be quiet and peaceable.

St. Paul appealed to the "brethren, by our Lord Jesus Christ and by the love of the Spirit, to strive together with me in your prayers to God on my behalf, that I may be delivered from the unbelievers" (Romans 15:30-31). He urged believers to "Pray at all times in the Spirit, with all prayer and supplication... for all the saints, and also for me, that utterance may be given me in opening my mouth boldly to proclaim the mystery of the gospel" (Ephesians 6:18-19; See also, Philippians 1:19).

Our prayers can have a great impact on outcomes because God's Sovereign power chooses to accommodate and fulfill man's participation by prayer. Yet, that involvement places a great responsibility on believers to pray and act as they are expected to, according to the plan and purpose of God. We are blessed with comfort, strength, and endurance, knowing that other believers in the Body of Christ can intercede with God in our behalf, just as Jesus and the Holy Spirit intercede for us (Romans 8:26).

When we are aware another person has been inspired by the Holy Spirit to pray for us, and we realize they are devoting their precious time and Godly service to improve our lives, that knowledge cannot help but motivate us to more noble, loving, and useful pursuits. It is much like responding to our Mother's prayers by trying to live up to her hopes and faith expressed in her prayers for us. Our lives are enriched and flooded with joy, as we see the love of God manifested in the prayers of another lovingly offered in our behalf. And it becomes increasingly difficult to squander our time vainly, when we know someone else is simultaneously seeking to enhance our wellbeing.

Widespread belief in the efficacy of prayer is confirmed by experiential knowledge that personal prayers are answered by God. And answered far too often and too precisely to be mere coincidence. The impress of His hand on events becomes unmistakable. Thus, God's responses verify and attest to His intervention in time and the world in answer to prayer.

Eventually, we will learn how foolish it is to think that we are too busy doing God's work to take time to pray. We will learn that the more we turn over to God in prayer, the more He will do to spare us from spending time and effort. For example, when we entrust our witness to God in prayer, he will make all arrangements for evangelism, including facilities, and ready-made receptive audiences, to hear the Gospel. The more we pray, the less we need to accomplish by our own power and organization. Martin Luther taught that the busier we become, the more we need to entrust matters to God in prayer. For, God will intervene in answer to prayer, with a loving concern for every significant detail of our lives.

When we do not offer up intercessory prayers for others, just as when we do not exercise our gifts of the Spirit for the edification and growth of the Body, then others may be denied the healing, deliverance, prosperity, and even the salvation, which God grants by the prayers of His people. As a member of Christ's Church, as a part of His Body, we are called to minister to, witness to, and pray for others, both saved and unsaved. When we fail in our ministry on behalf of Christ, His Body suffers at the hands of unredeemed men, whose lives have never been elevated materially; nor their hearts softened in response to our prayers; nor their spirits transformed by the miracle of New Birth in response to the Gospel ordained to be witnessed by us. In the stewardship of witnessing, our talking to God about men is as important as talking to men about God. Preparatory and intercessory prayer in isolation or in gatherings with others, is as important as public ministry to fulfill the Great Commission.

Because God has left us in the world as His legates to change sinners by our mercy, example, and witness in the name of Christ, we are exposed and susceptible to persecutions by, and the evil of, unsaved men in the world. Since God is aware of this consequence, the blessings of our participation in evangelism must be too precious to remove us from the midst of unredeemed men, despite their penchant to harm believers. Likewise, our participation in developing personal holiness is too important to remove us from the presence of other men. For, how could we learn unselfishness, tolerance, patience, concern for others, or loving stewardship without being in the midst of our brothers in the Lord, and the needy?

God keeps us in the world, despite the fact natural men with evil motives of greed, hatred, lust, and pride are capable of inflicting harm on others. Psalm 27:12 petitions: "Deliver me not over unto the will of mine enemies: for false witnesses are risen up against me, and such as breathe out cruelty." Psalm 37:14 adds: "The wicked have drawn out the sword, and have bent their bow, to cast down the poor and needy, and to slay such as be of upright conversation."

The panoply of evil is outlined at 2 Timothy 3:2-5: "For men will be lovers of self, lovers of money, proud, arrogant, abusive, disobedient to their parents, ungrateful, unholy, inhuman, implacable, slanderers, profligates, fierce, haters of good, treacherous, reckless, swollen with conceit, lovers of pleasure rather than lovers of God, holding the form of religion but denying the power of it." See also, I Peter 2:18.

Satan and the demons he rules are not the only creatures who initiate suffering, by acting independently of God. Since God has given freedom to men to believe, choose, and obey God voluntarily, it follows that each one, as well as other men, will be principal sources of suffering in the world whenever there is laxity in personal responsibility.

Since God has given freedom to men to believe and choose God voluntarily, it follows that oneself and other men will be principal sources of suffering when they corrupt that freedom. These categories of free beings are tolerated by God, within His permissive will, even though they produce much of the evil, torment, tribulation, travail, persecution, and suffering in the world. A terrorist or drunk person operating a vehicle can produce much harm to others, but this is clearly not God's will or desire. It is the corruption and distortion of one human's freedom bringing harmful consequences to others.

Other men can cause pain by perverting their freedom, initially at the instigation of Satan, and afterwards by the devices of their own vile, carnal inventions. Satan's demonic hierarchy also is free to foment persecution, temptation, and privations in the world's natural and material environments, through the instrumentality of other men. Persecutions by other men are also done freely, according to the evil of their unredeemed nature. A great deal of trouble originates from other beings, and is beyond our power to prevent or avoid, due to the freedom of others to do wrong or neglect to do what they ought. There will be no deliverance from these evils unless and until we are removed from this world, or God supernaturally transforms their unredeemed hearts through belief in the transmitted Word of grace.

SUFFERING FROM HUMAN PERSECUTION

Jesus recounts Satan's five weapons for attacking the Word at Mark 4:17-18: (1) tribulation; (2) persecution which arises on account of the Word; (3) the cares of the world; (4) the delight in riches; and (5) the desire for other things. Persecution or tribulation which Satan inflicts through other men "arises on account of the Word," because a believer's steadfastness in the Word is such a strong weapon against Satan.

Even the hundred-fold return of Mark 10:30, which is so eagerly embraced as a promise of prosperity, warns that disciples "receive a hundred-fold... with persecutions," from other men who recoil from godliness. New-Born men are aliens in a hostile environment, and the struggle for spiritual survival in the world is triggered by the world's contempt, persecution, and temptation (Matthew 5:10).

Jesus, Himself, as the very embodiment of God's Word, was subjected to suffering, vilification, and the agony of the Cross. At John 15:18-20, Jesus warns: "If the world hates you, know that it has hated me before it hated you. If you were of the world, the world would love its own; but because you are not of the world but I chose you out of the world, therefore, the world hates you... If they persecuted me, they will persecute you." Jesus also foretells torments inflicted by men: "they will deliver you up to tribulation, and put you to death; and you will be hated by all nations for my name's sake" (Matthew 24:9; and see also, Matthew 5:11-12, 10:22; Luke 21:22; John 15:20-24, 16:30, 17:14,16; Acts 5:41; I John 3:12-13; Hebrews 11:35-38; Philippians 1:29; 2 Thessalonians 1:5; 2 Timothy 2:9; I Peter 2:19, 3:14, 4:14,16). "Indeed, all who desire to live a godly life in Christ Jesus will be persecuted" (2 Timothy 3:12).

Jesus is an offense to the world because His righteousness convicts it of sin, and His way condemns the values and pursuits of the world. The powers and principalities of evil struggle to assert dominion over the world because they are aware they have been defeated by Jesus, and must surely relinquish control at His Second Coming (Luke 10:19; Colossians 2:15; Revelation

12:12). The carnal man may be happy enough to receive Christ's love and salvation, but he rebels against the obligations to serve by obedience, holiness or by witnessing, tithing, and loving others. The vested interests of worldliness resist being joined to Jesus' yoke, however light.

Carnal men in the world will resist the spiritual difference so readily detectable in Christians. They will seek to hamper the witness of a Christian life, or inflict trials and persecutions in retaliation against followers of Christ. The derision of friends and family about one's healing have sometimes driven a believer from the haven of divine deliverance back into ill health in the world. A businessman who openly praises his Lord may suddenly find the world shunning him as an extremist, and be persuaded to abandon his commitment to Jesus as a matter of commercial expediency.

The world's attacks may involve ridiculing the irrationality of faith, or subtle invitations to delight in the world. Their objective is to pull down righteousness to the level of worldliness. They will use cruel persecutions to drive a believer away from faith in Christ. Because of your commitment to Christ, mistreatment at the hands of men will become part of your life, unless, by the authority of Christ you resist and bind Satan, the author of these misadventures.

Modern warriors for Christ may carry the Gospel to neighborhoods inhabited by addicts and alcoholics, and be beaten, robbed, and afflicted because of the Word. A Christian may become the innocent victim of a crazed assailant's tragic, random shooting spree. A publisher may suffer financially as a result of rejecting revenue from pornographic, tobacco or liquor advertising because of his spiritual convictions. If you once languished in a dead church out of inertia or misguided loyalty, but then moved on to a Spirit-filled church, you may have encountered disheartening opposition and ostracism from some of your family or friends. Even on the highway, a vigilant driver may be victimized by another driver's momentary carelessness, or selfish use of the road.

A child may be killed by a drunk driver, or while serving in the military, and a grieving parent might bemoan, "God took my son." Yet, the cause of that death was an action by another free human being, and the only "taking" by God was to claim His child after the fact. It is wrong to infer that God intended that death to accomplish any direct purpose of His. No earthly father would devise the death of his own child; and neither is our perfect, loving Heavenly Father capable of that. Why would He accelerate a child's death by a few score years when He has all eternity to enjoy Him? Our comfort is not in the thought of God taking a loved one, but in the assurance of His receiving and keeping those we cherish.

As a Christian grows in spiritual stature, love, and faithful service, Satan's attacks often increase in vigor and intensity. Satan is little concerned with lukewarm Christians engaged in harmless gestures, ineffective pursuits, or the toothless utterances of spiritual babes. He can ignore Christians preoccupied with personal blessings and gratifications. He is hardly bothered by surreptitious distribution of tracts. For he can often steal away the seed so casually and impersonally sown. However, he must respond to activist believers who reclaim the lost for Jesus Christ. If you witness personally and sincerely, or support a dynamic, soul-winning evangelist, Satan will recognize your genuine threat to his domain, and retaliate against you.

We ought not conclude that every human act of persecution or hatred has been directly instigated by Satan. Evil men constitute an independent, self-determining cause of evil inflicted upon believers, and can act without any prompting by Satan. An evil man, like Adolph Hitler or Joseph Stalin, served an apprenticeship under Satan, where he was trained by, and remained habitually and cumulatively hardened by sin. An evil man in his carnal state is a moral free agent against whom we contend. And he is so sinful apart from God, that he can sublimate his genocidal extermination of millions of people as worthy and necessary to purify humanity. One who persists in rebellious, habitual, and unrepented sin, will necessarily provoke suffering in his own life, and cause grief for those who encounter him.

COLLECTIVE RESPONSIBILITY FOR SUFFERING

Collective wrongs also produce misery, sorrow, and distress, which have as much impact upon the individual as the sins he has committed personally. God forgives the penitent, but may allow the rebellion and sin of a nation to reap the consequences ordained and foreseeable for corrupt and misdirected human freedom. In THE PROBLEM OF PAIN, C. S. Lewis estimated that eighty percent of human suffering is attributable to men hurting one another by instruments of torture, warfare, human avarice and stupidity, producing destruction, death, poverty, and overwork.

All the Old Testament Jews were collectively exiled to slavery in Egypt, and all wandered for forty years in the wilderness. When Israel disobeyed God in the desert, it had consequences for the children, who could not easily be separated from their parents, being punished by God: "And your children shall wander in the wilderness forty years, and bear your whoredoms, until your carcasses be wasted in the wilderness" (Numbers 14:33). However, God promises generally not to punish a child for "the iniquity of his father" (Ezekiel 18:17). The sins of many were imputed to all, although presumably small children were innocent and unaware of the adult infidelities which provoked God's displeasure (Jeremiah 9:13-26, 11:3-11). Surely, the German Christians who secretly detested Nazi atrocities in World War II, still suffered the same wartime and post-war deprivations as all other nationals in a defeated country.

In speaking of the Body of Christ, I Corinthians 12:26 observes: "If one member suffers, all suffer together; if one member is honored, all rejoice together." This interrelationship, mutuality, and solidarity of the Body of believers is revealed at 2 Corinthians 1:6-7: "If we are afflicted, it is for your comfort and salvation; and if we are comforted, it is for your comfort, which you experience when you patiently endure the same sufferings that we suffer... for we know that as you share in our sufferings, you will also share in our comfort."

Both Old Testament Israel and the New Testament Church were formed by God from scattered individual existences, to create a people for Himself, and for Jesus.

In modern times when a parent sins by yielding to alcoholism, gambling, or adultery there will always be consequences for other family members. Disobedient children cause untold grief for countless parents. Adam and Eve sinned with consequences for all their progeny. When the kings of Israel were evil, the whole nation suffered their punishment, and when modern leaders disdain, forsake, and expel the values of God, the whole body politic shares the dire consequences of God's eventual withdrawal.

In the Old Testament, Jeroboam became so evil, idolatrous, and corrupt that "this thing became sin unto the house of Jeroboam, even to cut it off the face of the earth' (I Kings 13:34). His wickedness corrupted the nineteen Kings of Israel who followed him, and affected their subjects for two centuries (2 Kings 13:2, 15:9, 17:9, 24:19). Moreover, his evil and idolatry so corrupted Israel that the Lord was provoked to abandon the nation (I Kings 14:16).

The wickedness of King Manasseh corrupted his nation, Judah, provoking God to bring evil against it (2 Kings 21:11-12). David's pride was stirred by Satan to conduct an unauthorized, intrusively provocative census of the armed men in Israel (I Chronicles 21:1). Consequently, "God was displeased with this thing; therefore he smote Israel;" and killed seventy thousand men with pestilence; and partially destroyed Jerusalem (I Chronicles 21:7-15).

In Judaism one gains identity and significance as a member of the community, while in Christianity one is converted as an individual, and the community emerges as the joining together of all converted individuals.[91] A person is both an individual and a part of the corporate unity of his culture, and each member bears responsibility jointly and severally for collective acts.

We are all part of, and confined within, a closed system in our world. Where ever sin originates, it must eventually wash upon our shore. An auto accident which results from a moment's inattention and causes the death of an innocent bystander is the result of human negligence, although Satan may have distracted the driver with personal worry, fear, or intoxication.

Some themes in Jewish thought hold that if man is to accept the benefits of communal living by taking advantage of all its good, there is nothing unjust about the individual sharing in retribution imposed on his community as punishment for society's unrepented iniquities. After all, man is part of all mankind in relation to God, and if human society collectively needs expiation for its sins, the individual should shoulder his share of the responsibility in the community which needs repentance.

Jewish tradition holds that every person is responsible in some way for the injustices perpetrated by the state, economy or institutions of which he is a part. If he does not actively commit the act, or benefit directly from it, the individual is at least guilty of passive acquiescence by tolerating it instead of effectively opposing and protesting the injustice. Hence, the modern notion that unless one is actively engaged in the solution, he constitutes part of the problem. Indeed, if one part of a body sins, we do not say only that member has sinned, but rather, the entire body is guilty and reaps the consequences of iniquity. We do not say that the criminal's offending hand is guilty because it wielded the weapon involved, but we regard the entire person as guilty.

The sight of innocent suffering summons Christians to serve God by alleviating, and if possible removing, the cause of others' afflictions. Can American Christians who have stood by silently, escape the condemnation for public policies which sanction, encourage, and accommodate divorce, sodomy, out-of-wedlock children, disintegrated families, and abortion, the murder of pre-born babies? If the nation deserves to be punished for its transgressions, are not those who have acquiesced by silence also culpable? Has not Christian America passively concurred in its own deterioration?

Individuals will die from various ills abroad in the world until collective mankind learns, and someone masters new skills of medicine and pharmacy. Until we learn and apply the love of Christ to principles of economics, sociology and government, we can expect crime, war, free markets and bureaucratic programs to bungle the distribution of wealth because of greed, selfishness, ignorance, and social confusion. Collective free choices motivated only by selfishness and personal gain, must lead to social inequities on a large scale.

It is inconsistent for Christians to lift up and restore one alcoholic, prostitute, or gambler and leave the system unchallenged and beyond correction, which nurtures their sins. It is naïve to help a slave, while tolerating a system of slavery or any social or economic system which produces individual suffering and injustice. Christians need both to help the individual and to rectify inequities in the system, until individual men are changed by the New Birth. We need both an individual Gospel and a social Gospel which weaves Christian values of love and service into the national tapestry. We should not let militancy or tactics of dissidents dissuade us from listening to their grievances and evaluating the legitimacy of their complaints. Christians need to be fair-minded and evaluate the claims of the disenfranchised among us, who exhibit hatred toward our institutions and policies. Some are called by God to serve by changing world conditions through social legislation and policies to reflect His love.

If a disciple makes no effort to witness for Jesus in his community, he ought not be surprised when an unsaved neighbor breaks the law and robs him of property or supplies drugs to his children. A disciple may languish in a vapid, unedified church, if he fails to engage in intercessory prayer, or lovingly reprove sinning brothers. Godly values and a relationship with a personal Saviour would do much to solve social ills, but the individual Christian and the Church must first fulfill their duty of evangelism. There would be a noticeable reduction of suffering if the Church would only fulfill its ministry of loving service and evangelism by better following Jesus' example.

In the same passage where Jesus tells us: "Do not resist one who is evil. But if any one strikes you on the right cheek, turn to him the other also," Jesus also gives His prescription for overcoming evil: "Love your enemies and pray for those who persecute you" (Matthew 5:39,44). If we fail to pray for the transformation of others who persecute us, we will not see their conversion in this world, which can be accomplished only by the Holy Spirit's supernatural power. If we fail to love our enemies, we will do nothing to turn their hatred into reciprocal love, in the name and by the power of Jesus Christ. If we respond to hostility with hostility, we will never break the cycle of retaliatory hatred. If we did not deserve their hatred initially, we will have earned it later by re-cycling their evil, and failing to obey Scripture's prescription for facilitating the changed hearts of our enemies.

In much the same spirit, Galatians 6:1 counsels: "Brethren, if a man is overtaken in any trespass, you who are spiritual should restore him in a spirit of gentleness. Look to yourself, lest you too be tempted." What man means for evil, God intends for good, and uses believers to accomplish that good. Thus, I Thessalonians 5:15 says: "See that none of you repays evil for evil." This does not require Christians to offer no resistance or self-defense when passivity would endanger self-preservation, but reason and peaceful negotiation should always be our first resort.

God has chosen to leave us in the society of other men, rather than allow us to serve him in monastic isolation. We are called by the Great Commission to be His agents in proclaiming the Gospel to the unsaved. We are joined inseparably as members of one Body, the Church, of which Christ is the Head, and made totally dependent upon one another as instruments in administration of spiritual gifts by the Holy Spirit. The proximity, relationship, and interdependence among social beings exposes us to endless afflictions and persecutions at the hands of others. Very little we do is in isolation, or without consequences for others.

Famine in the world is not attributable to God, since by any standard He has provided earthly fecundity capable of supplying the needs of the billions inhabiting the planet. There is enough food to feed everyone, but human political regimes and economic structures have greedily imposed inequities in the distribution system. Famine in Russia or India is balanced by abundant production in Canada and the United States, which is provided by God for the benefit of all.

The selfishness of man, or the poor stewardship of Christians can delay the Providence of God within the unified family of man and the Body of Christ. God will not usually interfere when His plan for abundance and sharing is thwarted by corrupted human freedom. God seldom explains suffering, but teaches and convicts wrongdoers of their sin, once he gets their attention, He enables and sustains endurance by afflicted victims, until His church acts in His behalf.

God has constituted a family of man, and not opted for isolationist, separatist individualism, but ordained society as best for man. We may have the burden of caring for others, but it also entitles us to receive support, encouragement, instruction, and edification when we need it from others. Nothing undeserved would ever reach us within a rugged individualism of selfishness and hostility, but we would never share in the love, nurture, inventions, arts, or accomplishments of others in society. If we accept such benefits from the family of man, should we not also bear the consequences of our family's ignorance, folly and greed?

God logically can provide only one choice among alternatives. And membership in the family of men was chosen to accomplish greater benefits for the individual while living on earth. We cannot reap the joys and advantages of family life without its sorrows, obligations, and liabilities. God expects us to depend on one another, and satisfy another's reliance on us. If two consequences flow from a particular arrangement, we cannot elect to have only the good one without the other. Yet, if we were to abolish proximity and social interdependence with other persons, simply because they are capable of afflicting us, we would also lose the blessing of human society, intercourse, support, and encouragement.

A father could stop quarrels and fights among his sons by separating them permanently, but then they would never have the opportunity to know, help, and love one another as brothers, or enjoy the special bond of family unity, when they have shared, united against, and weathered the storm. Our caring for others' needs makes us vulnerable to their rebuffs and persecutions. But without the joy of human friendships and togetherness we would lose far greater blessings. And how many of our friendships develop over time through clashes and disagreements, as iron sharpens iron, and we learn, mutually and unselfishly to fashion our own actions to accommodate our friends, and lovingly limit our own freedom in order to expand theirs.

The causes of blessings may also carry the potential for our sufferings, but these blessings both define and nurture the human condition. Which is probably one reason why God does not eliminate suffering from our midst, or constitute the world differently. A perfect world is not simply a world without sin, but a community also filled with love and opportunity for ministry and service. A perfect field is not simply a plot free of weeds, but also a garden filled with fruit-bearing plants and flowers.[92]

Jesus has established the Church as the body which resolves conflict between believers, and removes that source of suffering. He instructs at Matthew 18:15-17: "If your brother sins against you, go and tell him his fault... But if he does not listen, take one or two others along with you... If he refuses to listen to them, tell it to the church; and if he refuses to listen even to the church, let him be to you as a Gentile and a tax collector." So the Church serves a unique function of keeping the peace between members, and by asserting its authority, of chastening wrongdoers and turning them toward righteousness.

CHAPTER 10

GOD'S BLESSING OF PARTICIPATION IN HOLINESS

"My son, do not regard lightly the discipline of the Lord, nor lose courage when you are punished by him. For the Lord disciplines him whom he loves, and chastises every son whom he receives."

– Hebrews 12:5-6.

God loved us while we were still sinners. And because He already loves us, He labors to make us lovable in fact. Because love intrinsically seeks the perfecting of the beloved, God calls His children to His holiness, and His love desires our fulfillment. His loving purpose is "that the church might be presented before him in splendor, without spot or wrinkle or any such thing, that she might be holy and without blemish" (Ephesians 5:27). Re-created in divine holiness, we can become worthy objects of God's love. God's Sovereignty will give us what we need to become fully lovable, like Christ, rather than what we may think we desire. God calls us to introspection; to grow spiritually, as well as to public ministry to serve and witness.

We have seen how the love of God blesses men with freedom to participate in divine processes of loving ministry to others and overcoming the world's allures and persecutions. In these matters, He entrusts the extent and pace of our involvement to us, treating each as a mature child. He pursues, persuades, encourages, and is ready to respond, comfort, answer prayer, intercede, and deliver, as quickly as we petition and act. In this process, our failure to utilize our spiritual gifts by invoking the power, love, and wisdom of God on behalf of our endeavors, may result in continuation of worldly evils which beset us. If we do not cooperate in these Divine initiatives, we will sacrifice growth and the benefits of fellowship which accompany maturity. So also our divine summons to be holy has consequences.

The initial goal of mortal life is to find God in Jesus, and be saved by grace through faith. Thereafter, the goals of Christian life on earth are to become spiritually like Christ, and to worship and glorify God. God has so blessed us that although He works the transformation, He entrusts our upbringing and development of holiness to our collaboration. His call to "Be Holy" blesses us with the dignity of accelerating our growth in holiness and facilitating our capacity to serve and fellowship with God. To the extent we fail or neglect to cooperate, our ministry, joy, and communion will be diluted, and our susceptibility to the assaults and iniquity of the world will be unrelieved. The blessing of human participation in development of holiness inherently involves individual suffering in the process, whenever we deviate from God's direction for our own well-being. Sometimes a spanking by a concerned Father may be purposefully administered by a loving hand to promote the supernatural process of transforming Christians to holiness in the likeness of Christ.

God's power is what transforms the New-Born man into the image of Christ and into a useful servant and collaborator for Christ. Yet, to say that "God does it all" is not to say that man does nothing whatsoever to facilitate the process. The very least we must do is pray for God to activate His power on our behalf, and then have faith He will answer this prayer. It is just as wrong to do nothing at all, as to seek to accomplish our desires by our own strength, without God. All is done by God's power, but God has chosen to work His power through man's cooperative effort. God is not a genie substituting His accomplishment for yours, but rather an Empowerer accomplishing many things through you and according to your willing collaboration. You are to cooperate in doing what God rightly calls you to do, while refusing to connive or contrive your own solutions. Yet, it is not you, but Jesus in you. You are not so much made powerful, as infused with Jesus' power, to be employed and applied on His behalf by you.

As we delve further into the phenomena of suffering in God's creation, it is well to remember that God has expressed His grace by allowing a believer to participate freely in his spiritual development. Growth in holiness glorifies the Father if and when the child freely chooses to become, and be made holy to please God. A believer also glorifies God by the obedient good works he does, and the manner in which he serves as God's steward. When we glorify God on earth it is not to cater to His vanity, but to show our loving respect, and lift Jesus up, so He will draw all men to Him (John 12:32).

A child's proper development by the grace of participation dignifies the child, and in that way glorifies the Father. Participation by man in no way detracts from God's grace when the collaboration, itself, is the very gift of grace. It is consistent with God's parental love when man is exalted or blessed with dignity, which comes from the grace of God, and ends in glorifying the Father, when man willingly responds to grace in the way God has ordained.

GOD'S BLESSING OF DIGNITY THROUGH COLLABORATION IN HOLINESS

At the New Birth, one is made into a new spirit-being and regenerated with the very character of Christ. Yet the New-Born man is still capable of sin because of his attachment to the flesh. He is no longer under bondage to sin, since Christ has set him free from Satan's control, and he can resist sin because of his new nature. It is paradoxical that on one hand God works the transformation to holiness, called regeneration, in Born-again believers, and yet requires a believer's cooperation in the lengthy process of sanctification to become like Jesus.

The Bible gives no specific reason why God chooses not to equip regenerated men with ready-made, unlearned, and unearned qualities of fully Christ-like character. We can infer that God's consideration for human dignity bestowed the gift of participation upon man to collaborate freely, or not, in his progress toward holiness. Allowing man's participation is a blessing of love and grace bestowed by God upon imperfect children, divinely empowered to grow toward spiritual perfection.

God transforms the character of believers at the New Birth, and then provides, through the Holy Spirit, ongoing sanctification so that by the time of their glorification they freely and inerrantly choose only good. God eventually makes believers incapable of evil choices, with their full concurrence. This transformation is based on the desire and obedient consent of a believer to be changed into the likeness of Christ. Freedom of choice is exercised initially by a believer to surrender evil choices forever in exchange for the privilege of right-standing and fellowship with God in Christ. We cannot do this without freely asking Jesus to enter our lives and transform and fulfill our character to be like Jesus. For this to be accomplished, we need to submit to Christ to be trained and shaped in His image. We must trust the Potter in His shaping of the clay. Discipline does not exist to deny or restrict freedom, but to train and restore us to the responsible use of enlarged perfect freedom.

God has ordained that we progress in holiness and that our progress may be initiated or accompanied by suffering. If God did away with the blessing of developed holiness so that men are simply constituted holy and have no need to learn by suffering, we would lose some human personality. We would lose the gracious exhilaration of accomplishment in cooperation with the working of the Holy Spirit. We would lose the precious opportunity to develop faith, if we never needed to depend completely upon God's grace to provide our needs. We would not be able to express our faith that the Spirit begins and perfects our spirituality, as our cooperative effort facilitates or accelerates our transformation.

If our holiness avoided the process of maturing, there would be no challenge to courageous living; no overcoming of worldly obstacles; no developmental experiences, but loss of variety in life. We might become robot-like automatons, with no need for learning, and no joy of labor's achievements or intellectual accomplishments.[93] Growth is a gift of love from an omnipotent, gracious Father to imperfect children, who are made capable of perfection only through His gift. Salvation is by grace, but successful Christian living requires cooperation with the grace God gives us to grow in holiness and achieve spiritual maturity on earth.

In this growth cycle, the Bible says we start out as 'babes in Christ'. We should then progress from little children to young men, able to invoke supernatural powers available to believers. We finally should become spiritual fathers who know God, capable of imparting His wisdom to others (I John 2:12-14). In the journey to spiritual maturity, we must feed on the Word, progressing from spiritual milk to solid food (I Corinthians 3:1-3; Galatians 4:19; Ephesians 4:12-13; Hebrews 5:12-13. 6:1; and I Peter 2:2).

Jesus compared growth of the Kingdom of God operating within individual believers, as well as the entire Body, to a grain of mustard-seed (Matthew 17:20), according to a seed-principle of fruition which takes place through a process of husbandry, gradual growth and development. Mustard seed is the smallest of all seeds on earth, "yet when it is sown it grows up and becomes the greatest of all shrubs and puts forth large branches" (Mark 4:32). Patience is necessary to let any seed grow into a "blade, then the ear, then the full grain in the ear" (Mark 4:28). The harvest cannot come until the grain is ripe (Mark 4:26-29). Although the Kingdom of God pervades a Christian's life silently, invisibly, and inwardly, there is a necessary interval of time between planting the Word and harvesting. Actual holiness is a continuing work to mature, develop, grow, and bear fruit worthy of repentance.

The spiritual process of perfectibility which begins with the New Birth and progresses until we are called home to be with the Lord, also uses the transforming agency of suffering for our sanctification. Romans 8:17 says we are children of God and joint heirs with Christ, "provided we suffer with him in order that we may also be glorified with him." 2 Thessalonians 1:5 says that persecution and affliction "is evidence of the righteous judgment of God, that you may be made worthy of the kingdom of God for which you are suffering." The same causal connection appears at I Peter 4:13; 17: "rejoice in so far as you share Christ's sufferings, <u>that you may also rejoice and be glad</u> when his glory is revealed... For the time has come for judgment to begin with the household of God." We are judged and chastened here, so we may be perfected and avoid judgment Hereafter. Indeed, faith, strength, courage, and a maturer appreciation of life's blessings will be found in the crucible of sorrow and affliction. God "disciplines us for our good, that we may share his holiness" (Hebrews 12:10). The transformation takes place in our will, to bring us into conformance, so we will choose to seek God and reflect His glory in the fruit of the Spirit.

Since God is sowing seeds of instruction in our times of trouble, then we should look forward to the times of reaping the blessings of Christ-like character which must follow; when patience has completed our perfection. Psalm 4:1 puts it: "Thou hast enlarged me when I was in distress." Psalm 126:5-6 adds: "They that sow in tears shall reap in joy. He that goeth forth and weepeth, bearing precious seed, shall doubtless come again with rejoicing, bringing his sheaves with him." One occasion for weeping is over the plight of the unsaved sinner. Yet, motivated by this concern, our witness to the Gospel will bear fruit and joy. Likewise, our efforts to cooperate in spiritual growth may be stressful, but will eventually produce joy and a harvest.

Think of those experiences where your creativity and direct participation in some process or event filled you with delight, peace, and joy of accomplishment. God has blessed us with the privilege of participation in creative spiritual processes for application in the world, using His materials and empowerment. Of necessity, when we fail to collaborate in recognizing and responding to God's instructions, He lovingly trains and prods us to renounce and turn from error toward righteousness. He will use methods of deterrence to evoke and persuade our willing compliance and change in accomplishing God's handiwork. We may be jostled, pinched, turned around, or thrown down to provoke our recognition we were headed in the wrong direction.

THE PAIN OF DETERRENCE BY DISCIPLINE

We are all familiar with God's work in chastening, chastising, and training believers to influence voluntary change in behavior and promote transformation to Christ-likeness. The pain is inherent in God's process of changing, pruning, refining, polishing, shaping, and molding us to conform to the image of Christ. The human will which has embraced sinfulness, rebellion, or disobedience, needs to be deterred, stopped, stilled, and re-directed by the intentional correction of a loving Father.

The child who lacks judgment to appreciate the harm which results from undisciplined freedom, and persists in running out into busy traffic, must be restrained and eventually forcibly taught obedience for his own safety. A loving parent may first invoke love and expressions of parental concern to elicit a response by promise of reward or appeals to the child's desire to please. If that motivation fails, the parent may threaten some punitive deterrence, such as loss of privilege. And if that fails, some slight physical discomfort, judiciously applied to the backside may be employed, all in the interests of the child's safety, and to preserve the opportunities for proper development.

After all, God is more concerned with character than comfort, and ordains Christ-likeness, not the absence of pain, as the highest good of the Christian life.[94] The purpose of earthly life after the New Birth is developing Christ-like character to fit us for God's society; not enjoyment of worldly blessings. Joy, or true happiness will be a result of that character, which is an eternal, spiritual blessing, and may not be attainable without the possibility and actuality of pain in producing character. An infinite being cannot find fulfillment in finite things. This life is your opportunity to know God and embrace Him for eternity, by responding to His one way to salvation, by grace through faith in Jesus Christ, the Saviour.

For, without Christ-likeness, we would be lacking in the fullness of loving service, ministry, witness, and ability to glorify God. We are privileged to bear correction because we are the special object of God's personal attachment. We have been sanctified as His children (John 1:12-13; Hebrews 2:11; I John 3:1). We are being trained for God's Kingdom and educated for an eternity in His presence. Consider how wretched we would be if God did not count us worthy of His chastisement, once He has ordained our cooperative participation in the process of spiritual growth.

Discipline is a sign of belonging to God, and of His love, for which we should be grateful. Correction is the badge of sonship by which God's family is identified. Without God's prodding you would never recognize your spiritual poverty or your neglect of God's fellowship. You would never fully appreciate the need to forsake worldly life-styles and traits for the higher spiritual calling. We cannot be completely spiritually transformed in the world without God re-working us, which is intrinsically painful. God is like a sculptor, using the trials of life as a hammer and chisel to shape believers from a featureless block of stone into the splendid form intended for them; the replication of Christ.

No parent is glorified by a permanently dependent adult child, who still waits to be dressed and have his shoe laces tied by daddy. Basically, power is the ability to achieve intent and purpose, and God daily demonstrates the absolute nature of His power. Yet, He relinquishes that power to allow our development by practice and training. He pushes us from the nest of security, so we can experience the joys of flight. He does not always coddle the baby crying for attention, but may allow the infant to "cry himself out," to realize he does quite well without constant parental presence. Parental withholding of aid can allow children to strengthen character, development, skill, and experience the joy of achievement, while knowing that God's forgiveness, comfort, and deliverance are always near.

Since God's supervening goal is the establishment of His Kingdom, populated by transformed children in the image of Christ, He may not insinuate His power to achieve lesser objectives, such as freeing us from momentary distress. His power is asserted to accomplish our highest good according to His plans and purposes. He has yielded His power so as to fashion character through free exercise of cooperative human will. Such self-imposed limitations are an expression of God's power and not a denial of it.

Without free will to make difficult choices, a man would never experience the joy of collaborating in his spiritual transformation, moral progress, or mature fellowship with God. Each is free to govern the pace of his own transformation to perfect holiness here on earth; free to impede his training, or facilitate the development of Christ-like character and access to all the blessings and gifts of grace it opens up for mature believers. We can yield to the sin of which we are still capable, and corrupt our privileges of freedom and participation, or we can overcome temptation, tribulation, and persecution by God's grace. Augustine put it: "Without God, we cannot. Without us, God will not." All holiness is accomplished by God's grace and power, but our embrace of sin will deter holiness, as sin reflects our rejection of God's call to obedience and submission.

Our sanctification necessarily follows the New Birth and justification. It is designed for God to supply all the motive power and transport us as in a car or plane. We need not struggle for our transformation, but simply rest in it. We are able to slow progress by putting on the brakes by sinning, or dragging our feet to provoke slowing down, but progress to glorification is ordained and inexorable for one Born-Again.

God is glorified when believers re-produce His holy character, as we are called to do, and share His loving nature with others in a tangible way. He is also glorified when we remember to thank Him for His grace in blessing us.

2 Peter 1:3-4 confirms that one purpose of blessings is to promote a disciple's holiness as he takes on the very character of Jesus: "His divine power has granted to us all things that pertain to life and godliness... by which he has granted to us his precious and very great promises, that through these you may escape from the corruption that is in the world because of passion, and become partakers of the divine nature."

Believers are to cooperate in seeking holiness, in order to be assured a continuous supply of blessings. In speaking of food and clothing, Matthew 6:33 says: "seek first his kingdom and his righteousness, and all these things shall be yours as well." The Kingdom of God consists in power (I Corinthians 4:20), so we are to seek God's power to serve His righteous purposes. Your citizenship in the Kingdom is evidenced by the righteousness, or fruit of the Spirit, which you exhibit by God's power (John 15:8). Our part in the process is receptivity to God's workings, and focusing on the spiritual blessings as we "look not to the things that are seen but to the things that are unseen: for the things that are seen are transient, but the things that are unseen are eternal" (2 Corinthians 4:18).

We would be beyond redemption if God chose to leave us in the sin and death into which we were born. Therefore, we ought to rejoice that a loving Father is concerned enough to work our transformation so we may share His very character. His orchestration of our suffering gives hope for our future. He has not despaired of us, but continues to shape new features in us. The mighty Creator of all the universe now lovingly condescends to re-create us. And He uses trials to develop steadfastness, by which "you may be perfect and complete, lacking in nothing" (James 1:4).

Samuel Rutherford observed: "God is no idle husbandman; He purposeth a crop," and God wills that suffering shall bring out the best in us, not the worst. God's objective for His children is not that they suffer, but that they become transformed to the image of Jesus; that in suffering they collaborate in developing personal holiness. God's objective is not punishment of His children, but their human spiritual growth. Man's purpose in the world is not to provoke God's wrath, but to engage with Him in creative alliance which produces Godly personality. What we become is as important as what becomes of us. Adversity is the corridor of our transformation and growth, and furnishes the passage from what we are to what we ought to be, by bringing us closer to God, His will, and His purpose for us. It is a teaching process by grace, in which believers gratefully, reliantly, and obediently must collaborate willingly to please the gracious Father who permits participation by granting the gift.

The promise of loss or punishment must be carried out if it is to remain an effective deterrent. A child's motive to obey disappears the moment he detects that promises of punishment are merely empty threats. By the same token, children must be able to rely on rewards of increased blessing for right conduct, as much as they can depend upon pain as a consequence of wrong actions. We would live in a world of chaos and anarchy, and God's chastisement would be purposeless, unless we had certain knowledge that spiritual maturity and reward will be the portion of faithful conduct.

God is constructing a spiritual edifice in believers, and the higher and grander He purposes to erect the structure, the wider and deeper He must dig the foundation. This is a principle of architecture: The higher the skyscraper, the deeper the foundation must go to bedrock, and the wider it must be dug to sustain the height. The planning and digging which go into a foundation is seldom visible, and far from dramatic, but it is essential to construction of anything which stands tall. How many Christians frustrate their spiritual growth by resisting the digging and blasting which must go into God's laying the foundation. How often do we fail to attain God's best for us because we question His painful methods and the apparent lack of measurable progress in our ascension. When God's work is unglamorous and painful in preparing our foundation, and we seem to be standing still in our spiritual development, we need to encourage ourselves in the Lord, and endure in His benevolence, providence, and sovereignty.[95]

We must accept God's correction in a spirit of gratitude that He cares enough to fit us for His companionship. Proverbs 29:17 offers this insight: "Correct thy son, and he shall give thee rest; yea, he shall give delight unto thy soul." Psalm 119:67,71,75 affirms that God lovingly afflicts believers to discipline and correct them; He is faithful and afflicts us to bring us back to obedience, toward the end of holiness. What better Teacher and Friend than God! "He is in the way of life that keepeth instruction: but he that refuseth reproof erreth" (Proverbs 10:17). "Poverty and shame shall be to him that refuseth instruction: but he that regardeth reproof shall be honored" (Proverbs 13:18). "A reproof entereth more into a wise man than an hundred stripes into a fool" (Proverbs 17:10). While "the kisses of an enemy are deceitful," "faithful are the wounds of a friend" (Proverbs 27:6), when they speak the truth for our correction. For only one who loves us cares to correct us.

Fortunately, God's Word discloses that His correction, chastening and chastisement involve discipline for deterrence of sin and rehabilitation for holiness. The sinner is driven to act rightly in holiness by deprivations provoked by his sins. Such deterrence involves learning that a penalty must be paid every time a rule is broken. God's Justice, law, and order must be reliable if His children are to grow as moral personalities. When we do prohibited acts, we must know there is a consequence which fashions and achieves deterrence and correction of wrong conduct. And we must be able to rely upon God's promised grace that life is joyful, despite setbacks, because they ultimately develop and lead to incomparable spiritual rewards, both here and Hereafter. We must know that goodness and mercy surely follow us all our days (Psalm 23:6), and that deprivation of some privilege, or even slight physical pain judiciously applied as a consequence of disobedience is essential to spare a child the greater pain inflicted by the perils of unrepented sin.

St. John Chrysostom believed that sorrow is given us on purpose to cure us of sin. And many a life has been transformed for the better in reaction to trouble and sorrow which drove out and replaced faults and failures, and produced faithful obedience with gratitude for God's grace.

We are visited with suffering so we can make the best of it, as it makes the best of us. With God in Sovereign control, there is no needless suffering. Its measures are precise and its durations exact. No part of it can be spared. God, as any loving father, dispenses instructional reproofs to His children when needed, to cultivate desirable personal and social characteristics.

God's infinite power will make His chastisements work effectively. Our loving Father will not scourge us without assurance He will turn it to our account and advantage by His infinite ability (Ephesians 3:20). In His exercise of perfect wisdom, we can be sure that God has chosen exactly the right moment, extent, intensity, and method of suffering each child needs to profit most from training. He is faithful in exposing each dark defect to His perfect light, in a loving remonstrance which seeks our spiritual perfection. Mature character results from modified behavior on man's part in response to effective stimuli. This is no doubt a trial to the frustrated child whose temporal or material demands have not been gratified or fulfilled. Yet, the future good from a cooperative, helpful, spiritual being, fit for the society of God, far outweighs the occasional unpleasantry resulting from necessary discipline.

God will use adversity to elicit a believer's cooperation in growing holy. Affliction can make us examine every nook and cranny of our lives to see how they conform to Jesus, and discover any dark sin which might be the instigator of our suffering. God graciously shows us our flaws and defects so that we may cooperate in removing them, whether or not they were the cause of our afflictions. Trouble serves that purpose, if it drives us to seek out the sins in our lives, in order to expel them. The objective of such chastening is reformation and transformation to the nature of Christ.

God clarifies the purpose of His chastisement at Amos 3:2-3: "You only have I known of all the families of the earth: therefore I will punish you for all your iniquities. Can two walk together, except they be agreed?" Israel had been chosen by God, and received intimate revelations of His love and character, as well as promised blessings of prosperity, privileges, and protection. God's special commitment to Israel should have elicited their desire to love, know, and serve Him better. When Israel's response was disobedience, God chastised them so they would learn to be in agreement with Him, and be able to walk in the fellowship with which He had blessed them. Because His Providence is so great toward them, God's people must be holy, and God provides His precise motivation through His chastisements.

THE BIBLE'S PROMISE OF CHASTENING

Chastening is not punishment, but has as its objective, making us chaste or holy. For, God "disciplines us for our good, that we may share his holiness. For the moment all discipline seems painful rather than pleasant; later it yields the peaceful fruit of righteousness <u>to those who have been trained by it</u>" (Hebrews 12:10-11). Throughout the Scriptures, man is asked to recall his collaborative part in responding to the lessons and training of chastisement and chastening. Certainly, this affects his enjoyment of spiritual blessings in this world and possibly, in the Hereafter.

Moses told the Israelites that the purpose of their wilderness experience was for chastening by God: "And he humbled thee, and suffered thee to hunger... that he might <u>make thee know</u> that man doth not live by bread only, but by every word that proceedeth out of the mouth of the Lord <u>doth man live</u>" (Deuteronomy 8:3). The connection between chastening and motivation to obedience is again made at Deuteronomy 8:5-6: "Thou shalt also consider in thine heart, that, as a man chasteneth his son, so the Lord thy God chasteneth thee. Therefore thou shalt keep the commandments of the Lord thy God, to walk in his ways, and to fear him."

Job observed that although the presence of God was not always readily apparent to him, he had no doubt that God was still working good for him: "But he knoweth the way that I take: when he hath tried me, I shall come forth as gold" (Job 23:10). Job 5:17-18 says: "Behold, happy is the man whom God correcteth: therefore despise not thou the chastening of the Almighty: For he maketh sore, and bindeth up; he woundeth, and his hands make whole."

Psalm 30:9-11 prays for deliverance by God from sin: "I was dumb, I opened not my mouth; because thou didst it... I am consumed by the blow of thine hand. When thou with rebukes dost correct man for iniquity, thou makest his beauty to consume away like a moth." Yet, God's remonstrances are always productive of growth in holiness: "For thou, O God, hast proved us: thou hast tried us, as silver is tried. Thou broughtest us into the net; thou laidst affliction upon our loins... we went through fire and through water: but thou broughtest us out into a wealthy place" (Psalm 66:10-12). Psalm 71:20 adds: "Thou, which hast shewed me great and sore troubles, shalt quicken me again, and shalt bring me up again from the depths of the earth."

Psalm 94:12-13 calls God's training and instruction a blessing: "Blessed is the man whom thou chastenest, O Lord, and teachest him out of thy law; That thou mayest give him rest from the days of adversity, until the pit be digged for the wicked." Psalm 119:67 applauds affliction administered by God: "Before I was afflicted I went astray: but now have I kept thy word. Thou art good, and doest good; teach me thy statutes." Psalm 119:75 acknowledges: "I know, O Lord, that thy judgments are right, and that thou <u>in faithfulness</u> hast afflicted me."

Proverbs 3:11-12 teaches: "My son, despise not the chastening of the Lord: neither be weary of his correction; for whom the Lord loveth he correcteth; even as a father the son in whom he delighteth." When we see God's Sovereign hand thus at work, we can give thanks for the suffering, because it makes us humble and teachable.

Proverbs 6:23 says that the "reproofs of instruction are the way of life." Proverbs 13:24 adds: "he that spareth his rod, hateth his son." Proverbs 22:15 expands that idea: "Foolishness is bound in the heart of a child; but the rod of correction shall drive it far from him." Proverbs 23:13-14 states plainly: "Withhold not correction from the child: for if thou beatest him with the rod, he shall not die. Thou shalt beat him with the rod, and shalt deliver his soul from hell." Proverbs 29:15,17 adds: "The rod and reproof give wisdom: but a child left to himself bringeth his mother to shame... Correct thy son, and he shall give thee rest."

We gain instruction and insight through the suffering we are sure to encounter "And though the Lord give you the bread of adversity, and the water of affliction, yet shall not thy teachers be removed into a corner any more, but thine eyes shall see thy teachers" (Isaiah 30:20). Adversity will bring us to an obedience which heeds the Prophets. At Isaiah 48:10, God uses language of refining precious metal: "Behold, I have refined thee, but not with silver: I have chosen thee in the furnace of affliction." Jeremiah 18:6 says: "O house of Israel, cannot I do with you as this potter? saith the Lord. Behold, as the clay is in the potter's hand, so are ye in mine hand." Lamentations 3:32 says: "But though he cause grief, yet will he have compassion according to the multitude of his mercies."

Malachi 3:3 also uses language of affliction unto righteousness: "And he shall sit as a refiner and purifier of silver: and he shall purify the sons of Levi, and purge them as gold and silver, that they may offer unto the Lord <u>an offering in righteousness</u>." See also, Job 7:18; Psalm 102:8-10; Proverbs 17:3; Isaiah 1:4-5, 1:25, 4:4, 43:2, 45:3, 48:10. and Jeremiah 9:7.

The New Testament also affirms that as we progress along the path of holiness, we can expect to be broken, pruned, and chastened to fashion character and grow spiritually in the image of Christ. The process of pressure, shaping, purging, hardship, or chastening is intended by God to elicit a spiritual response, so that holy character can develop by the inner workings of the Holy Spirit, in conjunction with the training of our faculties by man's practice of good, and willing exercise of holiness. Romans 5:3 teaches: "we rejoice in our suffering, knowing that suffering produces endurance, and endurance produces character, and character produces hope, and hope does not disappoint us." Romans 8:18 puts it: "I consider the sufferings of this present time are not worth comparing with the glory that is to be revealed to us." The blessed hope of Heaven can thus sustain a believer amidst any worldly sufferings.

God uses adversity for good, so that we can "be conformed to the image of his Son" (Romans 8:29). I Corinthians 11:32 says: "But when we are judged by the Lord, we are chastened so that we may not be condemned along with the world." Chastening is God's way of preserving us from sin after we are saved. 2 Corinthians 3:18 reveals that we "are being changed into his likeness from one degree of glory to another," and 2 Corinthians 4:16-17 explains: "Though our outer nature is wasting away, our inner nature is being renewed every day. For this slight momentary affliction is preparing for us an eternal weight of glory beyond all comparison." (See also, Colossians 3:10).

The process of adversity fits us for divine life, "eternal in the heavens. Here indeed we groan, and long to put on our heavenly dwelling... for while we are still in this tent, we sigh with anxiety... so that what is mortal may be swallowed up by life. He who has prepared us for this very thing is God, who has given us the Spirit as a guarantee" (2 Corinthians 5:2-5). Affliction and grief lead us to self-examination, "For godly grief produces a repentance that leads to salvation and brings no regret, but worldly grief produces death. For see what earnestness this godly grief has produced in you, what eagerness to clear yourselves, what indignation, what alarm, what longing, what zeal, what punishment" (2 Corinthians 7:10). Adversity opens us to receive the power of Christ, prompting St. Paul to say: "For the sake of Christ, then, I am content with weaknesses, insults, hardships, persecutions, and calamities; for when I am weak, then I am strong" (2 Corinthians 12:10).

2 Thessalonians 1:5-7 reveals that persecutions and affliction produce endurance and steadfastness: "This is evidence of the righteous judgment of God, that you may be worthy of the kingdom of God, for which you are suffering... and to grant rest with us to you who are afflicted, when the Lord Jesus is revealed from heaven with his mighty angels in flaming fire." Hebrews 12:5-6 declares: "My son, do not regard lightly the discipline of the Lord, nor lose courage when you are punished by him. For the Lord disciplines him whom he loves, and chastises every son whom he receives. It is for discipline that you have to endure." Adversity provokes our desire to change for the better, and cooperate with God in the transformation.

An ancient Greek proverb says that the root of education may be bitter, but its fruit of goodness and virtue is sweet. And God measures out suffering with specific intent to sweeten our lives with improved character for eternity. According to James 1:2-4, desired character is perfected by suffering, which allows us to share God's holiness: "Count it all joy, my brethren, when you meet various trials, for you know that the testing of your faith produces steadfastness. And let steadfastness have its full effect, that you may be perfect and complete, lacking in nothing."

I Peter 4:1-2 says: "whoever has suffered in the flesh has ceased from sin, so as to live for the rest of the time in the flesh no longer by human passions but by the will of God." I Peter 4:12-16 adds: "Beloved, do not be surprised at the fiery ordeal which comes upon you to prove you, as though something strange were happening to you. But rejoice in so far as you share Christ's sufferings that you may also rejoice and be glad when his glory is revealed. If you are reproached for the name of Christ, you are blessed, because the spirit of glory and of God rests upon you... yet if one suffers as a Christian, let him not be ashamed, but under that name let him glorify God."

The heat and flames of the refiner's fire are also used to illustrate how suffering strengthens spiritual consciousness and refines and purifies virtue, just as intense heat tempers metal on a forge, or flames separate gold from dross. I Peter 1:6-7 reveals refining as a process by which God's own people are identified and purified: "In this you rejoice, though now for a little while you may have to suffer various trials, so that the genuineness of your faith, more precious than gold which though perishable is tested by fire, may redound to praise and glory and honor at the revelation of Jesus Christ." Affliction is gold in the making for believers, and the refining process takes time, supervision, and direction, as well as intense heat to produce the precious metal.

Zechariah 13:8-9 predicts that two-thirds of mankind will be cut off and die, but God "will bring the third part through the fire, and will refine them as silver is refined, and will try them as gold is tried: they shall call on my name, and I will hear them: I will say, It is my people: and they shall say, The Lord is my God."

In the Old Testament, God also uses imagery of sifting his people as corn in a sieve, to remove impurities and coarse particles (Amos 9:9), which is similar to panning for gold, using water to sift and rinse out the dross. God alone, recognizing our potential holiness, can transmute the sorrows of this life to the gold of Heavenly blessings. He knows exactly how much adversity we need to grow progressively into the likeness of Christ and He never overtrains us by allowing too much affliction in our lives (I Corinthians 10:13).[96]

The New Testament also uses imagery of pruning; the sharp pain of cutting away what is old and useless, so that divine energy flows powerfully, and new and valuable branches may develop and thrive. Pruning is a horticulturist's method to elicit growth and stimulate fruit production by removing superfluous parts. Then the vitality of the vine is not dissipated in dead or unfruitful branches, but can concentrate on fecundity in what is spiritually valuable.

John 15:2 teaches that Jesus is the vine and God is the vinedresser: "Every branch that does not bear fruit he prunes, that it may bear more fruit." The very flowers we may regard as the luxuriant beauty in our lives may be pruned away by the Heavenly Husbandman because they are mere distractions and drains on our spirituality. Worldly loss of temporal pleasure and diminution in earthly blessings must occur before they can be replaced by fullness of life, exemption from pain, and heavenly gain in eternal joy. The fruit we are to bear, which Jesus mentions, refers to Christ-like character, the fruit of the Spirit outlined at Galatians 5:22-23. However, when man fails to cooperate, and is disobedient, then God may suspend the process of pruning His vineyard (Isaiah 5:5-7).

Scripture also speaks of chastening by the use of pressure to transform spirits to the image of Christ. The Greek word for tribulation connotes the pressure used to squeeze olives to extract oil, or crush grapes to bring forth juice. God does whatever is necessary to crush the energy of the flesh, so that man's spirit might emerge and thrive. Our afflictions for Christ's sake produce increasing levels of maturity and ability in handling trials, which promote our character and holiness. A grindstone's pressure grinds you down while it polishes you up. Our love, fruit, and strength will be stimulatcd by pressure, challenge, and trials.

There is stress and heat applied in the Potter's production of useful vessels. The clay must be beaten, worked, and squeezed to be shaped and given form. Then it must be baked in the oven's heat for structural integrity. After desired colors are applied, they must be baked in again or they will not last. The beating and heating are essential to achieve a useful, desired end product.[97]

It has been said that strong storms make strong trees. Unless man has something to resist, push against, or fight off, he may never exert any effort or invoke the divine power of the indwelling Holy Spirit to sustain him. Harsh and cruel challenge provides an adversary. It imposes a struggle without which there could be no victory over evil. It forces a contest calling for concentration on spiritual values, without which there could be no growth or profiting by experience. Jesus wants us spiritually strong so we can resist the material temptations of the world (Matthew 26:41).

This is why Jesus can teach: 'Blessed are those who are persecuted for righteousness' sake, for theirs is the kingdom of heaven. Blessed are you when men revile you and persecute you and utter all kinds of evil against you falsely on my account" (Matthew 5:10-11). When we are righteous in the Lord's service and withstand the contumely of other men, the first blessing of our submissiveness is a humble and improved character. God allows hardship so that we can overcome iniquity, and proceed to truly Christ-like character. Unless we have trials, testings and opportunities to obey and overcome, our character cannot be fully motivated, corrected, shaped, or trained.

Resistance to weight is what builds muscle. You can place body-building weights on your chest and let them crush you, or use them to advantage by movement and exertion which resists the weight and builds muscle through slow, but steady repetitions. Trials and the weight of burdens challenge our spiritual muscles of faith. They prevent atrophy and stimulate growth. They compel us to work harder and draw upon the Lord's strength to increase our own. Difficulties lift us to a higher level of faith, holiness, and Christian accomplishment. Trials purify you, strengthen your spiritual muscles, and produce a greater level of holiness.[98]

Just as the body's organs and muscles will degenerate or atrophy when they encounter no resistance because of dis-use, so one's spirit will lose healthy vigor if unexercised. Further, yielding to temptation weakens moral fiber and will recall one's human weakness, rather than divinely empowered strength, the next time it is necessary to resist temptation or combat evil. Every victory must begin with combat, and without battles a disciple could experience no victory over the world's adversity. This may be part of the reason Jesus teaches how difficult it is "for those who have riches to enter the kingdom of God!" (Mark 10:23). Their riches make their lives soft and inviting, and abundance gives no motivation to seek God or sacrifice comforts to follow Jesus.

Monumental victories require battles of epic proportions, and scars attest to surviving the cutting edge of combat. The more severe the test, the greater the triumph and rejoicing. The greater and longer our bondage to sin, the greater our victory over it. The traditional football rivalry which has been vigorously contested is usually a more meaningful victory than a romp over a weak adversary.

Another kind of pressure is exerted whenever our aims and intentions are thwarted, or our efforts frustrated because we are resisting the direction God would lead us. When a shepherd uses the rod and staff as prods to guide the sheep along the right paths, the wayward sheep persists in pursuing his own way until forcibly restrained. If a sheep starts to stray toward the edge of an undetected cliff or toward any unperceived danger, the shepherd must use whatever force is necessary to prod it back to the safety of the herd. If the sheep persists in its obstinacy, its leg may even be broken, to keep it close to the shepherd.

The spiritual man recognizes that the Good Shepherd's gracious nudging is a true blessing because it re-directs him along "the paths of righteousness" leading away from harm to fullness and contentment. The shepherd will also restrain the sheep's straying at night by physically laying across the opening of a sheepfold to keep the sheep safely in and predators out.[99] Thus, we can acknowledge "Thy rod and thy staff, they comfort me" (Psalm 23:4), since they are used not to beat us, but to protect, guide, deliver from harm, and drive away dangerous marauders which would prey upon the flock.

We may need to be trained or re-trained in <u>what</u> we should be doing to render loving service to others for God, and to be effective as a prayer warrior and witness for Jesus. We may learn the lessons of ill health, poverty, and denial of things prayed for, so that we can be entrusted with more responsible stewardship. God wants man's collaboration in producing a patient, generous, forgiving, and loving nature like Christ's. Adversity and affliction cultivate these qualities and sanctify the suffering overcomer when they elicit loving and faithful response in a Christian.

Although God's Word is the instrument and cause of our growth in holiness, we must long for it, ingest it, and internalize it. While God gives us prayer by which to communicate with Him, we will enjoy little fellowship if we do not initiate prayer, or at least sustain the conversation. God is the weaver of life's patterns, but He allows us to join in determining the fabric of our transformation, and we are enjoined to take care in our collaboration; use only materials provided by God; and employ only His techniques.

COLLABORATING WITH GOD'S GRACE FOR HOLINESS

Although regeneration is the start of our actual, progressive holiness, God has ordained that spiritual perfection be neither immediate nor automatic. He has promised spiritual perfection by the time we enter Heaven, but He has deemed it best to prolong the completion of our Godly character, while it is imparted by the Holy Spirit during our earthly sojourn. The New Birth enables us to obey God's command to be holy, and God furnishes all the power, if we will but receive it. When we confess our sins, God cleanses us of all unrighteousness (I John 1:9), which enables us to cooperate in refraining from sin.

Even though Jesus' righteousness is imputed to us at the New Birth, our actual transformation to His likeness is a gradual, lifelong process that takes time, and requires faithful, cooperative application by believers. Even after we "enter by the narrow gate," which is Jesus, we must still endure, and be firm in our resolve to traverse the hard way "that leads to life, and those who find it are few" (Matthew 7:13-14).

Thus, we are called to be active participants, rather than passive recipients, in our transformation to Christ-likeness. We must train ourselves to be Godly (I Timothy 4:7), and God fulfills our efforts by His power. If there is no effort, there will be no fulfillment in this world.

It is possible we may be saved and go to Heaven by grace through faith, yet sacrifice the fullness of holiness and joy in Heaven, because we have not obeyed, nor received what God proffered here on earth. We know a believer can suffer loss, when his work is burned, even though he himself is still saved (I Corinthians 3:15). We know the treasure we enjoy in Heaven is somehow impacted by the spiritual treasure we accumulate while here on earth (Matthew 6:21, 19:21; Mark 10:21; Luke 12:21, 12:34, 18:22; Romans 2:5-10).

Matthew 6:19-20 instructs: "Do not lay up for yourselves treasures on earth, where moth and rust consume and where thieves break in and steal, but lay up for yourselves treasures in heaven." God leads, and we follow. He commands, and we obey. He transforms to holiness, and we pursue righteousness. 2 Corinthians 6:1 says: "Working together with him, then, we entreat you not to accept the grace of God in vain." Jesus promises the blessings of His rest, if we obey His commands: "Come to me," and "Take my yoke upon you, and learn from me" (Matthew 11:28-29). But if we fail to act, or come to Him, or take His yoke, there is no promise of rest. See also, 2 Corinthians 3:5.

A Christian is to run, as in a race, and to exercise self-control in all things, as an athlete (I Corinthians 9:24,25). We must exert every effort, and do our all, but be constantly aware of, and relying upon, God's enabling power. We are to be purposeful and goal-oriented, not running aimlessly, nor beating the air, but bringing our bodies into subjection (I Corinthians 9:27).

Man is summoned to participate in the process of his spiritual growth: to "make holiness perfect in the fear of God" (2 Corinthians 7:1). Wishing for mature spirituality will not produce it. We must work hard to achieve it, in collaboration with the Holy Spirit. The balance between Divine and human input is spelled out in Philippians 2:12-13: "as you have always obeyed, so now... work out your own salvation with fear the trembling; for God is at work in you, both to will and to work for his good pleasure." We are to "work out" or practice, in our daily activities, the salvation God is working in us by the Holy Spirit. So man is responsible to cooperate with the power of God in him: to live externally in conformance with his spiritual transformation internally.

Jesus promises our effort will be rewarded: "Blessed are those who hunger and thirst for righteousness, for they shall be satisfied" (Matthew 5:6). Our salvation by baptism into Christ begins as we make "an appeal to God for a clear conscience, through the resurrection of Jesus Christ" (I Peter 3:21). The Greek word for 'appeal' is 'eperotema', which means agreeing to meet specified contractual conditions imposed by God before we are placed into the safety of Christ's Body. Man must desire to obtain a cleansed conscience from God, and have a willingness to meet the conditions of faith and repentance necessary to obtain it.[100]

After a believer's regeneration at the New Birth, we must collaborate with the Holy Spirit in an ongoing process of sanctification, leading to glorification after the Second Coming of the Lord. Colossians 1:21-23 reveals: "And you... he has now reconciled by his death, in order to present you holy and blameless and irreproachable before him, provided that you continue in the faith, stable and steadfast, not shifting from the hope of the gospel which you heard." God supplies all the enabling grace but a believer must cooperate by faith and hope in receiving the Spirit's transforming power!

God's summons to holiness confirms that man is required somehow to collaborate in the process, even though all motive power originates with God. Romans 12:2 exhorts believers: "Do not be conformed to this world but be transformed by the renewal of your mind, that you may prove what is the will of God, what is good and acceptable and perfect." Ephesians 4:1 calls us "to lead a life worthy of the calling to which you have been called." Leviticus 11:45 proclaims: "Be thou holy, for I the Lord your God am holy," and Hebrews 12:14, KJV concurs: "Follow... holiness, without which no man shall see the Lord."

I Timothy 4:6-8 urges believers to be "nourished on the words of faith and... Train yourself in godliness... godliness is of value in every way, as it holds promise for the present life and also for the life to come." At Genesis 17:1 God mandates: "walk before me, and be thou perfect." "Do all my commandments, and be holy unto your God" (Numbers 15:40). "Sanctify yourselves therefore, and be ye holy: for I am the Lord your God" (Leviticus 20:7).

Matthew 5:48 urges: "You, therefore, must be perfect, as your heavenly Father is perfect." Jesus healed sinners and adjured them to "sin no more" (John 5:14, 8:11). We are to "hate what is evil, hold fast to what is good" (Romans 12:9). We are to "Shun immorality" (I Corinthians 6:18), and "Make holiness perfect in the fear of God" (2 Corinthians 7:1). I Thessalonians 4:3,7 says: "For this is the will of God, your consecration, that you abstain from immorality... For God has not called us for uncleanness, but in consecration."

Holiness is defined by, and expressed in possessing the fruit of the Holy Spirit outlined at Galatians 5:22-23: "love, joy, peace, patience, kindness, goodness, faithfulness, gentleness, self-control." When we purpose to reflect the fruit of the Spirit in our corresponding acts of loving, enjoying and rejoicing; of making peace, exercising patience, or doing good, we collaborate in holiness in our lives. Thus, James 1:22 summons Christians to pursue and practice holiness: "put away all filthiness and rank growth of wickedness... But be doers of the word, and not hearers only." We are to seek holiness in "the things that are above, where Christ is" (Colossians 3:1), which include: "whatever is true, whatever is honorable... just... pure... lovely... gracious, if there is any excellence, if there is anything worthy of praise, think about these things" (Philippians 4:8).

2 Peter 1:4-7 teaches that we should "become partakers of the divine nature" by supplementing God's empowerment to overcome the world and be fruitful, by our pursuit of faith, virtue, knowledge, self-control, steadfastness, godliness, brotherly affection, and love; all of which are components of holiness. These things enhance effectiveness and fruitfulness in the knowledge of Christ; confirm a believer's call and election, and keep us from falling; "so there will be richly provided for you an entrance into the eternal kingdom of our Lord" (2 Peter 1:8-11).

Man's cooperation in the holiness worked by God is further clarified at I Corinthians 6:9-10: "The unrighteous will not inherit the kingdom of God... neither the immoral, nor idolators, nor adulterers, nor homosexuals, nor thieves, nor the greedy, nor drunkards, nor revilers, nor robbers will inherit the kingdom of God." Others barred from the Kingdom are men "full of envy, murder, strife, deceit, malignity, they are gossips, slanderers, haters of God, insolent, haughty, boastful, inventors of evil, disobedient to parents... We know that the judgment of God rightly falls upon those who do such things" (Romans 1:29-32); see also, Revelation 21:8,27).

"Sin is lawlessness" (I John 3:4), and "All wrongdoing is sin" (I John 5:17). James 4:17 adds: "Whoever knows what is right to do and fails to do it, for him it is sin." And James 2:9 reveals: "if you show partiality, you commit sin, and are convicted by the law as transgressors." Unredeemed, impenitent sinners are denied access to the Kingdom of God.

Thoughts are as damning as deeds. Jesus warns against the lustful thoughts of adultery, as much as the actual commission of the sin (Matthew 5:28). The seven deadly or capital sins of Medieval theology: pride, covetousness, lust, anger, gluttony, envy and sloth, are sins originating in the mind, and are evil whether or not such thoughts result in actions. They are the chief sources in human nature from which spring most human iniquities.[101] And God knows the thoughts of our minds (I Chronicles 28:9; Psalms 19:14, 139:2,4; and Matthew 12:34).

How much sin, entertained for how long, do you think will constitute unholiness? Under the ceremonial laws of the Old Testament, even a brief skirmish with sin contaminated one's holiness. A Jew believed he was unclean in the eyes of God if he simply touched a dead body or a diseased person (Leviticus 5:2,3, 11:24-28, 39). All sin is evil, because it transgresses, violates, disobeys and rebels against God's law. It deviates from a designated path of righteousness, and is crooked so that it misses the mark of rightness. Sin is wrong, and can never be depicted or rationalized as right. That is why Christians need to recognize, confess, and repent of sins, so they can be cleansed by God of them and of all unrighteousness (I John 1:9).

Sins of omission are as deadly for holiness as sins of commission. We sin by failing to do what we ought, as much as by doing what we ought not. At Matthew 25:41-42 Jesus says: "Depart from me, you cursed, into the eternal fire prepared for the devil and his angels; for I was hungry and you gave me no food, I was thirsty and you gave me no drink." Jesus reveals that the servant who knowingly fails to do his master's will "shall receive a severe beating, But he who did not know, and did what deserved a beating, shall receive a light beating" (Luke 12:47-48; and see Leviticus 4:12,13; 5:15; and Numbers 15:25-29).

We ought not become alarmed by the possibility of sin overwhelming us, and barring us from entering the Kingdom of God. Remember that God has determined to bring every New-Born Christian to the fullness of the measure of the stature of Christ until we are literally as righteous as Christ, Himself. We are called only to cooperate in the venture. For, while the New Birth does not make us immediately or completely holy, it does constitute and newly empower us to resist sin, whereas we could not before. We are "dead to sin and alive to God in Christ Jesus" (Romans 6:11). "We know that our old self was crucified with him so that the sinful body might be destroyed, and we might no longer be enslaved to sin" (Romans 6:6; and see also, I Peter 2:24). We are under grace, not law, and sin has lost its dominion over us, through God's grace and power (Romans 6:14).

The New-Born person is a new creation and a transformed, regenerated spirit, indwelt by God, Jesus, and the Holy Spirit. Sin has no power over a Christian because he is no longer a slave to sin. He has died to sin, and a consequential behavioral change of obedience has occurred, as God empowers and sustains man's desire, commitment, and purpose to do God's will. The New Birth is a creative alteration which makes one free, for the first time, to do right.

Thus, no Christian can willingly continue in sin and disobedience, with the excuse he cannot overcome it. Nor can he passively abide in sin the way he did before his conversion. That is why I John 3:9 can promise what seems at variance with experience: "No one born of God commits sin; for God's nature abides in him." Matthew 7:18 puts it: "A sound tree cannot bear evil fruit."

HOLINESS MUST OVERCOME THE FLESH

The victory we are called to win in the world is primarily of holiness over the flesh and worldly temptations. For whatever reason, God has chosen to leave New-Born believers in the world, but not of the world. James 1:27 teaches: 'Religion that is pure and undefiled before God and the Father is this.. to keep oneself unstained from the world." St. Paul knew that his mind served the law of God, but that his flesh was captive to the law of sin and death: "I see in my members another law at war with the law of my mind and making me captive to the law of sin which dwells in my members" (Romans 7:23; and see Romans 5:1-3).

The chastisements of the Lord, by which He applies the rod of correction, not surprisingly often involve deprivations of health and wealth, the blessings so earnestly sought by the faithful. God may allow us to be visited by sickness, so that the soul is operated upon through the body. St. Paul noted that delivering a sinner "to Satan for the destruction of the flesh" had the objective that the spirit may be saved in the day of the Lord" (I Corinthians 5:5). The soul is strengthened, invigorated, and quickened when the lusts and affections of the flesh are weakened. Physical illness exposes the vanity of the flesh, and the pride of worldly pursuits, restoring our focus upon God. Illness puts worldly frivolity in perspective, as it drives us to the Great Physician for healing. God may put us on our back in sickness, to force our abandonment of the world, and concentrate on Him with upward gaze. See Romans 5:3.

Giving up our attachments to alcohol, narcotics, sexual lust, and other diversions of the flesh are painful withdrawals for one who is addicted to them. Shedding pride, envy, ambition, or impure thoughts can be avoided by ignoring them, but the process of divestiture will produce suffering and discomfort, until they are replaced by the fruit of the Spirit. Images and concepts are easily burned into the mind, and memory impressions no longer need the stimulus of actual pornographic pictures. The entrenched memories of fleshly allures can continue to influence the mind without palpable reminders.

Suffering may be the very instrument which brings us to the point we prioritize spiritual values over worldly ones, and sever ourselves from all worldly attachments, so we may focus only on the Lord. Psalm 4:3 says: "But know that the Lord hath set apart him that is godly for himself: The Lord will hear when I call unto him." Godliness implies separation from the world, and God supplies and answers the prayers of those who determine to be Godly and are made so by Him. Nehemiah 9:2 says that the repentant in "Israel separated themselves from all strangers, and stood and confessed their sins, and the iniquities of their fathers." Communion in the presence of God requires disdaining one's worldly attachments, and the sins which teem amidst them.

At I Corinthians 3:3 Paul lovingly remonstrated with Christians whom he described as not yet ready for solid spiritual food: "for you are still of the flesh... while there is jealousy and strife among you." Galatians 5:16-17 urges us to "walk by the Spirit, and... not gratify the desires of the flesh... for the desires of the flesh are against the Spirit... for these are opposed to each other, to prevent you from doing what you would."

The Bible equates holiness with renouncing worldly pleasures, while defilement and death follow the ways of the flesh and world. At Romans 8:6-8, St. Paul exhorts Christians to think of spiritual things, and not the flesh, for: "To set the mind on the flesh is death, but to set the mind on the Spirit is life and peace... For the mind that is set on the flesh is hostile to God; it does not submit to God's law, indeed it cannot; and those who are in the flesh cannot please God."

301

St. Paul deemed conquest of the flesh so necessary, that he confided he had need to exercise "self control in all things... I pommel by body and subdue it, lest after preaching to others I myself should be disqualified." Born-Again Christians are to "Put off your old nature which belongs to your former manner of life and is corrupt through deceitful lusts, and be renewed in the spirit of your minds, and put on the new nature, created after the likeness of God in true righteousness and holiness" (Ephesians 4:22-24). Our new nature is totally sinless, renewed, regenerated, transformed, and endued by the Holy Spirit with the very nature and likeness of Jesus. We who "were baptized into Christ have put on Christ" (Galatians 3:27), and must continue to "put on the Lord Jesus Christ, and make no provision for the flesh, to gratify its desires" (Romans 13:14).

I Peter 2:11 beseeches us to avoid anything that panders to the flesh, depravity, or spiritual pollution, exhorting us: "as aliens and exiles to abstain from the passions of the flesh that wage war against your soul." We are called, and supernaturally enabled to "escape from the corruption that is in the world because of passion, and become partakers of the divine nature" (2 Peter 1:4). 2 Timothy 2:22 says: "So shun youthful passions and aim at righteousness." James 4:3 explains that our prayers will not be answered when they ask for divine power to feed our fleshly lusts: "You ask and do not receive, because you ask wrongly, to spend it on your passions."

Romans 7:14 identifies the flesh as imparting the original or inherited sin of Adam transmitted to every human being. The New-Born person can sin because sin dwells in his flesh (Romans 7:18). The quickened spirit lives in a "body of death," in whose members dwells "the law of sin" (Romans 7:23-24). The flesh, with its recollections of, and attractions to, sinful pleasures, is what drives Christians to sin, even while we will to do what is right (Romans 7:17-20). Since we have been made new, regenerated, and transformed spiritually by the New Birth, our new spirit does not need any additions from the Lord to be made perfect at death. Rather, a subtraction is necessary, releasing us from the flesh's sinful desires, and this is the Christian's occupation throughout his earthly pilgrimage. Once we have overcome the flesh, we can be raised up fit for God's society, totally receptive and enabled to embrace God's holiness.

Although sin has been dethroned from ruling man's New-Born spirit; and the old, carnal man has been subdued, deposed from reign, and no longer exists; sin is not yet exiled from the flesh, where responses to sin survive. Thus, we are assured of a sinless future, but in the world must still wrestle with sin, and are still prone to succumb to the sensuous flesh. The flesh has been trained for years in carnal pursuits, and retains natural man's affinity for carnal response, even after the New Birth.

A Christian's residence in a fleshly body complicates actual conformity to Christ's character and holiness. Natural man has left a legacy of strife to New Born Christians because the sinful tendencies of the flesh are not banished or eliminated by the New Birth. While rebelliousness and unbelief in Jesus are the principal causes of an unsaved person's alienation from God, the chief cause of a Christian's estrangement from holiness is the flesh.

That is why Jesus tells us to turn from temptations and cripple the power of the carnal flesh before it subdues the spirituality of the New Man: "And if your right hand causes you to sin, cut it off and throw it away" (Matthew 5:29-30). Jesus declares: "if your eye causes you to sin, pluck it out and throw it from you; it is better for you to enter life with one eye than with two eyes to be thrown into the hell of fire: (Matthew 18:9; and see, Mark 9:43-48). There is a sacrifice to be made in accepting the redemption of one's soul. We must struggle to put the flesh in submission to Christ. Loss of worldly advantages and benefits, in exchange for suffering, will be the price we pay to participate in the progressive process of holiness.

The source of suffering is the fact we can still sin if we choose to sin, and we are responsible to avoid exposing our flesh to temptations to sin. We must still exert our will to draw upon divine resources to resist sin which abounds in the world and still resides in the flesh's carnal recollections and habits. Our new nature does not prevent the worldly enticements which tempt the flesh, nor does it always avoid succumbing to sin in the world. The carnal remnant of man's evil inclinations in the flesh can draw us to sin, and permit the power of sin to reassert dominion in the body, despite the New Man's regeneration, unless we strive, struggle, and fight for holiness, while running from temptations.

The sooner we surrender to the Lord's reshaping of our lives, the sooner the process will be completed. The greater our cooperation, the sooner the result of a holy character like Jesus. The more willing our acceptance of the Potter's shaping, the sooner His planned transformation will be consummated. God cannot do much with us when we are hard-hearted as rock, complacently wealthy, proudly strong, arrogantly famous, selfishly powerful, or full of self-confidence and self-sufficiency. He might pulverize us down to dust so we can be re-fashioned into His image. Even though suffering accompanies the re-shaping of character, mature spirituality embraces it as an essential part of the process of holiness.

The natural man has long trained the flesh in baseness, pride, and ambition, and fostered unspiritual appetites, prejudices, and selfishness. Unless we are humbled, all these affectations will undo us. John Donne observed that "humiliation is the beginning of sanctification." Thus, God allows faith to be assaulted by pride, gluttony, rage, and despair so that our natural self-reliance can be humbled and worn down by the rough file of these assaults.[102] Without the holiness produced by humility and patient endurance, no man could see God because of the wall erected by his intellectual pride and arrogance.

Because "Great is the Lord... and his greatness is unsearchable" (Psalm 145:3), we must remember that God's ways are not our ways. His benevolence and beneficial outcomes become matters of faith in His Providence. You may ask for wealth or health to gain more happiness, and God may let you wallow in poverty or infirmity, that you might turn and find real joy in Him. Such victories by him over us, truly become our victories in Him. You may yearn for fame and popularity, and God may steer you into isolation so you learn to seek Him as your only consolation and far better reward.

Suffering may call us from unhealthy attachments to worldly wealth, and the destructive materialism which deters wealthy people from spirituality, for "it will be hard for a rich man to enter the kingdom of heaven" (Matthew 19:23). Unholy obsession with wealth and the acquisitions it permits will surely bar the blessing of prosperity, for "You cannot serve God and mammon" (Matthew 6:24). Attachment to his property kept the rich young man from following Jesus, when he was challenged to divest himself of wealth and give it to the poor (Mark 10:22). Denial of the blessing of prosperity, as well as afflictions which turn us toward holiness, serve to teach us that material possessions, fame, status, or power offer neither security in this world, nor a foothold for the world to come.

In the call to holiness, Scripture reminds us that "friendship with the world is enmity with God" (James 4:4). 2 Corinthians 6:14-15 queries: "For what partnership have righteousness and iniquity? Or what fellowship has light with darkness? What accord has Christ with Belial? Or what has a believer in common with an unbeliever?"

Suffering from sickness can be a great instrument for erasing pride. For, the man most boastful in his intellect or wealth will, when afflicted, quickly come to envy the poorest and most ignorant waif who possesses only good health. The pride of exalting oneself above other men is repugnant to God, Who "hateth a proud look" (Proverbs 6:17), and "resisteth the proud" (James 4:6). It is especially impertinent, ignorant, and conceited to think we ought to be exempt from suffering, because we deserve God's blessings, while others are more deserving of God's wrath. If one asks, "Why Me?" when visited with suffering, he implies there is someone else more deserving of punishment than he. Yet, we are all guilty of transgression, and true humility makes one aware he deserves nothing good, but receives blessings and exemption from pain only by the grace of God.

Humility is at the base of accepting suffering from God, for "Naked came I out of my mother's womb, and naked shall I return thither: the Lord gave, and the Lord hath taken away; blessed be the name of the Lord" (Job 1:21). Likewise, I Timothy 6:6 says; "There is great gain in godliness with contentment; for we brought nothing into the world, and we cannot take anything out of the world." Job clearly understood that God is the One Who had taken his blessings away. Job and Paul agree that no rights have been violated, because every blessing is a matter of God's grace; and not our just desserts. We have no basis for bitterness or protest when something is withdrawn to which we had no right originally.

We may have political rights of life, liberty and the pursuit of happiness against the state, but against God we have no claims, rights, or demands. Even "children are a heritage of the Lord: and... his reward" (Psalm 127:3). Yet, God makes it clear it is still His good pleasure to shower blessings upon His children, while providing endurance, evasion, and escape to overcome suffering in the world.

James 1:9 teaches that the universal need for a Saviour and the universality of suffering are great levelers: "Let the lowly brother boast of his exaltation, and the rich in his humiliation, because like the flower of the grass he will pass away." Poverty here does not impair the wonderful inheritance Hereafter, nor does worldly affluence guarantee the true inheritance. Suffering reminds all of us that our security does not rest in wealth or status, but only in God through Jesus Christ.

Our conversion and regeneration at the New Birth may have been painless, but our transformation to perfection cannot be accomplished so easily. God uses both love and the threat of punishment to induce His children's desired response to grow in Christ-like character. Correction would not be necessary, unless man was obligated to participate in God's process of sanctification.

God always gives us a warning in inner conscience to desist before the actual application of deterrence, force, chastening or punishment. Fortunately, His Word assures us that God administers discipline and the reproach of reproof lovingly, coupled with encouragement, hope, and the assurance of results divinely worked.

When discipline is designed and applied by God to accomplish a specific correction to assist spiritual growth, we would expect God's chastening to end when it has accomplished the reformation of character God intended. This presupposes that God will measure out exactly the right amount and extent of chastening necessary to work the transformation He wills. Implicit in the believer's release from chastisement is his collaborative effort to heed the lessons of suffering and attempt to remedy the defect or shortcoming in his character which suffering has pointed out. Our relief from any chastening initiated as correction by God, is connected to how we react to it in the shaping of Christ-like character in fulfillment of God's purpose. The sooner our response to correction, the sooner its surcease.

A believer cannot be undiscriminating in his spiritual life, for we govern the pace of our growth in holiness here on earth. Unrepented sin demonstrates an absence of cooperation and loss of spiritual cleansing, which will stunt spiritual development and fellowship with God. We can and should perceive an increase in righteousness when we have come through God's training.

However, while individual episodes of suffering are transitory, the process of learning from sufferings is for a lifetime. You may well have grown in one area of character development, but neglected others, or gone along without any substantial spiritual growth for years. Little habits such as pride or sloth may have become entrenched and affected other areas of character. Would we not expect God to insert training and its attendant correction into our lives to arrest our attention and convict us of the need to grow in holiness?

In cultivation of holiness, it is preferable to be and do what God wills for you, by your own choice and effort, freely and maturely, than to resist the chastisement of the Lord. When we cooperate, God helps those who help themselves, by supernaturally supporting their resolve, rather than sending trials. For, there is no longer any need for a particular discipline, once we have learned the spiritual lesson taught by that trial. So it behooves us to discern, accept, and apply the lesson as quickly as we can. Then, when we have passed the test, it need not be given repeatedly, as long as we retain and apply what we have learned.

Once suffering has driven us to recognize its divine purpose, and the lesson of affliction has been learned and heeded, there is no longer any divine love endorsing or motivating the need for that particular travail. When the discipline is completed, all a believer need do is recognize and receive the instruction; stop resisting the proddings of the Holy Spirit; repent; seek forgiveness and cleansing; and rush back to the protective arms of God. A specific chastisement from God ends when we have learned its lessons and conformed to the image of Christ in the New Man. Hence, at the first sign of torment we should rush boldly to the throne of grace, and ask God what He intends us to learn and gain by suffering, and then respond to the lesson.

A Christian knows that if he judges himself, the Holy Spirit can guide his conscience to examine, judge, and change his conduct. When we judge ourselves honestly, repent, and rectify that which needs correction, we are forgiven our sins and there is no need for God's judgment in those matters. I Corinthians 11:31-32 says: "But if we judged ourselves truly, we should not be judged. But when we are judged by the Lord, we are chastened so that we may not be condemned along with the world." If we change, we are not chastised. If we accept correction, our chastening ends.

On the other hand, if we distort our freedom and responsibility and refuse to respond to God's chastening, we can expect intensified activity until we do respond. Whatever drives us to rebellion we must first brake, and then break. Whatever puffs us up in pride must be deflated. God's arsenal of pulverization, devastation, disintegration, and vitiation can outlast and outperform whatever resistance we would offer to His chastening. The power of His love will outlast and outweigh our flimsy, unworthy assertions of self-regard and self-determination. Nothing in all creation, "will be able to separate us from the love of God in Christ Jesus our Lord" (Romans 8:39), although our intransigence might delay our requital.

Of equal concern, however, is our susceptibility to sin and temptation in the world because we have not yet achieved the level of actual holiness which can successfully resist temptation and combat iniquity. The Born-Again Christian who knows what he should be, will suffer terribly until he has attained it. Not only will he be shamefully aware of his spiritual shortcomings, but his compromise with the world will be a constant source of frustration and conflict in his life. We sin, and as Adam, we surrender the ongoing protection of God's grace, virtue, integrity, and ability to resist sin. Without these gifts of God's grace, for which we must pray, it is impossible to please God, and we become vulnerable to the flood of insatiable worldly appetites and sensual temptations. But God is faithful, and will always sustain and empower our determination to be holy; enable our obedience to His commands; and provide a way of escape from temptation.

God has privileged us to participate with him in many ventures, and when we do not do our part there will be failure and painful consequences, no matter how earnestly we pray, or depend upon God in faith. The Great Commission gives us the privilege of playing a part in bringing New Men into being when we witness to the Gospel. The Great Commission imposes a burden upon believers collectively to be God's voice, hands, and feet in sharing the Gospel with the unsaved. If we fail, they may remain lost for eternity. If we fail to witness to a lost soul, God's desire that all men be saved will be frustrated unless another witness is called and empowered by God to preach the Word.

God also allows us to share in ministering to the needs of other men, both saved and unsaved, as part of good stewardship and His Commandment to love others. If we fail to do our part in helping those less fortunate, whatever their need, there is no guarantee God will make other provisions for them. He has already entrusted the task to us believers, and our failure to perform our duty will affect others, if only by causing delay in God's deliverance.

When God, as Sovereign, decrees some blessing for another, and constitutes you as his agent to accomplish it, your failure to act requires God to use another instrumentality to transmit the blessing. He whom God intends to bless will be blessed. However, you have failed God, more than that other person. Hence David's plaint: "Against thee, thee only, have I sinned, and done this evil in thy sight" (Psalm 51:4).

We are privileged to share in developing personal holiness, by being receptive to the redemptive working of the Holy Spirit. No doubt all believers will be raised perfect at the Second Coming of Christ, but he who has neglected to cooperate in growing in holiness may be raised a perfect penny, while the believer who faithfully worked at growing Christ-like character may be a perfect dollar. Both a penny and a dollar are perfect specimens for what they are, but they may not necessarily share the same value or reward in Heaven.

The love of God in hastening our spirituality by chastening our sinfulness does not answer every question about suffering. But it does provide a vantage from which to regard trials God originates, initiates, directs, or orchestrates for our education, discipline, training, and correction. Such suffering is instituted because God loves us, not because He does not love us. While such suffering may end when it has served its purpose of warning believers away from sin, there is another facet of holiness involving suffering, which is inherent in the process, but not intended or calculated to teach us a lesson. It simply accompanies the rigors of training and practice which we must undergo to attain excellence, and is inescapable during the learning process. We turn now to this unavoidable suffering of training in holiness.

CHAPTER 11

THE UNAVOIDABLE SUFFERING OF TRAINING

"You need some one to teach you again the first principles of God's word. You need milk, not solid food; for everyone who lives on milk is unskilled in the word of righteousness, for he is a child. But solid food is for the mature, for those who have their faculties trained by practice to distinguish good from evil."

– Hebrews 5:12-14.

We have encountered many origins of suffering in our discussion so far. There is pain inflicted by Satan or other men, which is not intended nor necessitated by God, but is a possible consequence of genuine freedom to choose, originally conveyed by God to free beings. There is also pain intended by God as deterrence, and there is punishment for disobedient rebellion: what unrepented sinners can expect here and in Hell. We are heir to mainstream Jewish thought which stresses that a child is educated by parental correction of his mistakes and misdirections, through the application of chastisement. The infliction of suffering is intended to deter repetition of wrong, promote repentance, and effect the desired change.

We are also indebted to Ancient Greek thought, as well as Scripture, for the focus on suffering as an indispensable arena for struggle that increasingly develops constancy, strength, and conditioning to build one up for the prize of greater virtue.[103] This is a pain which accompanies God-ordained processes in which a believer participates, such as holiness, and is inherent in one's growth and progress toward Christ-likeness. It has no connection to personal sin, guilt, or defilement, and carries no message of correction or change. It is simply part of, and inherent in the process of maturing.

SUFFERING PROVOKES GROWTH IN HOLINESS

God does not explain why our holy personality is in a process of becoming, rather than a <u>fait accompli</u>. The reality is we are designated participants in the process of transformation to Christ-like qualities. Such a process would be incompatible with a perfect world, and only perfected holiness is suitable for a Heavenly environment. A world without suffering or pain would never provide challenge or need for God. It would not invoke the nobler aspects of human personality such as love, gentleness, kindness, generosity, or unselfishness. Such a world might provide maximum pleasure and happiness, but it could contribute little to the higher value of moral character.

If we are to participate in the working of holiness within, we must be in an outer environment which presents struggle, sacrifice, sorrow, danger, obstacles, and perils, which can evoke Godly responses. There will be less pleasure in such a world, and less intervention by God to snatch us from suffering. But such a world will best adapt us to grow in eternal, spiritual values of righteousness and holiness; by stimulating them in believers here on earth. Here, God eases our suffering by heightening our appreciation of His benevolent purposes.

The Scriptures make it clear we will encounter adversities which are inherent in, and indispensable to, growth in faith and holiness. Christ's way is described as a way of struggle, persecution, temptation, and challenge. There is a wrench of the flesh from the embrace of the world, which repeatedly produces pain for the believer who must abandon sinful ways. It is unavoidable in this process throughout one's lifetime, and pain is intrinsic to learning, applying, and practicing the faculty of good to conform us to our transformed inner man.

Jesus goes to great lengths to warn Christians about the reality of suffering, because to live in denial, as many faith advocates do, can jeopardize the very faith they assert. There is nothing incompatible between faith and suffering, if we recognize some suffering is ordained by God to provide or accommodate superior, spiritual joys, even though earthly blessings of health, wealth, and happiness may be temporarily interrupted or withheld.

Nothing is so helpless as a new-born babe. The progressive nature of human life means we begin our journey helpless, ignorant, and unskilled. Struggle attends our learning of motor skills and intellectual subjects. The parent who facilitates a child's learning to walk, stands by to ease the falls, but neither excuses nor dispenses with the child's efforts, which must be expended in learning to walk. A child will fall while he learns to walk, but the world is thereby opened to ever-expanding, delightful journeys.

Later, a father may assist his child in learning to ride a bicycle, which will maximize the child's enjoyment and scope of travel. The skill cannot be acquired without the constituent risk of falling and the possibility of injury. The father does not will, intend, or desire harm to his child, but it is an inherent, potential harm, incidental to the superior benefits of learning to ride a bicycle. The child must eventually be loosed to try his own control over balance and motion. His loving father will be there to instruct safety, encourage persistence, and mitigate spills. Moving from physical to mental pursuits, it may take months to master the multiplication table, but we can eventually progress to geometry and calculus. Learning the alphabet takes time and studying the rules of grammar may inflict real agony, but they enable us to read, understand words, grasp concepts, embrace ideals, and express them. The stress which accompanies learning effort is also an acceptable, collateral, and potential effect of a system which attains the highest good of man — freely choosing to grow in Christ-like holiness, and willing to be like Christ.

Even after a Christian is Born-again by grace through faith, suffering will continue since it is intrinsic to the process of spiritual maturation which God has instituted or allowed because of its transcendent spiritual values to man. Some suffering is endemic to the ongoing process of a believer's growth in Christ-like character. This process of spiritual growth inherently involves rigors and stress, which cannot be avoided for that very reason. To remove any aspect of spiritual growth simply because it involves pain, would cripple the spiritual maturity God requires.

To impress perfect holiness upon man as a <u>fait accompli</u> would rob man of the pleasure of accomplishment and creativity which accompanies the process of growth. The materials, instructions, and motivations for growth are provided by a loving Father to His developing adolescents. The process of participation promotes a higher purpose, and produces blessings of dignity and freedom in man, despite their perversion by those who choose wrongly and expose us to the bondage of pain. The specific good which God ordains as His purpose is conforming believers to the image of Christ. Romans 8:29 says: "For those whom he foreknew he also predestined to be conformed to the image of his Son... And those whom he predestined he also called; and those whom he called he also justified; and those whom he justified he also glorified."

These are some of the reasons God tolerates the suffering which results from the growing pains intrinsic to any process of maturing; why he allows suffering, and the occasional deprivation of other promised blessings, produced by deterrence, discipline, and training in holiness.

In cases of training for proficiency, where pain is an integral or constituent part of the process, we cannot say that God has intended specific suffering. Rather, it simply occurs because conditioning involves painful rigors. Your comfort lies in knowing God's purpose is your progress and development; not your punishment, deterrence, or chastisement. As He works all things for good, your change and spiritual maturation are the objectives rather than punishment. We need not conjecture that God is promoting some unknown good to our advantage, for His good purpose is known: to transform believers to the image of Christ.

The result of suffering, when accepted in the right spirit, now becomes a willing obedience, nurtured and enlightened by the experience of affliction, which we recognize as a companion of growth in holiness. In training, there is no plan or purpose on the part of the instructor to punish failure. Training seeks to provide incentives to learn and avoid conduct which thwarts learning, but suffering is incidental to, and inherent in, the very process of learning and growing. Perseverance will bring progress, but it also involves the discomfort intrinsic in training.

Do we need to be holy? We will soon learn that resisting temptation is exceedingly traumatic. Do we need to learn love and express it in unselfish care and concern for others? The intrusions upon our time and energy are initially painful sacrifices, albeit more than compensated by the joys of loving and giving. Do we need to practice loving others by sharing the Good News and witnessing our faith in Jesus, even at the risk of rejection? Sharing the Gospel is difficult because a believer exposes his deepest feelings and beliefs to another, and is especially vulnerable when his confidences are unwanted, uninvited, and rejected. But the joy of sharing God's love and light and seeing it gratefully received by a sinner, far outweighs any momentary travails in witnessing.

This suffering which accompanies training and discipline is not sent, directed, orchestrated, initiated, or caused by God with any intent to chastise or chasten us. These occasions of suffering are allowed by God's permissive will as incidental to human freedom, enabling us to participate in spiritual processes of growth. They are growing pains inherent in, and accompanying the processes which expand human dignity by man's collaboration in training, preparation, and commitment for holiness, loving service, and evangelism. Such pains reflect growth in strength and skill, as one is trained in fighting techniques for soldierly combat in the army of the Lord, and then tested for readiness and retention of what has been learned.

Someone has said that we need tears to wash out the grimy films that cloud our vision. We need occasional rain to sustain vegetation and flowers, because total sunshine would only produce a desert. This may be one meaning of Ecclesiastes 7:3: "Sorrow is better than laughter; for by the sadness of the countenance the heart is made better." The deepest insights are learned in sorrow, rather than amusement, as we are driven by loss to evaluate the unimportance of what once seemed significant in the direction of our lives.

Growing pains, physical or spiritual, are real and cause suffering. They are intrinsic to any process of training, and inherent in any progress, whether it be physical or spiritual growth. Our training in the Word involves correction to help us distinguish good and be equipped for every good work while in the world. The root of discipleship is discipline, or training which corrects error and perfects Christ-likeness. Discipline deals with eliminating sinful conduct in order to develop holiness in our lives. It uses training, trials, and tests to exercise our faith, strengthen our character, and develop perseverance, reliance on God, and focus on spiritual things. 2 Thessalonians 1:4-5 says when we are steadfast in faith through persecutions and afflictions, "This is evidence of the righteous judgment of God, that you may be made worthy of the kingdom of God, for which you are suffering." See also, 2 Timothy 4:5; and 2 Peter 1:4.

Spiritual training necessarily involves effort, deprivation, choosing alternatives, and abandoning undesirable pursuits; all of which can produce suffering. We are engaged in spiritual warfare, in which our flesh is weak, and responsive to the "wiles of the devil. For we are not contending against flesh and blood, but against the principalities, against the powers, against the world rulers of this present darkness, against the spiritual hosts of wickedness in the heavenly places" (Ephesians 6:11-12). We suffer because we must prepare to withstand the assaults which will inevitably occur from Satan and other men who are still his children, because still unsaved.

Victory over the flesh requires violent resistance toward sin before we can fully embrace holiness. "The kingdom of heaven has suffered violence, and men of violence take it by force" (Matthew 11:12). "The good news of the kingdom of God is preached, and every one enters it violently" (Luke 16:16). Dying to oneself is inherently painful, and St. Paul documented the incessant war between his fleshly recollections of sin and the new inner man being made over in the image of Christ (Romans 7:15-25). There is pain involved in withdrawal from any addiction, whether it be alcohol, narcotics, borrowing, food, sex, pornography, or any type of habitual sin. There is a wrench when the sinner wrestles with admitting his sinfulness in the throes of the Gospel's confrontation and conviction of sin.

Our training must toughen us for combat, much as resistance builds muscle, and strong winds make strong trees as their roots dig in to withstand the gale's force. The man who has known little suffering is often a man with much room to grow spiritually. Hence, the world is adapted to provide struggle, difficulties, and hazards in an environment which John Keats called the "vale of soul-making."

The practical application of what we have learned can produce pain from the effort of obediently doing our duty under actual conditions of spiritual combat. Endurance against the world will continue to exact pain and sacrifice, even though we have mastered spiritual techniques. After our training in spiritual warfare, the actual battles against sin and evil will involve stress and privation. There can be no heroic victory over the world without the suffering and struggle which accompany strife and epic battles.

THE WORD TRAINS US IN RIGHTEOUSNESS

God's Word contained in Scripture not only accomplishes our initial regeneration at the New Birth, but also accomplishes our sanctification and growth in holiness. While we can do nothing to earn our salvation, we can accelerate the pace of our growth in holiness in the occasions of adversity, by positive and faithful collaboration in obedience to the Word. God's Word revealed by the Holy Spirit, exists to instruct believers and provide the standard by which we measure our growth. It teaches us what to be and what to do, and accomplishes the transformation. It brings joy by encouraging, fulfilling, and creating perfect life by the power of God. It reveals what we can expect from God. 2 Corinthians 13:5 calls Christians to "examine yourselves, to see whether you are holding to your faith. Test yourselves... Jesus Christ is in you — unless indeed you fail to meet the test." Galatians 6:4-5 says: "But let each one test his own work, and then his reason to boast will be in himself alone and not in his neighbor. For each man will have to bear his own load."

In the realm of cooperating with the Word's instructions, the principle of sowing and reaping definitely applies. The more we sow the Word, the more we learn holiness and reap its harvest. The measure of obedience to the Word which we sow, will definitely correlate to the measure of fruit in spiritual growth we will reap. It applies to the learning process, since the speed, constancy and intensity with which we choose to learn, will determine our rate of growth by the power of the Word. The Holy Spirit is at work in you, even when you engage in non-Christian pursuits, but His efficacy and celerity is greatly enhanced by our immersion in the Word, and the measure of faithfulness with which we follow its teachings in pursuit of holiness.

If you plant anything spiritual for the Lord, you will receive back spiritual blessings, even to the extent of a hundred-fold (Matthew 13:8). If we recognize in the Word our need to be more loving, we will cooperate by sowing more active love, consideration, care, and concern for others. Then we will reap an increasing, conscious awareness of God's love in our lives, which in turn gives us access to the inexhaustible supply of divine love and enablement with which to love others even more.

If you seek restoration of your own health, pray for and minister to the health of others, then you will reap as you sow. If you wish to reap prosperity, then sow by giving liberally to the needs of others. If you wish to grow in holiness, sow with liberality your obedience to the Word which guides you in righteousness.

Discipline, which seeks to do right in pursuit of actual righteousness, begins with Scripture, which issues from God and is called to our remembrance by the Holy Spirit. Simply knowing Scripture is not enough. Training requires us to respond by internalizing, applying and practicing these Scriptures to live holy lives. Training involves the practice of holiness we have learned from the Bible. Hebrews 5:13-14 compares superficiality in the study of the Word to being "unskilled in the word of righteousness... But solid food is for the mature, for those who have their faculties <u>trained by practice to distinguish good from evil.</u>" We are required to practice what the Word teaches to train our faculties in righteousness. God's power through the Word accomplishes the transformation, but believers have a part in studying, internalizing, and obediently applying the Word.

When a disciple appropriates the Word in this manner, he puts treasure in his storehouse, to be drawn upon when needed. Jesus says at Matthew 13:51: "every scribe who <u>has been trained</u>

for the kingdom of heaven is like a householder who brings out of his treasure what is new and what is old." Training consists in learning the Word, so it can be applied when needed during the course of ministry and service. Training builds and fills a spiritual storehouse by the Word knowledge you put in, so it is available for use when the real assault comes or intensifies via satanic and worldly attacks. "Thy word have I hid in mine heart, that I might not sin against thee" (Psalm 119:11). The Holy Spirit will assist you in remembering what Jesus said, but it is helpful if you have already heard it.

Scripture is "inspired by God and profitable for teaching, for reproof, for correction, and for <u>training in righteousness, that the man of God may be complete</u>" (2 Timothy 3:16-17). I Timothy 4:7 exhorts: "Train yourself in godliness," and see Joshua 1:8; and I Corinthians 9:24-27. Suffering drives us back to the Word for guidance in holiness. Psalm 119:67 puts it: "Before I was afflicted I went astray: but now I have kept thy word." Suffering reminds us to grow in faithful obedience, which cooperates with, and leads to holiness. I Peter 4:1-2 adds: "whoever has suffered in the flesh has ceased from sin, so as to live for the rest of the time in the flesh no longer by human passions but by the will of God," which is expressed in the Word.

GROWTH COMES BY TRAINING

Even after we have examined and judged ourselves; after we have recognized our short-comings and resolved to reform, there are still areas that we are not able to change without prolonged training and practice. Head knowledge — knowing what is right to do — is not the same as learning a lesson by acquiring skill to perform rightly, as practice makes perfect. Learning is a gradual and arduous process. It generally takes long, repetitive sessions before what one has learned becomes second nature and one's personal, automatic, habitual response to worldly problems.

It is not enough to appreciate that borrowing or drinking is wrong and is the cause of one's trouble. Upon the next worldly assault, it is too easy to return to borrowing or drinking as the solution to a problem. It may take a long time before we actually learn that we need to depend on Jesus for strength to overcome temptation. We are not able to resist under human power, even though we may devoutly wish to avoid sinful conduct. Just as physical maturity is neces-sary to accomplish some physical tasks, so spiritual maturity is necessary to perform certain spiritual acts.

One with natural talent does not become an accomplished artist, musician, athlete, or typist simply by desiring to be so, or by registering for a course which teaches those skills. Will, skill, and learning still need practice and training. A tyro may have studied and even performed the rudimentary actions of piano playing, but still needs practice before he gains proficiency. An immature child cannot be entrusted with operating the family automobile, even though its use would greatly enhance his mobility. He lacks physical size and strength to perform the task. He must first acquire knowledge how to drive, as well as skill in driving, through practice. He may understand the mechanics of operating a bicycle or driving a car, but still needs to develop skills in its management, and judgment to proceed safely. These are acquired only through actual experience in supervised driving or bicycle riding.

If a physician's child earnestly sought to have his father's knowledge of medicine and surgical skills, the physician could not oblige him instantaneously, no matter how much both willed it. Even after hours of instruction and intellectual grasp of operative procedures, only a fool would submit to surgery at the hands of the child. The father must not only educate the child, but help him grow in wisdom, skill, and experience. Training must be embellished with practice, application, and sustained effort, as the neophyte voluntarily and obediently follows instructions and gains experience through supervised performance.

In spiritual maturation, the pain and rigors of disciplined training cannot be avoided, even though both God and His child jointly wish the immediate rendering of mature and efficient service. The effort and regimen of training and performance exact a price, as unspiritual excrescences are ripped off, pruned, cut away, and rough edges are made smooth by abrasion, refinement, purification, and growth.

One does not ordinarily graduate from kindergarten directly to college in one year, no matter how bright or well intentioned he might be, or privileged his family may be. Learning is cumulative and sequential in any worthwhile endeavor. One must first master the alphabet and sentence structure before becoming accomplished in composition and rhetoric. The multiplication table and algebra must precede calculus and quantum physics. If you quickly dump water into a glass, the contents will splash out of the receptacle and be lost. But if the water is poured gradually, we can fill the glass to the brim and everything imparted will be retained.

Likewise, a boxer cannot sally forth as a championship contender, no matter how superior his natural ability, until he is fully conditioned and thoroughly prepared in every way to meet his opponent. Indeed, as he grows in experience and is ratcheted up to a higher level of competition, the skills of his opponents are also likely to increase. Like the prizefighter, a long-distance runner, competitive ice-skater, or marine at boot camp will all collapse under pressure without conditioning and training in simulated combat or competitive conditions.

These trainees will experience pain and exhaustion during training, inherent in building strength, stamina, and skill through their regimen and routine. They cannot avoid or be excused from the rigors of striving and struggle in the process, lest they delay or cripple the desired result of accomplishment. The athlete who thinks it is clever to skip practice and repetitions because the coach is not watching, will soon find his unprepared shortcomings exposed on game day. God puts you into His training program, and determines precisely how much you need to be ready.

In military service, as well as in the army of the Lord, one does not become a general overnight but must usually work his way up through the ranks, learning the techniques of performance in dutiful service at every level. A military trainee will not survive actual combat without thorough, advanced preparation and toughening to meet his opponent. Only time and practice can develop the resiliency, proficiency, and stamina needed for success. And the training process is accompanied by pain, because only practice makes perfect, and the rigors of correction are built into the process.

A believer's spiritual growth is likewise a lifetime process, rather than an accomplished fact at the New Birth's regeneration. The growth in holiness we are called to develop is ongoing, and suffering inhabits and cannot be separated from the process. God will not deliver us from what He has built into the cultivation of spiritual character, and painful practice will be needed to perfect even what we know intellectually. It takes time to grow to physical maturity, and it takes just as much time to develop actual holiness and grow to spiritual maturity. Both processes involve practice, sacrifice, seasoning, experience, and effort. We acquire spiritual knowledge and instruction from God's Word, and learn there the character we are to study, emulate, rehearse, cultivate, practice, and apply before we acquire proficiency, The Spirit works the transformation, but works better with our collaboration. His power is not limited by our disobedience, but is facilitated by our obedient response to Him. This is the accompanying consequence of participation granted by God to His children.

The New-Born spiritual babe must learn to walk the Way of Jesus before he can run the race set before him. He must be trained to resist worldly temptation before he can stand fast, hold true to his course, or guide others along the narrow path to righteousness. We become good servants only by serving; good prayer warriors only by praying; and we become effective witnesses only by witnessing, all as empowered by the Holy Spirit through the Word.

Like a prizefighter or soldier, a spiritual tyro is too precious to sacrifice or destroy because of inadequate training and preparation for combat. Attaining combat-readiness for spiritual warfare is arduous, burdensome, and frequently an unavoidable cause of suffering. Only when he is prepared and made skillful by the experience of dozens of fights under his belt, will he be most effective. He has 'learned the ropes,' learned how to avoid being hit by his adversary, how to counterpunch, and how to deliver the knockout blows he has painstakingly developed. God protects His own from premature exposure to spiritual warfare and evil. Not every soldier can serve in the front lines all the time. A veteran may be recalled to train new recruits, and the supply quartermaster at the rear is also essential to the unit's success.

God is the source of all our strength and provision; our instructor in survival tactics; and His glory is the object of all our efforts. A disciple's devotion to God's service must be so single-mindedly committed to pleasing Him that no worldly enticement can distract him, nor trial deter him, from dedicated service in the army of God. Throughout our preparation we must never forget we rely on God to accomplish the desired result, but we are also obligated to be cooperative and receptive to the Holy Spirit's work in us. Participation in this joint venture of spiritual development is a blessing from God which requires our serious application. 2 Timothy 2:3-4 enjoins: "Take your share of suffering as a good soldier of Christ Jesus. No soldier on service gets entangled in civilian pursuits, since his aim is to satisfy the one who enlisted him."

To be an effective "good soldier of Christ Jesus," we must learn the tactics, skills and strategies of discipleship by a regimen of arduous training. We must daily take and follow our marching orders from our Commander-in-Chief. All training involves instruction: teaching, and learning, practice and performance, including simulated combat conditions, until the techniques of training have been learned and mastered for active duty. Only then is one regarded as combat-ready, and prepared to be entrusted with the battle, both for the safety of himself and his comrades, and for the assurance of victory over the world. We must be faithful in little things before we can be entrusted with bigger affairs (Matthew 25:23).

The battle to which we are called is one of loving service to the Body of Christ; ministering to the unsaved by our witness; relieving want and suffering where possible; and serving as prayer warriors to intercede on behalf of others. Christians may not be able to eliminate recurrent epidemics of moral sickness, but we can fight a holding action and occupy against Satan until the Second Coming of Christ (Luke 19:13, KJV). Then the source of evil will be abolished, and spiritually infirm men will be freed, cured, and made whole.

In the meantime, Jesus has ordained His followers to be a holy priesthood (I Peter 2:5), ministering to those stricken by moral pestilence. The healing prescription is the Gospel's Word that Jesus is the only way to spiritual health. He is the cure for the ravages of sin, and the vaccine against future temptations to sin.

Even after we have graduated from basic training in discipleship, we can expect refresher courses and continuing education from time to time, in order to sharpen and perfect our performance in the service of the Lord. In all warfare, self-sacrifices are necessary to produce victory. The learning process of discipleship is hazardous: as trials expose the weakness and sin in us, at the same time they invite the power of God to overcome them by grace.

Indeed, every progression from glory to glory involves the loss of a former condition, however congenial it may have been, in order to gain a better position. The precious toddler who is so dearly attached to his parent, will outgrow his dependency, and progress to self-sufficiency and manhood. There is the death of a child in the maturation to adulthood, with its different, albeit superior, consolations. The blasé High School Senior who enjoys status and comfort, will be transplanted, to find diminished importance as a college Freshman. Yet, he crosses the threshold to exciting and challenging newness, which would be impossible without severance. The championship season will recede from great importance to fond recollection, as we mature and weightier considerations assume their proper roles.

Testing is an integral part of the process of development to complete our sanctification. James 1:2-4 encourages us: "Count it all joy, my brethren, when you meet various trials, for you know that the testing of your faith produces steadfastness. And let steadfastness have its full effect, that you may be perfect and complete, lacking in nothing." Testing, and the suffering it necessarily involves, will occur throughout one's lifetime because spiritual growth is on-going while we are in the world. It exposes, and helps us to recognize, the flaws in our character that must yet be removed.

Even after we have reached spiritual maturity through training and suffering, or enjoyed prodigious blessings, we may still expect the suffering that accompanies testing. Our training never ends on earth, because one's Christ-like character is not perfected here. As we move from glory to glory, we can also expect to move from suffering to suffering as long as we are in the world.

Even in physical growth, we cannot mature without occasional risk. Our loving Father cannot let us progress from milk to solid food without the risk of choking, but He will be there to prevent harm. We are allowed to be exposed to risks of actually doing things by our Father because He loves us, and they are an essential part of our training and development. Ice-skaters and gymnasts routinely run the risk of sprains to arms and legs. Yet, they continue to practice and perform with bandaged limbs, because the challenges of excelling, conquering the discipline, and winning a medal by a flawless performance, make the risk acceptable. At the same time, God shares and provides strength, wisdom, guidance, and instruction to endure any travails which may befall us in the process of maturing. Even more, he will not allow us to be exposed to anything beyond our capacity to cope or endure (I Corinthians 10:13).

SUFFERING CULTIVATES THE FRUIT OF THE HOLY SPIRIT

In addition to the gifts of the Holy Spirit given the Church for the common good, the fruit of the Spirit is given individual believers to work actual holiness and transformation to the likeness of Christ. Fruit involves the cultivation of divine seeds growing in your new spirit because of the life of Christ within. Galatians 5:22-23 teaches that "the fruit of the Spirit is love, joy, peace, patience, kindness, goodness, faithfulness, gentleness, self-control." These traits reflect the Christ-like holy character to which we are called, as enabled by the Holy Spirit.

Jesus teaches: "I am the vine, you are the branches. He who abides in me, and I in him, he it is that bears much fruit... If you abide in me, and my words abide in you, ask whatever you will, and it shall be done for you. By this my Father is glorified, that you bear much fruit, and so prove to be my disciples" (John 15:5-8). Manifestation of the fruit of the Holy Spirit identifies us as Christ's own. The traits of the fruit of the Spirit will reflect a holy character which corresponds to "no self-conceit, no provoking of one another, no envy of one another" (Galatians 5:26). In the Spirit's fruit "God is at work in you, both to will and to work for his good pleasure" (Philippians 2:13).

The fruit of the Spirit has to do with spiritual holiness and character, and begins with God's love growing out of your heart toward others through the Holy Spirit. "God's love has been poured into our hearts through the Holy Spirit" (Romans 5:5). I John 3:14 says: "We know that we have passed out of death into life, because we love the brethren." Our love responds to God's gift of love to us, and we requite God's love "because he first loved us" (I John 4:19). I Thessalonians 4: 9 notes: "You, yourselves have been taught by God to love one another." Just as fire consumes a log and transforms it into fire, so God's love ignites the human soul and transforms it into love, itself.[104] Deuteronomy 30:6 forecasts: "And the Lord thy God will circumcise thine heart, and the heart of thy seed, to love the Lord thy God with all thine heart, and with all thy soul, that thou mayest live." (See also, Jeremiah 24:7; and Ezekiel 11:19, 37:14, 37:26).

The Spirit's fruit of love fills us with divine life because God not only has love, but is love (I John 4:8). Whoever confesses that Jesus is the Son of God, "God abides in him, and he in God" (I John 4:15). God's indwelling presence in your spirit means: "the darkness is passing away and the true light is already shining" (I John 2:8).

When we love one another, God abides in us (I John 4:12). Love is fulfilling because it infuses us with satisfaction, gratification, and joy by the very act of dispensing it toward others in obedience to God. We discover that imparting loving kindness toward others simply feels good, even if it is unrequited, unappreciated, unrecognized, or unknown by them. Love is intrinsically joyful because it shares a fruit of the Spirit, and revives, vitalizes, and refreshes what might otherwise be routine and prosaic. This is one reason Jesus observes: "It is more blessed to give than to receive" (Acts 20:35).

In the unselfish ministrations which alleviate physical or spiritual distress, we find fellowship with God, with our brothers in the Lord, and with the unsaved. As a bonus, if love is requited by others, it fills life with meaning, ease, and joy in the most congenial environment possible. And if other Christians fulfill their duty of love toward us, our lives are joyful, indeed. Love in a believer, as part of the Body of Christ, "grows with a growth that is from God" (Colossians 2:19).

When Christ dwells "in your hearts through faith," then "you, being rooted and grounded in love... may be filled with all the fullness of God... who by the power at work within us is able to do far more abundantly than all that we ask or think" (Ephesians 3:17-19). Love, as virtue, is its own reward.

Christ-like character is the object and the result of much human suffering. The fruit of the Holy Spirit for which we pray is synonymous with holiness, and its cultivation regularly exacts some sacrifice of worldly values in exchange for the holiness such fruit reflects. If we would love, we must be prepared to give of ourselves, our time, talent, and treasure to others, even when our love is unrequited or unappreciated. We cannot learn loving generosity without learning to share, and this often involves sacrifice and privation for fledgling benefactors. Love is the divine instrument by which God's blessings are dispensed to others, to alleviate suffering.

Experiencing our own pain develops humility and compassion toward the suffering of others. Man-made tragedies as well as natural ones can evoke love and compassion for the unfortunate victims we might otherwise overlook in our busy-ness. A good dose of poverty and humility, as men are broken and re-shaped under the pressure of torment, will do much to cure the contumely and unconcern of the proud and rich toward those less fortunate. The man whose health is failing will suddenly envy the poorest street urchin who still has youth or health. If we, ourselves, are victimized, the experience can produce sweeter and softer dispositions, which make us more compliant, vulnerable, and humble, and develop concern, compassion, sympathy, love and tolerance for the less fortunate of every kind.

We are better able to love, console, comfort, and minister to others when we have known the torments and anguish of their pains. The recovered cancer patient or alcoholic can best encourage the present victim of such affliction because he is eminently qualified by experience to counsel him. The ex-drug addict can speak authoritatively about the evils of narcotics to youthful users and impart insights in survival and the reliability of God's deliverance. Once-bereaved parents can authentically commiserate with the young couple who have just lost their child. The vulnerability and openness of the battle-scarred can help heal the broken hearts of the newly wounded. A redeemed sinner can offer convincing testimony about Jesus as the Author of his redemption. One who has also known suffering and trials is best equipped to understand and minister to another who struggles with the same problem.

Disasters which befall others may serve no good purpose, except to bring out love, sympathy and brotherhood in those spared, and expand our horizons to encompass others, as the injured are ministered to by an outpouring of Christian concern and compassion in action. Not only is our own love developed by response to another's tragedy, but our suffering may serve the same purpose in others and bring us opportunity to receive the communication of another's love. Suffering can help us to experience God's love flowing to us through the care and comfort of others, who receive His strength to minister to our suffering.

The Body is truly the family of God, and all families are strengthened by shared challenges which bring them together in common endeavor. Suffering becomes an opportunity for the Body collectively to trust God and confront each new adventure He has given us as a family. For, "If one member suffers, all suffer together; if one member is honored, all rejoice together" (I Corinthians 12:26).

Suffering makes us more effective in our ministry, and more believable as a teacher of others, because we can share consolations which we have previously received from God. God will send suffering people to us so we can love them, demonstrate His comfort, and tell about God's love for them. God will use us as a channel of His love: to replace sorrow with joy, despair with hope, discouragement with edification, and defeat with victory. We will choose to love them, as enabled by God's love, even if they are unloveable, because God's inexhaustible love will be flowing in and out of us toward others.

Our ability to edify and comfort others is enhanced when our own suffering has created awareness, appreciation and sympathy for their pain. Suffering makes us more prayerful and caring for the relief, comfort and healing of the afflicted ones who have given us an example of enduring faith or caused us to appreciate our own exemption from pain. Adversity reminds us that disciples hold all gifts of health, wealth, and wisdom as stewards of God's good gifts, for the benefit of others, as well as for our own joy.

The light of God's Word, for example, is meant to benefit others as it benefits us. We are not given divine light to hide it under a bushel (Matthew 5:15). Thus, 2 Timothy 3:16-17 says that "All scripture is... profitable for teaching, for reproof, for correction, and for training in righteousness, that the man of God may be complete, equipped for every good work." (See also, Hebrews 13:21).

The Word will remind us of our call to preach the Good News as witnesses for Christ, and deliver the Word, from which all faith comes, to others. When Jesus has delivered us from our own problems, we will not hesitate to share the priceless pearl we have discovered. If we have experienced His deliverance from adversity, we are equipped to witness for Jesus and comfort others by sharing Him as the solution to every problem, But if we have never troubled to know His comfort, our recollections of high hopes through Jesus, will be callow, hollow, shallow, and low.

Suffering fits us to express our love for others by actually sharing life with them: to rejoice when they rejoice, and to weep when they weep (Romans 12:15). Our suffering teaches us compassion to share the suffering and weeping of others. Your tears in God's bottle (Psalm 56:8) will proliferate as your love shares the pain of others, and accumulates tears of sympathy for others, as a parent cries with a hurting child. Because Jesus, "himself has suffered and been tempted, he is able to help those who are tempted" (Hebrews 2:18), and so suffering will operate in us to serve and minister to others.

God uses suffering to equip our character with the Spirit's fruit of divine love in yet another way. True agape love for others cannot be perfected in us without exercise and testing, and sometimes suffering sharpens our compassion, care, and concern for others. Even though we are regenerated and converted by the New Birth, we have not perfected the holiness essential to caring for others. We need to divest ourselves of self-centeredness, selfishness, and even jealousy of others. I Peter 5:5-6 says: "God opposes the proud, but gives grace to the humble. Humble yourselves therefore under the mighty hand of God, that in due time He might exalt you." We need to be broken so that God can reconstruct the loving disposition needed in the Body of Christ. Self-renunciation, selflessness, and crucifixion of the self proceed only from brokenness and submission to the will of God. Only when we are subdued by suffering can we make room for divine love, compassion, and tenderness. Only tribulation decentralizes the self, prepares the soul for agape love, and hides us behind the Cross that only Christ may be seen in us.

God's chastening for holiness centers on the Spirit's fruit of love, and we can be taught and matured in love by suffering. 2 Thessalonians 1:5 notes that persecutions and afflictions which one endures are "evidence of the righteous judgment of God, that you may be made worthy of the kingdom of God for which you are suffering." As we cultivate the imparted fruit of the Spirit, we grow in Christian character which predisposes us to obedience in helpful and edifying service to others, to the glory of God. We are saved by grace through faith, but develop love by grace through our suffering. Life is not made for pleasure, but for learning and dispensing sacrificial love, and we should not waste our sorrows in the world's classroom by ignoring their lessons.[105] We learn and practice selflessness in marriage, in the family, in church, and in all social relationships. It is God's grace which empowers loving, forgiving responses in all circumstances, and suffering is often the transport of that grace. Relationships gone sour may illuminate our own selfish and unloving nature, and develop in us a loving character. "Whoever has suffered in the flesh has ceased from sin" (I Peter 4:1).

In the spiritual realm, we have little control over misfortunes which befall us. We can control only our response to them, either allowing them to subdue our spirit, or regarding them as opportunities for growth in character and love. Our response makes the suffering a source of resentment and rebellion, or a cause of blessing. Suffering produces endurance, character, hope and the blessing of God's love "poured into our hearts" (Romans 5:5). Trials are to make us rejoice because their testing of faith makes us steadfast, and its effect is "that you may be perfect and complete, lacking in nothing" (James 1:4). Suffering fits us for eternity, where a loving character is essential, so it is understandable that much of this training is not appreciated or fulfilled until we are near life's end.

Joy, as the second named fruit of the Holy Spirit, makes our holiness complete, as it enables us to focus on God's revealed love, and sustains our cultivation and expression of the other fruit and gifts of the Spirit. We have just seen how joy is connected to the fruit of love, and accompanies active love, both received and imparted. In all our obedient acts of loving and witnessing, we experience joy as a fruit of the Spirit as we give ourselves to others. Our obedient, loving acts are expressions and translations of our love for God, by glorifying Him in compliant submission to His will. We act as obedient children, dutifully respecting the wishes of a loving Father, because we desire to honor, glorify, and please Him by actions which make Him proud of us. Loving obedience demonstrates our devotion and gratitude for His grace, blessings and gifts. Enhancing God's pleasure becomes the desire of our hearts, as we act obediently for the inherent joy of serving Him. We find intrinsic joy in generating happiness for others through loving acts, because a deed done in God's name is done for God.[106]

Joy is a blessing as it helps us to cope with worldly temptations and persecutions and constitutes and sustains our spiritual life in the earth. Joy helps us withstand worldly allures by exposing their transience in comparison to the true riches of the joy of the Lord. It not only helps us resist temptation to sin in our quest for holiness, but it sustains us to endure and put into proper perspective any worldly suffering produced by sin and persecution. Joy is a supernatural blessing which makes any torment bearable.

Jesus affirms God's will that we have fullness of joy, connected with obedient intimacy with the Lord. He says at John 15:5-11: "apart from me you can do nothing... If you abide in me, and my words abide in you, ask whatever you will, and it shall be done for you... If you keep my commandments you will abide in my love... These things I have spoken to you that my joy may be in you, and that your joy may be full." Abiding in the Lord necessitates conforming to His will and obeying His commandments in the Word, and joy is derived from this obedience. We are also directed to pray in Jesus' name that our joy may be full: "hitherto you have asked nothing in my name; ask, and you will receive, that your joy may be full" (John 16:24). Again, asking in the name of Jesus necessitates coinciding with His will, and joy is derived from devotion to the Master's purposes.

Jesus attests to the Disciples' faith and obedience, from which their joy proceeded, at John 17:6-7,13: "they have kept thy word, Now they know that everything that thou has given me is from thee... and they have believed that thou didst send me... and these things I speak in the world, that they may have my joy fulfilled in themselves."

I Thessalonians 1:6 recalls that the Holy Spirit is the agent through whom we experience joy as a fruit of the Spirit: "you received the word in much affliction, with joy inspired by the Holy Spirit." (See also, John 14:16, 16;7; Acts 5:32).

Joy comes from obedience because it directly shares in the divine personality. If we faithfully seek holiness by obedience to God's command to "be holy," then we will draw closer to God because we have acted in conformance with His character. Since God is perfect love (I John 4:8), faithful obedience in love connects the soul with God. I John 2:5 says: "whoever keeps his word, in him truly love for God is perfected." In the unselfish ministrations which alleviate another's physical or spiritual distress, we will find fellowship not only with God, but also with our brothers in the Lord, and the unsaved.

Since Heaven pursues and rejoices over one sinner who repents (Luke 15:7,10,20; Hebrews 12:2), we will have joy whenever we lovingly share the Gospel with a convicted sinner in obedience to the Great Commission of Mark 16:15, because it reunites a lost soul with God. Like Paul, we can recognize the privilege we have of gathering fruit and bringing unsaved persons to Christ, seeking no recompense from the Church, but confident our reward is "that in preaching I may make the gospel free of charge" available to the unsaved, "... that I may share in its blessings" (I Corinthians 9:18,23). Because Paul was obedient to God's will, he could describe himself as "always rejoicing... making many rich; as having nothing, and yet possessing everything" (2 Corinthians 6:10).

When we are filled with joy, we will have no room for occupation with temptations to sin, and we will be fortified by joy to endure any suffering inflicted upon us. We will see that obedience to God's Word puts us in harmony and communion with God, and joy comes from such intimacy according to Psalm 16:11: "in thy presence is fullness of joy."

Since Jesus is the Word (John 1:1), and the Word found in Scripture is the key to finding and knowing Jesus as a person, it follows the greater our familiarity with, immersion and saturation in the Word, through familiarity and obedience to it, the greater will be our contact and presence in the Lord, from Whom we receive joy. Since God is light (I John 1:5), and His Word is a lamp unto your feet and a light unto your path (Psalm 119:105), following the Word in obedience will lead to the presence of the Lord, as we dwell with the Word and reflect upon it prayerfully.

When we regard the life of the Lord we can see how joy contributes to deliverance. The joy of the Lord, and the prospect of deliverance by him help us endure temptation. When we look to Jesus, we can "lay aside every weight and sin which clings so closely, and... run with perseverance the race that is set before us, looking to Jesus, the pioneer and perfecter of our faith, who for the joy that was set before him endured the cross" (Hebrews 12:1-2). Psalm 126:5 agrees: "They that sow in tears shall reap in joy."

The lives of the Apostles also teach us that worldly torment can be surmounted by the fruit of joy in the Lord, After Paul and Silas were punished for speaking in the name of Jesus, they departed, "rejoicing that they were counted worthy to suffer dishonor for the name" (Acts 5:41). Paul and Silas could also pray and sing hymns of praise to God from their prison cell, rejoicing in the midst of suffering (Acts 16:25-30; and see Acts 13:52; Luke 24:52). Jesus did not explain much about why there is human suffering, but He did overcome it, and graciously shares the victory with His Church.

God's grace provides rejoicing as an antidote to weariness from resisting sin, enervation, and disinterest, "for the joy of the Lord is your strength" (Nehemiah 8:10). Joy comes from knowing God delivers His people, and turns all things to good for those who love Him. Psalm 28:7 observes: "The Lord is my strength and my shield; my heart trusted in him, and I am helped: therefore my heart greatly rejoiceth; and with my song will I praise him." We rejoice, therefore, because the Lord blesses us with His protection. Prayers of praise to God are superior to petitions for things, because praise brings the immediate blessing of joy in the recollections of God's love. Joy is not only a blessing for overcoming the world, but has intrinsic value for fullness and quality of life.

Suffering in the world is a fact of Christian life, and directly contributes to the development of spiritual joy in several ways. First, suffering drives us to the Lord for surcease, comfort, and deliverance. Seeking God focuses our attention on God's presence, so that in His communion and companionship we find fullness and quality of life. If our earthly life consisted of nothing but enjoying the glory and love of God, in His companionship and fellowship, it would be Heaven on earth, since God's presence is the essence of heaven. Scripture relates that our joy is generated whenever we look to our beautiful Lord; contemplate His holy character; find hope in His promises; offer praise for His works in creation, nature and man, and worship His flawless character for Who He is.

Joy comes from appreciating God's blessings, through reflection upon, and communion with, the very presence of God. According to Psalm 16:8, 11: "I have set the Lord always before me... Therefore my heart is glad... Thou wilt shew me the path of life; in thy presence is fullness of joy; at thy right hand there are pleasures for evermore." As we praise God and delight in His character and Providence, we will experience the joy of fellowship with God and abiding in Christ. The Bible says that joy is cultivated by praising God, during which we recall all our blessings and reprise the joy we have known in the Lord's love. Psalm 5:11 details joy from comfort in contemplating the Lord's benevolence and protection: "let all those that put their trust in thee rejoice... For thou, Lord wilt bless the righteous; with favor wilt thou compass him as with a shield." See also, Psalm 2:11, 27:6, 33:1, 37:4, 48:2, 96:4-12, 118:24; Isaiah 29:19; and Jeremiah 15:16.

The connection between praise and joy is affirmed at Psalm 27:4,6: "One thing have I desired... that I may dwell in the house of the Lord all the days of my life, to behold the beauty of the Lord... therefore will I offer in his tabernacle sacrifices of joy; I will sing, yea, I will sing praises unto the Lord." Psalm 35:9 adds: "And my soul shall be joyful in the Lord: it shall rejoice in his salvation." See also, Psalms 9:1, 17:15, 32:10-11, 35:10-18, 42:4-11, 43:3-5, 50:14-15, and 51:8-13. Acts 2:25-26 says: "I saw the Lord always before me... therefore my heart was glad, and my tongue rejoiced... thou wilt make me full of gladness with thy presence." We are urged to "Rejoice in the Lord always" (Philippians 4:4).

We trigger the praise and worship which produce joy, when we meditate upon God's goodness, wisdom, and power; that He is Sovereign in control, and intervenes in His exercise of dominion in the affairs of men; that he answers prayer; that He has promised our good, here and Hereafter, materially and spiritually. We can praise God because He has promised to deliver us from suffering as soon as it has served its purpose. We can praise Him because one blessing is often deferred while another is developed in us; and we can know that what causes pain now will, in God's good time, develop the superior blessing God has chosen for us. We can be certain that if God allows it, suffering will be for our good, because God loves His children, and is not careless with the circumstances He allows into their lives.

I Peter 1:2-6 confirms that believers rejoice, despite trials, because we depend upon our New Birth in Christ; that we are "chosen and destined by God the Father and sanctified by the Spirit for obedience to Jesus Christ and for sprinkling with his blood," for our "inheritance which is unperishable, undefiled, and unfading, kept in heaven for you, who by God's power are guarded through faith for a salvation ready to be revealed in the last time."

Suffering may be an indispensable part of joy, for we can only make time for spiritual things by relinquishing other time-consuming pursuits of worldly pleasures. We must be prepared to give ourselves to God and others to cultivate and accomplish fulfillment of the higher spiritual joy which accompanies service and fellowship. In a convoluted way, suffering can produce joy of thanksgiving when we are delivered from it as our pain or anxiety is relieved. We can rejoice after our endurance through pain is rewarded, or because the presence of suffering makes us appreciate all the blessings we have enjoyed in other areas and occasions. Then we are reminded to give God praise and thanksgiving, from which joy is derived. Thus, deprivations of joy may occur until we recapture the joy of recalling all the blessings we still retain or know are yet to come. Joy becomes the antithesis of fear, depression, discouragement, and surrender to the world's sorrows.

Often, we will not appreciate peace, the third fruit of the Holy Spirit, until we are hurled into turmoil or bellicose circumstances. This is not to say that we cannot appreciate peace in the midst of plenty and freedom from pain, but sometimes we do not seek peace until strife reminds us of our need for it. Then, peace is always found in the assurance that God has established forgiveness and salvation in Jesus, and promises eventual deliverance from suffering. Isaiah 26:3 acknowledges: "Thou wilt keep him in perfect peace, whose mind is stayed on thee; because he trusteth in thee." Peace is found in harmony with God's plan, through our obedience (Isaiah 48:18). We have peace as God reveals, and teaches us what He wishes (Isaiah 54:13). We have peace primarily in the certainty that Jesus has overcome the world (John 16:33), and that peace "which passes all understanding, will keep your hearts and your minds in Christ Jesus" (Philippians 4:7). Romans 8:6 agrees: "to set the mind on the Spirit is life and peace," and see also, Colossians 3:15. Isaiah 26:3-4 puts it: "Thou wilt keep him in perfect peace, whose mind is stayed on thee; because he trusteth in thee. Trust ye in the Lord forever: for in the Lord Jehovah is everlasting strength."

We have peace from trusting in God's assurance that if we hearken to His commandments, we will have peace and righteousness (Isaiah 48:18). If we will learn from the Lord, "all thy children shall be taught of the Lord; and great shall be the peace of thy children" (Isaiah 54:13). Psalm 29:11 adds: "Great peace have they which love thy law: and nothing shall offend them." Love of God's Word makes one impervious to worldly assaults. Psalm 29:11 says: "The Lord will give strength unto his people; the Lord will bless the people with peace." Inner peace allows us to endure any transient travails the world may inflict, as well as alleviate the anxiety of others, as the Lord's peace is imparted.

Our peace is judicial, or "peace with God" (Romans 5:1), because Jesus has made us righteous and justified. Our peace is also personal because we are given the peace of God" (Philippians 4:7). And this peace is kept, or supernaturally guarded against external intrusion or internal confusion.[107]

Thus, God's peace comes from the knowledge that we have been reconciled with God; freed from guilt; and justified by the Blood of Jesus. We are secure in trusting that "Blessed is the man unto whom the Lord imputeth not iniquity" (Psalm 32:1-2). Peace comes from the assurance that our sins are forgiven and forgotten when we confess them, and God cleanses us from all unrighteousness, so we are restored to the Christ-likeness of our regeneration. We find peace in the affirmance of glorification at Philippians 1:6: "And I am sure that he who began a good work in you will bring it to completion at the day of Jesus Christ."

Peace also comes from knowing you are right with God; that you serve and glorify the Lord; obey His Word to His glory; and as a result, supernatural peace comes as a fruit of the Spirit. This peace with God is made "by the blood of his cross" (Colossians 1:20), and securely guarded by the reconciliation and salvation which grace through faith assures.

Jesus warns disciples that we will have disruptions in the world and be scattered, but He has overcome the world: "yet I am not alone, for the Father is with me. I have said this to you, that in me you may have peace. In the world you have tribulation; but be of good cheer, I have overcome the world" (John 16:32-33). Our peace comes from strength in the perfect love of Christ which casts out fear. We are assured of God's deliverance (Psalms 34:17,19; 37:39-40; 91:3; 97:10), and this trust sustains our endurance of affliction.

We are directed to "Have no anxiety about anything, but in everything by prayer and supplication with thanksgiving let your requests be made known to God. And the peace of God, which passes all understanding, will keep your hearts and your minds in Christ Jesus" (Philippians 4:6-7). We cannot sin when our mind is occupied with the presence of Jesus. We can find peace in entrusting all our cares to Jesus, staying focused on His loving mercies, because "he who is in you is greater than he who is in the world" (I John 4:4).

We need only entrust the concerns of worldly life to Jesus, and He gives us His peace, rest, and serenity. We need only turn over control and direction of our lives to Christ, and he will turn them to righteous excellence in His image. Peace comes through Jesus, because of our salvation. "Peace I leave with you, My peace I give you," says Jesus at John 14:27. "Since we are justified by faith, we have peace with God through our Lord Jesus Christ" (Romans 5:1). It is God's own presence which provides peace to endure temptation without apprehension or trepidation, confident that by God's power we will overcome the tempter: "I will fear no evil: for thou art with me; thy rod and thy staff comfort me" (Psalm 23:4). "Perfect love casts out fear" (I John 4:18).

Paul could write to the Philippians from prison: "I have learned, in whatever state I am, to be content... I can do all things in him who strengthens me" (Philippians 4:11,13). Paul's secret of contentment was his awareness of the presence of God, and His long-term plan of deliverance, despite ongoing torture, strife, and struggle. He had inner peace in Christ, knowing that everything was under God's sovereign control. God's constancy is dependable, even though circumstances and environment might vary from day to day.

Patience is the fourth enumerated fruit of the Spirit, and trusts God to fulfill His promises, in His own providential time and according to His plan. This helps us to endure any affliction, knowing if we truly believe God's promise to bless us and deliver good; even if only ultimately in Heaven where all suffering and tribulation is banished, we can bear with any temptation or travails. For, we know God is using them to develop Christ-like character and bless us in a spiritual, rather than earthly way. When we are endowed with the supernatural fruit of patience, we can endure the world's assaults. We may still have pain, but it is no longer suffering, for all our attention is focused on the joy of the Lord which we are experiencing. God enables believers to overcome any suffering through the fruit of patient endurance.

Patience develops when suffering illuminates our character, and we await God's deliverance and expulsion of the flaws which must be remedied in our spirituality. We cannot learn patience without experiencing denial and delay. God may have to withhold blessings until we learn that worldly things are of no value, compared to God, Himself. We may have to undergo suffering to learn patient endurance, discovering that God eventually delivers, no matter how long the wait, if only we will persevere in faith. James 1:3-4 says of trials: "Count it all joy... when you meet various trials, for you know that testing of your faith produces steadfastness and let steadfastness have its full effect, that you may be perfect and complete, lacking in nothing." Philippians 1:6 says: "that he who began a good work in you will bring it to completion at the day of Jesus Christ."

Wounds may not heal instantly, even when the cutting edge has been withdrawn from us. We may have won victory over a struggle, but still need time to re-build and restore the damaged areas sustained in combat. This is one reason why God has established patience as a fruit of the Spirit. We can have patience because we know God will fulfill His vision, though he delay for a time: "For the vision is yet for an appointed time, but at the end it shall speak; and not lie: though it tarry, wait for it; because it will surely come" (Habakkuk 2:3).

We can patiently endure because God promises to supply whatever we need to accomplish that for which we are called. St. Paul attested that in his tribulation "the Lord stood by me and gave me strength to proclaim the word fully" (2 Timothy 4:17; see also, I Peter 4:14, 5:10; 2 Peter 1:4; I Corinthians 10:13). God supplied what Elijah needed to do God's will and discredit Baal's prophets by sending down fire from heaven to consume their sacrifices, and by empowering Elijah to slay them (I Kings 18:38).

When Elijah feared Jezebel's threats to murder him, and became so exhausted and dispirited that he prayed for death (I Kings 19:2,4), God refreshed, restored, strengthened, encouraged, and provided for His prophet, using His Spirit, angels, and other believers as instruments of restoration. Elijah was in a valley of despair, and God instructed him to sleep to regain his strength, and sent an angel with food and drink sufficient to sustain him on a forty day journey to Horeb, the mountain of God (I Kings 19:5-8). God supplies what His servants need to ascend to His mountaintop, and strengthens them in His rest. God may not remove the storms of life, despite our entreaties. He may choose to give us peace and security to weather the storm, which He uses to perfect us.

Jesus says: "Come to me, all who labor and are heavy-laden and I will give you rest... and you will find rest for your soul" (Matthew 11:28-29). I Peter 5;10 gives the assurance: "And after you have suffered a little while, the God of all grace, who has called you to his eternal glory in Christ, will himself restore, establish, and strengthen you." Isaiah 40:29-31 promises God's provision: "he giveth power to the faint: and to them that have no might he increaseth strength... But they that wait upon the Lord shall renew their strength; they shall mount up with wings as eagles; they shall run, and not be weary; and they shall walk and not faint." Lamentations 3:26 observes: "It is good that a man should both hope and quietly wait for the salvation of the Lord."

Patience is synonymous with endurance and perseverance by which we withstand the world's incitations to sin, or endure suffering caused by sins of oneself or others. We need patience to minister to the needs of other people. We may encourage, educate, counsel, serve, mentor or witness to them, but working with other people can be a tedious and arduous occupation. A great deal of time may be necessary before others bear fruit, and the virtue of patience well serves the disciple who sows, and eagerly awaits the appearance of another's spiritual blossoming.

The fruit of the Spirit imparts, coincides with, and constitutes the very characteristics of Christ which identify His holiness. I Corinthians 13:4, 7 says: "Love is patient and kind... Love bears all things, believes all things, hopes all things, endures all things." Endurance is as much concerned with patience while God works His will to transform believers to the image of Christ, as it is with our efforts to persevere in holiness and obedience throughout temptation and suffering.

The Bible says that we can <u>always</u> depend on instant grace to empower us fully to overcome the world, and then do God's will after we have withstood temptation or endured suffering for a little while. Whenever God makes a demand on us, we can expect to receive sufficient grace to endure it.[108] God's grace may rid us of pain, deaden discomfort, or simply enable us to bear our afflictions by God's strength.

God rewards patient endurance of temptation and suffering, for we "through faith and patience inherit the promises" (Hebrews 6:12). "For you have need of endurance, so that you may do the will of God and receive what is promised" (Hebrews 10:36). James 1:12 teaches: "Blessed is the man who endures trial, for when he has stood the test he will receive the crown of life which God has promised to those who love him" and see also, Lamentations 3:25; 2 Corinthians 1:6; Colossians 1:11; James 1:4, 5:11; and Revelation 3:10. The Bible's call to "wait on the Lord" (Isaiah 40:31) confirms that He is working, has a plan; and will deliver on His promises in <u>His</u> time.

The trials we have test our faith and produce patience, while we faithfully await God's deliverance from them. Faith only operates while we are being denied or deprived of some blessing. We have no need of faith or patience when our wishes have been gratified and our needs met. We are to "Count it all joy... when you meet various trials," because trials help us to grow in holiness as well as patience. We are exhorted to be patient because holiness and witnessing take time to bear fruit.

Patience, serenity, and calm also help to endure pain; for suffering is more difficult to bear if we revolt and refuse to accept it when it is sent by God. Irritation and impatience increase our suffering and retard its intended benefit to us. Resignation with suffering does not prevent our praying earnestly and persistently for God's consolation and deliverance from suffering. Patience puts us in harmony with God's will, for He provides the Spirit's fruits of patience and faith, which result from denials and persecutions. When we accept them, we act within the framework of submitting to God's will and timetable, as He develops these character traits in us. This redounds to the benefit of others we would serve, and reduces their needs.

It is true that some time and travail must pass before we can progress in our spiritual maturity, just as there must be an interval of time as we grow physically from infancy to puberty to adulthood. However, if a disciple learns quickly by cooperative, devoted service, he can minimize the pain of advancements, failures, trials, and errors in the process of spiritual maturing.

Even sincere, but ill-conceived prayers can evoke suffering for Christians. Someone has said, "Be careful what you pray for; You may get it." If you pray for patience without cooperating in its embrace, God may send affliction, trial, or despair, by which patience is developed, in answer to your prayer. For, we cannot learn patience without the sacrifice of denial and postponement of our desires. Longsuffering may come from suffering long.

If you pray for humility or meekness without making any effort on your own to cultivate that virtue, God may place you in humbling circumstances, from which you will learn humility. He may have to break you in order to reconstruct you. Prayers to be delivered from the sin of pride, which is hateful to God, may be answered by the temptation of fame and the praise of other men. Proverbs 27:21 says: "As the fining pot for silver, and the furnace for gold; so is a man to his praise." True humility is tested by the compliments of others, and how we react reveals whether our pride is properly in our Saviour, or wrongly in ourselves.

St. Paul had received extraordinary insights from Jesus when he visited the third heaven, and such knowledge could have made any man proud and boastful because of these privileged revelations. God used or allowed Satan to inflict a thorn in the flesh to remind Paul of his total dependence upon God for every blessing, including spiritual knowledge. As Paul relates: "And to keep me from being too elated by the abundance of revelations, a thorn was given me in the flesh, a messenger of Satan, to harass me, to keep me from being too elated" (2 Corinthians 12:7). Paul was allowed to suffer, as part of his training in true humility, to prevent the pride of self-importance, and maintain his reliance on God.

Paul possibly thought that without affliction he would be most effective in preaching and evangelism, to the glory of God. But God provided supernatural enabling for Paul's ministry, and added the perfecting of humble, Christ-like character in Paul. Paul sought natural strength, and God provided divine power made perfect in weakness, to strengthen Paul and overcome his suffering. Instead of altering circumstances and conditions, as Paul might have desired, God transformed Paul.

Goodness, kindness, and gentleness emerge from the crushed and broken hearts of sufferers, as pride and self-sufficiency are distilled and extracted by the pressure of affliction, and we increasingly share a common humanity in the knowledge and personal experience of universal suffering. Goodness, as righteousness, may blossom only in the midst of temptation and testing. Kindness may be exhibited only in demanding, time-consuming circumstances of giving oneself to others, regardless of personal sacrifice. Gentleness develops when we are exposed to cruelties which have crushed the esteem and discouraged the aspirations of another person. The fruit of goodness, kindness, and gentleness all directly bear on a believer's sharing of blessings and reduction of privation in others.

Faithfulness, as a fruit of the Spirit, cannot be developed without delay and denial of something sought, in order to let faith be tried and proved. Suffering develops faithfulness when it draws us to entrust our deliverance completely to the Lord, casting all care on him, and relying upon His solutions, rather than our own constructs, devices, and contrivances. As God's constancy and faithfulness are proved as we overcome suffering, our faith grows and provides a foundation for entrusting the next level of affliction to the Lord.

The Spirit seldom dispenses fully ripened fruit to a believer. He is more likely to plant a seed, and entrust it to us to pray for the fullness of the Spirit in His fruit. God's enlightened Word expels fear by creating faith, because we believe the Word, but we must put ourselves in a position to hear and receive that Word, by which faith comes (Romans 10:17). God may put us in uncomfortable situations to drive us to the point we see the need for His blessed consolation, and willingly seek it.

Faith in God overcomes fear according to Proverbs 29:25: "The fear of man bringeth a snare: but whoso putteth his trust in the Lord shall be safe." John 14:27 says; "Let not your hearts be troubled, neither let them be afraid," because Jesus leaves His peace with us as assurance of our righteousness and reconciliation in Him. When we know God will deliver believers from torment, such knowledge frees us from fear. John 8:32 says: "If you continue in my word... you will know the truth, and the truth will make you free." Faith brings freedom from fear, as we depend upon God's promised deliverance.

The Word is also God's pre-packaged answer to our prayers which seek His divine guidance. There is no need to pray to God for His blessing in a divorce proceeding, fornication, or homosexual liaison, when His Word has already answered in the negative (Malachi 2:15-16; Matthew 5:32, 19:9; Leviticus 18:22 Romans 1:24-27; I Corinthians 6:9; I Thessalonians 4:3). Faith in, and obedience to, the Word's instruction will be the true blessing, as it nurtures spirituality and opens us to spiritual knowledge and blessings. "Blessed are those who hear the word of God and keep it" (Luke 11:28). St. Paul said that spiritual knowledge, or "solid food is for the mature, for those who have their faculties trained by practice to distinguish good from evil" (Hebrews 5:14).

God has provided the Word in advance to give us, as needed, a repository of blessing in His comfort, protection, guidance, enlightenment, strength, fruit of the Spirit, rest, answers to prayer, direction in right conduct, spiritual growth, communion, and fellowship.

The more we look and seek to know God, the more we will know Him. The more we understand God's ways, the more we will appreciate His faithfulness, accept His initiatives, and unconditionally trust His goodness, leading to praise and joy through this knowledge. God was displeased with the Jews in the wilderness because they "do err in their heart, and they have not known my ways" (Psalm 95:10). But the more we praise Him, the weaker our pain becomes, and the stronger our awareness of the presence of Christ, and His peace, joy, and love. The more we praise God for His Providence, the more we will rejoice in the realization He is finishing and perfecting our faith.

Once we recognize that God always has a good reason and outcome for allowing circumstances of suffering to reach us, the stronger will be our faith. And we will express our faith by praising and thanking God for the situation, itself.[109] When we can have these attitudes and act according to these principles, then truly our faith in God will be active during, through, and because of suffering. The greater our faith that God will deliver us according to His eternal plan and purpose unto spiritual, eternal blessings, the sooner His power will transform us. The sooner we are transformed, the better we are able to receive the guidance which God is transmitting. Thus, suffering increases our faithfulness when we trust God and believe that He is perfectly good, all-wise, and all-powerful.

The fruit of faith comes because of Jesus, through the Holy Spirit, and originates with God as His way and instrument to help us endure. Romans 12:3 confirms we can "think with sober judgment, each according to the measure of faith which God has assigned him." St. Peter says believers "have obtained a faith of equal standing with ours in the righteousness of our God and Savior Jesus Christ" (2 Peter 1:1).

Jesus says this available faith is sufficient to move mountains, though it be small as a grain of mustard seed, and we have no need to ask the Lord to "Increase our faith" (Luke 17:5-6). Rather, we should seek the Lord to strengthen our faith so we might endure temptations. Persistence, tenacity, and perseverance are expressions of faith, because Jesus says at Luke 18:1 we ought not let our faith waver, but "ought always to pray and not lose heart."

All faith originates with God. Saving faith comes from God's prevenient grace, for Jesus teaches at John 6:44: "No one can come to me unless the Father who sent me draws him."

Hebrews 12:2, KJV identifies Jesus as the Pioneer and Perfecter, "the author and finisher of our faith." (See also, Luke 17:5; Romans 1:6, 10:17; Ephesians 2:8; and Philippians 1:29).

Self-control is the last-named, ninth fruit of the Holy Spirit, by which we develop the faculty of being content with the portion in life God has given us. St. Paul says at Philippians 4:11: "I have learned, in whatever state I am, to be content... I can do all things in him who strengthens me." See also, I Corinthians 9:24.

Self-control comes by taking the lesson of the Parable of the Vineyard to heart. In the Parable, Jesus teaches that a householder hired laborers at the start of the day to work in his vineyard, and continued periodically to hire laborers throughout the day, even to the eleventh hour, long after the first laborers had begun work. At the end of the day, the householder gave the same amount of wages to those who had worked least as he gave to those who had worked all day (Matthew 20:9-10). The natural mind would argue this was unfair because the first laborers had worked much longer and harder than the last, who worked but a little. However, the point of the Parable is that the wages paid were a matter of grace on the part of the Master, and the work and effort of all the laborers fell short of earning or deserving the reward.

All men who are saved receive the same wage: Grace; and their reward is not based on their works, whether as a missionary for decades, or the thief on the cross with Jesus for a day. Consequently, we have no right to expect anything, nor do we deserve anything, no matter what our works. We must work to please our Lord, because we love Him and enjoy working in His vineyard; not because we will be rewarded with benefits. We can accept our lot because whatever it is, it is more than we deserve, and the Creator of the universe can do whatever He wants, judging men however He pleases.

Self-control, or temperance, almost demands temptation and testing in order to be perfected. It is our response to suffering, empowered by God, by which we cooperate in curtailing the sinful traits which have produced disobedience to God and our consequent pain. Thus, it would seem that every fruit of the Spirit is cultivated, nurtured, fertilized, and harvested by circumstances of privation or stress. It behooves Christians to use self-control in collaborating with the working of the Holy Spirit to transform us to Christ-likeness. We are assured we will be glorified in the Hereafter, but while we are here, our holiness will affect the quality and extent of our faith, obedience, prayer, loving service, witnessing, and fellowship with God.

CHAPTER 12

THE LORD'S SUFFER

"For as we share abundantly in Christ's sufferings, so through Christ we share abundantly in comfort too."

–2 Corinthians 1:5.

"Beloved, do not be surprised at the fiery ordeal which comes upon you to prove you, as though something strange were happening to you. But rejoice in so far as you share Christ's suffering."

–I Peter 4:12-13.

In a world where the natural progression of life ends in death, it should not be surprising that for most of recorded history, worldly life has been brutish, nasty, and short, making it natural to turn in hope toward a Hereafter free from pain and suffering. The possibility of achieving Heaven on earth, where the promise of blessings becomes reality, amidst health and prosperity, was a 20th century phenomenon, confined mainly to America and Europe. For Christianity's first nineteen centuries, life for most was one of privation worldwide.

Even in the 20th century, millions of Christians throughout the world lacked health and wealth, and had no prospect of ever realizing them in this life. Prosperity implies freedom from financial suffering. Health implies freedom from debility and pain. The absence of these blessings is not far removed from suffering, whenever lack of wealth becomes the affliction of poverty, and lack of health becomes the distress of illness. When we lack prosperity or health, we often find we have not only lost the promised blessing, but also graduated to financial ruin or ill-health. Blessings of joy and felicity have then been replaced with the pain and suffering of privation.

One does not escape suffering by virtue of natural advantage, the New-Birth, holy living, wealth, or health. This human phenomenon is neither curse, nor accident, but produces a blessing from God to work good in a believer's life. We may not be able to discern whether God's blessing originated in human freedom, which produced poor choices and suffering; or whether God initiated travails as training and discipline to promote our holiness. We can, however, be sure that in the end God will work all things for our good advantage.

There is also punishment imposed upon unrepentant sinners, who suffer. Romans 2:9 warns that "There will be tribulation and distress for every human being who does evil." "For the wages of sin is death" (Romans 6:23). Evil men will suffer for their wrong, and faithful men will suffer despite their right, but we are assured all will suffer, either here or Hereafter. As someone has irreverently said, 'Christians must go through hell to get to Heaven,' while stubborn, impenitent sinners will end in hell.

The universality of suffering indicates that even one blessed with health and prosperity can experience other ills which interfere with, or detract from, the enjoyment of these blessings. Even worse, one may endure intense suffering without enjoying blessings in any area whatsoever. Degrees of suffering may range from physical torture, with varying torments and afflictions, to privations of indebtedness and social ostracism. We may concentrate on faithfulness and obedience to the Lord, and be persecuted for it. We may suffer when our loving-kindness is unrequited by an indifferent spouse or antagonistic child. We will sorrow over the death of loved ones. One cause of suffering may be removed by the grace and power of God, only to be succeeded by different, more complex varieties of suffering.

The Bible makes it clear that suffering, self-denial, persecution, and even the valley of the shadow of death, are required of every believer. Suffering originated with the Fall of Adam and Eve, when sin was introduced into the world. Suffering resulted from sin and God's condemnation of it: "Unto the woman he said, I will greatly multiply thy sorrow and thy conception... And unto Adam he said... cursed is the ground for thy sake, in sorrow shalt thou eat of it all the days of thy life" (Genesis 3:16-17).

Satan was able to convince Eve that she lacked something because she knew only good. He deceived her into thinking it was better to be like God and know good and evil. But evil can produce only pain and loss. Eve was out of fellowship not only with God, but also with Adam. Adam's choice was a deliberate one, preferring to fellowship with Eve, more than desiring to fellowship with God. His choice put him on Satan's side and made him the enemy of God.[110]

Romans 5:12-15 explains: "Therefore as sin came into the world through one man and death through sin, and so death spread to all men because all men sinned — sin indeed was in the world before the law was given... many died through one man's trespass." Since all men are under this sentence of death, suffering is simply an early manifestation of death, and it comes in slow stages, earlier and more intense to some than to others. Suffering is a part of the human condition since, and because of, the Fall.

In the Old Testament, Job 5:7 observes: "Man is born unto trouble, as the sparks fly upward." Job 14:1 adds: "Man that is born of a woman is of few days, and full of trouble." Job 2:10 inquires: "Shall we receive good at the hand of God, and shall we not receive evil?" Job 15:20-24 notes: "The wicked man travaileth with pain all his days... in prosperity the destroyer shall come upon him... Trouble and anguish shall make him afraid; they shall prevail against him." Psalm 22:11 petitions: "Be not far from me; for trouble is near." Ecclesiastes 2:23 bemoans the condition of man: "For all his days are sorrows, and his travail grief; yea, his heart taketh not rest in the night."

The Christ Whose example we are pledged to follow, is not only our substitute, Ransomer, Rescuer, Regenerator, Redeemer, Perfect Man, Preacher, Healer, Comforter, Lord, and Saviour. He is also the consummate Sufferer and Man of Sorrows, of Whom St. Paul said: "For I decided to know Christ and him crucified" (I Corinthians 2:2). The Christ Who Paul sought to know was Christ on His Cross, Who teaches by His loving sacrifice and substitutionary Atonement. The suffering and death of Christ was not a frustration of God's plan, but was His foreordained purpose brought to fruition. Jesus is the sacrificial "Lamb slain from the foundation of the world" (Revelation 13:8, KJV). Jesus was "delivered up according to the definite plan and foreknowledge of God" (Acts 2:23).

In addition to Job, other Old Testament saints were visited with grief, anguish, and great torment. Joseph unjustly languished in a well at the hands of his brothers and in prison because of Potiphar's wife. Moses was not allowed to enter the promised land. David was exposed to physical danger and exile by Saul; rebellion by his son; and the death of his children. Elisha witnessed lepers healed and the dead raised during his ministry, and even after his death his body miraculously healed a dead Moabite, whose body "touched the bones of Elisha... revived, and stood up on his feet" (2 Kings 13:21). Yet, Elisha himself was not exempt from worldly afflictions, and became "fallen of his sickness whereof he died" (2 Kings 13:14).

The Great Hall of Faith contained in Hebrews 11 exalts the faith of Old Testament saints such as Gideon, Barak, Samson, Jephthah, David, Samuel, and the prophets, yet reminds us that these paragons of faith became so because they "were tortured... suffered mocking and scourging, and even chains and imprisonment. They were stoned, they were sawn in two, they were killed with the sword; they went about in skins of sheep and goats, destitute, afflicted, ill-treated... And all these, <u>though well attested by their faith, did not receive what was promised</u>" (Hebrews 11:35-39). Despite their enduring faith, they were denied the earthly blessings they desired. New Testament saints have the added blessing of the indwelling Godhead in this life, but that does not guarantee exemption from suffering. Faith in God and His promises meets with God's approval and blessings, but not necessarily recognized in this world. Christian martyrs suffer here without earthly pleasures, in exchange for the joys of Hereafter.

SUFFERING OF THE APOSTLES

In the early Church Christian martyrs underwent persecution, punishment and death as the cost of their faith. Many knew no joy except to know Christ, love Him, and serve him by their faith in dying for Him. Jesus owned nothing to divide at his death, and even His seamless purple robe had been furnished by soldiers (John 19:2). He declared His poverty of worldly goods: "Foxes have holes, and birds of the air have nests; but the Son of man has nowhere to lay his head" (Matthew 8:20). Peter confessed to the lame man at the temple: "I have no silver and gold, but I give you what I have; in the name of Jesus Christ of Nazareth, walk" (Acts 3:6). Jesus promises to him who seeks the Kingdom of God, only sufficiency of food and clothing (Matthew 6:33). Paul, too, died penniless, hardly a testament to a Gospel of wealth for disciples.

It is true there were many occasions when Jesus encountered the sick and "he healed them all" (Matthew 8:16, 9:35, 12:15, 14:36; Mark 6:56; Luke 4:40, 6;19, 9:11; Acts 10:38). Peter, likewise had occasion to heal all the sick and afflicted (Acts 5:16). On the other hand, there "lay a multitude of invalids, blind, lame, paralyzed" at the pool of Bethesda (John 5:3), yet Jesus also chose to heal only one lame man, and then withdrew from the crowd (John 5:13). During all the preceding years an angel had stirred the waters, but only "whoever <u>stepped in first</u> after the troubling of the water was healed," among the multitude of invalids assembled (John 5:4).

Nor did Paul, who worked many miraculous healings (Acts 19:11-12), transmit divine healing to every other suffering Christian. Trophimus was "left ill" when Paul departed Miletus (2 Timothy 4:20). Paul's fellow worker, Epaphraditus, "was ill, near to death" and 'nearly died for the work of Christ" (Philippians 2:26-30). St. Paul relates that Timothy had "frequent ailments," for which Paul prescribed: "use a little wine" (I Timothy 5:23).

The cost of discipleship to follow Jesus includes abjuration of worldly ties and disavowal of worldly standards. Peter and John braved persecution before the Jewish Council in order to preach (Acts 4:20). Peter, Andrew, James, and John forsook the security of their occupations, homes, and families to follow Jesus' call faithfully (Matthew 5:18-22). Saul of Tarsus relinquished prestige and status among the Pharisees in order to serve the Lord as a transformed St. Paul (Acts 26:5).

Jesus told Ananias to seek out Paul, "for he is a chosen instrument of mine... for I will show him how much he must suffer for the sake of my name" (Acts 9:15). Knowing what lay ahead of him, Paul submitted to God and suffered from whippings, beatings, stoning, imprisonment, robbers; his own people, Gentiles, cities, wilderness, hunger, cold, and exposure (2 Corinthians 11:24-27). Paul endured "afflictions, hardships, calamities, beatings, imprisonments, tumults, labors, watching, hunger" (2 Corinthians 6:4-5; see also 2 Corinthians 4:8-9). Paul was arrested in Jerusalem, chained, tried, and left to languish in prison for two years at Caesarea (Acts 21:22-27, 24:27). He was nearly killed on several occasions (Acts 21:30-31; 23:12-33); and was shipwrecked (Acts 27:41). We believers, as Paul, are warned Christ's way is hard, so that every bump we encounter on the road is a reminder we are on the right road.

After Paul caught a glimpse of "the third heaven," he was sent "a thorn... in the flesh, a messenger of Satan" to keep Paul from "being too elated by the abundance of revelations" (2 Corinthians 12:7). Some believe Paul's thorn was a figurative one, such as his disappointment with Corinthian backsliders (I Corinthians 1:11, 3:3). However, conventional scholarship attributes Paul's suffering to physical symptoms from epilepsy, headaches, malaria, or his blindness originating on the Damascus road; any one of which could have affected his vision. Paul exclaims at Galatians 5:11: "See with what large letters I am writing to you with my own hand," possibly characterizing the over-sized script of a person with poor vision.[111] Paul also acknowledges that the Galatians if possible, "would have plucked out your eyes and given them to me" (Galatians 4:15); again suggesting an ongoing problem with his sight. Paul related to the Galatians that his "bodily ailment" was "a trial to them; yet they did not scorn or despise," or spit upon him, as his contemporaries might have reacted to an epileptic (Galatians 4:13-14).

Did Paul escape most suffering? His summary remarks suggest not: "For the sake of Christ, then, I am content with weaknesses, insults, hardships, persecutions, and calamities: for when I am weak, then I am strong" (2 Corinthians 12:10). Paul's suffering had nothing to do with punishment for sin, but was to deter him from pride or self-exaltation, and strengthen his resolve to submit to God for His glory. For two years Felix let Paul languish in prison, "desiring to do the Jews a favor" (Acts 25:27)., until Festus sent Paul to Rome, where he finally, as predicted, was "preaching the Kingdom of God and teaching about the Lord Jesus Christ" (Acts 28:31).

At Philippi, Paul and Silas had been unjustly imprisoned (Acts 16:23-30). Paul's imprisonment at Rome interrupted the most fruitful years of his ministry and evangelistic witness. Since God had forgiven Saul's persecution of the Church and blessed his Apostleship, it is inconceivable that Paul's imprisonment occurred as God's punishment for sin. Paul's imprisonment at Rome ended in his decapitation.[112] Why God did not intervene to prevent this human injustice toward Paul, the other Apostles, and the multitude of martyrs, is beyond our comprehension. Perhaps they serve as examples of the possibility of any believer enduring and overcoming worldly affliction in the joy and power of the Lord.

It is related that all the Apostles suffered severe trials, leading to their martyrdom. Peter, John and Stephen were falsely accused before the Sanhedrin (Acts 4:1, 7). Except for John, who died in exile, they all underwent violent deaths for the sake of the Gospel: hardly suggestive of a tribulation-free life for those who follow in their footsteps and build on their foundations. Peter, Andrew, James, the son of Alpheus, Simon, Bartholomew and Philip were crucified. James, the son of Zebedee, Thomas, Thaddeus, and Matthew were killed by sword, spear, or arrow. James, the brother of Jesus, was stoned to death.

SUFFERING REQUIRED OF ALL BELIEVERS

The New Testament reveals that suffering is inextricably connected with a Christian's attempts to be faithful, obedient, and holy to the Lord. So intense is the struggle against the world for spiritual survival in faith and holiness, and so difficult is the regimen of training in holiness and loving service, that the Bible depicts the Christian vocation in terms of affliction, persecution, tribulation, travail, trouble and torment because of one's faith.

Indeed there are verses which seem to make suffering as Jesus did a door to glory. Rewards seem to be promised if only we endure human persecution. Affliction seems to be rendered an obligatory duty or precondition to a Christian's final deliverance. If we maintain constancy, trust, and faithful obedience here, human suffering can be glorified as an instrument preparing us for the glory Hereafter. God uses suffering, even sends it, so we may grow in faith, holiness, and fellowship with Him. God calls us to eternal glory through sufferings along the path of affliction.

Romans 8:17-18 says we are "fellow heirs with Christ, provided that we suffer with him in order that we may also be glorified with him. I consider that the sufferings of this present time are not worth comparing with the glory that is to be revealed to us." 2 Corinthians 4:17 puts it: "For this slight momentary affliction is preparing for us an eternal weight of glory beyond all comparison." And "if one suffers as a Christian, let him not be ashamed, but under that name let him glorify God" (I Peter 4:16). "The same experience of suffering is required of your brotherhood throughout the world" (I Peter 5:9; and see I Thessalonians 3:3-4; Revelations 1:9). Suffering shares with, identifies with, exposes us to, and helps us to know, Jesus Christ.

Paul says at 2 Timothy 2:10: "Therefore, I endure everything for the sake of the elect, that they also may obtain the salvation which in Christ Jesus goes with eternal glory." At Colossians 1:24, 27, Paul says: "Now I rejoice in my sufferings for your sake, and in my flesh I complete what remains of Christ's afflictions for the sake of his body, that is the church... To them God chose to make known how great among the Gentiles are the riches of <u>the glory</u> of this mystery, which is Christ in you, <u>the hope of glory</u>." Suffering as Christ did, is an identification with Him in the crucible of affliction, emerging unto glory.

Scriptures which promise eternal joy through the divine mechanism of suffering, both here and Hereafter, include Romans 5:3: "we rejoice in our sufferings, knowing that suffering produces endurance, and endurance produces character, and character produces hope." "For this slight momentary affliction is preparing for us an eternal weight of glory beyond all comparison" (2 Corinthians 4;17). "If we endure, we shall also reign with him" (2 Timothy 2:12).

Matthew 5:10-12 says: "Blessed are those who are persecuted for righteousness' sake, for theirs is the kingdom of heaven. Blessed are you when men revile you and persecute you...

Rejoice and be glad, for your reward is great in heaven." Acts 14:22 reminds us: "through many tribulations we must enter the kingdom of God."

What is going on here? Affliction is working or literally creating our "eternal weight of glory." Our righteousness is fashioned by affliction, as it drives us to God's Word for instruction in living: "Before I was afflicted I went astray: but now have I kept thy word... It is good for me that I have been afflicted; that I might learn thy statutes... I know, O Lord, that thy judgments are right, and that thou in faithfulness hast afflicted me" (Psalm 119:67, 71, 75).

James 1:12 puts it: "Blessed is the man who endures trial, for when he has stood the test he will receive the crown of life which God has promised to those who love him." (see also, Matthew 10:22; Philippians 1:30, 3:8-10; I Thessalonians 3:3-4; and Revelation 2:3, 22:9). James 5:10-11 adds: "As an example of suffering and patience, brethren, take the prophets who spoke in the name of the Lord. Behold, we call those happy who were steadfast." (See also, Luke 6:22; Acts 5:40-41; Colossians 1:24).

Eternal joy is linked to suffering at I Peter 4:12-14, 19: "Beloved, do not be surprised at the fiery ordeal which comes upon you to prove you... But rejoice in so far as you share Christ's sufferings, that you may also rejoice and be glad when his glory is revealed. If you are reproached for the name of Christ, you are blessed, because the spirit of glory and of God rests upon you... Therefore let those who suffer according to God's will do right and entrust their souls to a faithful creator." I Peter 3:17 also speaks of suffering according to God's will: "For it is better to suffer for doing right, if that should be God's will, than to suffer for doing wrong." I Peter 5:10 then gives assurance: "And after you have suffered a little while, the God of all grace, who has called you to his eternal glory in Christ, will himself restore, establish, and strengthen you."

I Peter 2:20-21 calls us to suffer for doing right: "For what credit is it, if when you do wrong and are beaten for it you take it patiently? But if when you do right and suffer for it you take it patiently, you have God's approval. For to this you have been called, because Christ also suffered for you leaving you an example, that you should follow in his steps."

2 Corinthians 1:5 notes: "For as we share abundantly in Christ's sufferings, so through Christ we share abundantly in comfort too." At Philippians 1:29-30 St. Paul teaches: "It has been granted to you that for the sake of Christ you should not only believe in him but suffer for his sake, engaged in the same conflict which you saw and now hear to be mine." The "granting" of suffering implies a kingly gift from God, delivered and packaged in both believing and suffering. The words, "for his sake," imply "instead of," or "in the place of;" as a daily outworking of Christ's suffering in His absence, laboring and loving on behalf of others.

After the Apostles were beaten by the council of Israel for preaching in the name of Jesus, "Then they left the presence of the council, rejoicing that they were counted worthy to suffer dishonor for the name" (Acts 5:41). A Christian is summoned to empty his life of selfishness to make room for occupancy by the life of Jesus in him. 2 Corinthians 4:8-11, reveals Christians are "afflicted in every way, but not crushed... persecuted but not forsaken; struck down, but not destroyed; always carrying in the body the death of Jesus, so that the life of Jesus may also be manifested in our bodies. For while we live we are always being given up to death for Jesus' sake, so that the life of Jesus may be manifested in our mortal flesh."

Revelation 2:10-11 gives comfort: "Do not fear what you are about to suffer. Behold the devil is about to throw some of you into prison, that you may be tested, and for ten days you will have tribulation. Be faithful unto death, and I will give you the crown of life... He who conquers shall not be hurt by the second death." The need to overcome temptation, persecution and suffering and die to the flesh in order to be rewarded, is also noted at Revelation 2:7, 17, 26, and 3:12, 21.

Jesus is our greatest example of suffering for righteousness' sake, and the persecutions He endured did not end with His death. The world which so persecuted Him continues to resent and hate His Body of believers with the same intense dedication and dark passion. If we are to share in Christ's victory and rewards, we are also ordained to share, imitate, and actually participate in His sufferings, for John 16:33 plainly says: "In the world you have tribulation, but be of good cheer. I have overcome the world."

Jesus leaves no doubt that suffering at the hands of other men, the environment, and the natural world will befall Christians. At Luke 21:8-17 Jesus recounts multiple occasions of suffering at the end of the age, from which we are not exempt: "Take heed that you are not led astray; for many will come in my name, saying, 'I am he!'... And when you hear of wars and tumults, do not be terrified... Nation will rise against nation, and kingdom against kingdom; there will be great earthquakes, and in various places famines and pestilences; and there will be terrors and great signs from heaven... they will lay their hands on you and persecute you, delivering you up to the synagogues and prison, and you will be brought before kings and governors for my name's sake... You will be delivered up even by parents and brothers and kinsmen and friends, and some of you they will put to death; you will be hated by all for my name's sake."

Persecution and suffering for believers is also forecast at Psalms 34:19, 27:12, 37:14 and 118:18; Proverbs 3:11, 14:13; Matthew 10:24, 13:21; Mark 10:30; Luke 21:12, 16; Acts 5:40-41, 14:22; Romans 8:35-36; 2 Corinthians 1:6, 4:17, 7:4; Ephesians 3:13, 5:20; Philippians 3:9-10; I Thessalonians 3:4, 5:18; 2 Thessalonians 1:5-7; 2 Timothy 3:12, 4:5-8; Hebrews 10:32-34; James 5:10-11; I Peter 1:7, 9, 2:20-21, 3:17, 4:14, 16, 19, 5:9; and Revelation 13:7.

Jesus predicts suffering for Christians during end-time tribulation, amidst the confusion of spiritual claims by counterfeit messiahs, which will spread uncertainty into every aspect of life. Wars and conflicts in human society will cause death, sacrifice, and displacement, among both military and civilian populations. Physical calamities in nature, such as earthquakes will inflict casualties and deprivations. Famine and pestilence will deny the twin blessings of wealth and health. After the Rapture, which removes believers from the world, suffering accompanies fearful events and great signs from heaven, depicted as hail and fire mixed with blood, volcanic eruptions, death of sea creatures, a fallen star named Wormwood poisoning the oceans, and darkness from the sun, moon, and stars (Revelation 8:7-12).

Jesus also warns believers about suffering caused by one's own family and friends, as well as secular and religious authorities, because of faith in Jesus, and association with His Church. And death pervades all these calamities, as well as the natural progression of human life and aging. (Matthew 10:17, 34:36).

The believer who strives to follow the way of Christ will be incessantly assaulted by the world, the flesh, and the devil, with temptations to sin; confrontations with evil; and constant challenges to spiritual survival. The devil not only works to entice us into sin with the allures of the world, but also provokes the world's hostility against followers of Christ. The world which rejected Christ will hate and persecute believers because their holy lives are a reproach to worldly sin. Our very obedience to the Word will provoke contempt and hostility by the unsaved. Every disciple must contend with personal suffering at the hands of Satan and other men, as his faith is challenged by false accusations, scourging, rejection, hatred, and martyrdom. Consequently, in a world in bondage to Satan, Christians will suffer more than unredeemed non-believers because they endure persecutions from worldly men. As we shall see in a moment, transformed believers also wrestle with the flesh; a second struggle of little concern to the unsaved who embrace, serve, and pander to the world system.

At Matthew 10:22-23 Jesus warns the twelve apostles: "and you will be hated by all men for my name's sake. But he who endures to the end will be saved. When they persecute you in one town, flee to the next" (see also, Matthew 10:16-18, 24:9; John 15:18-22). In warning His disciples that a servant is not above his Master, Jesus says: "Blessed are you when men revile you and persecute you and utter all kinds of evil against you falsely on my account. Rejoice and be glad, for your reward is great in heaven, for so men persecuted the prophets who were before you" (Matthew 5:11-12; see also Mark 13:13; Luke 6:40; John 15:18-20, 16:2; 2 Timothy 3:12 and I John 3:12-13).

Man desires happiness and peace, but just the opposite are found in a disciple's worldly walk. Jesus says: "Blessed are the poor in spirit, for theirs is the kingdom of God. Blessed are those who mourn, for they shall be comforted... Blessed are those who are persecuted for righteousness' sake, for theirs is the kingdom of heaven" (Matthew 5:3, 4, 10).

The fact that we are pilgrims, aliens, and exiles, confined to a sinful world no longer adapted to our spiritual nature, explains much of the suffering endured by Christians. We suffer both because the world mentality resents, and even hates Christian spirituality, and we suffer because our flesh still longs for the world, and the wrench from its bonds is a painful one for even the most spiritual Christian. The world system purrs with its promises of illicit pleasures, and the earth groans in the aftermath of sin's travails.

We suffer because the world is a sinful place which groans in travail in tandem with a fallen mankind, and produces enough evil to vex and besiege everyone. Romans 8:22-23 observes: "We know that the whole creation has been groaning in travail together until now; and not only the creation, but we ourselves, who have the first fruits of the Spirit, groan inwardly as we wait for adoption as sons, the redemption of our bodies.

The New Testament refers to believers and their exile: "conduct yourselves with fear throughout the time of your exile" (I Peter 1:17); "Beloved, I beseech you as aliens and exiles to abstain from the passions of the flesh that wage war against you" (I Peter 2:11). "But our commonwealth is in heaven, and from it we await a Savior, the Lord Jesus Christ" (Philippians 3:20).

The Old Testament cites the example for our instruction (I Corinthians 10:11) of the Israelites wandering for forty years in the wilderness, and refers to God's people as transients and tenants in the world. "For the land is mine; for ye are strangers and sojourners with me" (Leviticus 25:23). "For we are strangers before thee, and sojourners, as were all our fathers" (I Chronicles 29:15; Psalm 39:12). "I am a stranger in the earth" (Psalm 119:19).

We are also a people sanctified by our new Birth, literally called out of the world: left in the world, but not to be of the world (John 17:14). Sanctification, being of the royal priesthood, imposes a duty on Christians to be Holy; to bring no shame on the Lord, but to renounce worldly attachments. And this involves substantial pain since we are still in the flesh which sinfully desires the world. We are chosen people to receive God's precious grace, and administer it for the benefit of others: to share it with the unsaved: "in thee shall the families of the earth be blessed; (Genesis 12:3; and see also, Exodus 19:6, Zechariah 8:23; I Peter 2:5, 9; Revelation 1:6, 5:10).

Jesus demands total allegiance to Him, and imposes an urgency to our quest for holiness, which calls for constant and regular effort and application by believers. First, we must relinquish the lifestyle of the world, even if it means renouncing adult movies, off-color jokes, binge-drinking, sexual promiscuity, attitudes of condescension toward religious values, or the former friends who persist in such pursuits. "Do not be mismated with unbelievers. For what partnership have righteousness and iniquity? Or what fellowship has light with darkness? What accord has Christ with Belial? Or what has a believer in common with an unbeliever?" (2 Corinthians 6:14-15).

Jesus makes it plain that a disciple's renunciation of worldly values is not something which should be postponed at the outset; nor abandoned once undertaken. It is an ongoing process, requiring constant reception and application of Holy Spirit resources and power. At Matthew 10:34-35 Jesus cautions: "Do not think that I have come to bring peace on earth; I have not come to bring peace, but a sword. For I have come to set a man against his father."

Total allegiance to Jesus is demanded before a disciple finds life: "He who loves father or mother... son or daughter more than me is not worthy of me... He who finds his life will lose it, and he who loses his life for my sake will find it" (Matthew 10:37-39). Jesus must occupy the primary place in a disciple's life. "If any one comes to me and does not hate his own father and mother and wife and children and brothers and sisters, yes, and even his own life, he cannot be my disciple" (Luke 14:26). Matthew 5:29-30 and 18:9 call for self-immolation of hands and eyes which tend to sin, to avoid being drawn by them to evil and damnation.

Moreover, Jesus reveals an immediacy to the response of forsaking the world for spirituality: "Another of the disciples said to him, 'Lord, let me first go and bury my father.' But Jesus said to him, 'Follow me, and leave the dead to bury their own dead.' (Matthew 8:21-22). It does not matter whether this was a command signifying that nothing, not even literal bereavement, was to come before commitment to Jesus, or whether it responded to a colloquial request to defer discipleship and stay at home until one's father had died. In either case, nothing must come before Jesus, nor postpone discipleship, despite the wrench from relinquishing worldly involvements.

In speaking of the end days, Jesus counsels His followers to remember Lot's wife, because while being saved she became lost by wistfully looking back toward her worldly attachments (Genesis 19:26). Jesus warns: "On that day, let him who is on the housetop, with his goods in the house, not come down to take them away; and likewise let him who is in the field not turn back. Remember Lot's wife. Whoever seeks to gain his life will lose it, but whoever loses his life will preserve it" (Luke 17:31). Her heart was still in the world, and the world was in her heart. Despite her privileges and angelic rescue from Sodom (Genesis 19:15), temptation dulled her holiness, so that she died in her nostalgia and thereby confounded grace.

Luke 9:62 and Matthew 24:18 also warn believers not to "look back" longingly at the world, but to look ahead to Christ. When you come boldly out of the world, the world will lose its hold on, and attraction for, you. At Matthew 6:19 Jesus counsels: "Do not lay up for yourselves treasures on earth, where moth and rust consume and where thieves break in and steal, but lay up for yourselves treasures in heaven" (See also, Luke 12:33; James 5:1-3). This total disenchantment with the world is clearly supported by John 12:25: "He who loves his life loses it, and he who hates his life in this world will keep it for eternal life." Thus, Jesus warns us of hardships when we follow His way of life, and intimates there is no Gospel of ease for true believers.

There will be times God does not end suffering, even for believers, which has nothing to do with punishment for unrepented sin. There is a regimen of training in holiness which is accompanied by suffering. Marines in bootcamp and athletes in training are intimately familiar with the pain and stress of conditioning and growing, which is necessary to attain their goals. No matter how much a believer may will to learn the lessons of training, there are certain disciplines which can only be mastered by practice and experience, and the attendant suffering cannot be distilled out of the development process, or avoided in any way. In such a case, merely knowing what is required and resolving to do it are not enough to end the pain of training, because it is necessary to accomplish one's transformation to holiness in God's plan of sanctification.

Jesus also asserts: "Whoever does not bear his own cross and come after me cannot be my disciple" (Luke 14:26-27). Jesus affirms at Matthew 16:24 and 10:38 that bearing a cross involves self-denial and hardship when we follow His way. Luke 14:33 makes it all-inclusive: "whoever of you does not renounce all that he has cannot be my disciple." To renounce is to act: to turn from the world and henceforth live one's life according to the way of Jesus. Discipleship is no passive learning experience, but an active, cooperative effort in striving for the Kingdom, running the race, waging the battle, counting the cost, and paying the price.

Separation from the world can also impose so much sacrifice, that a disciple is instructed to weigh the cost even before undertaking to follow Jesus as Saviour. One considering discipleship needs carefully to appraise his commitment to the venture before acting, just as a prudent man estimates the cost of a building to see that "he has enough to complete it" (Luke 14:28). Likewise, no king enters into war without determining whether he can successfully wage and win it with the resources at his command (Luke 14:31). A Christian must pay the price of acting dutifully and obediently throughout his lifetime. Jesus charges no admission fee to salvation, but the annual membership dues are costly. It costs nothing to become a Christian, and everything to remain one.

STRUGGLING TO ESCAPE THE WORLD IN PURSUIT OF HOLINESS

Suffering is involved in the Christian quest for holiness because believers are not perfect on earth, even though converted, Born-Again, regenerated, and continually sanctified by ongoing spiritual transformation to the likeness of Christ. The very process of maturing spiritually involves "growing pains" inherent in sacrifice and rigorous efforts, as we are chastened, chastised, trained and shaped in the image and way of the Lord. We will sometimes be tested in our faithful application of what we have learned, with attendant privations.

The slide down to Hell is effortless and natural, while the road to Heaven is necessarily an uphill battle; a spiritual pursuit involving struggle, strife, sorrow, combat, and violence. Matthew 7:14 prepares us: "For the gate is narrow and the way is hard, that leads to life, and those who find it are few." It is not difficult to see that Jesus is the narrow gate leading to life, for He explains He is the only way to God: "I am the door; if any one enters by me, he will be saved" (John 10:9). Yet, there is nothing 'hard' about the New Birth's occurrence, which involves a responsive mind set of sincere commitment to repent; have faith in Jesus as Saviour; and submit to Jesus as Lord.

The hard way is in submission to Christ, which requires everything one has, and is fulfilled by a total abnegation of the self in order to serve the Lord lovingly and fully. A believer must stop asserting control over the direction of his life and turn it over to God for growth in holiness. One's progress upon the hard way is inherently difficult as the Christian walks in the world, because dying to the self is intrinsically painful.

Because the world is sinful and under control of Satanic forces, we suffer spiritually when we yield to temptation, and we also suffer at the hands of the world when we successfully resist the allures of sin. Because we are finite, limited beings in a physical body of flesh, the pursuit of our holy calling to be like Jesus necessarily excludes enjoyment of some worldly pleasures otherwise attractive to the flesh. Throughout the process of spiritual training, Satan stirs the fleshly desires of Christians to war against the spirit (Romans 7:17-20). And one's carnal recollections would happily embrace and readily collaborate in these illicit adventures, but for the power of the Holy Spirit.

There is no question that Jesus warns His disciples they will endure suffering, just as He did: "The cup that I drink you will drink; and with the baptism with which I am baptized, you will be baptized" (Mark 10:39). Jesus explains that His sufferings are what He refers to as His cup (Matthew 26:39) and His baptism (Luke 12:50). Paul welcomed the same suffering of Christ, and experienced it (2 Corinthians 1:5, 6; Philippians 3:10; Colossians 1:24). We tend to attribute our suffering to worldly temptations of the flesh and persecutions by Satan. But Jesus' primary suffering was occasioned by vicariously taking on the sins of mankind, for which He endured the wrath of God and paid the full penalty. Perhaps our suffering can concentrate on easing the burden, or sharing the pain, of another sufferer. However, only Jesus could offer satisfaction to God, and our suffering draws us closer to Him by appreciating better what He endured, without our providing any literal atonement for sin.

Jesus calls His followers to emulate His life, and grow fruitful in death, as He did; explaining: "unless a grain of wheat falls into the earth and dies, it remains alone; but if it dies, it bears much fruit. He who loves his life loses it, and he who hates his life in this world will keep it for eternal life. If any one serves me, he must follow me; and where I am, there shall my servant be also" (John 12:24-26).

Jesus is here referring to the death of self involved in obedient submission, exemplified by baptism, at which a believer is lowered and raised symbolically in Christ's victory over the grave and death. He is also referring to the death of self involved in relinquishing selfishness for Jesus' sake, by ongoing devotion to the needs of others, both saved and unsaved. Fruitfulness comes from death. A seed which stays alive has potential, but produces nothing. Only when it falls into the ground, dies, and transforms to a plant, does it multiply. We cannot effectively serve others, love them unselfishly, or witness the Gospel to them, unless we first die to the self, with whatever suffering that sacrifice involves. Sudden death may be painless, but the extended process of dying often involves prolonged suffering.

Dying to oneself may take many forms. We may die to comfort by sacrificing the life style of our generation in order to provide for, or be closer to, those we serve. We may die to popularity and acclaim, as we embrace the truths of the Gospel which the world rejects. We may die to our pride, by casting upon the Lord all concern connected with loving service and witness, in total dependence upon Him. There is no room for Lord Jesus in our lives until we purposefully desire and cooperate in the death of self for the sake of receiving Him, with all the sacrifices and deprivation this entails. At Philippians 3:10 St. Paul hopes: "That I may know him and the power of his resurrection; and may <u>share his suffering</u>, becoming like him in his death" (See also, Romans 8:17).

There is an element of sacrifice and suffering for others as we give ourselves to the saints and the unsaved in a ministry of personal evangelism, witness, intercessory prayer, and sharing our possessions. St. Paul disclosed: "Now I rejoice in my sufferings for your sake, and in my flesh I complete what remains of Christ's afflictions for the sake of his body, that is, the Church" (Colossians 1:24). Paul again speaks of "the Gospel for which I am suffering... I endure everything for the sake of the elect, that they also may obtain the salvation which in Christ Jesus goes with eternal glory" (2 Timothy 2:9-10; and see also, Ephesians 3:1, 13). Paul recounted all his sufferings and persecution, and then exhorted Christians to imitate him, as he imitated Christ and shared His suffering (I Corinthians 4:11-13, 16; Philippians 3:8-10, 17).

We share in the suffering of Christ when we share in the sufferings of other Christians in the Body, and experience their anguish. We enter into it when we minister to and comfort others in their sorrows, in the name of Christ, Who sympathetically suffers with each beloved sufferer, just as a mother shares the pain of her child.

We are called to patience and perseverance in holiness, to resist temptations to sin, because the process of spiritual maturity inherently takes time. Since this situation persists for a life-time, we may expect our suffering in the struggle against sin, though progressively abating, to last for a lifetime, as well. Holiness requires a constant walk in faith which conforms to Jesus' way; abides in Him; comes to fellowship with Him; and resists the residual demands of the flesh. That is why the way is hard that leads to life, and our efforts to glorify God, triumph in holiness, render loving obedience, and witness for Jesus, will exact a price in suffering, pain, and tribulation, as the spirit of a believer is violently wrenched by God's sure hand from the flesh's grasp. Consequently, Romans 12:12 says: "be patient in tribulation."

As we collaborate in God's training program, we must exercise self-discipline; sacrifice through worldly relinquishment; selfless devotion to the Lord; and struggle in forsaking home and family. There is a forcible separation from the world as we regulate our freedom of choice, sacrifice self-will for submission to Christ; replace self-sufficiency with faithful dependency; and learn to seek eternal, spiritual goals instead of temporal, worldly values.

Wartime demands ongoing sacrifice, and a Christian's carnally inclined flesh must be re-trained to conform to his re-created spirit. Denial, loss, and failure are all part of the growing process and rigors of training. No matter how enlightened and learned a student may be, he will not competently drive a car, type an essay, or perform surgery, without extensive training and practice. Failures and frustrations accompany every learning process, and can produce agitation and despair, though the Christian's disciplinary regimen is actually meant to be joyful because it works patience and perfection (James 1:2-4).

In nature, baby birds must sometimes be pushed out of the nest when they are ready to fly and survive in the world, because they do not know their time has come. The initial nudge from the nest must be a source of momentary consternation, if not terror, to the fledgling, which soon changes to soaring confidence as it learns to accept the risk and challenge of trying its wings. A bird allowed to languish in the nest after its maturation becomes a useless burden to its parents, and worthless to the world in which it lives.

Likewise, baby Christians may draw nurture in the nest while it is appropriate, but must eventually be pushed into independence to survive in, and minister to, the world in which they live. The disquieting separation from the comfort of the nest is itself a source of apprehension and suffering, and is aggravated and prolonged by our resistance to the process. But just as a bird must learn that it is able to fly, so believers must be pushed to discover the developing God-given spiritual strength of spiritual ascent. Hence, the struggle, effort, and education of Christian life-style is a regular part of the human condition. Conflict inheres in the cultivation of Christian character and witness. The child who is left to enjoyable play, and nothing else, will not learn virtues of cooperation, selflessness, diligence, or responsibility.

Anyone called to bear the cross of Christ must expect suffering as a result of, and inherent in, his training in holiness, the rigors of spiritual education, and preparation for spiritual works. Just as athletes train because they are motivated, in part, by their identification as, and efforts to be, athletes, so Christians are called to do no less.

On the other hand, when we do yield to sin, fall, and fail, we generally reap the worldly consequences of what we have sown. God is forgiving and forgetting when we repent, but the world must still exact its vengeance, retribution and penalties in natural consequences. "For he who soweth to his own flesh <u>will from the flesh</u> reap corruption" (Galatians 6:8). God has warned us of the inexorable consequences resulting from violating this moral law He has ordained. Man is responsible for effects when he chooses freely to disobey God's laws. Thus, pre-marital, or extra-marital sex can produce horrible diseases, as well as unwanted pregnancies, presenting dreadful choices of abortions, rearing unwanted children, or entering unhappy marriages. The irony is that Satan is he who tempts men to sin with promises of pleasure, and then rewards them with worldly penalties, even though God has forgiven one who repents. For, Satan is implacable and unforgiving because he has only hatred arising out of jealousy for men.

God does not re-create us spiritually perfect at the New Birth, but allows the transformation to occur gradually on earth, leaving it to each believer to collaborate and govern the pace of his God-given growth and progress in Christ-like character. The only time freedom from suffering and affliction is guaranteed is after our glorification in the New Jerusalem (Revelation 21:10, 27). According to Revelation 21:4, God "will wipe away every tear from their eyes, and death shall be no more, neither shall there be mourning nor crying nor pain any more, for the former things have passed away." (See also, Revelation 22:3).

Even while we endure affliction, we are assured of God's imminent deliverance. Psalm 34:19 observes: "Many are the afflictions of the righteous; but <u>the Lord delivereth him out of all of them</u>." What we need to remember is that God always and eventually delivers His people from affliction. "They that sow in tears shall reap in joy. He that goeth forth and weepeth, bearing precious seed, shall doubtless come again with rejoicing" (Psalm 126:5-6). "Blessed are those who mourn, for they shall be comforted... Blessed are those who are persecuted for righteousness' sake, for theirs is the kingdom of heaven" (Matthew 5:4, 10).

Jesus says at John 16:33: "I have said this to you, that in me you may have peace. In the world you have tribulation; but be of good cheer, I have overcome the world." And Jesus proclaims His victory is ours! God is in control and His consolations and rewards for faithful endurance are marvelous. He enables us to persevere in the quest to become holy and stand faithfully, and His grace brings our glorification to completion.

STRUGGLE AND WARFARE PRODUCE STRIFE AND CASUALTIES

Jesus summons His disciples to endure in, and hold fast to saving faith, in dramatic terms of battle, struggle, race, contest, conquest, strife, and sacrifice. These terms obviously call for persistence in, rather than an isolated, initial expression of, faith in Jesus. There would be no need for the Bible's call for steadfastness and diligence in faith, unless there were trials and temptations to be encountered, and sustained efforts to be exerted by men. Waging warfare will number casualties and wounded believers.

The sources of man's struggles in the world are many. Christians are called to resist evil and overcome the world to sustain faith and holiness; something non-believers are not required to do. Christians must strive in warfare against Satan in fulfillment of the Great Commission to take the Gospel to all the world, and we will suffer in the travail of witnessing to bring New Births out of lost souls. Christians are required to seek the Kingdom, with all the rigors of training, discipline, and renunciation of the flesh which are involved, and we will suffer as we try to exemplify Christ's life to a world in the embrace of sin.

The Bible forecasts the "good fight of faith" for believers (I Timothy 6:12), so we can expect to encounter adversaries and obstructions to faith in the world. If we are so urgently called to conquer faithfully, then we can expect trials and opposition in this world, which must be overcome by faith. Jesus characterizes the Christian struggle at Matthew 10:34-36: "Do not think that I have come to bring peace on earth; I have not come to bring peace, but a sword. For I have come to set a man against his father... and a man's foes will be those of his own household." Even one's own family can become a source of strife. Indeed, a Christian may be most defenseless against tribulation and opposition inflicted by those persons closest to him.

In preparation for war and contention, we are counseled: "Put on the whole armor of God, that you may be able to stand against the wiles of the devil. For we are not contending against flesh and blood, but against the principalities, against the powers, against the world rulers of this present darkness, against the spiritual hosts of wickedness in the heavenly places. Therefore take the whole armor of God, that you may be able to withstand in the evil day...And take the sword of the Spirit, which is the word of God" (Ephesians 6:11-17). Jesus instructs: "let him who has no sword sell his mantle and buy one" (Luke 22:36). I Timothy 1:18 calls us to "wage the good warfare." "Take your share of suffering as a good soldier of Christ Jesus" (2 Timothy 2:3). I Corinthians 6:13 adds: "Be watchful, stand firm in your faith, be courageous, be strong."

The exertion of holding fast and racing toward the goal of faithful holiness can also produce suffering. After calling for the exercise of self-control in subduing the flesh, St. Paul teaches that we are running a race for the prize of immortal life, which requires striving for, and enduring in, the faith. I Corinthians 9:24 queries: "Do you not know that in a race all the runners compete, but only one receives the prize? So run that you may obtain it. Every athlete exercises self-control in all things. They do it to receive a perishable wreath, but we an imperishable."

The duty to run a race for constancy in faith is confirmed at Hebrews 12:1, which tells us: "Let us also lay aside every weight and sin which clings so closely, and let us run with perseverance the race that is set before us." The Christian's reward for faithful endurance in life's race will be "the crown of righteousness," according to 2 Timothy 4:5-8, which calls for sustained exertions, and their consequences: "always be steady, endure suffering, <u>do the work</u> of an Evangelist... I have fought the good fight, I have finished the race, I have kept the faith."

Hebrews 3:6 says that we are Christ's "house if we hold fast, firm to the end, our confidence and pride in our hope." We are rewarded for faithful effort, as much as the actual accomplishment of virtue and obedience. We are rewarded not for our own willful attempts, but for our faithful receptivity to God's grace. We are to endure in faith against the world's hostility, but we are not expected to abolish sin, only resist it.

I Timothy 6:12 exhorts Christians to "<u>take hold</u> of the eternal life to which you were called when you made the good confession in the presence of many witnesses." A believer's initial confession of faith has 'called' him to eternal life, but he has need to persevere and secure a firm hold on it while he is in the world, constantly maintaining his faith, and bearing spiritual fruit. The purpose of collaborative endeavor is to fortify us in apprehending the holiness to which God calls us.

Hebrews 10:22-23 exhorts: "let us draw near with a true heart in full assurance of faith... Let us <u>hold fast</u> the confession of our hope without wavering, for he who promised is faithful." Hebrews 12:14 counsels: "<u>Strive</u> for the consecration without which no one will see the Lord." Jude 3 instructs Christians "to <u>contend</u> for the faith which was once for all delivered to the saints." James 1:12 adds: "Blessed is the man who <u>endures</u> trial, for when he has stood the test he will receive the crown of life which God has promised to those who love him."

2 Peter 1:10-11 urges: "Therefore, brethren, be the more zealous to confirm your call and election, for if you do this you will never fall; so there will be richly provided for you an entrance into the eternal kingdom." If a Christian does not heed, confirm, and sustain his faith, by implication he can fall and forfeit a "richly provided" entrance into the Kingdom.

In the Parable of the Dishonest Steward at Luke 16:1-9, Jesus teaches us to emulate, not the dishonesty, but the zeal, of a thieving employee who schemed and contrived many ways to survive his impending discharge from employment because of his dishonesty. Christians should apply the same single-minded determination in striving to secure their eternal habitation. Such effort implies stress and strain in achieving one's goal, which can produce suffering.

Although we are to seek and share the peace of the Lord, we are also summoned to strive violently to take the Kingdom of God, if we would receive deliverance, and replenish our faith and holiness on a sustained basis, despite worldly afflictions. Indeed, there is violence whenever a believer pursues holiness; resists, and expels Satan's influence from his life. There is violence when an evangelist struggles against Satan to "take" or deliver the Gospel to the unsaved. And there is violence when an intercessor stands in prayer on behalf of others to snatch them from the power of evil forces. The idea of coercion or compulsions to draw free souls to the Kingdom, especially our children, is suggested by Luke 14:23; "Go out to the highways and hedges, and compel people to come in, that my house may be filled." And Jude 23: "save some, by snatching them out of the fire."

This struggle by the Church to take the Kingdom against evil forces was forecast in Daniel's vision of four beasts, or earthly kings, who dominate the earth for a time. "But the saints of the most High <u>shall take the kingdom</u> and possess the kingdom for ever" (Daniel 7:18). Clearly, more than passive receptivity to the Gospel is indicated in the call to forceful exertion. There is a victorious violence against unrighteousness, during which we must don the full armor of God. We must contend, compete, and combat to suppress and overcome our lusts and sins.

Luke 16:16 alludes to this contest against worldly distractions in the fight to stay faithfully at Christ's side: "The law and the prophets were until John; since then the good news of the kingdom is preached and <u>every one enters it violently</u>." Matthew 11:12 concurs: "From the days of John the Baptist until now the kingdom of heaven has suffered violence, and men of violence <u>take it</u> by force."

Although these passages have many levels of meaning, including a reference to Jesus' own imminent, physical capture, they also summon disciples to vie with all their might, self-discipline, and constancy to achieve the literal Kingdom. Those who struggle valiantly to sustain their faith by violent combat against sin, will actually 'take' the blessings of the Kingdom they so earnestly and demonstrably desire. Only Jesus saves us by a New Birth by grace through faith, and delivers us to the Kingdom of God (Colossians 1:13; Ephesians 2:4-6). However, the blessings of the Kingdom on earth are available through man's cooperation in receiving or harnessing the work of the Spirit. Heaven 'suffers', that is 'permits' or 'allows for' man's violent struggle against sin and its instigator Satan, in the divine economy of salvation. Our commitment to Jesus will be tested by strife, with the world, the flesh, and the devil, as well as by yielding to the Lord.

The message of Jesus to the end-time churches is to repent of evil works and conquer sinfulness, or lose their lamp-stand from their places. He promises if they repent, "<u>To him who conquers</u> I will grant to eat of the tree of life, which is in the paradise of God;" "Be faithful unto death, and I will give you the crown of life;" "He who conquers and who keeps my works until the end, I will give him power over the nations... and I will give him the morning star;" "He who conquers shall be clad thus in white garments, and I will not blot his name out of the book of life;" "He who conquers, I will make him a pillar in the temple of my God;" "He who conquers, I will grant him to sit with me on my throne" (Revelation 2:7, 2:10, 2:17, 2:26, 28, 3:5, 3:12, 3:21).

We must have victory over the world's temptations, to gain a full reward. We must overcome our own passions and desires of the flesh. We must withstand persecution and suffering. We must resist the devil and make him flee from us. A believer must either conquer or be overcome. If we prefer Jesus over the self, we will overcome the world, the flesh and the devil by faith in Jesus: "And they have conquered him by the blood of the Lamb and by the word of their testimony, for they loved not their lives even unto death" (Revelation 12:11).

This battle to remain faithful and holy is unavoidable. We cannot sit passively after we are saved by grace through faith, but must fight to remain in the faith. There is no neutrality, armistice, or non-intervention for one who rejects Jesus. For Jesus says: "He who is not with me is against me, and he who does not gather with me scatters" (Matthew 12:30; Luke 11:23; but cf. Mark 9:40). James 4:4 teaches: "friendship with the world is enmity with God." There is no alternative or option in choosing sides initially, or in defending our choice, once made. Appeasement toward Satan is tantamount to surrender. There is no peace in a world which inflicts constant warfare upon believers. There is only the lesson that the best defense is a good offense. If a Christian would be holy and stand with the Lord, then he must fight, using the protective armor of God, for Satan strongly contests our walk with Christ.

STRUGGLING FOR THE UNSAVED

We will have struggle as we strive to fulfill the Great Commission to take and witness the Gospel to the unsaved, and free the captives from their bondage to sin. We are called to fight in this spiritual warfare, using the methods and armament God provides. We are free to take the offensive and destroy the ramparts of the enemy by giving the light of the Gospel to the unsaved who are in dungeons of darkness. "For the weapons of our warfare are not worldly but have divine power to destroy strongholds. We destroy arguments and every proud obstacle to the knowledge of God, and take every thought captive to obey Christ, being ready to punish every disobedience, when your obedience is complete" (2 Corinthians 10:4-5).

We are to demolish the arguments and pretensions of the Gospel's foes. We are to occupy until Jesus returns. We are to overcome evil with good. And we are to take every thought captive to obey Christ, so that we are disciplined, as good soldiers fighting in a war. We are to be obedient, and punish our own disobedient thoughts and actions to complete our transformation to Christ-likeness.

Have you ever been frustrated by the stony hearts of the lost, which refuse to be softened by the Word of the Gospel? If so, you have had a taste of spiritual warfare. "Satan disguises himself as an angel of light" (2 Corinthians 11:14) to deceive men. Satan "has blinded the minds of the unbelievers, to keep them from seeing the light of the gospel of the glory of Christ" (2 Corinthians 4:4). Our foe is Satan, and we must use the Word, faith, and prayer to drive him off, so that the light of the Word can shine through to the unsaved. Preaching the Gospel, alone, will not always convert the unsaved, unless it is sandwiched between prayer and faith.

Satan steals the seed of the Word when it is sown (Matthew 13:19), so that no illumination can come into the heart of the unsaved. Wishing the devil would depart will not make him flee. It is necessary to drive off Satan by prayer, and invoking the authority of Jesus over Satan as a vanquished foe. Otherwise, Satan will remain and disguise himself as an angel of light to further blind the unsaved from the truth. No Crusade is ever successful without prayer in advance, which rids the atmosphere of Satanic forces so the Word of God can take root in the hearts of unsaved men.

So desperate is the plight of the unsaved, that we are to contend for their souls. We cannot force them physically, but with the persuasion of the Word and our warfare by faith and prayer, we can at least gain an audience to hear the Word. We are indeed involved in spiritual warfare when we ally ourselves with Christ. And the purpose of our warfare is to make men obedient to Christ, not to subject them to other men (Luke 22:26; 2 Corinthians 11:20). Our concern is with impenitent rebels; the souls of the lost, which are destined for eternal punishment and damnation unless they repent of their sin, and turn to Jesus for salvation by God's grace through faith.

Pain, suffering, and stress are not the greatest evils in the world, but loss of God's fellowship, peace, holiness, enlightenment, and saving grace are. Our ultimate blessing here and hereafter is in the Kingdom of God.

It should be comforting to know that all the faithful who have gone before us traversed the same dark path of affliction, and the throngs of martyrs in heaven came through worldly tribulation to enjoy eternal bliss. Where they were, we are, and by God's grace, where they are we shall be.[113] We will be glorified in Christ. We will be what we should be. We will be where we would be. And we shall have done what we could do.

CONQUERING MALARIA: VANQUISHING EVIL

At the close of the 19th Century, malaria was the principal cause of death throughout the world. Then, in 1897 an English physician, James Ross, discovered that malaria originated from plasmodium parasites transmitted by the bite of anopheles mosquitoes. Prior to that discovery, the cause of the contagion was unknown, and medical science had developed neither vaccines to prevent malaria, nor cures for it. Physicians could only ease the symptoms and distress of its victims.

However, once the cause of malaria was identified, it became possible to forestall the onset of the disease by preventive measures. First, proper screening of buildings was introduced to exclude mosquitoes from human habitation, and limit man's exposure to them. Next, quinine derivatives were developed as preventive vaccines. Finally, epidemics were eliminated, as the swamps which bred pestilence were cleansed by burning the insects at their source.

Public health medicine had progressed from treating the symptoms of afflicted sufferers, to screening the public from exposure; then to vaccination for personal protection; and finally to annihilating the mosquitoes at their source.

This comparison may shed some light on the redemptive work of Jesus Christ, the Great Physician and Healer of mankind. The First Advent of Jesus did not immediately eradicate the source of evil, nor establish an ideal earthly Kingdom, much to the disappointment of the Jewish Zealots of the time, who rejected Him because they expected an all-conquering Messiah who would reign in victory. He did, however, identify Satan as the source of evil, and proclaim His ultimate victory over the world (John 16:33).

Demonstrably, Jesus has not sequestered His followers from exposure to the world's travails. He has not isolated us from the spiritual hosts of wickedness which rule the world (Ephesians 6:12). He compassionately fed the multitudes, but also revealed that the poor would always be with us (Matthew 26:11). At his First Coming, Christ exorcised demons and healed countless afflictions, but He did not eliminate Satan, the author of disease in the world. Rather, He gave Christians the power of the Holy Spirit and the Word, with which to overcome temptation and resist the fiery darts of the evil one (Ephesians 6:16). He brought divine love by which to endure all things (I Corinthians 10:13, 13:7). We are not called to end the darkness of the world, but to share the divine light we have. Jesus will eliminate the dark when He returns.

Jesus has provided His Word, articulated in the full armor of God, by which we screen out the enticements of satanic evil. He has inoculated us against sin by the New Birth and the indwelling Holy Spirit, so that while we are still capable of relapsing into sin just as carnal men, we are constitutionally able to resist the pestilence of sin, and the affliction of temptation. We despise sin, and cannot persist in it because of this spiritual transformation worked by the Holy Spirit. We are no longer under dominion or compulsion of sin, no longer serving, living in, or continuing in sin. And Jesus reveals that evil will be annihilated at His Second Coming and purged from God's Kingdom. Jesus has saved us from the penalty of sin and sickness, but He does not promise to spare us from the assault of satanic evil, persecution, and humanly inflicted tribulations in the world.

Certainly, Satan can provoke unsaved men to oppose the Church of Christ; to harass and injure Christ's disciples in His Body. He can bruise the heel, but he cannot harm the head. Satan can torment us along our way to holiness, but he cannot conquer or overcome believers. Every believer will have a personal, life-long fight against evil, but the victory is already won in Christ. Our bodies may be imprisoned or destroyed by Satan's henchmen, but never our souls. Our church buildings may be burned, but nothing done by evil men can cast us out of the true spiritual Church of Christ. Satan is a vanquished foe, and we share the victory in Christ. "Thanks be to God who in Christ always leads us in triumph" (2 Corinthians 2:14).

GOD'S FORBEARANCE TOWARD SINNERS ALLOWS SUFFERING

There is yet another way that God's mercy toward sinners in granting them a lifetime to respond to grace, is a blessing with inherent possibilities for human suffering. While God condemns sin, and his Justice ordains punishment for inveterate, unrepentant rebels, His mercy recognizes that man is incapable of righteousness without God's grace. He has established Jesus Christ as man's One Way to escape the just consequences of his personal sin, and he has established His Church as the messenger of that Good News. God's grace establishes that the promise of salvation and the warning of eternal consequences for rejecters of God's grace, be communicated to men before they are irrevocably condemned. He establishes His witness in the Creation and individual conscience. This is consistent with God's will that all men be saved by their own consent from the Judgment of destruction due sinners.

While the saga of human choice for Christ is played out on the world's stage, ironically one of the consequences of freedom's corruption continues to be injustice, persecution, and harm by unregenerate men toward others. Yet, so important is the blessing of opportunity to be converted and changed, that God forbears in punishing these perpetrators of evil. The injustice, harm, and persecutions inflicted upon, and endured by, believers at the hands of unsaved men are evil works. Nevertheless, God temporarily tolerates this suffering inflicted upon others through sin, in order to allow all unsaved men every opportunity to choose God, even though it allows for evil-doing by unredeemed free men.

In the world, one's confession leads to conviction and punishment in the name of justice. In Heaven's plan, confession follows conviction of sin, and leads to pardon and total forgiving, forgetting, and erasing of the sin, as God's gift of love and mercy.

Even though God foreknows every individual choice from His vantage which overlooks all of time, genuine freedom requires that man must still play out his actual acceptance or rejection of God's grace on the world's stage and in time. Otherwise, the fact of free human choice could not occur, and serve as the basis for God's Justice toward sinners and mercy toward the faithful.

God's grace toward sinners is further manifested by his patient long-suffering in suspending the execution of His Judgment against sinners. He is "forbearing toward you, not wishing that any should perish, but that all should reach repentance" (2 Peter 3:9). With a new generation every thirty years, God's forbearance could be perpetual, if He so willed, since "He desires all men to be saved and to come to the knowledge of the truth" (I Timothy 2:4). He is "ready to pardon, gracious and merciful, slow to anger" (Nehemiah 9:17). "For his anger endureth but a moment" (Psalm 30:5; and see Psalm 78:38; Isaiah 12:1, 54:7; Hosea 11:9). "He retaineth not his anger for ever, because he delighteth in mercy" (Micah 7:18). God blesses all men in the interval of history in which they are to choose, and "makes the sun to rise on the evil and the good, and sends rain on the just and unjust" (Matthew 5:45; see also, Ecclesiastes 9:3).

Romans 2:4 cautions men not to: "presume upon the riches of his kindness and forbearance and patience. Do you not know that God's kindness is meant to lead you to repentance?"

God extends the time to respond to salvation until the final moment of one's last breath, valuing the last penitent equally with the first one who responds to mercy, according to the parable of the Laborers in the Vineyard (Matthew 20:1-16). God waits to condemn evil men until the last moment before death, allowing reclamation of even the worst sinner in the eleventh hour. He intends to give every sinner an opportunity to be converted and transformed from iniquitous weed to righteous wheat, willingly, by grace through faith in Jesus. He defers punishment of the wicked, and preserves their freedom, until "night comes, when no one can work," and the opportunity to choose Jesus is over (John 9:4).

Christ's own directive in the Parable of the Tares is that worthless weeds or tares should be allowed to exist alongside the wheat until the harvest, "lest in gathering the weeds you root up the wheat along with them" (Matthew 13:30). In nature, roots of wheat become intertwined with roots of weeds. They start out looking identical, as all men start as indistinguishable sinners, and by the time the difference is perceptible, the roots are so intertwined that the removal of the weeds is deferred to harvest, lest the healthy wheat become damaged or destroyed in the process of removing the weeds. Since we are all evil while unsaved, God's forbearance in removing evil people from the world, has redounded to every person's benefit at one time or another. This may be why the tares or weeds abide with the wheat until God's harvest time (Matthew 13:30).

There is good in the worst of us, and some bad in the best of us. Every man, in the early stages of his life, resembles an unfruitful weed, and his final character may not be formed until just before harvest time, when the wheat is revealed. If unbelievers were snuffed out upon commission of their first sins, none of us would have an opportunity to come to Jesus. If God eliminated all evil which was extant at any given moment, He would also exterminate unsaved sinners who would otherwise freely come to repentance, forgiveness and regeneration, eventually. For, every man begins in the category of evildoer, from which he must emerge through Jesus, if he is to be saved.

No human parent would destroy his child for repeated disobedience, but would make every effort to regulate and reverse his rebellion. Should we expect any less of God, Who provides the New Birth's regeneration in Christ to all who would have it. Free moral agents need opportunity and time to judge Satan's rebellion by the example of Christ, and then decide in favor of Jesus' way to reconciliation and salvation. Thus, no sinner is irretrievably lost or destined for destruction until his final, unrepenting moment. For, his conversion is possible until then.

Even if God extirpated every sinner He foresaw as impenitently unredeemable, the evil committed by natural men destined eventually to be saved by faith, would still be pervasive and generate abundant suffering until they experienced the New Birth. For, we all start out as tares: "Among these we all lived in the passions of our flesh... and so we were by nature children of wrath, like the rest of mankind" (Ephesians 2:3; see also, Acts 26:18; Romans 6:17; I Corinthians 6:9-11; Colossians 1:13; and I Peter 2:9-10).

Nor is anyone totally evil his entire life. The unsaved physician may have opportunities to save the lives of many Christians. The unredeemed bus driver and restaurateur may frequently ease the lives of believers, and an unbelieving firefighter may rescue Christian occupants from flaming structures. Certainly, God used unsaved agents, such as the heathen conquerors,

Pharaoh, Nebuchadnezzar, and Cyrus, as instruments of chastisement against Israel to accomplish His purposes (Genesis 9:16; Daniel 1;2, 11:36).

God prefers to transform sinners into sons, rather than eliminate them as enemies. In the Parable of the Fig Tree at Luke 13:6-9, Jesus teaches that the unfruitful fig tree is given a last chance to bear fruit, but persistent barrenness will lead ultimately to destruction. God honors His promises to spare a people from destruction. He always puts conditions before the dire consequences He threatens are fulfilled. If we continue to pursue evil ways, unrepentant, then we will be destroyed, but if we repent the evil, we will be saved.

God promises and delivers painful consequences to the evil-doer, but He always gives the condemned a choice in advance (Deuteronomy 11:27-28), and He predicates punishment on continuing rebellion and impenitence. He tolerates each man's flickering moments of earthly imperfection to afford him an opportunity freely to choose God and goodness over evil; but such forbearance is not forever. God tolerates the evil which human freedom incidentally produces, so that every person has every opportunity to be redeemed through the Blood of Jesus.

It is also possible that God refrains from destroying an evil person because of the negative impact it might have upon some believers, such as the loving parents of the transgressor. Even a pet animal affords some pleasure for the family to which it is attached, and the loved ones of an unsaved person may not themselves be spiritually mature enough to cope with early punishment of a wicked loved one. They would suffer punishment along with him, creating a new set of painful consequences.

Even more, to which man could God entrust the judgment of how much evil identifies or determines when and which weeds are to be uprooted? The religious leaders of Judaism, including Saul of Tarsus, clearly, but erroneously, regarded Jesus as a dangerous evil-doer. The bloody trail of martyrs throughout history attests to the human fallibility of majority passions. If God delegated the task of eliminating evil to His Church, its coercive enforcements might also uproot some of its kindness and tolerance, and detract from its love and witness. The Spanish Inquisition, Crusades, and Salem witch-hunts all demonstrate how extreme preoccupation with evil can produce evil exploits by professing believers. It is sometimes better for believers to concentrate on the divine goodness which Jesus bestows, and leave the handling of evil to God at the harvest, when wheat will not be harmed by the weeds' separation and destruction.

There is also good which can result from brotherhood and solidarity among men of salt and light who continue in contact and relationship with the unsaved. Men are capable of learning by hearing and example and seeking God's enabling and conversion. Intercessory prayers of a righteous man, given sufficient time, may elicit the miracle of spiritual transformation in another, by invoking divine grace and power. When Moses interceded for the Israelites, "the Lord repented of the evil which he thought to do unto his people" (Exodus 32:14). A reluctant Jonah successfully preached repentance to eighty thousand Ninevites (Jonah 4:11). When Abraham interceded for a corrupt Sodom, the Lord agreed not to destroy the city if as few as ten righteous men could be found there (Genesis 18:32). Likewise, Jesus reveals at Revelation 2:20-23 that He will give the end-time Jezebel opportunity to repent, but will destroy her children when she refuses to be contrite. Men are capable, by God's grace, of learning by example, and seeking divine conversion and enabling. The promise of the Great Commission is that some weeds can respond to the witness and example of Christian wheat, and themselves be changed supernaturally before the harvest time.

Ironically, when God exercises restraint in punishing evildoers, they continue to wreak iniquity and persecution against the righteous during the time of forbearance. Apparently, the value of their immortal souls outweighs the earthly afflictions.

EXAMPLE OF SUFFERING

As the world attained a capacity to provide material prosperity, improved health and longevity, Born-Again Christianity recaptured the joy of the Lord in this life, and new emphasis was placed upon the joyful aspects of Jesus' life on earth. The example of a Biblical Jesus which we are called to follow, does not reflect a pattern of suffering, except in very special, limited ways. It seemed no longer necessary for Christians to put themselves in bondage to suffering by equating pain and deprivation with holiness.

It was never necessary for Christians to express sanctity by looking as if they survived on a diet of sour pickles and lemons. One need not go about with a long face, lest someone resent his happiness or infer he has enjoyed something sinful. Suffering is not a badge of honor attesting that one's service has been sufficiently significant to attract the attention and assaults of Satan. It is true that Satan contests one's effective service to the Lord by inspiring persecutions and deprivations against faithful servants. However, there is no need to be in love with suffering for its own sake, and there is nothing inherently wrong with pleasure in this life. Nor is the world necessarily ugly, wretched, and distressing for Christian pilgrims who are destined to suffer nobly. The better life which Jesus promises His followers is attached to this world, as well as the next. The mark of a Christian is not his stigmata, but the faithful trust in God which empowers his endurance, and allows him to rejoice in the New Covenant Blessings, here and Hereafter. It is not necessary to seek out opportunities to suffer, and perpetuate them, allowing suffering to endure, rather than one's self enduring the suffering. It is wrong to interpret "Sufficient unto the day is the evil thereof" at Matthew 6:34, as imposing a mandate to seek sufficiency of suffering if it has not yet sought one out. We need not seek out pain simply because I Peter 2:20-21 sublimates our suffering: "But if when you do right and suffer for it patiently, you have God's approval. For to this you have been called, because Christ also suffered for you leaving you an example, that you should follow in his steps." Suffering will always find us without our help.

It is clear we are to follow in His steps, but Jesus' suffering on the Cross does not make constant suffering normative for His disciples. Indeed, there are three aspects of Jesus' suffering which are unique to Him and incapable of duplication by believers. First, we are personal sinners, while Jesus never committed sin. We suffer for sin at times because we have sinned and deserve to be punished while we persist in it. Jesus was called to render vicarious or substitutionary atonement through suffering and death for the sake of all mankind, as our only Saviour and Redeemer to bring men to glory after we are made new and transformed to the image of Christ (Isaiah 53:10-11; Mark 10:45; Galatians 1:4; Hebrews 2:10). Jesus' suffering and death on the Cross was necessary for the Redemption of mankind; but not so individual lives which have been redeemed by that suffering. God's grace would be denied if we thought our suffering was necessary to accomplish or complete our own salvation.

The suffering endured by Jesus was necessary to effectuate and demonstrate His obedience to God, and make His sacrifice perfect through His obedience, for He learned obedience through suffering, without which He would not have had the challenge essential to sacrifice.

Hebrews 2:10 says Jesus was "made perfect through sufferings." Hebrews 5:8-9 adds Jesus "learned obedience through what he suffered; and being made perfect he became the source of eternal salvation to all who obey him." Luke 24:26 teaches it was "necessary that Christ should suffer to enter into his glory." Therefore, we might reasonably expect that following the example of our Lord will produce similar results, as Psalm 119:67,71 reveals: "Before I was afflicted I went astray: but now have I kept thy word... It is good for me that I have been afflicted; that I might learn thy statutes." Suffering arrests the attention of sinners, and leads them to the bench of repentance for their sins (Psalm 32:4-5; 2 Corinthians 7:9-11).

None of us can declare redemptive work "finished" from the Cross, as Jesus did, nor is there any need for us to attempt it. Believers are called to faith, and Jesus bore our suffering so we could avoid it: "Surely he hath borne our griefs, and carried our sorrows" (Isaiah 53:4-5; I Peter 2:24). As Saviour, Jesus could endure the Cross "for the joy that was set before him" (Hebrews 12:2) of a redeemed mankind. We endure for the joy of the promises He will deliver.

Secondly, believers suffer because we are learning to be holy, and growing pains are intrinsic to the learning process. Jesus was holy throughout His earthly sojourn, and he "knew no sin," despite suffering every worldly temptation (2 Corinthians 5:21 and see Hebrews 4:15; I Peter 2:22; I John 3:5). He bore mankind's sins on the Cross, and paid our penalty for sin, so we would not have to pay our own debt. Jesus ended eternal punishment by accepting it for us in the world; He overcame the finality of death by dying, and disposed of sin's consequences by bearing the sins of mankind. His example of good vanquished evil. His love overcame hate, and the way of the Cross and the Resurrection overcame the world. Thus Jesus proclaims: "Now is the judgment of this world, now shall the ruler of this world be cast out; and I, when I am lifted up from the earth, will draw all men to myself" (John 12:31-32).

The time of Jesus' greatest suffering was the time of His greatest triumph, and this is a lesson to sustain us in our own suffering difficulties. The greater our travails, the greater will be our victory in faith and holiness. His suffering calls us to bear our own cross and feel its weight upon our shoulders.

Thirdly, aside from the Cross, Jesus' suffering involved resisting temptations to sin, and intense mourning over the lost who continued to defy God and reject the salvation by grace which he proffered through faith. Yet, Jesus' suffering from worldly temptations can have little application for men, apart from His example in resisting sin, since His exposure was in preparation for His High Priesthood, by encountering, understanding and sympathizing with human temptation in the world. His office as eternal High Priest and Intercessor was fashioned by suffering temptation, according to Hebrews 4:15: "For we have not a high priest who is unable to sympathize with our weaknesses, but one who in every respect has been tempted as we are, yet without sinning." Jesus suffered by experiencing all our temptation to sin from the human vantage point, so He could perfectly intercede on behalf of our weakness as sinners. Temptation was also used as a foil to highlight His perfect sacrificial innocence and sinlessness. "In all their affliction he was afflicted, and the angel of his presence saved them" (Isaiah 63:9).

When we speak of "completing what remains of Christ's affliction for the sake of his body" (Colossians 1:24), it does not mean His Atonement was incomplete, and our suffering can add one thing. It means that Christ suffers and is concerned with each generation of men as they suffer in this world. Christ's reason for accepting the Cross was to relieve the agony of mankind's bondage to sin, and we are to love one another as He did, and weep over the lost and share His concern for the unsaved with the same love as He. We are to share His compassion and feeling for the suffering and persecution of others. He has constituted us to console, comfort, and encourage sufferers in His name, whereby we complete His suffering for the sake of his Body, by sharing and bearing its ongoing persecutions, sorrows, and tribulations.

An interesting lesson for us about human suffering is that Satan's efforts to tempt Jesus were aimed at by-passing God through solutions that were self-reliant, rather than dependent on God. Satan's enticements were to escape suffering and human limitation by invoking supernatural means apart from God's power or God's plan. Jesus had fasted for forty days, so Satan attempted to persuade Jesus to act independently of God by turning stones to bread to feed Himself. But Jesus retained his meekness and reliance only on God's Divine power, and responded by quoting Scripture. He accepted the suffering of hunger, rather than abandon humility and feed himself supernaturally, as the Son of God could have.

Satan's second temptation for Jesus was to rule the world through Satan's power, rather than by God's endowment. Again, Jesus answered with the Word: "You shall worship the Lord your God, and him only shall you serve" (Luke 4:8). Jesus would not exalt Himself above mankind by receiving rulership of the world before the appointed time and without God's blessing. Jesus refused to gain the world by using worldly methods instituted by Satan, or by obeying the ruler of the world, as other men did. Jesus would suffer the Cross and death in order to be our Redeemer. He did not seek to be saved <u>from</u> suffering, but knew He was ordained <u>for</u> suffering.

By voluntarily and vicariously bearing the suffering, pain and death rightly due sinners, Jesus satisfied God's justice. Yet, because Jesus was without sin, and His punishment was personally undeserved, he could be sure the Righteous Judge would vindicate Him as righteous, and reward his substitutionary sacrifice by letting Jesus completely save sinners from the penalty they deserved.[114]

Satan's third temptation taunted Jesus to prove His divinity by leaping from the pinnacle of the Temple, so the angels would bear Him up, and the world would acknowledge He was the Son of God. Again, Jesus answered with the Word, and refused to act in self-reliance apart from God. His Kingdom was ordained to be future, rather than present, as offered by Satan, and the only way was through the suffering of the Cross. Jesus never avoided His suffering, or relinquished His humanity. He refused to set Himself apart from men, but intended to provide an example of ability to endure and overcome suffering by relying upon God's power. Jesus taught that death to the self was the way to life and glory (John 12:24; Romans 8:17; 2 Timothy 2:11-12), but the man who loves his life will lose it. A kernel of wheat dying in the ground would produce many fruits and seeds, for death must precede harvest (John 12:24), and Jesus knew His death was the way for Him to be the first-born of many brethren.

Jesus was led to the wilderness by the Holy Spirit (Luke 4:1), and fasted forty days there before being tempted by Satan, with all the suffering involved in those events. Yet, He did not bear assaults passively. He refuted Satan's temptations three times with the Word of God (Matthew 4:1-10), and he has empowered us to do likewise by using all the armor of God (Ephesians 6:11-17), and the Word to resist the devil who must then flee from us (James 4:7).

There are other ways we can profit by sharing Jesus' suffering, as we are called to do. We can know Him better as we experience intimately how He responded to temptation and suffering. We can share His innocent suffering when we endure unjust persecution by others because we are Christians. When we are the objects of undeserved hatred, anger, envy, or hostility we suffer because of the sins of others. By sharing Christ's persecution and condemnation, we have the same opportunity to respond in love to those who sin against us. By patterning our response to sinners, as Jesus did, we may draw others to him by our example of loving forbearance. We can also learn His love, care, and sympathy for the suffering of others.

Jesus' love for others made Him vulnerable to the suffering of mankind, and caused Him to weep. He wept at Lazarus' death (John 11:35), as he shared the grief of all mourners. His passionate love for mankind caused Him to suffer over the lost souls who rejected His love. Thus, Jesus wept over Jerusalem's hardness of heart in refusing to repent and turn to God (Luke 19:41; and see Hosea 11:8). Hebrews 5:7 notes: "In the days of his flesh, Jesus offered up prayers and supplications, with <u>loud cries and tears</u>, to him who was able to save him from death, and he was heard for his godly fear." The fervor of His prayers for the lost expressed Jesus' love, as well as recognition of God's fearsome justice, and made Him vulnerable to suffering because of the ordained fate of impenitent, rebellious men.

When we share Jesus' suffering, the joyful burden for saving the lost will also bring us grief over the plight of the unsaved who persist in rebellion. Dwight L. Moody opined that no evangelist ought to preach to the unsaved without first crying for them. The overseer of the flock is susceptible to: "affliction and anguish of heart and with many tears" because of love for the ones ignoring correction (2 Corinthians 2:3-4; and see also, Hebrews 6:11, 12:5).

If we are to heed the example of Jesus, His advice was both to avoid suffering, and avoid wasting resources on unresponsive sinners. In fact, when we study the life of our Lord, we find that He endorses passivity and the exercise of restraint only to the extent of being struck twice: "To him who strikes you on the cheek, offer the other also" (Luke 6:29). But when it comes to real harm, His advice and example is to depart from danger (Matthew 10:23; 24:15-16; Luke 4:30; John 7:30, 8:59, 10:39; Acts 13:50-51; Proverbs 27:12).

Jesus sent the Apostles out as missionaries, and directed them to avert harm: "When they persecute you in one town, flee to the next" (Matthew 10:23), which is exactly what Paul and Barnabas did in fleeing to Iconium from Antioch (Acts 13:50-51). Jesus advises End Time survivors: 'when you see the desolating sacrilege... then let those who are in Judea flee to the mountains" (Matthew 24:15-16), and remove themselves from impending peril.

Nor was Jesus passive in letting evil go unchallenged around Him. He preached a Gospel of love, but ejected the money-changers from the Temple, and boldly condemned the Scribes and Pharisees (Matthew 21:12, 23:13). He counsels disciples not to destroy themselves; nor to give unappreciative dogs what is holy, nor cast pearls before swine, lest they be trampled under (Matthew 7:6, see also Matthew 10:14, 10:23; Acts 13:51).

Since too much suffering can repress spiritual growth, it would be counterproductive to use excessive affliction as a means of training, and would work contrary to God's purposes to love, heal, and deliver us. When physical or emotional suffering reaches such intensity that it destroys one's fruitfulness and ability to serve the Lord, we should expect God, according to His promise, to provide a literal escape and removal from the situation, rather than continued endurance. The battered wife, for example, serves no purpose of the Lord in absorbing destructive or paralyzing abuse to the point she is of no use to herself or her children. The key is always sustaining, and survival of, one's devotion to the higher service and glory of the Lord. Love sometimes needs to be tough in the interests of self-preservation, or to motivate the wrongdoer to turn from sinful ways (I Corinthians 5:5; I Timothy 1:19-20).

If we study the life of Jesus, we see that the Bible notes as many instances of Jesus enjoying a feast, festival, banquet, or wedding celebration, as it notes His suffering. His life-style was sufficiently involved with the world and its pleasures that he regularly feasted in the company of sinners. (Luke 7:36, 10:38-40; John 2:2, 12:2), and was criticized by the Pharisees for it (Matthew 11:19; Luke 7:34). Scriptural references to His first thirty years include triumph, joy, and fellowship with God (Luke 2:46-48, 52).

During the thousand days of His public ministry, Jesus enjoyed the company of all kinds of persons, and found joy and fulfillment in doing His Father's will. He taught the Word, healed all suffering believers He encountered, and was perfectly fruitful in His ministry, except when He was rejected by unbelief (Matthew 13:58). He found joy in applying His life selflessly to the welfare of others.

He knew in advance He was called by God to suffer and die (Matthew 16:21), and was prophesied as a "man of sorrows and acquainted with grief" (Isaiah 53:3). Yet, even the two days from the Garden of Gethsemane until His death on the Cross (Matthew 26:37, 27:26; Luke 22:44), though the most horrible, intense, and worst suffering in the history of the world, was relatively brief and limited when it occurred.

Thus, the example of Jesus' suffering teaches purposeful suffering: in selfless sacrifice and ministry for others; in pursuing personal holiness; and in preaching the Good News of salvation to the unsaved. In taking up our cross, we are not called to follow the road to the Crucifixion, except figuratively, as we die to the self to be transformed into new persons. The dregs of the cup Jesus was given to drink cannot be shared by us, though we will drink of the cup (Matthew 20:22-23), and be given both the duty and privilege to emulate some of His suffering (Philippians 3:10; Revelation 1:9).

As Jesus, we can be fitted for our purpose in life by the suffering we endure as we are trained in obedience, loving service, and growth in holiness. By suffering in His service, we will have a unique opportunity to acquire Christ-like character through a God-oriented life of submission, spiritual preparedness, and growth, with victory over the world. We will replace sin's pleasures with celebrations of new life in Christ, experiencing supernatural joy and genuine happiness in spiritual virtues.

If we use Job as an example of suffering, his travails are also illustrative of a relatively speedy deliverance, and full restoration in the Lord. God did not allow Job to be destroyed, but used adversity to drive Job to "die to the self," and place all his confidence in the Lord. There is no longer any need for adversity if a Christian asserts himself and spiritually fills what has been emptied and cleansed with the things of the Lord. When he awakens, comes to himself, repents, learns, grows in holiness, and resists the devil, he may find his travails have ended.

The example of Job encourages believers' faith not to waver when we undergo suffering. Every trouble comes with its own blessing and Sovereign grace, and we ignore its teaching and opportunity for growth, only at our peril. God sends milder trials first, to provoke repentance and spare us more severe troubles. Our prolonged ignoring of them moves God to increase the intensity of our travails until he has our attention.

God appointed Jesus to suffer, that we might succeed to the glory He has prepared for us in Him. If God thought our salvation was worth divine suffering, we should not expect exemption from some suffering in our ordained pursuit of that same glory by grace (Romans 8:18).

The Christian attitude toward suffering does not ask the question, "when am I going to get out of these troubles?" until it has first asked "what am I going to get out of them?" We recognize that our extreme circumstances are God's opportunity to work in us; that we can grow rich by our losses; brought erect by our falls; filled by being emptied; and embrace eternal life by dying to self. Sorrow will continue to be an underground river of darkness, but we will not emerge from its caverns until we have traversed and tasted of its waters. We will not escape affliction's corridors until we have mined the precious ore of its veins. We will not depart the orchard of torment until we have sampled its fruits of righteousness.

Our faithfulness is certain, despite suffering, because of the providence, constancy and benevolence of God's love: "For I am sure that neither death, nor life, nor angels, nor principalities, nor things present, nor things to come, nor powers, nor height, nor depth, nor anything else in all creation, will be able to separate us from the love of God in Christ Jesus our Lord" (Romans 8:38-39).

CHAPTER 13

SUFFERING WHEN GOD PUNISHES EVIL

"The Lord revengeth, and is furious; the Lord will take vengeance on his adversaries, and he reserveth wrath for his enemies:"

— Nahum 1:2

Because God has revealed His character as indefectible and perfectly good, we can be sure He is, by nature, incapable of anything evil. Whenever our loving Father imposes punishment to satisfy His Justice, we can be sure it accomplishes some higher good for Creation, which blesses His faithful. Yet, the application of God's Justice, which necessitates punishment for evil-doers, no doubt appears to be a real evil to the transgressor being punished and his loved ones.

It is a comfort to the righteous whenever God demonstrates His Sovereignty over Creation and intervenes in history to remove wickedness from their path, or promises an eternity without the presence of evil. Only a fool would claim to know God's specific purpose when He exercises His Sovereign prerogative of punishment. However, traditional penology suggests several motivations for punishment, which occasionally coincide with God's revealed purposes.

First, punishment may be administered as implacable Justice, exacting a penalty for sin, and stressing vengeance, recrimination, retaliation, or retribution by taking away the freedom, property, or life of the wrongdoer. Second, punishment may focus on restoration or restitution to the one injured by imposing payment of damages. Third, punishment may seek to imprison, segregate, or remove the wrongdoer from the presence of free society to preserve and prevent further harm to the righteous. Unredeemable rebels are removed from our midst to prevent harm, corruption, or destruction by a "bad apple" in the barrel.

Fourth, punishment serves as an instructive example of the dire consequences of wrongdoing, to deter such conduct by observers, both contemporary and in later generations. Finally, punishment may seek to instruct, chasten, reform, chastise, and rehabilitate the wrongdoer, by correcting a fault and training him in righteous conduct. The threat of punishment often is used in conjunction with the promise of reward to provide full motivation to act rightly.

A few thoughts are worth repeating before we begin our study of punishment in depth. He who seeks God's way is blessed by the good of His deliverance from evil. All evil which besets man is committed by human or demonic agency. God has ceded some control over human affairs by a partial relinquishment of power to free beings in order to bless them with participation in processes of holiness, ministry, stewardship, intercessory prayer, and witnessing to the unsaved. In the interests of that free choice which exalts man, God tolerates some corruption of freedom and the evil and pain it produces, until the hearts of evildoers are transformed to the image of Christ.

Consequently, all evil may be causally attributable to God as the First Cause or Creator of institutions or processes allowing freedom, which in turn permits evil corruption by creatures of the Creation God had originally declared "very good" (Genesis 1:31). However, we cannot conclude that God intended or willed any evil resulting from corruption of free choice simply because He allows freedom's intrinsic potential to produce evil. His wish is that all come to faithful obedience and eternal bliss. His will is that recalcitrant rebels be punished if they will not come.

This contingency, but not necessity, which allows evil to result from freedom is the prism through which we should regard passages such as Proverbs 16:4: "The Lord hath made all things for himself: yea, even the wicked for the day of evil." Likewise, Isaiah 45:7 acknowledges God's Sovereign, original creativity: "I form the light, and create darkness: I make peace, and create evil: I the Lord do all these things." At Isaiah 54:16 God declares: "I have created the waster to destroy"; though surely He will only destroy what is evil in God's perfect sight. Ecclesiastes 7:14 confirms God's absolute and limiting control over evil: "In the day of prosperity be joyful, but in the day of adversity consider: God also hath set the one over against the other, to the end that man should find nothing after him." Job 9:22 says of God: "He destroyeth the perfect and the wicked."

God reveals His total Sovereignty by the original impress of His hand on all creation: "Who hath made man's mouth? or who maketh the dumb, or deaf, or the seeing, or the blind? have not I the Lord?" (Exodus 4:11). Likewise, God declares at Deuteronomy 32:39, 41: "there is no god with me: I kill, and I make alive; I wound and I heal: neither is there any that can deliver out of my hand... I will render vengeance to mine enemies, and will reward them that hate me." God asserts His connection with suffering at Psalms 51:8; 102:10-11; and I Samuel 2:6-7.

God reveals He sometimes uses evil instrumentalities to accomplish His good purposes. He "put a lying spirit in the mouth" of all king Ahab's prophets to encourage him to go into battle, where he would be killed by the Syrians for his evil (I Kings 22:19-23).

I Samuel 18:10-11 relates that just before Saul tried to kill David with a javelin: "the evil spirit from God came upon Saul... And Saul cast the javelin; for he said, I will smite David." Later, in contemplating God's interventions on his behalf, David recognized they were all done to draw David closer to God, Who had "done all these great things, to make thy servant know them" (2 Samuel 7:21). Psalm 78:41, 49 says that when the Israelites tempted God and turned from Him, then "He cast upon them the fierceness of his anger, wrath, and indignation, and trouble, by sending evil angels among them." God allowed a messenger of Satan to harass St. Paul with a thorn in the flesh to keep him from becoming too elated by all the revelations he had received (2 Corinthians 12:7).

Whenever God hardens a heart unto condemnation, it is not an arbitrary appointment orchestrated by God, but a judicial determination acknowledging the consequences of man's wrongful free choices already made. Pharaoh had hardened his heart against God five times in denying the departure of the Israelites from Egypt. The sixth time, God simply acted upon and retaliated against Pharaoh's cumulative, free determinations to rebel against God (Exodus 9:12).

2 Thessalonians 2:10-11 speaks of wicked men who refused to love the truth and be saved. They consequently succumbed to Satan's lies: "Therefore God sends upon them a strong delu-

sion, to make them believe what is false, so that all may be condemned who did not believe the truth but had pleasure in unrighteousness." God did not cause their disbelief, but eventually accepted what they had irreversibly chosen, and no longer convicted them of sin, nor sought their conversion. Psalm 82:5 explains this hardening of the wicked: "They know not, neither will they understand; they walk on in darkness." When men become inveterate and hardened in their rebellion, God ratifies their decision and eventually confirms their delusions. Their own acts sealed their fate of destruction. Whether a man's heart is pliant or hard determines the reaction God's touch works on it. The same sun softens wax and hardens clay, but it is the composition of wax and clay that determines the sun's effect upon them. When God gives sinners up to their own choice, His grace is withdrawn from them, and they are alienated from God in accordance with their own stubborn decisions.

Inveterate sinners may become so stiff-necked and hard-hearted that God abandons "them up in the lusts of their hearts to impurity, to the dishonoring of their bodies among themselves, because they exchanged the truth about God for a lie and worshiped and served the creature rather than the Creator... For this reason God gave them up to dishonorable passions... God gave them up to a base mind and to improper conduct" (Romans 1:24-28; see also, 2 Corinthians 3:14). Ephesians 4:18 explains unbelievers "are darkened in their understanding, alienated from the life of God because of the ignorance that is in them, due to their hardness of heart; they have become callous and have given themselves up to licentiousness, greedy to practice every kind of uncleanness."

Whenever we encounter some apparently unloving act of God in Scripture, let us keep in mind God's declaration of His love, goodness, and desire that all men be saved. Let us evaluate what God does in light of His omniscience and foreknowledge that some men will not repent evil during their lifetimes, but will remain stubbornly unredeemable, as the Antedeluvians in the time of Noah. Let us focus on the fairness of God's constant warnings to sinners to change their ways so they might avoid the consequences of disobedience, coupled with the loving alternative of repeated mercy, forgiveness, second chances, and opportunities to repent.

God warns us of the consequences of sowing and reaping, so we can avoid the inevitable results which sin breeds. Rebellious abandonment of God's protective grace leaves sinners open to the enticements of Satan and the world. Moral sloth and carelessness lead to sin. Hardness of heart produces unloving selfishness, as one reaps what he has sown. A loving Father admonishes His children to avoid sin for their own good, so they can escape the harm of worldly consequences. It is foreseeable that sexual promiscuity in a world of disease may produce personal illness. It is difficult in such a case to charge that God has ordained illness as a punishment for the sinner's disobedience, simply because He has warned against the natural penalties of sin resulting from corrupted freedom in a damaged world.

Above all, let us remember that God in His infinite love has provided Jesus as the atoning sacrifice to satisfy God's Justice. He has provided sinners with a way out of their predicament of personal punishment by His grace through the sinner's faith in Jesus. God has provided Jesus as a vicarious substitute to bear the sins of man, though Himself sinless, and redeem sinners from the consequences of sin. Jesus was the only possible satisfaction of God's Justice, short of destroying each sinner for his own sin. However, if God's mercy is spurned, a sinner must bear his own penalty for sin, since he has rejected his only hope of redemption. When you faithfully present the Gospel that the penalty for sin is God's wrath and eternal damnation, you are like a physician who follows the bad news with the good news that Jesus is the complete cure for the malady of sin.

God gives sinners every opportunity to embrace Him, and desires none to perish (Acts 2:21; I Timothy 2:4; 2 Peter 3:9), but those who consistently rebel against God's law and order are stubbornly signing their own death warrant. This means that responsibility is personal, and individual accountability is the basis for Judgment. God does not predetermine who responds to Him, but allows for free choice in His economy of salvation.

REJECTERS OF JESUS BEAR THEIR OWN PENALTY FOR SIN

It is well to remember that every unsaved person qualifies as an evil sinner, but is free and fully able in that unregenerate state, to collaborate in his salvation by divine grace. God calls first, but man must answer and choose divine help for conversion and transformation by the New Birth. However, if a sinner corrupts his exercise of freedom, and repudiates Jesus' loving Atonement, then he must bear his own condemnatory, but rightly deserved, penalty for sin. He has chosen to embrace faithless disobedience, sinfulness, naturally wicked inclinations, and worldly advantage. He has chosen to bear his own penalty and pay his own debt. His fate is to be punished; to suffer the penalty of eternal damnation, and the painful cognizance he has forfeited God's presence.

Faithless disobedience is directly productive of suffering or loss of blessings when a sinner refuses to accept redemption through Jesus and collaborate in his own salvation. If mercy is rejected, then God cannot extend forgiveness or grant pardon. Without Jesus, the penalty for sin is not remitted, and retributive justice demands punishment and personal atonement for sin. A merciful God destroys only those who refuse to receive His grace. He must execute the sentence of damnation against those who stubbornly choose to remain unsubmissive, unregenerate, and evil by rejecting Christ.

Because God has granted free will to men, there is nothing unloving or vindictive in God's justice if He honors man's exercise of free choice and power of decision, even if it disdains grace and rejects God. We ought not let our faith waver that God is good and does only good, when seeing evil men destroyed, or personally undergoing suffering. God does nothing evil, but He will assuredly transform suffering into ultimate good for the faithful sufferer and for His Church in the world and throughout eternity.

If God's love has not motivated transgressors to repent, then knowledge of Judgment should move them to self-examine and consider their position: to judge themselves, recognize their sin; and receive Christ, so they will not have to be judged sinners at His Second Coming. Unsaved sinners will be pursued and persuaded by God's love to abandon the world and embrace salvation. No heart is too venal, too unworthy, or too hardened to withstand penetration by God's love. Only the sinner's stubborn, rebellious will can reject God's overtures. Unsaved sinners who are unmoved by the sacrificial love of God, must be alerted to God's impending Judgment upon sin and the consequences of eternal damnation in Hell, so they will seek to embrace salvation out of dread and anxiety: if not love.

Judgment is based on God's Justice in holding each human responsible and accountable for his actions on earth. This requires human decisions in which one's choices are freely made, and not commanded or orchestrated by God. Judgment for non-believers occurs after Jesus returns and administers total and literal justice, based upon one's own acts and choices to bear his own penalty for sin. We cannot become so occupied with God's love and mercy that we overlook His justice, which necessitated satisfaction for sin at the Cross.

Unrighteous sinners know "no fear of God before their eyes" (Romans 3:18; citing Psalm 36:1). They are spiritually dead, rotting in the coffins of their unrepented sins; entombed in their habitual transgressions; entwined in their grave-clothes of rebellious unconcern. They will not escape Judgment by wishing for annihilation or nirvana at death. If they have not received Jesus, put on His righteousness, and been cleansed of sin by His Blood, they are still evil, spiritually dead, and condemned by their own choice.

The destruction of the wicked, which gives urgency to evangelizing the unsaved, imperils all who refuse to embrace God's grace and pardon in Jesus Christ. Even though God wishes all men to be saved, He has not ordained unconditional and automatic salvation for all men. Salvation becomes a spiritual reality only for believers. God's gift of salvation is for all, but only to those who believe and receive that gift, by grace through faith in Christ, "because, if you confess with your lips that Jesus is Lord and believe in your heart that God raised him from the dead, you will be saved. For man believes with his heart and so is justified, and he confesses with his lips and so is saved" (Romans 10:9-10).

God's holy nature can neither tolerate, nor compromise with sin. If sin is not washed clean with the Blood of Christ, and forgiven in response to confession and repentance after we are converted, then God will not overlook our transgressions. God hates sin intensely (Psalms 5:5, 7:11), unless it has been remitted through Jesus' intercession, in which case it is forgiven and forgotten, removed "as far as the east is from the west" (Psalm 103:12).

Yet, in most cases, God gave Israel warning of consequences for sin, and conditioned punishment upon continued intentional pursuit of evil. If Israel repented and returned to God, then He would relent and be merciful. Only if Israel persisted, would she be punished, pursuant to God's warning. Israel's suffering was always deserved, always shrouded in willful rebellion against God, and the certainty of punishment for impenitence always communicated and understood.

Each one who rejects God's forgiveness and mercy must bear personally the consequences of punishment and loss, "For each man will have to bear his own load" (Galatians 6:5). "And if a soul sin, and commit any of these things which are forbidden to be done by the commandments of the Lord, though he wist it not, yet is he guilty, and shall bear his iniquity" (Leviticus 5:17; and see also Leviticus 5:1, 7:18, 17:16, 19:8, 20:17,19; Numbers 14:34; Deuteronomy 24:16 and I Kings 17:17-18). There is a time of resurrection for all the dead, both good and evil, "when all who are in the tombs will hear his voice and come forth, those who have done good, to the resurrection of life, and those who have done evil to the resurrection of judgment" (John 5:28-29; see also, John 5:27; Romans 2:16; Hebrews 9:27; Jude 15; James 2:13, I Peter 4:5; I John 4:17).

I Peter 1:17 says that unrepented, irresponsible conduct invokes divine judgment, and since God "judges each one impartially according to his deeds, conduct yourselves with fear through the time of your exile." If you ignore the call of Jesus now, you will most certainly respond and come forth at the Judgment. There is no escape for sinners from the Last Judgment. If you will not have Jesus as your Saviour, you will most certainly have Him as your Judge.[115] If you despised His grace, then you must taste of His wrath. If you spurned His love, you will be introduced to His judgment, and partake of His punishment.

Sin deserves punishment, and if rebellious men freely persevere in habitual sin and faithless disobedience, God allows the execution of His perfect and righteous Judgments upon such a sinner. The consequences will occur which He predicts and warns for unrepented sin. The man who refuses to embrace the loving Lord has determined to pay the penalty and satisfy God's justice by his own resources. God prefers to conquer sin through salvation and regeneration for faithful penitents, rather than by judgment for unrepentant sinners. God forgives only because the penalty of sin was paid by Jesus, and only when His sacrifice has been accepted by sinners.

There would be no genuine mercy for penitent believers unless wrath were truly reserved for sinners who stubbornly persist in rebellious disobedience, and refuse to embrace mercy by God's grace through faith in Christ. Their ultimate separation from God and heaven is strictly the result of their own choice.

Moreover, if God forced reconciliation upon impenitent sinners it would be inconsistent with their free choice, and irreconcilable with a holy Heaven. Indeed, how could a rebel, contemptuous of grace be joyful in Heaven, where all God's subjects joyfully glorify and submit to Him? The rebel would have nothing in common flocking with birds of such disparate feather. Thus, all men will understand the destruction of unrepentant sinners, because their stubbornly unchanged characters are totally incompatible with a Kingdom which honors God. That is why all will recognize and concede the justice of God's Judgments upon the unsaved sinner who chooses to be judged in his own unrighteousness.

God's treatment of evildoers reveals remarkable constraint, consistent with His goodness and mercy tempering His Justice. He withholds punishment until man's choice is irrevocably sealed. Only then He honors the choice freely made by man, knowing that an inveterate unrepentant sinner would not and could not be happy with God and His Church in Heaven.

PUNISHMENT AS VENGEANCE OR RETRIBUTION

Retributive justice is strictly punitive and exacts loss of benefits and reparation or satisfaction to God, because sin reflects pride and flows from dissatisfaction with God's provision. This recrimination or vengeance is literally the payment of a "life for a life, Eye for eye, tooth for tooth,... wound for wound, stripe for stripe" (Exodus 21:23-25). It is primarily retrospective and focuses on irreparable wrongdoing because of a broken command willfully, rebelliously, and impenitently flouted in the face of God's Justice and mercy.

By way of contrast, chastening of God's children is basically prospective and seeks to correct and deter fault and wrongdoing. This punishment is motivated by love for the child. It intends to train and instruct him in obedience and holiness for future blessings. Such chastisement has nothing to do with revenge against evil, but with deterrence of future wrongdoing by the one involved, or other observers who may learn from his example.

We will see that God uses punishment in a destructive or vengeful way in many categories. Satan and fallen angels or demons know punitive retribution for their rebellion. The nations which scorn God and pursue other idols know His vengeance. Israel has been punished for its disobedience, rebellion and idolatry despite being the apple of God's eye (Zechariah 2:8), although in Israel's case, vengeance is combined with a large dose of deterrent instruction.

God's expulsion of Satan and his rebellious angels from heaven (Isaiah 14:22-25) is the first example of strict punishment or vengeance for prideful rebellion. Reason compels us to infer that Satan's punishment was necessary because his disobedience was unredeemable and could not have co-existed with the righteousness of God in Heaven. However, God did not initially separate Satan from Creation but left him at large, roaming the world, even though he could freely tempt men to sin. At the final consignment of Satan and his demons to the Lake of Fire's torment (Revelation 20:10) the saints will enjoy evil's removal and segregation. Demons are apparently aware of their fate, asking Jesus: "Have you come here to torment us before the time?" (Matthew 8:29).

The Old Testament is clear that one's unrepented personal sin, as well as the corporate infidelity of the nation, always provokes punishment and suffering. The original sin of Adam and Eve chronicled at Genesis 3:15-17 is identified as disobedience, pride of self-determination in sampling the forbidden fruit, and not trusting God's directions. I John 3:4 explains: "Sin is lawlessness." Adam and Eve descended to a fallen state in knowing evil after they disregarded God's prohibition not to eat "of the tree of knowledge of good and evil... for in the day that thou eatest thereof thou shalt surely die" (Genesis 2:17).

Scripture affirms there is personal responsibility for one's own sin. Eve tried to blame Satan for tempting her to eat the forbidden fruit, but God held her accountable, along with Satan. Adam tried to blame Eve for his sin, and even accused God indirectly, with the extenuation: "the woman whom thou gavest to be with me, she gave me of the tree" (Genesis 4:12). However, God declared it was Adam's sin, as well as Eve's, because he had been present, but stood mute, throughout Eve's temptation, and then joined in the transgression.

Mercifully, God removed Adam from the Garden "lest he put forth his hand, and take also of the tree of life, and eat, and live for ever" (Genesis 3:22). God had planned man's redemption before the beginning of time, but He did not want Adam and all his descendents to exist eternally in their fallen state. They needed to be saved and transformed to the image of Christ before becoming immortal by grace through faith in Jesus. Expelling them from Eden preserved mankind against being permanently scarred by evil's corrupting influence.

The Bible discloses various levels of God's wrath, vengeance, or destruction against unrepentant sinners who persist in disobeying and rebelling against God. Eternal punishment, agony, and loss are forecast for the wicked when they are consigned to the flames of Hell and final separation from God. There is the eschatalogical torment of the End Times, when God's wrath is poured out upon unrepentant rebels in the Last Days. There is the wrath of abandonment, where God gives up unrepentant sinners to reprobate minds and removes the restraints of reason upon their sinful lust (Romans 1:28). There is catastrophic wrath, as in the plagues poured out upon Pharaoh's Egypt when the Israelites were captive there.

Some passages reveal God's concern and special zeal by retaliating against unbelievers who wrong His children. At Deuteronomy 7:15 God promises to spare his people from diseases, but to "lay them upon all them that hateth thee." Deuteronomy 24:23 says: "he will avenge the blood of his servants, and will render vengeance to his adversaries, and will be merciful unto his land, and to his people." We are not to avenge ourselves, but entrust it to God according to Psalm 94:1. At Isaiah 54:14-15 God forecasts his retribution for the evil committed against His chosen: "whosoever shall gather together against thee shall fall for thy sake... and I have created the waster to destroy."

As if on some dread sortie through the alphabet, lest the Israelites be destroyed by evil, God either delivered Israel from, or directed preemptive strikes against, the Ammonites, Amorites, Anakims, Amelekites, Assyrians, Babylonians, Chaldeans and Cananites, sometimes to the extent of eliminating all women, children, and even livestock (Exodus 17:14; Jeremiah 49:2; 50:13; Deuteronomy 20:17; Joshua 10:8, 11:4; 14:12; 2 Kings 19:35; and Isaiah 43:14). When sinfulness is unredeemable, it must be destroyed completely, lest it overcome the righteous. God told Saul to "go and smite Amalek, and utterly destroy all that they have, and spare them not; but slay both man and woman, infant and suckling, ox and sheep, camel and ass" (I Samuel 15:2). When Saul disobeyed God, he was punished and lost all his kingdom (I Samuel 15:3, 9, 26).

God "slew all the firstborn in the land of Egypt," when Pharaoh would not let the Israelites go (Exodus 13:15), but He passed over the Israelites whose doors were marked with blood (Exodus 12:26,29). God freed Israel when He destroyed Egypt at Passover, and brought about Pharaoh's capitulation. God's favor on Israel then motivated the Egyptians to give them jewels, silver, gold, raiment, and flocks to pacify God, lest He destroy more than every firstborn child (Exodus 12:29-38). God then drowned Pharaoh's army in the Red Sea as it pursued the fleeing Israelites (Exodus 14:28).

In the New Testament, Romans 12:19 says: "Beloved, never avenge yourselves, but leave it to the wrath of God; for it is written, 'Vengeance is mine, I will repay, says the Lord'." Colossians 3:25 forecasts: "For the wrongdoer will be paid back for the wrong he has done, and there is no partiality." I Corinthians 4:17 says: "If anyone destroys God's temple, God will destroy him. For God's temple is holy, and <u>that temple you are</u>." Christians are assured: "he who is troubling you will bear his judgment, whoever he is" (Galatians 5:10). St. Paul relates at 2 Timothy 4:14: "Alexander the coppersmith did me a great harm; the Lord will requite him for his deeds."

At the time of Judgment, those who have persecuted Christians and not repented, will be repaid, according to 2 Thessalonians 1:5-6: "And this is the evidence of the righteous judgment of God... God deems it just to repay with affliction those who afflict you... inflicting vengeance upon those who do not know God... They shall suffer the punishment of eternal destruction and exclusion from the presence of the Lord and from the glory of his might."

Hebrews 2:2 notes: "every transgression or disobedience received a just retribution." Revelation 6:10 relates that the blood of the martyrs will be avenged against those who persecute the righteous. In Revelation 19:2, the multitude in Heaven shout: "His judgments are true and just; he has judged the great harlot... and he has avenged on her the blood of his servants."[116]

Scripture is clear that God uses rulers as His instrument to punish evildoers and preserve the righteous. I Peter 2:13-14 declares: "Be subject for the Lord's sake to every human institution, whether it be to the emperor as supreme, or to governors as sent by him to <u>punish those</u> who do wrong and to praise those who do right." Romans 13:3-4 reminds us: "For rulers are not a terror to good conduct, but to bad... for he is God's servant for your good. But if you do wrong, be afraid, for he does not bear the sword in vain; he is the servant of God to execute his wrath on the wrong-doer."

THE ETERNAL DAMNATION OF THE WICKED

Jesus' Atonement is evidence that God's justice requires satisfaction, and those who reject God's grace and mercy in Jesus must meet God's Justice by themselves. Psalm 9:17 forecasts: "The wicked shall be turned into hell, and all the nations that forget God." Ezekiel 18:4, 20 warns: "the soul that sinneth it shall die." Jesus warned the Pharisees at John 8:24: "you will die in your sins unless you believe." "For the wages of sin is death" (Romans 6:23), "and sin when it is full-grown brings forth death "(James 1:15). See also, Numbers 15:31; Deuteronomy 24:16; 2 Kings 14:6; and 2 Chronicles 25:4).

Evil will be removed from the earth in the end days, when the Lord, in "wrath and fierce anger" lays "the land desolate; and he shall destroy the sinners thereof out of it " (Isaiah 13:9). At the end of the age, the followers of the beast will be destroyed by the sword of the Lord, and the beast and false prophet will be thrown into the lake of fire and brimstone (Revelation 19:20-21). At the close of the Millennium, God will destroy Gog and Magog by fire which "came down from Heaven" to consume them, and will cast the devil, Death and Hades into the lake of fire (Revelation 20:8-14). The Great White Throne Judgment of Revelation 20:11 is the final consignment of sinners to eternal damnation.

Several other passages describe the sinner's destruction in terms of hell-fire. At Matthew 5:29-30 (paralleled in Matthew 18:8-9 and Mark 9:43-48), Jesus commands His disciples to avoid hell by avoiding sin: "If your right eye causes you to sin, pluck it out and throw it away. And if your right hand causes you to sin, cut it off and throw it away; it is better that you lose one of your members than that your whole body go into hell."

Whether Jesus was advocating a literal amputation, which seems unlikely, or dramatizing the importance of actual righteousness, it is clear that He intended to depict the horrors of sin which result from faithlessness and make "your whole body go into hell." Sin in one part of a man's body could easily become fatal faithlessness in the whole body. A limb can become so painfully infected or leprous that our whole body constantly lacks peace, driving us to amputate the gangrenous member. A diseased appendix can rupture and disperse poison throughout the entire body, resulting in death. Our salvation is such a serious matter that we must save the whole body at any cost, even if it requires removal of a sinfully offending member. Personal sin can be so destructive that it threatens one's very spiritual existence.

Jesus describes the Judgment following His Second Coming where human works of those then living on earth are weighed. There, Christ teaches that He will come in His glory with the angels and sit on His glorious throne or Judgment seat. Before Him will be gathered all the nations, and He will separate the sheep from the goats. Those who failed to act lovingly or minister to their fellow men by good deeds, are labeled 'goats' by Jesus. They have denied love to Him and to others, and are therefore condemned: "Depart from me, you cursed, into the eternal fire prepared for the devil and his angels" (Matthew 25:41). They "will go away into eternal punishment, but the righteous into eternal life" (Matthew 25:46; See also, Matthew 13:41-50; James 5:3; and Hebrews 10:26-27).

Revelation 20:12-15 speaks of the Great White Throne Judgment, or Last Judgment of the wicked dead, based upon their deeds: "And the dead were judged by what was written in the books, by what they had done... and all were judged by what they had done... and if anyone's name was not found written in the book of life, he was thrown into the lake of fire." The records of personal conduct kept in the books confirm the justice of the disobedient unbeliever's damnation and reflect his lack of faith, so he is not covered by the Blood of Christ. Revelation 22:14-15 closes with a warning for sinners: "Blessed are they that do his commandments, that they may have the right to the tree of life, and may enter in through the gates into the city. For without are dogs, and sorcerers, and whoremongers, and murderers, and idolaters, and whosoever loveth and maketh a lie." (See also, Matthew 5:22; I John 3:14-15, 20; 2 Thessalonians 2:11-12; Revelation 3:2-5).

Jesus also reveals that at the "close of the age," God will send angels as reapers to "gather out of his kingdom all causes of sin and all evil-doers, and throw them into the furnace of fire; there men will weep and gnash their teeth" (Matthew 13:41-42). We may not presently know why God does not correct nature's aberrations which cause disease or why He allows other sufferings originating with men. We can be sure, however, that God does intervene whenever creaturely freedom threatens God's purposes and objective of salvation and good for His children.

Judgment is meted out on a personal basis, according to one's iniquity. Those who reject Christ will be punished, and "it shall be more tolerable on the day of judgment for the land of Sodom and Gomorrah than for that town" (Matthew 10:15; 11:24; Mark 6:11, Luke 10:12). Jesus warned about Hell in the cities where most of His mighty works had been done, but they were not moved to repent: "it shall be more tolerable on the day of judgment for Tyre and Sidon than for you" (Matthew 11:22; Luke 10:14).

GOD'S PUNISHMENT OF ISRAEL

God was especially concerned in preserving the integrity of the nation by chastening the people collectively and individually for their sins. The fate of the nation and of individuals were intertwined and interdependent. When Israel suffered from widespread iniquity and idolatry, a righteous individual like Moses bore the same suffering and shared Israel's wandering in the wilderness. The Jews were God's chosen people (Deuteronomy 7:6), and the apple of His eye (Zechariah 2:8); the only people He has ever known (Deuteronomy 14:2; Amos 3:2). Yet, God punished them whenever they departed from belief in Him.

God used the Egyptians to chasten the Israelites in captivity (Exodus 5:5-14). His displeasure with their ingratitude resulted in their punishment, overthrowing them in the wilderness (Numbers 11:33, 14:29). At I Corinthians 10:5-11 St. Paul recounts Israel's example, which instructs us concerning five freedoms given the Israelites liberated from Egypt, which were abused by them and resulted in their deaths. They craved the pleasures of Egypt, such as meat, and after God had indulged them, they were struck by a plague (Numbers 11:13, 33; Psalm 78:18, 34); They were idolaters, worshipping a molten calf, for which God killed them with a plague (Exodus 32:1, 28, 35; Psalm 106:19, 29); They indulged in immorality, for which they were slain (Numbers 25:1, 4, 9; Psalm 106:39-40); They put the Lord to the test and questioned His benevolent intent, for which they were killed by snakes (Numbers 21:5-6); and they grumbled rebelliously against God's anointed, Moses and Aaron, for which they were killed by a plague (Numbers 14:2, 35; 16:41, 49). God then used Nebuchadnezzar, King of Babylon, to "make the multitude of Egypt to cease" (Ezekiel 30:10).

When God's anger was kindled against the Israelites because "they forsook the Lord, and served Baal and Ashtaroth... he delivered them into the hands of spoilers that spoiled them, and he sold them into the hands of their enemies round about, so that they could not any longer stand before their enemies" (Judges 2:13-14).

Habakkuk was a Prophet of God who bewailed the constant evil which ran rampant in Judea, yet went unpunished. When he queried of God how He could countenance such evil, God revealed He would "raise up" the Chaldeans as an instrument of His justice, and "ordained them for judgment; and... established them for correction," and permitted the Chaldeans to continue the chastisement of Judah by conquering the land and devouring their substance (Habakkuk 1:6-13). He established the Assyrians as the rod of His anger and staff of His indignation against an idolatrous Israel (Isaiah 10:5). God was so disappointed with Judah's refusal to repent of its sinful disobedience that He instructed Jeremiah: "Therefore pray not for this people, neither lift up cry nor prayer for them, neither make intercession to me, for I will not hear" (Jeremiah 7:16). When the Israelites relapsed into sin and Baal-worship, God warned: "I will send a sword after them, till I have consumed them" (Jeremiah 9:16).

Yet, in His grace, God promises pardon to Jerusalem after retribution has been exacted: "Comfort ye, comfort ye my people saith your God... that her iniquity is pardoned: for she hath received of the Lord's hand double for all her sins" (Isaiah 40:1-2).

Conversely, individual sin could impact and bring condemnation on the entire nation, as individual wrong was attributed to all Israel. God "gave Jehoiakim king of Judah" into "the hand of Nebuchadnezzar, king of Babylon" because of his unrepented evil (Daniel 1:1-2), bringing all Israel into captivity. Mercifully, a century later God "raised up" Cyrus (Darius), king of Persia in righteousness, and directed all his ways so he would depose Belshazzar and let God's people go from the Babylonian captivity (Isaiah 45:13; Daniel 5:28).

King Jeroboam, the son of Solomon was so wicked and idolatrous that his evil "became sin unto the house of Jeroboam, even to cut it off, and to destroy it from off the face of the earth" (I Kings 13:34). Worse, he so corrupted Israel with his evil that the Lord smote and scattered the nation, and gave Israel up "because of the sins of Jeroboam, who did sin, and who made Israel to sin" (I Kings 14:16).

God ordered the swift execution of Achan and his family for personally taking some of the spoils from conquered Jericho, despite being commanded by God not to (Joshua 6:18; 7:15). Achan's disobedience condemned all of Israel and provoked their defeat at Ai, until he was exposed and punished as a thief (Joshua 7:5).

The Israelite example is also instructive in illustrating how individual sin received summary judgment and even death for disobedient children, adulterers, idolaters, and sinners of every stripe. Even Moses received direct punishment for his disobedience, as we shall see at the end of this Chapter, when he was denied entry into the promised land because he angrily struck the rock instead of speaking to it as he had been instructed (Numbers 20:8; 11-12). His anger misrepresented God's mercy and forgiveness, which God extended even to sinners through Jesus Christ, the Living Water, which would have been prefigured had Moses spoken to, rather than struck, the rock.

Samson lost God's Spirit because he sought to marry out of the faith in disobedience to God's law (Judges 14:2-3). He suffered blindness, purposeless life, and then death. God declares His intent to send sure and certain punishment upon unrepentant sinners: "the wicked shall not be unpunished" (Proverbs 11:21); "Every one that is proud in heart is an abomination to the Lord... he shall not be unpunished" (Proverbs 16:50); "he that is glad at calamities shall not be unpunished" (Proverbs 19:5). John the Baptist warned the Pharisees and Sadducees not to presume they were personally immune from punishment for their evil, simply because they were lineal, or national descendents of Abraham (Matthew 3:9).

Angels struck blind the lustful men who sought to attack them at Sodom (Genesis 19:11), and an angel of the Lord smote Herod for his pride in thinking he was like God (Acts 12:23). Ezekiel witnessed six angels scatter glowing coals upon the wicked in Jerusalem, while the righteous were rescued from the city (Ezekiel 9:2-8; 10:2,7). When God condemned idol worship because it rejects His holiness, He warned that deserved punishment for unrepented sin would visit "the iniquity of the fathers upon the children unto the third and fourth generation of them that hate me" (Exodus 20:5, 34:7; Numbers 14:18; and Deuteronomy 5:9), "for I the Lord thy God am a jealous God" (Exodus 20:5). That is, God is 'jealous' of His integrity and destroys all those who stubbornly and impenitently oppose Him. The consequences flow from the sinner's own choices. See also, Deuteronomy 23:3; 2 Kings 10:30; Psalm 37:1-2; Isaiah 34:10; Ezekiel 39:25; and Nahum 1:2.

The Old Testament threatens punishment for unrepented rebellion and disobedience at Leviticus 26:18: "And if ye will not yet for all this hearken unto me, then I will punish you seven times more for your sins." Deuteronomy 24:16 adds: "Every man shall be put to death for his own sin." Joshua 23:15 promises re-payment for evil: "so shall the Lord bring upon you all evil things, until he have destroyed you from off this good land which the Lord your God hath given you."

Psalm 32:10 forecasts: "Many sorrows shall be to the wicked,' and Psalm 91:8 concurs: "Only with thine eyes shalt thou behold and see the reward of the wicked." Isaiah 3:11 says: "Woe unto the wicked! It shall be ill with him; for the reward of his hands shall be given him." God promises to punish the unrighteous at Genesis 38:7; Leviticus 26:18; Isaiah 3:10-11, 10:12, 13:11, 24:21, 26:21 and 27:1; Leviticus 26:15-38; Proverbs 12:21; Jeremiah 21:14, 25:29, 30:11, 46:28, 49:12 and Hosea 4:9.

Lamentations 3:32-39 provides insight and affirmation that God is good; permits, but does not practise evil; and that divine affliction is the consequence of personal sins: "But though he cause grief, yet will he have compassion according to the multitude of his mercies. For he doth not afflict willingly nor grieve the children of men... Out of the mouth of the most High proceedeth not evil and good? Wherefore doth a living man complain, a man for the punishment of his sins?"

God exhibited little mercy for corrupters, and ordained that any Israelite cursing or blaspheming the Lord should be stoned to death by the congregation (Leviticus 24:14-16). God commanded the sons of Levi to "kill every man his brother, and... friend, and... neighbor" who had forsaken God and worshipped the golden calf (Exodus 32:27-29). God commanded that a murderer be executed by "the elders of his city... that it may go well with thee" (Deuteronomy 19:11-13). The spirit of revenge was enunciated by Lamech at Genesis 4:24: "If Cain shall be avenged seven fold, truly Lamech seventy and seven-fold."

To preserve order in Ancient Israel, God exterminated disrespectful children: "If a man have a stubborn and rebellious son, which will not obey the voice of his father, or the voice of his mother, and that, when they have chastened him, will not hearken unto them: Then... all the men of the city shall stone him with stones, that he die: so shalt thou put evil away from among you; and all Israel shall hear, and fear" (Deuteronomy 21:18,21). An equally harsh penalty was reserved for adulterers, who were to be stoned to death for their sin (Leviticus 20:10). You may recall that Jesus interceded on behalf of the woman taken in adultery (John 8:11); contended with her accusers; and would not himself condemn her.

Proverbs 29:1 warns unrepentant sinners who have been repeatedly admonished against sin: "He that being often reproved hardeneth his neck, shall suddenly be destroyed, and that without remedy." Exodus 21:28-29 extends personal responsibility for one's possessions. An ox which gores a person to death shall be stoned to death, and if its owner knew of the vicious propensity, the owner, himself, shall be stoned to death.

Divine fire devoured the priests, Nadab and Abihu when they offered strange sacrifice to the Lord (Leviticus 10:2). They were destroyed because their rebellious self-assertion could corrupt other priests to disobedience, at a time when the priesthood was in its inception, and the Lord sought to impress upon successive priests how important was the holiness of their office. God has executed swift judgment at such turning points in history, in order to set an example for His people, and insulate them from wickedness.

Psalm 37:7,9 confirms that sin produces loss and denial of blessings: "fret not thyself because of him who prospereth in his way, because of the man who bringeth wicked devices to pass... For evil doers shall be cut off." Isaiah 59:2 agrees: "But your iniquities have separated between you and your God, and your sins have hid his face from you, that he will not hear." Jeremiah 5:25 adds: "Your iniquities have turned away these things, and your sins have withholden good things from you."

When Uzzah laid hold of the ark, contrary to the Law which forbade touching it, God smote him for his irreverence toward God's holiness (2 Samuel 6:7).

The Ancient Israelites believed that God employed a death angel, called Samael, Meshachith, or Mashhith, as an executioner of divine vengeance to terminate the physical lives of the un-Godly.[117] St. Paul appears to validate this Rabbinic tradition at I Corinthians 10:10, where he cautions believers not to "put the Lord to the test... nor grumble, as some of them did and were destroyed by the Destroyer." See also, Exodus 12:23; 2 Samuel 24:16; I Chronicles 21:15; Psalm 78:41,49; Hebrews 11:28; and the Apocryphal Wisdom 18:20.

SIN AS THE CAUSE OF SUFFERING

The widow whose son had fallen sick connected illness with sin when she queried of Elijah: "art thou come unto me to call my sin to remembrance and to slay my son?" (I Kings 18:18). By the time of Jesus, the belief was common that infirmity was somehow equated with punishment for one's own sin. The disciples inquired of Jesus, upon seeing a blind man: "Rabbi, who sinned, this man or his parents, that he was born blind?" (John 9:2). Although the question seems fatuous because it attributes sin to a baby born blind, remember that Jewish thought regarded a fetus as conceived in iniquity and born into personal sin (Psalms 51:5, 58:3). Jesus revealed that in this case "it was not that this man sinned, or his parents, but that the works of God might be made manifest in him" (John 9:3).

When Jesus healed the sick man at Bethesda He declared: "See you are well! Sin no more, that nothing worse befall you" (John 5:14). He healed a paralytic at Capernaum, and directed him to "Rise, take up your pallet and walk... that you may know that the Son of Man has authority on earth to forgive sins" (Mark 2:9-10; Matthew 9:2). In both cases, healing was equated with forgiveness of sins, which suggests a relationship between sin and sickness or paralysis (See also, John 8:11). Additionally, Jesus demonstrated His divine healing power to authenticate His authority to forgive sins. Jesus also showed, by relieving suffering wherever He found it (Matthew 4:24), and by extending mercy according to God's will, that affliction was not always to be regarded as punishment for sin, imposed by a vengeful or retributive God (John 9:3).

Modern preaching seldom focuses on Hell or eternal damnation for sinners, but prefers to be inoffensive, focusing upon God's love, which has deflected punishment for sin from the sinner and placed it upon Jesus. Yet, Scripture is clear there is a Hell and a penalty of "everlasting justice", with literal Hellfire for impenitent sinners (Psalms 9:17; Isaiah 66:24; Daniel 12:2; Matthew 3:12, 5:29, 13:41-42, 18:9, 23:33, 25:46; Mark 9:47-48; John 5:29, 15:5-6; Luke 12:5; I Corinthians 15:25; and Revelation 4:2, 20:13,15, 21:8).

In the New Testament, Jesus promised "greater condemnation" for the insincere and hypocritical scribes, who "for a pretense make long prayers" (Mark 12:40; Luke 20:47). He cleared the temple of those who desecrated it by commercial dealings (John 2:15), although the loss of profit must have seemed an evil to the moneylenders and merchants He expelled. Ananias and Saphira were disciples of the Lord and took to heart His teaching that wealth held in stewardship should be shared with those less fortunate. They willingly sold some property to give to charity, but gave only a part of the proceeds to the Apostles, while representing they had brought the entire sale proceeds to the Church. They were under no compulsion to sell the house or to donate all the revenue to the Church. Yet, pride drove them to exaggerate the extent of their gift, and they were struck dead because they lied to the Holy Spirit by misrepresenting to Peter the extent of their charity, to create a false impression of piety and generosity (Acts 5:3).

We cannot know whether their deaths were meant as punishment for this sin of pride; to prevent their further degeneration by sin; as instructional deterrence for subsequent givers; or as a quarantine to protect the Body of Christ, lest their contagion, duplicity, and self-indulgence contaminate others and work incalculable harm to the early Church. But there is a definite connection between their lie about charity and their deaths.

In another incident, New Testament believers were killed for irreverently partaking of the Lord's Supper: "For anyone who eats and drinks without discerning the body eats and drinks judgment upon himself. That is why many of you are weak and ill, and some have died" (I Corinthians 11:29-30). The example of punishment must have also intended a deterrent effect for our instruction, since the passage goes on to say: "But if we judged ourselves truly, we should not be judged. But when we are judged by the Lord, we are chastened, so that we may not be condemned along with the world" (I Corinthians 11:31-32). Lamentations 3:40 urges: "Let us search and try our ways, and turn again to the Lord".

James 1:15 reveals the general principal that "desire when it has conceived gives birth to sin: and sin when it is full-grown brings forth death." James 5:19-20 makes it clear that this principle applies to the worldly death of believers: "My <u>brethren, if any one among you</u> wanders from the truth and someone brings him back, let him know that whoever brings back a sinner from the error of his way will save his soul from death." The sinner may not lose his salvation, but if he refuses to repent of sin, even when warned and chastised by God, his earthly life may be prematurely ended to forestall the sinner's deeper, irretrievable descent into sin (see I Corinthians 11:30). Jesus says the unsaved are cursed when they fail to feed the hungry, give drink to the thirsty, welcome the stranger, clothe the naked, and visit the prisoner: "as you did it not to one of the least of these, you did it not to me. And they will go away into eternal punishment, but the righteous into eternal life" (Matthew 25:42-46).

The idea that personal sin is the cause of suffering is paralleled in other world religions. The Hindu concept of suffering posits that we are responsible for wrongdoing and injustice committed in previous lives which accounts for, and is transferred to, subsequent suffering. Our sins in the present life will be projected into successive reincarnations. Thus, reincarnation's equivalent of Hell allows for eventual redemption through a worldly process of repetition with progressive improvement. According to the law of Karma, our unworthy deeds produce suffering; and justice both compensates for good in the next life, and punishes personal wrong-doing with suffering.[118] The poor and infirm deserve their condition because of what they did in a previous life. Escape from one's suffering is found ultimately in unity with Brahma or Being, by forsaking desire, deeds, and relationships in order to end the cycle of re-births and enter into bliss. Individual identity is finally extinguished as it is merged into eternal consciousness, much as an egg is combined with and indistinguishable from other eggs in an omelet, or a drop of water is indistinct from all other drops in a stream.

Buddhism also relates suffering to earthly desires which motivate our actions and produce suffering as the fruit of our deeds. Suffering is inextricably tied up with existence, and the only way to avoid suffering is to suppress desire and pursue deeds of compassion. Borrowing from Hinduism, Buddhism says we continue to experience re-births, fueled by our passions and desire, under the law of Karma.[119] As we purge desire from our successive reincarnations, we progress to a higher state of Nirvana, in which all passion, action, and personality are eventually subdued, and all pain and existence are extinguished.

While much suffering is the consequence of sin, we cannot assume that all suffering is a direct product of personal sin, or that every sinner suffers, or every believer is exempt from tribulation. The righteousness of Job repudiates the idea that all affliction in the world is the result of sin (Job 1:8), and Jesus pointedly denied that all suffering stemmed from personal sin. Suffering can originate with acts of other men inflicted through their evil intent or negligence. Jesus declared that the Galileans who suffered at the hands of Pilate were not punished because they were "worse sinners than all the other Galileans." Nor were the eighteen men who died under a collapsed tower in Siloam "worse offenders than all the others who dwelt in Jerusalem" (Luke 13:2, 4). The Apostles were despised, buffeted, and homeless, as related in I Corinthians 4:9-13; and 2 Corinthians 11:23-27, because of their witness for Christ, not for their sin. Paul was given a thorn in the flesh, not to punish him, but to suppress undue elation over the divine revelations which God had imparted to him (2 Corinthians 12:7).

RESTITUTION

Sometimes, making the injured victim whole is the dominant purpose of God's punishment, designed to make restitution or reparations to an innocent party harmed by a wrongdoer. Reparations by criminal perpetrators to wronged victims are intended primarily as compensation for injury.[120] At Proverbs 6:31 the thief is required to restore what he has stolen "seven fold; he shall give all the substance of his house." See also, Exodus 22:1 and 2 Samuel 12:6; and Luke 19:8. Ephesians 4:28 prescribes: "Let the thief no longer steal, but rather let him labor, doing honest work with his hands, so that he may be able to give to those in need."

PUNISHMENT AS DETERRENCE OF SIN

Both the threat of punishment and the actual application of corrective measures can serve to deter future misconduct. Genuinely loving parents must occasionally incorporate actual punishment: the deprivation of reward as well as the infliction of pain, to deter sin and promote

Godly behavior. In a penal system, measures which seek to deter and dissuade the evildoers from future misconduct by motivating reformation and rehabilitation, can include torture, hard labor, imprisonment, monetary fines, rendering public service, parole, and probation.

I remember as a boy whenever my older sister was punished, it always made a vivid impression on me, as well. Both the wrongdoer and witness can be taught a strong lesson in obedience by the punishment of the sinner. Both will be instructed by the experience, and motivated to follow the ways of righteousness thereafter, deterred by the example.

God's punishment can serve to instruct, chasten, and discourage the sinner from future misconduct. If God's vengeance destroys one rebellious wrongdoer, that example can serve to instruct many survivors; dissuade them from sin; and inhibit tendencies toward a like fate. The Old Testament serves as an example for us under the New Testament. I Corinthians 10:6 speaks of the faithless sinning of the Israelites, and reveals: "Now these things are warnings for us, not to desire evil as they did." See also, Hebrews 2:2 and Jude 7, which refer to the cities of Sodom and Gomorrah, "which likewise acted immorally and indulged in unnatural lust, serve as an example by undergoing a punishment of eternal fire."

Ecclesiastes 8:11 observes the deterrent benefit of sure punishment: "Because sentence against an evil work is not executed speedily, therefore the heart of the sons of men is fully set in them to do evil." In this sense, punishment is essential to affirm the very nature of morality and the goodness of God throughout eternity. Because God's work employs the threat of punishment to influence behavior, His justice requires real infliction of punishment for sin. Otherwise, there would be no deterrent effect on conduct unless unrepentant sinners perceived loss as real because God means and enforces what He says.

How can a just God allow evil and injustice to go unchecked? Once God has ordained reward for good and punishment for sin, both here and Hereafter, then His justice requires fulfillment of the promise, or it would be faulty and untrue. If God overlooks disobedience, it would confirm Satan's lie in the Garden: "Ye shall not surely die" (Genesis 3:4), implying that God does not mean what He says and man can disregard His Word with impunity. Evil would be left unchallenged if God allowed inveterate evil-doers to despise His mercy and scorn His Justice. It would condone the unrepentant sinner's disdain for God's revelation that man is a sinner in need of a Saviour.

God must occasionally confirm the threat of punishment by administering some pain, lest an apparently empty warning lose its deterrence. However, pain's primary deterrence is its vivid reminder that God can deliver the real thing eternally to those who resist Him here. Because of carnal man's weakness, he must be convinced that God's punishment for sin, here and Hereafter, is certain and unrelenting. Otherwise, man may sin more readily, presuming and relying upon God's unlimited supply of love and mercy, and assuming with impunity his immunity from any penalty for sin (Romans 6:1,15). St. Thomas Aquinas thus called tribulation a necessary evil to achieve the greater good of escaping condemnation and preserving spiritual life. Our conduct is often shaped by the desire to avoid pain. Pain motivates holiness by reminding us of the far worse pains of Hell, and thereby deters us from sinning. Sometimes, only pain will drive us to the Great Physician for total healing.

A good scare can be equally as memorable a lesson as loving admonition. When a parent keeps extending kindness to a rebellious, intransigently disobedient child, his benevolence becomes counter productive and self-defeating. Where a child persists in destructive ways and repudiates the rules and values of the family, tough love requires ending any support which merely perpetuates the rebellion. If the prodigal calls from jail asking for bail and parental help to retain a lawyer, his parents may accede initially, but eventually they will recognize that repeatedly granting his requests only strengthens his weakness and self-destruction.[121]

John the Baptist did not preach the popular modern message on the love of God, but warned of fleeing the wrath to come by repenting of sin. Half of the Gospel message is how horrible Hell will be for the unsaved, to deter those who need the stimulus of fear in order to respond to God's love by grace through faith in Jesus. Indeed, the deterrent force of a threat is the certainty it will be carried out. Without belief in actual Hell for rebellious sinners, men would lose some motivation for embracing Jesus as Saviour.

Punishment vindicates God's Law and confirms that His Commandments are important and just; that breaking them leads to more serious consequences, including dire harm to the lawbreaker, himself. We punish the child who persistently seeks to set off fireworks because of the real possibility of physical harm to the child and others if such conduct is allowed to continue undeterred. God cannot overlook disobedience, because it leads to expanded spiritual destruction. God sometimes visits the chastisement of suffering upon sinners for rehabilitation to deter future violations of his Law and the damning consequences of unrepented sin.

Children are motivated to behave rightly by the fearful prospect of punishment, in addition to expectations of reward. God recommends punishment to parents as an effective deterrent against wrongdoing by children: "he that spareth his rod hateth his son" (Proverbs 13:24). The way of the Cross leads to the resurrection of a transformed person, conformed to the image of Christ.

If suffering is visited upon unsaved sinners (or backslid disciples) to draw them to God, then what is apparently an evil to man's faulty perceptions, is in reality the necessary stimulus and process to man's transformation. For, if carnal man was left content and prosperous in worldliness, he would have no incentive to turn to Jesus. The pain inflicted upon a sinner is the assurance and confirmation of divine retribution and demand for satisfaction. If man's unrepented evil went unpunished in the world, he would lose some motivation to be and do good.

God seeks to win our love and allegiance by His benevolence. But if we rebel against His love, then we will encounter loss of blessings, denial, and discipline until we seek a return to right relationship with Him. We do not respond with perfect obedience, though submission is a sign of repentance, but with a softened heart, totally dependent upon God's grace and enabling, through, by, and because of Jesus. The practice of holiness then reduces the need for further deterrence and suffering.

The use of discipline, chastening, chastising and punishment serves to deter and discourage repetition of wrong conduct, rebellion and sin. It supplies motivation to return to submissiveness; to seek and accept God's will and way. It is a call back to obedience and embracing His plan for man's salvation. The application of corrective penalties and deprivations; of sure and certain punishment; is a deterrence against wrongdoing and succumbing to temptation. However, the mere threat of certain deprivation, harm, or punishment can also serve to deter rebellion and sin, once the actuality of punishment has been established.

To motivate man's free choice for God, the threat of punishment for sin is added to the hope engendered by His love. The threat of punishment incorporated in the idea of Hell where all evil is paid for, is a tremendous deterrent to sin, when used as a supplement to loving exhortation, vicarious satisfaction, and forgiveness.

The Old Testament uses the threat of earthly and eternal pain and suffering to deter evil, and influence man's actions for good in the future. Deuteronomy 19:20 directs that when a murderer is executed, then "those which remain shall hear, and fear, and shall henceforth commit no more any such evil among you" (See also Deuteronomy 6:2,12). Job 28:28 says: "the fear of the Lord, that is wisdom, and to depart from evil is understanding." Psalm 25:14 reveals: "The secret of the Lord is with them that fear Him, and He will show them His covenant", (see also, Psalm 103:11). Psalm 130:3-4 explains that the fear recommended to believers is not terror, but reverential, adoring devotion, out of appreciation for God's goodness, grace, pardon, loving forgiveness, and almightiness.

Proverbs 1:7 teaches: "The fear of the Lord is the beginning of knowledge." When we know enough to respect God's might, we will know enough to live obediently as children. Proverbs 16:6 summarizes the interplay of love and fear: "By mercy and truth iniquity is purged: and by the fear of the Lord men depart from evil." Proverbs 28:14 adds: "Happy is he that feareth always, but he that hardeneth his heart shall fall into mischief."

Jeremiah 32:39-41 says: "I will give them one heart, and one way that they may fear me for ever... And I will make an everlasting covenant with them, that I will not turn away from them, to do them good; but I will put fear in their hearts, that they shall not depart from me." The Apocryphal Ecclesiasticus 7:40 advises: "In all thy works, remember thy last end, and thou shalt never sin" (See also, Psalms 31:19, 112:1-3, 128:1-4; Proverbs 8:13; Isaiah 11:3; and Lamentations 1:9). This healthy fear of consequences is related to the actuality of punishment for sin by a sovereign God who exercises absolute dominion. Fear of losing touch with God, of alienating His friendship, and fear of Judgment and punishment dissuade misconduct as much as the incentive of love motivates obedient conduct. Thus, both love and fear help rouse the conscience to choose rightly.

The New Testament re-enforces the revelation that God will motivate holiness by using fear as well as love, focusing our attention on Judgment and loss of reward, as well as upon salvation in a loving Christ. Because faith must be nurtured constantly, Jesus warned His twelve Apostles, who had already vowed their faith, that there was still need to fear God: "fear him who can destroy both soul and body in Hell" (Matthew 10:28; paralleled at Luke 12:5). The early Church was "built up; and walking in the fear of the Lord and in the comfort of the Holy Spirit it was multiplied" (Acts 9:31).

2 Corinthians 7:1 exhorts believers: 'Since we have these promises, beloved, let us cleanse ourselves from every defilement of body and spirit and make holiness perfect in the fear of God." Ephesians 5:21, KJV calls for "Submitting yourselves one to another in the fear of God." You are to "work out your own salvation with fear and trembling; for God is at work in you" (Philippians 2:12-13). As Christians you are to "conduct yourselves with fear throughout the time of your exile", because "you invoke as Father him who judges each one impartially according to his deeds" (I Peter 1:17). 2 Peter 3:14 focuses our attention on the coming of the day of God: "Therefore, beloved, since you wait for these, be zealous to be found by him without spot or blemish, and at peace." (See also, Colossians 3:22; Hebrews 12:28; and Revelation 14:6-7, 15:4).

The prospect of rendering an account for a believer's life before the Judgment Seat of Christ should also act as a deterrent, since even the faithful can suffer loss because of disobedience. Unrepented sins will be recalled and produce loss of reward at Christ's Judgment. Our failure to render works of loving service to others will be judged and punished with loss of reward. Matthew 16:25 foretells: "the Son of man is to come with his angels in the glory of his Father, and then he will repay every man for what he has done." 2 Corinthians 5:10 confirms that believers "must all appear before the judgment seat of Christ; so that each one may receive good or evil, according to what he has done in the body."

Romans 14:10-12 queries of believers: "Why do you pass judgment on your brother? Or you, why do you despise your brother? For we shall all stand before the judgment seat of God... So each of us shall give account of himself to God." I Corinthians 4:5 explains that the Bema Judgment seat of Christ is a place of reward for believers, not criminal judgment: "do not pronounce judgment before the time, before the Lord comes, who will bring to light the things now hidden in darkness and will disclose the purpose of men's hearts. Then every man will receive his <u>commendation</u> from God" (See also, I Corinthians 3:13-15). Ideally, our motive for good works should not be fear of loss, but longing to hear the commendation: "Well done, good and faithful servant... enter into the joy of your master" (Matthew 25:23). Yet, God has elected to yoke motivation to please God out of love, with deterrence which fears loss because of disobedience.

Nor will we be ashamed or resentful as our hidden sins are laid bare before the assembled saints in heaven. For, the emphasis will be on God's love and mercy, magnified by forgiving every wretched deed we have done, and we will spend eternity glorifying God and rejoicing in His unfolding glory revealed to the saved in Christ.

The righteous should also be motivated by fear of the consequences for all sinners, which includes unsaved loved ones. That fear should lead us to constant prayers of intercession and empowerment to witness by our speech and by the faith of our lives, lest our loved ones die before receiving Jesus as Lord and Saviour. For, he that believeth not is condemned already, but he who escapes from condemnation now, by grace through faith in Jesus of Nazareth, will escape damnation forever. The idea of Purgatory, which we encounter in a moment, can stimulate the concept of intercessory prayers for others: not for the dead, but for the living. Indeed, it is our dead loves ones who are with the Lord, who hopefully intercede on our behalf if we are unsaved, that we might be convicted unto salvation, and not we who can do them any good if they died unsaved. In all matters, Jesus is the Intercessor for us who are saved.

PURGATORY'S DETERRENCE OF SIN

No study of deterrence would be complete, nor the effect of deterrence appreciated, without some reference to the Roman Catholic concept of Purgatory, recognized by a third of Christendom. Even after the debt of eternal punishment is remitted by Christ for repentant sinners, there remains a debt of temporal punishment to be discharged "either in this world or in Purgatory" (Council of Trent, 1547, Canon XXX). God does not always pardon the whole penalty for sin, but even with the new life of repentance, His Justice and Sanctity require penance through punishment, borne by the priest, or individuals voluntarily undertaking fasting, prayers, almsgiving, and other works of piety.[122]

The punishment by fire for the sins of those in Purgatory is suggested by I Corinthians 3:13,15: "each man's work will become manifest; for the day will disclose it, because it will be revealed with fire, and the fire will test what sort of work each one has done... If any man's work is burned up, he will suffer loss, though he himself will be saved, but only as through fire." Jesus' narrative of the beggar, Lazarus, and Dives the rich man also depicts a status immediately following death, where Lazarus is delivered to Paradise, or Abraham's Bosom, as his immediate reward; and the rich man is consigned to a place of fiery torment in Hades as his punishment (Luke 16:23), which apparently is permanent, since Abraham tells the rich man: "None may cross from there to us" (Luke 16:26).

The transient state of the dead is also suggested in the Apocryphal 2 Maccabees 12:46: "It is therefore a holy and wholesome thought to pray for the dead, that they may be loosed from sins." This passage has been interpreted to imply the living can assist the dead to depart Purgatory by offering prayers and penance for them. The Eastern Orthodox Church, while not sharing belief in Purgatory, does offer prayers for the memories of the dead and repose of their souls.[123]

The Roman Catholic Council of Trent in 1563 declared that the souls detained in Purgatory can be aided by the "suffrages of the faithful, and chiefly by the Acceptable Sacrifice of the Altar." The living can suffer so the merit of their suffering can relieve the anguish of the dead in Purgatory, by vicarious penance, as well as by indulgences which apply the spiritual riches accumulated by the Church to the dead; and by the Holy Sacrifice of the Mass.[124]

Hundreds of saints, canonized by the Roman Catholic Church for their holy and trust-worthy lives, have attested to visitations by Poor Souls in Purgatory, who tell of being punished in a most uncompromising way for every minor transgression they ever committed. God can see stains even in that which appears most pure to man. Some of the transgressions committed by those in religious orders, for which they suffered in Purgatory, include failing to observe the rules of strict poverty; interrupting habitual prayer to dwell on worldly cares; having wicked sentiments of jealousy; uncharitable words for others; amassing worldly objects contrary to a vow of religious poverty; being indifferent to another, or to the holy mass; proudly seeking the status of a public office; speaking inconsiderately in order to be clever; and failing to edify others.[125]

While God forgives confessed sin (I John 1:9), punishment in Purgatory for routine breaches of duty which were unconfessed is required because they were overlooked or forgotten, and hence the perpetrator never sought forgiveness and cleansing of these sins. Having failed to judge themselves, they must be judged by God for their unrepented sins (I Corinthians 11:31-32). Purgatory is the condition of souls which, at the moment of death, are in a state of grace, but have not completely expiated their sins, nor attained the degree of purity necessary to enjoy the vision of God.

Believers in Purgatory argue that Judgment does not occur until after the return of the Lord. Opportunity to work continues until we stand before the Judgment Seat of Christ described in Matthew 25:31. The event is future, "for the hour is coming when all who are in the tombs will hear his voice and come forth, those who have done good to the resurrection of life, and those who have done evil, to the resurrection of judgment" (John 5:28-29). Thus, contemporary prayers and penance for the dead can still be added to the mix throughout Purgatory.

Those who do not believe in Purgatory rely on John 9:4; where Jesus says: "We must work the works of him who sent me, while it is day: night comes when no one can work." Ecclesiastes 9:10 warns: "Whatsoever thy hand findeth to do, do it with thy might; for there is no work, nor device, nor knowledge, nor wisdom in the grave whither thou goest." 2 Corinthians 6:2 says: "Behold, now is the acceptable time: Behold now is the day of salvation." These passages are construed to mean that at death the opportunity to repent and embrace Jesus is ended, and faith or works are no longer possible.

Christians who do not believe in Purgatory, focus on God's forgiveness because of Christ's intercessions on our behalf, which cover unknown or unconfessed sins. We feel freed from punctilious obedience because we can rely on God's promise to transform us to the image of Christ despite our actual sins. We are still required to cooperate in holiness, but we are no longer penalized for our failures because we have the full assurance of salvation in Christ. This provides a full freedom to serve Christ because of the security of believers. The motive of our responsive love, in recruiting the love and mercy of God, dispenses with any need for fearful anxiety as a motivation for obedience unto holiness.

Still, it cannot be denied that expecting a personal accounting for one's sins by measured punishment and penance for even the slightest faults, will provide a different perspective of the minor sins we often presume will be forgiven and forgotten by God, when we confess and repent them. It is a most effective deterrent, through the constraints of fear, for those who believe in the reality of Purgatory and its pains. Little acts of pride, envy, sloth, and lust, would get more than a second thought, if the perpetrator believed he will receive literal and severe punishment in this world, or in the flames of Purgatory, until he had given full acquittal and expiation. We will also be driven to greater self-examination, and pray for divine illumination of forgotten and unknown sins so we can repent them now, and give satisfaction and atonement for our sins in this life rather than in the fires of Purgatory. We will gladly accept the sufferings of this life to avoid the far more intense suffering of Purgatory.

We will not presume upon the mercy of God, if we believe He will hold us accountable for every sinful word and deed. Romans 14:10,12 says: "For we shall all stand before the judgment seat of God... So each of us shall give account of himself to God." Jesus warns at Matthew 12:36: "on the day of judgment men will render account for every careless word they utter... and by your words you will be condemned."

If we know God is keeping precise accounts of sin, which we must pay, we will think twice before indulging in a sinful, transient pleasure. I will serve God with an exact fidelity, to avoid the punishment of just expiation, for even the faults which seem most trivial to us are monstrous defects and imperfections which offend God's sanctity. But we will not be deterred by the prospect of punishment, unless we believe it is real and irrevocable, even though repented. God's mercy operates to allow a penitent sinner to give penance, but this added cost of sin here, and in the fires of Purgatory, can be a tremendous deterrent, added to the love of God which motivates us to please Him by obedience.

Those who believe in the severity of Divine chastisements for every sin one commits will also redouble efforts of intercessory prayers for the living, and on behalf of delivering relief to the souls in Purgatory from their great need, by expiations offered on their behalf. Indeed, by this view, non-Catholics will languish longest and suffer worst among Christians in Purgatory, because they do not have anyone offering penance for them on earth, or offering their pain as a substitute to expiate and alleviate the pain of those in Purgatory.

PRESERVATION THROUGH SEGREGATION

In the world we incarcerate criminals who have abused their freedom, removing them from society to preserve victims from infliction of further harm. Likewise, God's punishment of the wicked is at times to preserve His Church against them; to accomplish quarantine, confinement or removal of the wrongdoer to protect God's people from contamination. In the world, the good and pure are corrupted by evil, while evil is seldom cured by exposure to good. Add muddy water to clear water, and the clear will become muddy, but adding clear water to the muddy will not make it clear. Nor will a healthy child's presence heal a sick child, but the sick child will likely infect the healthy one. Perfume added to manure will not overcome the odor, but perfume infused with manure becomes useless. The redeemed in Christ are to present the Gospel to the unsaved, and witness by the example of their lives, but only Christ can transform the evil nature of men.

Sometimes God promotes a higher good of preserving creation from evil's contamination and corrupting influence, by destroying unrepentant rebels. God destroyed the last remnant of sinful societies whenever they became so permeated by evil that even childish innocence could not survive in such an unyielding, rebellious environment. An unchecked propensity toward evil will accelerate, not diminish. Children who have only an example of evil, will learn, imitate, and exercise the same uncontrolled lust, anger, and evil as their parents. Lacking any temperance or adult restraints to control their natural degeneration, and without examples of righteousness, even children would eventually be corrupted, unless they were exterminated with mature sinners. They would reach the point where they reject redemption and become unredeemable by self-choice (Psalm 21:8-11).

Holiness cannot long co-exist alongside sin, which is why Christians are cautioned to be in the world, but not be of it (John 17:16-18). We must be in the world to reach the unsaved or afflicted, and minister to their specific needs, but we must live moral lives of righteousness, sanctified or apart from them. There is a point where worldliness can begin to corrode holiness, if admitted into holy environments, and its example left unchallenged. If human evil were allowed to continue unrestrained in creation, it would eventually contaminate everything it touches. Thus, God occasionally extirpates sinners from the world, to spare the unspoiled remnant from infection by disruptive, irresponsible, and unholy influences.

To sustain the felicity of His faithful followers for eternity, God will not permanently mingle saved believers with 'rotten apples' who set bad examples and despoil faith of believers. God prevents the spread of decay, harm, or degradation to the community of believers by purging and removing the corrupting influence of unregenerate sinners from the main Body of believers.

Clearly, if a surgeon operates to remove malignant tissue from an organ in order to save the whole body, no-one would regard the elimination of cancerous cells as evil, for they tend to grow insidiously and destroy the entire organism. Every cell in the body must function and contribute to the well-being of the whole, or it must eventually be cut out to preserve the whole body.

The perfect good in God and His glorified Church could not coexist eternally with the pernicious influence of unrepented satanic and human evil. Unrepentant sinners cannot co-exist with the redeemed in eternity, because sin will not be enveloped and embraced by God. There is a special urgency to heed the warning of 2 Corinthians 6:2: "Behold, now is the acceptable time; behold, now is the day of salvation." One moment after man's last breath is too late. Then, God's perfect good must necessarily eliminate any evil which it touches. His perfect love must repel all hate, His perfect life must destroy all death; and His perfect light must extinguish all darkness. Nor could recalcitrant sinners be joyful, nor coexist with God as long as they refuse to abandon their darkness, death, and hate.

If separation from God constitutes a penalty for the rebellious persons choosing to reject Jesus, it serves a higher good by preserving the decency of creation, the sanctity of the redeemed, and the harmony of heaven, while confirming the justice of God and the genuineness of free choice. Out of love for faithful men, God may remove from earth, and must exclude from Heaven, all sinful men who adamantly refuse to be loving, in order to spare from contamination those who wish to love God. Thus, the redeemed will receive God's undiluted and uninterrupted benevolence for eternity.

DOES GOD PUNISH THE RIGHTEOUS FOR THEIR SINS?

Because the motives of God are complex and multiple, it is difficult to say whether God ever punishes believers to satisfy His justice in the sense of retaliation, reprisal, retribution, or revenge against the wrongdoer.

God will use pain as punishment when stubborn, rebellious evil-doers refuse to repent and turn from their sins. Likewise, when a child of God backslides and refuses to relinquish his pattern of sin, the purpose of pain may be punishment in a vengeful or punitive sense, until the backslider repents and turns toward God's grace and mercy for forgiveness and cleansing. Scripture warns Christians that we will suffer despite our status as God's children, and we will suffer persecution because we are His.

While rebellious, unbelieving sinners and impenitent Christians will undergo punishment of wrath and reprisal for their sin, we find that repentant Christians usually will not. Of course, to the one suffering it may be inconsequential whether the pain he endures is punitive, exemplary, or instructive deterrence, if the experiential consequences are the same. Indeed, a believer can expect an increase in suffering until he responds to a caring God's persuasions to change. His tolerance to endure will be greatest when correction is administered by a loving Father. Chastisement is sent for the well-being of God's children because of His love, but reprisal is to vindicate God's Justice, rather than for the good of a sinner.

God's people certainly do suffer, but usually at the hands of other free beings. Job suffered at the instigation of Satan and suffered for his righteousness, not his sin. Joseph bragged about his revelations from God and was sold into slavery by his jealous brothers, not because he had angered God.

Yet, we know that God inflicts or allows suffering to befall His own people, to chasten, chastise, rehabilitate, train, or test by way of instructional reproof and as a deterrent example to observers.

As long as a believer persists in wrongdoing he can expect the pain of punishment, whether it originates in God's anger, the desire to return His child to ways of righteousness, or provide a deterring example for others of sin's consequences. But does God ever punish His penitent child for mere reasons of retribution? Some Old Testament examples suggest that God is unrelenting in punishing even those who repent and seek God's forgiveness, but we will see that these examples do not necessarily apply to New Covenant Christians.

God's punishments of Moses, Achan, and David, provide three Old Testament illustrations of suffering inflicted for strictly punitive reasons; which provide mighty instructional deterrents against sin for any reader of the Bible stories. Moses had been instructed to speak to the rock to bring forth drinking water for the Children of Israel (Numbers 20:8). This was to pre-figure God's grace, which would bless believers with living water from Jesus, simply by asking for it. However, Moses became angry at the Israelites' lack of faith, and struck the rock instead of speaking to it (Numbers 20:11), thereby misrepresenting God's mercy and forgiveness, extended even in the face of human faithlessness. Moses also appropriated God's glory by drawing attention to his own feelings and actions, rather than the grace of God, in bringing forth the blessing of water.

As a punishment, God said to Moses: "Because ye believed me not, to sanctify me in the eyes of the children of Israel, therefore ye shall not bring this congregation into the land which I have given them" (Numbers 20:12). God's anger persisted, despite Moses' favored position and his entreaties to see "the good land." God was wroth with him and finally warned: "Speak no more unto me of this matter" (Deuteronomy 3:26). Moses was allowed to gaze upon the promised land from Mt. Pisgah, but he lost the blessing of entering it with his beloved nation, Israel. He was privileged to witness how God honored His Covenant promise, but he was not allowed to participate in it.

Achan was a soldier serving under Joshua at the battle of Jericho, and violated God's ban against personally taking any spoils, by appropriating gold, silver, and clothing from the enemy. God consequently punished the entire nation of Israel for Achan's disobedience, by allowing it to be defeated at Ai. God directed Joshua to seek out the sinner, and Achan confessed he had "sinned against the Lord God of Israel" (Joshua 7:20), and thereby profaned the nation. Despite his confession and recovery of the loot, Achan and his children were stoned to death as punishment for his sin, and as cleansing for the nation.

Then there was King David, a man after God's heart, but a sinner like us all. David was forgiven by God when he repented his adultery with Bathsheba and the murder of Uriah, her husband, but he was also punished: "because by this deed thou hast given great occasion to the enemies of the Lord to blaspheme, the child that is born unto thee shall surely die" (2 Samuel 12:13-14). David beseeched God for seven days of prayer and fasting to spare the child. He was no doubt aware that God had withheld His judgments in the past when His people truly repented. Nevertheless, "The Lord struck the child... and it was very sick... And... the child died" (2 Samuel 12:15,18). God denied David's petitions, and visited sickness and death on the child, despite David's complete repentance. Still, God forgave David and later blessed him with another child, Solomon, the wisest man who ever lived.

Despite these Old Testament examples, their punishment may not be a valid comparison for sin consequences to the righteous in Christ, since we are distinguished by, and operate under a New Covenant of reconciliation and forgiveness; the benefits of which they did not have. Hebrews 8:6-7 says: "Christ has obtained a ministry which is as much more excellent than the old as the covenant he mediates is better, since it is enacted on better promises. For if that first covenant had been faultless, there would have been no occasion for a second." No man can assert dogmatically that God does not punish believers vindictively. However, a number of developments suggest deterrence, example, or training as more likely reasons for New Testament punishment of believers.

First, we are told that Old Testament examples are for our instruction, "warnings for us, not to desire evil as they did... Now these things happened to them as a warning, but they were written down for our instruction, upon whom the end of the ages has come" (I Corinthians 10:6,11). If God's Justice punished an Old Testament believer, then that example can serve for survivors' instruction and have a beneficial deterrent effect against our repeating such sins. The fact that God punished Moses and David, or summarily killed Ananias and Sapphira in the New Testament for misrepresenting the extent of their giving (Acts 5:1-5), does not mean He will always repeat those punishments for every person in every age. Their penalties may be far more severe than anything God would send to us, because they are established Biblically as persuasive examples to deter our conduct from sinning, whereas our example to others are likely to be less notorious or influential.

Secondly, at the New Birth we are drawn into the imputed righteousness of Jesus because His vicarious sacrifice has occurred prior in time to our sinning; but not so the Old Testament believers. Jesus had not yet offered propitiation for human sins in Old Testament times, and Moses, David, and Achan could not plead the new Covenant retroactively, when they committed their sins. But our sins are covered prospectively by the Blood of Christ. Since Jesus' Atonement for our sins has occurred, God's Justice has been satisfied by Christ's bearing of all our sins, and would be violated if He imposed the penalty for sin again. Forgiveness and exemption from punishment are compatible with God's Justice because Jesus vicariously bore all your sins and punishment, past, present, and future in relation to your time on earth, since all your sins were yet to be committed at the time Jesus walked the earth. This forgiveness depends on your receiving Him as your Saviour, and seeking forgiveness of sins in, by, and through him. Jesus has already satisfied God's Justice by paying the penalty of sin for all who receive him as Lord and Saviour (Isaiah 53:4-6), and God has already accepted the substitutionary work of Christ in full satisfaction, redemption, and ransom of a sinner's debt. Even when specific sins deserve punishment under Justice, we can claim deliverance by the imputed righteousness of Jesus.

In love, Jesus lived a perfect life of obedience, so that His righteousness might be attributed to us. Our debts have been paid by Christ on our behalf and cannot be collected twice by a perfectly just God. If Jesus suffered the condemnation, and paid the penalty to satisfy God's justice, then God will not punish a repentant child for the same sins a second time, for then He would be unjust. This is verified by Hebrews 10:14, 17 which says of Jesus: "For by a single offering he has perfected for all time those who are consecrated... then he adds, 'I will remember their sins and their misdeeds no more.' Where there is forgiveness of these, there is no longer any offering for sin." Romans 8:12 agrees: "There is therefore now no condemnation for those who are in Christ Jesus. For the law of the spirit of life in Christ Jesus has set me free from the law of sin and death."

If we are redeemed, it means that whatever has been lost by disobedience or ignorance has been restored in Christ, and God intends to replace all you have lost.[126]

When Jesus has paid the penalty for even our most despicable sins, how could God, Who is perfect love, allow one of His beloved children, who has confessed sin and repented, to continue in affliction when God has promised to forgive the sin and cleanse the sinner of all unrighteousness? The Passion of the Cross was designed by God so we could escape wrath because Christ bore it for sinners. Atonement originated in love for sinners, not in a desire to impose wrath upon them.[127] "In this was manifested the love of God among us, that God sent his only Son into the World, so that we might live through him" (I John 4:9; see also, Romans 5:8; I John 3:16; 4:10).

Jesus' Atonement stresses God's love and grace toward man, not His wrath and justice. By God's benevolent will "we have been consecrated through the offering of the body of Jesus Christ <u>once for all</u> " (Hebrews 10:10). The sacrifice of suffering is not repeated if Jesus accomplished it "once for all." Otherwise, Jesus' suffering and death would serve no purpose.

John 3:36 says: "He who believes in the Son has eternal life; he who does not obey the Son shall not see life, but the wrath of God rests upon him." Faithless, impenitent sinners receive the wrath of God (Romans 1:18, 3:8-9; Ephesians 5:6; Colossians 3:6), but his wrath no longer rests on believers. I Thessalonians 5:9 speaks of wrath and destruction of sinners, but not for God's faithful; "God has not destined us for wrath, but to obtain salvation through our Lord Jesus Christ."

On what basis would a God of perfect love inflict pain on a Christian to avenge wrong in the name of Justice? The answer is, He would not, and does not! Instead, God promised a New Covenant of mercy at Jeremiah 31:34, reprised at Hebrews 8:12 and 10:17, under which "I will forgive their iniquity, and I will remember their sin no more." God promised by everything He is and has: "That I will not turn away from them, to do them good... Yes, I will rejoice over them to do them good" (Jeremiah 32:40-41). This New Covenant was accomplished in Jesus.

A third advantage of the New and better Covenant of Jesus is the literal transformation to the character of Christ which is established under the New Testament. We are made new in the image of Christ, and are no longer under compulsion to sin (Romans 6:17) since our new nature is no longer inclined to commit sin, but to resist allures of the flesh and world. While Christ's future sacrifice covered the <u>salvation</u> of Old Testament saints retroactively, and they could anticipate His deliverance, they did not have the blessing of the indwelling Holy Spirit available, as we do. It is possible God's other graces, blessings, virtue, and integrity, were not fully available to relieve them of worldly torments, by supernaturally enabling endurance and righteousness. On the other hand we are constantly receiving imparted holiness through the Holy Spirit, and supernatural empowerment to resist sin and please God by a righteous life.

God was with the Jews in the wilderness, and Jesus was with His disciples for the years of His public ministry. Following His death and resurrection, Jesus covenants that the Godhead will be <u>in</u> us, a fellowship far greater than accompaniment with us. God provided for the Jews in the wilderness, but under the New Testament, in Christ "all things are yours...and you are Christ's; and Christ is God's" (I Corinthians 3:21, 23). God guided the Jews in the wilderness and gave them His law to establish standards of righteousness. Under the New Testament He has written the law in our hearts, and provided the Holy Spirit to explicate His will, and transform our new spirit being to actual righteousness and obedience.

Under the New Birth of the New Covenant, the fruit of the Holy Spirit which is imparted to believers endows us with divine power to resist sin in order to glorify God, rather than because we fear the consequences of sin (Galatians 5:24-25; I John 3:7,9, 5:2, 5:18-19). In fact, the first fruit of the Spirit, love, provides insight into God's mercy toward repentant sinners. One's own experience as a parent suggests that God the Father is not inclined to punish His repentant child. I might momentarily be angry with my son for being disobedient and unloving toward me, but I am no longer able, because of God's love in me, to sustain such feelings toward him. I could not leave him to suffer when he has asked for forgiveness and reconciliation, because I love him, despite what he might have done. What I know of love is imperfect, and I have learned it from God's perfect love toward me.

Remember that all men, both under the Old and new Testaments, "were dead through the trespasses and sins in which you once walked, following the course of this world, following the prince of the power of the air, the spirit that is now at work in the sons of disobedience. Among these we all once lived in the passions of our flesh, following the desires of body and mind, and so <u>we were by nature children of wrath,</u> like the rest of mankind" (Ephesians 2:1-3; and see Colossians 1:12-13). Our new, Christ-like nature contributes to sparing sinning Christians from God's wrath, because we are supernaturally enabled to be submissive and obedient to God once we have repented our sin.

Fourth, our regeneration is continually maintained whenever a sinner confesses and repents his sins. I John 1:9 teaches that a penitent Christian's sin is immediately forgiven and remitted. He is freed from guilt or punishment for sin because God promises not only to forgive him, but also to <u>cleanse him of all unrighteousness</u> by the Blood of Jesus. Forgiveness eradicates the sin and cleansing restores us to right-standing with God, provided our confession is genuine and includes a repentance which intends to turn away from the confessed sin. The sinner's repentance and changing have satisfied the deterrent, instructive, and chastening purposes of punishment. That being the case, there is no reason for God to punish a Christian's past sins, for which Jesus has already atoned.

A fifth grace of the new Covenant which redounds to the benefit of sinners is their access to total forgiveness because Jesus and the Holy Spirit intercede on our behalf and assure our restoration to righteousness, as adopted sons of God, in and through Jesus Christ. Jesus "holds his priesthood permanently, because he continues forever. Consequently, he is able for all time to save those who draw near to God through him, since he always lives to make intercession for them" (Hebrews 7:24-25). Under the Old Testament, a human High Priest, and animal sacrifices were but pre-figures of Christ, and could not provide the full atonement and intercession available under the better promises of the New Covenant.

Furthermore, the Holy Spirit "helps us in our weakness; for we do not know how to pray as we ought, but the Spirit himself intercedes for us with sighs too deep for words... because the Spirit intercedes for the saints according to the will of God" (Romans 8:26-27). He not only prays for us as we ought, but the Spirit's indwelling transforms our desires so that we come to seek only what we ought in conformance with God's will. He thereby enables our literal compliance and obedience to God's will, and empowers conformance to our repentance.

All this suggests that the punishment of the righteous is not the same as for unfaithful rebels who choose to reject Jesus as Saviour, and therefore must personally bear their own penalty for sin. Nevertheless, earthly consequences of sin are not always remitted, nor immediately removed, even for the saints, but may continue to operate and affect the life of a believer, as we see in the next Chapter. Christians must be careful to avoid Satan's incitations to doubt the benevolence and forgiveness of God, when it is actually the world system exacting its penalty, demanding you reap what you have sown. For example, a child born out of the momentary lust of adultery will not be erased by God as an accommodation to the sinning Christian. Unacceptance, resentment, hardship, and mortification may persist in the world, despite God's forgiveness of the transgression.

A believer who remains sinfully impenitent, has also refused to accept God's mercy in Christ, and can expect to suffer continued discipline, correction, training, restitution, or chastisement until he repents and responds to rehabilitation, and spiritual purification. God must correct unrepentant believers until they repent. Loving parents are familiar with natural world situations where punishment must be administered to protect the wayward child and preserve other family members.

The child addicted to drugs, who becomes disobedient and disruptive of the household, who steals from his parents to support his habit, must be punished, even to the point of exile by the family or society, to avert his self-destruction and maintain family integrity. The alcoholic who repeatedly relents his drunken abuse of others, only to break his promises to change, must somehow be deterred from harming himself and others. Such children cannot be rewarded with money to feed their sinful habits, nor given access to the haven they would pillage and destroy, while they remain in rebellious impenitence.

A sinning Christian may be forgiven and his sins forgotten when he repents, but he may still need correction and training to deter him from unsurrendered fleshly tendencies to repeat his sin. Easy forgiveness may be counterproductive, despite good intention, by making it easy to presume upon God's forgiveness the next time temptation beckons. God's wisdom may see the need for suffering or deprivation to accomplish the deterrence which loving forgiveness alone, has not. This is training to eliminate the sinful tendency until it is judged conquered in a believer's own, faithful turning from sin. For "if we judged ourselves truly, we should not be judged, But when we are judged by the Lord, we are chastened so that we may not be condemned along with the world" (I Corinthians 11:31-32).

If we fail to judge ourselves by determining to stop an habitual sin unconditionally, then God must do the stopping for us. Turning from sin is an indispensable part of repentance. Repentance begins with intent and commitment to change. It must be carried forward with conduct consistent with one's purpose, which entrusts obedience to God, Who always empowers a believer's faithful desire to act rightly. Weakness in succumbing to sin is no excuse, since God empowers His children to resist sin, which admits no excuse or further presumption upon God's mercy. If we neglect or are unable to make this commitment, then "it is impossible for those who were once enlightened... If they shall fall away, to renew them again unto repentance" (Hebrews 6:4,6 KJV). We do not lose our salvation, but our inveterate backsliding has made it more difficult, if not impossible, for repentance to rescue us from worldly consequences. Each relapse or repeated reversion disobeying God's will results in a weakened conscience, and reduces one's power to respond rightly the next time. It is far better to ask God immediately for strength to turn from sin than to ignore one's recidivism.

Praise God that He is faithful and answers our prayers to be strengthened by His might in our resolve to resist sin. He will always provide a deliverance from sin if we are faithful in seeking it. Once we make the penitent determination to obey God, by His strength, He will empower our obedience and enable circumstances to escape sin and its consequent chastisement.

When the instructional reproofs of chastisement have succeeded in motivating repentance, and when divine forgiveness, cleansing and turning from sin have occurred, one would expect the suffering to end. Affliction which chastens or chastises a sinner is intended to subdue stubborn willfulness and compel obedience. When the lesson of suffering is learned, the rationale for it disappears, and the deprivation and discomfort of that training should be over. The deterrent effect of pain or fear of threatened punishment has accomplished its objective of changed behavior.

God chooses to forgive and empower obedience for the penitent who seeks to amend his ways. The woman taken in adultery was completely forgiven by Jesus, Who confronted her accusers, and then charged her to turn from sin: "And Jesus said, 'Neither do I condemn you, go and do not sin again" (John 8:11). After Jesus healed the invalid at Bethesda, He directed: "See, you are well! Sin no more, that nothing worse befall you" (John 5:14). Whenever Jesus delivered someone from infirmity He dispensed unconditional grace and forgiveness; and confirmed His empowerment to resist sin. He still does, for He "is the same yesterday, today, and forever" (Hebrews 13:8).

God is more than a loving father. God <u>is</u> love, and His character and loving nature are revealed at I Corinthians 13:4-7: "Love is patient and kind; love... does not insist on its own way; it is not irritable or resentful; it does not rejoice at wrong, but rejoices in the right. Love <u>bears all things</u>, believes all things, hopes all things, <u>endures all things</u>." Love is expressed for the benefit of the beloved; bears with shortcomings, and overlooks failures. It exalts and encourages, rather than destroys. The reformed sinner in Christ has the love of God, and has no need for punishment once he repents and opts to change the error of his ways, relying on God's enabling power to overcome sin, and pledging His full cooperation to obey.

In the parable of the weeds sown among wheat, Jesus affirms that the weeds will not be gathered up and burned until the wheat has grown to fullness and is ready for harvesting, "lest in gathering the weeds you root up the wheat along with them" (Matthew 13:29). Thus, God's loving and merciful nature declines to punish even the wicked who deserve destruction, if that would result in harm to the faithful connected with them. How then could we conjecture that the same considerate and protecting God would inflict harm upon the righteous because of the sins for which Jesus has already paid the penalty in full?

Jesus revealed that a tax collector who "confessed his sinfulness and implored: 'God be merciful to me a sinner!'... went down to his house justified" (Luke 18:13). The word "justified" is a precise term and denotes full pardon and remission of sins, including escape from any penalty for them because of God's grace and forgiveness through Christ. James 5:19-20 agrees: "if any one among you wanders from the truth and some one brings him back, let him know that whoever brings back a sinner from the error of his way will save his soul from death and will cover a multitude of sins."

When the Prodigal Son repented and returned, he was not punished, but publicly and fully restored to status as a son. He was given 'the best robe" and "a ring on his hand", the emblem of family entitlement, and "shoes on his feet", along with a celebratory feast of public proclamation (Luke 15:22-23). Why would Jesus give the example of the Prodigal Son if not to illustrate that God is totally forgiving to his children who repent and return to him. A loving Father does restore full status, privilege, and blessings to His repentant child. A forgiving Father does not punish His child who is covered by the Blood of Christ, to exact vengeance, reprisal, and justice after the fact.

CHAPTER 14

EVIL AUTHORED BY FREE BEINGS

"Woe unto the wicked! It shall be ill with him: for the reward of his hands shall be given him."

–Isaiah 3:11.

While we are rewarded for obeying God's Word, we can also suffer for our disobedience, by acting as we ought not when we commit proscribed sins. Such suffering is the result of perversion of God-given freedom, outside the will of God, but permitted by His providential gift of freedom. God may be glorified when a believer suffers as a Christian for the name of Christ (I Peter 4:14, 16), yet one ought not "suffer as a murderer, or a thief, or a wrongdoer, or a mischief-maker" (I Peter 4:15), for such suffering is not approved by God, but is an affront to His trust in us.

Man is responsible personally for most of the suffering he endures, because of his failure to obey God's laws which prescribe the good life for man. Since disobedience is the articulation of irresponsible freedom, there is a direct connection between obedience and the absence of affliction.

A believer, himself, can be the principal cause of his own adversity by sinful, wrong choices which irresponsibly use his freedom and produce dreadful consequences. There is not the slightest possibility God puts sinful thoughts into our minds when everything he does intends to provoke a righteous response, build resistance, demonstrate His grace, and strengthen man's resolve not to sin. Evil originates in our own flesh and weakness, and is initiated by "sin, which dwells within me" (Romans 7:15-20).

The New Birth truly transforms us into a new spirit being, but we are still the same person, with the same failings as far as the recollections and temptations of the flesh are concerned. Even though divine forgiveness converts and establishes a Christian in spiritual righteousness, we can still respond, and subject ourselves to the dictates of the flesh while we await our glorification and complete transformation by God. The trials, allures and vexations of the world will continue to operate within a believer's own desires.

Suppose that a man yields to lustful temptations to commit adultery. Is it conceivable that God could have encouraged an illicit relationship which contradicts His righteousness, and causes guilt and destruction of two families? How could we believe it is God's implanted thought to sin, when Jesus tells us that Satan's ideas are what incite us to sin? And if God is 'guilty' of leaving us free to commit harmful sins, at what point should He be excluded or exonerated as a cause of sin, when we are the ones who eagerly and willingly choose to pursue it?

Psalm 107:17 says that "Fools because of their transgression, and because of their iniquities, are afflicted." Ecclesiastes 7:17 puts it: "Be not over much wicked, neither be thou foolish: why shouldest thou die before thy time?" James 1:14-15 teaches "each person is tempted when he is lured and enticed by his own desire... and sin when it is full-grown brings forth death."

Other passages confirming that man is often the author of his own hardship when he sins rebelliously, and disobediently departs from God's Law are 2 Kings 17:7-24; Nehemiah 9:26-27; Proverbs 11:24, 27, 29, 13:20, 19:16, 22:3, 27:12, Psalms 7;14-16, 37:1-2, 38:3-5, 52:1-5, 92:7; Ezekiel 18:4; and Revelation 20:13-14. As Isaiah 3:11 forecasts: "Woe unto the wicked! It shall be ill with him: for the reward of his hands shall be given him." Moses prophesied to the Israelites that if they did not obey God's commandments, then "all these curses shall come upon thee, and overtake thee" (Deuteronomy 28:15).

In the New Testament, James 5:15-16 implies that sin is connected to physical sickness: "Is any among you sick? Let him call for the elders... and if he has committed sins, he will be forgiven. Therefore confess your sins to one another... that you may be healed." I Corinthians 11:29-30 warns that sinful disdain for the Lord's Supper at Holy Communion causes sickness: "For any one who eats and drinks without discerning the body eats and drinks judgment upon himself. That is why many of you are weak and ill, and some have died."

When God sends some suffering or deprivation to deter sin, it is reasonable to assume that such affliction will end as soon as we respond to His correction. If God sends sickness as chastisement for unconfessed sin, we would expect confession and repentance to restore healing.[128] God has promised forgiveness and cleansing of unrighteousness to His children who repent. When we are thus freed to walk in the light of God's Word, the Blood of Jesus enables us to continue in obedience: "if we walk in the light, as he is in the light... the blood of Jesus his Son cleanses us from all sin... If we confess our sins, he is faithful and just, and will forgive our sins and cleanse us from all unrighteousness" (I John 1:7, 9).

Even though divine forgiveness converts and re-establishes a Christian in spiritual righteousness and restoration, there may still be a worldly penalty to be exacted for our succumbing to sin. Even a faithful Christian, whose repented sins are remitted in heavenly places, may suffer the consequences of iniquities committed before conversion. Even after the new Birth, one who has carnally sown self-indulgence in alcohol, tobacco, sexual promiscuity, gluttony, torpor, and other violations of proper living which God has prescribed, can reap physical problems of cirrhosis of the liver, lung cancer, AIDS, heart attack, diabetes, and gout.

When we covet what we do not own, buy what we cannot afford, satisfy our appetites, or plant the sins of the flesh, we will eventually harvest their worldly physical consequences. Despite the fact that God wishes health, prosperity, and blessings for His children, Christians plant the seeds of affliction whenever they abuse their bodies with overweight, malnutrition, tobacco, drugs, and other toxins. Departing from God's way leads to calamitous consequences. We cannot presume upon God's grace and forgiveness to excuse us from the world's penalties, even though God exercises Sovereign dominion over creation, and intervenes in answer to prayer in any way it pleases Him. God's forgiveness is no guaranty of escaping worldly consequences. His Sovereignty moderates man's possible abuse of freedom by always giving advance warning of consequences.

REAPING NATURAL CONSEQUENCES

It is possible for a person to repent of, and abandon sinful ways; be forgiven and cleansed by God, and still have consequences played out in his life. While God sometimes uses suffering to perfect His children spiritually, we need to recognize that some occurrences are due to the operation of physical laws and the inevitable aftermath of acting in certain ways in the natural world. The denial of blessings and the pain which accompanies loss may not be intended as punishment by God, but simply be the result of reaping what we had sinfully sown earlier.

We are free to choose an action, but we are not free to choose its consequences, for these flow from physical and moral laws of God's universe. If we intentionally leap off a high building we will fall toward the ground, and one ought not tempt God by asking his deliverance from self-inflicted peril. One who is severely injured in defiance of physical laws, cannot argue that God intended or orchestrated the resulting harm. The law of gravity blindly, routinely, and naturally produced the consequences.

Neither should one expect or seek God's deliverance from the operation of ordained spiritual laws by intentionally subjecting himself to more subtle, but equally devastating spiritual perils. We cannot sin with impunity, for evil actions always breed evil consequences, according to the principle of reaping what one sows. Colossians 3:25 warns: "For the wrongdoer will be paid back for the wrong he has done, and there is no partiality." Proverbs 26:27 puts it: "Whoso diggeth a pit shall fall therein: and he that rolleth a stone, it will return upon him." The spiritual law of sowing is reflected in the worldly wisdom which asserts that lady Luck smiles best on those who work hardest: that God helps those who help themselves. On the other hand, indolence, lack of diligence, and neglect to perform one's duty will result in personal misfortune and poverty.

The child who puts his hand in the fire after being warned not to by a loving parent, will be burned and possibly scarred permanently. The parent will forgive the disobedience and facilitate the healing, but the resulting disfigurement, pain, and fright from playing with fire remain realities. He who breaks God's law will be broken somehow by it and against it, along with innocent victims of the wrongdoing, who also reap what the sinner sows. That is why abortion, sexual promiscuity, divorce, gay life styles, gambling, drugs and alcohol are all sins; as heinous as murder or stealing, which God forbids because He knows how devastating and destructive all sins are to the participant who makes his own rules and abandons God's.

Sin always has worldly consequences both to the sinner and those close to Him, even though spiritually forgiven. That is why God works so faithfully to deter His children from sin. Consequences may be personal shame, fear, regret, or loss, or one's family could be affected if the sinner is exposed openly, or the congregation or whole denomination disappointed or embarrassed by the sins of a member.

As we have seen, freedom incorporates the risk of evil-doing by oneself and others, and God will not always interfere with the perverse actions of free men. Worldly consequences may make it impossible for God to alter painful circumstances, even though Jesus has paid the full spiritual price for the sin, and God has forgiven the sinner who repents his excesses. But how can God remit the worldly pain inherent in facing up to the circumstances of a blameless infant being conceived in adultery or outside wedlock? He who engages in pre-marital sex or fornication, in disobedience to God's commands in I Corinthians 5:9, 6:9; I Thessalonians 4:3; Ephesians 5:3; and Colossians 3:5 is exposed to sexually transmitted disease, illegitimacy, and choosing between the dreadful temptations of abortion or loveless marriage. He who flirts with adultery will see his marriage suffer, whether as a result of discovery by the betrayed spouse, guilt by the sinner, or an unintended child.

Certainly, God has not planned or desired these harmful worldly consequences. On the contrary, He has prohibited sex outside of marriage to spare us from such results. God will comfort, ease, and strengthen penitent believers to cope, when beset by difficult circumstances, but He will not always avoid worldly effects flowing from corrupted human freedom. He will re-direct the evil we do to produce greater virtue, wisdom, or good, but may not remit worldly suffering initiated by human freedom.

What has God to do with chemical plants which spew out cancer causing particles, or the cigarette smoke inhaled willingly by smokers, despite the warnings of lung cancer and emphysema? If we disregard God's caution to honor our bodies as His temples, we cannot expect to be healed while we continue smoking, and contaminate our lungs with tar and nicotine. The obese smoker, flaccid from sloth and inactivity, cannot expect good health when his bodily systems finally break down.

A husband on the brink of divorce cannot continue to belittle, ignore, abuse, antagonize, or cheat on his spouse and expect his prayers for reconciliation to be honored. What has God to do with the driver who drunkenly loses control of his car, or becomes careless for a moment, resulting in a collision? What is God's involvement with buildings, bridges, and structures which collapse from poor maintenance or shoddy construction? Not only has a free man exposed himself and others to these tragedies, but God has abundantly warned us of the dangers from irresponsible, careless, or sinful living which lead to emotional and physical degradation. The problem is not lack of warning from God, but rebellious disobedience by men to the warnings God has imparted.

Jesus has paid the price for your sins, and established your right-standing with God, but the natural world may also have a price to exact for worldly activities. Just as the Born-Again believer can still sin, so he can also still become physically infirm as a result of sinning in the flesh. The prisoner in jail who becomes spiritually transformed will not find himself physically released from prison because of his spiritual New Birth. A disciple who is unequally yoked in marriage to an unbeliever will continue to know sorrow, as long as her spouse persists in stubborn rejection of the Lord. Even the most fervent intercessory prayers may go unanswered because God does not, and a woman cannot, force real belief on anyone. It must be personally expressed as part of personal conviction.

Just as you must sill pay for the car or home you purchased before you were Born-Again, so you must continue to pay the worldly costs of folly or degeneracy incurred while a carnal citizen of the world. We must learn, and be governed by, God's laws, or we will suffer until we understand that they must not be violated.

If we pursue only worldly objectives, take in no spiritual nurture, and sow nothing spiritual, we will reap nothing spiritual. We can bar ourselves from the protection and power of the Holy Spirit by neglecting to remain open to receive Him. In human relations, one who freely violates God's law of love toward other men will inspire a reciprocal lack of good, and invite retaliatory unloving treatment. At the very least his attitude will block the love of others from reaching him.

If we fail to obey God's directives and will, our rebellion can bar the blessings He has promised. We will still be saved, but our earthly enjoyment of the fuller life has been jeopardized.

Why do we believe the promises of reward for obedience, but ignore the clear teaching that obedience is a pre-condition of God's blessings? If disobedience leads to unholiness, and God chastens His children to recall them to holiness, why would we be surprised when He reproves the sin in our lives, and gets our attention by withholding blessings as part of chastisement?

Like the Prodigal Son who wallowed in the misery and degradation of rebellious attachment to the world, we will reap the consequences of choosing sin rather than God, until we come to our senses and return to our new, true nature. All men are called to walk in divine light rather than darkness. Jesus says: "he who walks in the darkness does <u>not know where he goes</u>. While you have the light, believe in the light, that you may become sons of light" (John 12:35-36). Jeremiah 13:16 calls men to "Give glory to the Lord your God before he cause darkness, and before your feet stumble upon the dark mountains" (See also, Isaiah 59:9-10).

It is better not to enter the strange caverns of darkness, at all. For if we wander or remain in darkness, we are vulnerable to accidents, stumbling, and harm. If we follow the dark road, it may not be easy to escape the darkness, much less the consequences of moving in it. You may rue darkness, but you are in the blackness which you have chosen, until you turn to the light, and follow Jesus' way out of darkness. Only the individual actor, by succumbing to the enticements of the world, is responsible for this type of suffering in his life. Often, the sharpest pain will accompany the revelation that one's own sin, infidelity, carelessness, or inconstancy has caused the tragedy of unnecessary loss, and initiated one's own suffering. Then, there is only the love of Jesus to console and restore.

DISOBEDIENCE AS A BAR TO BLESSINGS

A believer may have complete faith in a Bible promise; claim it by truly trusting faith; and yet still be denied the blessings for which he has prayed, because of misperceptions about the promise. For example, John 15:7 and 16:23 seem to promise that a believer can pray for, and receive, 'anything' he prays for in faith. John 14:14 says: "<u>Whatever</u> you ask in my name, I will do it, that the Father may be glorified in the Son; if you ask <u>anything</u> in my name, I will do it." The language appears to be an absolute, unconditional promise by Jesus to answer any prayer of a disciple asked in his name. Yet, we do not receive everything for which we pray, and lack of blessing can sour into suffering because of loss and denial of desires.

Common sense tells us that Jesus will not negate His specific commands established elsewhere in Scripture, simply because their antithesis is now sought in His name. If an adulterer prays for the Lord's blessing on his new relationship, when adultery is prohibited in the seventh Commandment (Exodus 20;14), can he really expect John 14:14 to countermand the condemnation of adultery because it grants "anything" asked in Jesus' name? If we pray for the rewards of any sin which Jesus has condemned, how can we expect such prayers to be answered?

The Bible literally says in two places: "There is no God" (Psalms 14:1, 53:1), but anyone could readily determine from the context, in a Bible which reveals the existence of God throughout, that this phrase standing alone is misleading, and cannot be interpreted to contradict other Scripture. Indeed, the complete passage declares: "The fool hath said in his heart, 'There is no God'." There is a principle of hermeneutics, or Bible interpretation, that Scripture interprets other Scripture, so that the entire Bible clarifies, particularizes, explains, and gives meaning to specific passages. The sense of any passage which seems to make a broad statement is often elucidated by a parallel verse which creates exceptions and narrows the language.[129]

Consequently, we find Scriptures which impose obedience as a prerequisite to blessings, and disobedience as an inhibitor to answered prayer. Deuteronomy 11:26-28 says: "Behold, I set before you this day a blessing and a curse; a blessing if ye obey the commandments of the Lord your God, which I command you this day: And a curse if ye will not obey... but turn aside out of the way which I command you this day." We saw earlier how obedience was rewarded with blessing. Conversely, disobedience frustrates blessings. Psalm 34:16 warns: "But the face of the Lord is against those that do evil to cut off the remembrance of them from the earth." Psalm 38:3 reveals turmoil as the consequence of sin: "There is no soundness in my flesh because of your anger; neither is there any rest in my bones because of sin."

Proverbs 1:28 teaches: "sinners shall not hear or find God." If we ignore or actively try to hide our sins, we will not prosper according to Proverbs 28:13: "He that covereth his sins shall not prosper, but whoso confesseth and forsaketh them shall have mercy." Isaiah 59:2 explains: "But your iniquities have separated between you and your God, and your sins have hid his face from you, that he will not hear." However, our sins are forgiven when we confess them (I John 1:9), and are "blotted out" when we repent and turn from them, and we are refreshed from the presence of the Lord (Acts 3:19). Fortunately, the sanctification of a believer, carried on by the Holy Spirit, continues to empower obedience.

At Luke 12:35, Jesus speaks of three categories of servants who failed to perform in their master's absence, and are denied any rewards because of their unfaithful service. They receive different, severe consequences based upon the egregiousness of their infidelity, either as punishment or deterrence from future wrongdoing. The servant who regarded the master's absence as an opportunity to carouse and abuse his fellow servants will be punished for his evil and will be put with the unfaithful (Luke 12:46), which is tantamount to damnation. Another servant who knew his master's will, but did not "act according to his will," receives a severe beating (Luke 12:47). The third, who did not know the master's will, but did "what deserved a beating, shall receive a light beating" (Luke 12:48). Conversely, the servant who was faithful and wise will be set over all the master's possessions (Luke 12:44; see also, Matthew 25:21, ff).

Inheriting God's Kingdom is denied those who practice: "the works of the flesh: immorality, impurity, licentiousness, idolatry, sorcery, enmity, strife, jealousy, anger, selfishness, dissension, party spirit, envy, drunkenness, carousing, and the like... those who do such things shall not inherit the kingdom of God" (Galatians 5:19-21). Ephesians 5:5-6 urges the saints to avoid "immorality, impurity or covetousness," for "no immoral or impure man or one who is covetous (that is, an idolater), has any inheritance in the kingdom of Christ and of God... for it is because of these things that the wrath of God comes upon the sons of disobedience." Specific sins of immorality, impurity and faction are elucidated at Galatians 5:19-21; Ephesians 4:31; Colossians 3:5-17; James 4:17; Mark 7:21-22; and Romans 1:26-31.

I John 2:4-11 warns us that hatred puts us in darkness and inclines us to falling, by separating us from Jesus, Who is the truth and the light of the world: "He who says 'I know him' but disobeys his commandments is a liar, and the truth is not in him... He who loves his brother abides in the light, and in it there is no cause for stumbling... he who hates his brother is in darkness and walks in darkness, and does not know where he is going, because the darkness has blinded his eyes." He who disobeys the commandment to love has put himself in darkness; separated from the love and power of God, which reflect His light.

I John 3:14-16 says: "He who does not love remains in death. Any one who hates his brother is a murderer, and you know that no murderer has eternal life abiding in him... and we ought to lay down our lives for the brethren." Death does not necessarily abide in one who hates, but he who hates abides in darkness and death, removed and remote from divine blessings and companionship, just as Lot resided in Sodom for a time. Without love, we are bereft of eternal life, spiritual light, or God's communion in us. Without love, a Christian forfeits spirituality and the spiritual blessings connected with it. Thus, hate is the moral equivalent of murder because it wars with and destroys the spirit of another, in the absence of love. Hate usually originates in fear or resentment of another, but we should remember that perfect love, which resides in God, Who is Love, casts out fear and incipient thoughts of murder.

Just as hatred puts us into darkness, removed from the light of Christ, so disobedience and immorality generally tend to block us from divine illumination. Christians can shut themselves off from God and His friendship, blessings, and grace, by persisting in disobedience, rebelliousness, licentiousness, pride, greed, and uncleanness. Sinners can become hardened of heart, and "darkened in their understanding, alienated from the life of God because of the ignorance that is in them, due to their hardness of heart" (Ephesians 4:18). Unrepentant sinners shut out the perfect life and light of God when they most need vitality and illumination. And they rebuff God's perfect love because they prefer the momentary gratifications of sin.

When one impenitently erects a wall of sin, shutting him off from God, God allows man's choice of separation, and will persuade, but not compel the willful sinner's return, as long as such disobedience continues unrepented. Ongoing sin is the same as refusing to demolish the barrier which the sinner has himself erected, with the result that: "your iniquities have separated between you and your God, and your sins have hid his face from you, that he will not hear" (Isaiah 59:2).

SINFUL ATTITUDES STIFLE BLESSINGS

Faith and obedience won't work when your attitude is wrong. An unforgiving nature, an unrepentant heart, and proud self-righteousness are impediments to receiving God's love. They block our effective prayer and communion with a holy God. God may not hear or answer prayers which come from disobedient, rebellious, and unforgiving hearts, regardless of the faith invested in a specific Bible promise.

The Lord's Prayer at Matthew 6:12 teaches us to petition: "And forgive us our debts, as we also have forgiven our debtors." Jesus explains the spiritual dynamics of forgiveness at Matthew 6:14: "For if you forgive men their trespasses, your heavenly Father also will forgive you; but if you do not forgive men their trespasses, neither will your Father forgive your trespasses." The unforgiving servant who did not have mercy on his fellow servant, as his master had shown mercy to him, was "delivered to the jailers." Jesus warns: "So also my heavenly Father will do to every one of you, if you do not forgive your brother from your heart" (Matthew 18:35). If Jesus has already suffered punishment and earned forgiveness for the sins of all men (Ephesians 1:7; Colossians 2:13); and God stands ready to forgive them for Christ's sake, then we are obligated to forgive others. For, we cannot presume to know whom God has forgiven, only that He calls us to forgive others because we know He loves all men, and He has forgiven us.

The Parable of the Unforgiving Servant also teaches that failure to forgive the debt someone owes you, will revoke the forgiveness previously extended to you by your Lord (Matthew 18:23-25). Also, we must affirmatively seek reconciliation with our alienated brother, before presenting an offering at God's altar (Matthew 5:23-24; See also, Matthew 18:21; Romans 12:18; Ephesians 4:32; and Colossians 3:13).

Judging another harshly brings the same harsh judgment upon oneself. Matthew 7:1-2 says: "Judge not, that you be not judged. For with the judgment you pronounce you will be judged, and the measure you give will be the measure you get." Romans 14:10-12 reminds us: "Why do you pass judgment on your brother? Or you, why do you despise your brother? For we shall all stand before the judgment seat of God... So each of us shall give account of himself to God."

Jesus proclaims at Mark 11:24: "Whatever you ask in prayer, believe that you receive it, and you will." He immediately qualifies such general language, with the admonition: "And whenever you stand praying, forgive, if you have anything against any one; so that your Father also who is in heaven may forgive you your trespasses" (Mark 11:25). Indeed, 2 Corinthians 2:10-11 says that if we are unforgiving, Satan gains advantage over the Church, either through disunity among us, despair in the one unforgiven, or hardness in the unforgiving heart. We must live in a condition of forgiveness if we want to experience the miraculous power of prayer and blessing.[130]

I Timothy 2:8 says that prayer is to be offered "lifting holy hands without anger." For, holy petitions cannot rise out of unholy petitioners. Your spirit is degraded and your hands stained by anger or wrath. You must be washed clean by the Blood of Christ through confession and genuine repentance which actually turns from sin. And when thus made holy, your hands can be lifted again in an appeal for God's help for the supernatural blessings promised. Psalm 66:18 puts it: "If I regard iniquity in my heart, the Lord will not hear me." "Let all bitterness, and wrath and anger and clamor and slander be put away from you, with all malice." (Ephesians 4:31).

Strife and jealousy are also special extensions of an unloving nature, and prevent the Word from operating in one's life. They cut a disciple off from spiritual blessings because they bring him to the level of an unbeliever. I Corinthians 3:3 admonishes Christians: "For while there is jealousy and strife among you, are you not of the flesh, and behaving like ordinary men?" This is not good, for St. Paul explains that ordinary men, to whom Christians in strife are compared, are cut off from blessings: "The unspiritual man does not receive the gifts of the Spirit of God, for they are folly to him, and he is not able to understand them because they are spiritually discerned" (I Corinthians 2:14).

Christians who are quarrelsome or in strife are consequently unloving, and have lost effectiveness to minister to unrepentant sinners who are in the "snare of the devil, who are taken captive by him at his will" (2 Timothy 2:26, KJV). Perhaps the absolute need to share the light of Christ by obediently abiding in Him, is the reason why God commands love. The Church must exhibit the love of Jesus and be readily seen in the light, if it is to attract the unsaved.

Envy blocks our blessings because it disputes the rightness of God's blessings lavished upon another person. Envy may lead to irrational behavior, as in the case of King Saul, who sought to kill David with spears because he resented the public infatuation with David's military victories, expressed in the popular refrain: "Saul has slain his thousands, and David his ten thousands" (I Samuel 18:7-11, 19:10). The one who envies is always the one most affected by the venom of jealousy. God departed from Saul because of all his wickedness, and Saul lost the kingdom to David (I Samuel 28:16-17). Proverbs 6:34 discloses how serious a sin is jealousy: "For jealousy is the rage of a man: therefore he will not spare in the day of vengeance."

Pride and self-righteousness are also at odds with faithful petitions for blessing. "A proud look" is among the seven things which are an abomination unto the Lord (Proverbs 6:16-17). Jesus says that the proud, self-righteous prayers of the Pharisee were worthless, "for he who exalts himself will be humbled," while the penitent tax-collector who humbly sought and trusted in God's mercy, was justified (Luke 18:14). James 4:6 puts it: "God opposes the proud, but gives grace to the humble." See also, Proverbs 8:13, 11:2, 13:10, 16:5, 16:18, 29:23; and Daniel 4:37).

We are familiar with the idea of fire testing our endurance and refining our character by burning off the dross of sin, to produce the pure gold of character (I Peter 1:7, 4:12). But pride can also be tested in the furnace of praise, according to Psalm 27:21: "As the fining pot for silver, and the furnace for gold; so is a man to his praise" (see also Psalm 17:3). God also tests us with praise from other men to see if we are humble, modest and ready to handle more serious stewardship requiring mature spirituality. If praise puffs us up and inflates our ego, then we may be denied substantial blessings until we are ready to serve God selflessly to His glory.[131]

The Old Testament details several other mental states which frustrate or deny the blessing of fellowship with God, Who is not in communion with men who offer unworthy service to Him (Malachi 1:7-9); who turn a deaf ear to the Law (Proverbs 28:9; Zechariah 7:11-13); who worship other gods (Jeremiah 11:10-11; Ezekiel 8:15-18); who hate God and His people (Psalm 18:41); who hate goodness and God's people (Micah 3:2-4); who are hypocrites (Job 27:8-9); or who are proud and evil (Job 35:12).

When the Israelites offered imperfect sacrifices unto the Lord, which reflected their selfishness and ingratitude, God rejected them: "I have no pleasure in you, saith the Lord of hosts, neither will I accept an offering at your hand" (Malachi 1:10). "Though ye offer me burnt offerings and your meat offerings, I will not accept them" (Amos 5:22).

Lack of obedience to God will deprive the sinner of blessings since disobedience reflects a basic mistrust of God's Word and goodness, while obedience is evidence of faith in God's commands and benevolent intelligence behind them. Obedience reflects and sustains faith, while disobedience vitiates faith and the blessings of faithful trust in God, and also brings the punishment of pain and suffering on the sinner.

We may sin by wrongly seeking to use God to transform circumstances into the conditions we wish. Selfish petitions are not necessarily pleasing to God, simply because they are prayers. They assume that God is vicariously pleased when we are pleased; is automatically responsive to our entreaties; and that our happiness is all that pleases Him. While our happiness is very important to God, there is often a great gulf between seeking what pleases oneself and what delights God. We should seek to make God happy, rather than ourselves, and "speak, not to please men, but to please God who tests our hearts" (I Thessalonians 2:4). And God favors motives and prayers that are loving, concerned, and intercessory for others, emerging from a tender, forgiving heart, which seeks to please God, most of all.

God promises deliverance to one who keeps his vow or pledge to the Lord, according to Psalm 50:14, 15: "Offer unto God thanksgiving; and pay thy vows unto the most High: And call upon me in the day of trouble; I will deliver thee, and thou shalt glorify me." Even the mere promise of keeping a vow has secured God's deliverance. Jephthah vowed that if God would deliver the Ammonites into his hands, he would make a burnt offering to the Lord, "and the Lord delivered them into his hands" (Judges 11:32). Likewise, Hannah vowed that if the Lord would give her a baby son, she would dedicate him to the Lord, and Samuel was born to her (I Samuel 1:27-28). Job 22:27-28 suggests that if you pray and "pay thy vows, Thou shalt also decree a thing, and it shall be established unto thee." Simply intending and promising to "pay that that I have vowed" was sufficient for God to deliver Jonah from the fish and to dry land (Jonah 2:9-10).

Conversely, failure to keep one's vows "would be a sin in thee," "for the Lord thy God will surely require it of thee" (Deuteronomy 23:21). Failure to keep vows represents reckless indifference toward God's sanctity, and presumption that we can ignore the injunction of Psalm 15:4: "he honoureth them that fear the Lord. He that sweareth to his own hurt, and changeth not." Ecclesiastes 5:4-5 adds: "When thou vowest a vow unto God, defer not to pay it; for he hath no pleasure in fools: pay that which thou hast vowed. Better is it that thou shouldest not vow, than that thou shouldest vow and not pay." If love of money and the things it buys has kept you from honoring a pledge to God, it may result in God dishonoring your reward.

Fortunately, Jesus' sacrificial Atonement has paid the penalty for all our sins, past, present, and future. From our vantage point in time, every one of them had yet to occur when Jesus bore them on the Cross — including failure to have a right motive, or to pay our vows. Thus, genuine confession and repentance will bring forgiveness and cleansing "from <u>all</u> unrighteousness" (I John 1:9).

SUFFERING FROM FAITHLESS BORROWING

An equally distressing explanation for a believer's failure to receive blessings is when a Christian succumbs to doubt and unbelief, and no longer has faith or motivation to pray for a blessing he once believed was promised and intended by God for him. Losing faith is equivalent to never having had faith, for in either case, petitions are not offered, or they are presented, but without any confidence they will be answered.

At Nazareth, Jesus was treated with contempt by his townspeople because they were so familiar with Him as "the carpenter's son," and with His family. They had no faith in Him and had even attempted to throw Him off a cliff for his perceived pretensions (Luke 4:16-29). Although Jesus willed to help them, He could "not do many might works there, <u>because of their unbelief</u>" (Matthew 13:58).

A common scenario for lost faith begins with a Christian in debt, who begins praying faithfully for solvency, but remains crippled by debt, and ends up doubting the prosperity promised in Scripture. Mired in self-doubt and defeatism, he may suspend tithing and all giving in order to meet worldly obligation, even though that means he is no longer sowing seed to the Lord's purposes, from which he would reap prosperity.

A believer confronted with a loved one's terminal illness may soon lose faith that Bible promises of healing are meant for all believers or for modern times. He may feel betrayed because God has not brought deliverance according to human expectations and timetables, but allowed him to be exposed to worldly ridicule, contempt, or distress.

Prayer time may diminish as the disappointed Christian resents the futility of petitions which have gone unanswered for so long a period. He becomes disgruntled by frustrated desires, and submerged in a malaise of alienation from God. His feeding from the Word becomes perfunctory because its comforts seem too remote, and its powers too removed, to solve the immediate demands of worldly crises. The erstwhile believer has come to walk in the same dark unbelief in which skeptics constantly struggle. The Christian who no longer believes God's promises are intended for him, can have no faith and receive no blessings, except what God elects to provide in a system geared to reward a believer's collaboration by faith.

A pernicious form of faithlessness is when we become impatient, or despair of waiting for God to provide, and attempt to take matters into our own hands. It is harmful because our self-reliance automatically stifles any true dependence or reliance upon God. We hinder any channel by which God would meet our need, as we attempt to manipulate circumstances to accomplish our desires. We put ourselves outside of God's plan and the place where He purposes to send blessings, and usually end up with more needs, until we are driven back to depend exclusively and faithfully upon God as our last resort.

When we refuse to rely on God because of false pride in ourselves, we cannot have faith, and without faith it is impossible to please God. When we attempt to do things by our own contrivances, it is as if we expel an unclean spirit, which only returns "and brings with him seven other spirits more evil than himself" (Matthew 12:45), because we have not relied upon the Lord to fill the desires which we have gratified. We have relied on our promises to pay in the future rather than on God's promise to provide.

This impatience with God to supply our material wants often leads to borrowing so we can have things which God has not yet authorized us to acquire or afford. The Christian who borrows sows financial irresponsibility and will reap the burdens of re-paying both the debt and unproductive interest. When we borrow to provide that for which we lust, we will end up with greater lack, because resources intended by God for enjoying life and serving Him are diverted to pay off what was prematurely acquired. By appropriating blessings God has not yet provided, we can forfeit access to the best God was preparing for us.

One can reverse the process of debt only by working longer and harder to pay his way out of it. What was sowed in the past to satisfy desires beyond one's means will interfere with what is sown and reaped in the present and future. For, much of a debtor's effort and wealth must be misdirected and applied to paying off the indebtedness of the past. Borrowing always reduces total satisfactions by gratifying cravings which should not have been indulged, but which now must be repaid at the expense of genuine needs.

Borrowing indebtedness has become one of Satan's vilest devices for entrapping Christians in the thicket of subservient obligation to other men. Proverbs 22:7 says: "the rich ruleth over the poor, and the borrower is servant to the lender." Despite the clear mandates to avoid debt: "owe no man anything, save to love him' (Romans 13:8 KJV), and the assurances "I will make you the lender and not the borrower" (Deuteronomy 15:6, 28:12), which imply God will give us resources to accomplish His will without recourse to borrowing, we find Christians falling into the debt trap.

Even worldly wisdom grasps the advantage of not borrowing. "Neither a borrower, nor a lender be; for loan oft loses both itself and friend, and borrowing dulls the edge of husbandry," was the sage advice of William Shakespeare in Hamlet I, iii, 75.

Borrowing is wrong because it reflects a worldly desire for immediate gratification of desires, without waiting to earn them, or receive them by the providential hand of God. Borrowing repudiates trust in God's promise to fulfill all our needs, and instead yields to the blandishments of creditors to trust in our own power and exhaust our borrowing potential. Yet, you cannot buy your way to significance or happiness with borrowed money. Borrowing steals from legitimate purposes for one's wealth, by diverting income to interest repayment, rather than enabling savings for gradual and eventual acquisition of wants. Borrowing by credit cards has driven many Christians to bankruptcy; betrayal of promises to pay cheated creditors; and reproach to Christian honor and the sanctity of one's word. And when we don't keep the promises we make to other people, our reputation suffers; we discredit the Lord we serve; self-respect is lost and replaced with guilty self-condemnation.[132]

Christians have even borrowed for religious purposes, in misplaced reliance upon promises of divine returns upon funds sown or invested in ministry programs. Even then, one's focus becomes worldly, concentrating on making money to repay loans, rather than upon joyful service to the Lord by serving others. God seldom endorses borrowing to accomplish His purposes, and the very necessity for borrowing to accomplish a desired goal, is evidence God has not blessed the endeavor. Certainly, God can finance His own plans, without resort to human lenders solicited by misguided Christians. Patience is the virtue which waits for God's timing.

God will forgive the carnal indiscretion of Christians who have repented borrowing. He will reinstate blessings, and if the lesson has been learned not to borrow, will even enable repayment over a period of time, often accompanied by severe fiscal pangs. But the world will continue to demand and collect the interest on money loaned, and dilute the joy of financial blessings God continues to endow. Psalm 37:21 notes: "The wicked borroweth, and payeth not again: but the righteous sheweth mercy, and giveth." Worst of all, we shut ourselves off from the joy of sharing, when we have no surplus from which to bless others because of foolish debt.

The worst part of borrowing for many Christians is that all of one's disposable income is applied toward debt repayment. It is very easy to stop tithing when God's money becomes encumbered by your lenders' demands. If tithing stops, then God's whole system of blessing grinds to a halt, and you can never produce increase because your seed is never planted, but devoted to paying debt. Yet, you will not readily emerge from debt until you resume tithing and give the first part of your harvest to God.

When we have borrowed, we are beset by despair, as no prospect of surcease is evident. We can be overwhelmed by the size of our obligations; resentment against the lenders to whom we initially were grateful, especially if it was a friend; and the interminable period of time to complete repayment. Our only hope is to be driven to God for endurance as we entrust the matter of deliverance from debt to him. We should be encumbered by sorrow and remorse for failing God; aware of our poor stewardship as we accumulated debt. Borrowing is enervating and emotionally draining under the burden of debt. It encourages deceit and concealment with one's spouse, and leads to duplicity, rather than transparency, in one's relationships.

Borrowing gives Satan a foothold, and steady intrusion into your life, because you have lost some of the joy in your work. You no longer have enough money to give obediently for God's work, and you have no present reward for your own efforts at work. This is coupled with the fact government has already taxed you to pay for charitable activities it has arrogated and turned into entitlements of the recipient, so that you have no joy in giving through government, although it is still God's money channeled through you to others, by redistribution of wealth via taxation.

The pressure from owing builds as interest compounds and accumulates, and you are not easily extricated from debt. When you are saddled with debt, your finances control you. You have encumbered your future at the expense of Christian freedom. You have become a slave to mammon instead of Christ.

The Christian who disobeys the commandment to stay out of debt, will soon suffer from his poverty and lack of prosperity. Modern borrowing is the door to lose the blessing of prosperity, and there is nothing saintly in the contrivance to "borrow from Peter to pay Paul," descending in a downward spiral of increased debt. Then, we suffer spiritually by losing the joy of giving, intended and embodied, in God's blessing of loyal, obedient stewardship; by inability to give help to the poor; and lack of funds with which to finance missionary evangelism; not to mention the loss of material comforts, as our income is diverted to interest payments on debt. We sacrifice the joy of spiritual fellowship, as we increasingly apply our time to production of wealth to pay debt.

Nor is there time or money to spend with our children, or create quality opportunities, because our time and treasure is diverted to repayment of debt. We lack the means to bless our own family with things we would prefer to give them. We may suspend intercessory prayers for others because we are pre-occupied with seeking our own deliverance from debt.

EXAMPLES OF LOSS BY SOWING DISOBEDIENCE

The Old Testament is replete with examples of men beloved by God, who sustained loss of blessings as a result of specific disobedience. We cannot know whether God intended their loss as a direct punishment or retribution for their sin; whether it was intended as a chastisement, deterrence or rehabilitation for them; or whether it occurred to provide an example for us, as so many Old Testament narratives do, illustrating the consequences of sinning. We begin with the original sin of Adam and Eve, which produced loss of the blessings in the Garden of Eden, with multiplied sorrows and accursed ground for them (Genesis 3:16, 17). The next generation saw Cain punished with exile for slaying Abel, and the earth cursed for him (Genesis 4:11-12).

Many believe Abraham may have been punished with a quarter-century's delay in the birth of Isaac, because he and Sarah conspired to force God's Covenant by siring a child in the flesh when Abraham committed adultery with Hagar and produced Ishmael (Genesis 16:15).

Sodom and Gomorrah suffered the ultimate loss, as they were destroyed by the Lord for their iniquity (Genesis 19:24). God's clear intention during the destruction of Sodom was to save Lot and his family by providing for their flight. Yet Lot's "wife looked back from behind him, and she became a pillar of salt" (Genesis 19:26). Lot's wife was free to frustrate God's mercy toward her by wistfully yearning for the evil city, and she suffered ultimate loss by her disobedience.

God denied entry to the Promised Land to the whole generation of Israelites in the wilderness, because they refused to trust God and obey His commands (Deuteronomy 1:32, 35). When the Israelites later attempted to obey God "and fight according to all that the Lord our God commanded us" (Deuteronomy 1:41), God did not relent but denied victory, despite their tears and belated trust. He decreed that Israel's punishment was to wander in the desert for forty years, as an instructive chastisement, to teach Israel a lesson in faithfulness that would serve them well for all time.

The Jews fleeing Egypt clamored for some food spicier than the manna God provided in the wilderness, and ended up dying over their appetites. The Israelites "lusted exceedingly in the wilderness, and tempted God in the desert, and he gave them their request; but sent leanness into their soul' (Psalm 106:14-15).

When Israel coveted the human kings who ruled neighboring pagan lands, God warned them they would suffer great loss because they already enjoyed God's benevolent reign over them. God instructed Samuel to warn Israel: "ye shall cry out in that day because of your king which ye shall have chosen you; and the Lord will not hear you in that day' (I Samuel 8:18). The people insisted on a king, and Samuel anointed Saul with God's blessing, but Saul turned into a terrible tyrant, as predicted (I Samuel 22:17).

When King Saul disobeyed God's directive to destroy completely the sinful Amelekites, he sought to mitigate his rebellion by offering a sacrifice to the Lord. The prophet Samuel reproved him: "Behold, to obey is better than sacrifice, and to hearken than the fat of rams... Because thou has rejected the Word of the Lord, he hath also rejected thee from being king" (I Samuel 15:22-23). Saul's disobedience prevented him from retaining the blessing of kingship.

Samson eventually lost God's Spirit because he sought to marry out of the faith in disobedience to God's laws (Judges 14:2-3). He was blinded, enslaved, and never fulfilled the promise of His gifts.

As we saw in the last Chapter, both Moses and David, despite being specially chosen, favored, and blessed by God, suffered loss for their sinful disobedience. By striking the rock, instead of speaking to it, as he had been instructed, Moses destroyed God's paradigm intended to depict God's mercy and forgiveness to unfaithful Israel (Numbers 20:11). Despite his fervent prayers of remorse to see the Promised Land, Moses was punished for his disobedience, and denied entry (Numbers 20:12; Deuteronomy 3:26).

David lost his son conceived in adultery, to sickness and death, despite his complete repentance and prayers that the child be spared (2 Samuel 12:13-18). Further, because David had killed Uriah by the sword, God established appropriate punishment; "Now therefore the sword shall never depart from thine house" (2 Samuel 12:10), and David lost the blessing of peace among his family. His son, Absalom, fulfilled the prophecy by slaying all the others sons of David (2 Samuel 13:30), bringing grief to David. Then, Absalom was "thrust through" by Joab and his armor bearers (2 Samuel 18:14-15), destroying all of David's sons then living.

Because David's sin of adultery weakened the foundations of the family, his punishment from God extended into his family. He contended for the kingdom against his son, Absalom. His daughter Tamar was raped by his son, Amnon. His son Absalom hated Amnon for this, and eventually killed him (2 Samuel 13:14, 22, 30). The penalty for adultery was established as death by stoning, so God was merciful in not sentencing David to death. But the sin of adultery produced loss for David: "he that doeth it destroyeth his own soul... and his reproach shall not be wiped away" (Proverbs 6:32-33).

Even more, because David had "shed blood abundantly" and "made great wars," God denied him his desire to build the House of the Lord, though He approved David's intentions. Despite the sorrow such denial brought to David, God left it to Solomon to build the temple (I Chronicles 22:7-9).

King Uzziah was punished with leprosy until his death, because he disdained God's laws and pridefully appropriated the priest's function of burning incense upon the altar (2 Chronicles 26:16-21).

Jeremiah was an ordained Prophet of the Lord, and yet sustained horrible calamities which he perceived as punishment for his sins: "Wherefore doth a living man complain, a man for the punishment of his sins?" (Lamentations 3:39). Jeremiah understood that God was the cause of his suffering, making him "the man that hath seen affliction by the rod of his wrath" (Lamentations 3:1). Jeremiah recounts that God put him in darkness; visited him with gall and travail; shut out his prayers; brought desolation and bitterness; broke his teeth with gravel stones; and denied Jeremiah peace, prosperity, strength and hope (Lamentations 3:5-18). He lamented that God "hast utterly rejected us; thou art very wroth against us" (Lamentations 5:22).

Other verses teaching that sinful, disobedient servants, as well as rebellious unbelievers are separated from God and will forfeit some or all of God's blessings, include Deuteronomy 5:29, 28:15-68; 2 Samuel 3:39; I Chronicles 22:13; 2 Chronicles 15:7; Job 22:23, 28; Psalms 34:7, 10, 34:15-16, 37:3-5, 58:11, 66;18, 112:103; Proverbs 10:3, 11:18, 6:20, 24:12; Ecclesiastes 5:6, 13-17; Isaiah 1:15; Amos 4:6-9; Habakkuk 3:18; and Nehemiah 8:10.

In every instance, the pain of loss from the harvest of evil quickly eclipsed the transient pleasures of the sin sown: important lessons for our instruction. We can assume, and in David's case we know, that these Old Testament saints prayed for mercy and exemption from penalty, yet their petitions went unanswered (2 Samuel 12:13-18). Jeremiah probably believed he was praying according to God's will, and still his desires were denied.

It is important to identify our disobedience to God's commands, since continuing unrepented sin may bar access to blessings until we have put sin out of our lives. God may withhold blessings strictly to punish unrepentant sinners; to chasten, deter, or rehabilitate sinful conduct; or to motivate self-examination and obedience. When we commit any sin, we are barred by our own act from blessings which might otherwise be received from God, and suffer loss accordingly.

We can put ourselves out of the way where God has stored up blessings in advance for us. We can wander into barren places under our own power and guidance. Sometimes, God does not grant new revelations which might benefit us, because we have consistently and rebelliously ignored His counsel which answered previous prayers. If God has revealed His will for our lives, and illuminated the way we are to go, or directed our attention to certain sins we should repent, yet we persist in not responding, God may not say anything else until His original command is obeyed, and His Lordship re-established.[133] God may use any inducement, including denial of blessings, to draw us to Him, and build Godly character. We would do well to heed His instructions.

Disobedience cuts our supply line even to our true needs, because God cannot condone or reward ongoing, unrepented sin. If we are fortunate, denial of blessings will motivate us to repent our sin and drive us back to God. But when we disobediently fail to do our part, as directed by God, out of idleness or rebellion, we will smother or deflect our blessings, for God cannot validate or bless our slothfulness. Jonah did not enjoy many blessings while he dodged and squirmed to avoid God's clear directions to go to Ninevah. He jeopardized the safety of others while he attempted to flee God's directives (Jonah 1:13-15), and was the author of his own misfortunes along the way.

When we rebel at following God's directions, or refuse to go through a door God has opened, we will retard, and perhaps forfeit the blessings God intends for us. Without a track record of reliability, achievement, and good stewardship, how can a Christian expect to be entrusted with greater responsibility? Jesus says that you will not be set over much until "you have been faithful over a little" (Matthew 25:23; Luke 19:17). Jesus concludes at Luke 16:12: "And if you have not been faithful in that which is another's, who will give you that which is your own?" Only God knows how many blessings and opportunities have been lost because we stubbornly sought to fulfill our will, rather than obediently seek out and comply with God's.

The Prodigal Son was granted his request, and certainly given wide latitude to squander his prosperity and blessings. He experienced vile circumstances which made him appreciate the benefits he already possessed, but had scorned, in his father's house (Luke 15:11-32). It is possible to become so enmeshed in the pursuit or love of the gifts, that we forget the Giver. We may lose our keenness for obedience, loving service, evangelism, or growth in holiness. We may forget to thank God for our blessings, or fail to inquire into what He would have us do with them. Such faithless stewardship will not invite further entrustment of the real riches (Luke 16:11).

Natural man is easily surfeited, and even when God gives us what we pray for, we would eventually be dissatisfied and even complain about it. Ralph Waldo Emerson said that if the stars came out once each year, we would rush to watch them, as we do a comet. But since stars are commonly familiar on a nightly basis, we hardly ever look at them. So it is with human reactions to any blessing from God; we become accustomed to it; and tend to take it for granted unless we are denied it, or focused to appreciate it by an act of will. We must resist being disgruntled over what we do not have, and concentrate instead on being thankful for all that we do have.

SATAN AS THE SOURCE OF EVIL AND PAIN

If there is much suffering which is neither intended nor originated by God, we need not look far for an explanation of evil. Jesus declares He "came that they may have life, and have it abundantly" (John 10:10; and see also, Hebrews 2:14). Jesus came to free the natural man from his bondage and compulsion to sin (Galatians 5:1). Jesus identifies Satan as the thief who comes "only to steal and kill and destroy" (John 10:10; Hebrews 2:14). Jesus further describes Satan as "a murderer from the beginning, and has nothing to do with the truth, because there is no truth in him" (John 8:44).

As a thief and murderer, Satan steals the Word of salvation sown by Jesus before it can take root in those who hear it, in order to abort the New Birth in unsaved men (Mark 4:15). He delays and steals human accomplishment by hindering human endeavor (Daniel 10:12, 13; I Thessalonians 2:18). As a liar, Satan would have us believe that evil and suffering originate with God, rather than with him. If Satan can be successful in depicting God as the initiator of pain, then faithful men will not resist what Satan inflicts, and will not use divine resources to overcome Satan's efforts to immobilize us spiritually and kill our spirit, faith and love for God.

One who believes that God is intentionally harming him may withdraw from, resent, and even hate God, rather than draw near to God with trust and love for Him and His benevolent Providence, beautiful character, and deliverance. If the New Testament emphasizes that Satan is abroad in the world, seeking whom to devour (I Peter 5:8), how could we possible attribute to God the evils identified with Satan? Does it really make sense to believe God orchestrates every suffering to teach some lesson, and uses demons and men as His instruments of evil, even to the point of persuading the drunk driver to take his first drink, lose control of his car, and destroy a group of innocent children standing at the curb? Perhaps we blame Sovereignty as the source of pain and reason for evil because we dislike admitting Satan is the prince of this world, and he is allowed to afflict us, and employ unsaved men to persecute us.

As a thief, Satan seeks to steal our witness for the Gospel or ministry to any needs of others, by removing all incentive to help other sufferers, lest we interfere with God's intent to test and train them in righteousness through the instrument of suffering. We would cease to evangelize because God will save whom He will, regardless of what men do, and this facilitates complacency, inertia, and irresponsibility. If we accept as God's action the evil Satan initiates and does, we may become resigned, passive, fatalistic, and immobilized; forsaking the resources which God has given us to resist and overcome evil. For, if God's sovereignty necessitates His orchestration of every evil, then grumbling is unbelief, and undue concern is a faithless questioning of God's benevolent direction for every life.

If we accept Satan's lie that every suffering is an explicit instrument of God, then we will accept stoically the suffering inflicted by evil, and seek no other blessings, nor expect our prayers for deliverance to be answered. We would fatalistically accept whatever occurs because we believe it to be God's will and irrevocable decision for purposes of deterrence, instruction, or chastening. If all suffering originates with God and is meted out according to an individual's tolerance to bear it, then prayer would be futile. For, God would not answer prayers to remove the suffering until it has served its purpose of strengthening faith and righteousness. We could not pray for deliverance, but only for insights to understand and learn from the experience we are enduring. If a believer understands that every one of his torments is visited by the express intent of God and through agencies God purposes to employ, there would be no rejection of the sufferings not actually sent by God.

Indeed, if God has promised to provide our needs, then he will do so, and there is no reason for anyone to pray in faith for what God has already intended, and chosen to do. We would have no need to plant in faith in order to reap God's promised blessing of prosperity. We would assume that every affliction was sent by God to strengthen our character, and prosper our growth in holiness, and we would unnecessarily occupy much of our time trying to endure nobly, rather than serve or fellowship with the Lord in more useful ways.

As a murderer, Satan seeks to destroy Christian witness and service by creating despondency, discouragement, disillusion, and depression. Satan's tactic is to trouble Christians with worldly concerns and immobilize their service to the Lord by occupying their time with worry and fear of worldly consequences. Satan knows care is numbing and can sink a man into the quagmire of worldly involvement and despair. An equally effective ploy to distract men from spiritual values is catering to their pride and vanity by assisting them in accumulation of worldly success and acclaim. This is a more subtle form of suffering inflicted by Satan, since the worldly man's hardened heart is not even aware of his loss of eternal benefits while he pursues carnality.

Scripture makes it plain that Satan comes against Christians with every resource at his command. Even when we strive to be obedient and holy, or more accurately, _because_ we try to be, Satan inflicts the torment of temptation and persecution upon believers. We dare not neglect to resist his temptations and fiery darts of doubt and despair. Make no mistake that the real enemy of Christians is Satan, who visits tribulation upon believers because they have chosen God. In fact, Jesus teaches that "tribulation or persecution arises on account of the word" (Matthew 13:21), which is clearly something God would not initiate to confound His expressed, revealed purposes in the Word.

Satan operates as an independent, free agent, visiting the oppression of sickness upon the faithful. Acts 10:38 relates that Jesus went about "healing all that were oppressed by the devil." Sickness can become a major preoccupation of the flesh, when passively accepted as a normal part of living in the world. It can take one's mind off spiritual joy in the Lord, and interfere with focusing on Jesus, and living unselfishly and lovingly, for Christ. The Gospels speak of "a man with an unclean spirit" (Mark 1:23 and 5:2); of men besieged directly by Satan. Jesus referred to a woman, "a daughter of Abraham whom Satan bound for eighteen years" (Luke 13:16). Jesus makes it clear the woman's suffering originated with Satan, as evil, and was not God's choice, even though He permitted it.

Jesus healed every sufferer He encountered, and sent His Apostles and disciples out with a commission to heal in the same way. Sickness reflects the world's bondage to Satan, the thief who steals man's health and originates all earthly distress and illness (Luke 11:14-18; Acts 10:38). However, "the reason the Son of God appeared was to destroy the works of the devil" (I John 3:8). Disease, "every sickness, and every plague" was the curse of the Law under the Old Covenant (Deuteronomy 28:58, 61), but Galatians 3:13 reveals that "Christ redeemed us from the curse of the law, having become a curse for us," thereby relieving believers of "every sickness and every plague."

2 Timothy 2:26 speaks of men in "the snare of the devil, after being captured by him to do his will." Satan imprisons and enslaves his own subjects, but wars against the liberated saints. I Peter 5:8-9 exhorts us to "Be sober, be watchful. Your adversary the devil prowls around like a roaring lion, seeking someone to devour. Resist him, firm in your faith." Satan is the thief and poacher who arrogates worldly finances and politics by default. He does it without lawful authority, but with the tacit consent of every generation's unconcern, non-involvement, and ignorance.

Satan may also be responsible for obstructing God's revelations and answers to one's prayers for blessing. When Daniel prayed for an explanation of a vision given by God, God immediately answered the prayer by sending an angel with the answer (Daniel 10:14). Yet, the angel was detained by a demon, the prince of the kingdom of Persia, for three weeks, until Michael, one of the chief princes, came to help the angel (Daniel 10:13). The angel then disclosed he was returning "to fight with the prince of Persia: and when I am gone forth, lo, the prince of Grecia shall come" (Daniel 10:12), but the victory is assured through "Michael your prince" (Daniel 10:21).

Satan, the thief also steals the Word sown by Jesus, to prevent it taking root in hearers. Matthew 13:19 reveals: "When any one hears the word of the kingdom and does not understand it, the evil one comes and snatches away what is sown in his heart." Not only does Satan try to steal the Word received or rooted in a believer's heart when it is not well prepared or tended (Mark 4:16, 18), but he blinds the hearts of unbelievers by stealing the light of the Word out of their hearts (Mark 4:15; 2 Corinthians 4:4; Ephesians 4:17-18), by making them doubt the efficacy of the Word to bear fruit. He tries to provoke one's words to express doubt and evil, and tries to empty man's heart by using worldly distractions to separate him from prayerful communication with God.

Another proof God does not send evil against men is that He provides believers with spiritual resources to resist Satan. We are told to "take the whole armor of God, that you may be able to withstand in the evil day... above all taking the shield of faith, with which you can quench all the flaming darts of the evil one" (Ephesians 6:13, 16). God would not equip us to deflect anything He has sent for our good. Therefore, equipping us to resist Satan proves that God does not use Satan for evil purposes against His children, which would be totally inconsistent with His nature. When we pray the Lord's Prayer, we petition that God "lead us not into temptation, But deliver us from evil" (Matthew 6:13). Jesus would never prescribe a futile prayer for His disciples. Therefore, God's will must always be to keep us from temptation and deliver us from evil.

One may well ask, if God has given us weapons to withstand Satan; to claim Jesus' victory over him and overcome, how can these blessings be reconciled with blind acceptance that every travail comes from God? Why would God give us the Word, guardian angels, the name of Jesus, belief in prayer, God's hedge of protection, God's armor, and promises of deliverance from travails, unless these spiritual instruments served God's purpose to bless believers by overcoming evil.

It is true that sometimes God sends trials to strengthen the resolve of our faith and trust in God, and to inspire reliance on divine spiritual resources. God may, having fortified us with divine defenses, then use Satan to test us by trials and temptations to strengthen our faith by resistance. However, there are specific activities of Satan, which are labeled as evil. They deal with temptations to sin, which only produce misery if we succumb to them. If the activities of Satan were not actual as well as illicit, why would James 4:10 direct us to "Resist the devil and he will flee from you?"

You see, a Born-Again Christian has been given the integrity of a free and sovereign will, and Satan cannot impose his will, usurp authority over your will, or get into your life, unless you stand in your own strength; permit him by your consent to be deceived; or by the carelessness of your words confessing doubt and faithlessness.

In the case of the long-suffering Job, we know that Satan instigated the mischief which produced Job's travails. However, it could not have happened without the permission of God, Who told Satan that everything Job had in the world, except Job's life, was then vulnerable to Satan's power for a time (Job 1:12, 2:6). Significantly, Satan sought with evil intent to embarrass God by exposing the shallowness of human faith, by destroying rather than testing or benefiting Job. If God provoked or initiated the use of Satan as His instrument, we would expect the story to relate such an important detail. But God did not originate Job's trials, although He had to concur in the testing of Job before the trials through Satan could occur.

Why God allowed Job to be tested is never explained to Job or to us. We do know that Old Testament examples are related for our benefit, and Job is an illustration of faithfulness for every Christian who comes under attack from Satan. The story of Job confirms that God is in control, and does work all things for good for those who faithfully trust and love Him. Satan instigated and initiated the evil which befell Job, but it was God Who restored him after the trials.

A spiritually effective Christian who has committed all his efforts to the battle against evil will soon find his service and witness under attack by inimical demonic powers seeking to reduce, dilute, and divert his effectiveness. In self-defense, Satan will contest you when you fight the good fight of faith as a soldier in the Lord's service. If you strive for holiness, he will tempt you. If you witness for Christ, he will come to steal the Word from your audience. If you minister to others lovingly, Satan will try to undercut your base of wealth; rob your peace by sowing divisiveness; and distract those who would support you prayerfully.

This is because one's life, when immersed in the Word, reflects devotion and commitment to God's purposes. Warriors for Jesus, by their love, prayer and witness, seek to win others to Christ and destroy the very foundations of worldliness. Such faithfulness provokes a defensive reaction from the ungodly, who are both attracted to, and uncomfortable around spiritual lives which reflect Jesus' glory and attest to a believer's renunciation of the world and reproach toward evil.

Satan effectively visits torment upon Christians through his posterity, comprised of all natural men not yet born-again spiritually by grace through faith in Christ. Jesus characterizes natural men as "of your father the devil, and your will is to do your father's desires" (John 8:44). King David lamented: "Behold, I was shapen in iniquity; and in sin did my mother conceive me" (Psalm 51:5). Ephesians 2:3 confirms that all men were once carnal, including Christians, who formerly "lived in the passions of our flesh, following the desires of body and mind, and so we were by nature <u>children of wrath, like the rest of mankind</u>."

Satan is "the prince of the power of the air, the spirit that is <u>now at work in the sons of disobedience</u>" (Ephesians 2:2). I John 5:19 says: "the whole world is in the power of the evil one." And the principal weapon Satan uses in spiritual warfare against believers and the Church is to <u>undermine their confidence</u> in the Gospel and the Word.[134] In his quest to distract and oppress disciples, Satan communicates with the sons of disobedience through the air, transmitting, insinuating, and implanting evil thoughts and moods into their minds and attitudes to provoke them to disobedient acts and words, harmful to self and others. James 3:6 describes man's resulting destructive speech as a tongue aflame, "set on fire by hell."

Ephesians 6:12 warns us to use the strength of the Lord and the whole armor of God to stand against the wiles of the devil: "For we are not contending against flesh and blood, but against the principalities, against the powers, against the world rulers of this present darkness, against the spiritual hosts of wickedness in the heavenly places." 2 Corinthians 4:4 says of those who are perishing: "the god of this world has blinded the minds of the unbelievers, to keep them from seeing the light of the gospel in the glory of Christ."

2 Corinthians 10:3-5 identifies the arena of our struggle, and our part in harnessing God's power for victory: "For though we live in the world we are not carrying on a worldly war, for the weapons of our warfare are not worldly but have divine power to destroy strongholds. We destroy arguments and every proud obstacle to the knowledge of God, and take every thought captive to obey Christ, being ready to punish every disobedience." We are to cooperate in self-control, destroying contentiousness and pride because they are obstacles to the knowledge of God. We are to conform our thoughts to the thoughts of Christ. We are to accept and apply reproofs and chastenings when we disobey the commandments of Christ. We must seek to be children in whom God can take pride, while we renounce our own conceits. For, among the instincts in carnal man to which Satan can appeal, is human vanity or self-sufficiency.

The righteousness which a believer exhibits by divine enablement, becomes an example which reproaches the sins of the unsaved, and can make them uneasy, resentful, and hostile. Christians are hated by the world because we do not belong to the world (John 15:18-19). When we follow Jesus, our submission points to the humiliation of the Cross, which is a stumbling block to Israel, and folly to unbelievers (I Corinthians 1:23). Thus, other men are easily incited by Satan to become the worldly instrument of evil in persecuting Christians.

Indeed, there are some Christians who take pride in the suffering they endure, regarding it as a badge of holy service; a scar from their war with evil; or a sign of special involvement with God's work. They reason that Satan attacks only the righteous and active warrior for Jesus. Hence, the absence of suffering indicates you are not part of the Church-militant and are so tepid on behalf of the Lord you are not worthy of Satan's attention. Otherwise, Satan would have contested your success and effectiveness in the Lord's work; his attacks thereby confirming your righteousness.

The question is not 'Why doesn't God do something about evil?" Because He did when He sent Jesus to pay the price for sin. Rather, the question is, Why does God continue to tolerate evil until Jesus returns? God has revealed that He rids Creation of Satan at the end of time (Revelation 20:10), so it is never a question of God's power or ability to defeat Satan and terminate evil whenever He pleases. The fact that God tolerates Satan until the End Time of history suggests that Satan may have some sanctioned part to play in the unfolding sequence of the emergence and completion of Christ's Church.

WHY DOES GOD PERMIT SATAN'S EVIL?

It is easy to obey God in isolation, unchallenged by temptation. But in a fallen world, obedience will be tested by temptations abundantly supplied by Satan. It has always been difficult to understand God's tolerance for Satan's evil operations in the world, which so hinder the obedience and holiness demanded of believers. Certainly, God does not put up with Satan for the same reason He tolerates human freedom: to preserve every opportunity for man freely to respond to God's love. Satan is unredeemable, and God expelled him from Heaven for his corruption of free choice in prideful rebellion. Satan is fore-ordained to be consigned to "the lake of fire and brimstone" for eternity (Revelation 20:10). God's tolerance of Satan has something to do with freedom, but with man's freedom, not Satan's.

Perhaps God tolerates Satan's evil presence on earth to honor Adam's and Eve's choice to believe Satan's lie, rather than God's truth. This may account for how Satan originally obtained dominion over the world God had given to Adam. God may be preserving human freedom as the pre-eminent value in creation by honoring Adam's transfer of allegiance from God to Satan, despite its obvious potential to work harm.

Having once determined that freedom for man is of paramount importance and value in the economy of salvation, God's probity honors His transfer of decision to man, even though it resulted in Adam choosing wrongly to submit to Satan's authority, or in other free men inflicting suffering and persecution on God's people. When Adam and Eve first corrupted freedom; they departed from faith in God and trust in His Word, by believing Satan's lie that they would not die if they ate of the forbidden tree, but "be as gods" (Genesis 3:4). By their faith in Satan's false assurances, Adam and Eve transferred their allegiance from God to Satan, and also assigned to Satan the gift of dominion over the earth which God had given them (Genesis 1:26).

God's gifts to man of freedom and dominion over the earth had been violated and disgraced by Adam's rebellion, pride, and infidelity. Yet God, because of His integrity, honored the gifts to Adam and Adam's transfer of allegiance and rights to Satan. From that time on, Satan has ruled over "all the kingdoms of the world and the glory of them," as he boasted without contradiction, when he offered them to Jesus in exchange for His submission (Matthew 4:8). Adam and Eve's original sin brings every man born afterwards under the rule of Satan until each personally comes willingly under the rule of Christ by the New Birth by grace through faith (John 8:44; Romans 3:9, 8:9).

Some have explained God's tolerance for Satan because he sometimes serves as a divine instrument of punishment; a temporary chastener to effect permanent good; a kind of Heavenly agent or enforcer operating with evil intent outside the pale of goodness, but employed for God's good purposes. The Old Testament relates that evil spirits are sent by the Lord to motivate human actions in scenes directed by God. I Samuel 16:14 tells us that "the Spirit of the Lord departed from Saul, and an evil spirit <u>from the Lord</u> troubled him," leading Saul to seek out a musician, David, who later replaced Saul as King.

Later, I Samuel 19:9-10 explains: "And the evil spirit <u>from the Lord</u> was upon Saul... And Saul sought to smite David even to the wall with the javelin." Saul became insanely jealous of David; was suspicious of his priests and slew them; stripped off his clothes; consulted with the witch of Endor to conjure up the spirit of Samuel; and finally committed suicide (I Samuel 18:11, 19:24, 22:13,19, 28:14, and 31:4). Consequently, the argument has been made that our Sovereign God orchestrated all of Saul's acts in order to facilitate David's ascendancy to the throne as Saul's successor.

Satan remains the principal instigator of human evil. He provoked Eve to question God's directions. And I Chronicles 21:1,7 says: "Satan stood up against Israel, and provoked David to number Israel... And God was displeased with this thing; therefore he smote Israel," because taking a census was a prideful act by David. God's punishment was sure, but He gave David a choice of one of three penalties God could impose against Israel (I Chronicles 21:12).

The Book of Job is clear that Satan, not God, instigated Job's suffering. Yet the same Scripture suggests that Satan cannot approach a believer, nor inflict any satanic harm without God's express permission, since Satan could not attack Job while God had "made an hedge about him, and about his house, and about all that he hath on every side" (Job 1:10). God permitted Job's tormenting by Satan, suggesting His Sovereignty in total control, by replying: "Behold, all that he hath is in thy power" (Job 1:12). Whether God intended the incident for good, or rather turned Satan's evil to good, Satan's activity proved Job's faithfulness; and made Job aware of God's Providence and deliverance. It also demonstrated to Satan and believers through the ages, who draw courage from the instruction of Job's example, that faith and total trust in God's Providential goodness will endure and overcome Satan's attacks.

Jesus told Peter: "behold, Satan demanded to have you, that he might sift you like wheat, but I have prayed for you that your faith may not fail; and when you have turned again, strengthen your brethren" (Luke 22:31). Satan's 'demand' was apparently acceded to by God, since Peter denied Jesus three times (Luke 22:61), before he was strengthened and "turned again" to serve the Lord.

Judas was entered into by Satan to accomplish his betrayal of Jesus (Luke 22:3), and became the instrument to facilitate the salvation of mankind through the death of Jesus, ordained and orchestrated by God. Those who extend God's Sovereignty to intend and manipulate every incident which occurs on earth, will conclude that God chose Judas to betray Jesus, at the instigation of Satan, as a necessary part of God's plan for the salvation of mankind. Others will conclude that God's plan for Redemption was unalterable, but Judas' part in it was unplanned, since God's intelligence could predict that some man would betray Christ to set crucifixion in motion, leading to the Atonement.

Satan was also involved in the wickedness of Ananias and Saphira, for Peter asked Ananias: "why has Satan filled your heart to lie to the Holy Spirit and to keep back part of the proceeds of the land?", upon which Ananias "fell down and died" (Acts 5:3-5). Whether God instigated Satan's assault on Ananias, or turned Satan's independent evil act to good, Satan had a part in precipitating reverential fear in the early church, when "great fear came upon all who heard of it" (Acts 5:5).

Paul, himself, suffered at the hands of a "messenger of Satan... a thorn in the flesh... to harass me, to keep me from being too elated by the abundance of revelations" (2 Corinthians 12:7). We must assume that Satan would delight in any pride felt by Paul, and not do anything to suppress it. Consequently, only God would use a messenger to encourage appropriate humility in Paul. Self-esteem or pride in serving the Lord was prevented from taking root in Paul in this way. It was a reminder to Paul that all power and goodness come from God, who enables us to minister to others, and that divine knowledge is imparted to enhance loving service for others.

There are some instances where backslidden believers are treated like unbelievers, and abandoned to Satan to chasten and correct their blasphemy, unholy living, and dissipated faith; else they will perish, unrepentant, destroyed by the very world they have refused to renounce. At Corinth, Paul condemned a man living with his step-mother; directed the Church to remove him from their midst, and "deliver this man to Satan for the destruction of the flesh, that his spirit may be saved in the day of the Lord Jesus" (I Corinthians 5:5). In similar vein, St. Paul relates that "certain persons have made shipwreck of their faith, among them Hymenaeus and Alexander, whom I have delivered to Satan that they may learn not to blaspheme" (I Timothy 1:19-20). God's protection is removed by putting them out of the Church, allowing Satan's access to their persons, so they might be saved by exposure to the true nature of evil.

In these instances, the evil to which the impenitent sinner clings becomes the instrument by which both chastening and retributive punishment are exacted. Presumably, the dreadful, intense evil a sinner encounters outside the protection of the Church will cause him to see his error, turn him from his evil ways, and accomplish correction.[135]

We know the Lord uses hardship to chasten, shape, train, or test believers in their development of Christ-like spirituality. There are indications God uses Satan to strengthen character by providing resistance to worldly challenges and temptations to accelerate spiritual growth. Thus, we can give thanks in and for every situation, despite its apparent destructiveness, because God has ordained an ultimate benefit of strengthening faith through its use. At Revelation 2:10 Jesus assures the martyrs at Smyrna: "Behold, the devil is about to throw some of you into prison, that you may be tested, and for ten days you will have tribulation. Be faithful unto death, and I will give you the crown of life." Jesus had foreknowledge of Christian tribulation, which He shared with His Church, but allowed it for reasons not disclosed. Revelation 6:11 likewise forecasts coming martyrdom for new believers, throughout the Great Tribulation.

Even if God permits Satan's affliction or men's persecutions, we need not conclude that God intends or orchestrates each incident specifically. Rather, God's concurrence may occur only in an indirect and general sense. He has authorized the system of freedom because of its general value, without authorizing specific evil acts which can result within a network of genuine freedom. The fact that God sometimes uses Satan as His instrument to promote God's purposes, does not mean that God always uses Satan as His agent in everything Satan does.

Moreover, God's occasional use of Satan as an agent to accomplish good results desired by God, does not seem to justify tolerance of Satan's freedom to do real evil. God can alternatively accomplish all instruction through the Holy Spirit, our Inner Guide Who reveals what is right to do. God's Word and Law can teach that sin is failing to do what God prescribes as right (James 4:17). God once deployed the Holy Spirit as the messenger to lead Jesus into the wilderness to undergo temptation by the devil (Matthew 4:1). God has legions of angels at His call, capable of serving as agents of the End Time destruction of the wicked (Revelation 20:7-9), who could readily eliminate or transform evil into good.

Another explanation for evil is that human choice would not be real without some genuine alternative to good, or to choosing God. Satan must have some attraction with which to assert genuine opposition which competes against Heaven's promise. If God and good were the only choice available to man, where is willful choice which so ennobles his response? Without sin and evil, which provide immediate temptation and gratification for the physical senses, there would be nothing to challenge or rival God's spiritual and eternal attraction, and hence, no genuine choice. In any event, since Jesus triumphed completely over Satan on the Cross, and "disarmed the principalities and powers and made a public example of them, triumphing over them"(Colossians 2:15), any Satanic activity since the Cross can only be by God's permission.

Some feel that evil must actually exist in order to be contrasted with good. They argue that man could not appreciate good without first understanding what evil is, and for this reason God allows Satan to exist in history. Philosophers have posited for centuries that we cannot truly appreciate a mountain's height until it is contrasted with its valleys' depths. We cannot fully experience joy until we have first experienced pain. Thomas A□ Kempis observed that sometimes God withdraws Himself so that, in the aftermath of loss' bitterness, we might know the sweetness of His presence when He returns.

Philosophy offers a related human explanation for suffering — that we cannot fully grasp the ideas of good, prosperity, or health, unless we are exposed to contrasting concepts of evil, poverty, and sickness. As light must produce a dark shadow; as 'long' or 'wet' necessitate opposites of 'short' or 'dry'; as a mountain by definition must have valleys, so the idea of good logically requires the idea of evil to be apprehended. The focus of many paintings is illuminated by light, which requires dark shadows, else there would be no contrast. The dark strands of a tapestry exist to highlight and counterbalance the bright colors. The underside has no pattern, but turn the weaving over and a beautiful creation is apparent, invigorated and improved by the dark threads woven in.

Denial and delay of promised blessings can also enhance your eventual enjoyment of them. When you are not very thirsty, a glass of cool water offers slight refreshment, but when you are dehydrated, the same water is deliciously satisfying. So it is with blessings which are withheld for a time, and then served up to a parched spirit who will more deeply appreciate the sweetness of deliverance when it emerges against the bitterness of tribulation and suffering. If we have never know privation, we will never fully appreciate what the harvest means. Indeed, constant worldly contentment would obscure our need for God and cloud our humility, vigilance, and spirituality. We must occasionally experience loss, anxiety, disappointment and darkness to appreciate fully their opposites. The miner working deep underground best appreciates the sunlight. The long-distance runner most appreciates the pause which rests an exhausted body; and the facets of a diamond are best illuminated against a jet black background. Sight is more joyful to a just-cured blind man than to one who has always had vision. The starving man enjoys his bread more than one already surfeited with food. Likewise, the relief of ending pain surpasses routine freedom from pain.

Yet, even if contrast were necessary to appreciate what is good, would not a much smaller sampling serve to stir the memory? After all, one painful session in the dentist's chair suffices for a lifetime to remind us what pain is like. We ought not need daily reminders to appreciate freedom from pain.

Scripture does teach that the Law exists to identify what sin is by way of contrast to how we should live (Romans 7:7-11). Romans 9:22-24 suggests that harsh comparisons exist to highlight goodness, grace and mercy: "What if God, desiring to show his wrath and to make known his power, has endured with much patience the vessels of wrath made for destruction, in order to make known the riches of his glory for the vessels of mercy, which he has prepared beforehand for glory, even us whom he has called?"

However, as evidenced by God's original ordinances for Eden, it is not necessary to have contrasting evil in order to know good. All Adam and Eve needed originally was to depend upon God's guidance, and consult God for revelation of His will. Then, they would inerrantly know and do good, without any reference to evil. The knowledge of the distinction between good and evil is ironically what God withheld from Adam, and what destroyed man's blissful existence in the Garden. We can anticipate Heaven's blessings beyond our wildest imaginations, by recollecting the good we have experienced on earth, rather than the evil we have encountered. A monastic in isolation from the world, does not need cancer or any other worldly affliction to turn his attention toward God. He is capable of learning by God's instruction through the Holy Spirit and the Word, and he can sustain his endeavors by praying for God's enablement. We may understand Heaven as a place free from pain, but that creates no appreciation of blessings in a positive sense. Even the world recognizes, as Plato observed in the Republic, that the pleasures of taste and smell could exist and be appreciated independently of any prior awareness of their absence.

CHAPTER 15

GOD'S CREATIVE USES OF SUFFERING

"Those whom I love, I reprove and chasten."

–Revelation 3:19

"Call upon me in the day of trouble: I will deliver thee, and thou shalt glorify me."
–Psalm 50:15

In the world's view, suffering is evil, and the occurrence of suffering is regarded as objective proof of one's infidelity or disobedience to God, or simply accounts one as unlucky or star-crossed. Even to Christians, withholding of blessings and abundance is regarded as punishment, and afflictions seem neither light, nor momentary, but heavy, intrusive, and constant. However, a Christian understands that suffering which is intended, orchestrated, designed, or initiated by God can never be evil, but is a blessing which works spiritual change and draws us closer to God. God does not author or encourage evil, but does use suffering as His transforming agency, instrument, and corridor for blessings to train, correct, and grow in holiness. God uses trials and tests to perfect and steadfasten our faith, love and obedience.

Affliction so employed is instructive and chastening, intended by God to work a change in man's will, and induce correction in behavior here to accomplish our approach to perfection Hereafter. His remonstrances by way of affliction re-direct us to right thinking and living, and deter repetition of spiritually harmful conduct. Trials and testings sent by God become opportunities and motivations to obey and overcome. They prod us into paths of righteousness to help us find the hard way that leads to life.

In God's hierarchy of values, developing the character of Christ is a higher purpose of earthly life than the absence of pain or the presence of worldly pleasures. Relieving our momentary distress is a lesser priority with God than achieving Godly character, fellowship with Him, harmony with His purposes, and all the benefits attached to spiritual maturity. Thus, God lovingly disciplines His children to accomplish correction in spiritual conduct.

God's seventh way by which man eases suffering is to learn quickly the lessons of instruction, chastisement, and correction encapsulated in the adversity God has sent or allowed in the exercise of His Sovereign will. The sooner we recognize, change, and rectify our spiritual poverty and renounce our dark, sinful ways, the sooner we forsake the worldly circumstances which have pushed us into distress. The sooner we rush boldly to the throne of grace to confess, repent, and turn from sin, the sooner we claim and benefit from forgiveness, cleansing, and the creative reproofs of instruction with which we have been blessed. The sooner we accept and obey God's will, with a loving and faithful response, the sooner the joy of His presence displaces our discomfort. The sooner we discern, accept, and apply the creative alliance of man's obedience with God's Sovereignty, and sever ourselves from worldly attachments, the sooner we will avoid the rigors of chastisement and correction.

Even if pain is inherent in the process of reforming character to the image of Christ, the sooner we cooperate in the change, the sooner the pain of transformation is abated. Even if suffering is vengeful or retributive, rather than corrective or deterrent in nature, our responsive obedience, repentance, and cooperation in changing will best express our petition for surcease.

Still, there are some sorrows which are not set right in this world, even though God offers comfort and relief. The death of a little child is irreversible in the earth, and can be endured only if it helps focus our attention on some Heavenly explanation, assurance, or ultimate reconciliation. We speak here only of afflictions originating with God, not those of a malfunctioning, decaying world system which inflicts incurable arthritis, cancer, dystrophy, AIDS, or sudden destruction. These evils can be transformed to good results, and as God works them for good we can delight in their occurrence, not because of intrinsic good, but because we expect to encounter God's deliverance emerging through the process.

Nevertheless, the creative uses of suffering by God to accomplish and facilitate the growth and development of His children, reveal that suffering is not necessarily an evil instrument, but can promote a different and superior blessing of increased faith, holiness and spiritual perfection. I Peter 5:10, KJV notes how God's grace uses sufferings, as they: "after... ye have suffered a while, make you perfect, stablish, strengthen, settle you." (See also, Hebrews 2:10). God makes us rich in eternal and spiritual blessings, which may replace, and are of far greater value than transient and worldly advantages.

Once we see that genuine evil instigated by Satan and other men is always regulated and transformed by God to help believers develop Christ-like character and purity, then we can "count it all joy" when we meet various trials, because the testing of our faith produces steadfastness, which makes us "perfect and complete, lacking in nothing" (James 1:2-4). Our faith is re-directed into an assurance that when trouble first strikes, God turns suffering to our account, regardless of its origins, by transforming it to the good of "an inheritance which is imperishable, undefiled, and unfading, kept in Heaven for you" (I Peter 1:4).

Suffering intended or orchestrated by God for our chastisement, chastening, and instruction, is also consistent with God's benevolence because it addresses our ultimate happiness and abundant life, rather than our immediate gratification of fleshly desires. We can focus on the higher blessing and prosperity of fashioning character for eternity, and receiving the fruit of the Holy Spirit, even when we are not enjoying health or wealth during our suffering.

Even where there are natural disasters sent by God, or punishments intentionally and retributively meted out by God to destroy inveterate, impenitent sinners, God uses their examples as warnings for our good, to instruct and motivate our obedient submission. In all these cases, and even in the inherent hardships in the process of spiritual growth, suffering is more readily eased by our response of faithful obedience, as we heed God's warning instructions and therapeutic directives.

SUFFERING REVEALS GOD'S SOVEREIGN OMNIPOTENCE

God can use affliction and natural disasters as occasions to reveal Himself, and remind both faithful and unfaithful men of His almighty, providential Sovereignty. He uses trials, tests, and suffering both to make us aware of our spiritual progress as well as our persistent shortcomings which require further remediation. He may use suffering to divert a believer's attention from worldly, transient preoccupations back to spiritual, eternal realities in Him. He may use pain to reveal the need for spiritual change, and drive us back to Him for healing and strengthened character. Even natural disasters can be used to demonstrate human frailty before a fearsome God, and prompt conversion by alerting sinners to an impending Day of Judgment, which is both personal and universal.

God has revealed that He would prefer to teach us by the instruction of His Word, and the conviction of the Holy Spirit, without the use of suffering, as long as we heed His Word. Deuteronomy 4:30-31 teaches: "When thou art in tribulation... if thou turn to the Lord thy God, and shall be obedient unto his voice... he will not forsake thee." See also, Proverbs 8:1, and 15:19. Psalm 25:9 adds: "The meek will he guide in judgment: and the meek will he teach his way." (See also, Psalms 32:8, 73:24; Isaiah 30:21).

God's first call to correction is by knowledge, wisdom, conviction and persuasion, but if we fail to respond, His next loving measure may be by the chastening of suffering. Hosea 5:15 predicts the fate of a disobedient Israel, which God would tear as a lion, then depart from their iniquity, and use affliction to turn them: "I will go and return to my place, till they acknowledge their offence, and seek my face: in their affliction they will seek me early." God indicates He requires three things before He returns in mercy to Israel: There must be a sense of guilt and repentance; there must be an awareness of man's misery in the wretchedness of sin and self-sufficiency; and there must be an awareness of their need for God to help them, as affliction drives them to seek God quickly for mercy and healing. See also, Leviticus 26:40-42; Psalm 42: 6, 9; and Amos 4:6, which reveals God's use of deprivation to turn men back to Him: "And I also have given you... want of bread in all your places; yet have ye not returned unto me, saith the Lord."

God raised Pharaoh up, and then exposed his hardened heart (Exodus 4:21), as he afflicted Israel and refused to acknowledge God. God used Pharaoh's own inclinations to build to a climax and prove God's total power over Egypt, so that unbelievers seeing Pharaoh's down-fall, would honor God and know that He is the Lord, "And they did so" (Exodus 14:4). Indeed, Rahab the Harlot received and aided Joshua and the spies in Jericho because she had heard how God delivered Israel from Pharaoh and parted the Red Sea (Joshua 2:9-10). Rahab helped preserve and advance Israel because she was drawn to God through knowledge of His love, power, faithfulness, and mercy toward His Chosen People (Romans 9:4).

God first sent plagues upon Egypt as "my signs and my wonders in the land of Egypt," and promised to remove them if Pharaoh let the people go, "to the end thou mayest know that I am the Lord in the midst of the earth" (Exodus 7:3, 8:22). If Pharaoh had let God's people go, God would have extended grace to Egypt, and Pharaoh's obedience would have accomplished God's purpose of redeeming Israel in the Promised Land to God's glory. However, Pharaoh persisted in dishonoring God, provoking evil plagues of frogs, flies, locusts and darkness which afflicted Egypt (Exodus, Chapters 7-10). God's purpose was to demonstrate His singular sovereignty, glory, and power; to draw unbelievers to Him for deliverance. Romans

9:17, quoting Exodus 9:16, says: "For the Scripture says to Pharaoh, 'I have raised you up for the very purpose of showing my power in you, so that my name may be proclaimed in all the earth.' So then he has mercy upon whomever he wills, and he hardens the heart of whomever he wills." See also, 2 Thessalonians 2:11-12.

God did not make Pharaoh's heart hard, but simply exposed its pre-disposition to be rebellious and disobedient. We know that the same sun hardens clay even as it melts wax. The properties of the sun are impartial and consistent: it is the composition of the substance upon which it acts that determines hardness or softness. Thus, God uses circumstances, as the sun, to impact men to reveal their true nature. Clay which is already predisposed to rebellion will continue to be hardened when exposed to testing, but impressionable, tender-hearted wax will be melted by the contact and respond submissively to God.

The instrumentalities God used on Pharaoh simply brought out the latent character of the substance upon which they acted. Thus, when Scripture relates that "God hardened Pharaoh's heart" (Exodus 7:3; 8:19; 9:12, 34, 35; 10:27), He simply provided the catalyst which exposed Pharaoh's already-developed tendency to rebel and disobey God. Exodus 8:32 affirms Pharaoh's own, free act: "And when Pharaoh saw the rain and hail... he sinned yet more, and hardened his heart, he and his servants" (See also, 2 Corinthians 2:15). As the divine twisting or wringing of Pharaoh's heart revealed the wicked sentiments it contained, God withheld His grace and softening influence where it was unwelcome. God caused Pharaoh's heart to harden only in the sense His mercy excites contempt, and His threat of judgment provokes resistance, in one who has declared rebellion. When Pharaoh rejected the spiritual light he had been given, he consigned himself to the darkness he preferred. Had he responded to the light he had, he would have been given more light and revelation.

A proud Nebuchadnezzar focused on his own power in creating Babylon the great, and lost his kingdom. He lived with the beasts of the field for seven years, and was restored when he acknowledged God as the source of all power; that "the most High ruleth in the kingdom of men, and giveth it to whomsoever he will" (Daniel 5:27-32). One purpose of suffering is to make proud men aware of their beastly level of existence, until they are eventually driven back to God.

God provides circumstances of testing, but man provides his reaction. God neither tempts man, nor provokes man to evil. Romans 1:24-25 speaks of rebellious wicked men who chose to dishonor God and became futile in their thinking. Their minds became darkened so that they worshipped idols; "Therefore, God gave them up in the lust of their hearts to impurity... because they exchanged the truth about God for a lie and worshipped and served the creature rather than the Creator." God did not intend their wickedness, but gave them up because of their willful choice to rebel against Him. They already belonged to Satan and served him, so God simply left them in their chosen predicament with its dire consequences.

Jesus adds yet another dimension to the Christian's affirmative reactions to suffering. We are to acknowledge the reality of calamities and natural disasters, and use them as an occasion for giving testimony. Jesus warns his disciples of a time of wars, earthquakes, famines, pestilences, terrors, great signs from heaven, and persecutions of His people, and concludes: "This will be a time for you to bear testimony" (Luke 21:13). We are not simply to escape trouble, deny its reality in the surrounding world, or merely bear it as the will of God. We are to be thankful for the trouble, and use the calamity as an opportunity to glorify God as the eternal answer to suffering. A Christian learns to use any suffering to promote the purposes of God's

Kingdom with the unsaved.[136] Disasters give us an opportunity for loving service and comfort to help victims overcome tragedy's consequences, and thereby demonstrate God's working all things for good, even natural catastrophes.

Jesus turned the Cross into a testimony of God's benevolent intent to save repentant sinners by grace through faith in Jesus. Jesus used His Crucifixion as an occasion to demonstrate God's love and forgiveness of even those who had been the instruments of His death. Likewise, Stephen turned his stoning into a lesson in forgiveness as he prayed for God's mercy toward his murderers (Acts 7:60). Paul turned his thorn in the flesh into an opportunity to glory in infirmity, because such weakness made room for God's strength to take over and accomplish far more than Paul could have done in his own power.

Catastrophes are an alert to every witness and bystander to be ready to die because he could be, but for God's grace, the victim of the next calamity. Being spared does not mean a survivor is better or more deserving than a victim. God's mercy in sparing him is to give yet another opportunity to face eternal Judgment and repent. Perhaps he will be alerted to the suddenness of death, and appreciate the urgent need for present action to save himself and others. Perhaps this reminder of vulnerability and mortality will be a reminder that death comes to all, sooner or later.

Calamities are a clarion call to repentance, a graphic lesson on the brevity of life and a last opportunity to respond to God's salvation. Pain directs our attention to God's judgment and eventual punishment for sin, and warns us of the Day of Judgment. Suffering reminds us that man is responsible and answerable to a God who punishes rebellion and disobedience. Natural disasters do not happen only to people who are more sinful than others, but tend to remind all sinners that without God, worse is yet to come to indifferent, impenitent sinners. For, all are headed toward eternal death, unless they are covered by the Blood of Jesus.

Suffering and disaster thus can be used as barriers to deflect sinners from the path to Hell. A sinner recognizes he is not entitled to defer his decision about Christ to some future time, indefinitely. There is no certainty or security about existence, when any life can be snuffed out in a moment, without warning. The demonstrated fragility of life gives a new urgency and immediacy to personal decision about salvation in Christ.

At the same time, the Church is struck by the reality that witnessing cannot be deferred indefinitely. The unsaved souls we do not reach in loving evangelism are doomed to spend eternity in Hell apart from God, unless His grace somehow delivers them through some other instrument. Praise God He has provided a merciful way of escape for sinners by grace through faith in Jesus, and allowed believers to present the Word of salvation to the unsaved. Thus, disasters can be a reminder that nature has been corrupted by man's sin, and indiscriminately visits pain and suffering on believers as well as evildoers, so that the unsaved recognize their urgent need of a Saviour.[137]

Defects in nature, cataclysm, and diseases are warnings of malfunction in creation which shout for man to seek reconciliation with God. Disease and disasters are God's warning that sin, rebellion and disobedience ruin a man's life. Calamity may be sent or used by a wise Providence to arouse a wicked and indifferent world to embrace God's righteousness and power, which is made perfect in weakness. A natural disaster is always a reminder to put our values and priorities in proper order and start appreciating what is really important: people, not possessions; eternal things, not temporal or worldly. Jesus remind us of what is important: "Heaven and earth will pass away, but my words will not pass away" (Matthew 24:35).

Even natural disorders which are not intended by God, can drive an afflicted man and those around him to the healing power of the Great Physician, and to God's Word for confirmation that His love, support, and strength are dependable to overcome the world's suffering. The great natural disasters and monumental tragedies can be so overpowering in their impact on human resources, that they make us aware of our inadequacy and reliance upon God. They force us to turn to God and throw ourselves on His mercy because we recognize our total inability to solve them. God may not cause the problem in the sense of initiating it specifically for human instruction, but He does use mass calamities and natural catastrophes to remind us He alone is big enough to solve them.

Natural disaster, like any pain, can show man his pettiness, ignorance, weakness, and insignificance, and direct him to a sovereign, all-powerful God, Who is also infallible in His workings and judgments. Without these cataclysms, man could easily fancy he is competently managing the world, and never recognize his need for God. Man's utter helplessness in the face of natural forces drives him to the God Who created and controls them.

On the other hand, there are instances where defections from belief in God are attributable to the random harm and evil inflicted by natural disasters upon both good and evil men in a world corrupted by sin. They cause us to ponder why God permits nature to produce harmful phenomena, even if He does not orchestrate them.

If God spared us the results of natural disaster, would we turn to Him in gratitude more often? America has enjoyed prodigious blessings and been spared much of the famine, disease, and destruction occurring in most of the world. Yet, despite our abundance, our ease has made us self-reliant, sinful, and indifferent, rather than turned us toward God. Even when God supplied Israel's every need in the wilderness exodus from Egypt, the nation scorned God's provision of manna from Heaven, and longed for the Egyptian meat and condiments they no longer had, in an egregious show of ingratitude.

Consider that if God rushed to correct man's mistakes in his use of freedom just before they produced tragic results, He would not be credited with the rescue. Man would think he is in control, does not need God, and that he is exempt from the judgment of God.[138] God has given men His Word for their guidance and instruction in righteous, peaceful, and satisfying life, and lovingly warned of harmful consequences from disobedience. If man chooses to ignore God's admonition, then the only way man can learn from his mistakes is if God lets their immediate consequences ensue. Then, man will repent his mistakes, seek God's grace and deliverance, and thereafter seek to shun disobedience.

SUFFERING REVEALS GOD'S LOVE AND DELIVERANCE

God's Sovereign omnipotence is equally evident in His deliverance of man from afflictions. St. Paul queries at Romans 9:22-23: 'What if God, desiring to show his wrath and to make known his power, has endured with much patience the vessels of wrath made for destruction, in order to make known the riches of his glory for the vessels of mercy, which he has prepared beforehand for glory?"

There are some instances in Scripture where adversity serves as an instrument to glorify God and exhibit His love by His deliverance from suffering. At John 9:3, in response to a query whether being born blind was evidence of sin, Jesus answers: "it was not that this man sinned, or his parents, but that the works of God might be made manifest in him." Jesus then proceeded to heal the man's blindness, and when the man proclaimed the miracle, God's love and power were demonstrated to unbelievers by the man's testimony. God was glorified by the healing He worked in the blind man through Jesus.

Two days before Lazarus was raised from the dead, Jesus had been informed of his illness, and said: "This illness is not unto death; it is for the glory of God, so that the Son of God may be glorified by means of it" (John 11:4). He told His disciples: "Lazarus is dead: and for your sake I am glad that I was not there, so that you may believe" (John 11:14-15). Jesus then said to Martha, the sister of Lazarus: "Did I not tell you that if you would believe you would see the glory of God?" (John 11:40). Jesus' purpose was not to heal a sick man, but to raise a dead one.[139]

By arriving after death, Jesus worked a far greater miracle than healing Lazarus' sickness. Jesus thanked God publicly, before the resurrection event, for hearing and answering His prayer: "on account of the people standing by, that they may believe that thou didst send me" (John 11:42). God was the only explanation for the miracle, and His greatness was revealed, to His and Jesus' glory. Hence, when Jesus raised Lazarus, "Many of the Jews therefore, who had come with Mary and had seen what he did, believed in him" (John 11:45).

Jesus also healed a paralytic lowered on a pallet through the roof, "that you may know that the Son of man has authority on earth to forgive sins" (Mark 2:10). John 9:3 also relates that Jesus was given healing power to confirm He was the Messiah invested with divine power to forgive sin (See also, 2 Kings 5:15, and I Corinthians 1:27-30). Indeed, Jesus' ministry included forgiving sins, and healing was the divine confirmation of His power to cleanse and free sinners. God's mercy was evident as it was extended in healing, as well as by enabling endurance to bear the affliction.

A believer is assured, while executing the Great Commission and witnessing to the Gospel, that the Word will be accompanied by signs of the sick healed and demons cast out (Mark 16:17-18). These signs confirm the divine origins of the Gospel message, and thereby inspire belief in the Word of salvation. In these instances where God turns suffering to good by alleviating it, men are drawn to Him. It is not that God's ego needs to be fed by man's praise or gratitude, but that God uses miracles to confirm the authenticity of the Gospel message, and these inspire our worship.

When a Christian glorifies God, it is not to cater to His vanity or need for recognition, but so the world can understand He is the source of all comfort and endurance. Likewise, when a Christian has emerged from affliction, sustained by the comfort of the Lord, God has given him a testimony, and means of confirming faith. Without affliction and the personal knowledge and comfort to endure until delivered, one could not testify about the Lord's goodness with the same authenticity of triumphant experience. Thank God, He still heals the afflicted person who turns to Him for deliverance from spiritual and physical ills.

Elymas the magician wrongly tried to dissuade the proconsul, Sergius Paulus from the faith, by disputing the Word of God. For his evildoing, he was temporarily blinded (Acts 13:8, 11). As a result of this, the "proconsul believed, when he saw what had occurred" (Acts 13:12). King Herod was smote by an angel of the Lord because he accepted his subjects' worship as a god, and "did not give God the glory... But the word of God grew and multiplied" (Acts 12:23-24). As a consequence of the punishments which befell Herod and Elymas, God's glory and power were demonstrated, and belief was fostered in observers, resulting in greater good.

If we become preoccupied with ourselves or the world, God can use suffering to remind us of His presence and trustworthiness, if only we would perceive them. The storm which continues to rage is used by God to demonstrate He is still Sovereign in control, that He provides His deliverance and loving kindness if we would only depend on Him (Joshua 23:14; I Kings 8:56; and Psalm 107:28). Ecclesiastes 7:14 teaches: "in the day of prosperity be joyful, but in the day of adversity consider: God also hath set the one over against the other, to the end that man should find nothing after him."

Any suffering or disaster can divert our attention to God, make His Word and presence more meaningful, and produce a closer fellowship, far greater than in untroubled times. Suffering reveals how God gives of Himself; how He can be entrusted with our pain and perplexity; how He yearns to embrace us as His children. We draw closer to God in friendship as we recognize His love in chastening us, His grace in teaching us, and His blessing in turning every travail to our advantage. Pain, when abated, makes us aware of the grace of relief, and all other blessings from God. It makes us appreciate all we have been blessed with, and still have, and keenly reminds us of the good God has bestowed in the past without pain.

The warmest time of fellowship is when we are illuminated by the Holy Spirit and enfolded in the mind of God through His Word. The destruction of Sodom was catastrophic by any measure. God confronted and challenged Abraham with the knowledge He intended to destroy Sodom. He allowed Abraham to experience the grace of God, and to intercede for the righteous in Sodom (Genesis 19:17-33). The crisis led to knowledge of the loving-kindness of Him Whose friendship we would seek. Abraham was moved to communicate with God, and elicit His promise that if there were fifty righteous persons within the city, God would not destroy Sodom. Abraham then posited the presence of forty-five, forty, and as few as ten righteous men in the city, and each time God replied He would not destroy Sodom if that number of righteous persons could be found in the city.

God demonstrated a side of His character to Abraham in this encounter, which might not otherwise have been revealed, and he rescued Lot and his family from the city. By involving Abraham in a dire situation, God presented an opportunity for Abraham to learn about, and embrace Him. God longs for this interaction with His children, and to have their prayers invite, and perhaps even elicit, His interventions.

Pressure building up will either come between us and God or push us closer to Him. Our travails should always turn us in humble reverence toward God. Hudson Taylor observed that the amount of worldly pressure was of no significance unless we somehow let it come between us and God. Otherwise, no matter how much pressure was applied, it serves beneficially to press us closer to the Lord.[140] Even adverse winds can be harnessed in the sails to push you closer to God, rather than blow you away from His safe haven.

There are times I prayed with fervent heart to grow closer to the Lord. Sometimes He answered me with pain or distress which drove me to Him for surcease and comfort. And there, in sweet surrender to His Sovereign will, I found perfect peace in His care, and new awareness and appreciation of His suffering for my sins.

God will use adversity to draw us closer to Him for the special blessing of fellowship. Suffering summons and recalls to us the need for God's presence and companionship, to enjoy the beauty, integrity, and intellect of His character, immeasurably worthy of worship and glorification. God's painful proddings to return to Him are because He wants to embrace you as His child. He values your friendship, companionship, and intimacy in a personal relationship with

Him. Jesus offers friendship to His disciples at John 15:14-16: "You are my friends if you do what I command you. No longer do I call you servants, for the servant does not know what his master is doing: but I have called you friends, for all that I have heard from my Father I have made known to you. You did not choose me, but I chose you and appointed you that you should go and bear fruit."

Sometimes, even our gifts and blessings may be withdrawn to return our focus to the Giver. If we have regressed from seeking Him to rendering service, our focus may have slipped to trying to serve God through activity, rather than simply longing for Him and trying to find Him. We may have sought manifestations of speaking in tongues, being slain in the Spirit, or the inner experience of power, joy, or peace, rather than hunger for God, to see and know Him.[141] God may use suffering to demonstrate that what is missing in our lives is the presence of God, rather than His gifts.

Suffering brings us into a tension with God, so that we are prodded to encounter Him and discover the depth and dimensions of His grace and love. As the parent who prompts a baby to start walking, God will initiate challenge and hardships so we seek Him out, discover, and bond with Him in our dependency. God's grace begins with us where we are, and then draws us where He wants us to be, in the best position for fellowship and communion with Him. Like Abram, we must 'Get thee out of thy country... unto a land that I will shew thee" (Genesis 12:1). We may need to be provoked to move cooperatively toward God's direction, in total faith, awaiting the outcome of the promise of reconciliation.

Even when we think we are successfully in the midst of God's favor, enjoying His Providence, He may be beckoning us to a more congenial venue, where He may be encountered more readily, in a closer relationship. We may be so pre-occupied with serving Him or studying what the Word says about Him, or what He says in the Word, that we have never known Him as the Life. We may never have enjoyed Him as the total object of our affections, or experienced His friendship.

We may be thrown into darkness so we will resume or intensify our search for the light. We may be broken and weakened so we will turn to the strength and comfort of Christ's companionship. God may hide from our sight (Job 23:3, 8-9; Psalm 104:29; Isaiah 45:15) to drive us in our despair to seek Him out and walk with Him. God may forcefully remove our distractions from faith and shatter our attachments to other idols, so we can concentrate our attention exclusively on Him. God provided manna in the wilderness one day at a time, to remind the Israelites their survival depended upon trusting in God's deliverance (Exodus 16:16-21).

SUFFERING TEACHES US GOD IS TRUSTWORTHY

God uses suffering as an occasion to strengthen hope and trust in Him. We are to rejoice in suffering because it produces endurance, enabled by God, which produces experience and proof of God's presence, which produces hope, "and hope does not disappoint us because God's love has been poured into our hearts through the Holy Spirit which has been given to us" (Romans 5:5). The hope which results from affliction is encouraged by God's pouring out of His love into our hearts. The Holy Spirit confirms the reality of God's love, and gives assurance that hope in God, His grace and glory is not misplaced, and will not fail. God's love is our guaranty that we will be delivered from suffering in His good time.

In the Old Testament, Deuteronomy 33:27 puts it: "The eternal God is thy refuge, and underneath are the everlasting arms." Psalm 145:14 says: "The Lord upholdeth all that fall, and raiseth up all those that be bowed down." Trust is pleasing to God, according to Psalm 147:11: "The Lord taketh pleasure in them that fear him, in those that hope in his mercy." Psalm 42:5 proclaims: "Hope in God, for I shall again praise Him for the help of His presence."

Jesus' faith extended to every aspect of His ministry, as He trusted God for all things. Before He raised Lazarus from the dead, Jesus confessed God would do it, and thanked God for hearing Him and responding, so He could act in total confidence and reliance on God (John 11:41).

Jesus, as always, provides our supreme example of meekly trusting God: "when he suffered, he did not threaten; but he trusted to him who judges justly" (I Peter 2:23). Jesus' example teaches us to submit to suffering orchestrated by God, as He did, in total reliance on God's righteousness. Jesus' last words from the Cross were: "Father, into thy hands I commit my spirit!" (Luke 23:46).

Faith acknowledges that God's wisdom, omniscience, omnipotence, and ability to perform His will are trustworthy because in His love and benevolence God has already given us Jesus. Hence we can be confident that "He who did not spare his own son but gave him up for us all, will he not also give us all things with him?" (Romans 8:32). If we belong to Jesus, He will give us all things we need, because God has already given us His promise of "all things" at Calvary when He "did not spare his own son." Conversely, if God withholds something we desire, it follows it was not anything we really need, or He would bestow it.

Moreover, we can be assured God's blessings are always His best, since He gives us "all things with him" (Romans 8:32), and we know Jesus enjoys only the best of Heaven. We receive because of grace, not our worth, so we can continue to approach the throne of grace with confidence. We can endure in faith, and finish the race, because we cannot be separated from the love of Christ by anything (Romans 8;38-39). Moreover, as a token of forgiveness from birth, God continues to bless us, as all men, despite His foreknowledge we will sin after we are blessed, and even after we are saved.

When we cannot understand any purpose in suffering or pain, we need to trust God's benevolence to keep us eternally safe with Him. God has promised us victory, and faithful trust knows that every moment brings us closer to the winner's circle. "Thanks be to God, who in Christ always leads us in triumph" (2 Corinthians 2:14). God promises at 2 Corinthians 4:17 that "this slight momentary affliction is preparing for us an eternal weight of glory beyond all comparison."

Psalm 55:22 says: "Cast your burden upon the Lord, and he shall sustain thee: he shall never suffer the righteous to be moved." I Peter 5:7 teaches: "Cast all your anxieties on him, for he cares about you." I Peter 5:10 assures us that if we will resist the devil, firm in faith, then "after you have suffered a little while, the God of all grace, who has called you to his eternal glory in Christ, will himself restore, establish, and strengthen you." God created us and can be trusted to sustain and deliver us. I Peter 4:19 urges: "let those who suffer according to God's will do right and entrust their souls to a faithful creator."

Until we realize how much we need Him, how completely we depend upon Him for every good and perfect gift, God's presence may be unapparent. Yet, Psalm 22:24 tells us that "he hath not despised nor abhorred the affliction of the afflicted; neither hath he hid his face from him; but when he cried unto him, he heard." Nothing "in all creation, will be able to separate us from the love of God in Christ Jesus our Lord" (Romans 8:39). He is always present, always watching over us, though sometimes unseen. He is Immanuel, "God with us." We are reminded to pray to God whenever we are in need or besieged by misfortune (James 5:13-14).

Suffering evokes our faith that Jesus' words are true: "I am the way, and the truth, and the life; no one comes to the Father, but by me" (John 14:16); "apart from me you can do nothing" (John 15:5); and that "every perfect gift is from above" (James 1:16). Like John the Baptist, we must welcome the death of self involved in the magnification of Jesus: "He must increase, but I must decrease: (John 3:30). Like St. Paul, we must acknowledge: "to live is Christ, and to die is gain" (Philippians 1:21).

C. S. Lewis observed that periods of prosperity are great campaign weather for the devil. We tend to place too much emphasis on success and personal affairs when we enjoy health and prosperity, while neglecting to center our lives around God. God alone is the true source of spiritual fulfillment for believers. When we ignore God in our complacency and self-sufficiency, we leave Him no alternative but to seize our attention by removing the sources of our worldly contentment. If we will not pay attention to God in the midst of plenty, He may introduce us to poverty so we will recognize our need for Him and eternal values. If we squander good health in pursuit of worldly pleasures rather than God's work, we may be disabled for a season to turn us back to God and higher spiritual life. As Psalm 55:19 says: "Because they have no changes, therefore they fear not God."

SUFFERING DRIVES US TO DEPEND ON GOD

There will be times God uses suffering constructively to arrest our attention, curb our self-reliance, and force us to recognize our need to depend upon Him, and not on our own strength or power. An unbeliever who does not know Jesus as His personal Lord and Saviour is without access to the Kingdom of God and its prodigious blessings. So we might expect God to use, initiate, or allow difficulties in unsaved lives to reveal man's inadequacy, convict him of sin, and persuade him to turn to God for his own good. Even Christians can lean to their own understanding and recklessly attempt to function under their own power, losing the spiritual battle without understanding that victory is won only by the power of God.

Jesus sets the standard of dependent submission to God for His Disciples: "The Son can do nothing of His own accord, but only what He sees the Father doing... I can do nothing on my own authority... I seek not my own will but the will of Him Who sent me" (John 5:19, 30).

St. Paul experienced suffering to the point he and his companions were "utterly, unbearably crushed that we despaired of life itself. Why we felt we had received the sentence of death; but that was to make us rely not on ourselves, but on God who raises the dead" (2 Corinthians 1:8-9). At 2 Corinthians 12:9-10 St. Paul records God's comfort: "he said to me, 'my grace is sufficient for you, for my power is made perfect in weakness'... I am content with weaknesses, insults, hardships, persecutions, and calamities; for when I am weak, then I am strong." We must wait for God's good time and pleasure to receive blessings, but in the meantime we must pray, ask, seek, and knock as Jesus directs (Luke 11:9-10). God calls us to "pray always and everywhere" (Luke 11:18; I Timothy 2:8), and we pray, not to advise Him of our needs, but to remind us of our total reliance upon Him. He already knows our need before we do, and before we articulate it in prayer. He is in sovereign control. Yet, we are commanded to pray and are advised: "You do not have, because you do not ask" (James 4:2). Thus, prayer for deliverance from suffering is our acknowledgement that only God can assuage our predicaments.

God may send a storm so we will realize that the anchor of our soul is secure only on the Rock.[142] A potent and triumphant faith is a blessing to be derived from suffering. Hebrews 6:13-19 recalls God's promise to Abraham: "Surely I will bless you and multiply you... So when God desired to show more convincingly to the heirs of the promise the unchangeable character of his purpose... we who have fled for refuge might have strong encouragement to seize the hope set before us. We have this as a sure and steadfast anchor of the soul."

God may test us with suffering to prove that we are willing to relinquish control over the situation to Him, because He really knows best and regulates our affairs better than we. Disappointment by unanswered prayer may be God's appointment to bring us to Him in total surrender to His rule. God truly desires what is best for us according to His perfect will, and seeks to bring us into conformance with His will. God knows that without Him we focus on the problems and obstacles. Like the spies sent to Canaan, we forget God and give an evil report, fearing giants, and regarding ourselves as grasshoppers in their sight (Numbers 13:32-33). We need David's victorious, positive mentality when confronting Goliath; that nothing can withstand the living God (I Samuel 17:26).

Proceeding in our own strength can breed fear, anxiety, diffidence, and even rebellion against God. The children of Israel turned their backs on God, murmured against Moses and Aaron, prepared to stone Moses and Joshua, and then, when they were ready to believe God and obey Him, it was too late to take the Land of Canaan. The battle was lost, and they were returned to the wilderness (Numbers 14:40-45). In any endeavor, even when we are committed to spiritual warfare and running the race, fatigue will be a constant reminder that strength to persevere is supplied only by God.[143]

God may use and allow suffering resulting from sins to draw us back to Him and His protective arms. God may allow a believer to suffer the consequences of wrong choices and rebellious actions until he learns to heed God's voice and withdraw from the folly of error. In this way, the evil of suffering accomplishes a higher good of focusing attention on the need for change; for deeper trust in God; for wisdom and strength to submit to God's direction; and for spiritual growth for fellowship and communion with God. Often, suffering is God's path to know Him better, and rely fully on Him.

Sometimes, God allows us to withdraw from Him, and fall into the suffering of our own stubbornness, that we might come to recognize the paucity and failure of our self-governance, and appreciate the sweetness of His presence and the blessing of His resources. His love allows even distorted freedom to teach us true happiness when we are driven to find it in His protection, law, and order. Only His patience can conquer human rebellion, restore ruined lives, and empower rejoicing.

Pains, like natural disasters which expose human frailty, remind us that we are fragile and mortal, and perfection and immortality must be found outside man.[144] Pain reminds us that we need God's strength to endure and become faithful and fruitful (Psalms 78:34, 119:67-75; Job 33:19-20; Hosea 5;15; 2 Corinthians 1:5-10). We will find God wherever we are driven by suffering. When the great tribulation of the end time comes, Jesus advises that "those who are in Judea flee to the mountains" (Matthew 24:16). Adversity drives us from the valleys to the mountain-top, where we can look toward God and more clearly see His grace and love.

However, trust is much more difficult to sustain in the midst of denial, withholding, privation, and apparent abandonment by God. Waiting for God requires complete trust in His promises, and no longer relying on our own devices, but emptying our spirit of self-determination so we can be filled with God's direction. We leave all our concern to God, and cast the care on Jesus, relying on His power alone. We trust in God's goodness and wisdom for deliverance, since the Scriptures give no assurance of immunity from suffering. God chooses to develop faith, rather than give unconditional promises of exemption from pain; to see us <u>through</u> the storm, rather than around it.

Only trials reveal that we can and must rely upon God, rather than ourselves; that we must flee to the fuller discovery of God's abounding grace, healing, and forgiveness. There is no way we can be sure of God until He is put to the test and delivers us from trial. It is easy to trust God while He is blessing abundantly. Often, God may sustain baby Christians with extraordinary blessings and insulate them from overwhelming tests, to encourage and fortify their incipient faith. But eventually the moment of mature response must occur.

The curious fact about God's tests is that we appear at the outset to be taking them on our own, without any help from God. Then, the initial reliance upon, and failure of, our own devices will invariably highlight the need for God's power and wisdom. The realization of our inadequacy is often intended to draw us to God as we recognize our complete dependency upon Him. Even after God prepares, enables, and encourages us for testing, there will be times He apparently abandons a sufferer, despite His unquestioned power to assert His Sovereign will, intending to evoke man's reliance on God. This was the experience of a suffering David, who inquired of God: "How long, O Lord? Will you forget me forever? How long will you hide your face from me?" (Psalm 13:1; and see Psalm 77:7-8).

The apparent abandonment by God only heightens our anguish and despair amidst torment. Job endured all his losses, pain, and suffering, until he lost the sense of God's presence, and only then fell into despair and anguish (Job 23:9). God dried up the brook from which Elijah drank, and then provided nourishment through an impoverished widow, so that Elijah would appreciate his dependency on God, rather than the brook (I Kings 17:7-16). King Hezekiah was blessed abundantly, and was then tested in his faith: "God left him, to try him, that he might know all that was in his heart" (2 Chronicles 32:31).

Even Jesus, our exemplar in all things, cried out to God from the Cross: "My God, my God, why hast thou forsaken me?" (Mark 15:34). Earlier, Jesus had watched unseen, as the disciples struggled against strong winds and high waves. When they cried out in terror, He comforted them, entered the boat, and the wind ceased (Mark 6:48-51). Jesus did not intervene immediately, although He was aware of their needs but He finally came to their aid and quelled the storm when they cried out to Him.

God may keep us waiting until we learn patience, and realize He is our only salvation; that we are truly dependent upon Him for all things; and that He is more than sufficient to meet every need we may have. Natural man is so perverse he may disdain or despise an easy grace which is too readily available. God may use absence to make the sinner's heart grow fonder for the presence and deliverance which comes only from God.

Adversity likewise re-directs our gaze upon the Lord when we suffer loss of prosperity, fortune, esteem, or worldly honor. Earthly blessings may be too great a distraction against Godly values. God says at Jeremiah 22:21: "I Spoke unto thee in thy prosperity; but thou saidst, I will not hear... that thou obeyedst not my voice." Only as we lose these things are we driven to the reliable, precious friendship of Jesus. We may have poverty in the world, but He is the true riches. By losing earthly advantage we are driven to seek our entire portion, in God, Himself.[145]

Bereavement, although not necessarily initiated by God, may be used by Him to restore eternal values in the lives of the faithful. Sorrow over a departed loved one creates an emptiness that drives us to seek fulfillment in the Lord. The desolation of mourning leaves us thirsting for the Water of Life, as God makes room for Himself in hearts that had been engorged with other desires and engrossed in other loves. The death of an unsaved friend turns our thoughts to eternal purposes, and the death of a saved one makes us see that Heaven is the real family home to which our treasures have been transferred, and where reside those with whom we will spend eternity by the grace of God.

God has endowed America with such prosperity that we can easily take it for granted and expect its automatic continuance. Worse, one might easily and wrongly forget that God "giveth thee power to get wealth," and not "My power and the might of mine hand" (Deuteronomy 8:17-18).

God may allow His children to abuse their freedom and pursue what they think is the better way, until they experience loss and suffering and appreciate it is easier and better to conform faithfully to His way. Sometimes experiencing the folly of our errors is the best way to learn how to avoid them next time. The Father of the Prodigal Son allowed him freedom to roam the alien world, squander his inheritance, and endure degradation and oppression, until this abject misery eventually drove him back to his Father's house, filled with remorse and right resolve.

Believers must learn to surrender any hope of independently accomplishing objectives by our own power, and entrust it to God, alone, "For while we live we are always being given up to death for Jesus' sake, so that the life of Jesus may be manifested in our mortal flesh" (2 Corinthians 4:11). As the Jews suffering in the wilderness, we must appreciate that the manna God provides on a daily basis is to heighten our awareness of total dependence upon Him for our needs.

Indeed, a great deal of suffering is endured because we foolishly neglect turning in faith to Christ for guidance and relief, entrusting all to His care. We should recall the hymn which summons us back to Jesus: "What a friend we have in Jesus, All our sins and griefs to bear!... Oh what peace we often forfeit, Oh what needless pain we bear, All because we do not carry, everything to God in prayer!" Faith in God gives us the wisdom to entrust all to his divine providence, and the courage to be what God calls us to be as Christians.[146]

Pain, disease and deformity make us see that we are not capable of managing our lives without God. When adversity drives us to the depths of despair, we will find God waiting patiently at the foundation of all things to lift us back into the sunlight and fresh air. God may allow us to suffer from our own folly, and may even delay in answering prayer, so that when He does respond, we will have exhausted all human contrivances and there can be no question our deliverance is by His hands.

When human burdens accumulate to the point they are unbearable, a man will recognize his own inadequacy and need for God's grace and power. The evils that befall us provoke us to listen for the voice of God, and to seek in Him the recovery of health, the safety of loved ones, deliverance from tribulation, provision of material sufficiency, wisdom, benevolence, comfort, and every good and perfect gift which comes from above.

There will be a moment of desperation, a nadir of despair, when a man relinquishes control; when worldly concerns are so overwhelming and beyond human capacity or determination, that he abandons any attempts or responsibility for their solution. That is the moment we mortals turn to the eternal Sovereign of the universe, especially if we know Him as Our Father, Whom we can boldly approach for grace.

Painful circumstances knock down the walls of pride and independence we erect; and demolish misplaced confidence in our own ability to handle a situation. We come to realize that our real power comes from Christ dwelling and growing within us, and we will understand that God is all we have, yet in Him we have all. There is no yieldedness whatever in self-governance. The 'self-made' person is a prime candidate to learn reliance on God by transformation worked through trials. Without suffering we would never feel the need to entrust our cares to the Lord. And we can never learn the lesson that God can be trusted, unless we first entrust the matter to Him. We will never know God does not saw off the limb of faith on which we sit, until we have trustingly crawled out on that limb.[147]

There is nothing like a little suffering and misery to break our spirit, crush pride, admit defeat, expose the poverty of our own resources, and bring us to total reliance on God as the only possible answer to our problems. When we reach the depths of despair and get rid of self-reliance, we are poor in spirit, but we are also blessed because we now appreciate our need for God and His willingness to meet our every need. Matthew 5:3 proclaims: "Blessed are the poor in spirit, for theirs is the kingdom of heaven." Pride and vanity keep us from crying out for help or seeking the prayerful intercessions of our fellow believers in the Body of Christ. However, humility and poverty in spirit free us to seek the ministrations of our Great Physician. We may need the helpful prod of humility to surrender control of our lives to God. Sometimes, we need to be put on our backs so that our gaze will be re-directed upwards.

It may become necessary for God to strip you of all self-reliance and pride by removing the strength of your will and the comfort of your possessions. As you are denied this last refuge, even evidence of God's presence may vanish with it. Every avenue of escape or rescue seems barricaded, and the longer you struggle, the weaker you become, until in the complete surrender of defenselessness, you embrace the Lord as your only refuge and deliverance. Until you come to realize that all is to be found in God, you may lose every blessing, develop all sorts of weakness, become powerless to protect yourself, lose the ability to pray, find no rest or sanctuary in your own spirit, believe God to be angry, and find temptations on every hand.[148]

We may have to sink in the slough of despond so that we can touch the bedrock of divine comfort. God may bring us to the dead end of our wisdom, power, alternatives, inventiveness, dreams, and ability to cope, so that we know not where to go, which way to turn, or what to do, except it be God.

Sometimes we may believe we are patiently waiting for God's timing, when in fact we have become slothful and lazy, so that God uses discomfort to alert us to our need for renewed zeal and vigor. If we have become smug in the complacency of our spiritual accomplishments, vain, arrogant, or self-satisfied in faithful service and good works, then God may withdraw His sustaining power and blessings, to drive us from self-sufficiency back to His arms and rest. If we have embraced primarily the approval of fellow Christians, or sought assurance in temples or schools, and neglected Almighty God, then God may withdraw their nurture to revive our dependence on Him. God may use suffering to create an environment in which we are gradually compelled to face our inability to continue by human strength. God may authorize suffering to challenge us to new levels of experience in divine fellowship.

By dissolving, dismantling, and removing your own self, you will make room for the growth of God's life within you, that His strength may be made perfect in your weakness. Your image takes on His form and stature, as you succumb to, and are overcome by, God's loving kindness. His life flourishes by your death to self. You are able to sense God's love and presence because you have become inured and insensitive to suffering and all other worldly distractions. His glorious light has dissolved the dark recesses of your worldly habitat. His sovereignty has replaced your willfulness, and His Providence has supplanted your spiritual poverty.

By focusing on Jesus, you reclaim His eternal perspective against the transience and insignificance of any worldly trouble which has besieged you.

God uses suffering to strip us of our artificial supports, to make us aware He is all we need. We may secretly find comfort and delight in fame, wealth, financial security, intellectual achievement, or popular acclaim, but these are not contributors to spiritual survival. Joy, security, and life, itself, are found in God alone. When suffering and privation persist, we are driven to seek and find God to obtain His healing love and comfort. 2 Corinthians 4:7 says we are afflicted, perplexed, persecuted, and struck down in the flesh "to show that the transcendent power belongs to God and not to us." No matter how much we may want to divest ourselves of worldly attachments, we cannot appreciate how strongly we cling to objects, until they are removed from us by the wise hand of God. Powerlessness becomes pleasant, rather than painful, when we are full of the life and power of the Lord. We are in union with Him, wanting to think what He thinks, desire what He desires, and act as He acts. The sufferings you have endured become cherished mementos of what God is accomplishing in your life. You are attached to, and anchored in, those travails of blessedness which over time have crowded out worldliness, and allowed God to rush in. His presence reaffirms that nothing can ever overcome you, because God has promised always to provide a way of endurance, escape, victory, and the security of His love.

Occasionally, we will need the training of trials to remind us of our impotence, and the need to depend absolutely upon God if we are to be made suitable for His intended habitations. Some men may need to fall before they realize they stand only by depending upon God for all things. Some men need to experience the degradation of inadequacy and failure before they are driven to turn back to God for more abundant life. Spiritual maturity is a process of experiencing trials and overcoming them by God's power.

Just as the atom has to be smashed before its power can be released, re-directed, and controlled, so a Christian may need to be broken by the death of self, to be fully resurrected in the power of Christ. Affliction destroys self-reliance and re-directs attention to God for deliverance. It brings man back to reality and awareness of his total dependence on God. Trials force us to seek and find God in prayer and in His Word. Man is not very teachable nor receptive to God's call while entertaining delusions of self-sufficiency or preoccupied with worldly dalliances.

By suffering, we learn to rely upon God's faithfulness, deliverance, and protection for victory over the world. Humility and teachableness come from abandoning pride and self-reliance. We learn to entrust the success of every venture to Him, rather than our own stratagem, connivance, or contrivance. We secure ourselves in His rest and peace. When we wait for

Him, and endure until relieved, we receive staying power by focusing on Him rather than ourselves.

Trials and tests may be permitted to remind us that we are not self-sufficient, but totally dependent upon God's love and mercy. Affliction provokes self-examination to expose our own sinfulness and God's greatness. It reminds us to submit to God's purposes regardless of the consequences, to trust God, and surrender to His will, even though we may not understand the purpose of our suffering.[149]

Without sorrow and mourning, we would never look for and experience the comfort and encouragement of God. God uses evil, once it touches us, to show He can destroy sin and eliminate evil. "Blessed are those who mourn, for they shall be comforted" (Matthew 5:4). At first blush, this sounds like putting your hand in the fire so you can enjoy the relief of withdrawal from the pain. But in point of fact, discovering God and His power to sustain you opens doors to permanent fellowship with Him after you have been comforted. Moreover, mourning is a reality of the world and mortality. The promise of God's loving comfort is the blessing of the Holy Spirit coming to inspire you with new courage, enthusiasm for life, and selfless service to others who suffer and who need your comfort, to the glory of God. "He shall give you another Comforter, that he may abide with you for ever" (John 14:16, KJV).

Without persecution, we could never know the comfort of Jesus' presence, or experience the full envelopment of His love. "Blessed are those who are persecuted for righteousness' sake, for theirs is the kingdom of heaven" (Matthew 5:10). Jesus has overcome the world, and persecution for His sake will stimulate the joy of knowing Christ is risen; make us more than conquerors; and verify our resurrection in Him. Persecution becomes an honor by sharing the same persecution as our Lord, though not to the same degree.

The man who has achieved worldly success by human wisdom and energy is a prime candidate needing to learn how to trust in God. For, his own resources will eventually fail him as victims at the hands of time. God can get his attention and begin to deal with him when the world completely loses its attraction and becomes unsatisfying and even negatively repulsive. And when a man puts the Kingdom of God first, God promises to restore worldly things, but then they will be in proper perspective, subordinate to the blessings of the Kingdom.

We would not hesitate to rely on God if we remembered He is willing and desires to guide us in all His ways, and have us depend upon Him for everything. Your doubt may not be about God's power and benevolence, but about your unworthiness to be blessed, your unfitness to serve the Lord, or be used by Him in any way. You may feel guilty when you repeatedly and constantly turn to Him for every need. Yet that is His very plan: to free His children from furnishing their own needs, so they may concentrate on His will and work. This is consistent with Jesus' instruction to "pray always" (Luke 18:1), so God's involvement, concern, and underlying power are never forgotten, but always sought.

We need to remember that God would not tell us to entrust our suffering to Jesus, if He could not be trusted to control and deliver us from it. "Cast all your anxieties on him, for he cares for you" (I Peter 5:7). Jesus will take the shattered and broken remnants of life, and restore them to wholeness and more abundance. Psalm 57:1 declares: "my soul trusteth in thee: yes in the shadow of thy wings will I make my refuge, until these calamities be overpast." When the five loaves and two fish of the boy were turned over to Jesus, He prayed over them, blessed them, and transformed them into enough to feed five thousand people, with leftovers to distribute (Mark 6:38-44). When we turn what we have over to Jesus, we can trust Him to intercede with God, and bless it unto good and multiplied abundance.

Our faith may be at a very low level because we have never practiced using it in total reliance on God. Then we need to take a leap of faith, entrust a matter completely to God, and experience a spiritual adventure with Him. You may entrust the development of a specific character trait to God. You may offer up a sacrifice and forbearance of something you cherish in the world; so that your faith in action becomes the substance of things hoped for. You may give to the Lord's work beyond your usual generosity. In every case you are entrusting the matter completely to God, and will share the joy of mastery and progress with Him as He works the change or growth in you. You can ask for the means to give something to someone else in need, and watch as God provides it in some unique way so that the impress of His hand is unmistakable. Offerings and tithes are a great way of sharing activity with God, as He directs your good and faithful stewardship.

With trust, we will not expect to know all of God or His ways, but to accept the results He allows, confident He works all things for good. We sincerely wish that God's will be done, not our own. We enjoy the peace that comes with awareness that God is in control, and genuinely loves us.

Trials soften us so we may receive the transforming impressions of God's grace. We dare not harden our hearts, lest we repel God's chastening. God delivers His faithful, and His direction of our lives is so clear through the prism of retrospection that it is readily identified and resembles no other imprint. We may even discover that while we did not receive what we prayed for, we are more blessed by what we have received and learned to desire according to God's will.

DELIVERANCE STRENGTHENS AND DEVELOPS FAITH IN GOD

God may use suffering to divert our attention to Him, and embrace the opportunity to recognize Him as Deliverer. Each deliverance confirms His Sovereign, Almighty power, and gives us direct knowledge of His love, grace and goodness, which strengthens our trust in Him for our care and deliverance on future occasions. If relief is not immediately forthcoming, faith is strengthened by the enabling God provides to endure suffering, along with the eventual extrication by way of escape. Whenever we see other saints enduring their afflictions by the Holy Spirit's gift or fruit of faith, our own faith is fortified.

Tests or trials which involve suffering will inherently develop faith as they stimulate resistance, by which the sinews of faith grow. Pain points out our need to remedy deficiencies in holiness. Trials are sometimes necessary as an instrument to develop faith and character by providing force and resistance to spur spiritual growth. When we are aware that suffering provokes increase in faith or spiritual character, we can hasten the process by our willing collaboration. When a test reveals the genuineness of our faith as we withstand some torment or affliction, our faith grows in the knowledge of God's deliverance by enabling patient endurance, which is productive of virtue, knowledge, self-control, steadfastness, godliness, brotherly affection, and love (2 Peter 1:5-7). Finally, pain is a warning, when our faith wavers or fails, that we need to cooperate in receiving this fruit of the Holy Spirit, so that our endurance may be supernaturally strengthened.

Suffering is the pressure which breaks the patterns of old ways, produces discontent with familiar comforts, and pushes backsliders on to rehabilitation and mature development. Parents do not permit their child to lie in the crib forever, but prod the baby into maturity, using challenges and triumphs over obstacles as stepping stones to advance in virtue and achievement. Discomfort alerts us to the existence and availability of new grace, love, and resources which we may use, but which we might not otherwise find without being motivated by need.

Without the challenge of difficulty which provokes resistance and marshalling of resources, we would not evoke the noble virtues of heroism, courage, selflessness, benevolence, perseverance, or sympathy. Without a battle, there can be no splendid triumph or conquest over hardships. The life of ease is what prompts degeneration of body, mind, and spirit, while use and exercise tones and develops muscle. Moral good can emerge from worldly evil. This does not justify evil which originates in free beings, but explains how God uses it to produce good for believers. God trains and equips us by adversity to grow in righteousness. He shows His love for us, since He will not let us continue in sin, and allow us to forfeit the blessings of obedience here or Hereafter.

When we protect a child from doing difficult things, we deny him the development of strength and resourcefulness to meet the challenges of life. If we shield him from problems, he will never build up the spiritual strength and confidence to withstand suffering. Daily confrontations fit us for the more demanding intrusions of life's trials. Then, adversity gives opportunity to react with courage and dignity, for we have had occasion to procure and develop our gallantry, valor, and the encouragement of others.

A fractured bone when properly knit together, is stronger than it originally was at the point of breaking. A tree growing on the side of a mountain, grows strong in extending its roots, as it resists the mighty winds which beset exposed altitudes. A tree on arid soil has of necessity sent out long and deep roots over the years, and is conditioned or adapted to survive the droughts of nature. Hard times strengthen our toughness for the crises of life. This does not explain why the hard times come, but how God works them for good in strengthening us.

Only after suffering can we appreciate that we endured tribulation by God's grace, and were faithful through the ordeal; that the sustained exercise of faith overcame the world. Only then is the assurance of faith vindicated from the vantage point of deliverance, and we are absolutely positive of God's total dependability. Only then do we have verification of His faithfulness, on which to base our reliance during subsequent encounters with suffering. There is no substitute for the experience that proves God is trustworthy. You will best learn to live by faith by successfully having lived by faith.

Only when suffering has finished, can we perceive that God truly limited the nature of our temptation and the intensity of our suffering, always providing a way of escape. By hindsight, we see that we were able to endure by prayer and faith, claiming the promises of His Word, and invoking the name of Jesus. Above all, we understand we were able to endure and overcome by the merciful and gracious power of God, the Sovereign ruler of the universe. God never gave any explanation of suffering to Job, but instead made him aware of God's Sovereign righteousness, and of Job's acute need for God's mercy. Job's attitude is what changed as he was overwhelmed by God's greatness and goodness, which forestalled any questions men might have about their suffering. Once Job appreciated God's magnificent providence, he could entrust any problem or suffering to God's care.[150]

The familiar principle of sowing and reaping, applied to deliverance from suffering, confirms that the greater your reliance upon God, the greater and more remarkable your deliverance. If you sow one hundred percent faithful reliance upon God, He will deliver you one hundred percent. For God's grace is solely from Him, and His favor follows man's faith. Without faith it is impossible to please Him. And there is no way to trust God except to turn every care over to Him in faith, and wait patiently and confidently for His deliverance, whether it be in the realm of prosperity, health, or any other blessing.

If you will simply trust Him, you too can recognize and delight in the Lord's operations, rather than your own contrivances. This trust is a volitional act which chooses to depend upon a loving, all-powerful Father. Even though we may lack understanding, we confidently trust He knows what He is doing, and acts benignly.

Our deliverance from suffering confirms the foolishness of focusing on the extent of our suffering, when we should concentrate on the source and strength of our faith. After we have emerged from trials, we can appreciate how God has kept His promises, prepared our way, picked us up after we fell; worked the situation for our advantage; and produced holiness out of suffering; that our Sovereign Father accomplishes everything He intends, independently of His creature. Just as we do not resent God revealing our sins so we can turn from them in repentance, so we no longer resent God's constructive criticism expressed in suffering, which produces spiritual improvement, and a closeness to God superior to any worldly benefits.

Indeed, after God has crushed us, and reduced us to total dependence upon Him, He invariably reveals that what we originally desired is of little eternal importance. We are given wisdom to apprehend that His process to transform us to Christ-likeness was perfectly appropriate. He literally transforms our desires to conform to His, and we willingly rejoice in the knowledge that we now prefer something vastly superior to the worldly benefit which we once desired. Resentment of God's methods dissolves because we can apprehend the rightness of God's working, and are absolutely convinced that what God did has promoted spiritual blessing.

At the end of such experiences, having drawn closer to God, we can actually perceive the growth God has worked, advancing us from glory to glory. Sometimes, we will not recognize how God's hand has moved, shaped, and directed suffering until the ordeal is over, and faith has progressed to actual deliverance and fulfillment. Only then can we see how involved God has been, and how much closer we have drawn to God.

We come to understand that even in the midst of suffering, trial, or tribulation, we are enjoying our promised blessings, only at a higher level, and we can be confident God will work affliction for good for all those who love Him and follow His way.

When we understand God's uses of suffering, we will see that His chastening may bring momentary pain to hasten our mature discipleship, and we will wish only to cooperate in devoting God's gifts of time, treasure, and talent to His purposes. When we understand that God's benevolence in suffering is divinely ordained to modify behavior, and call our attention to the need for change, we can respond to God properly, rather than resent Him or recoil from His discipline. Suffering can give us light to examine our conduct in terms of God's will for us, as well as heat to burn off the dross of un-Christ-like character in us.

Whenever God's grace provides deliverance, a result of fulfilled faith in Him is the strengthening of faith for the next occasion of suffering. Whenever we are freed from affliction, our exercise of faith is strengthened to expect God will provide blessings according to the promise of His Word. Then, when inevitable affliction recurs, we will look for God's empowerment to endure suffering patiently, confident He still cares for us and will re-mold suffering into good, even as He delivers us. Our faith focuses on the spiritual, eternal blessings which will result from trials and disciplines. Our faith desires and expects grace, even at the expense of worldly benefits, for we depend on God's eventual deliverance and perfecting, even though His presence may not be obvious. Mature faith has grown in faithful submission and obedience, despite loss of worldly blessings, out of love for God's perfect plan and purposes.

Growth then fits believers for advanced spiritual benefits, and appreciation of God's presence. By making us grow, suffering increases our ability to praise, honor, and glorify God, which will enhance our service to the Lord throughout eternity. Through suffering, "the genuineness of your faith, more precious than gold which though perishable is tested by fire, may redound to praise and glory and honor at the revelation of Jesus Christ" (I Peter 1:7). 2 Corinthians 4:17 says: "this slight momentary affliction is preparing for us an eternal weight of glory beyond all comparison." Jesus relates His own suffering to His glory: "Was it not necessary that the Christ should suffer these things and enter into his glory?" (Luke 24:26).

Jesus' suffering makes possible our entry into glory according to Hebrews 2:10: "For it was fitting that he, for whom and by whom all things exist, in bringing many sons to glory, should make the pioneer of their salvation perfect through suffering." See also, Hebrews 5:8-9. Jesus' path to glory was suffering, and His example of endurance shows us how to respond to suffering (I Peter 2:21).

We see that the Author and Pioneer of our faith uses suffering to perfect and finish our faith. What appears to be an evil of persecution, pain, or humiliation is only incidental to a benevolent divine purpose which ultimately produces the fullness of blessings and joy in the Lord. We can see that discipline is spiritual training, mercifully administered by a loving Father to hone His children's techniques of defense, as well as offense, to initiate attacks against evil: to accomplish a change in attitude and skills to shape a new, Christ-like character so that one desires to pursue good, both to please God, and because one recognizes his own advantage in doing so.

Jesus teaches us not to rejoice "that the spirits are subject to you; but rejoice that your names are written in heaven" (Luke 10:20). Our salvation is that which causes our rejoicing, and for which we give thanksgiving. You rejoice in the certainty God will reveal His presence, make known His intent for you, and bless you beyond all expectation. You give thanks because you are sure God will always show up in your behalf at His appointed time; that He will use every misfortune, whether originating with Him or initiated by others, to achieve some special blessing in your life.

Proverbs 30:5 bases reliant trust in God on His Word: "every word of God is pure: he is a shield unto them that put their trust in him." Faith originally comes by hearing the Word of God in Scripture, and relying upon the express promise of God to deliver us from death and suffering (Romans 10:17; I Peter 1:7). Faith is strengthened as a fruit of the Spirit, as He recalls to memory the words of Jesus which we have heard. Then, faith for the future is marvelously strengthened by actual deliverance, and recollection of each previous instance when God has kept His promise and actually provided deliverance from suffering according to His Word. Suffering not only reveals and proves our trust in God, but confirms God's trustworthiness. By experience, a believer learns and enforces his trust in God, just as a trapeze artist develops assurance that his partner will catch him in mid-air, once he has leaped out in faith. Past reliability increases confidence that a fall to destruction will be intercepted and averted by the secure grasp of his partner's hands.

Equipped with the remembrance of God's trustworthiness, ensuing trials will quickly bring us back to God for His power and protection, as experience reminds us to seek His caring involvement. In this way, faith in God is developed and called forth to advantage by successive difficulties. The spiritual fruit of faith develops by a process, often beginning with suffering. For, we cannot develop trusting faith without circumstances which create conditions through which trust in God is elicited.

Romans 5:3-5 teaches that we can rejoice in suffering because it produces endurance, which produces character, which in turn produces hope, "and hope does not disappoint us, because God's love has been poured into our hearts through the Holy Spirit." Suffering drives disciples to hope, and we learn that our hope is not disappointed because we are made aware of God's grace, and re-introduced to God's love and promised deliverance. Without earlier trials, God's constancy could not have been demonstrated, and His promise of deliverance could not be confirmed as trustworthy. Thus, suffering from which we have been delivered, fortifies our trust for the next round of adversity.

Just as faith for any blessing is strengthened by performance, faith is amplified whenever God proves His Word is trustworthy by performing it. Our hope in God is increased as successive trials confirm the experience that God's grace and power actually sustain believers in the realm of suffering. Jesus compared faith to a seed which grows, and this comparison helps us patiently to endure suffering with undiminished faith God will eventually deliver us. No farmer plants a seed and expects it to come forth immediately. Nor does he dig it up repeatedly to see how it is progressing while hidden from view, for he knows it requires time to grow and bear fruit — in this case the fruit of deliverance from suffering and the restoration of blessings. Our faith in God will be unshakeable as long as we envision the seed we have planted as continuing to grow steadily, albeit imperceptibly.

By experience, we can learn that when we are denied our prayers, but relinquish our own desires and yield to God's superior Providence and knowledge, we are suffused with the peace of God. We understand that when we surrender control of our lives to God we will begin to feel His love, and recognize all the other blessings He provides us; past, present, and future.[151] When we release care and tension to God, He will replace them with the peace and comfort of resting content in Him. Man has no part in the result of faith, except to confess and rely upon God's promises and His ability to fulfill them. True faith necessarily exalts God, as a believer senses and appreciates that all accomplishment comes by the grace of God.

God's faithful performance of His Word heightens our perception that God is always right and to be relied upon, even when His ways are beyond comprehension. We have experiential confidence that any pain God allows to reach us will do us no permanent harm, but will be worked for our good, even though it may hurt temporarily. We are certain that God's control will be administered lovingly and in a way it can be endured. He may not have initiated or intended our pain, but His Providence will use it to work our good.

Going through trials teaches us that God alone is totally trustworthy, and the only One upon Whom we can rely; that God's operations justify our staying the course, even when His timetable does not coincide with our anticipations. We have confidence that some suffering is necessary or useful to God in perfecting our sanctification.

God's dependability allows our insight that trust in God's perfect love relieves us of anxiety; dissolves stress; dispels nervousness; and casts out fear over outcomes. There is no way we can be certain that God is too loving to hurt us, and too wise to err in His chastening, unless we are exposed to trials. Trials teach us that God alone is totally trustworthy, and the only One upon Whom we can rely. They affirm God's paternal love and grace, as we recognize in retrospect that He uses the tools of affliction to shape and fashion Godly character in us.

We emerge from suffering with proof God answers our faith in Him; that He has enabled steadfastness and spiritual growth through the experience of suffering; and that we have been divinely empowered to endure suffering by God's grace. We have received proof that nothing in all creation can separate us from the love of God in Christ. We have realized that God's Word does not fail; that His promises are met, but always in His way and according to His purposes, and these are mighty causes for Christian rejoicing.[152]

We will understand that trusting means to put the matter in God's hands for safekeeping. I entrust myself to Him, with the assurance He will enable, fulfill, and bless according to the integrity of His promises. I have learned to overcome fear on the basis of who He is, rather than what I am. I know that He is in me, and I in Him. I have learned to focus on Jesus, the solution, rather than concentrate on worldly causes of the problem. I can appreciate that when Peter focused on Jesus, he walked on water, but when worldly winds and waves distracted him, he started sinking (Matthew 14:29-31). Because of God's faithfulness in the past, we can confidently reject Satan's lies accusing God of withholding blessings, and identify Satan as the instigator of evil. We do not abandon prayer or fatalistically and passively accept all affliction, but do everything in our power to learn the lessons of chastisement to reform our character, and avoid them in the future. Only then, will we accept with resignation what we cannot change by prayer.

The perspective of our faith shifts from asking for things in the world to total reliance that God's sovereignty has already solved the problem of our suffering. We are confident our faith will be rewarded, and that God's dominion over Creation implies a purpose in allowing pain, which He may not originate, but will always convert to our advantage.

The Bible may not reveal ready answers to withstand every crisis, nor give explicit directions for solving every problem we encounter. Our travails give us an opportunity to stretch our faith, and trust in God, until He gives us divine enlightenment and understanding. God does not always give us escape or evasion from trials, but His strength and comfort to endure them by faith.

Suffering enables us to trust God to do <u>whatever</u> He chooses to accomplish His purposes, regardless of sacrifice or cost to us. It fosters willing reliance upon His constancy in love and goodness, which can work only good for His children. And when we submit unconditionally to God, we make ourselves fully available to Him for achieving His good purposes in our lives, despite the worldly loss.

Jesus made it clear His Kingdom was not of this world, and His eternal concern was with eliminating human pride and sin, more than bringing physical healing and prosperity. He brought faith and spirituality to make believers like Christ, more than he brought solutions for worldly problems of poverty, disease, or political oppression.

We can have peace in the faith that even suffering unintended by God is worth the final result of what God produces, because all difficulties are useful tools in the hands of God. Our faith acknowledges that God's forbearance in allowing evil to remain in the world is consistent with his benevolence in remarkably turning it to our benefit. Our portion is spiritual joy and the peace of the Lord, instead of the world's ease and abundance, or freedom from pain or deprivation.

We may even come to appreciate, once we have endured and overcome our suffering, that the temporary loss of blessings of health or prosperity was indispensable to the vastly superior spiritual blessings and joys discovered through the course of suffering, and the eternal redemption yet to come. We have come to discern that there are many joys to be found whenever the suffering of ourselves or another turns our attention to God in thanksgiving and appreciation for the blessings He has actually bestowed or will yet deliver. There is joy when suffering redirects our focus to glorifying God and appreciating His companionship; when it reminds us of our dependency upon Him, or drives us in our affliction back to the Great Physician for comfort and healing. We rejoice that the faithful are called here and for all eternity to glorify God by our obedience, righteousness, and love (Psalm 22:23; Matthew 5:16; John 13:31-32, 21:19; Romans 15:6, 15:9; I Corinthians 6:20; 2 Corinthians 9:13).

Indeed, suffering reaffirms God's loving kindness and forgiveness, as He blesses sinners despite knowing we will commit sin, and as He proves His trustworthiness through endurance and deliverance from suffering, after we have entrusted the torment to God. We are especially moved to glorify God when He delivers and remits us from suffering by His grace and power, according to Psalm 50:15: "Call upon me in the day of trouble: I will deliver thee, and thou shalt glorify me." (See also, Leviticus 10:3; I Chronicles 16:28, 29:11; Joshua 7:19; I Samuel 6:5; Psalm 86:9, 12; Isaiah 24:15, 25:3; Jeremiah 13:16; and Malachi 2:2).

I Peter 4:16 says: "If one suffers as a Christian, let him not be ashamed, but under that name let him glorify God." I Peter 4:13 says: "rejoice in so far as you share Christ's sufferings, that you may also rejoice and be glad when his glory is revealed." Much of this glory is in the world (Luke 13:17; 2 Corinthians 3:18; Ephesians 3:16-19; and Colossians 1:11), as well as in the Hereafter (2 Corinthians 4:17). When infirmity is healed, God's deliverance is an occasion for rejoicing and glorifying God. When Naaman, the leper sought to heal his leprosy at the hands of Elisha, he was sent to bathe in the Jordan river seven times to be healed. When he did this and his flesh was restored, Naaman returned to Elisha, and confessed: "Indeed, now I know that there is no God in all the earth, except in Israel... Your servant will no longer offer either burnt offering or sacrifice to other gods, but to the Lord" (2 Kings 5:15-17).

In the end-time tribulations of Revelation 11:13, a great earthquake destroys a tenth of the Holy City, Jerusalem, and kills seven thousand people, "and the rest were terrified and gave glory to the God of heaven," driven to submissive repentance by the devastation around them. The elders who worship God in Heaven for eternity proclaim: "worthy art thou, our Lord and God, to receive glory and honor and power, for thou didst create all things" (Revelation 4:11; and see also, Revelation 15:4). Let us rejoice that suffering gives us opportunity to glorify God here, and prepares us for our eternal task of praising and glorifying God Hereafter, in harmony with the twenty-four elders in Heaven, and every creature in Heaven and earth (Revelation 4:8-10, 5:13-14).

CHAPTER 16

SUFFERING AS GOD'S INSTRUMENT OF GRACE

"Come, and let us return unto the Lord; for he hath torn, and he will heal us; he hath smitten, and he will bind us up... and we shall live in his sight. Then shall we know, if we follow on to know the Lord: his going forth is prepared as the morning; and he shall come unto us as the rain."

–Hosea 6:1-3

God may also use suffering to teach us to appreciate what we already have and enjoy. He works change in us, by transforming our attitudes, rather than changing the circumstances around us. He draws us closer to Him, and carries us through trials, rather than around or away from them. The man who bewails his lack of shoes will realistically appreciate his circumstances when he meets a man with no feet. One with impaired vision must count himself still fortunate when he sees another who is totally blind. Current deprivations of our own, or observed in another, tend to make us appreciate all the blessings we have enjoyed, but taken for granted, in the past.

SUFFERING REMINDS US TO APPRECIATE BLESSINGS

The tribulations which we personally endure, as well as what we see afflicting others, not only make us appreciate the blessings we have already received, but also inspire us to be sensitive to our complete dependence upon God for future blessings, guidance, and protection. We may be driven to regret the ungrateful or cavalier attitude which took for granted or squandered the precious gifts and blessings bestowed by God in the past.

God sometimes allows believers to experience pain and deprivation to understand that we deserve nothing from God, but that everything He gives us is a matter of grace. In the crucible of suffering, we also learn that many of the temporal, worldly acquisitions which seemed so valuable before our troubles are actually debris we can do without, and only eternal, Godly values are of any importance. Deprivations can show us just how insignificant worldly acclaim, status, or wealth have become in the course of spiritual development and friendship with God; that "It is well with my soul" because serving Christ is the only importance, the only worthy endeavor and magnificent privilege of this life.

When we see the suffering of others, we are made to appreciate our own blessings of exemption from severe affliction. The contrast in our own lives, when we see infirmity in

437

another, should prompt us to be more grateful for our own unafflicted condition. The unsaved may be motivated to choose God, and the faithful will be moved to glorify God, for the grace He has demonstrated in sparing us.

We may regret taking our blessings for granted and ignoring the gifts we already possess by God's grace. We may stop complaining about the material things we lack, and concentrate on the greater spiritual abundance which God has already provided. We can take pleasure in what we formerly took for granted, such as the sweet simplicities of life; a sense of humor; the joy of generosity to and in others; and gratitude for the soundness of mind and body we enjoy.[153]

There is a tendency for human psyches to dwell in ingratitude, much as the nine lepers healed by Jesus failed to give thanks, while only one of the ten expressed his appreciation (Luke 17:17). Often, beneficiaries are so wrapped up in enjoying the gift, they forget the Giver. We tend to take for granted our health and material sufficiency, the possession of physical and mental faculties, until we have lost them. Perhaps we fall prey to the conceit that we have accomplished the blessings by our own power, or deserved them because of our culture, heritage, or personal merit. Whatever the cause, ingratitude reflects a selfish failure to appreciate God as the source of all blessings. The vision of chronically deprived throngs of poor, hungry, diseased, homeless and displaced persons should make us grateful and humble before God.

How often does seeing a blind man inspire fresh resolve to utilize one's own gift of sight more productively? We seldom appreciate our faculties fully until we are forced to consider the lack of them. The multi-millionaire who is terminally ill will envy the vitality of the penniless waif who takes her good health for granted, or the slave enjoying sexual vigor. The poorest person in America is still better off than the poor of India, Africa, or South America.

And if we encounter a blind man whose sight has been restored, we rejoice in his understandable gratitude to God, and empathize with his keen desire to serve forevermore the Lord Who delivered him from darkness. Seeing another's recovery of sight can help us recover our own insight and appreciation for the vision we have continually enjoyed. And we, who have received our own sight daily, should be equally willing to dedicate our precious gift of vision exclusively to the service of the Giver, with the same zeal as a blind person enjoying sight for the first time. No matter what we lack, we are always better off than many others, and we should remember this, as we regard their appropriate gratitude to God when blessed or restored after years of deprivation.

When a believer's prosperity has dwindled, do his prayers petition only for restoration of finances, or do they thank God for the children, health, and spiritual assets God still bestows? If health declines, do his prayers seek only physical restoration, or also express gratitude for the privilege of boldly coming to the throne of grace, and for our blessed hope of Christ's return? A loss can prod us to appreciate what we still possess, but have taken for granted. We can be grateful that a temporal blessing has been replaced by eternal blessings of Christ-like character.

I Peter 1:8-9 says: "You believe in him and rejoice with unutterable and exalted joy. As the outcome of your faith you obtain the salvation of your souls." We are counseled to lay up our treasures in Heaven, "For where your treasure is, there will your heart be also" (Matthew 6:21). Colossians 3:2 agrees: "Set your minds on things that are above, not on things that are on earth." Thus, Philippians 4:8 urges believers to think about whatever is pure, lovely, gracious, excellent, and worthy of praise. Focusing on the Kingdom, glory, and excellence of God will help sustain our Christian walk and our endurance of suffering.

When a person loses something he has taken for granted for many years, he will either wrongly resent the loss and turn against God, or hopefully start appreciating those lost blessings he has taken for granted, as well as the blessings God still provides. Look at what you still have, rather than what you have lost. Count your blessings, not your lack; your joys, not your heartaches; and the flowers in your garden, not the weeds.

Things of the world enjoy their place, but they are nothing compared to eternal values. The world may destroy one's health, wealth, fame, reputation, status, and possessions, but it can never destroy one's soul or eternal blessedness prepared for us before the foundation of the world. We can lose our lives to the world by a process of pain and suffering, but not our souls.[154] It is this blessedness of Heavenly reward which overcomes all suffering by the peace and joy of God's assurances, as we look to Jesus. Gratitude for these blessings of grace and mercy, as we praise God for them, becomes a wellspring of joy and our haven against despair or fear.

Whatever we may lose as the encrustations of worldliness are removed, we still have the Lord! He is everything and all things, and He sustains us. As we traverse paths we may not understand, we need only rest in the Lord, Himself, not the blessings. doctrines, or anything less than Jesus.

Perhaps the ultimate lesson to be learned from the travails of Moses, David, Job, St. Paul, and all other sufferers is the insignificance of worldly blessings in comparison to the spiritual blessing of ascertaining God's trustworthiness and fellowship, here and Hereafter. After the lessons of submissiveness, transformation and faithfulness have been learned, we are left with the assurance that possessing God is everything that is important in one's life. What does it matter how many earthly possessions or positions we may lose, as long as we still know God and are entitled to the eternal reward of being with Him. Praise God for these examples of faith!

It may seem sad at first that Moses was denied entry to the Promised Land because he struck the rock rather than spoke to it. Yet, all he lost was presiding over Israel for the brief period of earthly time remaining to him. He was privileged to see the Israelites he had loved and led for so long, blessed with restoration to their homeland by his God. He was privileged to rejoice in the integrity of God's Providence, expressed in love and deliverance for the nation, Israel. How Moses' loss of entry into the Promised Land pales in significance to these genuine blessings for eternity. God's love for Moses never diminished, and he buried Moses in a valley in a hidden tomb: "but no man knoweth of his sepulcher unto this day" (Deuteronomy 34:6). Moses may have lost the worldly blessing of the Promised Land for fleeting moments in time, but he did not lose the spiritual blessings of knowing God and His continuing fellowship; of relying on the integrity of His Word, the beauty of His character; and the fulfilled promises of eternity.

David's loss of a child, a tragedy shared by Job, was terrible in worldly terms, yet David appreciated immediately that losing a child was nothing compared to possibly losing God. And so David worshipped God when he realized his child was dead (2 Samuel 12:20). While children are a gift from God, we should never prefer the gift to the Giver. Jesus' first commandment is: "you shall love the Lord your God with all your heart, and with all your soul, and with all your mind" (Matthew 22:37). Jesus adds at Matthew 10;37: "He who loves son or daughter more than me is not worthy of me."

David continued to worship and love God, and rejoice in the knowledge that because of God's benevolence, there would be a resurrection and reunion with his son for all eternity, not just a few years on earth: "I shall go to him, but he shall not return to me" (2 Samuel 12:23). Job likewise glorified God in the midst of his torments: "the Lord gave, and the Lord hath taken away; blessed be the name of the Lord" (Job 1:21); "Though he slay me, yet will I trust in him" (Job 13:15).

Tests and trials borne on wings of affliction not only make us appreciate what we already have as blessings from God, but can be used to develop, measure, strengthen, and verify our faith and holiness, revealing their progress and sufficiency. The test of faith can be as simple as requiring obedience to seemingly inane directives to compass the walls of Jericho for seven days; end the siege with a great shout; and see the walls fall by Gods power collaborating with man's faith (Joshua 6:6-21). Confronting difficulties enables a believer to develop confidence in faith that man can be enabled to act by the grace of God, by the power of the Holy Spirit, in the wisdom revealed in God's Word (Psalm 119:67, 71, 75, 86, 92, 134, 153, 170).

The testing of Noah's, Abraham's, Joseph's and Job's faith was a revelation to them, and an example for other men, of their mature faithfulness to God and their ability to serve Him. Trials proved the integrity of their faith in God and His unwavering benevolence toward them. God proved Noah's unwavering faith in God by allowing him to suffer the ridicule of men while he labored for 120 years to build the ark on dry land, without vindication, and in apparent futility (Genesis 6:3). God summoned Abraham to sacrifice Isaac as a burnt offering (Genesis 22:1), to test Abraham's trust in God's promises that he would father a great nation through this child's bloodline.

Joseph was tested by his brothers selling him into slavery; by Potiphar's wife falsely accusing him of seducing her; by the chief butler's ingratitude which left him languishing in prison: "Whose feet they hurt with fetters: he was laid in iron: Until that time that his word came: the word of the Lord tried him" (Psalm 105:18-19). Joseph endured and overcame all his trials, grew in holiness rather than bitterness, and learned that he had been purified through his ordeal, and fitted for God's service because "The Lord was with him" (Genesis 39:2, 23; 41:38).

Just as miracle healing and deliverance can reveal the power of God to His glory, so the faithful enduring of difficulties can show faith to advantage to the glory of God, when an afflicted Christian endures and overcomes suffering by the power of God, with unwavering trust and reliance in the benevolent, absolute sovereignty of God to work a blessed result. Believers and unbelievers may experience the same afflictions, so the world might see the difference in their responses, as a believer endures in faith and overcomes by the grace of God.

GOD IS ALSO EXALTED BY FAITHFUL ENDURANCE

When a believer's deliverance from suffering is not immediate, and we are perplexed with the question why a good person continues in affliction, one may wrongly assume that God is not glorified by patient endurance of ills. He may believe God can be glorified only by restored health or status which fully overcomes the works of the devil, and allows believers to serve God with full capacity and effectiveness. Indeed, it is hard to reconcile unrelieved suffering with the idea that the Head of the Church can be well served by an enervated, effete Body, as much as by Christians who are "complete, equipped for every good work" (2 Timothy 3:17), and "with everything good, that you may do his will" (Hebrews 13:21).

Although we may not understand why, we can recognize that God does not heal every infirmity or remove every adversity for believers. Yet, saintly persons who witness for God from their infirmity, do inspire us by the example of their unwavering faith in the face of adversity. Their constancy somehow ennobles our own intercessory prayers to seek their speedy deliverance and reward. For, we can be comforted in their suffering by the assurances of I Peter 5:10: "And after you have suffered a little while, the God of all grace... will himself restore, establish, and strengthen you."

Indeed, how many Christians have been comforted through adversity by the strength and faith of Helen Keller, born deaf, dumb and blind; or Corrie TenBoom, sharing Nazi oppression to save Jewish lives; or Joni Erickson Tada, overcoming paraplegia; or Fanny Crosby, the brilliant, but blind hymn writer? Often, others who see such Godly response to suffering, will be encouraged to respond with the same faithful endurance, and may even by led to Christ by such examples of faith overcoming adversity. Clearly, the supernatural provision of patient, faithful endurance is as much a testimony to God's power and goodness, as supernatural intercessions of physical healing. Both ways can glorify God.

The Bible gives many noble examples of faith enduring in the face of agonizing torment, trusting God will do what is best, despite transient occurrences or temporary losses which seemingly disprove His dependability. The story of Job teaches many lessons about the character and faithfulness of God. He allowed Satan to inflict suffering, but within limits. God did not originate the idea of persecuting Job, nor perpetrate the actual affliction. God allowed Job to suffer to prove Job's loyalty and faithfulness to God by his perseverance through suffering. Job was the principal witness in a cosmic trial of faith. God allowed the universal reality of faith to be established and proved by a human agent. Adam and Eve had failed the first test of faith for mankind by disobeying the authority of God. But Job remained faithful to God based on God's character; not the things which God could give him.

If Job had listened to his wife and cursed God, or heeded his friends and focused on his own failures, rather than God's reliability and trustworthiness, the result would have been quite different. But Job vowed his confidence in God, regardless of all his suffering or loss: "Though he slay me, yet will I trust in him" (Job 13:15).

Similarly, the Israelites fleeing from Egypt had been led by God to an impasse so they could learn to trust Him. At the sea their progress was blocked and the Egyptian pursuers were closing in. The Israelites were fearful, but Moses assured them: "Fear ye not, stand still, and see the salvation of the Lord" (Exodus 14:13). Then, the Lord parted the sea, allowing their escape, and afterward closed up the sea, so that the pursuing Egyptian hordes were drowned.

When Shadrach, Meshach, and Abednego were condemned to the furnace, they proclaimed to Nebuchadnezzar: "If it be so, our God whom we serve is able to deliver us from the burning fiery furnace... But if not, be it known unto thee, O king, that we will not serve thy gods, nor worship the golden image which thou hast set up" (Daniel 3:17-18).

It is the same faith as Jesus at Gethsemane, and on the Cross, seeking reprieve, but also professing absolute faith in God: "My father, if it be possible, let this cup pass from me; nevertheless, not as I will, but as thou wilt" (Matthew 26:39); and "Father, into thy hands I commit my spirit" (Luke 23:46). Jesus suffered, or "became a servant to the circumcised to show God's truthfulness, in order to confirm the promises given to the patriarchs, and in order that the

Gentiles might glorify God for his mercy" (Romans 15:8-9). When Paul and Silas prayed and sang for joy in prison, following hours of torture and pain, their faithful witness inspired their jailer to seek salvation in Jesus (Acts 16:25-30).

In the great Hall of Faith of Hebrews, Chapter 11, examples of unique faithfulness to God are recounted, attesting to the truth that their courageous perseverance, ending in the blood of the martyrs, is the seed of the Church: "Others suffered mockings and scourging, and even chains and imprisonment. They were stoned, they were sawn in two, they were killed with the sword" (Hebrews 11:36-37). God honored their faith, but did not deliver them from suffering. They did not receive the things promised. Their witness of faith encourages: "Therefore, since we are surrounded by so great a cloud of witnesses, let us also lay aside every weight and sin... and run with perseverance the race that is set before us, looking to Jesus" (Hebrews 12:1-2).

Scriptures calling for sublimation of suffering to the glory of God include I Peter 4:16: "yet if one suffers as a Christian, let him not be ashamed, but under that name let him glorify God." The use of suffering to glorify God results in rejoicing, as I Peter 1:6-7 explains: "In this you rejoice, though now for a little while you may have to suffer various trials, so that the genuineness of your faith... may redound to praise and glory and honor at the revelation of Jesus."

Paul's thorn in the flesh had been given him "to keep me from being too elated by the abundance of revelations" which had been taught by Jesus (2 Corinthians 12:7). Perhaps it was too much for Paul to resist pride and exaltation without the constant prodding and reminder of his thorn in the flesh, but for whatever reason, God denied Paul's triple entreaties for relief (2 Corinthians 12:8). Paul learned to trust God, Who gave Paul sufficient grace and enabling by His perfect power to endure, make life sufficient, and overcome the thorn. God revealed: "My grace is sufficient for you, for my power is made perfect in weakness: (2 Corinthians 12:9); and Paul could say: "when I am weak, then I am strong" (2 Corinthians 12:10).

The faith which pleases God is not faith for earthly advantage or blessings, but faith God can be trusted totally, even when earthly blessings have been withdrawn. Psalm 84:12 says: "O Lord of hosts, blessed is the man that trusteth in thee." Faith begins with relying on God to deliver on the promises in His Word. Then faith matures to trusting God to accomplish good, even when He delays in fulfilling His Word of promise. Faith is obsolete when all that God has promised becomes actual reality. Faith, based on the Word, encompasses reliance that God is preparing us for eternity with Him by spiritual growth while in the world.

Indeed, we have everything that truly matters as long as we have God, can know Him, and have insight into the beauty, love, integrity, and providence of His character. We will rejoice as long as we focus in thanksgiving, praise and worship on what we still have in God, rather than what we have lost in the world. Putting worldly advantages in this proper perspective is the essence of our victory over the world: "nevertheless do not rejoice in this, that the spirits are subject to you: but rejoice that your names are written in heaven" (Luke 10:20). Focus on "the hope to which he has called you, what are the riches of his glorious inheritance in the saints, and what is the immeasurable greatness of his power in us who believe... which he accomplished in Christ" (Ephesians 1:18-20).

Others are drawn to Christ when we praise God, rather than grumble and complain as ungratefully as non-Christians. Our reaction to delay, frustration, difficulties and emergencies should reflect the joy and peace of God in our lives, because He is in control. We should also reflect an obvious, attractive, and winsome difference from unbelievers because our relation to

Christ allows confident trust, security, and commitment. It is easy, though we often forget, to glorify God in the midst of blessings. But real, honest glorifying occurs amidst suffering.

When a creature glorifies God, it is God-centered activity, rather than self-centered. When you praise and thank God for everything, God will use your praise to attract anxious, unhappy, and despairing people to Jesus, and He will transform their cares into unperturbed peace and joy, as they understand God's Providence in upholding His creation, exhibited by the example of your life.

One who endures suffering provides an example of patient confidence in God's deliverance, and makes his preaching and witness believable. One who remains joyful in the midst of affliction demonstrates how supernatural joy is a grace beyond fleshly concerns or worldly assaults. Enduring faith attests that our New-Born spirit is indeed a "treasure in earthen vessels, to show that the transcendent power belongs to God and not to us. We are afflicted in every way, but not crushed... struck down, but not destroyed... so that the life of Jesus may also be manifested in our bodies" (2 Corinthians 4:7-10).

Philippians 2:14-15 says: "Do all things without grumbling or questioning... in the midst of a crooked and perverse generation, among whom you shine as lights in the world." An example of faithful trust in God during adversity will do much to strengthen the faith of others. For God never allows anything to reach us beyond our power to endure. He never calls us to His service without placing appropriate resources at our disposal. He never encumbers us without giving us the power to pull the load, and He always gives strength equal to the struggle.

If we recognize His love in chastening us, His grace in teaching us, and His blessing in turning every travail to our advantage, we must warmly embrace Him. As suffering teaches that God is the source of power for courage and strength; of knowledge for insight into His character; and of substance for fulfilling faith, our closeness grows to friendship. As God provides comfort and strength to endure suffering, that interaction cements trust and reliance in Him.

When we, ourselves, are visited with affliction, or tormented by the suffering of a loved one, or burdened by empathy for the agonies of others, we should take comfort in the assurance that endurance of suffering always produces ultimate blessing and reward. Indeed, most good things promised Christians require patience before they are fulfilled, and nothing comes to pass without it. We must occupy and endure, with fervor, hope, and expectation, until the Lord's return, the Coming of God's Kingdom, and our perfecting in the image of Christ (Romans 5:3-4, 15:4; Ephesians 6:18; 2 Thessalonians 1:4-5; Hebrews 6:11-12; James 1:3-4; and Revelation 1:9).

We must follow the advice of Hebrews 10:35-36: "do not throw away your confidence, which has a great reward. For you have need of endurance, so that you may do the will of God and receive what is promised." Trust in God's all-loving Providence is what allows us to pray for grace to endure, as well as for illumination and termination of suffering. We will know it is sufficient to rejoice in the Giver, even if all the gifts on earth be taken from us.

Deliverance from suffering will have taught us that we can rely on God's benevolence; abandon dependence on our senses and feelings; trust His Word; and believe His love will always provide what is best for us. Without suffering we would never learn to rely on God, even to the point of thanking Him for our trials, which cannot reach us unless God allows them.

We will have learned that God not only fulfills His promises, but provides us with the faith necessary to have such confidence. Whenever God imposes a test of faith, He always gives us the faith and the means we need to pass the test, not fail it. First the test, then man's faithful response, and then God's provision for fulfilling its requirements. Abraham demonstrated his faith in all God had promised by his willingness to sacrifice Isaac on the Altar. Then God delivered what He had promised, and provided "himself a lamb for a burnt offering" (Genesis 22:8), to produce good for His faithful servant.

If you continue to love God and live for Him in the midst of affliction, then your constancy proves God must be worth loving and living for. The unsaved person may be driven to wonder how such endurance, triumph, and happiness are possible, and thereby be drawn to the revelation of God's love. One's witness for Jesus to a hurting world is more effective when God's power is the only explanation for overcoming and enduring tribulations. Deliverance because of and through divine presence becomes a public display of the power of a caring Christ, and redirects attention to eternal values.

A healthy and wealthy Christian proves God's greatness by His grace in granting blessings as a reward for faithful trust in Him, and can be an effective witness in that way. But a handicapped believer who overcomes His affliction, evidences the empowerment of God when he lives and works to the glory of God. His life verifies that spiritual vitality transcends physical health, and that someone without God is the truly handicapped person; that moral sickness is more tragic than physical ailment. He is proof that God is loveable because of Who He is, and not just for what He gives His children.

Without injustice, suffering, and pain we would never have an opportunity to demonstrate our free choice to love God. If every good act produced a reward, we would be conditioned to respond to God because we felt good and won rewards. God uses the world's imperfections and pain as a test of faithful endurance in our commitment and love for God. The question is still pertinent for every age: "Nevertheless, when the Son of man comes, will he find faith on earth?" (Luke 18:8).

Suffering befell Job to verify the validity of his virtue and faith in the Lord. Satan sought to destroy Job's faith by visiting afflictions upon him, but Job's faith endured, and was strengthened by God's ultimate deliverance. At the outset of his trials, Job, one of the Biblical exemplars of faith, was able to assert: "Though he slay me, yet will I trust him" (Job 13:15), because he could recall God's previous love and kindness. Through the suffering, God reminded Job that His ways may be unknowable and unaccountable to man, but are nevertheless righteous, good, and sufficient to promote a believer's welfare (Job 38:2-7; See also, Isaiah 40:14 and Romans 9:19-23).

GOD USES PAIN TO ALERT US TO DANGER AND THE NEED FOR CHANGE

Whenever God initiates suffering, He may be using pain as the ultimate warning of spiritual malfunction and the need for corrective change. God sometimes intends pain to warn us in the same way a train sounds a whistle to alert us to its approach so we can get out of harm's way, or a doctor warns us of the need for an operation now so we can avoid future complications. When God has authored pain, it demands an attentive response for one's own good. The wise person will heed God's first alerts of danger to avoid more stringent rescue measures later. Pain shares the same Latin root, poena, as do the words 'penalty' and 'punishment', and we connect God's pain with the discipline of a spanking lovingly administered for misbehavior which needs correction.

God can apply pain to reveal our need to change some undesirable condition in our lives, and drive us to seek its cure in God. Pain can summon us to recognize spiritual malfunction and the need to obey God and eliminate distress by conforming to His purposes. The chastening of pain can guide God's children back to Him and His Word, so we can be trained in His way and develop His character (Deuteronomy 8:2-3; 2 Chronicles 33:12-13). Painful lessons teach that God must be put in control because our own contrivances and machinations are such wretched failures. God alerts us to deficiencies in character and shortcomings which require remediation, by chastening us and drawing our attention to the problem, by showing how far we have yet to go. Pain ultimately calls us to healing and a change in our excesses of pride, sloth, and unloving acts, as we come to entrust the transformation to Him.

Deprivations get our attention, calling us to change life and pray for fellowship and Christ-like character as essential needs and wants. Pain is the messenger which proclaims we have overexerted, overextended, or malfunctioned either physically or spiritually; that we are not acting as we are meant to. Pain is an integral part of the life process, as an alert or warning of imminent danger, and later can be an accompaniment to physical degeneration and infirmity leading to death, which ultimately liberates us from pain. Saul of Tarsus (St. Paul) was under conviction to stop persecuting Christians. At Acts 26:14, KJV, Jesus says to him: "why do you persecute me? It hurts you to kick against the goads." The hurting conscience is a warning of the need to have something fixed, lest one sustain more serious harm. When Saul stopped resisting the pricks and changed direction in response to them, he became of real use to the Lord, just as we will.

God uses pain to evoke awareness of the carnality we still embrace, and to show the need for improvement in holiness in our relationship with God. Suffering is a tool to deter wrong conduct, and trials are God's way of recapturing our attention. Trials put us to proof of faithfulness, and we then discover our retained sins, concealed and unsuspected in each of us. In ignorance, we may not appreciate the rage and passion harbored, and secreted within, but trials will expose the sojourn of our unwelcome guests. A calm sea gives the appearance of purity on the surface, but when it is roiled by storms, all the sediment and debris beneath the surface emerge, and only then are we motivated to seek purification of what had become contaminated.

We might not appreciate the paucity of our faith without the revelation we lack blessings or experience pain because we lack faith. Pain can fire up our loving service and witness. Illness, be it physical or moral, produces symptoms which cry out for a cure. God's grace uses pain to call us to self-examination, repair, and change so the underlying defect can be remedied. Without the agony of mortification, condemnation, and guilt we might never be driven to seek tranquility, forgiveness, and reconciliation.

Thus, pain can be the friendly alarm bell which warns us that we are being burned by fire; bitten by a snake, stung by a wasp, or developing clogged arteries, leading to stroke. Without pain we would be ignorant of symptoms and allow them to become festering, gangrenous, infected, and baneful. Without persistent pain, we might ignore its first warning, but we cannot overlook pain which continues, until we respond by identifying and removing its cause.

Pain has been provided as a safeguard to health, both physical and spiritual. Imagine if a man put his hand on a burning log or the cutting edge of a knife, but felt no pain. He would soon lose his most useful tool for living because of the damage inflicted. Leprosy is so pernicious because it attacks the pain cells of skin, numbing and anesthetizing them to pain. A wound to a hand or foot then goes untended because no pain is felt, and leads to infection, ulceration, and deterioration because the warning system of pain has been silenced by leprosy. Safety often depends on one's ability to feel pain and respond to it appropriately. We dare not ignore suffering when it is God's instrument prodding us to respond. C. S. Lewis observed that God whispers in our pleasures, but shouts in our pain.

Without the pain of correction, we might never have any warning signs of illness, or be prompted to take preventive measures to arrest its progress. Sensitivity to pain exists in the human body to preserve it from harm. Sensory nerves are designed to transmit valuable warning signals to the brain, to protect human existence and survival.[155]

Conformably, spiritual pain is a prick or goad to prompt man's reaction by alerting him to danger and the need to alter behavior. As in the physical body, pain from suffering can be a warning of some malfunction requiring treatment and spiritual rehabilitation. Testing can reveal one's iniquity, the diluted quality of faith, estrangement from God, and the need to reform life. When we wander from God, or neglect to pray, praise, glorify Him, or feed on the Word, we put ourselves in the midst of temptations. When we ignore or shed the armor of God, we expose ourselves to the fiery darts of the evil one (Ephesians 6:13-17).

If God allowed us to control pain after it had given its initial warning, humans would opt to turn their sensory alert off, rather than fix the underlying problem, If God used anything other than pain to alert us to danger, such as buzzers or flashing lights as warnings to cease certain activity, it would be too easy to presume on God's grace, ignore the warning, and persist in whatever one purposed to do. Without pain, some men would simply not heed nor respond to the stimulus which God has provided to warn us of danger.

Some men find it easy to ignore internal bleeding and other painless signs of physical disorder or distortion. However, it is more difficult to ignore pain as a warning indication of the need for corrective action. Physicians are quite familiar with the phenomenon of patients who are finally motivated to relieve the underlying problem, but only after pain has produced enough suffering that painful treatment which remedies the cause of pain becomes the lesser of two evils. In this way, pain can be an unmistakable identifier of weak or defective elements in one's character. It can indicate the need to change, improve or reorder our priorities; and expose our remaining shortcomings or inadequacies which require further transformation. Pain can be our best friend when it speaks God's truths.

TESTS MEASURE SPIRITUAL PROGRESS

Trials provoke, expand, prod, and accelerate faith in God's dependability for our spiritual growth; while tests reveal our growth in faith and spirituality. We will never know how strong our faith has grown until it is put to the test, and we totally and confidently entrust God with the solution to our problem. We will never have confidence or appreciate how much we have grown in holiness until we are tested by temptations and are able to resist by the grace of God. 2 Corinthians 4:17 reminds us: "For this slight momentary affliction is preparing for us an eternal weight of glory beyond all comparison."

How many children have learned they are able to swim, by necessity, after being thrown into the water by a loving parent, and discovering they can apply the swimming lessons they were taught on dry land. Like the baby bird pushed by its parent from the nest and forced to fly, we may never learn how much we have grown in faith and holiness until actually confronted with a need to test our wings. Both trials and tests may involve terror, anguish, and pain, until we learn God has qualified us to conquer new challenges.

God may be able to see how a believer has grown, and what is the intent of his heart (I Samuel 16:7; Proverbs 21:2; Luke 16:15; John 6:6; Acts 1:24; and Hebrews 4:12), but believers need to be tried and tested from time to time so they can discover that the regeneration of the inner spiritual man is working the transformation intended by God.

Only actual circumstances will reveal if you are capable of sustaining or losing trust in God. Only when you have committed yourself to act specifically in submission, despite the cost or consequence to what you once held dear, will your devotion to selfless service be proved. Unconditional, submissive obedience and good behavior can prove, express, and evidence your faith and the actual realization of holiness. We are directed primarily to "please God who tests our hearts" (I Thessalonians 2:4). Vows of allegiance are but intentions, until verified empirically by performance (James 1:25-26).

We can profess to trust God, but until He has led us to the sacrificial altar, and we stand with knife poised to strike, like Abraham over Isaac, we will never have certain proof that our faith in God's benevolence is unconditional. God may be testing our submission, obedience, and willingness to worship Him at any cost, so that our faith can be verified to us. He may know our hearts, and even foresee our faithfulness, but the act must yet be played freely on the stage of history, before it can confirm God's foreknowledge. God may impose specific trials, such as leading His steward to the brink of bankruptcy, to push him to break through to the other side to discover the superior prosperity God has in store for true believers. We may need to test our humility, patient endurance, wisdom, skill in spiritual combat, or faith in God and His Word.

Trials give us an opportunity to practice our profession of faith by totally committing our needs and problems to Jesus. Our total measure of faith means total reliance, dependence, and entrustment of care to Him, with abandonment of our manipulations to solve the problem or achieve the result. Only adversity or sorrow can prove our total commitment to trust in God's goodness, and position us for new revelations of grace, love, and blessings we might not otherwise know. Hence, Psalm 139:23-24 petitions: "Search me, O God, and know my heart: try me and know my thoughts; and see if there be any wicked way in me, and lead me in the way everlasting."

Trials are to be expected because intentions to act, however worthy, are not determined or fulfilled until a believer chooses to act. What a great chasm exists between vows intending to serve and submit to the Lord's will, and the actual surrender of one's own desires to His. You cannot be sure you have submitted until the choice is clearly before you, involving sacrifice, family disruptions, and even humbling, in order to obey the revelation of God's will for you. Actual effort, privation, and commitment of resources far exceed mere mental intent or purpose.

We have no trouble understanding the function of tests in education, or in processes where a new drug is developed, or in the military where a weapon's effectiveness is measured. Studies and experiments lead to accuracy, improvement, efficiency and eventual realization. Testing helps researchers identify and eliminate defects, structural weakness, and inadequacies. Testing is the way to develop improvements and reliability in commercial products. Only in trials involving simulated, or actual conditions, are we called to judge our own expectations, maturity, sin, and faith, rather than question God's love, benevolence, wisdom, or power. Only in trials can we learn not to question God's Word, but our application of it.

Every test or trial exacts a moral resolve and exertion, involving some degree of deprivation, conquered by joy in obedience and righteousness. Without demands upon submissiveness, we will have no opportunity to focus, fortify, and exercise the moral strength we have developed. Real faith is revealed in difficulty when you resolutely seek and trust God completely, and rush to His open arms for safe harbor. Like a sponge, we may have to be squeezed from time to time, so that pressure can reveal, and we can discover, what is really contained inside us.

Hardships drive us to examine ourselves to see if we are still stubborn and unyielding, encrusted with sin, unready to receive and properly employ that which is holy. A test reveals how we have studied, prepared, learned, and applied what has been assigned us. A test will tell a believer how his faith is doing, and give him the satisfaction of confirming genuine spiritual progress and status in the Lord.

An athlete may be trained by arduous conditioning and practice to compete in a boxing match or a race, but he is never sure of his prowess until he is tested and motivated under actual conditions. The significant thing is that passing a test measures achievement, certifies accomplishment, and indicates one's readiness for promotion and graduation to greater spiritual responsibility. Competence in a test emboldens believers to try more difficult, complex, and advanced tasks they might not otherwise attempt. The more difficult the challenges we overcome, the more courageous we become to assume more mature responsibilities.

We are not likely to experiment with dexterity in our left hand until our right hand in incapacitated or restrained, and we are challenged to discover, develop, and test our potential capability. The believer may need to be shown how his faith has developed; how his resolve is firmly set; and how qualified he is to serve the Lord (2 Corinthians 7:12). He may be the sleeper who needs to be awakened or stirred to action.

Tests often show us how far we have progressed on our journey of faith, but tests can also involve failure, and show how far we have yet to travel; hopefully motivating a response to our need for instruction and improvement. Adam and Eve were monumental failures in faith when they disbelieved God's instructions, and ate of the tree of knowledge of good and evil in the Garden. God had designated one tree 'off-limits' as a test of their loyal submission through free and loving obedience, and they failed the test (Genesis 3:3, 11-19).

Deuteronomy 8:2 says that God left the Jews in the wilderness forty years "to prove thee, to know what was in thine heart, whether thou wouldest keep his commandments or no." God indicated He would rain manna from Heaven upon the Israelites, which they were to gather, "that I may prove them" (Exodus 16:4; see also, Deuteronomy 8:16; 2 Chronicles 32:31). Unfortunately, the people failed the test by balking at eating the manna, and lusted after flesh to eat. Their faithfulness was not proved. They failed in the obedience and discipline so necessary for survival in a strange land. So God sent quails in answer to their grumbling, and "smote the people with a very great plague" (Numbers 11:13, 33; and see also Psalms 78:18 and 95:8-10). It fell to the next generation to enter the Promised Land, because of that failed test.

God then promised the Israelites that if they took possession of Canaan, He would go with them and assure their success. Ten of the reconnoiterers were frightened by the giant sons of Anak who occupied the land, and counseled the people not to enter Canaan (Numbers 13:33). Only Joshua and Caleb expressed faith in God's promise to overcome the giants. But the Israelites listened to the ten faithless spies, and initially refused to enter the Promised Land.

Then, when they relented, it was too late; for the moment of God's timing and window of opportunity had passed. Consequently, they were soundly defeated when they tried to enter Canaan under their own power (Numbers 14:42-45; Deuteronomy 1:41-45).

Without severe trials, we would never experience the great opportunities to endure and grow in faith. We could never be tutored by humility and failure to seek and depend upon God. Faith is a matter of making your mind up to trust God, as He enables faith, which is a fruit of the Spirit and comes through hearing the Word of God. Elementary faith is confidently expecting God to give us what we ask for according to His promises in the Word. Mature faith is knowing that God is infinitely wise, caring, good, loving, and benevolent, even in the wake of permanent loss or tragedy. Mature faith is putting all our trust in Him, even when ignorant of why He allowed one type of loss to occur, while accruing another gain or alternative blessing to our account, greater than any denial or loss which might tempt us to doubt His power or wisdom. Without trials or tests, we might never heed God's call to turn to Him; discover His absolute dependability and confirmation of faith; or reveal specific areas for chastening.

Even failing a test presents God with new opportunities to express His forgiveness and love, by trusting us again in His service. Peter, and all the disciples failed the test of loyalty to Jesus, when they all fell asleep three times at Gethsemane (Mark 14:37-41; Luke 22:45), and when Peter denied Him three times at the court of the high priest (John 18:25). Yet, Jesus forgave and constituted Peter as the shepherd of His Church to feed His lambs, and re-commissioned all disciples to preach the Gospel throughout the world. When Abraham was faithless to God's promise, by seeking to accelerate the birth of a son with Hagar (Genesis 16:4), God forgave him, and delivered His covenant promise in Isaac. God even gave Abraham a second test of faith to sacrifice Isaac (Genesis 22:2).

God never abandons His people, nor stops loving, fulfilling, and increasing them, simply because of failures. He is the great Restorer of the soul, of joy, comforts, health, prosperity, and paths to dwell in (Psalms 23:3, 51:12; Jeremiah 30:17; Joel 2:25; Isaiah 57:18, 58:12). Edward Markham has observed that sorrows come to enlarge spaces in the heart to accommodate more joy.

God purposes a goal of true fellowship with those who are in Christ Jesus, and may use suffering to accomplish that result, drawing us to Him in our brokenness; driving us to Him despite our stubborn rebellion. John 17:3 reveals: "And this is eternal life, that they know thee the only true God, and Jesus Christ whom thou hast sent." God's love longs for the fellowship of true believers, and we have an obligation to present ourselves for His enjoyment, no matter how spiritually immature we may be, for God will never rebuff His penitent child. He may know the good intentions of our hearts, but that is not the same as sharing fellowship with Him. We are saved to be glorified and made perfect so we can glorify God and share His companionship for eternity.

New Born Christians are beneficiaries of God's special favor. We are put into God's presence positionally in Jesus, so we can experience His presence in actuality, now in this world. While the Old Testament promises that he who seeks God shall find Him (Deuteronomy 4:29; Proverbs 8:17), it is clear that Jesus is the One Way to reconciliation. Natural men in the flesh, who do not know Jesus as their Lord and Saviour are "strangers to the covenants of promise, having no hope and <u>without God in the world</u>" (Ephesians 2:12). Hebrews 12:14 confirms this, as believers are commanded to "Strive for peace with all men, and for <u>the consecration without</u>

which no one will see the Lord." Holiness, received by the imputed righteousness of Christ, is essential to any increased fellowship with God.

GOD'S GRACIOUS OFFER OF FRIENDSHIP AND SONSHIP

God is love, and He has revealed how He longs to have us in His presence, not only to glorify Him, but for the mutual enjoyment of fellowship. The nature of love is to enjoy the beloved in direct contact, and share pleasure in his presence; almost to possess or have the beloved for oneself. Jesus came lovingly to restore God's people to His fellowship, even to the point of giving Himself on the Cross to satisfy God's longing for us.

Before we can begin our walk with God, we must be confident such intimacy coincides with His wish. Like all belief, friendship starts with, and comes by, faith in the Bible promises that God wishes to fellowship with us. Like any blessing, base your faith on the Word of promise, which reveals that we can fellowship with Him because He first loved and desired us.

Friendship with God is an inheritance and privilege, as heirs to God's Covenant with Abraham, who "was called the friend of God" (Genesis 15:6; Isaiah 41:8; James 2:23), and with whom God established His Covenant: "and thy seed after thee in their generations for an everlasting covenant, to be a God unto thee" (Genesis 17:7).

Direct fellowship with God was the privilege of His people in Old Testament times. Genesis 5:24 relates that "Enoch walked with God." God assured Jacob: "And behold, I am with thee, and will keep thee in all places whither thou goest, and will bring thee again into this land; for I will not leave thee, until I have done that which I have spoken to thee of" (Genesis 28:15). God again promised Moses: "My presence shall go with thee, and I will give thee rest" (Exodus 33:14). Moses reprised that promise at Exodus 33:16: "For wherein shall it be known here that I and thy people have found grace in thy sight? Is it not in that thou goest with us?" Exodus 33:11: relates that "the Lord spoke unto Moses face to face, as a man speaketh unto his friend," and Moses prayed "show me thy glory" or presence, and God obliged him to the extent Moses was able to receive the vision (Exodus 33:18).

Psalm 16:11 convinces us that God wishes to fellowship with us: "Thou wilt show me the path of life: in thy presence is fullness of joy; at thy right hand are pleasures for evermore." If we would walk with God, we must be in agreement with His direction: "Can two walk together, except they be agreed?" (Amos 3:3). God declares at Jeremiah 9:24: "let him that glorieth glory in this, that he understandeth and knoweth me, that I am the Lord which exercises loving kindness, judgment, and righteousness in the earth."

Plumb the depths of Micah 6:8: "what doth the Lord require of thee, but to do justly, and to love mercy, and to walk humbly with thy God?" Our attachment to the presence of God is required of believers! Our walk in God's company is to be humble, obedient, and aware of the reverential awe to which our Creator is entitled. We can express love for our Daddy, even as we respect and admire our Father for His excellence, loveliness, creativity and power.

God has created in us this desire for Him. John Calvin said "A sense of deity is inscribed on every heart:" a God-shaped vacuum which we are driven to fill. Psalm 37:4 says: "Delight thyself also in the Lord; and he shall give thee the desires of thine heart." Delighting in the Lord is possible only with the intimacy of contact and familiarity, which God graciously allows. Obviously, our desire and delight in God will vary from time to time, according to our spiritual condition, obedience to God's will, and our walk in the light (I John 1:6). However, once we delight in the Lord, we discover that He and delighting in Him have become the desires of our hearts. Psalm 73:25 queries: "Whom have I in heaven but thee? And there is none upon earth that I desire beside thee."

The delight is apparently reciprocal, for Zephaniah 3:17 declares: "The Lord thy God in the midst of thee is mighty; he will save, he will rejoice over thee with joy; he will rest in his love, he will joy over thee with singing." God is capable of delighting in us, His children, so much that he expresses His joy by singing! Psalm 40:5 says that God's thoughts of us "cannot be reckoned up... they are more than can be numbered."

When a Christian is made new by grace through faith in Jesus Christ as Lord and Saviour, he receives an intimacy with the indwelling Godhead, which establishes a shared identity or community as the essence of, and basis for fellowship. God lives in a believer through Jesus, and goes with him wherever he goes. Jesus reveals that the Holy Spirit "dwells with you, and will be in you" (John 14:17). He promises disciples: "you will know that I am in my Father, and you in me, and I in you" (John 14:20; see also, John 14:23). Jesus may have ascended into heaven to be with God (Acts 1:9), but they are in our hearts by the Holy Spirit.

Jesus ordains the ongoing intimacy of union at John 15:5: "He who abides in me, and I in him, he it is that bears much fruit, for apart from me you can do nothing." Jesus reveals that fellowship inhabits abiding in Him, which is accomplished by obedience: "As the Father has loved me, so have I loved you; abide in my love. If you keep my commandments, you will abide in my love, just as I have kept my Father's commandments and abide in his love" (John 15:9-10; and see James 4:4). So through obedience we abide in Jesus' love, and in that love, we abide in God's love. At John 15:4 Jesus adds: "Abide in me, and I in you. As the branch cannot bear fruit by itself, unless it abides in the vine, neither can you, unless you abide in me."

Jesus prays God for our unity: "that they may be one, even as we are one... that they may all be one; even as thou, Father, art in me, and I in thee, that they also may be in us... that they may be one even as we are one, I in them and thou in me, that they may become perfectly one, so that the world may know that thou hast sent me and hast loved them even as thou hast loved me" (John 17:11, 21-23). I Corinthians 6:15 confirms our shared identity that Jesus is in us, and we are in Him: "Do you not know that your bodies are members of Christ?"

Jesus professes His faithfulness at John 6;37: "All that the Father gives me will come to me; and him who comes to me I will not cast out." When the Prodigal Son's father welcomed him back, it provided a remarkable insight into the loving forgiveness and restoration of God toward His repentant children. Yet, God's transparent generosity, and willingness for unbroken fellowship is equally evident in the father's revelation to his elder son: "Son, you are always with me, and all that is mine is yours" (Luke 15:31). Scripture tells us that God is always near, ever present, bestowing every good thing a loving father gives, including the full light and blessing of His thoughts for each of His children.

Jesus establishes obedient disciples as His friends: "If you keep my commandments, you will abide in my love,... Greater love has no man than this, that a man lay down his life for his friends. You are my friends if you do what I command you. No longer do I call you servants, for the servant does not know what his master is doing; but I have called you friends, for all that I have heard from my Father I have made known to you" (John 15:10-15).

I Corinthians 1:9 reveals: "God is faithful, by whom you were called into the fellowship of his Son, Jesus Christ our Lord." I Corinthians 3:21-23 tells us: "For all things are yours, whether... the world or life or death or the present or the future, all are yours; and you are

Christ's; and Christ is God's." Ephesians 3:12-13 discloses that in Christ "we have boldness and confidence of access (to God) through our faith in him." See also, Ephesians 3:19 and Hebrews 10:19-22. Ephesians 1:4-5 explains: "even as he chose us in him before the foundation of the world, that we should be holy and blameless before him. He destined us in love to be his sons through Jesus." 2 Peter 3:18 commands: "grow in the grace and knowledge of our Lord." "Come boldly to the throne of grace" (Hebrews 4:16).

I John 1:3-6 confirms: "that which we have seen and heard we proclaim also to you, so that you may have fellowship with us; and our fellowship is with the Father and with his Son Jesus Christ. And we are writing this that our joy may be complete... If we say we have fellowship with him while we walk in darkness, we lie and do not live according to the truth." I John 2:23 adds: "No one who denies the Son has the Father. He who confesses the Son has the Father also." And I John 3:24 says when we obey Jesus' commandments, "by this we know that he abides in us, by the Spirit which he has given us." I John 5:20 puts it: "And we know that the Son of God has come and has given us understanding, to know him who is true; and <u>we are in him who is true</u>, in his Son."

Our eternal destiny is to be in God's presence: "Behold the dwelling of God is with men. He will dwell with them, and they shall be his people, and God himself will be with them... He who conquers shall have this heritage, and I will be his God and he shall be my son" (Revelation 21:3,7). Revelation 4:11, KJV confirms we exist to give God pleasure: "Thou art worthy, o Lord, to receive glory and honor and power: for thou hast created all things, and for thy pleasure they are and were created."

Jesus proclaims His willingness to share the most congenial fellowship of dining with believers: "Behold, I stand at the door and knock; if any one hears my voice and opens the door, I will come in to him and eat with him, and he with me" (Revelation 3:20). Hebrews 13:5 recalls the words of Jesus: "I will never fail you nor forsake you," and Jesus also promises; "and lo, I am with you always to the close of the age" (Matthew 28:20).

God's intent to be a God to His people and fellowship with them, is also documented at Exodus 6:7, 33:13; Numbers 18:20; Deuteronomy 7:6, 29:13; 2 Chronicles 20:7; Psalms 27:8, 34:8, 61:4, 65:4; Isaiah 41:8; Jeremiah 3:24, 31:33, 32:38: Micah 7:9; Matthew 5:8; John 16:5-7, 10:27; Acts 13:17; I Corinthians 15:28; 2 Thessalonians 2:13; and Hebrews 8:10-11, 10:19).

HOLINESS THROUGH SUFFERING FITS US FOR FRIENDSHIP

We have observed that the same sun melts wax, as it hardens clay. A trial will quickly reveal our true substance, and how we respond is determined by us. If we purpose to submit to God's decision, we will seek His will for our next move. If we end up bitterly resenting God, we will lose the advantage we would have gained from the trial. Job "praised" God in his travail and was rewarded (Job 1:21), while the end-time victims of a terrible plague of hail "cursed God" and died (Revelation 16:21). The same winds of adversity can be harnessed to push one ship north and another south, depending on how each sets its sails and rudder. Even adverse winds can be used to push you closer to God, rather than blow you way from His safe haven.

Like any friendship, our friendship with God is fortified by shared hardships which cement the relationship and forge mutual trust through the crucible of suffering. The flames which engulfed Shadrach, Meshack and Abednego did not harm them in the fiery furnace, but revealed

Jesus was there with them, and ended up freeing them as their bonds were burned off (Daniel 3:25). A believer is seldom so close to God; so happy in His communion; so safe in His haven; or so aware of the transience and superficiality of all else, as during adversity. Tribulation deepens a man's prayer life, reveals how totally dependent he is upon God's mercy, and gives God opportunity to supply His deliverance. Trials push us to recognize that God is man's only dependable, loving, constant companion and gentle comforter.

God wants children who have an intimate, familial relationship with Him, not just intellectual knowledge about Him. Jesus is the highest and only value, and doing His work in our power is no substitute for His friendship. Pursuing truth does not replace knowing Him Who is the truth. Embracing redemption cannot supplant knowing the Redeemer. God does not desire sacrifice, nor delight in burnt offerings, but "The sacrifices of God are a broken spirit: a broken and contrite heart... the sacrifices of righteousness" (Psalm 51:17, 19). God wants us in a personal relationship with Him, in a condition transformed to the image of Christ, accomplished through the crucible of suffering, as necessary.

Thus, another way God uses suffering as an instrument to advance friendship is by developing holiness through affliction, which fits us for fellowship with God. Suffering increases, shapes, and is indispensable to Christ-like character, which in turn fits us for the society and companionship of God. God reveals at Isaiah 48:10: "Behold, I have refined thee, but not with silver; I have chosen thee in the furnace of affliction." Holiness is a process involving suffering, as our new nature disentangles from the unspiritual attachments of the flesh to the world. Worldly dross is extracted from our character by travails, and spiritual gold is produced by pain's refining process. Much that is good in us will be born through our suffering, patiently borne.

There must also be a connection between obedience and spiritual growth which fits us for fellowship; otherwise suffering will simply turn our attention to God. The transformation to the likeness of Christ is worked only by the Holy Spirit in the inner man. But if we are to change and grow spiritually, then obedience must cooperate with God's workings to transform us to the image of Christ. Knowing God intimately motivates obedience as proximity reveals His perfect character in clearer detail, while His light exposes our own dark imperfections. Without our collaboration, persisting in sin would neutralize or retard God's transforming power. With our cooperation, God leads us from glory to glory spiritually (2 Corinthians 3:18). God's fellowship leads us to spiritual fruitfulness, as proximity leads to emulation and enablement, so we become more like Him in character and the witness of our lives. The result of spiritual maturity is fuller enjoyment of God's society.

Parenthetically, God does not give us more friendship or responsibilities than we can bear to receive. Jesus told the eleven Apostles, His closets friends: "I have yet many things to say to you, but you cannot bear them now. When the Spirit of truth comes, he will guide you into all the truth" (John 16:12-13). All truth is available to believers, but the Spirit gives revelation according to our spiritual capacity, maturity and receptivity.

Jesus is our model, and we profit by emulating Him in every respect, including His intense suffering. "Although he was a Son, he learned obedience through what he suffered; and being made perfect he became the source of eternal salvation to all who obey him" (Hebrews 5:8-9). Jesus certainly knew the meaning of obedience before He rendered it to God in His humanness. Yet, suffering is the ultimate evocation of obedience, as pain would otherwise tend to drive us to escape, rather than endure it. Jesus rendered as much obedience as was humanly possible, since the severity of His test exacted fully perfect obedience.

Jesus experienced what obedience demanded in terms of the suffering it entailed, and was perfected for His role as sympathetic High priest and Intercessor for His people. Jesus acquired knowledge about the human condition because He was genuinely human. Thus, Luke 2:52 tells us that "Jesus increased in wisdom and in stature," even though He was mysteriously and divinely perfect in wisdom as the Son of God. Hebrews 2:18 puts it: "For because he himself has suffered and been tempted, he is able to help those who are tempted." See also, Hebrews 4:15.

Like Jesus, Who obeyed and was perfected through His obedience in suffering, we likewise can increase in holiness, victory over Satan, and deliverance from evil, by obediently bearing with the suffering which befalls us. Our character cannot help but improve when we model our behavior after Jesus, including enduring suffering parallel to His, for the obedient love of Him. A believer's salvation is based only upon faith, but his sanctification and perfection in glorification is facilitated by obedience. This is consistent with Jesus' admonition: "If any man would come after me, let him deny himself and take up his cross and follow me. For whoever would save his life will lose it; and whoever loses his life for my sake and the gospel's will save it" (Luke 8:34-35). Romans 8:17 says we can be heirs of God with Christ, "provided we suffer with him in order that we may also be glorified with him."

SUFFERING ENHANCES CHRIST-LIKENESS

Another way suffering promotes friendship with God is when we share the same activity as Christ by enduring suffering as He did. For, shared experience is the means to cement friendship and to gain insight into what events have shaped our friends. We will know Jesus better when we gain appreciation, and even share in and cultivate, His character traits. By sharing the fellowship of His suffering, we will see how He reacted to and overcame travail, and in that way come to know Him.

Philippians 3:8-11 extols suffering loss as a way of knowing Jesus: "For his sake I have suffered the loss of all things, and count them as refuse, in order that I may gain Christ... through faith in Christ... that I may know him and the power of his resurrection, and may share his sufferings, becoming like him in his death, that if possible I may attain the resurrection from the dead." Suffering makes us receptive, and opens us to the same power which resurrected Christ; which transforms us to His likeness; and prepares us for reunion with Christ at the resurrection of the dead. 2 Corinthians 4:8-10 says: "We are afflicted... always carrying in the body the death of Jesus, so that the life of Jesus may also be manifested in our bodies." When we suffer as Jesus did, we gain insight into the depth of His limitless love for us.

I Peter 4:12-13 calls us to welcome "the fiery ordeal which comes upon you to prove you... But rejoice insofar as you share Christ's sufferings, that you may also rejoice and be glad when his glory is revealed." In context, Peter is referring to contemporary suffering more easily endured in the knowledge of future glory at Christ's return (I Peter 1:7, 5:1). However, sharing the sufferings of Christ produces, in this world as well as the next, shared joy with Him (Hebrews 12:2); fellowship with Him (Philippians 3:10); glorification with Him (Romans 8:17); and reigning with Him (2 Timothy 2:12). Romans 8:18 observes: "I consider that the sufferings of this present time are not worth comparing with the glory <u>that is to be revealed in us.</u>"

Suffering prepares the unsaved, driven by privation, to find Jesus, and appreciate the depth of His loving sacrifice, so they are drawn to Him by His suffering on the Cross. When we experience what Christ endured, and understand how He responded to suffering, we will be able to react the same way He did when we encounter comparable suffering in the world. When we suffer persecution as He did, emboldened by His example, we can practice the depth of His love and the nobility of His grace in forgiving His persecutors from the Cross. We will better understand the strength of His endurance when we encounter tribulations which we must endure. Peter and the Apostles were beaten for preaching about Jesus, yet "they left the presence of the Council, rejoicing that they were counted worthy to suffer dishonor for the name" (Acts 5:41).

Without suffering, we could not comprehend St. Paul's comments: "Now I rejoice in my sufferings for your sake, and in my flesh I complete what remains of Christ's afflictions for the sake of his body, that is, the church" (Colossians 1:24). This is not to suggest that Christ's sacrificial suffering on the Cross is ongoing, or was incomplete to accomplish our salvation, for it is sufficient and efficient (Hebrews 10:10, 14, 32). Rather, it relates to the afflictions which are continually sustained by the members of Christ's Body, the Church, which we are called to relieve that Christ might be exalted. We share the suffering of Christ when we bear the burdens, or share the grief, mourning or affliction of another, as Jesus did, by offering aid, relief or comfort in their travails. Missionaries bear our burden to witness to the unsaved, acting on behalf of all believers. Helpers who provide any need of another, at the sacrifice of their own comfort or provision, share the suffering of Christ, and are enriched by their loving emulations.

Christ suffers with us when we are afflicted, and is affected by what affects us. God sorrows over our rebellion and the consequences of sin for us. Jesus reveals that He shares intimate union and identity with His Body when He queries of St. Paul, a tormentor of the early Church, "Saul, Saul, <u>why do you persecute me</u>?" (Acts 9:4). Our suffering prepares us for the privilege of ministering to, caring for, enduring, and alleviating the contemporary suffering of others in the Body of Christ. Philippians 1:29 discloses: "For it has been granted to you that for the sake of Christ you should not only believe in him but also suffer for his sake."

We will never fully appreciate Jesus' resistance to temptation until we experience it, and through that come to understand His strength of character. We will not learn how to be dead to sin like Jesus until we also suffer for the sake of righteousness, and are crucified to sin as Jesus was crucified <u>for</u> our sins. We cannot atone for the sins of mankind by suffering as Jesus did, but we can learn the depths of His love when we endure our pains. We may even imitate Christ's work by offering up our suffering to glorify God, as Jesus did, who offered His suffering sacrificially and lovingly on behalf of others. Our own suffering must be ennobled by the same motive of loving service, if we are to be like Jesus. When we pattern our response to suffering after Jesus' we will be sensitive to the needs of others, rather than concentrating on our own.

Suffering teaches us to respond to life the same way Jesus did: in love, acceptance of persons, and understanding toward others. We will learn how Jesus was sanctified or separated from the world by experiencing what He did in affliction. We will gain comfort in sorrow: "For as we share abundantly in Christ's sufferings, so through Christ we share abundantly in comfort too" (2 Corinthians 1:5; see also Psalm 23:4; Isaiah 40:1, 49:13, 51:3, 61:2; Matthew 5:4 and Acts 9:31).

When we, ourselves, suffer we will learn the love of Christ in His Body, as our brothers and sisters in the Lord minister to our needs, and help us overcome grief and tragedy by their very presence. They will remind us that there is still a life to be lived, and much in the world for which to be thankful; that we are left with much, even though we may have suffered a great loss. Their human ministry, as the hands and words of Christ, inspired by Him, will remind us that more good things happen in the world than bad things. And our example of endurance may encourage others to bear their burdens faithfully.

We first love God because He first loved us, and demonstrated that love through grace, mercy, and blessings. However, God wants us to love, enjoy, and cherish Him for Himself and Who He is, not just because He gives us things. God wants us to rejoice, celebrate, and enjoy our objects and gratifications which Daddy brings home, but tempered by remembering and worshipping Him as Almighty God, from Whom every good and perfect gift comes. Jesus teaches that if we "first seek the Kingdom of God and His righteousness," then we shall be blessed with food, drink, and clothing (Matthew 6:31, 33).

When things go well, it is easy to remember God in thanksgiving for a moment, and then rush to share our happiness with the world. Conversely, in the midst of our grief or privation we are driven to spend more time looking for God. Acts 17:27 explains that God made men "that they should seek God, in hope that they might feel after him and find him. Yet he is not far from each one of us." When we seek the Lord, Himself, and His righteousness, rather than His gifts, we will begin to appreciate that His fellowship and the eternal blessings He is working are superior to any other perquisites of our sonship. Making room for God's governance by evicting self-reliance from one's life explains the promise of Matthew 5:3: "Blessed are the poor in spirit, for theirs is the Kingdom of Heaven."

In the world, suffering accompanies seeking and finding the Kingdom of God, "and every one enters it violently" (Luke 16:16), "and through many tribulations we must enter the kingdom of God" (Acts 14:22). Seeking God and His Kingdom at the expense of worldly pursuits, requires strength of desire and commitment. It calls for earnestness, firm resolve, supreme effort, and intensity, appreciating the great rewards of fellowship, righteousness, and laying "up for yourselves treasure in heaven" (Matthew 6:20).

We may be involved in reading the Scriptures, practicing faith, or ministering to the needs of others, but unless we focus on fellowship with God as the object of our endeavor, our efforts will lack direction. We are called to single-mindedness of focus and purpose, not running aimlessly, nor striving "as one who beats the air" (I Corinthians 9:26). We must persist, and overcome opposition and difficulties in our pursuit of the Kingdom of God and His righteousness, for there is struggle in much of our Christian walk, discouragement, suffering from loss of worldly things, and temptations to waver in our resolve.[156]

Pain and suffering play a part in the poverty and abnegation of worldly things, for Jesus says: "If any man would come after me, let him deny himself and take up his cross and follow me" (Matthew 16:24). The flesh will mourn its severance from worldly temptations and feel the pain of such loss. But the way to deeper knowledge of God and possession of all things spiritual is by renouncing the oppression of worldly lusts. Jesus puts it: "whoever loses his life for my sake will find it" (Matthew 16:24).

James 4:4-8 reminds us: "friendship with the world is enmity with God. Therefore whoever wishes to be a friend of the world makes himself an enemy of God... Draw near to God and he will draw near to you." The way to approach God is to divest oneself of all attachment and attraction to the world; to sever oneself from all distractions which turn our attention from God. We must repudiate our fleshly, fallen nature of self-glorification and self-sufficiency. The man who has God at the center of his life, has all things in One. Everything else is external and meant to serve man.

Our goal is no longer possession of things, but possession of God and by God; not slavery to the tyranny of things, but liberation in the presence and right service of the Master. Worldly treasures may be lacking, or in abundance, but they make no real contribution to the joy of one who knows God as his first, total, and only pleasure; his sole delight and satisfaction. Only then, can God reign supreme and unchallenged in the heart of a believer, who seeks to possess nothing except God. Though one may continue to have and use his earthly blessings in their proper place, they no longer control him. Indeed, whatever we entrust to the Lord is best maintained and preserved by Him as our treasure laid up in Heaven.

If we rid ourselves of pride, we will have no concern for the world's judgments or persecutions. Our only concern will be how we stand in the presence of God. We free ourselves from the world by deriving all status and worth as a child of God. We will have no pride in ourselves if we recognize everything we are is in God, and comes from Him. We will have no room for pretense or artificiality, because we draw our genuineness from membership in the Body of Christ. Jesus determines where we are, what we are, and who we are, and the world's opinion of us is put in its proper place; all is of secondary importance to what God thinks of us.

We can serve God "with a perfect heart and with a willing mind" (I Chronicles 28:9), when we seek perfect integrity in total submission to God's perfect will. May God grant each of us the grace to respond to God's call; to turn to Him earnestly; and seek to develop spiritual receptivity to His holiness in total obedience, trust, and humility.[157]

CHAPTER 17

PORTALS TO FELLOWSHIP WITH GOD

"You are my friends if you do what I command you."

–John 15:14

"That which we have seen and heard we proclaim also to you, so that you may have fellowship with us; and our fellowship is with the Father and with his Son, Jesus Christ."

–I John 1:3

God pursues us all the days of our lives. He persuades and convicts us in righteousness; and He is always there for us in grace, mercy, guidance, and love. But He will not force Himself upon any free being, and if we persist in rebelliously rejecting Him, He will honor our choice, though it result in the death of us. Through all of this, He gives us the privilege of participating in friendship with Him by inviting us to seek him so He may be found. God both draws us to Him and rushes to meet us, as the Father of the Prodigal Son did when he saw him approaching (Luke 15:20). Communion is initiated by God, and is mostly His activity, not ours. So we can depend upon Him to reveal Himself so we can experience Him, as long as we remain open and receptive.

GOD INITIATES COMMUNION WITH MAN

From the dawn of history, men have been aware of God's existence, presence, power, glory, and benevolence, communicated then, as now, in the firmament and beauty of His Creation (Psalm 19:1; Romans 1:20). Primitive men believed His displeasure was expressed in natural calamities and departures from ordinary phenomena. However, for the past 6000 years, God has communicated with men through the Scriptures, declared to be His Holy Word, in which He reveals His love, concern and benevolent intent toward men, both in history and for eternity. From the Garden of Eden, Passover, the deliverance of Israel from Egypt, Christ's redemption and Resurrection, to the present, God's people have experienced His Providential grace, deliverance, forgiveness, and blessings.

God's Word details the beauty and excellence of His character, exemplified in the life of Christ; His desire that we emulate it; and His promise to empower faithful men as agents to transact His plans and purposes. God communicates through His Word by prescribing our submissive obedience which pleases Him and promotes our well-being as well as His objectives and purposes for us. He uses the Word not only to guide our thoughts and conduct, but also to transform and grow us spiritually through obedience to, and practice of, the Word (John 6:63; Mark 4:14-32; 2 Peter 1:4). In this, the Holy Spirit recalls and explains the Word to us, guides us into all truth, and shows us Jesus (John 14:26; 16:13-14; I Corinthians 2:12-13; I Thessalonians 2:13). "We have access by one spirit unto the Father" (Ephesians 2:18, KJV).

The reward of knowing Christ is articulated at 2 Peter 1:3: "His divine power has granted to us all things that pertain to life and godliness, through the knowledge of Him who called us to His own glory and excellence, by which... you may... become partakers of the divine nature." The more we know Him, the more we have access to all things. Our growth in holiness is intimately involved in Christ, and is a form of communion with Him. Ephesians 2:5 says that God "made us alive together with Christ." God provides the immortal, spiritual life of Jesus in the Word which builds up believers; in the Holy Spirit, Who indwells believers and recalls the words of Christ; and in Christ, Himself, Who is the Vine in Whom we reside, and from Whom we draw spiritual strength and nurture. The Holy Spirit builds believers together for the habitation of God (Ephesians 2:22), and strengthens us with inner might (Ephesians 3:16), to strive for the holiness without which no one will see the Lord (Hebrews 12:14).

Through the Holy Spirit, the Word activates and imparts divine life to believers, and fashions their holiness: "the words that I have spoken to you are spirit and life" (John 6:63). The Kingdom of God originates in the Word, germinates and grows in a believer, and "produces of itself" (Mark 4:14; see also, Joshua 1:7-8; Psalms 19:7-8, 119:71; Matthew 13:18-23; Acts 20:32; 2 Timothy 3:15-16; Colossians 3:16; I Peter 2:2; 2 Peter 1:4). James 1:21 speaks of "the implanted word, which is able to save your soul." Jesus teaches: "You are already made clean by the word" (Ephesians 5:26), which brings "forth fruit with patience," when held fast in a good heart (Luke 8:15).

Even more, "God is at work in you" to accomplish your spiritual transformation (Philippians 2:13), through a mutual indwelling by which He enters believers' lives in the most intimate manner and union, no longer a God 'out there' or simply 'with us', but present in us, as a Person. Jesus reveals: "I am in my Father, and you in me, and I in you" (John 14:20, 23; see also, John 10:38, 15:9, 17:11, 21). As constituent parts of His Body, we are in Jesus, and He is in God, just as God is in Jesus, which allows us to be in God. Like a drop of water in the sea, we are constituently in the whole, even as the sea contains all the drops of water. We retain our own individuality and identity, as a grain of sand on shore, while we are integrated parts of the whole. During this merger, absorption, mingling, and synthesis of the divine and human personalities, God communicates a shared identity which imparts the perfect life and likeness of Christ to the faithful.

We do not change God in any way, nor lose our own identity, but are incorporated into, and complete the Body of Christ, of which Jesus is the Head; enjoying interaction, interdependence, and exchange of energy, much as cells and nerves interact in a physical body (Romans 12:5; Galatians 3:28). Because we share the same indwelling Holy Spirit with them, we have an affinity for every other member of the Church through the New Birth (2 Corinthians 13:14; I John 4:13). God communicates and blesses believers through the ministrations, spiritual gifts, encouragement, edification, and counsel of other Christians. Each believer both imparts to, and draws strength from, the other members of the Body, for each is established and delegated as an agent of the Lord. Each is given a gift from the Holy Spirit, with which to serve 'the common good" (I Corinthians 12:7-11).

God communicates to us through the Church, directing us to "stir one another to love and good works" (Hebrews 10:24), and fellowship in our interconnection and brotherhood in Christ, using our spiritual gifts "until we all attain... to the measure of the stature of the fullness of Christ" (Ephesians 4:13). God is present in and through His Church: in communal praise and worship, prayer groups, Bible study, mentoring, Christian television and radio broadcasts of the Gospel, expository preaching, hymns, and in the company of those who demonstrate a close walk with Him.[158] Jesus promises God will answer our joint prayers: "if two of you agree on earth about anything they ask, it will be done for them by my Father in Heaven" (Matthew 18:19). Jesus is in our midst where two or more are gathered in His name (Matthew 18:20).

In communal sharing of the Holy Eucharist, God is especially close in presence, whether we believe He is in the sacrament of Holy Communion as in transubstantiation; or present at the Eucharist, as in consubstantiation; or imparting a special sense of His life during a remembrance ceremony. Jesus says at John 6:56: "He who eats my flesh and drinks my blood abides in me, and I in him," confirming a divine Blood Covenant which strengthens and sustains the partaker.

In the beginning, God spoke directly to Adam, and then to Abraham in directing him to leave for a land God would reveal later (Genesis 12:1). Jesus spoke directly to the Apostles, Disciples, and crowds in the First Century. Saul of Tarsus learned he had persecuted Jesus by direct communication from Him (Acts 9:4). God spoke through dreams as He revealed empires to David, and victory to Gideon through the dream of another (Judges 7:13). God spoke through angels to Daniel, Lot, Mary and Joseph, and countless others. He communicated through His Prophets, and speaks through circumstances which deny, frustrate or disappoint our desires in affliction, failure, loss and grief.

There may have been a time God revealed His will through urim and thummin (Numbers 27:21), or by moistening Gideon's fleece as a verification of support in victory (Judges 6:39-40). But primarily God speaks to us by His Holy Spirit in our inner man or conscience (Romans 8:14, 16). Since the Holy Spirit indwells believers, we can expect His leading to be more by inner consciousness than outward signs.[159] And we have communion with the Spirit as we receive His testimony. Romans 9:1 says: "my conscience bears me witness in the Holy Spirit," and is reliable because our spirit is in harmony with, and bears the life of the Holy Spirit (I John 5:9-10, see also, John 16:13; Acts 16:6). The Spirit articulates "the gifts bestowed on us by God" and interprets spiritual truths to believers (I Corinthians 2:12-13). He reminds us to do what pleases God by doing right, for "no one comprehends the thoughts of God except the Spirit of God" (I Corinthians 2:11).

The Holy Spirit communicates to us our own needs and shortcomings, so we can take these to Christ for rectification and remediation. The Spirit "helps us in our weakness, for we do not know how to pray as we ought," and intercedes for us "according to the will of God" (Romans 8:26-27). He not only re-directs our prayers by His intercession, but inspires in us a recognition of our true needs and infirmities so we can pray to God as we ought, guided by the Spirit, Who alone knows the mind of God.

God responds to our praise, and in fact inhabits the praises of Israel (Psalm 22:3); Israel being the root of Covenant which Gentiles share, and into which they have been grafted by faith (Romans 11:17, 23). The presence of God in our praises is reflected in the joy we experience when we recount the blessings from God which are worthy of praise, and recollect every good and perfect gift God provides (Psalms 5:11, 27:6, 28:7, 32:11, 33:1, 35:9, 42:1, 43:4).

Reverence for God, also referred to as fear of God, helps us seek and know the Lord. "The secret of the Lord is with them that fear him; and He will shew them His covenant" (Psalm 15:14). In the sense that God's Word provides insight into the character and mind of God, the revelations of the Word are invited by fear of the Lord. Proverbs 1:7 teaches: "The fear of the Lord is the beginning of knowledge." See also, Proverbs 9:10, 15:33, and 31:30.

God responds to our confessions of sin with mercy, forgiveness, and cleansing from all unrighteousness (I John 1:9). God provides peace, deliverance, and freedom from anxiety when we entrust our cares and concerns to Jesus (I Peter 5:7). God wants to relieve the fear, anxiety, concern, tension, and worldly weariness of believers. Let your best friend be in control and take over your cares, and He will deliver you from any evil influences in your life. He will help you to focus on Jesus' all-sufficiency, grace, and mercy, rather than your failure or inadequacy. If you cultivate the Sabbath habit of resting in the Lord, and cease your own labors and self-direction, God will begin when you stop. But you must trust Him, rest in Him, and stay secure in Him. Offer yourself completely to God, and be willing to obey Him unreservedly, and He will renovate you into what you ought to be, according to His will. Faith is trusting God to do what His Word promises, and abiding His good and perfect timing.

In fact, God responds and communicates His pleasure in our submissive obedience, whenever we participate in the tasks God has delegated to believers, in which we serve as His ambassadors and agents here on earth. When we obey the Great Commission to witness the Gospel to the unsaved, amidst prayer for their divine conviction, and a lost sinner repents and turns toward Jesus, God and all of Heaven respond by rejoicing (Luke 15:7). Furthermore, we have collaborated in adding another member to the Church, who may dialogue, serve, and share with us, as God's newest representative.

When we pray for guidance and direction, God responds with wisdom and counsel (Proverbs 2:3-5; James 1:5). When believers pray and seek God's face, and turn from their wicked ways, then God promises He will: "forgive their sin, and will heal their land" (2 Chronicles 7:14). I Chronicles 28:9 has a double promise: "if thou seek him, he will be found of thee; but if thou forsake him, he will cast thee off forever." See also, 2 Chronicles 15:2; Proverbs 8:17; Jeremiah 29:13; Lamentations 3:25; and Amos 5:4, 6. Deuteronomy 4:29 proclaims: "seek the Lord thy God, thou shalt find him, if thou seek him with all thy heart and with all thy soul."

God is especially responsive to intercessory prayers for the well being of others, because they accomplish His purposes, and coincide with His love, mercy, care, and concern for others, rather than self. He is present, not only because He hears our prayers, but also because He is pleased by our submissive obedience in seeking to fulfill our part, incorporated into His plans, to benefit others. And because He is love, He is thus present and entwined in our loving intercessory prayers, just as He is in our loving acts toward others.

Because our reliance on God's promises for the future is based on His faithful fulfillment of past promises as recorded in His Word (Romans 10:17), and empirically verified to us, we can faithfully pray for and enlist His intervention in, and transformation of, this world. God factors in, and responds to, our faith, when it directly expresses agreement with His plans and purposes, and He applies it to the substance of things hoped for, and the evidence of things unseen (Hebrews 11:1).

When Peter saw Jesus walking on the water in the midst of a storm, he said: "Lord, if it is you, bid me come to you on the water," and Jesus empowered Peter to walk on the water and come toward Him (Matthew 14:28-29). But Peter's faith was necessary to heed Christ's call to draw near and when Peter was distracted by the storm and failed to keep his focus on Jesus, his faith failed, and he began to sink. Jesus saved him despite his lapse of concentration; "reached out his hand and caught him," and drew Peter to His side (Matthew 14:31-32).

We must also intend to be like Christ if we wish to be near Him, and this calls for obedience and holiness. Amos 3:3 asks: "Can two walk together except they be agreed?" 2 Chronicles 15:2 promises: "The Lord is with you, while ye be with him; and if he seek him, he will be found of you." Our encounters with God in obedient service, love, witness, holiness, prayer, and praise, are more than communication with God; they rise to a level of union with Him and collaborative sharing of His interests and purposes. There is a special awareness of His close observation, knowing our obedient acts are pleasing to God, even as they lay up treasure in Heaven. We are blessed with goodness, and hidden in the secret of God's presence, when we obey and fear God (Psalm 31:19-20; see also, Jeremiah 9:24; Isaiah 64:5).

Jesus promises to reveal Himself to obedient believers (John 14:21). Our obedient love for God especially attracts His love and companionship as a reward. Jesus says: "If a man love me, he will keep my word, and my Father will love him, and we will come to him and make our home with him" (John 14:23; see also, Proverbs 8:17; 2 Corinthians 13:11; I Peter 4:14; and I John 4:12). When we minister lovingly to the needs of others, Jesus says it is the same as ministering to Him (Matthew 25:40), as a point of direct contact. We cannot love God without loving our brothers (I John 4:20, 21). But while we have the capacity to love God by loving men, we must not fail to love, glorify, and dote on Him at least as much and as often.

The Holy Spirit makes us new creatures in Christ, sharing His very nature, and we cooperate in developing our transformation on a sustained basis by pursuing holiness and not quenching, grieving, or resisting the Holy Spirit by ingratitude or disobedience. Hebrews 12:14 tells us to "Strive for... the consecration without which no one will see the Lord." We are enjoined to "walk in the Spirit" (Galatians 5:25), which means conforming to His holy way, by the power of His indwelling presence. In these ways, we learn God's very nature, and fit ourselves for meaningful dialogue with our Father. No one can "ascend into the hill of the Lord" or "stand in his holy place," without clean hands and a pure heart (Psalm 24:3-4).

As we behold the glory of the Lord, we "are being changed into his likeness from one degree of glory to another; for this comes from the Lord who is the Spirit" (2 Corinthians 3:18). The Holy Spirit speaks as he calls, converts, regenerates, indwells and infills us with His presence, gives spiritual fruit to us, and gives gifts to perform the work of Christ. He communicates by illumination and discernment to understand and share in the process, and empowers our conscious receptivity; all of which proceeds only from our earlier attachment to the Vine, Who is Christ (John 15:4-5). Hence, we have "the mind of Christ" (I Corinthians 2:16; see also, James 1:5).

Our discussion would not be complete in a book on God's easing of suffering, without noting that God speaks through suffering to communicate our need to change, and as a deterrent against future sinful conduct. The Holy Spirit gives comfort, in the special fellowship of consolation and counsel, which helps us endure affliction while we learn its lessons. The Holy Spirit's comforts are everlasting, enabling, and powerful (Acts 9:31; 2 Thessalonians 2:16; and Hebrews 6:18), imparted in His fruits of love, joy, peace, faithfulness, patience, goodness, kindness, gentleness, and self-control in our lives.

God may use suffering as an instrument to develop holiness through affliction, which fits us for the society, companionship, and fellowship of God. Hosea 6:1-3 recognizes that God intends and sends some suffering so we may discover Him in and through it: "Come, and let us return unto the Lord; for he hath torn, and he will heal us; he hath smitten, and he will bind us up... and we shall live in his sight. Then shall we know, <u>if we follow on to know the Lord</u>: his going forth is prepared as the morning; and <u>he shall come unto us</u> as the rain, as the latter and former rain unto the earth." God's reliability and providence shall be revealed "if we follow on" to know him. The Spirit reveals God's hand in suffering, so we can rejoice in His loving summons to repent and turn to Him for restored fellowship (Ephesians 5:20; I Thessalonians 1:6, 5:16).

When God has faithfully helped us endure suffering, or delivered us from its afflictions, he directs us to share our example and experience, and communicate His love and concern to others who need encouragement, edification, and His strength. Each of us is God's agent to share the instructive lessons learned in the crucible of suffering: of God's forgiveness, cleansing, and spiritual growth, and thereby ease the burdens of other sufferers. Even revealing your punishment for sin can deter others from self-inflicted pain, or edify them by attesting to God's faithfulness in overcoming affliction, and providing forgiveness and cleansing. The example of Paul suffering in prison, yet enduring by the grace of God, is not a lesson about punishment for Paul, but of encouragement for us who have need of God's comfort and strength.

MAN'S PART IN FELLOWSHIP

It is true that "God does it all," but man's willing collaboration can ease and accelerate the process of friendship. It is well to remember that every human friendship is built, nurtured, and cultivated by discovering someone else is willing to entrust His friendship to you, based on shared attraction, aspiration, attitude and experiences. Friendship is then built and nurtured by shared activity or association; by spending time together.[160] Friendship's foundation develops common interests; the open exchange of and attention to, what each regards as important in word and deed. Friendship bolsters one another's empowerment and mutual regard; expressed in support, affection, admiration, and acceptance of one another, tempered by appropriate reproofs out of loving concern for the best interests of one's friend.

God has already communicated His unfailing love for us by approving, accepting, and affirming us because of Jesus, and making everything He has available to us in Christ Jesus. In turn, we love God because He first loved us since we are in Jesus and He in us, and despite our natural imperfections, character defects, failures, or lack of merit. We love Jesus and recognize Him as our best friend because he gave His life to save us and restore us to right relationship with God. "He delivered me because he delighted in me" (Psalm 18:19), and did that in our most wretched and unlovable state, before we were even aware of His grace. We remain secure in His love because He continues to draw us to Him; rushes to embrace us as the father of the Prodigal Son did; accomplishes our illumination, spiritual transformation to glorification; enables our response, and reveals Himself so we can know and trust Him.

Once we have been drawn to the Lord, experienced Him through the Word, and grasped His accessibility, our initial responses are likely to be petitionary prayers, expressing needs and desires, exploring aspirations to glory, and freely discussing apprehensions and anxieties with a loving parent, without feeling self-conscious or inhibited. These will be interspersed with utterances of thanksgiving, adoration, praise, and worship for everything which reveals His benevolence, control, involvement, beauty, and creativity (Psalm 19:1-4; Romans 1:20). We would have unlimited and ongoing opportunities for fellowship with God if we were to give thanks whenever He blesses us, especially when He blesses us extravagantly. We can start with the air we breathe and the heartbeats which sustain life, and proceed to appreciate each grace and kindness He shows us, our loved ones, and our nation. We may discuss salvation, spiritual growth, and preparation for Heaven. We can admit shortcomings and difficulties, without fear of rejection or rebuke, and honestly seek God's help in exposure of forgotten sins, improvement, overcoming, and deliverance from temptations to sin. We have unlimited opportunities to seek wisdom and instruction for daily living.

Fasting is another fruitful source of communication with the Lord. While Jesus did not command fasting, He legitimated its practice by His example preceding the temptations by Satan, and "fasted forty days and forty nights" (Matthew 4:2; Luke 4:2). He identified certain evil spirits as "This kind cannot be driven out by anything but prayer and fasting' (Mark 9:29). He ordained fasting by saying: "when you fast, do not look dismal... that your fasting may not be seen by men; and your Father who sees in secret will reward you;" (Matthew 6:16; see also, Matthew 9:15). St. Paul and the early Church practiced fasting (Acts 9:9, 13:2-3; 2 Corinthians 6:4-5; Luke 2:37).

The essence of fasting is mourning or repentance, evidenced by one's humbling of self through denial or sacrifice (Joel 2:16). It is the "chastening" or the "affliction of the soul" (Psalm 69:10; Ezra 8:21; Isaiah 58:3). When we invoke God's mercy by fasting, our penitent prayers are amplified and answered (I Kings 21:27-28; Joel 1;14; Ezra 8:23; Isaiah 58:9; cf. Jeremiah 14:12). Often, God responds to fasting by counsel and guidance (Judges 20:26-27), heightened awareness, insight and understanding (Daniel 9:3, 21; 10:12). Isaiah 58:11 says the reward of fasting is "the Lord guide thee continually and satisfy thy soul in drought, and make fat thy bones." Fasting brings peace; looses the bands of wickedness; undoes heavy burdens; frees the oppressed; and rewards one with "the glory of the Lord" (Isaiah 58:6, 8).

Through fasting, God motivates believers "to deal thy bread to the hungry, and...bring the poor that are cast out to thy house" (Isaiah 58:7). As a result of fasting, "Then shall... thine health spring forth speedily" (Isaiah 58:8). If we would be spiritual, fasting can help to reject the indulgence of the flesh, and reassert the soul's dominance over the body (I Corinthians 9:27); making fasting both a spiritual weapon and enjoyable blessing.

As we seek understanding of suffering, or express gratitude for exemption, release, or deliverance from it, we may discuss why affliction exists to burden others, or ask the reason for our own travails or freedom from them. Intercessory prayers for afflicted men offer unlimited opportunity for discourse and active collaboration with God. When you thank God for the faculties He has freely given you, you will also come to sympathize with the burdens of those who are blind, deaf, or lame, and offer special prayers to God to help, sustain, or bless them in other ways, especially with Heavenly rewards for their example of faithful endurance.

You become more open to God's blessings through faithful intercessions. Job 42:10 relates: "And the Lord turned the captivity of Job, when he prayed for his friends: also the Lord gave Job twice as much as he had before." You will never lack for intercessory prayers, once you expand them to include family, neighbors, service providers, clergy, missionaries, broadcasters, leaders in authority, persecuted saints, widows, prisoners, the infirm, poor, downtrodden, their families, and the unsaved, not necessarily in that order.

As we expand our circle of concern for others, we will discover countless occasions for points of contact with God about their needs. Likewise, we will find God when we seek to minister lovingly to the needs of others. Tell God you are ready to do things His way, and seek His marching orders and guidance every step of the way, and you will never run out of topics for conversation. If you pray the prayer of Jabez: "Oh that thou wouldest bless me indeed, and enlarge my coast" (I Chronicles 4:10), you will have unlimited topics of conversation with God about how He intends to expand your ministry and blessings; and then you will have opportunities to give thanks as God grants that which you requested. Keep a journal of God's responses for days of wavering faith, as a reminder, verification, and assurance of God's faithfulness. We increase our love for God when we gratefully recall how much He loves and blesses us.

When we submit obediently to the Word, which is God's direct communication to us, and consciously intend obedience as a means of pleasing our Father, we present and communicate ourselves as living sacrifices to the Lord (Romans 12:1). Jesus defines friendship with Him as doing what He commands us to do (John 15:14), and promises to reveal Himself to obedient believers (John 14:21). When we seek to do God's will, He guides and teaches us in His righteous ways (Psalms 18:28. 25:9, 25:14; Proverbs 1:7, 2:6-9, 9:10, 16:3, 22:4; and 2 Timothy 2:7). It is more than merely wishing to be associated with Him or grasp the benefits of relationship with Him. For, Jesus told many who sought to follow Him that He never knew them (Matthew 7:23). Friendship requires submissive obedience; wanting to please Jesus by imitating His Holy thoughts, words, and deeds.

Your interest in the welfare of any friend deepens in proportion to your involvement in His interests. When you are drawn to a friend by his character, you go out of your way to discover, digest, and discuss subjects and activities which please him. You seek to give him joy in you by reflecting and sharing his interests and desires. With God, we can share His noblest character and perfect capacity to enjoy holy thoughts, subjects, and actions, even as He develops them in us.

There will also be Sabbath days when we rest in Him from all activity, simply to enjoy the consolation of His presence and companionable silence. We must stop and be still to appreciate His ever-constant presence, wishes, and transforming work in our lives, making Him the object of our affection, meditation, and activity. Every hour of the day, concentrate on loving and obedient things to do, and you will never lack opportunities to embrace Him and enjoy intimate communion with God.

When we collaborate in the Great Commission to bring the Gospel to all the world, we share God's desire that all men come to repentance and be saved. The Holy Spirit will anoint our words, prepare the hearts of the unsaved to receive the saving Word, and convict unbelievers of sin, making them aware, based on their own choice, that they must meet Jesus now as Lord and Saviour, or later as Judge of the damned.

Friendship is turning your life over to the Lord and submitting to Him; making Him the center and purpose of your life. It is expressed in works; not works to earn salvation, but to please Him. Our obedience seeks the attainment of God's objectives, empowered by, and collaborating with Him as His ambassador or agent, to His glory. Once we have submitted to God for direction, we should pray for enablement and fulfillment of what God has revealed as His will for us. If we will simply cultivate the habit of consulting God for His counsel on major decisions in life, we would regularly multiply the opportunities for communion and occasions for fellowship, as we explore the mind of our Heavenly Father. If we would go to Him for direction and advice in every significant decision of our lives, we would enjoy His constant company. We will be in communion because we are completely yielded to God and surrender full control over our daily activities to Him as Lord.

Our obedient, loving actions in loving service to others afford us joy because they involve God's loving presence. If we will only surrender our self-centered assertiveness to God's power, He will respond by anointing our stewardship with His perfection and power. Let every approach to God and every petition for fellowship with Him be borne by a complete surrender to Him to transform you to the image of Christ.[161] We are called to "Become partakers of the divine nature" (2 Peter 1:4), and our receptivity to God working the transformation to the divine image of Christ is a major part of our communion. We need to be soft and pliable, and change our attitudes and actions to want what God wants and do what God does, so that we can be transformed by God. It is only in God's presence, positioned where he would prefer us; focused and receptive to His leading, that we can be rightly situated to be guided by Him. This conscious cooperation to practice obedience, receive, and facilitate holiness is preliminary and ongoing communion with God.

Especially seek the fullness of the Holy Spirit (Acts 2:4; Ephesians 5:18), so that your whole life may be spiritual all the time, and God will conform your desires to His, and empower you to work according to His will (Philippians 2:13). God expresses His love for believers by making available to us in Christ Jesus, everything He is and has, including the gifts and fruit of the Holy Spirit, for the asking (Luke 11:13). He fulfills His promise that believers "Be filled with all the fullness of God" (Ephesians 3:19). Indeed, the objects of fellowship with God are to glorify him; have more of Him in our lives, to focus on our privileges in Jesus by access to God's grace, love, and heart; and see Christ formed in us. Our regeneration and sanctification remove the defilement of our natures and actual sins; transform us to the likeness of Christ; sanctify us with the Lord's actual thoughts, words, and deeds; and empower us to seek His fullness, works, fruits, and gifts.[162] "God's love has been poured into our hearts through the Holy Spirit which has been given us" (Romans 5:5).

God is glorified when we walk with Him in this way, and yearn for His righteousness. He is glorified by our avowals that without Him we cannot render obedience or attain holiness. For, in all matters God provides everything, and man can only cooperate to receive His grace. We will find Jesus where He is, walking in righteousness, and we will not abide in or near Christ unless we walk with Him. While we are engaged in sin, God will not fellowship with us. Neither will the Holy Spirit choose to dwell or thrive in the worldly cesspools of corruption which we allow to seep into our lives through sin. So our cooperation in obeying God's commandments is useful in facilitating spiritual growth. We cannot grow in character by God's power if we retard its operations by returning like dogs to the vomit of our sin (2 Peter 2:21-22). So we must follow His lead, for He will not walk with us in sin or join in foolish pursuits; nor will we when we walk His way. You can sit and watch secular television alone or with friends, but not with God. You will do your thing, or God's, but if your activities are not His, He will not be in them, though He will still be in you. Stop operating without God, and take on His activities and change your life. If you are not aware of God's presence, it is because you are not doing Godly things. Love somebody. Witness to somebody. Be holy, and when you do what God has called you to do, you will sense His presence.

Even the tedium of secular, repetitious work can be sublimated by devoting every act of daily labor to the glory of God. The humble stitches of Brother Lawrence, the tailor in monastic isolation, can be as holy an act of worship acceptable to God as the witness of a great evangelist preaching to an assembly of thousands, for God is glorified by both. And He holds us accountable only for the positive use of our abilities, not the lack of our limitations. Speak His words, and let your actions sincerely flatter Him with imitation. In short, "whether you eat or drink, or whatever you do, do all to the glory of God" (I Corinthians 10:31).

We glorify God by keeping our physical body clean and free from entanglements with worldly lusts, for "your body is a temple of the Holy Spirit within you... you were bought with a price. So glorify God in you body" (I Corinthians 6:19-20). Confessing sin also glorifies God by acknowledging His Sovereignty and right to be obeyed (Joshua 7:19). Our part is to deal with sin through confession, in order to worship God.[163] Our commitment to spiritual restoration and righteousness will lead to introspection and repentance, bringing a significant opportunity to turn to God and dwell on His grace, promise of cleansing, and forgiveness. God then responds to the penitent believer by granting forgiveness and cleansing as the divine part of dialogue (I John 1:9).

We respond to God's revelation of His excellence and glory by glorifying Him in love and obedience. Psalm 50:23 says: "Whoso offereth praise glorifieth me." We focus on God and devote everything to His glory by sacred acts of praise, worship, piety, and prayer, ministering to the needs of others, including witnessing to the Gospel. It may well be that you will not experience fellowship with God until you have entrusted the entire matter to Him, to initiate your thoughts of Him. Do not hesitate to ask God to keep you in constant remembrance and awareness of Him. There is no substitute for divine power in any part of your life, including fellowship with Him, and He is far better equipped to draw near to you and billions of others, than you are to approach Him. Jeremiah 9:24 teaches: "But let him that glorieth glory in this, that he understandeth and knoweth me, that I am the Lord which exercises loving kindness, judgment, and righteousness in the earth; for in these things I delight, saith the Lord."

A Bible verse placed strategically over a mirror or refrigerator can trigger our recollections, and ignite our thoughts of God, leading to fellowship with Him. If one word, such as 'pray' or 'love'; can stimulate and focus our thoughts on God, imagine how memorizing or visualizing God's actual Word can open us to awareness of God's presence. The more we know the Word, the more readily we will recognize God's voice, and distinguish it from Satan's. God never contradicts His Word, and expresses Himself through His Word.

We learn, recall, and concur in God's purposes and plans for our lives by studying the Scriptures which recount everything God has done for us; detail His Sovereign intentions; and reveal the excellence of His character. The better we know the Word of God, the better we will know the God of the Word. Man's part is to receive God's revelations in the Word, by which He communes with us as we immerse ourselves in it; seek God and heed His counsel; memorize and meditate upon it; and allow it to enfold, teach, nurture, and transform us to Christ's holy likeness. We memorize, visualize, and appropriate the Word by etching it into our hearts and souls; in our good works for the Lord; and incorporating His Word into our house, thought, speech, and acts. (Deuteronomy 11:18-22; Luke 8:15). We need to inspire and ignite our thoughts of God throughout the day: to initiate and direct our focus on God and dwell on what Jesus would do, by scriptural reminders posted strategically at work and home.

This immersion in, and absorption of, the Word is the key to fruitfulness as the result of Christ's life being reproduced in believers. Jesus speaks of abiding in Him like a branch attached to the vine, from which we draw strength and nurture: "He who abides in me, and I in him, he it is that bears much fruit, for apart from me you can do nothing" (John 15:4-5).

Abiding in Christ means remaining in Him; to sustain and persist in faith in Him in obedient love (John 8:31, 15:9-10; I John 2:24). Isaiah 64:5 teaches: "Thou meetest him that rejoiceth and worketh righteousness, those that remember thee in thy ways."

Jesus reveals that we abide in Him by response, reception, and obedience to the Word: "If you keep my commandments, you will abide in my love, just as I have kept my Father's commandments and abide in his love: (John 15:10). "By this we may be sure that we are in him: he who says he abides in him ought to walk in the same way he walked" (I John 2:5-6; and see John 14:15-23, 15:7; I John 1:6, 2:3, 2:27, 3:22, 3:24, 5:3 and 2 John 9. Obedience to the Word assures us of shared activity with God: "Let what you heard from the beginning abide in you, then you will abide in the Son and in the Father" (I John 2:24).

The unity which Jesus seeks is a unity of love; obedience to God; and a shared commitment to His will and glory. Psalm 25:4 reveals: "The secret of the Lord is with them that fear him; and he will shew them his covenant." 'Fear' of God is based on reverential awe and respect for His wisdom and Sovereign power, and for His gracious Providence which inspires obedience. "The fear of the Lord is the beginning of knowledge" (Proverbs 1:7; and see also, Psalms 18:28, 25:9; Proverbs 9:10, 16:3; 2 Timothy 2:7; and James 1:5).

Since all vitality originates with the Vine, and the branches can do little except resist falling away from the Vine, and gratefully receive the grace of God which produces the fruit we bear, we should entrust the process to God, enjoy resting in Him, and avoid interfering with His perfect will. Of course, there will be times we need to cooperate in ministering for the Lord, witnessing to the unsaved, and doing the good works for which He has fashioned us (Ephesians 2:10). We need to be prepared to receive the goodness God has stored up for us, for if our gaze is focused on the world, or our hands are filled with material things, we will have no capacity to receive, and will miss the showers of, God's blessings.

We "put on our new nature, created after the likeness of God in true righteousness and holiness" (Ephesians 4:25), by setting our "minds on things that are above, not on things that are on earth" (Colossians 3:2); by striving to "hold fast what is good, abstain from every form of evil" (I Thessalonians 5:21-22). And we do this by meditating upon everything that is true, honorable, just, pure, lovely, gracious, excellent, and worthy of praise (Philippians 4:8), which is exemplified by Jesus. For, He alone, "is altogether lovely" (Song of Solomon 5:16).

Never forget that Jesus has promised to be with you always, for every moment of your earthly life: in Him is strength to be righteous; victory over sin; security in daily life; mercy in times of weakness and failure; and the joy of His unbroken fellowship.

Thank God that He does speak to the believer who takes time to listen. He will come to the believer who responds to His call and waits patiently for His appearance. God will be found by the believer who devoutly seeks Him. He will enter the door of human hearts that are opened to Him. In the enduring fidelity of His love, God has pledged to grow His life in you until, as part of the Body of Christ, you attain to the measure of the stature of the fullness of Christ. "For I am sure that neither death, nor life, nor angels, nor principalities, nor things present, nor things to come, nor powers, nor height, nor depth, nor anything else in all creation, will be able to separate us from the love of God in Christ Jesus our Lord" (Romans 8:38-39).

ENDNOTES

CHAPTER 1.

1 James Dobson, WHEN GOD DOESN'T MAKE SENSE, Tyndale House Pub., Inc., Wheaton, Ill, 1993, p. 110.

2 J.M. Pendleton, CHRISTIAN DOCTRINES, Philadelphia: American Baptist Pub. Soc., 1906, p. 130.

3 C.S. Lewis, "The Humanitarian Theory of Punishment," in GOD IN THE DOCK: Grand Rapids, Mich: Eerdmans, 1970, p. 288.

4 C.S. Lewis, THE PROBLEM OF PAIN, Nashville, TE: Broadman & Holman Pub., 1962, p. 114.

5 Maurice Berquist, THE MIRACLE AND POWER OF BLESSING, Anderson, Ind: Warner Press, 1983, pp. 100–104.

6 James Ryle, "Let There be Light," END TIME NEWS DIGEST, Medford, OR., Omega Ministries; Dec., 1996, p.5.

7 Paul Heinisch, THEOLOGY OF THE OLD TESTAMENT, Collegeville, Minn., The Liturgical Press, 1950, p. 49.

8 Alexander Cruden, CRUDEN'S UNABRIDGED CONCORDANCE, Westwood, NJ: Fleming H. Revell Co., 1961, p. 603.

9 Lester Sumrall, THE NAMES OF GOD, New Kensington, Pa.: Whitaker House, 1993, pp. 84, 105.

10 George F. Thomas, PHILOSOPHY AND RELIGIOUS BELIEF, New York: Charles Scribner's Sons, 1970, p.71.

11 William Strawson, JESUS AND THE FUTURE LIFE, Philadelphia: Westminster Press, 1959, p. 234.

CHAPTER 2.

12 Arthur Hertzberg, Ed., JUDAISM, New York: George Brazilier, 1962, p.22.

13 The Scriptures supporting this Reformed position are ably presented in James R. White, THE POTTER'S FREEDOM, Amityville, NY: Calvary Press Pub., 2000, <u>passim</u>.

14 Alexander Bruce, THE PARABOLIC TEACHING OF CHRIST, New York: A.C. Armstrong & Son, 1887, p. 477.

15 Dave Hunt, WHATEVER HAPPENED TO HEAVEN? Eugene, OR: Harvest House Pub., p. 236.

[16] Norman Geisler, CHOSEN BUT FREE, 2nd Ed., Minneapolis, Minn: Bethany House Pub., p. 196.

[17] William Arnot, PARABLES OF OUR LORD, Grand Rapids, Mich., Kregel Pub., No Date, pp 385-6.

[18] A RELIGIOUS ENCYCLOPEDIA, Philip Schaff, Ed., New York: Funk & Wagnalls Co., 1891, Vol. III, p. 2017.

[19] Billy Graham, THE HOLY SPIRIT, Word Books, Waco, Texas, 1978, p. 192.

[20] D. James Kennedy, TRUTHS THAT TRANSFORM, Grand Rapids, Mich: Fleming H. Revell, 1996, p. 87,98.

CHAPTER 3.

[21] Curtis Hutson, RESPONDING PROPERLY TO TRIALS, Murfreesboro, TN: Sword of the Lord Publishers, 1995, p. 8.

[22] Paul Tournier, CREATIVE SUFFERING, San Francisco: Harper & Row, 1982, p. 37.

[23] Carol Mayhall, HELP LORD, MY WHOLE LIFE HURTS, NavPress, Colorado Springs, Col., 1988, p.71.

[24] Kenneth E. Hagin, MUST CHRISTIANS SUFFER? Faith Library Pub, Tulsa, Okla., 1983, p. 3.

[25] George A. Buttrick, PRAYER, Nashville, Tenn.: Whitmire and Stone, 1942, p. 69.

[26] Rev. James Alberione, PRAY ALWAYS, Boston, Mass.: St. Paul Editions, 1966, p. 118.

[27] Albert Wieand, THE GOSPEL OF PRAYER, Grand Rapids, Mich: William B. Eerdmans Pub. Co., 1953, p. 151.

[28] Lawrence E. Lovasik, PRAYER IN A CATHOLIC LIFE, New York: The MacMillan Co., 1961, p. 99.

[29] William R. Parker and Elaine St. Johns, PRAYER CAN CHANGE YOUR LIFE, New York: Pocket Books, 1957, p. 125.

[30] John L. Rice, PRAYER, ASKING AND RECEIVING, Wheaton, ILL: Sword of the Lord Pub., 1942, p. 192

[31] Harry Emerson Fosdick, THE MEANING OF PRAYER, New York: Association Press, 1931, p. 75.

[32] Alexander Whyte, LORD, TEACH US TO PRAY, New York: George H. Doran Company, No Date, p. 201.

[33] John L. Casteel, REDISCOVERING PRAYER, New York: Association Press, 1955, p. 11.

[34] Harry Emerson Fosdick, PUBLIC PRAYERS, New York: Harper & Brothers, 1959, p. 7.

[35] Steve Brown, APPROACHING GOD, Nashville, Tenn: Random House, Inc., 1996, p. 165-172.

[36] F. B. Myer, THE GIFT OF SUFFERING, Grand Rapids, Mich: Kregel Publ., 1991, p. 105.

[37] Edgar N. Jackson, UNDERSTANDING PRAYER, New York: World Pub. Co., 1960, p. 128.

[38] D. Stuart Briscoe, WHEN THE GOING GET TOUGH, Ventura, CA: Regal Books, 1982, p. 11.

[39] Ron Lee Davis, GOLD IN THE MAKING, Nashville, TN: Thomas Nelson Publishers, 1983, p. 65.

[40] Philip Yancey, DISAPPOINTMENT WITH GOD, Grand Rapids, Mich: Zondervan Pub., 1990, pp. 134, 148.

[41] For example, see Roy H. Hicks, GUARDIAN ANGELS, Tulsa, OK: Harrison House, 1991, pp. 16, 25, and passim.

[42] R.C. Sproul, SURPRISED BY SUFFERING, Wheaton, Ill., Tyndale House Pub., Inc., 1988, p. 38.

[43] John MacArthur, Jr., HEAVEN, Moody Press, Chicago, Ill., 1988, p. 114.

CHAPTER 4.

[44] William D. Watkins, THE BUSY CHRISTIAN'S GUIDE TO THE DEEPER LIFE, Ann Arbor, Mich: Servant Pub. 1996, p. 51.

[45] Rev. Henry T. Sell, BIBLE STUDY BY DOCTRINES, Chicago: Fleming H. Revell Co., 1897, p. 49.

[46] J.I. Packer, EVANGELISM & THE SOVEREIGNTY OF GOD, Downers Grove, Ill., Intervarsity Press, 1961, p. 24.

[47] Andrew Telford, SUBJECTS OF SOVEREIGNTY, Philadelphia, Pa: Berachah Church, N.D., p. 63.

[48] Rev. Alexander Keith, PROPHECY, Waugh & Innes, Edinburgh, 1832, p.22.

[49] A. W. Pink, THE SOVEREIGNTY OF GOD, Edinburgh: Banner of Truth, 1961, p.22.

[50] Ben Patterson, WAITING, InterVarsity Press, Downers Grove, Ill., 1989, p.58.

[51] Philip Yancy, WHERE IS GOD WHEN IT HURTS, Grand Rapids, Mich: Zondervan Pub. House, 1996, p. 108.

CHAPTER 5.

[52] Harold S. Kushner, WHEN BAD THINGS HAPPEN TO GOOD PEOPLE, New York, Avon Books, 1981, p. 81.

[53] Other Old Testament passages confirming free choice by obligating men to resist sin are Deuteronomy 11:26-28; Joshua 24:33; I Kings 18:21; I Samuel 8:18; Psalm 119:45; Proverbs 1:29, 3:31, 29:1; and Isaiah 7:15, 1:18, 45:9, 55:6, 65:2, 66:4, 65:9.

[54] Charles Overton, THE EXPOSITORY PREACHER, London: James Nisbet & Co., 1850, Vol. I, p. 182.

[55] J. L. Mackie, in GOD AND EVIL, Nelson Pike, Editor, Englewood Cliffs, NJ: Prentice-Hall, Inc., 1964, p. 56.

[56] E.C.M. Joad, GOD AND EVIL, New York; Harper and Brothers, Pub., 1943, p. 30.

[57] C.S. Lewis, THE PROBLEM OF PAIN, Nashville, TE: Broadman Holman Pub., 1962, p.30.

[58] C.S. Lewis, MERE CHRISTIANITY, New York: Macmillan Co., 1952, p.49.

[59] Howard Clark Kee, THE RENEWAL OF HOPE, New York: Association Press; 1959, p. 64.

[60] John B. Magee, RELIGION AND MODERN MAN, Harper and Row, New York: 1967, p. 431.

[61] D. James Kennedy, TRUTHS THAT TRANSFORM, Grand Rapids, Mich: Fleming H. Revell, 1996, p.35.

[62] Fulton J. Sheen, FREEDOM UNDER GOD, Milwaukee: The Bruce Pub. Co., 1940, p. 32.

[63] Horatius Bonar, GOD'S WAY OF HOLINESS, Hertfordshire, England: Evangelical Press, 1979, p.87-88.

CHAPTER 6.
[64] Charles C. Ryrie, SO GREAT SALVATION, Victor Books, 1989, pp. 119 ff.
[65] John MacArthur, THE GOSPEL ACCORDING TO JESUS, Grand Rapids: Zondervan, 1988, p. 87.
[66] Louis Berkhof, SYSTEMATIC THEOLOGY, Grand Rapids, Mich: Eerdmans, 1941, p. 505.
[67] Robert Shank, LIFE IN THE SON, Minneapolis, Minn: Bethany House Pub. 1960, p.33
[68] Evelyn Christenson, WHAT HAPPENS WHEN GOD ANSWERS, Waco, Tex; Word Books, 1986, p. 11.
[69] Kenneth E. Hagin, BIBLE FAITH STUDY COURSE, Kenneth Hagin Ministries, Tulsa, Okla., 1985, p. 117.
[70] Roger C. Palms, BIBLE READINGS ON HOPE, Minneapolis, Minn: Worldwide Publ., 1995, p. 52.
[71] William P. Barker, WHEN GOD SAYS NO, Fleming H. Revell Co., Old Tappan, NJ, 1974, p. 146.
[72] Bruce Barron, THE HEALTH AND WEALTH GOSPEL, InterVarsity Press, Downers Grove, Ill., 1987, p.127, ff.

CHAPTER 7.
[73] Carroll E. Simcox, UNDERSTANDING THE SACRAMENTS, New York, Morehouse-Gorham Co., 1956, p. 63.
[74] J. Oswald Sanders, THE JOY OF FOLLOWING JESUS, Chicago: Moody Press, 1990, p. 13.
[75] Samuel Smiles in LIFE AND LABOR, 1887, quoted in John Bartlett, FAMILIAR QUOTATIONS, Boston: Little Brown and Company, 1968, p. 1100.
[76] John Avanzini, IT'S NOT WORKING, BROTHER JOHN, Tulsa, OK: Harrison House, 1992, p. 38.
[77] William Hendrickson, NEW TESTAMENT COMMENTARY: EXPOSITION OF THE GOSPEL ACCORDING TO JOHN, Baker Book House, Grand Rapids: 1953, p. 281.
[78] Nina Mason Bergman, COMFORT FROM THE CROSS, Colorado Springs, Co.: NavPress, 1990, p. 50.
[79] Leslie D. Weatherhead, WHY DO MEN SUFFER?, New York: Abingdom Press, 1936, p. 27.
[80] Hannah Whitall Smith, THE GOD OF ALL COMFORT, Chicago: Moody press, 1956, p. 76.
[81] D.R. McConnell, A DIFFERENT GOSPEL, Hendrickson Publishers, Peabody, Mass., 1988, p. 180.

CHAPTER 8.
[82] Richard J. Foster, CELEBRATION OF DISCIPLINE, San Francisco, Harper & Row, 1987, p. 88.
[83] Jerry Savelle, GIVING, THE ESSENCE OF LIVING, Harrison House, Tulsa, 1982, pp. 72,ff.
[84] T.L. Osborn, HOW TO HAVE THE GOOD LIFE, Osfo International, Tulsa, Okla., 1977, p. 194.
[85] Leslie D. Weatherhead, WHY DO MEN SUFFER? New York: Abingdon Press, 1936, p. 156.
[86] Jacques Ellul, HOPE IN THE TIME OF ABANDONMENT, New York: The Seabury Press, 1977, p. 118.

CHAPTER 9.
[87] Eusebius A. Stephanou, CHARISMATIC RENEWAL IN THE ORTHODOX CHURCH, Logos Ministry, Fort Wayne, Ind., 1976, p. 10.
[88] Helge Brattgard, GOD'S STEWARDS, Minneapolis: Augsburg Pub. House, 1963, p. 64.
[89] T.A. Kantonen, A THEOLOGY FOR CHRISTIAN STEWARDSHIP, Philadelphia: Muhlenberg Press, 1956, p.78 ff.
[90] Jerry White, CHOOSING PLAN A IN A PLAN B WORLD, Billy Graham Evangelistic Assoc., 1987, p. 169.
[91] Martin Buber, TWO TYPES OF FAITH, London: Routledge and Kegan, 1951, p. 9.
[92] Robert Schuller, KEEP ON BELIEVING, Garden Grove, Cal: Hour of Power Pub., 1976, p. 44.

CHAPTER 10.
[93] James D. Bryden, GOD AND HUMAN SUFFERING, Broadman Press, Nashville, Tenn., 1953, p. 71.
[94] SUFFERING: A BIBLICAL SURVEY, Worldwide Pictures, 1980; #13, issued in conjunction with Billy Graham Association film, Joni.
[95] Joel A. Freeman, GOD IS NOT FAIR, San Bernardino, CA: Here's Life Pub., Inc., 1987, p. 106.
[96] Jerry Bridges, TRUSTING GOD, NavPress, Colorado Springs, 1988, p. 122.
[97] H. Beecher Hicks, Jr., PREACHING THROUGH A STORM, Grand Rapids, Mich: Ministry Resources Library, 1987, p. 109.
[98] John MacArthur, Jr., HOW TO MEET THE ENEMY, Victor Books, Wheaton, Ill., 1992, p. 127.
[99] Roger C. Palms, BIBLE READINGS ON HOPE, Minneapolis, Minn: World Wide Publications, 1995, p. 24
[100] John MacArthur, Jr., THROUGH SUFFERING TO TRIUMPH, Chicago: Moody Press, 1991, p. 69.
[101] Rev. M.V. McDonough, THE CHIEF SOURCES OF SIN, Baltimore, Md., John Murphy Co., 1910, p. 8.
[102] Michael Molinos, THE SPIRITUAL GUIDE, Christian Books, Gardiner, Maine, 1982, p. 33.

CHAPTER 11.
[103] Charles H. Talbert, LEARNING THROUGH SUFFERING, The Liturgical Press, Collegeville, Minn., 1991, p. 20.
[104] John of the Cross, THE DARK NIGHT OF THE SOUL, E. Peers, trans., Garden City, NY: Doubleday, 1959, p. 1127.
[105] Paul E. Billheimer, DON'T WASTE YOUR SORROWS, Fort Washington, Pa: Christian Literature Crusade, 1977, p. 79.
[106] William Barclay, THE LETTERS TO THE CORINTHIANS, Philadelphia: The Westminster Press, 1975, p. 83.
[107] Stephen F. Olford, THE SWORD OF SUFFERING, Chattanooga, TN: 2001, p. 21.
[108] Blaine Allen, WHEN GOD SAYS NO, Thomas Nelson, Pub., Nashville, 1981, p. 36.
[109] Merlin R. Carothers, POWER IN PRAISE, Logos International, Plainfield, NJ, 1972, p. 83.

CHAPTER 12.
[110] Thedore H. Epp, WHY DO CHRISTIANS SUFFER?, Lincoln, Neb: The Good News Broadcasting Association, Inc., 1970, p. 20.
[111] William Barclay, THE LETTERS TO THE CORINTHIANS, The Westminster Press, Philadelphia: 1975, p. 258.
[112] W. J. Conybeare, THE LIFE AND EPISTLES OF SAINT PAUL, New York: George H. Doran Co., No Date, p. 847.
[113] F.B. Meyer, THE GIFT OF SUFFERING, Kregel Pub., Grand Rapids, Mich., 1991, p. 14.
[114] Alan Stibbs, THE FIRST EPISTLE OF PETER, Grand Rapids: Eerdman's Press, 1971, p. 119.

CHAPTER 13.
[115] Charles H. Spurgeon, TWELVE SERMONS ON THE RESURRECTION, Baker Book House, Grand Rapids, Mich., 1968, p.53.
[116] Examples of God's vengeance also appear at Genesis 4:15; 38:7; Exodus 9:8-10, 15:26; Numbers 11:33, 31:2-7; 35:19: Deuteronomy 6:22, 7:10, 28:15-68, 32:35-43; Joshua 23:15; Judges 7:22, 11:36; I Samuel 2:6-7, 17:14; 2 Samuel 22:48; I Kings 9:9. 14:10, 21:21; 2 Kings 15:5, 6:33, 9:7-8, 22:16; 2 Chronicles 26:20, 34:24,28; Job 1:16,22, 2:3, 5:13-14, 17-18; Psalms 11:6, 38:3, 39:9-10, 58:10, 66:10-11, 73:27, 79:10, 94:1,23, 102:8-10, 119:75; Proverbs 16:4; Isaiah 1:24, 30:20, 31:2, 61:2; Jeremiah 4:6, 11:11,23, 16:10, 19:3,15, 23:12, 24:12, 25:29, 32:42, 35:17, 36:31, 40:2, 45:5, 46:10; Lamentations 3:32; Ezekiel 25:14,17; Daniel 1:2; 5:21; Amos 3:2-6; Micah 1:12, 5:15, and Nahum 1:2.New Testament passages proclaiming God's vengeance on sinners include Luke 1:20, 18:7-8; John 3:36; Acts 12:21-23, 13:8-11; Romans 1:18, 11:22, 13:4; I Thessalonians 4:6, 17:15-17; 2 Thessalonians 1:8; Hebrews 10:30; Jude 7: and Revelation 6:10, 16:6, 18:20, and 19:2.
[117] C.K. Barrett, HARPER'S NEW TESTAMENT COMMENTARIES ON THE FIRST EPISTLE TO THE CORINTHIANS, Peabody, Mass: Hendrickson, Pub., 1968, p. 226.
[118] Joseph Gaer, THE WISDOM OF THE LIVING RELIGIONS, New York: Dodd, Mead and Co., 1956, p. 116.
[119] Charles S. Braden, THE WORLD'S RELIGIONS, New York: Abingdon Press, 1949, p. 123.

[120] Henry Davis, MORAL AND PASTORAL THEOLOGY, New York: Sheed and Ward, 1938, Vol. I, p. 262.

[121] Leith Anderson, WHEN GOD SAYS NO, Bethany House Pub., Minneapolis, MN, 1996, p.80.

[122] Council of Trent, 1551, Canon 13; St. Thomas Aquinas, SUMMA THEOLOGICA, III, Qu. 87, Art. 3.

[123] George H. Demetrakopoulos, ORTHODOX THEOLOGY, New York: Philosophical Library, Inc. 1964, p. 147.

[124] John M.T. Barton, PENANCE AND ABSOLUTION, New York: Hawthorn Books, 1961, p. 138.

[125] F. X. Schouppe, PURGATORY, Rockford, Ill., 1986, pp. 116-157.

[126] Maurice Berquist, THE MIRACLE AND POWER OF BLESSING, Anderson, Ind: Warner Press, 1983, p. 51.

[127] William Kinkade, BIBLE DOCTRINE, Dayton, Ohio: Christian Pub. Assoc., 1908, p.238.

CHAPTER 14.

[128] Curtis Hutson, GOD'S CHASTENING OF BELIEVERS, Murfreesboro, TN: Sword of the Lord Pub., 1982, p. 9.

[129] Milton S. Terry, BIBLICAL HERMENEUTICS: Grand Rapids, Mich.; Academie Books, Zondervan Pub. House, No Date, p. 222.

[130] Pat Robertson, THE SECRET KINGDOM, Nashville, TN: Thomas Nelson Pub. Co., 1982, p. 188.

[131] Warren Wiersbe, GOD ISN'T IN A HURRY, Grand Rapids, Mich.: Baker Books, 1994, p. 60.

[132] George Fooshee Jr., YOU CAN BE FINANCIALLY FREE, Fleming H. Revell Co., Old Tappan, NJ, 1976, p. 103.

[133] Charles Stanley, HOW TO LISTEN TO GOD, Nashville: Thomas Nelson Pub., 1985, p. 130.

[134] Michael Horton, IN THE FACE OF GOD, Dallas: Word Pub., Inc., 1996, p. 97.

[135] Homer Kent, THE PASTORAL EPISTLES, Chicago: Moody Press, 1896, p. 94.

CHAPTER 15.

[136] E. Stanley Jones, CHRIST AND HUMAN SUFFERING, New York: Abingdon-Cokesbury Press, 1933, p. 72.

[137] Philip Yancey, WHERE IS GOD WHEN IT HURTS?, Grand Rapids, Mich: Zondervan Press, 1977, p. 84.

[138] Brian H. Edwards, MAKING SENSE OUT OF SUFFERING, Evangelical Press, Hertfordshire, England, 1982, p. 19.

[139] Anne and Ray Ortlund, YOU DON'T HAVE TO QUIT, Nashville: Thomas Nelson Pub., 1986, p. 50.

[140] Howard Taylor and Mary G. Taylor, HUDSON TAYLOR'S SPIRITUAL SECRET, Chicago: Moody Press, 1932, p. 152.

[141] Roy and Revel Hession, WE WOULD SEE JESUS, Fort Washington, PA: Christian Lit. Crusade, 1958, p. 11.

[142] Henry G. Bosch, RAINBOWS THROUGH SORROWS, Grand Rapids, Mich., Zondervan Press, 1947, p. 70.

[143] Ron Mehl, MEETING GOD AT A DEAD END, Sisters, OR: Multnomah Books, 1996, p. 64.

[144] C. S. Lewis, THE PROBLEM OF PAIN, New York: The MacMillan Co., 1955, p. 83.

[145] Horatius Bonar, WHEN GOD'S CHILDREN SUFFER, New Canaan, Conn: Keats Publ., Inc., 1981, p. 41-48.

[146] Dennis A. Anderson, JESUS OUR BROTHER IN SUFFERING, Minneapolis, Minn: Augsburg Pub. House, 1977, p. 46.

[147] Steve Brown, APPROACHING GOD, Nashville, Tenn: Random House, 1996, p. 58.

[148] Madam Guyon, UNION WITH GOD, Christian Books, 1981, p. 44.

[149] Gleason Archer, THE BOOK OF JOB, Grand Rapids: Baker Press, 1982, p. 18.

[150] Joel A. Freeman, GOD IS NOT FAIR, San Bernadino, CA: Here's Life Pub., 1987, p. 54.

[151] Robert A. Schuler, WHAT HAPPENS TO GOOD PEOPLE WHEN BAD THINGS HAPPEN, Grand Rapids: Fleming H. Revell, 1995, p. 63.

[152] Horatius Bonar, WHEN GOD'S CHILDREN SUFFER, Keats Pub., New Canaan, Conn., 1981, p.30.

CHAPTER 16.

[153] Lowell Russell Ditzen, THE STORM AND THE RAINBOW, New York: Henry Holt & Co., 1959, p. 50.

[154] R.C. Sproul, THE INVISIBLE HAND, Dallas, Texas: World Publ., 1996, p. 177.

[155] John R.W. Stott, THE CROSS OF CHRIST, InterVarsity Press, Downers Grove, Ill, 1986, p. 313.

[156] Jonathan Edwards, ON KNOWING CHRIST, Edinburgh: The Banner of Truth Trust, 1990, pp. 81-86.

[157] A. W. Tozer, THE PURSUIT OF GOD, Camp Hill, PA: Christian Pub. Inc., 1982, p.66.

CHAPTER 17.

[158] W.W. Sangster, CAN I KNOW GOD? New York: Abingdon Press, 1960, p. 24.

[159] Lewis Sperry Chafer, HE THAT IS SPIRITUAL, London: Marshalls, 1929, p. 115.

[160] John A. Redhead, GETTING TO KNOW GOD, Nashville: Abingdon Press, 1979, p. 9.

[161] Andrew Murray, THE DEEPER CHRISTIAN LIFE, Springdale, Pa: Whitaker House, 1995, p. 8-11.

[162] John Owen, COMMUNION WITH GOD, The Banner of Truth Trust, Edinburgh: 1991, p. 185.

[163] John MacArthur, Jr., GOD, Victor Books, Wheaton, ILL: 1993, p. 152.

Printed in the United States
113891LV00006B/77-86/A